James P. Cannon and
the Origins of the American
Revolutionary Left,
1890–1928

James P. Cannon and the Origins of the American Revolutionary Left, 1890–1928

BRYAN D. PALMER

UNIVERSITY OF ILLINOIS PRESS
Urbana, Chicago, and Springfield

First Illinois paperback, 2010
© 2007 by the Board of Trustees
of the University of Illinois
All rights reserved
Manufactured in the United States of America
2 3 4 5 6 C P 5 4 3 2 1
♾ This book is printed on acid-free paper.

Supported by Trent University.

The Library of Congress cataloged the cloth edition as follows:

Palmer, Bryan D.
James P. Cannon and the origins of the American revolutionary left, 1890–1928 /
Bryan D. Palmer.
p.   cm.— (The working class in American history)
Includes bibliographical references and index.
ISBN-13: 978-0-252-03109-0 (cloth : alk. paper)
ISBN-10: 0-252-03109-1 (cloth : alk. paper)
1. Cannon, James Patrick, 1890–1974.   2. Socialists—United States—Biography.
3. Communists—United States—Biography.   4. Socialism—United States—
History.   5. Communism—United States—History.   I. Title.
HX84.C2P35   2007
320.53'2092—dc22 [B]   2006036201

PAPERBACK ISBN 978-0-252-07722-7

For Bernard Goodman (1910–2003):
Revolutionary, Artist, Cannonist

Contents

Acknowledgments   xiii

Introduction: The Communist Can(n)on   1

Questioning American Radicalism   1

Stalinism: What's in a Name   4

American Communism: Histories of Ambivalence
and Accomplishment   7

At the Point of Embattled Historiographic Production:
The Meanings of Theodore Draper   8

The Three Drapers   11

Communist Biography and Stalinism: James P. Cannon
and the Origins of the American Revolutionary Left   15

1. Rosedale Roots: Facts and Fictions   21

An American Birth   21

Fin de Siècle Context: Kansas in a World of Change   22

In the Shadow of the Irish Diaspora: England
and America   24

The Industrial Frontier   27

Family Fortunes   29

A Boy's Life   31

Meanings   35

2. **Youth's Discoveries**   39

    Mothers and Fathers and Adolescent Work   39

    Early Encounters with Socialism   42

    Education and the Discovery of Desire   45

    The Limitations of Rosedale Socialism   50

3. **Hobo Rebel/Homeguard**   52

    A Soapbox Apprenticeship   52

    Traveling Man: A Vincent St. John Seasoning   57

    Anarchy in Akron: Rubber Workers and
    the Mass Strike, 1913   60

    Fast-Train Hoboing and Hell Popping in Peoria   67

    A Solidarity of the Jail Cell: Marriage   70

    Duluth and the Testing of Class-War Leadership:
    Gunmen, Kidnappings, and Beatings   71

    The Home Front: Cannon Back in Kansas   75

    World War I and Revolutionary Doubt   78

    The Personal Is Political: Radical Manhood   80

    The IWW: The Great Anticipation   85

4. **Red Dawn**   87

    1917: Revolution in the East; Repression in the West   87

    Socialist Revival   89

    A Revived Class Struggle   93

    Browder and Cannon   94

    A Revolutionary Press   96

    A Fractious Left Wing   98

    Foreign-Language Federations and the Dialectic
    of Revolutionary Mobilization   100

    Cannon and the Communist Labor Party   106

    The Agitator's Return: Kansas Coal Fields, 1919   107

    Caught in the Anti-Red Dragnet   109

5. **Underground**   113

    A Suit of Clothes   113

The Divided Communist Underground 114

Bridgman Brokering: The Emergence of Cannon
as a Potential Communist Leader 117

A Cleveland Sojourn: Challenging Ultraleftism 121

New York: Bohemians and Clandestine Communists 126

Cannon, Consolidation, and an Above-Ground Party:
Kansas Charm and the Politics of Revolutionary
Regroupment 128

6. **Geese in Flight 135**

Founding the Workers' Party 135

Undergroundism Unreconstructed 141

Cannon and the Struggle for an Activist
Communist Party, 1922 145

The Birth of the Goose Caucus and the Turn to Moscow 151

7. **Pepper Spray 166**

The Americanizer's Return to America 166

Cannon on the Road Again: The Push and Pull
of Party Assignment 168

Pogany/Pepper 175

Communists Outmaneuver Themselves: Farmer-Labor
Party Illusions and Intrigues, 1923 177

Cannon, Foster, and Trade Union Combination, 1923 188

Pepperism Rampant 192

The Romance of Politics 195

The Third National Convention of the Workers'
Party, 1923–1924 199

8. **Stalinist Suspensions 202**

Of Factions and Foreign Domination 202

Labor Organization, Communist Education,
and Sustaining Collective Leadership 206

Blind Spot: "Women's Work" 208

Race and Revolution 212

Pepper, Bureaucratism, and Permanent Factionalism 219

Farmer-Laborism, Again   222

Factionalism's Enigmatic Fulcrum: Ludwig Lore   224

Comintern Changes   225

Bolshevization and Electoral Campaigns   229

Lore, Escalating Anti-Trotskyism, and Factional
Stalemate, 1924   231

Return to Moscow and Comintern Degeneration, 1925   235

"Tearing Each Other to Pieces": Factional Gang War   239

Of Cables and Comintern Men: American
Communism's Decisive Subordination   242

9. **Labor Defender**   **252**

Bolshevization and Leninist Mass Work   252

Labor Defense and the Shifting Nature of Communist
Trade Union Work, 1923–1926   254

"Professionalizing" Nonsectarian Labor Defense   260

Press and Propaganda   268

Class-War Prisoners   272

Sacco and Vanzetti   274

Factionalism's Toll, 1927–1928   280

10. **Living with Lovestone**   **285**

A Cannon Faction to End Factionalism, 1926   285

Ongoing Stalinization   291

Regrouping a Collective Leadership   293

Ruthenberg's Death and the Lovestone Coup   297

Stalinism and Lovestone *Becoming Lovestone,* 1927   299

The Lovestone Regime: A Right Lurch, 1927–1928   304

11. **Expulsion**   **316**

Cannon and the Corridor Congress, 1928   316

The Temporary Eclipse of Foster   321

Cannon and a Canadian: Maurice Spector   322

Trotsky's Draft Program Surfaces   323

The Cannon-Dunne Split   327

A Clandestine Cannon   328

American Trotskyism Underground   331

Antoinette Konikow: Boston's Red Birth-Control Advocate and
Pioneer Left Oppositionist   332

Piecing Together Possibilities of an American
Left Opposition   334

Flushing the Trotskyists Out   336

Before the Court of Lovestone   338

"Three Generals without an Army": Under Attack   342

How Communist Party Repression Organized Early American
Trotskyism   344

Chicago and Minneapolis: Centers of a New Movement   347

Trotskyism and the Communist Party: An Uncertain
Future, 1928   349

**Conclusion: James P. Cannon, the United States Revolutionary
Movement, and the End of an Age of Innocence   350**

Revolution and Reaction   350

Communism's First Decade: The End of an Age
of Revolutionary Innocence   351

Stalinism at Work   353

Cannon and the Struggle for a Left Oppositionist Practice   355

Cannon's Legacy: The Theory and Practice of Building
a Revolutionary Party   360

Communist Continuity: The Significance
of Revolutionary Subjectivity   364

Notes   371

Index   527

Illustrations follow page   284

Acknowledgments

Jim Cannon found writing difficult. He was something of a master of procrastination. Were he looking over my shoulder at various times during the last decade, he would, I am sure, have found himself laughing at, and sometimes with, me, for this book has been a long time coming. This is not entirely my fault. Without the support and encouragement, help and good graces, and, above all, insistent criticisms and demands that new material be included, of a number of people, completion of this book would have taken fewer years and extracted a lesser toll, not just on my time, but also on my mental and physical well-being, than it already has. It would, however, have been a poorer product.

Like all historians, I owe a great debt to archivists. I am especially thankful to the following: Tamiment Institute, Bobst Library, New York University, New York (where Peter Filardo, Dorothy Swanson, Andrew Lee, and others were of great help); the State Historical Society of Wisconsin, in Madison (Harold L. Miller was always attentive to my requests); Wayne State University Archives of Labor and Urban Affairs, Walter P. Reuther Library, Detroit; the Oral History Research Office, Columbia University, New York; Special Collections and Archives, Emory University; the Special Collections Research Center, Syracuse University Library; and the United States Justice Department, Federal Bureau of Investigation, Freedom of Information/Privacy Acts Section. My work in the extensive James P. Cannon and Rose Karsner Papers, housed in the State Historical Society of Wisconsin, was facilitated by Jack Barnes, who is the owner of the copyrights in and to the James P. Cannon Papers, and who arranged for me to have uninhibited access to these materials, so obviously necessary to the research I was undertaking.

My greatest debt in the archival realm, however, is to the Prometheus Research Library (PRL), the archive and research institute of the Central Committee of the Spartacist League, USA. Its director, James M. Robertson; its librarian, Diana B. Karsten; and its archivist, Emily Turnbull, were gracious and accommodating. This book would not have been possible without their understanding and efforts on my behalf. Well before the archival holdings of the Center for Research and Preservation of Documents on Modern and Contemporary History, based in Moscow, were microfilmed and acquired by various universities and research institutes around the world, the PRL secured microfilm copies of the documentation housed in this Russian collection relevant to the communist movement in the United States in the 1920s. They helped me to work out an agreement with the Center so that I could research in the holdings of the PRL, rather than travel directly to Russia, where the only repository of much crucial United States communist material from the 1920s existed at the time I was conducting my readings of evidence. I therefore cite the microfilm reel numbers of the PRL holdings, but lead all citations with the precise document title and date, which should allow other researchers to compare sources that are referenced with the *fond, opis, delo,* and *listok* (general area, such as Comintern, or Red International of Labor Unions, subcategory, often chronological, individual file, and page reference) of the original organization of this material in the Moscow archives, which retains sole ownership rights to the wealth of documentation I and so many other historians of U.S. communism now rely upon.

Financially, I have been sustained in undertaking this project by a 1993–1996 Social Sciences and Humanities Research Council of Canada operating grant. I was allowed by the Council to shift away from an original research focus on Upper Canada in the 1830s, which proved unfeasible because of a lack of release time, parenting responsibilities, and administrative duties at Queen's University, to the study of Cannon and radicalism, which I could pursue more successfully with the help of Queen's Interlibrary Loan services. I was also fortunate to be the recipient of a 1997 Lipman-Miliband Trust Award that further offset costs of researching this project. At Queen's University and at Trent University I have been provided with material support, and from 2001 to the present I have been fortunate indeed to be sustained in my research endeavors by the Canada Research Chairs program. Without the time and funds provided by this latter federal government initiative, I would not have been in a position to complete this study and do the other work that I have been engaged with.

However much I appreciate funds provided by various programs and institutions, they have never been the ultimate foundation on which I have built my studies of political opposition and working-class life. Rather, what has always been central to me has been the encouragement and critical engagement with my writing of people who appreciate the ongoing dialogue of the Left. In writing on Cannon, I have been propped up in moments of flagging commitment, pushed to do better at the point I thought I had achieved what I wanted to, encouraged to rethink when I lapsed into contented complacency, and aided in countless other ways, including accommodations and sociability, research help and advice, and the selfless sharing of sources, by a broad array of men and women, many of whom constitute a part of the audience for this study.

Among those whose research assistance, varied supports, and sometimes hard-nosed prods to do better I have especially appreciated are Tom Reid and Cathy Neems, Michael Carmody and Cathy Anderson, Steve Brier and Terry Karamanos, Alan Campbell and John McIlroy, Emily Turnbull and James Robertson, Mike Davis, Paul LeBlanc, Peter Campbell, Steve Rosswurm, John Holmes, Murray Smith, Todd McCallum, Jerry Tulchinsky, Ian McKay, Ed Johanningsmeir, Jim Barrett, David Roediger, Herbert Romerstein, Alvin Finkel, Paul Buhle, Scott Molloy, Christopher Phelps, Alan Johnson, Robert Saxe, Patrick Quinn, Lisa Steffen, Julian Locke, Tom Mackaman, Jeff Balfour, Alan Wald, John Earl Haynes, Theodore Draper, Alan Draper, Peter Rachleff, Susan Weissman, Eugene Orenstein, Steven Sandor John, and Nicholas Rogers.

I met a number of figures from various tendencies on the non-Stalinist Left in the course of researching Cannon's life, some of whom I interviewed formally. Not all of them were of one mind on Cannon's strengths, weaknesses, and meaning, but they were a fascinating lot. Those who were particularly significant in my keeping at this project and writing of Cannon in his pre-Trotskyist years were Frank Lovell, Bernard and Pauline Goodman, Jean Tussey, Dorthea Breitman, Marshall and Walta Ross, Marguerite Horst Glotzer, Cynthia Cochran, Nora Roberts, Milt Zaslow (Mike Bartell), Sol Dolinger, Carl Cowl, Miriam Braverman, Walter Lippmann, and Jeanne Morgan. Tussey, Braverman, Breitman, and Morgan, in particular, were exceptionally generous in providing me with either access to or direct gifts of important documents and perspectives, and from Glotzer I was able to secure (in friendly cooperative competition with my friend, John Durham, of Bolerium Books) some important references that have been widely used in this book. Those researching the history of the Left Opposition know one thing well: its advocates keep the historical record alive, not only in their minds, but also in spare bedrooms, closets, and attics. I have been to as many of these as to official archives, and this study could not have been written without pressing my hands into these corners of people's houses, where well-thumbed volumes, brittle newsprint, boxes overflowing with internal documents, and dusty, disintegrating pamphlets speak to the struggles of the past and their relevance to our futures.

I benefited greatly from two very different readings of this manuscript for the press, where Dick Wentworth and Laurie Matheson have never let their interest in the book flag. Paul LeBlanc provided an extremely detailed and careful reading of my submission to University of Illinois Press, and his expertise on the history of international communism and sound judgment improved the published product immensely. He showed me where I had to cut out unnecessary detail, forced me to clarify specific points, and saved me from slipping into loose formulations or faltering in errors of detail or interpretation. Rare are the scholars on the Left as serious, supportive, and selfless as Paul. Through writing on Cannon, I have come to value his friendship as well as his energy and knowledge. A different kind of reading was offered by David Montgomery, who knocked me about a bit when I deserved it (and sometimes when I did not), challenged me to include more contextual material, and demanded that I rethink certain matters. Few historians know as much as Montgomery about the nature and range of United States working-class struggle and the complexities of the revolutionary Left in the twentieth century. I have been fortunate to have his generous, if often hard-hitting, counsel. If neither LeBlanc nor Montgomery will, in the end, agree with everything I say, they at least have made me say it better, and the book they will have before them is somewhat different from the version they were originally presented with.

All errors are, of course, my own. How they could survive the various readings given this manuscript by the legions of critics and helpmates mentioned above is beyond me, but mistakes do happen. For one deficiency, however, I take no responsibility. The University of Illinois Press asked for deep cuts in a book that was, admittedly, much longer than what is regarded as financially prudent in today's commercial marketplace. During the revisions and excisions that followed, much context and considerable referencing had to be shed. For those who would complain about a source not cited or an event that went unmentioned, please understand the limitations of academic publishing in our times.

My life with Joan Sangster began as I commenced to research James P. Cannon's development from a Rosedale youth to an international revolutionary. Relationships, like politics, are about commitments within change, and the continuities of passions expressed in old and new ways. Our loving attachment to one another has never been premised on an insistence that we both see the world in exactly the same way, and this has provided us with the capacity to share much and, on occasion, hold aloft our slightly different banners. She has, throughout it all, been an amazingly supportive partner, and a disturbingly productive scholar, publishing three marvelous books, a collaboratively edited collection of documents, and half a dozen important articles (not to mention heading a graduate program and a research institute) as I struggled to bring this book to a close. It is a race just to keep up with her. I take some solace in the fact that I don't need to surpass her, only to keep sight of her as she pulls further and further ahead.

Our children pull ahead too. Each in their own way goes their own way. Beth has lived with Cannon for many years, and has developed a healthy skepticism about my attachment to him. I enjoy her teasing, and watching her develop her ideas in ways that often challenge mine. Kate, Laura, and Rob prod me as well, and, along with Beth, bring me back to ways of anchoring life in the political ugliness of our times, which includes much that is threatening to their futures and those of their children, who will live, as Cannon did not and as I will not, into the next century.

I dedicate this book to one of Cannon's comrades. I came to know Bernie Goodman when he was in his eighties. I missed 85 percent of his life, but the 15 percent that I experienced was my good fortune. To have met him in the 1920s, when he was prize-fighting in the back rooms of New York taverns; to have crossed paths with him in the 1930s, as he protested unemployment or offered some defensive muscle against the threat of Stalinist violence to the beleaguered members of the Communist League of America (Opposition); or to have run up against him in San Francisco or New York, where he was a Trotskyist (often blacklisted by both the bosses and the "left" in the trade union bureaucracy) militant in the 1940s maritime unions, would, I am sure, have impressed me in particular ways. I doubt Bernie was known as a gentle soul in those days, though he was very much that in his later years. By the time Bernie became my friend, he was formally retired from life in the politics of the Left, which in the 1960s and 1970s had included important roles in anti-Vietnam War mobilizations and tenants' rights activism. He had taken up outsider art, and was producing wonderful collages of collective humanity, alive with color and a particular internationalist vision of the world. Perched on his stool in his studio high atop the Wall Street area courthouse building, his beret angled on the side of his head, gnarled fingers grasping brushes that made huge canvases and whatever he could salvage (linoleum squares and plastic light coverings) speak with the splash of Jackson Pollock and the ancient representation of petroglyphs, Bernie would talk softly and gently about what mattered and how the working class would rise again, because it had to. His attachment to Jim Cannon was a part of this long-standing commitment. It never waned: Bernie told me with pride how he used to walk the Socialist Workers Party leader home from the New York offices in the evening, fearing that Cannon might be accosted by those who were willing to harm him. On occasion, if my daughters were not around, and it was just Bernie and me, sipping a surreptitious glass of wine, or heading to the bus that he took from his studio to his 17th Street apartment, he would tell me how much he hated capitalism and what those who benefited from it deserved. He was a wonderful man. It saddened me greatly when this committed Cannonist died in 2003. To say that his passing was unexpected speaks to Bernie's vitality, for although he was ninety-three I think everyone around him thought he would go on forever. I'm only sorry I could not put this book in his hands, watch him make a fist, and bang it slowly but determinedly into the cover, his eyes sparkling, his smile the only review I would ever need.

James P. Cannon and
the Origins of the American
Revolutionary Left,
1890–1928

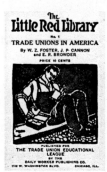

The Little Red Library

No. 1

TRADE UNIONS IN AMERICA

By W. Z. FOSTER, J. P. CANNON
and E. R. BROWDER

PRICE 10 CENTS

PUBLISHED FOR
THE TRADE UNION EDUCATIONAL
LEAGUE
BY THE
DAILY WORKER PUBLISHING CO.
1118 W. WASHINGTON BLVD.   CHICAGO, ILL.

INTRODUCTION

The Communist Can(n)on

Questioning American Radicalism

We ask questions of radicalism in the United States. Expectations and precon-
ceived notions of what radicalism should look like abound, and our queries
reflect this. Why is there no socialism in America? Why are workers in the
world's most advanced capitalist nation not class-conscious? Why has no third
party of laboring people emerged? Some want the questioning to stop; it seems
wrong-headed. Yet the interrogation continues, periodically sparking debate
and efforts to reformulate and redefine analytic agendas for the study of American labor radicals, their diversity, their ideas, and their practical activities.[1]

This book is not exercised by such concerns. It views socialism, syndicalism,
anarchism, and communism as minority traditions in United States life, just as
they have often been in other settings. The revolutionary Left is, and always
has been, a vanguard of the exceptional. Life in a minority is not, however, an
isolated, or inevitably an isolating, experience. In the late nineteenth and early
twentieth centuries, the United States gave rise to a significant Left, rooted in
what many felt was a transition from the Old World to a New Order. Populists,
anarcho-communists, Christian Socialists, early feminists, bohemian intellectuals, trade unionists, immigrant Marxists, exiles from failed European revolutions, Wobblies, co-operators, and countless other stripes of radical rubbed
shoulders in metropolitan centers, in the towns of middle America, and in
frontier settings, all of which sustained varied institutional and cultural spaces
in which the sociability and politics of the Left were generated and regenerated
over time. Weekly journals, like the Girard, Kansas, *Appeal to Reason* (which
Lenin considered "not at all bad"), had a readership of more than 760,000;
special theme issues associated with particular mobilizations sometimes

exceeded print runs of 4 million. A revered figure such as Eugene Debs could rally hundreds of thousands to the electoral standard of the Socialist Party of America. He polled an unprecedented 6 percent of the presidential vote in 1912, and eight years later, from a jail cell, Debs garnered nearly a million votes in his symbolic run to occupy the White House. It was a heady time for those who thought themselves revolutionaries, although it was not without its dangers, the latter most evident in the wave of repression that engulfed radicalism in the period from 1917 to 1921.[2]

Joseph Freeman, whose *An American Testament* (1936) was praised by Theodore Draper as "one of the few Communist human documents worth preserving," and by Max Eastman as the "best and most engaging book written by an American communist,"[3] recalled the developing radical politics of the United States in the early twentieth century vividly, capturing a sense of its disruptive, destabilizing impact on all aspects of life. Writing in 1934–1936, Freeman, like many who gravitated to the revolutionary Left in the period associated with World War I and the Russian Revolution, came to regard the Communist Party of the United States (CP), for a time at least, as the place where the struggle for the new radical order was to be carried out to best effect. An editor of the communist magazine *New Masses* and a teacher at the party's Workers' School when he penned his testament, Freeman was drawn to the inspiration of the party ranks, "selfless, incorruptible." From them he learned, and for them and for himself, he worked "to abolish poverty, ignorance, war, the exploitation of class by class, the oppression of man by man," and to create "the utmost imaginable freedom for the mass of humanity."[4]

Freeman's passionate communist commitment was not to survive the 1930s Red Decade of economic depression and social upheaval, which had done so much to steel his anti-capitalist convictions and dedication to socialist humanity. *An American Testament* was insufficiently critical of the exiled Russian revolutionary Left oppositionist, Leon Trotsky, whom the United States cultural radical had witnessed firsthand in one of the last Comintern debates of the 1920s. As a consequence, Freeman was, in his word, "excommunicated." Party leaders demanded that the communist author self-censor his own publication by barring mention or advertisement of it in *New Masses,* call off a promotional speaking tour, and cancel a large order placed by the Workers' Bookshop. That accomplished, and with the seemingly well-ensconced "captain of cultural activities" of the large communist movement sufficiently humbled, the Comintern then insisted that Freeman's CP affiliation be terminated. The ex-communist's next novel, *Never Call Retreat* (1943), sounded the inspirational cry of ongoing struggle with a predictable awkwardness, but an articulate voice of radicalism had been quieted.[5]

Another American communist, James P. Cannon—the main subject of this book—would be harder to sideline and impossible to silence. He had been drummed out of the CP a decade before Freeman was given his walking papers. Cannon never relinquished his attachment to the original Workers' Party, later renamed the Workers (Communist) Party (and, a few years thereafter, subsequent to Cannon's expulsion, the Communist Party, USA or CP), that he had very much helped to establish. Long after he himself had come to see the party as an impediment to revolution, Cannon saw as victims those won to its struggles through their sincere desire to create a better, socialist, world; to him, they were a radical generation motivated by the best of intentions but misguided by a squandering, Stalinist leadership: "The chief victim of Stalinism in this country was the magnificent left-wing movement, which rose up on the yeast of the economic crisis in the early Thirties and eventually took form in the CIO through a series of veritable labor uprisings. . . . The story of what happened to these young militants; what was done to them, how their faith was abused and their confidence betrayed by the cynical American agents of the Kremlin gang—that is just about the most tragic story in the long history of the American labor movement."[6]

How radicals like Cannon and Freeman came to embrace communism, and how that communism repudiated so much of itself in the 1920s, is the subject of this book. Such a treatment of the origins of the American revolutionary Left necessarily concerns itself with another question historians have often wrestled with. Was United States communism a genuine or natural expression of a native radicalism, or was it a foreign import, imposed on indigenous conditions from without, an external domination?

I end this journey of analysis and accounting with Cannon's expulsion from the Communist Party late in 1928, at least for the time being. In a future volume, I plan to pursue Cannon's history further, following him as he struggled to build Trotskyism as a political force and a party formation in the United States, and to develop an alternative to the Communist International around the world. That study, though, in effect takes us beyond the origins of the American revolutionary Left, which had built on the eclectic radicalisms of the nineteenth century and been consolidated through the discussions and debates of the 1900s. It was an atmosphere in which Marxism, social democracy, populism, socialism, syndicalism, anarchism, and other strands of dissident thought and practice contended for the hearts and minds of those on the Left. World events of momentous consequence and implication, encompassing war and revolution, altered the map of global politics in the next decade and, alongside particular repressive developments in the United States, ushered American communism into being.

Cannon allows us to view those beginnings with new eyes, forcing us to look where many have perhaps not wanted to see. The history of America's revolutionary Left, in its origins and in the uneasy years of communism's birth in the United States, cannot be understood, I suggest, without attention to the ways in which the communist project was transformed by Stalinism in the 1920s. Moreover, the varied historiographies that chart developments, accent particulars, and lay interpretive stress on specific parts of the Left experience in America are also understandable only if we begin to grapple openly with Stalinism's forceful historical presence. As the words and experiences of Cannon and Freeman suggest, Stalinism matters in what happened to twentieth-century American radicalism.[7]

Stalinism: What's in a Name

A profound unease marks both the history and the historiography of United States communism. Participants, advocates, and scholars—the lines of distinction by no means always clearly discernible—have found it difficult to address the complex meaning of what is surely one of the most influential segments of the American Left. Many who spent their lives in circles justifiably proud of their Bolshevism, and content to live attached to the considerable historical accomplishments of the world's first successful proletarian revolution and its state, the Soviet Union, never managed to adequately work through the experience of degeneration that lowered on the revolutionary drama of communism with Joseph Stalin's rise to power.[8]

As a shorthand term, *Stalinism* is not so much a personalized denunciation as a designation of political defeat. The aspirations and expansive potential of revolutionary communism were suffocated in bureaucratization, compromise of political principle, abandonment of theoretical and programmatic consistency, waning of commitment to socialism and its spread throughout the world, and a narrowing of agendas to the most defensive and mundane. Stalinism was, of course, guided in part by the subjective agenda of the individual whom Trotsky would come to conclude was capable of proclaiming "I am Society," but it was also determined to some extent by objective historical conditions and developments detrimental to sustaining the revolutionary cause, much of which took place in situations once-removed from Stalin's direct influence. The revolution's making in a political economy of backwardness, with its history of czarist autocracy and the class dominance of the peasantry, for instance, ensured that the road to Russian socialism would inevitably be a rough one. This original difficulty was complicated by the immense drain on the resources of the Russian/Soviet social formation during World War I and the subsequent containment of the first workers' state by a hostile grouping of powerful capitalist nations, all of which continued to oppose what Lenin and the Bolsheviks stood for well after the end of hostilities in 1918. In the crucible of civil war, the practice of governance in the world's first socialist state was inevitably hardened over the course of the years from 1917 to 1921, and many Bolsheviks faced the necessity of institutionalizing an apparatus of repression, centered in the Cheka, in order to preserve the revolution and its advances. Internationally, the failure of the socialist revolution in Europe and especially Germany, on which the healthy continuity of the Russian Revolution depended, first in 1919 and then in 1921–1923, constrained Soviet possibilities even further. All of this conditioned an internal regime within the Soviet Union in which a series of misplayed hands at the table of Russian revolutionary politics, some of them involving Trotsky himself, consolidated Stalin's power, weakened and marginalized his potential opponents, and, ultimately, culminated in the decimation of the Leninist Party that had registered such gains in 1917 and the immediate post-Revolution years.[9]

The practical consequence of this constellation of inhibitions and steps backward inside and outside the Soviet Union was thus formidable. Under Zinoviev, the Communist International (Comintern/CI), formed in 1919, was subjected to increasing bureaucratization after the defeat of the German Revolution precipitated the forces of revolutionary internationalism into problematic postures. The consequence was an unhealthy and arbitrary Zinovievist penchant for centralism that often overrode considerations of national contexts. Under the guise of a campaign for Bolshevization, first proclaimed in 1924, Zinoviev's CI addressed obvious problems inherent in the relations of various communist parties and the particularities of specific national struggles, grappling awkwardly with how to overcome a marked lack of revolutionary discipline and draw more from the organizational strength of revolutionary parties and their work to build communism. Unfortunately, the way the Comintern negotiated these relations in 1923–1925 erred on the side of heavy-handed, authoritarian intervention. To be sure, the ease with which Zinoviev transformed the CI, subordinating national sections and, indeed, in Deutscher's words, "shuffling, displacing, and breaking up at will" the once powerful Central Committees of the French, German, and Polish Communist Parties, suggests an unhealthy atmosphere of Russification within the Comintern—a slavishness that Lenin himself had expressed concern over. That the Polish and French committees protested in 1923 against the initial assaults on Trotsky, however, suggests that kernels of independence did exist within the CI. Nevertheless, the defeats of 1923, and the parallel campaigns of Zinovievist Bolshevization and early Stalinist moves in the consolidation of party power, fused for the moment in an anti-Trotsky defamation that was inadequately responded to by a nascent Left opposition, including Trotsky himself. The once-revered leader of the Red Army retreated into his own obeisance to the Comintern. He failed to gain election to the Executive Committee of the Communist International, and Stalin was voted the seat in his stead. A language of "monolithic Bolshevism" dominated the CI podiums in 1924; it was an ill wind that blew no good. Given that there were positive aspects to Bolshevization, which attempted to address genuine problems in the practices of communist parties and their constituencies, it is possible that had the Soviet Party retained a healthy revolutionary program, the wrongs of the mid-1920s Comintern could have been righted. But this was not to be. The parochialism and chauvinism of the constricting advocacy of "socialism in one country" replaced the proletarian internationalism and widening reach of a program of world revolution.

Within the degenerating revolutionary Soviet society, the ruthless elevation of the *lider maximo*, Joseph Stalin, produced an autocratic state eventually governed by terror. Stalin ordered the first Bolshevik shot in 1923, and between 1927 and 1940 he orchestrated the trial, exile, or execution of virtually the entire corps of revolutionary leadership. Beyond the boundaries of "socialism in one country," a series of defeats and international misadventures (beginning with the routing of the Chinese Revolution in 1926, and reaching through the debacles of fascism's rise to power in Germany and the bloodletting of the Spanish Civil War in the 1930s) haunted the revolutionary conscience in decades that might well have witnessed pivotal political advances and radical successes. This dismal record of opportunities tragically wasted was eventually blunted with the Stalinist brokering of a reconfigured Europe in the aftermath of World War II: a buffer zone of supposedly socialist economies being established in Eastern and Central Europe was the price the capitalist world was willing to pay for the monumental losses the Allied Soviets sustained in helping to liberate Europe from Hitler's awful designs. Such Iron Curtain socialism was born deformed, though, as would be the postcolonial regimes of national liberation, such as Cuba and Vietnam, that ended up taking both material aid and political inspiration from the Soviet Union.[10] From possibly as early as 1926, then, and certainly from the late 1920s and 1930s on, the forces of the international Left faced not only the resolute opposition of global capital and its considerable power, vested in nation-states and their militaries (as well as the widening material and ideological reach of hegemonic capitalist markets and cultures), but also the constraining defeatism of leaderships, structures of power, and political orientations committed, in their Stalinism, to anything but world revolution. Specific communist parties paid dearly in the process, as evidenced in Isaac Deutscher's and Pincus Minc's (Aleksander's) recollections of the sacrifice and destruction of the Polish Communist Party (KPP) which, in 1938, was dissolved by Comintern dictate.[11]

If we want a definition of *Stalinism*, then, we must look well beyond the usual commonplace understandings of Moscow domination and totalitarian politics, which have infused much scholarship on the United States Left with a certain moral revulsion. In a nutshell, *Stalinism* can be defined as the socioeconomic phenomenon of bureaucratized governance and political rule rooted in collectivized property forms that, in their origins, were ultimately meant to produce genuine workers' democracy. The governing ideology of Stalinism—again in stark contrast to the project of the revolutionary society that spawned it, the Soviet Union of 1917—proved to be the national parochialism of "socialism in one country." Stalinism stood the agenda of proletarian internationalism and working-class struggle against world capitalism on its head. Nothing less than the political antithesis of revolutionary communism and its internationalist embrace of ongoing proletarian revolution, Stalinism buried the Leninist party and early Bolshevism's political commitments and legacies, even though many genuine revolutionaries continued to take their stand against injustice and exploitation as members and advocates of official communist parties.[12]

American Communism: Histories of Ambivalence and Accomplishment

In the United States, from Harlem to southern sharecropping plots,[13] within the communities of arts and letters associated with writers' congresses and left-wing theater troupes,[14] in the Abraham Lincoln brigade mobilized to fight in the Spanish Civil War and through peace and anti-war movements,[15] as well as among housewives' organizations,[16] labor defense bodies, industrial unions, and unemployment protests,[17] communists fought for much that was honorable and achieved more than a little that was necessary and humane. If one realm of special oppression, women's subordination, has been regarded as "the question seldom asked"[18] of the American communist Left, there is still no denying that women in the ranks of the revolutionary party promoted progressive, feminist causes and struck important blows, not only for female emancipation, but also for women's public involvement in political struggle.[19] It is striking how much United States history in the twentieth century that is associated with the eradication of racism is inextricably entwined with the Communist Party, whatever its programmatic and practical lapses with respect to the meaning of the "color line" within advanced capitalism.[20] Internationalism, too, was undoubtedly fostered by communist parties and their members.[21]

Much post-1980 writing on these themes by New Left-influenced historians has presented the United States communist experience sympathetically, and with important insight, but almost all of this relatively recent interpretation both sidesteps Stalinism too easily and avoids the original decade of international communism's faltering steps into problematic defeats (and worse).[22] This unease, lived historically, has been reproduced in the memoir writing on American communism. Social and cultural histories, as well as reminiscences, have too often, in Geoff Eley's words, diminished "the significance of formal communist affiliations, leading in extreme cases . . . to a history of communism with the Communism left out."[23]

At the Point of Embattled Historiographic Production: The Meanings of Theodore Draper

It is not an overstatement to contend that the serious historiography of the origins of the American revolutionary Left begins with Theodore Draper. Draper joined the communist student movement in the 1930s, but left the party after he thought through the full implications of the Hitler-Stalin pact of 1939–1941. Thereafter, as did many ex-communists who came to regard the revolutionary Left as a "God that failed,"[24] Draper experienced something of a political transformation. His anti-communism, however, was liberal rather than reactionary, let alone neoconservative. Draper's obvious strengths as a historian were that he knew the CP well and had an eye for detail, as well as a keen sense of archival preservation; he gathered sources diligently and compiled extensive dossiers of communications/interviews with as many of the major figures in the formative years of United States communism as would engage with him. The former communist eventually produced two impressive volumes, researched and written over the course of the mid- to late 1950s, that addressed the founding years of United States communism in the 1920s. They are distinguished by their thorough scholarship as well as their relentless interpretive insistence that American communism, like all post-1921 communist experience, was a "made in Moscow" affair.[25]

As such, Draper proved a convenient target for a number of new histories of United States communism that emerged largely in the 1980s. His perspective flew directly in the face of those who accented social histories of rank-and-file particularity, emphasized the indigenous roots and Americanized character of communism, or asserted some kind of blend of international influence and national experience.[26] Few were the book prefaces or historiographic articles in the New Left revival of American communism's significance that did not dissent from Draper's characterizations of the CP and its meaning.[27]

Draper rapidly became the key figure in a school of communist studies labeled "political" or "institutional," a pioneer who inspired advocates in a revived 1970s traditionalist anti-communist cohort of writers headed by Harvey Klehr and John Earl Haynes.[28] Klehr and Haynes were as out of favor with the New Left-influenced historians as was Draper, but like their detractors they usually took as their subject discrete periods or aspects of communist studies that post-dated Draper's attentiveness to the origins of United States Bolshevism. In a 1992 overview jointly authored by Klehr and Haynes, *The American Communist Movement: Storming Heaven Itself*, the duo ranged broadly if rather brusquely over seventy years of communist history; Draper utilized the back cover of the book to declare that it would tell readers "as much as we are likely to know or care to know" about the tortured development of the CP. Haynes, in particular, continued the useful bibliographic initiatives that flowed from the original "communist problem" series, edited by Clinton Rossiter and financed by the Fund for the Republic, that spawned Draper's volumes.[29]

In the 1990s aftermath of the Cold War, Klehr, Haynes, and others found further ammunition for their cause in the opening of the Soviet archives, which proved a boon for books on spies and the "secret world" of that age-old shibboleth, "Moscow gold" (the financing of revolutionary activity by the Communist International), all of which merely confirmed the routinized notion of Soviet dominance. With respect to this book's concern with the origins of the American revolutionary Left and the establishment of the communist movement in the 1920s, the repetitious fixation on espionage and World War II and its immediate aftermath inevitably casts United States communism in a particular light, overshadowed by a later McCarthyism that takes on, for some readers of Klehr, Haynes, and their collaborators, a jaundiced justification: If the CPUSA was indeed so engaged in this "secret world" of laundering Comintern money, feeding intelligence to Soviet sources, pilfering state documents, and hovering around atomic research units, surely McCarthy was right and the anti-communist witch hunts of the 1950s were warranted. In fact, as the major New Left-inspired historian of anti-communism, Ellen Schrecker, has established in a considerable body of writing, nothing could be further from the political truth. As Schrecker states unequivocally, McCarthyism was an unnecessary violation of democratic rights, one that irrevocably bloodied the body politic of United States civil society. Even Klehr and Haynes do not disagree, although some who read them need to hear their words. For all that the traditionalist anti-communist camp has piled up evidence of what it considers CPUSA wrongdoing, two of this school's leading commentators conclude that nothing done by communists "offers any vindication for Senator McCarthy or McCarthyism."[30] Nevertheless, what is passed over rather too easily in this recent historiographic work is nothing less than the origins of communism's attractions for segments of the United States working class. The liberal anti-communism of Klehr, Haynes, and others, with its current fixation on communist subterfuge, Moscow domination, and Comintern funding of espionage and propaganda, overwhelms the indigenous history of American radicalism. Historians of the Left have faced a literal ordeal by spy historiography.

They have not always survived this medieval-style torture-test. This historiographic overproduction, when considered in conjunction with the shifting ground of the contemporary political terrain, has not been without effect. As the New Left waned and the climate turned decisively to the right in the 1980s and 1990s, some 1960s scholars shifted sides and lined up more directly with the growing ranks of academic anti-communism. Early bailouts included Ronald Radosh, whose growing conviction of the guilt of the Rosenbergs moved him directly into the anti-communism of the Klehr-Haynes camp.[31] More subtle, because they somewhat refused the binary oppositions and cloistered positionings of blunt communist/anti-communist designations, were the responses of New Left-inspired historians such as Maurice Isserman and Sean Wilentz, who became far more willing to entertain the prospect that not all in the anti-communist tradition was to be written out of a left-liberal coalition that increasingly wanted less and less to do with the belated discoveries of Stalinism's tainted past.[32] Although the Cold War was over (at least militarily), it continued among historians of American communism, where attachments to and repudiations of the Old Left remained as the twentieth century closed. If few older New Leftists were as willing to embrace United States communism in the 1990s as they had been in the 1970s, there remained those deeply committed to depicting the Communist Party in ways that challenged Draper. At the same time, the once-beleaguered traditionalists seemed buoyed by new evidence and a reconfigured political climate in which communism's reduction to an anachronism allowed longstanding hostilities to the revolutionary project an increasingly free rein.[33]

Nevertheless, a deep irony of meaning lies lost from sight in the evolution of this Draper–New Left clash. Until the mid-1990s, Draper stood virtually alone as someone who had actually written seriously about the formative years of American communism in the 1920s. It was as though Draper had closed the book on the subject, only to have those who insisted on opening new pages of communism's histories from the 1930s through the 1950s return to his 1920s perspectives to claim that Draper had been proven wrong by subsequent developments. Still, those years of the "Red Decade" of Depression, the Popular Front, and Browderism had their origins in the uneasy birth of United States communism in the 1920s, when a Stalinism that the New Left-leaning cohort of radical historians has largely passed over in silence took problematic root.

Both Draper and many New Left-influenced histories interpreted communism in the United States problematically because they constructed their understanding of Stalinism as nothing less than an ideological mirror image. For many American New Left-inspired historical writers, Stalinism was, for the most part, the association of communism and Comintern domination of American radicalism that studies of locale, particularity, secondary cadre, and Browderesque popular frontism were at pains to deny. New Left historians engaged with Stalinism, ironically, by not engaging with it: they simply reversed Draper's construction of "communism = Moscow domination" by declaring that "American communism = genuine, native-born radicalism." Their studies of specific places, people, and parts of the communist experience were, without doubt, valuable contributions to our knowledge of the revolutionary Left, but too often the histories produced lacked the important wider context that a grappling with Draper could have generated. If such New Left work was able to recognize, as much indeed did abstractly, that the Communist Party of the United States was inevitably a blend of national and international developments, it looked incompletely at Comintern influences and, perhaps most importantly, skipped almost entirely over the actual period of the development of Stalinism, and the way that it conditioned a particular party and program in the United States. Revisionist studies of the Communist Party that appeared in the 1970s and 1980s largely ignored the 1920s, concentrating their researches in the 1930s and 1940s of the Popular Front and World War II.[34] Its gaze too narrowly national and too often circumscribed by its appreciation of militancy and struggle, the American New Left largely averted its eyes from the troubling programmatic degenerations of the 1920s that were in some ways a prefatory analytic window into the show trials, repression, and terror of Stalin's USSR that were to occur in the same period during which revisionist writing would see communism mobilize the masses in a democratic United States. This ensured that the New Left in the United States, for all its deep commitments to the history of admirable communist organizing and humane resistance to oppression, would seem blinded by the light of its rediscovery of a politics of class struggle. It tended to miss not only a good deal of the meaning of Stalinism, but also the kernel of substantive research and a misnamed, bluntly formulated truth that lay at the heart of Draper's problematic histories.[35]

The Three Drapers

It is possible to discern within Draper's communist histories three different, if related, sensibilities. These are evident in the stages of Draper's *development*, which few New Left-influenced social historians and none of Draper's so-called institutional followers address.

First was the historian's Draper, a commentator who, whatever his anti-communist tilt, could be counted on to scrutinize evidence and present it. Draper's first volume, *The Roots of American Communism* (1957) commenced with statements of analytic direction that many New Left-influenced historians (not to mention others) could well have accepted, or should have. Draper concluded his introduction to this initial study of the origins of the American revolutionary Left with the improbable (in hindsight), if unchallengeably balanced, claim that, "Even in the days of Lenin—the period dealt with in this book—communism was not merely what happened in Russia; it was just as much what was happening in the United States." When one considers how Draper has been represented by New Left-leaning historical critique, as well as how Draper himself has come to put forward his later, more baldly stated, views of Moscow domination, this is a truly surprising claim with which to open his assessment of United States communism. Such a statement reveals that Draper's original research was conducted with more openness than his later fixed positions (on which New Left criticism focused) would suggest.

Draper ended his account of the early 1920s grappling with the seed of a degeneration he could not name: Stalinism. "For Moscow in 1923 was just entering on a period of fierce and ugly fratricidal struggle to determine the succession to Lenin's leadership in Russia. This struggle poisoned the life of the Comintern and seeped into the bloodstream of every Communist party in the world." Precisely because Draper's anti-communism was, at the time he wrote *The Roots of American Communism*, already sufficiently entrenched, the ex-communist could not address the possibility that communism per se was not the original problem, but rather that the difficulty lay in the transformation of the Soviet revolutionary process over the course of the 1920s. Unable to accept that a Stalinism he could neither name nor address politically and interpretively was *not* simply a more universal politics of timeless Moscow domination, Draper saw inevitability where historical contingency should have appeared.

This was the second Draper, the historian blinkered by an ideological short-sightedness that incapacitated him. He read the contests of 1923, when Comintern bureaucratization and Stalinist machination were in their nascent beginnings, in an exaggerated way, and he projected them both backward in time and forward into the mid- to late 1920s, which he was embarking on reconstructing in what would later appear as *American Communism and Soviet Russia* (1960). The result was a distortingly dismissive, almost biologically determinative, understanding of revolutionary internationalism as pure and simple communist dictation: "The first change of line was every other change of line in embryo. A rhythmic rotation from Communist sectarianism to

Americanized opportunism was set in motion at the outset and has been going on ever since. The periodic rediscovery of 'Americanization' by the American Communists has only superficially represented a more independent policy; it has been in reality merely another type of American response to a Russian stimulus. A Russian initiative has always effectively begun and ended it."

Draper's ideological antagonism to communism thus overwhelmed his scholarly insights. *The Roots of American Communism* ended on a note of prejudgment that would nevertheless capture something of the future trajectory of Comintern-U.S. communist relations: "something crucially important did happen to this movement in its infancy. It was transformed from a new expression of American radicalism to the American appendage of a Russian revolutionary power. Nothing else so important ever happened to it again." The Cold War warrior proved incapable of seeing the interpretive possibilities that an analysis of Stalinization would have provided, opting instead for an overly deterministic assertion of communism's inevitable reduction to Russian domination of the forces of world revolution, United States "reds" among them. The first and second Drapers thus struggled with one another in these two original Fund for the Republic volumes.[36]

The second Draper would, of course, win out. Stalin figured barely at all in *The Roots of American Communism,* understandably so given his less-than-central role in Russian revolutionary developments during the period 1917 to 1922 that formed the core of Draper's first study. In Draper's sequel, *American Communism and Soviet Russia,* however, it was inevitable that Lenin's successor would figure more prominently on the stage of Comintern politics and its meaning in United States radical circles. Draper concluded that Moscow domination of American and other communist parties was an inherent feature of the Communist International. Thus, there was no need to explore the nature of Stalinism, which, as a term used in this second of Draper's volumes, is more of a description of the wielding of communist power than a lever used to pry open a conceptualization of revolutionary degeneration. Moreover, in *American Communism and Soviet Russia,* Draper tends increasingly toward a reductionist view of United States communism, highlighting factionalism in a disembodied way and understating the extent to which such factional struggle involved critical questions of programmatic direction—some of which related directly to mass struggles in the United States and all of which figured in whether American communism would reach out to a wider constituency.

For Draper, the meaning of American communism was settled. This was not so much a product of Stalinist degeneration as it was a political *essence*: "Whatever has changed from time to time, one thing has never changed—the relation of American Communism to Soviet Russia. This relation has expressed itself in different ways, sometimes glaring and strident, sometimes masked and muted. But it has always been the determining factor, the essential element."[37]

It was for precisely this reason—Draper's predetermined judgment that communism was an organically flawed project destined to reproduce time and time again a subordination of American to Russian interests—that some communists who lived through the struggles of the 1920s rejected Draper's account. They recognized the strengths of Draper's histories, but insisted that their weakness was a failure to grasp that there was more to United States communism's uneasy formative years than Draper's "cocksure interpretations and summary judgements" implied. Even ex-communists with a profound, and rightward-leaning, aversion to Stalinism, prone to accept implicitly Draper's interpretive stamping of Comintern-American relations with a "Made in Moscow" finality, recalled the early to mid-1920s differently. Bertram Wolfe and Jay Lovestone, for instance, insisted that the Russian revolutionary leaders treated early American communists "as equals, with equal respect . . . They were big men, and because they were big men they did not act in little or small ways." If Russian influence was "decisive" and veneration of the Comintern leaders undeniable, Lovestone and Wolfe were adamant that Lenin, Zinoviev, Trotsky, and Radek never advocated or nurtured this.[38] Draper thus proved unable to draw a necessary distinction between advice and guidance from a Comintern healthy in its commitment to world revolution, developed through consultation and genuine regard for the advancement of the revolutionary forces in the West, as existed in the dialogue between United States communists and their Soviet comrades in the early years of the 1920s, and a Comintern that was drifting into bureaucratization by 1925.

When a former communist such as Steve Nelson, who developed from a youthful rank-and-file figure in the CP in the 1920s to a major influence in the party's New York leadership in the 1940s and 1950s, sidestepped the issue of American communism's degeneration by referring to communist "discipline" as perhaps making CP members "more vulnerable to Stalinism" (as if, over the course of the 1930s and 1940s, Stalinism were not an established foundation of party life and politics), Draper saw more than red. This was the birth of the third Draper, the liberal Cold War warrior gone ballistic. As historical writings in the 1980s increasingly castigated earlier accounts for their depiction of the CP as "a monolithic totalitarian organization whose history reflected the shifts and turns in the Comintern line," and instead posited the need for histories of U.S. communism as "an authentic expression of American radicalism," Draper moved into a crankier articulation of his hostility to the Communist Party and its meaning. If his critical engagement with so-called new histories of communism did indeed strike appropriately at many vulnerabilities, over time

Draper grew more and more likely to slip into attacks that, in their demand that Stalinist foibles and much worse be resolutely identified, often lapsed into complacent acquiescence with respect to the unsavoriness of the Cold War right. In the cause of anti-communism, Draper excused much.[39]

Scholarship in the last decade and more that has addressed U.S. communism has nonetheless relied heavily on Draper's original contribution. Some of this work has drawn somewhat mechanically from Draper's Soviet domination argument, as in the writing of the Klehr-Haynes traditionalist cohort, with its fixation on the "secret" and "soviet" worlds of U.S. communism as revealed in newly released Moscow documents.[40] Much other work has taken individual communists of long-standing significance in the American movement as its subject. Close examinations of the making of communists—their origins in specific kinds of class struggles and their attractions to the ideas, disciplines, and potential of a revolutionary party linked to the first successful proletarian state—illuminate the experience of communism with a sense of development and detail that is often lacking in more general studies. Such disciplined, archival-based, biographical study, reaching well beyond memoir, is relatively new within communist historiography, and is beginning to register both internationally and within the United States.[41]

This is especially evident in what are undoubtedly the best recent contributions to American communist studies: sophisticated biographies of the syndicalist turned communist, William Z. Foster, by Edward P. Johanningsmeier and James R. Barrett. Each text, moreover, addresses seriously the formative decade of American communism, the 1920s. Foster's history necessitates a return to this critical period, upon which Draper concentrated but few New Left histories probed. These histories now stand among the most accomplished accounts of United States communism in the 1920s, yet it would be fair to say that neither places Stalinism at its analytic core, although it is difficult not to see what they regard as the tragic dimensions of Foster's revolutionary life as in some senses framed by the political defeat that Stalinism designates. This takes us, inevitably, into an appreciation of the international meaning and making of communism, and the particularities of its expressions in the United States.[42]

Communist Biography and Stalinism: James P. Cannon and the Origins of the American Revolutionary Left

Few figures in the history of United States labor radicalism are more suited to chart a path in this direction than James P. Cannon. Enough can be excavated of his family background and childhood to explore how it was that a working-class youth with the capacity to make something of himself chose instead to

cast his lot with radicals and dissidents, becoming a professional revolutionary. A Midwestern, native-born Bolshevik whose parents were Irish immigrants, Cannon shared much with other centrally important individuals in the
communist milieu of the 1920s and beyond, among them William Z. Foster,
Earl Browder, and Jay Lovestone. Indeed, for a time, at different times, he
would be aligned with each of these revolutionaries in the early factional politics of the Workers' Party and its successors. If anything, he was more quintessentially American than Foster; seemingly more genuinely revolutionary
than Browder; and, by all accounts, eminently more congenial than the overly
clandestine and disingenuous Lovestone. His Rosedale, Kansas, upbringing
touched him forever with the social stamp of Main Street, in ways that Foster,
a child of the urban slum, could never have replicated. Unlike Browder,
another native Kansas radical who would rise within the Communist Party,
Cannon had the demeanor of a class-struggle militant, experiencing firsthand
the attractions and shortcomings of the pre-World War I Socialist Party of
Debs in his youth. More importantly, he served a stint as a hobo agitator in the
later to be larger-than-life army of the Industrial Workers of the World
(IWW); there a young Cannon rubbed shoulders with the likes of William D.
Haywood, Frank Little, and the revered Vincent St. John. An orator of almost
unrivaled eminence among the early communist elite, Cannon was sociable
and public, whereas Lovestone tended to cultivate the back rooms of inner-
party intrigue. Yet, for all his homespun Americanisms, rootedness in class
struggle, and experience of politics in the United States revolutionary Left,
Cannon was a confirmed internationalist, with a profound regard for what the
Bolshevik revolutionaries of 1917 accomplished and taught the radical workers
of the world.

Cannon's history, then, *is* the history of the origins of the American revolutionary Left, a red thread running from his youthful confrontation with
poverty, work, and inadequate wages through his apprenticeship and eventual
maturation as a professional communist revolutionary. He shows us how a
United States communism germinated, not in the pogroms of Eastern Europe
or in the metal works of early twentieth-century Russia (although these
locales, to be sure, did contribute ideas and experiences that fed, through
streams of immigration, the project of revolution in capitalist America), but in
the seeds of a native radicalism. As Cannon indicates, a background of alienation and disappointment rooted in class inequality, and watered with the
appeal to socialism provided by a discontented father (as well as the more
mainstream longings of a mother), proved to be a family setting in which a critique of the social order and an accommodating acquisitive individualism
clashed. Young Jim's upbringing was one in which collectivist protest con-

tended repeatedly with the appeals of church, nation, and the sociabilities of the street. Eventually won to radicalism, Cannon reveals how it was that difficult choices and the slow educational momentum that brought working-class autodidacts through various Left organizations, testing competing strategic directions for mobilization of labor's discontents, culminated, after years of development, in revolutionary communism.

Cannon's induction into the leading ranks of United States Bolshevism commenced not so much in the workplace as in the labor defense campaign: a sixteen-year-old Cannon joined the socialist movement with the 1906 agitation to free the Western Federation of Miners officials William D. Haywood and Charles Moyer from the clutches of the courts and the possibility of execution on the gallows. Cannon, like many others, cut his first mobilizing teeth on the cause of their freedom. Associated with the labor wing of the communist movement in the 1920s, Cannon had virtually no direct, card-carrying, trade-union involvement in American labor circles. Nevertheless, in the politics of class struggle he faced various baptisms by fire in the tumultuous World War I years and their immediate aftermath, as a Wobbly on his way to becoming a communist. He reentered the Socialist Party via the left wing with the Russian Revolution of 1917, and quickly found himself, somewhat by default, a major player in the emerging revolutionary underground that was struggling to reconstitute political opposition in the aftermath of the intense state repression of 1918–1920. Out of this upheaval would be born the first above-ground legal communist party in the United States, the Workers' Party, and Cannon played a pivotal role in bringing the new body into being, chairing its first convention in 1921. For the next seven years, few individuals rivaled Cannon in significance within the party of the American revolutionary communist Left.[43]

Of the leading cadre, only Charles E. Ruthenberg (who died in 1927), Lovestone, and Foster played roles comparable to Cannon's in the communist movement of the 1920s. Ruthenberg, whose authority rested on his long-standing significance in the Socialist Party, his executive and administrative ability, and his considerable time served in prison, actually lacked Cannon's breadth of involvement in early communist activities. Universally disliked across the spectrum of revolutionary leadership because of his unscrupulousness, Lovestone was approximately a decade Cannon's junior, a man who could never quite shed his background as the inveterate New Yorker, college-educated and petty bourgeois. Moreover, Lovestone, who headed the American Party for a brief period in the late 1920s, expelled Cannon for Trotskyism in 1928, only to find himself given the boot from the CP soon thereafter. Unlike Cannon, however, who remained a staunch communist revolutionary, deeply committed for the rest of his life to the United States Trotskyist movement that he had founded, Lovestone drifted (and then raced) to the right. He ended his days as an anti-Soviet Cold War spymaster, filtering operatives through the American Federation of Labor and cultivating his own intelligence operations with the CIA. Only Foster had Cannon's longevity on the Left, and he lived it out in increasingly stilted, Stalinist ways.

Cannon, then, seems a logical beginning if one wants to trace some of the paths that led a native American working-class radicalism toward communism and the United States revolutionary Left of the 1920s. That he was perhaps *the* highest ranking communist who had earned his credentials as a revolutionary in the near-mythical and resolutely American ranks of the Wobblies was an expression of this; his IWW experience was actually much deeper than that of Foster. Moreover, if we want to probe U.S. communism's wrestling with its "otherness"—its struggle to shed an insular skin as an immigrant import, the cause of Jews, Russians, Germans, Finns, and the like—Cannon again is an obvious starting point. For it was Cannon who battled against a range of naysayers to create an interface between these foreign-language Bolsheviks and the native American radicalism of the United States working class. No figure worked more diligently and more persistently to Americanize communism, to bring it out of its clandestine, alien underground into the public legal struggle that was the only vehicle capable of driving varied discontents and anti-capitalist impulses forward to a mass revolutionary party. It was Cannon who stood as the inspiration behind and the founding figure within the most successful communist mass activity of the 1920s, the International Labor Defense organization that bound native American radicals and the more oppressed immigrant workers together in common struggles.

Many roadblocks kept all of this from culminating in a successful mass party, not the least, in the end, being the Stalinization of the Comintern and the subsequent deformation of the United States Workers (Communist) Party in the mid- to late 1920s. Of all the critically placed leaders who stood as communists within the origins of the American revolutionary Left, only Cannon eventually broke decisively from this debilitating Stalinism, and for this he has suffered a rare, and lengthy, exile.[44] Cannon's formative place in the uneasy early years of U.S. communism has been shadowed by official Communist Party animosity and New Left indifference to a figure who founded the Workers' Party, but who faced expulsion before the economic collapse of the 1930s revitalized possibilities for the Left and propelled a thoroughly Stalinized party into a context of profound working-class radicalism that it was destined to squander. Returning to the origins of the American revolutionary Left via Cannon, then, can rediscover a history of labor rebellion, and turn pages of significance some have condemned as lost to our current struggles. Only by confronting how Stalinism constrained and ultimately suffocated the indigenous American revolutionary ranks that consciously gravitated to communism can we resurrect something of the meaning of the early twentieth-century working-class radicalism that remains absolutely necessary to the rebirth of the revolutionary Left. Cannon takes us in this direction.

Draper perhaps knew as much, although he could not bring himself to acknowledge it in his published pages. There is evidence, for instance, that in the first drafts of his second volume, *American Communism and Soviet Russia*, Draper followed Cannon's accents more closely than those of others. In subsequent revisions, however, pressured especially by Browder, Draper downplayed somewhat the role played by the former Wobbly who had come to be widely known as the leading Trotskyist in the United States. Draper rewrote sections to understate emphases Cannon had stressed. It was not the case, I suspect, that Draper privileged Browder (or anyone else) over Cannon, but rather that the Cold Warrior, consciously or unconsciously, had no desire to see his books read and reviewed in ways that might suggest too close an affiliation with a source that could be conceived as tainted, however highly Draper himself had come to regard Cannon's reliability. Thus the anti-communist historian covered the tracks of this informant, brushing a focus here into less prominence and changing a chapter title there so as to avoid allegations that he had been led into a dissident communist's lair.[45]

At first, Draper confessed, he had little hope that Cannon would even speak to him. Most acquaintances of Cannon's assured Draper in the 1950s that seeking out Cannon the Trotskyist was a doomed endeavor: "they were unanimously and vociferously certain that he would have none of me." But such pessimism proved wrong. As a correspondence developed between Draper and Cannon, the latter put aside his initial, somewhat taciturn, engagement with the distant historian, whom he knew to be no friend to the Left. Seeing the first Draper at work, Cannon undoubtedly grasped that for all his political biases, here was a scholar committed to evidence and marshaling it to present a narrative of the origins of United States communism, warts and all. Indeed, Cannon was under no illusions: he realized that the warts might well be painted with the bold strokes of a Cold War brush, but he was prepared to allow Draper his prejudgments, as long as they did not overwhelm the history itself. The old-time communist thus warmed to an individual with whom he shared no political common ground, but whom he came to trust in the vital activity of getting the facts right. For his part, Draper began to realize that Cannon was putting together his answers in a way that would form an invaluable commentary on the beginnings of the American communist movement. Cannon's capacity to recall events accurately soon registered with Draper:

"I learned from repeated experiences that his memory excelled by far that of his contemporaries with whom I [had] dealt in the same way." Why, Draper asked himself, did Cannon, almost alone among old-time revolutionaries, remember so well? Was it some "inherent trait of mind"? No, Draper concluded, Cannon remembered because, "unlike other communist leaders of his generation, Jim Cannon *wanted* to remember. This portion of his life still lives for him because he has not killed it within himself."[46]

Cannon's communism was alive because it had not been snuffed out by Stalinism; his memory, consequently, had not been subordinated to pressures to rewrite history, something that could not be said about either Foster or Browder, both of whom left published and unpublished accounts that confirm their unreliability as subsequent witnesses to the history that they both made and that would eventually make them. To Cannon, in contrast, there remained such a thing as truth—a revolutionary's last refuge, however uncomfortable. As difficult as it is to discern and develop, this is what I have labored to reproduce in this history of the origins of the American revolutionary Left, a project Cannon was central in developing, and to which he deserves to be restored.

Jno. Cannon & Sons

Insurance
Agency

1148 Kansas City Ave.

ROSEDALE, KANSAS

Resident Agents for The Standard Accident Insurance Co.,
of Detroit, Mich.

Bell Phone   Office. 94 Rosedale
             Res. 137X

Rosedale Roots:
Facts and Fictions

An American Birth

11 February 1890: A boy child is born in the working-class hamlet of Rosedale, Kansas. Childbirth does not occasion a great deal of fanfare in the poor industrial districts of the Greater Kansas City region, where Rosedale is situated adjacent to both of the Kansas and Missouri cities of the same name. In most working-class households, deliveries take place at home, rather than in a hospital. Neighbors help, large families rally, and a midwife undoubtedly attends at this Rosedale birth. The physician's role is almost certainly minimal, perhaps limited to reporting that a child has come safely into the world. However, even that level of involvement is unlikely, and no birth certificate is required to register the baby before the rather unwatchful eyes of the late nineteenth-century state.[1]

The parents of this newborn are recently arrived in the United States of America. The son they celebrate on this midwinter day will be as American as they are striving successfully to become. For certain "white ethnics" such as they, ultimate acculturation at this point in United States history is less a matter of citizenship's socially learned or politically bestowed credentials and more a reality of birthplace.

This is a native son who will carry his proletarian heritage, admittedly something of a choice, into the twentieth century. There it will rub up against the dominance of hegemonic powers in ways that persistently exhibit frictions and tensions: of the promise of equality tempered by injustice and material deprivation; of the lure and lore of family, so often constrained by want and need, the ties likely to be lost temporarily in the chaos of survival struggles; of labor and capital, contextualized in an ongoing battle where rural and urban mesh as development proceeds with a vehement unevenness; of a consciousness of belonging, cut to the bone by the displacements of being ever alien. The boy born with and socialized through this legacy of ambivalence will be a mix of the old and the new. He will, throughout his life, embrace orthodoxy and tradition as well as make deep commitments to fundamental change. Leaving Rosedale as a young man, this product of small-town Kansas will become an habitué of the metropolitan center (Chicago, New York, and Los Angeles), a revolutionary in a society long distanced from its eighteenth-century origins in revolution. A native son he was born, however, and a native son he would remain. This Rosedale boy is James Patrick Cannon.[2]

Fin de Siècle Context: Kansas in a World of Change

The 1890s, in which the infant Jim Cannon would grow to boyhood, was a period of profound destabilization. Cannon's birthplace, the United States, emerged as a pivotal power, becoming the premier industrial-capitalist nation in the world in 1894, turning out fully one-third of the recorded product of the globe. The business cycle nevertheless took a turn for the worse in the early 1890s; the state was challenged forcefully by an army of unruly tramps, and found itself seduced by a presidential pretender of populist persuasion. Strikes rocked the relations of capital and labor. Before his fifth birthday, a Rosedale boy would have heard talk of shootings at Carnegie's Homestead works; the pardoning of some of the Haymarket martyrs; and the infallible, salvation-like authority of Eugene Debs, who led American railwaymen—quintessential workers of the age—on a justice crusade for the laboring classes.[3] It was a time of trouble; it was a time of hope.[4]

The Kansas in which James Patrick Cannon was born was somewhat unusual. Nonetheless, it too was ravaged by change in the late nineteenth and very early twentieth centuries. The Greater Kansas City region, encompassing the border cities of Kansas City, Missouri, Kansas City, Kansas, and the adjoining enclaves of Independence, Missouri, and Rosedale, Kansas, had a history reaching back to the fur-trade era.[5] However, its dynamic growth was in the post-1860 period of economic expansion associated with the coming of railroads, and, most emphatically, the explosive upsurge of manufacturing that developed out of the 1880s and the depression of the 1890s. Productive output was paced by the meatpacking and grain/flour milling enterprises that drew on the livestock and crops of the surrounding agricultural hinterland, but leavened by coal mining and other, more obviously industrial, activity. The value of that output soared from roughly $6 million in 1890 to more than $218 million twenty years later. Located near the confluence of the Missouri and Kansas Rivers, straddling the state line, the Greater Kansas City area encompassed a territory of slightly more than seventy-five square miles in 1915: an area traversed by 25 percent of the nation's rail lines, which linked the district to every major metropolitan center in the United States. Booster publications proclaimed the Greater Kansas City region to be "The Heart of America."[6]

Yet the early heart of industrial-capitalist America could be cold indeed. In the early to mid-1880s, years of abundant rainfall sustained bumper crops in the Midwest. As railway fever added heat to the soaring land market, a speculative mania gripped town and country alike, driving property values upward in an inflationary cycle that fueled illusions of never-ending prosperity. Then, as suddenly as it had expanded, the bubble burst. Kansas was hit hard by a decade of declining rainfall, commencing in 1887–1888, and dry conditions were exacerbated by summers of scorching heat and moisture-robbing winds from the south. Crop yields declined and then shriveled to insignificance, land prices bottomed out, and many farmers faced foreclosure and destitution; 60 percent of the taxable acreage of the state was encumbered in 1890. Some eked out a marginal existence, but others gave up, their stoic resignation articulated in a stream of covered wagons heading out of the state with Conestoga canvas billowing the words, "In God we trusted, in Kansas we busted."[7]

What nature missed in its ravaging of the land, the financial institutions wanted to seize. Railroads, bankrolled by municipal and state taxes, began to raise their freight rates, which had originally protected local Kansas industry in diversified manufacturing sectors. Depression lowered over economic life in the early to mid-1890s. Particularly hard hit were a multitude of factories that existed in the shadows of large milling and meatpacking monopolies. Workplaces closed, unemployment rose, wages were cut back, living and working conditions deteriorated. Small wonder that Kansas was perhaps the core region of a United States populist revolt that raged against "the interests," and was sustained by a movement culture of programs, parties, itinerant organizers, open-air meetings, dissident newspapers, and generalized hostility to the unbridled acquisitive individualism of the age.[8]

On 12 June 1890, when young Jim Cannon was barely five months old, Topeka, Kansas, was the site of a political convention. Attended by ninety delegates representing the Farmers' Alliance, the Knights of Labor, the Farmers' Mutual Benefit Association, the Patrons of Husbandry, single-taxers, greenbackers, and the stillborn Union Labor Party, the Topeka gathering founded the People's Party. Their sights set on dethroning the reigning Republicans, the Kansas populists built coalitions, coaxed Democrats, and rallied the people. Out of the turmoil came Mary E. Lease, an indomitable Irish-American agitator who delivered 160 speeches in 1890 alone. Her reputed admonition, directed at the farmers of Kansas, to "raise less corn and more *Hell*," was a rhetorical coup, but her passionate message echoed wider oppositional meanings.[9] Two years later, Kansas voted the Wichita populist Lorenzo D. Lewelling into the governor's mansion. Lewelling railed against the robbery and enslavement of the people, deploring conventional politics as little more "than a state of barbarism."[10] As one historian of Kansas populism concluded, during the 1890s "the state served as a stage upon which the rest of the nation acted out its antagonisms, hopes, and frustrations."[11]

In the Shadow of the Irish Diaspora: England and America

For the Cannon family, Rosedale *was* this Kansas stage. It was not so much bounded by the nation as it was situated within movements and migrations of socioeconomic change associated with the English-speaking transatlantic world; at the same time, though, it was inhibited by a fundamental, and parochial, enclosure. One fragment of this process involved James Patrick Cannon's parents: John Cannon and his second wife, Ann Hackett.[12] Both were English-born children of Irish emigrants escaping the blight of the potato famine in the 1840s and 1850s. They coincidentally shared a common background in the English town of Bolton, where they were "city poor."[13] Bolton was a textile center of approximately 70,000 in 1860, associated with the traumatic changes of the Industrial Revolution.[14]

John Cannon was born on 14 January 1857 in nearby Chorley, a smaller enclave infamous for a riotous 1779 attack on one of the "dark, satanic mills" of early cotton-factory capitalism.[15] At eleven years of age Cannon left school, working a few weeks in a cabinet-making shop (the occupation at which Ann's father toiled), and later apprenticing four years with a tailor. Eventually he took up the trade of spindle flymaker,[16] a craft displaced in the final wave of technological innovations that revamped the cotton industry in the years after midcentury.[17] His apprenticeship being for nought, John Cannon settled, at the age of fifteen, for laboring jobs.

The industrial Lancashire in which Ann Hackett and John Cannon were raised was thus the archetypal locale of nineteenth-century proletarian immiseration. Over it rolled waves of intense labor-process transformation, orchestrated by powerful families of Tory mill owners.[18] With much of an expanding population made up of the dispossessed Irish—half of Bolton's population increase at mid-century came from in-migration—social dislocation rather than class solidarity was often dominant, with the attendant struggle of the state to manage various pathologies. Lancashire was thus scarred by the grim edifices and difficult adjustments of factory production and a range of regulatory welfare interventions, from the Poor Law to the institutionalization of modern policing and intrusive campaigns to improve the public health.[19] A congested demography of urban poverty, an occupational degradation composed of equal parts craft dilution and industrial paternalism, and the subterranean subordinations of ethnicity thus marked Victorian Bolton as a way station for those mobile Irish and their acclimatized offspring quick to see opportunities to be had in distant lands.

At the age of nineteen John Cannon married, and in the space of five years he fathered three children with his young wife, Kate: Edward (1877), Mary (1879), and Thomas (1882). His most constant work was as a foundry laborer; one of his brothers was an iron worker. Next to his family, John's consuming passion was the Bolton Irish Land League, where he served as secretary, organizing meetings and providing touring orators with a platform to denounce Irish oppression. John Cannon, a child of the Lancashire mill town, was nevertheless a convinced Irish Republican, a determined opponent of England's colonizing oppressions.

John Cannon's feet would never touch down on Irish soil, and even Bolton could not hold him long into adulthood. Work was seldom steady for any of the Cannon clan, and John's father, a skilled tailor noted for the fine fit of the suits he made, struck out for New York City with his wife, Catherine. Lines of communication and knowledge of family members' whereabouts and well-being were not always sure in the Cannon family circles, however. John Cannon departed for the United States in 1883, leaving Kate and the children behind in Bolton, thinking that he could make a better go of it in the new world that was now home to his father and mother. Upon arrival in New York, the Irish immigrant was disappointed to see his father living a wasted, dissolute life, in which drinking sprees were punctuated by periods of irregular return to tailoring. There was nothing for John, socially or economically, in the sprawling urban complexity of metropolitan enticements.

Making his way to the Providence, Rhode Island, vicinity, John Cannon reconnected with his foundry-working younger brother Jim; landed a job; and immersed himself in the local labor movement by joining the Knights of Labor (then at its peak) and becoming secretary of the Central Labor Council. A member of Prospect Assembly, No. 2971, a small Central Falls local of 38 carders and spinners in the mid-1880s, the congenial Cannon found the sociability of the Order attractive, especially in the period of separation from his family. He would be remembered by Providence radicals thirty years later, although his stint as a figure of note in labor-reform circles was brief. It is likely that John's stature in the memory of Rhode Island's working-class activists was enhanced by association with another Cannon, possibly John's younger brother Jim, who may have been the John T. Cannon (Bolton-born in 1867) who figured prominently in Rhode Island Lodge, No. 147, of the International Association of Machinists (IAM), which he joined in 1897 and of which he was soon elected president. This Cannon also played an active role in the American Federation of Labor-dominated Central Trades and Labor Union of Rhode Island, and was an outspoken advocate of labor-political action in the establishment of a 1902 Trades Union Economic League.[20]

His labor movement involvement facilitated by the absence of Kate and their children, John Cannon would apparently find family a brake on his later activity; he was destined not to play an ongoing role in the class struggles of the next decade. Nevertheless, his initial Providence/Central Falls sojourn, and involvement in the Knights of Labor/Central Labor Union, eased the newcomer's adaptation to his adopted land. Having settled into Rhode Island life and labor, he sent for his wife and children, who probably arrived in the United States sometime in 1885. Barely reunited, tragedy soon befell the family: Kate died in 1886.[21]

John Cannon's brother Jim had married one of two Hackett sisters, both of whom, with their mother, had emigrated to the United States from Bolton. Family ties and Old-World familiarities, not to mention a common enthusiasm for the radicalism of Irish Home Rule, brought John Cannon and Ann Hackett together. The dire predicament of a working father responsible for three children under the age of ten may have enhanced the attractiveness of his brother's sister-in-law for John Cannon. The couple married in 1887, eleven months after the death of Cannon's first wife, and around the time that John Cannon offered a toast to "the ladies" at a February social and Knights of Labor dance. John's mother, Catherine, either abandoned by her dissolute husband or liberated from responsibility for him by death or choice, moved west to Rosedale in this same period, drawn to Kansas because of the presence of four of her brothers, who had settled in Kansas City, Missouri, and nearby Shawnee County, within which Rosedale was situated. When word came that a large rolling mill or smelter might afford plenty of work, John Cannon and his brother Jim joined their mother and her brothers, moving across the country to partake of the economic bonanza that had drawn so many to the Midwest. Unfortunately, the Cannon exodus did not manage to catch even the tail-end of prosperity's promise; its timing, in 1887, could not have been worse, coinciding as it did with an economic downturn that would last a decade. The metal-working factory failed and was converted to a small foundry. In what was by then an oft-repeated disappointment in the Irishman's life, it afforded only casual employment and unskilled wages to John Cannon. His brother Jim likely returned in disillusionment to Rhode Island, joining the IAM as the nationwide depression lifted in 1897.[22] Industrial Rosedale thus looked as much the bust in the late 1880s and early 1890s as the drought-plagued farms of Kansas. The ideas and resentment that fueled the region's populist revolt found a ready reception in the Cannon household.

The Industrial Frontier

The Rosedale that drew so many Cannons to its environs in the mid- to late 1880s was but a step removed from what family members, driven by Irish destitution to the gritty slums of a mill town like Bolton, then later by constricted opportunities to the bustling metropolis of New York or the industrial sectors of Providence, must have regarded as a bucolic frontier. Originally plotted in 1872, Rosedale drew its name from the wild roses nestled in ravines and crevices of a peaceful river valley surrounded by high, tree-covered bluffs.[23] To be sure, within two decades, Rosedale undoubtedly lost much of its rustic appeal. Located a few miles southwest of downtown Kansas City, Kansas, it was physically separated from the activity and business of its much larger urban neighbor by the Kansas River and a smaller watercourse, Turkey Creek. These natural demarcations of bluffs, rivers, and small streams would, over time, be paralleled by a dense, interlocking network of rail lines, featuring tributaries of the Union Pacific, the Atchison, Topeka, and Santa Fe, the Missouri Pacific, and other systems. In the industrial core of Kansas City, known as Armourdale, clusters of large factories such as Procter & Gamble, United Zinc and Chemical, and Kansas City Structural Steel were but a few miles from Rosedale. What dominated the regional economy, though, was the massive, 207-acre complex of stockyards (only 59 acres of it under roof), situated directly north of the emerging working-class town of Rosedale, that serviced the Kansas City meatpackers—Swift's, Armour's, Cudahy's, and others. By the opening decade of the twentieth century, the slaughterhouses were butchering 70,000 head of livestock a day; the central market of the stockyards had a daily capacity of 66,000 cattle, 35,000 hogs, 34,000 sheep, and 5,000 mules and horses. A south wind would have blown no good into Shawnee Township kitchens on a hot summer day.[24]

Kansas City's population mushroomed in the decade 1880 to 1890, rising from 3,200 to 38,000, a phenomenal growth of 1,097 percent. Much of this demographic expansion was fed by migration, including an 1879 influx of southern blacks known as "Exodusters," and waves of English, Irish, Scottish, Welsh, German, and Swedish immigrants.[25] As Leon Fink has shown, by 1880 Kansas City was characterized both by the heterogeneity of its industrial population and by a marked racial/ethnic occupational hierarchy. Fully one-third of the workforce was first- and second-generation foreign born, and another quarter was African American. English, Scottish, Welsh, and German immigrants fared relatively well (although never quite attaining the privileged place of native Yankees) in the socioeconomic order. Irish Americans (42 percent unskilled) and blacks (86 percent unskilled) occupied the bottom rungs of the labor-force ladder, working as teamsters, porters, hod carriers, and other chore-runner jobs.[26]

Rosedale rode this general population wave: it grew from just under 2,000 in 1895 to a turn-of-the-century population of 3,000 to 4,000; in 1915 it claimed 6,700 residents. In 1895, approximately 44 percent of Rosedale's residents were foreign born. Among them, apparently, Irish laborers figured prominently, though they were concentrated on the lower rungs of the socioeconomic ladder.[27] When two demographers noted in 1936 that "[t]he shift from agriculture to industry as the stimulator of migration has thus saddled upon certain industrial centers of Kansas two of their most perplexing problems—racial conflicts and unemployed foreign workers," they were focusing on social tensions that had their origins in the settlement patterns of early Rosedale.[28]

It was precisely this configuration of race and class issues that animated a politics of urban city-building and social reform over the course of the 1880s in Kansas City, Kansas. A maverick Irish-Catholic stonemason, Thomas F. Hannan, built a powerful machine of civic improvement by drawing on support from the Knights of Labor and Republican and Democratic Party forces attuned to the possibilities of biracial electoral tickets that fused the interests of white ethnics and African Americans. Sustained in the aftermath of the class tensions associated with the Great Southwestern Strike on the region's railroads, pitting Jay Gould against coalitions of labor reformers and trade unions, Hannan's progressive initiatives pledged loyalties to working-class organizations in ways that spilled over positively into the black community. By the time of Cannon's birth in 1890, however, this alliance had largely run its course. With the class voice of the Knights of Labor quieted by the 1890s, Hannan's machine increasingly took on the trappings of a gang dedicated to the politics of ethnic brokerage. The cry of "Hannan and the Irish" sounded an increasingly narrow commitment to patronage, culminating in a scandal of skyrocketing debt associated with municipal works projects.[29]

The civic boosterism unleashed by Thomas Hannan registered only lightly in Rosedale. Electric illumination graced the borough's streets in 1890, but the neighborhood was still something of an outpost. It had no theaters, parks, or high school, and remained something of a winding valley and craggy hillside, despite its population of immigrant and laboring people dependent on the wages of meatpacking plants, factory labor, and work in the yards of railways and mills. There was no doubt an abundance of squalor, if the cramped frame houses of nearby Armourdale, sitting on twenty-five-foot lots, were at all comparable to those of Rosedale. As late as 1915, only 44 percent of Armourdale's homes were connected to water systems, and a mere 10 percent were linked to sewers. Refuse littered back alleyways, outhouses were inadequately and irregularly cleaned or emptied, and streets were often muddy or cluttered with filth. In Rosedale, though, unlike Armourdale, there was an escape to the open air and undeveloped land. To many new arrivals, whatever the shortcomings of its housing stock and lack of amenities, Rosedale would have had certain charms. John Cannon defended the place like a seigneurial knight, resisting the inevitable annexation of the neighborhood to Kansas City, a colonizing conquest that would eventually swallow Rosedale whole, leaving it, late in the twentieth century, criss-crossed with freeways.[30]

Family Fortunes

Settling in Rosedale, John Cannon and Ann Hackett wasted no time in starting a second family. The birth of their first daughter, Agnes, in 1887, was followed by the arrival of young Jim, in 1890, and, three years later, Phillip. The couple were the same age, thirty-five, when this last child was born, and their lives were undoubtedly difficult. Anything but affluent, the family now consisted of six children under the age of sixteen, an entourage that must have kept Ann's nose very much to the domestic grindstone. Jim recalled that the Rosedale house was quite cramped, laid out "railroad style, with the kitchen in the center of the front room." It lacked running water, which had to be hauled from a neighbor's well; the floors were soft, uncovered pine; and the routine responsibility of keeping the modest domicile clean and the household functioning undoubtedly consumed a large portion of the day and evening for Ann. Jim remembered with bitterness how she would ring the mop out, with hands scarred by protruding floor nails and back bent after repeated trips to the outside well. John Cannon found that work was intermittent and often seasonal, and one later family member recalled talk of his stints as a brickmaker, punctuated by winter unemployment. Ann apparently made her husband promise not to apprentice Jim to the trade, for she wanted no part of saddling any future daughter-in-law with a provider forced to "warm his feet by the stove" during long, cold months of idleness. Other comment suggests that John also worked as a carpenter, but this, too, was a trade disrupted by seasonal layoffs.

How much of this was the later construction of memories tilted in particular directions by a politics of class solidarity is impossible to tell, but Cannon came to embellish the oppressions of the moment, attributing his father's routine periods of unemployment to the blacklist: "My father was the first to be laid off and last to be hired because of his activities in the Knights of Labor," he told Harry Ring in 1973. There is, however, no indication that John Cannon played any role in Rosedale's single Local Assembly of the Knights of Labor, which had a brief lifespan from 1884 to 1888; it would have offered Jim's father scant opportunity for leadership, and there is little reason to think that he was sufficiently activist and militant to warrant employer harassment in the mid-1890s. A more likely cause of his persistent joblessness was the severe economic downturn of 1893–1897, which would have brought activity in the building trades to a halt. Nevertheless, young Jim did accompany his father to work-sites, where he saw his fill of rough labor and demanding supervisors. It was there that a heavy board smashed the child's right thumb. The local Rosedale doctor was insufficiently skilled to do anything but amputate, and all that remained of Jim's thumb was a short stump; proximity to an urban hospital would almost certainly have resulted in the appendage being saved.[31]

Limited means and material insecurities, compounded by the sheer number of mouths to feed, backs to clothe, and accommodations to sustain, must have exacerbated traditional stepchild/stepmother tensions, especially given Ann Cannon's character, in which emotional reserve dominated.[32] Within a few years, all three of John Cannon's children from his first marriage struck out on their own.[33] The eldest, Edward, possibly secured work in the Kansas City area (graduating from grocery clerk to collector/solicitor, and passing through the insurance business of his father); the youngest two, Mary and Tom, settled in Oakland, California. Young Jim had only the vaguest of recollections of his half-siblings as children, and in future years his contact with them was negligible to none.[34]

Obviously tired of eking out a bare living as a laborer, John Cannon shifted occupational gears in the mid-1890s. No longer would he work for others in low-paying and insecure jobs. John Cannon was commissioned as a notary public in 1894. He opened an insurance office and real estate business on Rosedale's main business thoroughfare, but his occupational eclecticism eventually reached into loans and collections; the elder Cannon may even have sat as a police judge and justice of the peace for a brief time. During the entirety of Jim Cannon's adolescent and early adult years, John Cannon, who would retire in 1918, lived his work days along a short stretch of Kansas City Avenue between his residence and his business office. His income could not have been large, but the pay was no doubt the equal of anything that John could earn working with his hands, the toil was not as taxing, and the cash flow was a little more regular. Also, his sons might learn a profession; indeed, there is an indication that by 1910 John Cannon's firstborn, Edward, was working with him in the insurance and real estate business. Jim's younger brother Phil also worked at the Cannon real estate business in 1909–1910, living in the family residence and clerking beside his father at the Cannon and Sons office. However, in the mid-1890s, all of this was a decade and a half away. As John Cannon switched from the uncertainties and class-marked daily rigors of physical toil, in the building trades or foundry shops of Rosedale, to the small-scale entrepreneurialism of handling documents and deeds, earning his living through his contacts and with his tongue, there was no doubt an expectation that life would take a turn for the better. The Cannon family, with half of its children now flown from the nest and its provider taking on a new career, appeared poised on the benign edge of more prosperous times.

Appearances proved deceiving. John Cannon's timing was, again, not the best. The middle of the 1890s depression was an unlikely moment to cash in on the land and housing markets. John was sufficiently parochial (he was known as a Rosedale "patriot") to limit his business to Rosedale's constrained offerings, which were largely tapped out by the turn of the century, and as a small operator he lacked the resources to challenge the larger, Kansas City-based competitors. It is possible that he continued to work as a laborer from time to time. His first years as an independent, then, hardly changed material circumstances for John Cannon, his wife, Ann, and their children. There is no indication, for instance, that at this time they were able to cross the economic threshold into home ownership, thus freeing the family from the fear of a landlord's threatening knock and upgrading the makeshift accommodations that were always regarded as a stepping-stone to more comfortable surroundings.[35]

A Boy's Life

Given these circumstances, for young Jim Cannon, the first decade of his life was therefore something of a contradiction. He knew poverty and economic hardship, but apparently suffered little. Indeed, young Jim reveled in the life of a carefree child. The dominant influence in Jim's life was his mother, Ann, whose devout Catholicism was translated to her son not through dogma and scriptural devotion, but as a sense of obligation: to do right, to treat people well, to practice honesty and decency. To be sure, Jim attended parochial school after one was built in Rosedale when he was nine or ten ("My God, you don't go to a school with Protestants when you can go to a school with your own kind!"); Ann and her children belonged to the Holy Name Parish Catholic Church, and Jim was an altar boy. Of these years he later recalled, with some derision, "Religion every day of the week and twice on Sunday." Cannon's sister Agnes and his brother Phil "remained devout Catholics till the end of their lives," but Jim was to become more his father's son. John Cannon, only nominally a Catholic, was something of a "maverick who didn't like anybody telling him what to think, not even the priest."[36]

To a boy not yet ten, however, the constant presence of religion during the school year was something that could be shed, like shoes, with the coming of summer. This was when Jim, as a child, *lived*. His world was one of meandering creeks, walks in the hills, and outings along the railroad tracks. Leaps off of train trestles, spontaneous foot races, or feet sinking into the cool slime of a brook on a hot summer day were the very stuff of young Jim's everyday life when school was out.[37] One comrade saw Cannon as "made in the cast of Huck Finn." To know how to engineer a swimming hole; to appreciate the place of an aggie in a game of marbles; to fashion a bean shooter from the fork of a sapling and strips cut from old tire inner tubes; to build a fishing pole from a rusty safety pin, some string, and a stick—these were skills never forgotten and not to be lost to the march of progress and maturity. Cannon's narrative repertoire included accounts of venerable Rosedale characters, such as the memorable "Baldy" Keegan, a boy with no hair, and he was known to be full of quips and oratorical tricks on a par with those of Mark Twain.[38] Cannon left a memory of these formidable years in the form of an unfinished, fictionalized tale titled *Iron City*. Penned sometime in the late 1950s, its story line bears a remarkable resemblance to the Cannon family's migrations and meanings, and buried within its understandings of how a child experienced his early years are suggestions about important themes in the making of a native son.[39]

Iron City opens with an image of Rosedale's beginnings, arising "in a blaze of glory . . . in the wave of industrial expansion that moved westward in the late Seventies." At the center of the drama was the Keystone Steel Company, which erected a rolling mill on a site purchased surreptitiously from an unsuspecting local skinflint. For a decade, "Iron City" prospered, only to fall victim to "the panic of '83." The Keystone Steel Company failed; a monopolistic competitor gutted the plant, moved the stock, and reduced production to "a small foundry employing only a few hundred as against the thousands of the old working force." Immigrants drawn to available work vanished; partly paid-for lots were foreclosed on; construction came to an abrupt halt, leaving homes half-built; gardens gave way to weeds. The Irish had to stay, too poor to move.[40] Periodically the promise of a railway shop rumored to be coming to town lifted speculative spirits anew, but the hopes of an economic score foundered on the failure of any such development to materialize: "Iron City became an ugly suburb of the thriving metropolis on the river across the state line. A poor man's town, it was called. A town for Shanty Irish, for Negroes, for the property-poor Welsh aristocrats."[41]

One of the Irish laborers drawn to this Rosedale-like setting was Hugh Dailey, Cannon's prototype for his father, John: "He was one of those credulous and impulsive Irishmen . . . born to lead forlorn hopes and fight for lost causes. His genius was for the impractical, for the inexpedient, the unprofitable. . . . He was concerned about injustice even when it interfered, as it continually interfered, with his making a good living. . . . In short, a dreamer and a sad misfit in the social scheme of dog eat dog." Dailey had been a leader of the Irish Land League in the old country, but fled his homeland under threat of arrest. His 1883 steerage crossing of the Atlantic was a hard one. Disembarking in New York City, Hugh endured hunger and police brutality, and worked sporadically, but could not bring himself to report to his anxious old-country family, keen to hear word of the successes that had yet to brighten his horizon. Eventually, with a few jobs under his belt and some money saved, Hugh moves to Rhode Island to take up a position as a spindlemaker, where his prosperity allows him to secure passage to America for his mother and two younger brothers. Hugh becomes a leader of the Knights of Labor, "an active agitator for its hazy ideal of the workmen's coming day." He marries Sophie, "a delicate blue-eyed colleen who worked in one of the textile mills," and they soon have a baby girl. After leading an unsuccessful strike, Hugh, blacklisted in Rhode Island, travels to Iron City, assured by a brother that work will be available. Of course, the Dailey family arrives after the boom has gone bust, "newcomers" who can neither achieve a social station nor a modicum of prosperity, forever stigmatized as those who missed out on the bonanza of Rosedale's beginnings.

It is here that Cannon's fictionalized self, Joe Dailey, is born, in the rented family home—a ramshackle abode plagued by winter draughts and merciless summer sun, invaded by flies and mosquitoes from the air, dirt and dust from the ground, and the smoke and din of the nearby railway. An unpainted structure, its windows and doors sagging, the nearest water a common well serving a dozen families 100 yards distant, the home was meant by Hugh Dailey to be temporary, until his lot in life improved. But it never did, and the indignities of poverty weigh heavily on Mrs. Dailey: "Hers was an undying ambition to live in a home of her own on higher ground, stoutly-built and painted and cozy-looking, with a well or cistern in her own yard and a bit of ground for a garden, and no landlord to call for rent and threaten eviction." She rails against her lowly place: "I won't raise my children in the mud with the railroad for a back yard," she declares defiantly, demanding that Hugh "bestir himself and quit trying to save the world until he had made some decent provision for his own family."

Young Joe sympathizes with his mother's daily drudgery, and does his best to help her with the chores. It is a proud moment when he grows strong enough to carry the water from the well, saving his mother's back a few of its aches, and he imagines that he will someday carry the burdens of the family on the shoulders of his affluent manhood, providing for Sophie Dailey a cottage on the hill. Joe never really understands his mother's grievances, though, for he knows no other houses, and he is in their shanty little enough. He particularly finds her antipathy to the creek unfathomable: "In summertime the mud was cool and soft to his bare feet and, so far as he could see, the proximity to the creek was a decided advantage. He was there most of the time, fishing or swimming, brown and naked in the sun. Life's fun and adventure were there; it was handy, he thought, to live so near."

Indeed, Turtle Creek is the center of Joe Dailey's universe. The site of drownings and other dangers, the creek is nevertheless alluring. Home to snakes, fish, frogs, and the locale of cool, refreshing depths in which teenage boys doff their clothes and, the protocols of decency be damned, frolic in the age-old practice of nude bathing, Turtle Creek is off-limits to "babies" and girls. It constitutes a rite of passage to be negotiated if one is ever to enter the "conditional citizenship" and "free spirit fraternity" of boyhood independence.[42] Joe's mother eases her son into the uses of the creek, first letting him fish with older boys, but refusing to humor his desire to parade his paltry catch through her kitchen and into her skillet. "I won't have the smell of Turtle Creek in my house," she scoffs. Once he masters fishing, Sophie Dailey knows her adolescent offspring will be "bathing," the act having the "emphatic disapproval" of Joe's rather austere-minded and uncompromising father. Joe is not long in breaking the taboo, succumbing to the banter and daring of the swimming hole. When a telltale sunburn, exposed by his irascible sister, informs his mother that the creek has indeed claimed her boy, Joe feels his time of retribution is upon him. His mother's scolding is followed by promises of a patriarchal thrashing when Mr. Dailey returns for the day from his foundry job. Before that feared arrival, though, Joe's mother skims cream from the milk crock and rubs a cool, soothing lotion over his burning skin. With the household asleep, she awakes to apply another home remedy, and the next morning she strikes a pact with her errant son, extending him the privilege of "bathing" as long as he takes care to keep out of the deep water until he has mastered swimming. "And we won't let your father know," she concludes, "you're getting big enough to take care of yourself and some day, maybe, you'll be saving us all from drowning." The bond between an immigrant mother and her native son was forged in secret alliances and shared recognitions. Ann Cannon clearly regarded Jim's ability to take on the creek and win, or at least battle it to a draw, as a life-course passage. In the face of her husband's material failures, she gave young Jim a sense that he could succeed where his father dared not go.[43]

In the story, Joe's father never relented in his refusal to countenance Joe's relation to the creek: it was "no place for a boy to play, winter or summer."

Somewhat out of touch with his son's daily activities, Hugh apparently failed to grasp that the boy was on and in the creek as much as any youngster in Shanty-town. His wife never disabused him of his innocence, and neither did Joe, who borrowed and cajoled skates from other boys for the price of a loaned sled. As he grew older, his daring increased: bonfires were built on the frozen stream, and on warm winter days, the ice weakening and bending, he skipped across the creek, daring others to follow in his tracks. On one occasion he fell through, and plunged into the icy water. Afraid to face his father's wrath, he stripped naked and partially dried his clothes at a bonfire on the bank of the creek, his friends howling their derision. Joe Dailey was twelve years of age as he stood shivering on the banks of the ice-bound stream that winter day, where the longest segment of *Iron City* (chapter 3, entitled "Turtle Creek") is about to end. Chapter 4 is little more than a two-page detour, an unfinished account of Prohibition and the saloons of Rosedale. There Cannon's "fiction" comes to a close.

What are we to make of these facts and fictions of Jim Cannon's childhood? On the one hand, it is apparent that the divide separating the genres is not large; indeed, they blur into one another. *Iron City* is so transparently autobi-ographical that in rare places, Cannon confuses the fictional Sophie Dailey with his own mother, calling her Ann. It is perhaps not insignificant that this occurs when he is recounting how a mother protected a son from a father's wrath, ensuring that her son's freedom would not be restrained by a man whose principled refusal to give ground on large matters of politics seemed to turn to rigidity with respect to his relations with his son, and the rules that governed that relationship. Equally important is the contextualization of this mother-son intimacy, a setting of poverty occasioned by the inadequacies of a father who never quite attained the status of male breadwinner.[44] In this sense, *Iron City* may well open out into the facts of Cannon's childhood as revealingly as any other source. Yet, it is equally apparent that there are some fictionalized constructions, embellishments, and distortions associated with Cannon's childhood that were undoubtedly products, not so much of overt lies or even mistaken impressions, as of understandable presentations of the past. To sift through these facts and fictions is to place the accent on a particular concep-tion of Cannon's Rosedale roots, one that appreciates two features about the complexity of James Patrick Cannon's childhood and his early relations with his parents.

Meanings

The first feature addresses Cannon's place as a native son. It was a background he could not shake—indeed, he made no effort to. This is not to say he was not conflicted by his origins. In later life Cannon consciously presented Rosedale in terms largely of its limitations. "God deliver me from small towns!" he exclaimed to Harry Ring in 1973, "I have no nostalgia for the place either as a piece of geography or as a small town." Cannon's only connection to Rosedale was slowly snuffed out, it seemed to him late in life, with his family's inexorable passing from the scene, as parents, aunts and uncles, cousins, and his full brother and sister died. "My own sister never got out of Rosedale," he lamented, adding that the world of Main Street had narrowed to "neighbors, friends, the people they liked and people they didn't like, the grocery store, the pool hall, the church, and a few other institutions." For Cannon, civilization was foreign to this milieu. "I can't imagine a sanely organized society perpetuating such an outmoded form of life as the small town," he concluded definitively. "The terrible limitedness!"[45]

There could be no political, scientific nostalgia for such a place, and Cannon would broach none. Nevertheless, fifteen years or so before posing such a condemnation, Cannon took the trouble to craft a fictional narrative of his childhood that was nothing if not nostalgic about a "piece of geography" such as "Turtle Creek," a thinly veiled pseudonym for the Turkey Creek that young Jim lived with so intimately for the first years of his life, and remembered with deep, symbolic fondness. In later years, Cannon never advocated Rosedale, but in his positionings and polemics Rosedale's homespun, experiential, deeply materialized midwestern American commonsense would often filter through arguments and articulations, voiced in a Missouri-Kansas border twang and drawing upon the wellspring of Rosedale lore, lending sociopolitical comment the authority of a rare revolutionary who was unmistakably a native son. He always spoke fondly of the Kansas motto, *Ad Astra Per Aspera* ("To the stars by hard ways"), and his speech was peppered with Rosedalian aphorisms such as, "A flood is as bad as two fires," undoubtedly learned in the arduous experiences of everyday life.[46] As his son Carl recalled at a memorial in 1973, Jim was a storyteller: "His tales came right out of Rosedale, Kansas, and were about things he had seen and done while a boy there."[47] A native son was, on many levels, not something to improve upon.

There were, however, realms that Cannon's later political commitments certainly structured in particular ways, especially those that related directly to his working-class background and the manner in which it could be credentialed with subtle shifts and accents. This conditioned Jim Cannon's facts and fictions as they have been elaborated on in this chapter. The central figure here was John Cannon, a father whose occupation, from the time Jim was four years of age, was that of a marginal real estate broker and insurance agent. John had had, to be sure, a surfeit of working-class occupations in his early life, none of which secured him steady employment, and it is certain that he gave a year or so during his Rhode Island sojourn to the labor movement of Providence in the 1880s. It is striking, though, that in all the interviews done with James Patrick Cannon, with all the references to his working-class father, John Cannon was never once identified as a real estate agent and insurance broker. Cannon's novel-like account of Hugh and Sophie Dailey stresses a father's failures to provide a home and an exit from poverty, as it fictionalizes his mother's prodding, even nagging, of her husband to secure a better life for her and the children. Cannon never mentioned this side of his mother to any interviewer, yet this obviously partially explains John Cannon's occupational movement into the ranks of the pettiest of men of the market. The more salient truth, however, was the fictional cloak that Cannon clearly did his best to drape over his father's working-class past.

No doubt Jim also exaggerated John Cannon's labor activism, the better to accentuate a parable of familial resistance to capitalist oppression. John Cannon was a man of radical, developing socialist conviction in the 1890s, but he lived his politics of class in the realm of ideas rather than at the point of production. It would be a practice of class that his son would also follow; it was no slight on John Cannon's convictions or his commitments to recognize this, but clearly Jim Cannon found it more comfortable to present his father in a slightly different light, as a man who, if fiction is to be believed, developed little intimate connection to his son during Jim's childhood years. The poverty within which Cannon fictionalized the Dailey household of *Iron City* probably captured something of the difficult straits the Cannon family found itself in during the years immediately following Jim's birth, but it is unlikely that conditions were quite as bad as this literary account suggests.

Just as Jim left out a part of his father's history (a previous wife, and their three children, for instance), he added dimensions to the story that could well have served his plot line. The loss of his thumb, widely believed to have been work-related in the radical circles in which Jim later traveled, was probably not, in fact, a consequence of something that happened on any paying job. That Cannon himself seldom recounted how the thumb was crushed, and then amputated, suggests that it was not at all easily adapted to an allegory of capitalism's rapaciousness. More likely, the accident, which happened when Jim was quite young and in his father's care, occasioned tense, possibly acrimonious, relations within the Cannon household; Ann would have been greatly upset by her son's pain and disfigurement. She might forgive her husband much, but a boy's suffering would not have sat well with her. Fact and fiction thus fuse, in complicated ways, as we unravel the childhood experiences of James Patrick Cannon.

Cannon's fictionalized account of his Rosedale roots ends on a somber note. *Iron City*'s core third chapter concludes with Joe Dailey facing the end of his "Turtle Creek" freedom: "He did not know it then, but the sterner duties of life were calling. The frolics of the following winter on the ice took place without him. Joe had become a worker."[48] As childhood passed from adolescence to early manhood, James Cannon's world reached beyond the creek, where the discoveries of youth were both bitter and sweet.

Youth's Discoveries

Mothers and Fathers and Adolescent Work

Ann Cannon died in 1904. No older than forty-seven, she had lived a hard life. It was her fate never to see her modest aspirations realized, or, at best, to experience them only partially and briefly. Her disappointments would have been evident to young Jim Cannon, who was a mere fourteen years old at the time of his mother's passing, and they no doubt nurtured a sense of injustice that eventually turned against wider issues of inequality, unfairness, and victimization. For the moment, though, Jim Cannon's hurt was a personal one.

That John Cannon's move into insurance and real estate did not pay large and immediate dividends was evident in his son's early entry into the workforce. In the summer of 1902, with school out, it was arranged, through a friend of the family who worked as a foreman at one of the Armourdale meatpacking plants, to secure Jim a job. Hopping a streetcar, the boy made his way to the 7:00 a.m. "shape-up" on the riverside docks, where people milled about, waiting for their names to be called. Stepping up politely, Jim was asked how old he was. After answering truthfully, "Twelve, sir," Jim got an apologetic response of, "Can't hire you. Come back when you're sixteen." Cannon insisted that he was doing nothing more than what he had been taught at home: "My parents were very honest people. They paid great attention to not lying and not stealing. That's not right according to the Church. Upon my return home I told my mother what happened and I never knew whether she felt more disappointed that I didn't get the job[,] because we needed the money[,] or whether she was prouder of my honesty." Young Jim had a summer's reprieve, but the scruples that kept him out of waged work were apparently set aside the next fall, when the routine was followed again, with Jim stating that he was six-teen and landing employment. For ten hours a day, every day but Sunday, Jim labored in the packinghouses, employed for two years at, alternatively, Swift's and Armour's. At first he opened and closed the large iron double doors to the coolers where meat was stored, but he soon graduated to all manner of other work, including a stint on "the hog's bed," where they "made use of all parts of what once had been a pig, even the bristles, tails and snouts; everything, as they used to say, except the squeal."[1]

Kansas City, Kansas, ranked as the second largest meatpacking center in the world in the opening decade of the twentieth century, its eight slaughterhouses processing $152 million worth of livestock annually and employing 12,500 workers—male, female, and child.[2] A boy's wages were a drop in the bucket of this local industry, capitalized at roughly $20 million, but they were crucial to the survival of many Kansas City families. A portion of young Jim's wages, which must have hovered around $7.50 a week (and certainly would not have topped $12.00), may well have contributed to the domestic economy; by 1905, Jim's father owned his home for the first time in his life, having purchased the modest domicile at 1709 Kansas City Avenue where he would reside for much of the early twentieth century. Ann's death occasioned her husband's temporary move to Rosedale's nearby Mill Street, where he shared accommodations with his mother for a part of 1904, while his daughter Agnes retained the family house on Kansas City Avenue. Jim's grandmother continued to live with her son and grandchildren when they relocated back to 1709 Kansas City Avenue in 1905, and no doubt shouldered some of the domestic tasks that had so bur-dened her daughter-in-law.[3] At seventy years of age, she could not have kept house with the fastidiousness of Ann, nor was this Irish matriarch likely to have been as indulgent with Jim and his siblings. It was not a happy time for a fifteen-year-old boy, and work offered few prospects. "I never had a job I was interested in or wanted to work up in," Cannon recalled, confessing that, like most teenage workers in meatpacking, he changed employment frequently.[4] After his spell at Swift's and Armour's, Jim ostensibly found work on the Mis-souri, Kansas, and Texas (KT, or Katy) Railroad, where the hours were longer than those of the slaughterhouses (seventy hours a week) and the seniority sys-tem locked him into night shifts. Years later, he told Ray Dunne and Farrell Dobbs, "You know, I went to work on the Katy. I was young, I was new, I was green. I had a night job. It was all you could get . . . when you were starting, and if you worked real hard and pleased the boss, and didn't ask for a raise too often, one day you'd get a day job."[5] Lesson One of the workplace came quickly: bow-ing and scraping got you little more than a change of venue for continued bow-ing and scraping. Jim did not linger long at the railyards, and sometime during this period found six months' labor in the printing sector. Again, the stint was night work, with Jim serving as a galley boy for the linotype operators, shuffling between the printers and proofreaders with setup print and corrections.[6]

However, with his days now his own, and wages to pay his way, Jim was free to pursue pleasures that his mother would have forbidden. Even before her death, he was becoming a handful, "willful and resistant" to the point of being difficult to control. He took up with a crowd of less-than-angelic youths, whose idea of a productive day was to hitch a ride on the back of the streetcar and lounge about the pool hall, perhaps cadging a taste of beer now and then from Rosedale's tavern clientele.[7] "Among [his] derelictions," Cannon later confessed to Theodore Draper, was membership in the Fraternal Order of Eagles, where the attractions of various insurance protections paled in comparison to "the club room." There Rosedale's "regular fellows" gathered, a congregation not of church and YMCA, but of saloon and billiard parlor. A sanctuary for male bonding at the lower end of the class hierarchy, the Eagles lodge was a place where "a deserving brother could get a glass of beer and play a game of pinochle in prohibition territory without fear of interference by the constables who respected the political influence of our noble order." Jim clearly knew the scene, and he also became quite proficient with a pool cue, as well as earning a reputation as a local cardsharp.[8] He was going nowhere fast, and this no doubt created problems at home, where his father and grandmother must have tired of his comings and goings and worried about his influence on younger brother Phil. His older sister, Agnes, following in her mother's footsteps as a devout Catholic, was likely impossibly censorious. Two of his aunts, Agnes and Emma, tried to exert a positive influence, but soon gave up in despair. To make matters worse, John Cannon, by then aged fifty, took another wife, Frances, aged thirty-nine, and they promptly had a son, John (later to be known as Jack), who was born in 1908.[9] Destined to be short-lived, John Cannon's third marriage would not last through the next state census, in 1915, but his courtship of Frances made him less available for Jim in the years immediately following Ann's death.

By this point, the rather rebellious teenager had probably already had enough of family women replacing his mother. Whatever the climate of his home life, Jim moved out on his own, finding accommodations in a series of railroad boarding houses along the Kansas City Avenue/Bluff Street intersection adjacent to his father's insurance offices (where he apparently worked briefly as a clerk in 1906) and the Cannon family home. "I would never have been a pool hall bum if my mother had been living, I'm sure," he later speculated, emphasizing how forlorn his life was at that time. "But I was on my own, then, very unhappy, melancholy, at loose ends."[10]

Work and the wages of sin provided little solace for Jim Cannon. He began to look to books and magazines for a window into a wider world, where the meanings of life consisted of more than an eight-ball pocketed with panache. He discovered the public library in Kansas City, Missouri, crossing the state line to spend hours in its reading rooms (as a Kansas resident he could not obtain a borrowing card), and he scouted second-hand bookstores, devouring everything he could get his hands on, developing a vocabulary and an ability to consume serious literature that marked him as "unique in the gang I was with." It was during this period, living first at home and then boarding out, that he began, for perhaps the first time, to know something about his father and to appreciate his ideas.

Early Encounters with Socialism

John Cannon and his wife Ann had shared almost nothing politically except their attachment to the cause of Irish Home Rule.[11] For Ann this was an almost instinctual politics of opposition, aligned comfortably with the Irish-situated Roman Catholic Church. John Cannon, in contrast, pushed this advocacy in ever-widening circles, being, in his son's eyes, "a natural sympathizer with every kind of underdog movement." He read works such as Edward Bellamy's *Looking Backward* (1888), and took their utopian socialist message to heart. Ann had no such inclinations, opposing socialism because it countered church teachings. As John moved with the radical tide of populist Kansas—aligning with Debs at the time of the great Pullman strike in 1894, endorsing Bryan during the 1896 campaign, and opting for Debs again four years later, declaring himself a socialist as he cast his 1900 presidential vote—Ann made sure that her children did not absorb the dangerous ideas of her husband. John eventually joined a small nucleus of about a dozen Rosedale radicals in the Socialist Party local. Many, like Jim's father, were struggling businessmen, who had graduated from a school of proletarian hard knocks to offer a working-class service, such as an ice-cream or lunch parlor. John Cannon subscribed to socialist publications (*The International Socialist Review, Wilshire's Magazine,* and, most importantly, *The Appeal to Reason*) and was one of those many stalwarts who used their spare time for "talkin' socialism" and their spare change to subsidize the movement. One of the classic "Jimmie Higginses" of the movement, John Cannon hawked socialist papers, set up chairs for meetings, and orchestrated speaking tours for SP national speakers' bureau figures such as Kate Richards O'Hare and Luella Twining.

Comrades in the movement, some of whom met John Cannon in Rosedale after his son had risen to prominence in the revolutionary Left, were impressed with how Jim had been "raised in a radical family." They clearly revered a genuine native son of socialism's American heartland. Max Shachtman, for instance, remembered John Cannon as "a fine sterling militant," whose socialism was a "religion" that elicited complete and total dedication, "night and day and every week in the year. And Cannon was raised in that atmosphere." This was based in fact, of course, but it ignored the apparent lack of socialist influence John Cannon had over Jim's brother and sister, and sidestepped the fact that Cannon actually learned of much of his father's labor and socialist activities only later in life. All of Jim's engagement with his father's dissident politics took place after Ann Cannon's death. One suspects that father and son went through some difficult estrangements, including Jim moving out on his own; it was not until then that his father introduced him to Bellamy and provided him with access to the socialist press. "My father was a socialist but he didn't convert me directly," Cannon later acknowledged. "The way he converted me was to have all the socialist papers come to the house." From there Jim graduated to Jack London and Upton Sinclair, often reading their works in serialized form. "Being a packinghouse boy," *The Jungle* (1906) "had a natural appeal," he later remembered. Cannon would claim in 1963 that Sinclair's muckraking account was "the first socialist book I ever read," adding that it "made the deepest impression on me of them all." Jim's appetite for London was also voracious, and he was especially drawn to *The People of the Abyss* (1904) and *The Iron Heel* (1908).[12] His early reading, less scientific and sociological than that of counterparts such as William Z. Foster, highlighted the more rapacious sides of capitalism and the inevitability of a proletarian Prometheus rising up in vengeance to attempt a righting of the wrongs of industrial injustice.[13]

The transition from mother's boy to father's son was a life shift associated with the gendered movement from the nurture and nature associated with home and an environment of play (sustained, of course, by hard domestic toil) to the world of dirty, poorly paid waged work and the politics of varied socialisms, and it was not made as an immediate leap. Rather, it evolved over a matter of years, a period of reading and working in which Jim Cannon wrestled with his mother's legacy of religious convictions and commitments to the values of decency and honesty; the alienating and taxing exactions of largely unskilled and uninteresting labor; the profane draw of the gang and the pool hall; the sensual lure of the printed page and the wider worlds that beckoned from it; and the promise of a New Jerusalem, however it was envisioned coming, that emanated from the newspapers in his father's home, socialist meetings, and radical speeches. It may have been the case that, discovering the lure of politics, as a teenager Jim was drawn briefly to the urban machine of the Kansas City, Missouri, Democratic Party bosses Tom and James Pendergast, whose mixture of patronage, paternalism, and progressive reform was warmly received in the riverfront stockyards. Like the Missouri-born U.S. president Harry Truman, Cannon once supposedly confessed, he had been "scooped up by the Pendergast machine for a while." Still, the "radical streak in his upbringing" rescued him from a life in corrupt, mainstream politics.[14]

It was relatively easy for Jim to come to his father's politics via his mother's religion, "Christian socialism" being a major wing of the radical movement.[15] Religion was a foundation of workers' lives, and Cannon recalled, from his days as a galley boy, hearing two printers discuss a lecture of the freethinker Robert G. Ingersoll. Ingersoll's agnosticism registered with one of the men, whom Jim heard say bravely, "I do not believe there is a supreme being whom men call God." Cannon equated this with declaring, "I don't believe the sun will rise tomorrow," and adding, for good measure, "Religious belief was very widespread, not necessarily active, but it was widespread." As Jim navigated his way into left-wing circles, he embraced religious socialism as a way of keeping the Christian ethics of his mother central to his worldview, considering himself a "Christian socialist" up to the age of twenty-one. He found the fit of religion and socialism somewhat ill-suited, though, especially as he grappled with the more philosophical questions posed by a resolutely materialist approach to existence. The turning point came in 1911 with a two-part Kansas City lecture on science and socialism by the famous socialist author and orator, Arthur M. Lewis. "His specialty was linking together the Darwinian theory of organic evolution and the Marxist theory of social revolution, culminating in revolution," Cannon remembered. "That's the first I had ever heard of it," he continued, "and I've never been the same since. I was raised as a Roman Catholic and he started me looking into this question of where we came from and so on. I was never able to be religious after that."[16]

If ideas pushed Jim toward the socialism of his father, active mobilizations played a larger part in his earliest political development, especially in easing him into the movement during his teenage years. Most decisive was the Moyer-Haywood defense campaign of 1906. A former governor of Idaho, and staunch opponent of the radical Western Federation of Miners, Frank Steunenberg, had been assassinated by an enigmatic drifter named Harry Orchard on 30 December 1905. The reason for the killing, as well as an explanation of why Orchard made himself so available for arrest to the sheriff, was never provided, but state and local officials were quick to pin the murderous deed on an "inner circle" of dastardly WFM officials. The two principals, Charles Moyer and William D. "Big Bill" Haywood, president and strike leader of the militant miners, languished in prison until a series of trial acquittals freed them in 1907–1908. In the process, the labor and socialist movements raised $140,000 to defend Moyer, Haywood, and others, all of whom were widely believed to be the victims of a capitalist frame-up. Eugene Debs toured the United States threatening a revolution if Haywood, targeted by the prosecution, was convicted, and the famed Chicago lawyer Clarence Darrow was appointed chief defense attorney.[17]

Perhaps nothing moved Jim Cannon as much in this period as Eugene Debs's manifesto of 10 March 1906, "Arouse, Ye Slaves!" a front-page *Appeal to Reason* call to arms in defense of Moyer, Haywood, and the others who faced execution in Idaho; an older Cannon would repeatedly allude to this Debs statement in his political writings and recollections.[18] In Rosedale, socialist circles were revived, ordering 500 copies of the paper, and Jim lent an eager hand in their house-to-house distribution. Cannon went to hear Debs speak, and came to love and revere him as did so many others in the socialist movement; he pored over the socialist press accounts, and took in new knowledge about the history of the United States workers' movement; he followed the drama of the trial breathlessly. Young Cannon was at that point on the periphery of the socialist cause, though not terribly well versed in the theoretical issues and organizational differences of the labor and radical movements. Two years later, in 1908, at eighteen years of age, he joined the Rosedale local of the Socialist Party.[19]

The Socialist Party (SP) in the United States of the pre–World War I years was a wide-ranging amalgam of immigrant Marxists, native-born radicals, and reform-minded farmers and workers. Founded in 1901, it had roots in the major urban centers as well as in small-town industrial America. Radical intellectuals, Christian socialists, and progressive small businessmen lined up with craft unionists, weather-beaten agriculturalists, and the casual laborers of the slums to hear its speakers, read its press, and contribute to its mobilizations. Factions formed, of course, and in the more vibrant locales of SP activity contingents polemicized against one another, debating reform versus revolution and petty-bourgeois versus proletarian leadership. In Rosedale, the small SP local seemed to lack a decisive theoretical core, and was likely composed of moderate advocates with little revolutionary, industrial, or trade-union focus, although undoubtedly figures associated with such politics passed through the small socialist circles.[20]

Education and the Discovery of Desire

Jim had nursed his intellect in this milieu and, in the process, discovered that he was more comfortable with a book than a pool cue. Nevertheless, he remained essentially uneducated, a young working-class autodidact stalled in a Rosedale rut. Driven to waged work by familial need, he had also been pushed into the packinghouses by a lack of educational facilities. Completing public school in Rosedale slightly after the turn of the century brought a working-class boy or girl to the end of the educational road, for there was no high school in town, although some classes were offered through the public school. This changed after Cannon had been out of school for four years. In 1906, a bene-factor, Albert Marty, donated land atop one of Rosedale's lofty, undeveloped hills and, at a cost of $25,000, Mt. Marty Rosedale High School was con-structed. Soon it had an enrollment of more than 100 students, and a new wing had to be added in 1913.[21]

Out of work, and lounging about the corner watching the girls with books in their arms walk to the new school in the spring of 1907, Jim turned to a friend of his father's and muttered, "Gee, I think I'd like to go to high school and see what it's like." Encouraged to do just that, he made the climb up the hill and applied to be admitted. Startled by his acceptance, he enrolled for the fall semester of 1907. It was no easy undertaking. His first two years were sustained by summer employment as a laborer for the Park Board, digging ditches, grad-ing roads, and breaking rock. Jim saved every penny beyond his $4.50 weekly room and board at the railroad tenant house. He accumulated $200, sold some clothes, and borrowed a few dollars from an aunt. It was enough, but during the third year his finances hit such a low that he was forced to take up waged work during the school year, get back on his financial feet, and then return to classes after an absence of two or three months. Jim apparently even tried his hand at selling real estate for his father, but the life of the salesman brought him few rewards and little income. In the end, it proved impossible, and Jim never graduated. Years later he recalled it with sadness: "I would say the most burning ambition of my youth was to go to college. To be educated. But it couldn't be done, it cost too much money and I didn't have it."[22]

Jim's worldview nevertheless widened as he was introduced to knowledge, subjects, and books that he had never known existed, from ancient history to algebra. The English instructor supervised the staging of two Shakespearean dramas in 1910: in *Julius Caesar* Jim played Mark Antony, and, in a role he remembered with much less fondness, he was Shylock in *The Merchant of Venice*. Sergeant-at-Arms of the 1910 junior class, Cannon was a popular stu-dent, and was featured prominently in high school assemblies, to which the townspeople were invited. His favored activity was the Rosedale Society of Debate, which, as one of a "few boys" he helped to found on 13 October 1908. The club took as its motto "Labor Omnia Vincit." Among the subjects debated with other Kansas and Missouri schools were Henry George's single tax, the doctrine of socialism, and compulsory arbitration of labor disputes. Jim became known in Rosedale as a supporter of woman voting, and debated that "hot issue" with great vigor. In 1910, when one of his classmates penned an anonymous tribute to the junior class, much was made of Tennyson's "Charge of the Light Brigade," where the lines "Cannon to right of them,/Cannon to left of them./Cannon in front of them," offered the irresistible temptation to pun Jim into the story line: "But luckily for us, there was one Cannon in the midst of them. And as this is an eulogy, although he is still alive (as he has not yet read this), we will modestly admit that he can 'volley and thunder' in a way that will make any noted orator sit up and take notice." Jim also developed a love of poetry which, through a disciplined regimen of memorization, allowed him in later life to draw on Rudyard Kipling, adapting the poet laureate of empire to the cause of the downtrodden and those who would struggle on their behalf: "not as a ladder from earth to heaven, not as an altar to any creed, but simple service, simply given, to one's own kind in their common need." Taking all of this into account, his diploma was not really what mattered: "I got swept up into that goddamn whole new world. . . . I became utterly absorbed in it. . . . [T]hat transformed my life. It opened up a whole intellectual world. I could never be a Rosedale patriot again."[23]

Jim was still relatively tight with his pool-hall buddies. They were willing to cut him some slack for his accomplishments, and they no doubt enjoyed the public exposure of one of their own as an ace debater. They could even stomach some of Cannon's politics, accepting the Moyer-Haywood defense work, strike support, and endorsement of trade unions, although they drew the line at socialism—"they didn't want any monkeying around with anything"—and were emphatically unmovable in their opposition to extending the vote to females. "'You give women the vote and first thing you know, they'll close up all the saloons and we won't be able to get any beer.' That was their argument." Nonetheless, Jim was becoming an increasingly idiosyncratic character. After all, he had commenced his high school education at an age when most students would have been graduating; he did not live at home, and he supported himself with his own labor. And if his gang friends were tolerant of his enthusiasm for school, which none of the rest of them shared, they were not above giving him a good-natured ribbing. Many was the day that Jim, his books strapped over his shoulder, "ran the gauntlet of his former chums." He had to physically rebuff their scoffing and show them that he would take "nothing but respect from them." At that point, Jim Cannon was marked as a native son oddly out of step with his environment.[24]

One of the taunts Jim faced as he sauntered past the billiard room was, "Hi, Jim, how's teacher?"[25] The joke may have had an edge. One of the teachers at Rosedale High School was a young, Iowa-born woman from the small town of

Melvern, Kansas, named Lista Makimson, who served as the faculty sponsor for both the debating society and Jim's 1910 junior class.[26] At some point she and Jim became more than student/teacher. There is a faint suggestion that Cannon was not sexually inexperienced when he first met Lista, as well as strong indications that what he felt for her was more than infatuation or passing sexual fancy.[27] Their relationship was obviously one that they kept very much under wraps, and it is possible that it was not at that time consummated sexually (although it soon would be), whatever the pool-hall gang might have surmised. Makimson, clearly older than her student, was decidedly uncomfortable with the age difference, and dating a student was about as far out of the question in Rosedale as it is possible to imagine. Even when it became apparent that Jim would not be continuing in school for the 1911 academic year, she could not countenance a public liaison, let alone anything more sanctified. When Jim broached the subject of marriage, Lista quickly scotched the idea, saying simply that it was "impossible."[28]

A mythology developed in the Trotskyist movement, perhaps sustained by Reba Hansen's innocent, twenty-five-year-old recollections of a 1948 conversation with Cannon, and repeated, more recently, in the writings of Alan Wald, of a considerable age gap, with Hansen juxtaposing Cannon's age when he entered high school and Makimson's age (gestured to wrongly) at their later marriage, embellishing the figures with an exaggerated ambiguity and a description of dashing physicality. "Jim was seventeen: Lista thirty—'some odds.' She was 'blond, fair, beautiful.'"[29] Makimson, however, was less blond and fair than she was brunette.[30] Students saw her as somewhat stern: "This motto of Miss Makimson:/Those gigglers, I could shake 'em some;/Aroused much dismay;/And of hope not a ray,/For her glance really seemed to bake 'em some."[31] Decades later, the facts of physicality seemed subject to fictionalized construction.

Nowhere was this more apparent than in the matter of the couple's age difference. In actuality, Lista, born in April 1883, the daughter of an engineer of Scandinavian (probably Swedish) descent, was less than seven years Jim's senior. This may have defied traditional age/gender boundaries of heterosexual relations, but it was less noteworthy than the couple's shared commitments and convictions.[32] An obvious if unaffiliated dissident, drawn to a mature student's support of the range of progressive positions Jim espoused with such ability, Makimson was as suitable a partner for Cannon at that time as any young woman his age in Rosedale. However radical their politics, though, the young lovers could not cross the boundaries of gender convention, which were apparently more rigid than those of politics in working-class Kansas.

Jim's youthful discoveries, then, took him a certain distance in the years 1904 to 1910. He confronted the harsh rigors of alienating labor, and he found, in the traditional male dissipations of the poor, little to sustain a sense of the future. In his reading and in his return to school, he cultivated the autodidact's confidence, a love of literature, and the tone and pace of the stage, as well as a hint of what a more cosmopolitan experience might offer. He discovered that he was a public speaker of some ability, and it was in this period that he dedicated himself to the orator's art, taking the lessons of high school and advancing them through meticulous and disciplined study of the methods and techniques of addressing an audience. He probed books on the subject assiduously, including manuals put out by the radical publishing house, Charles H. Kerr, especially the often-reprinted Arthur M. Lewis's *The Art of Lecturing*. Still, the experience of hearing an effective speaker was Cannon's best teacher: "Plunge deep the rowels of thy speech,/Hold back no syllable of fire."[33] Rarely did a campaign meeting, or even religious revival, come to Kansas City that did not see Cannon in the audience, watching the podium to discern the tricks of the trade and sizing up the "accomplished artists" of the day. From the evangelist Billy Sunday, from the heroic socialist Eugene Debs, from mainstream Republicans and Democrats, Cannon appropriated what he could, putting it to the use he thought best. "I was sort of a celebrity for a while—the great boy orator," he told his secretary in 1954.[34]

These years thus established a foundation upon which Cannon would build in the future. One part of this was the obvious psychological component of being willing to break out of the normal and the complacent, to endure ridicule and a kind of ostracism, bucking the tide of familiar friendships and established routine to strike out on a path that promised much but whose material end was nowhere in sight. For a boy of seventeen to go back to school, rubbing shoulders with twelve- and thirteen-year-olds, after four years of working and living on his own, where his contacts were with gang peers and older men, was an act of rebellious courage. "I think all my late life was to a certain extent shaped by this experience of going to high school, when I was already old enough to be a graduate," Cannon suggested a year before his death.[35]

In the process, Cannon also came to love defiantly, as his attraction to a woman of ideas who was both his teacher and his senior challenged deeply entrenched understandings of appropriate sexual behavior. The fruits of this dual discovery of learning and loving would be bittersweet as Cannon moved out of his teens and into adulthood. To be sure, he had been well disciplined in the constraints of orthodox propriety, and his love for Lista was, for the moment, circumscribed, but he had ventured into new realms, where few of his social station had gone before.

The Limitations of Rosedale Socialism

Jim's socialism of this time, however developed it may have seemed to his buddies from the street or his teachers at Mt. Marty, nevertheless remained embryonic and programmatically unfocused. Cannon would later come to appreciate that the Socialist Party he had joined in 1908 was caught on the horns of a dialectical dilemma. On the one hand, the all-inclusive nature of the American Socialist Party in the pre-1910 years was a "historically justified . . . experimental starting point," one that in its mobilizing heterogeneity captured the possibility of expanding radicalism's reach throughout broad sectors of the American population. "All hues of the political rainbow, from dogmatic ultra-radicalism to Christian socialism" were present in the early socialist movement, Cannon recalled. With agitators such as Debs thundering the message of revolution and earning the reverence of hundreds of thousands of committed opponents of capitalism, the future looked bright for the successful making of an alternative social order, at least to a young recruit like Cannon. On the other hand, as Cannon would come to see, the Socialist Party of his youth was also something of a "variety store," one susceptible to mercantile takeover:

> Droves of office-hunting careerists, ministers of the gospel, businessmen, lawyers and other professional people were attracted to the organization which agreeably combined the promise of free and easy social progress with possible personal advantages for the ambitious. In large part they came, not to serve in the ranks but to take charge and run the show. Lawyers, professional writers and preachers became the party's most prominent spokesmen and candidates for office. . . . The revolutionary workers in the ranks were repelled by this middle-class invasion, as well as by the policy that induced it.[36]

Socialist Party opportunities were perhaps decidedly limited for a small-town, midwestern revolutionary such as Jim, intuitively grasping for a chance to move himself to the Left through activity, analysis, and agitation, which in these years was increasingly associated with the question of industrial organization, class struggle at the point of production, and Marxist theory.[37] In Rosedale, there was little of any of this.

As he entered his twentieth year, Cannon had thus exhausted the possibilities of his home town. School, work, family, and his father's socialist circles were no longer able to bind him to the place of his birth or the limited social space of his class. Jim Cannon yearned for more. When the Rosedale High

School debating society held its first annual banquet on 10 September 1910, Cannon rose, like his peers, to many toasts. Some were sentimental ("Reminiscences"), others specific to the club ("The Debater's Policies/The Debater's Future"), and still others possibly unsettling to the talented public speaker who must have sensed that his own graduation was not to be ("Alumni Future"). And so Jim Cannon stood, his teacher/lover and his high school friends looking on, offering his final salutation, to "Insurgency."[38] In the Industrial Workers of the World he would find an avenue into which to channel this need for rebellion and agitation. It was a vehicle that, ironically, took him out of Kansas only to reconnect him to Rosedale, breaking down the barrier that separated him from Lista.

FELLOW WORKERS

Remember!

WE ARE IN HERE FOR YOU; YOU ARE OUT THERE FOR U!

3

Hobo Rebel/Homeguard

A Soapbox Apprenticeship

Jim Cannon dated his entry into the ranks of the revolutionary movement from 1911, rather than from 1908 when he joined the Socialist Party.[1] "I committed myself when I joined the IWW in 1911," he told Reba Hansen in 1948. "Before that I was a sympathizer. I make a distinction. When I joined the IWW, my life was decided." Cannon felt no hostility to the Socialist Party; he simply stopped paying dues, drifted away, and dedicated himself to a different and, in his view, more resolutely revolutionary wing of the movement.[2]

His father may well have had ties to the Industrial Workers of the World (IWW) while being a Socialist Party (SP) member,[3] but the Cannons, father and son, were anything but closely connected to the revolutionary unionism of the pre-World War I era. At twenty-one years of age, Jim knew nothing of the IWW until his father suggested that an old bricklaying friend, Tom Halcro, wanted the young radical to come to a Wobbly meeting. Halcro, a Rosedale "boomer" who followed the trail of available work wherever it took him, was prominent in IWW circles, being a member of the General Executive Board. His political base of operations was the soapbox community of Kansas City, Missouri, a street corner in the Market Square at Sixth and Main. Known as "skid row," the district was in actuality a marketplace for migratory workers, its string of employment offices attracting laborers who found themselves between jobs. Perched atop his soapbox, Halcro preached the cause of "one big union." A "new organization," the IWW, seemed to have the answers Jim Cannon was looking for: "get all workers into one big union and put an end to this whole damn capitalist claptrap. Make a society run by the workers and fit to live in."[4]

In a series of unpublished plot-outline fictions, written years after his conversion to the Wobbly creed (possibly in the 1950s), and encompassing both
plays and short stories, Cannon summarized the experience of a boy drawn to
the soapbox militants in Kansas City, Missouri, in the fall of 1911. In the first
scene of a play entitled "Trails of Glory," Cannon employed a crude trope of
oppression's physicality: the key speaker was "crippled, sinister-faced," while a
man selling radical papers bore the disfigurement of an industrial accident,
being "one-armed"; the crowd was composed of "rough faced, migratory
men"; the message was a bluntly materialized sermon of capitalist wrong and
simple, remedial working-class action. It was not long before the boy found his
way to the headquarters, which is named as an IWW building in the short
story "The Renegade." Sprawled leisurely about, twenty or so men were reading and arguing:

> Politics, evolution, natural science, birth control, poetry, religion, the Haymar-
> ket martyrs, the strike on the Harriman Lines, the controversies in the labor
> movement, all the large affairs of the world ... were dealt with by men ... with
> no less ease and sureness than the fellows in the railroad yards or in Bull's Pool
> Hall talking about the ball games. .... Here were educated people who knew
> things and knew how to talk about them.

It all "went to the boy's head like liquor." He signs on. In the absence of the
facts of Cannon's recruitment to the Industrial Workers of the World, these
fictions convey a sense of what it was like for a youthful rebel to encounter
experienced Wobblies and join their ranks.[5]

At the intersection of these facts and fictions lay the tragic figure of Kansas
City, Missouri's Max Dezettel, who, like Tom Halcro, exerted a powerful influence on a young, leftward-moving Jim Cannon in 1911. A stunning orator,
Dezettel had gone to jail during the famous Wobbly battle for free speech in
Spokane, Washington, where he was secretary of the IWW local. Well-read in
the classics of Marxism, the Wobbly leader impressed upon Cannon that there
was a need to "educate the workers," sustaining them with a "philosophy" that
would fortify them in periods of adversity. Originally affiliated with William Z.
Foster and the Syndicalist League of North America, Dezettel built Kansas City
into a militant stronghold of class actions; hooked up with the IWW and then
broke from it; continued his connection to Foster; and moved to Chicago,
where he edited the newspaper of a new Foster-led syndicalist organization, the
International Trade Union Educational League. According to Cannon's thinly
veiled fictional account, Dezettel soon repudiated the entirety of his past. He
flirted with spiritualism (in vehement opposition to his earlier atheism), turned
patriotic during World War I, and aided the raid on IWW headquarters in 1918.

In alliance with corrupt unionists, he challenged the progressive head of the Chicago Federation of Labor, John Fitzpatrick, forging a parasitic bureaucratized caste of labor officialdom that was "bound by a thousand cords to the employers and the capitalist politicians." Foster later claimed that Dezettel eventually died in an early morning accident involving a "scab" taxicab, his last night one of dissipation and debauch. However, in Kansas City, Missouri, in 1911, Dezettel seemed the very epitome of revolutionary industrial unionism, blurring syndicalist and socialist lines in a revolutionary practice that drew a twenty-one-year-old Cannon and others to the cause of "one big union."[6]

The Continental Congress of the Working Class first convened in Chicago's smoke-filled, perspiration-drenched Brand Hall late in June of 1905. Far to the left on the spectrum of trade union and socialist activity, the one big unionism of the new movement was oriented to the unskilled and the unorganized, and was relentlessly critical of craft union officialdom.[7] Over the course of the years 1905 to 1908, the IWW was wracked with factional fragmentation: its first general president, the rather nondescript Charles Sherman, was removed from office, and the stalwart Marxist, Daniel DeLeon, lost a bid for power, condemning the "Overalls Brigade" and "Proletarian Rabble and Bummery" responsible for his ouster.[8] In the process, the Wobbly rhetoric of antagonism to conventional politics hardened, and its so-called syndicalism, long debated by historians, seemed embedded in its program.[9] But appearances could be deceiving: most Wobblies, like the Socialist Party that some of them continued to support, were at home in a broad revolutionary Left that included various tendencies. Common struggles for workers' control animated both the Wobblies and significant sectors of skilled workers in the conservative, craft-dominated American Federation of Labor.[10] The IWW's fortunes in the years 1909 to 1912, following on the heels of frustrating efforts to organize workers in western mines, coastal and southern logging operations, and eastern mills,[11] were tied directly to the soapbox and a series of much-publicized clashes that pitted Wobbly street speakers against local authorities in Spokane, Fresno, San Diego, and elsewhere.[12] Though not orchestrated by the ballot, this was nevertheless politics with a passion.

At the very point that Cannon was drawn to Halcro, Dezettel, and other Wobblies, Kansas City, Missouri, caught the free-speech disease. It was an influential moment in the making of a young revolutionary, albeit not one that he would participate in fully. If Cannon's fictional account of Dezettel has any factual merit, he first saw the spirited Max agitating in the midst of this battle, hauled down from his soapbox at the corner of 11th and G Streets. Wobbly activist Frank Little was arrested somewhat later, on 6 October 1911, incarcerated for violating local prohibitions on open-air propagandizing. True to form, the IWW responded with an invasion of the city. Jailings and $500 fines followed, but the Wobblies forced concessions from the backtracking Kansas City authorities.[13]

The IWW's success in Kansas City in 1911 depended on the mass of hobo rebels that could be summoned by the organization to any locale. John Graham Brooks understood, as early as 1913, that the IWW represented a new sociology of class conflict in American life, one rooted in alienation and the militancy of the mobile:

> The I.W.W. taps labor strata not only lower than those of the trade union, but still lower than those from which socialism generally gets recruits. It appeals to youth, to the most detached and irresponsible, to those free to follow a life of adventure. It appeals to those who rebel at the discipline of the trade union. It easily becomes a brother to the tramp and the outcast. . . . We have consented to and encouraged the conditions out of which these *fondeurs* come. They are now integrally a part of us.

To ignore this newly emerging demography of the dangerous classes, warned Brooks, would be to breathe life into the IWW, to give its "fighting feature" a prominence that could only multiply "the unexpectedness and mystery" of "the inscrutable pageantry" that marked most Wobbly agitations.[14]

Jim Cannon took to the possibilities of the IWW immediately. With Halcro as his patron, the young Kansas radical got a taste of the revolutionary movement outside the Socialist Party for the first time, rubbing shoulders with a range of ultralefts—anarchists, "red" impossibilists, militant single-taxers—all of whom were friendly and attended the same meetings and Sunday-night forums as many Wobs. A small group of impossibilist socialists had a Sunday-afternoon class in Marxism, known as the Socialist Educational Society, where Jim experienced something of an intellectual baptism: "It was Marxist economics, that was all they knew in Marxism. *Value, Price and Profit*, that pamphlet of Marx, *Wage, Labor and Capital*. My first introduction to Marxism was there and I attended quite assiduously." Cannon's introduction to Daniel DeLeon's Socialist Labor Party (SLP) might well have come from this quarter, as its *New York Labor News* popularized Marxist economics in the United States. DeLeon's Marxism was a creative adaptation of the original texts of historical materialism, motivated by an "exemplary selflessness" and "complete and unconditional dedication to the workers' cause." Key texts in the IWW's propaganda campaign, such as important pamphlets on the history of United States industrial evolution and trade union development by Justus Ebert, were stimulated by DeLeonist conceptions of the revolutionary potential of the working class and printed on the SLP press. If, as Cannon claimed, DeLeon was perhaps "rigidly formalistic," and "sectarian in his tactics," he nevertheless exerted an unrivalled influence on the revolutionary Left in early twentieth-century America. To Cannon, he "towered above the primitive pygmies" of the mainstream socialist Left, and DeLeon's death in 1914 left the nascent Marxist movement searching for a replacement, condemning the SLP to a sect-like isolation. Many militants, Cannon among them, had been pushed and pulled toward revolutionary theory by DeLeon's much-castigated dogmatism.[15]

Once it was common knowledge among radicals in the Kansas City region that young Jim was a gifted public speaker and debater, his IWW comrades promptly hoisted him up on the soapbox. Over the next six to eight months, Cannon labored diligently at the vocation of outdoor agitator. The key was not to "read" a speech, but to arouse the masses. To do that, you first had to draw people. Jim learned the tricks of the trade from his Wobbly comrades. They would go in a group to the designated corner, usually located in down-and-out districts teeming with unemployed youth. Setting up their boxes and watching for other activity, particularly that of evangelicals like the Salvation Army or the Holy Rollers, the Wobblies awaited an opportunity to put on their show. Parody and irreverence were the IWW trademarks, song the announcement of their presence. Once the crowd was drawn to the theater, the soapboxer began, loosening up the street gathering with words, gestures, and humor before delivering the message of revolution. Comrades sold literature, enticing people to discussions and future meetings, and passing the hat for the movement. "You are either a soapboxer or you are not," Cannon later commented. "You are tested by whether you hold the crowd, by the literature sold, and the money given to the collection." It was the most demanding of agitational activity: "In indoor speaking, the crowd is captive and a poor speaker can get by, but you can't do it on a street corner."

At twenty-one, Jim Cannon was thus a professional revolutionary, albeit one without a salary. Moving out of his old, familiar Rosedale environs, Jim established a Kansas City address. As was now his pattern, he sustained himself with short-term casual employment, often finding work as a clerk, where his high school education, if unfinished, nevertheless proved of some utility. His purpose, though, as a member of the "bummery brigade," was to graduate to the status of a full-time agitator. Living off their take of 40 percent of literature sales, and the good graces of those IWW members fortunate enough to have some funds from a recent stint of employment, the soapbox fraternity worked the districts of industrial cities, speaking for their dinners on the street corners of Minneapolis, Kansas City, Omaha, Akron, and Chicago. Hanging out in dingy IWW halls and the dilapidated haunts where migratory workers congregated, the rebel army of Wobbly speakers always had an ear cocked for the welcoming words, "Did you eat yet?" "It wasn't much, but it would keep you alive," Cannon later reminisced. "What more do you want?"[16]

Traveling Man: A Vincent St. John Seasoning

Few soapboxers, especially those who were young and unmarried, stayed rooted in a single locale. Crowds grew stale and unappreciative if agitators overstayed their welcome. It was only a matter of time, therefore, before Jim finally moved more decisively away from his Rosedale roots. He was nudged from the nest in the summer of 1912. His talents as a Kansas soapboxer resulted in Wobbly comrades in Local Union No. 61 electing him their delegate (one of only forty-five from the entire country) to the Seventh National Convention of the IWW, held in Chicago from 16–26 September 1912. Cannon was taken under the wing of a legendary hobo agitator (elected as the alternative delegate by LU 61, and well-known at the IWW's Chicago headquarters), George Leppert, who schooled the Kansas City firebrand in the ways of the road.[17] Leppert utilized an old agitator's ploy, signing himself and Jim on with a skid-row employment shark. For two or three dollars they got a comfortable ride from Kansas City to their ostensible work destination—"rode the cushions all the way"—and then promptly hopped a freight to Chicago, leaving their would-be bosses in the lurch.[18]

The 1912 convention was the high-water mark of the accomplishments of the early IWW, orchestrated by the general secretary and direct-action centralizer, Vincent "The Saint" St. John. Perhaps the most loved figure among Wobbly soapboxers, St. John, whose origins (like Haywood's) lay in the radicalism of the Western Federation of Miners, guided the IWW through its early organizational traumas. He beat back the worst decentralizing impulses of the migratory ranks, some of whom wanted to severely curtail the right of the General Executive Board to orchestrate strikes, free-speech fights, and other IWW activities. Although the decentralizing bindle stiffs of the West would fight again at the 1913 convention, when the IWW met in mid-September 1912 the Saint's leadership was secure and the revolutionary forces were enthused by the prospects of new victories: the mass strike of 25,000 textile workers in Lawrence, Massachusetts, had already placed the direct-action body dramatically in the public eye.[19]

As was customary, the convention was preceded by soapbox meetings in Chicago, and Cannon was one of a number of Wobbly speakers who drew crowds of migratory workers to their street-corner pitches of revolution and industrial unionism. St. John listened to the Kansas agitator and was favorably impressed; he considered proposing Jim as chair of the convention. Cannon ended up acclaimed to the auditing committee, served as secretary of the convention in its last stages, and played an active role in the proceedings, voting in ways that suggest opposition to bureaucratization, advocacy of defending class-war prisoners, commitment to a centralized press, and refusal to buy into sectarian AFL/IWW antagonism. The Saint had made his assessment: he valued Cannon's ability, trusted his judgment, and began to "promote [Cannon] as much as he could." Jim was thus enrolled in St. John's "school of learning by doing,"[20] one of a few chosen cadre dedicated to educating the mass of workers in the revolutionary class struggle.

More than any other single individual, St. John put Cannon on the track of being a professional revolutionary. He introduced him to the agitational road, gave him responsibility, and let him mature. "My development as an organizer and speaker was in no small part due to him," the aged revolutionary told Harry Ring in 1973. For his part, Cannon saw the Saint as a model of revolutionary leadership: "The Saint lived his ideas and methods. He radiated sincerity and integrity, and unselfishness free from taint or ostentation. The air was clean in his presence."[21]

Immediately after the 1912 convention, St. John asked Cannon and Leppert to go to an auto workers' strike in Jackson, Michigan. "I had never seen a strike," Cannon confessed. The Jackson conflict was largely over, but St. John thought the young Cannon could do no harm, might possibly revitalize the conflict, and would learn something either way. The Jackson excursion proving a bust, Cannon and Leppert struck out east. Prodded by St. John, they rode the rails through Ohio, landing in Newcastle, Pennsylvania, where Ben Williams, a printer by trade and the movement's preeminent intellectual, edited the IWW newspaper, *Solidarity*. The footloose radicals found the famous paper's production facilities less than imposing: "a little hole-in-the-wall in the corner of an alley, a two storey shack with a creaky old press on the first floor. The print shop and offices were upstairs."[22]

Newcastle was a center of IWW-Socialist Party strength, although this did not mean that the radicals were able to hold court unopposed. The town had a socialist railroad brakeman, Walter V. Tyler, as mayor and a large, foreign-born working class, but its tone was prudish, and Sunday blue laws were rigidly enforced: nary a moving-picture show could be seen on the Sabbath. Local newspapers catered to an established Presbyterian upper crust, while municipal authority prided itself on its strait-laced familialism; it thus looked askance at IWW propaganda, most of which, though printed in Newcastle, quickly found its way through the mails to some 7,000 or 8,000 subscribers throughout the country. Williams and *Solidarity* were heavily involved in cases concerning freedom of the press and seditious libel throughout 1910–1911, their defiance of legal and social norms drawing judicial attack. Wobblies, however, found Williams and his somewhat rustic offices quite congenial, and many planned their travels around a visit to "the fellow workers" of *Solidarity.* Cannon and Leppert were two such itinerant knights of the road; "just travelling around," neither one of them had any intention of staying long in Newcastle.[23]

Williams, like St. John, appreciated what he saw in Jim Cannon, and convinced him to stay on at the paper as a kind of jack of all office trades. Jim typed some of Ben's letters, kept the books, filed materials, looked after subscriptions, and, on the day *Solidarity* went to press, helped Williams operate the cumbersome and unwieldy antiquated press. Living skimpily on about half of a laborer's wage, Cannon had "just enough to get by." The rewards were of the nonmaterial kind. Cannon took considerable pleasure in helping bring Emma Goldman to town, reveling in the notoriety of a free-speech address that tackled the town where it ticked. As announcements of Goldman's lecture appeared in various postings throughout Newcastle, the mainstream newspapers began to editorialize against her scandalous views. The preachers promised to appear in a denunciatory assembly, and actually showed up on the night of the lecture, planting themselves in the front row. "That was right down our alley," laughed Cannon. "The popular expression of [Goldman's] theory was 'free love,'" he explained, "which meant the terrible sin of men and women living together without the sanction of civil authority and without benefit of clergy. A terrible thing!" The lines were clearly drawn, with the Wobblies and anarchistically inclined Italian workers supporting Goldman, and the priests and their followers in disturbed opposition. "I will never forget the challenge she hurled at them," Cannon reported decades later. "You accuse us of free love, gentlemen," thundered "Red Emma," her stance one of unrepentant accusation. "Let me ask you, is there any other kind of love?" For Jim, "[i]t was very effective."[24]

In the IWW, particularly among the soapboxers, "it was considered enough just to speak," but St. John was of the opinion that Cannon could write as well, and "tipped off" Williams about this potential. Cannon's first contribution was a laudatory report on the IWW convention that appeared, initially, in a lengthy version in *Solidarity,* and later in abbreviated form in the *International Socialist Review.* Confident in the "young blood" of the delegates, 90 percent of whom were said to be under the age of thirty, Cannon was also proud of the "I Will Win" heritage and its pioneers. Cannon's report was a staunch defense of class-war prisoners, but he also tweaked the Socialist Party's formal repudiation of militant, class-struggle tactics, proudly drew attention to the IWW's conscious efforts to draw black workers to its cause, and insisted that the convention was an uncompromising statement of revolutionary commitment. "Every man was a 'Red'. . . . Here was an assemblage which, to a man, rejected the moral and ethical teachings of the existing order, and had formulated a creed of their own which begins with Solidarity and ends with Freedom." Such a "Proletarian Congress" would hasten the day when "the whistle will blow for the Boss to go to work!" In another contribution, a compilation of recent quotes and reports headed "Cannonballs," Jim provided snide comments on Bowery Mission preachers, dismissive barbs directed at the "white handed gentry who wants office," and pleas for workers in the Wobbly ranks to heighten their activity: "The place for a man is in the fight, and not on the fence."[25]

Cannon no doubt learned a lot from his stint at *Solidarity*'s offices, but settling into the routines of propaganda production was not his first priority. Sunday-night socialist lectures in nearby Youngstown, Ohio, were something to look forward to, but they were not likely enough to stem Cannon's agitational restlessness. He believed strongly that "[t]he shock troops of the movement were the foot-loose militants who moved around the country as the scene of action shifted." This "genuine proletarian movement growing indigenously in the soil of America" was what he strove to become a part of, and 100 days or more in Newcastle was perhaps enough of a sedentary layover for the aspiring hobo rebel. His Pennsylvania sojourn would end when the rubber plants of Akron, Ohio, boiled over early in the winter of 1913.[26]

Anarchy in Akron: Rubber Workers and the Mass Strike, 1913

Few cities in the United States epitomized the boom cycle of early twentieth-century monopoly capitalism, with its concentrated production, crossover economic sector dependencies, technological innovations, and massive drives to recruit labor—immigrant, African American, and the impoverished native born—and adapt it to the disciplines of the assembly line more than Akron, Ohio.[27] In fewer still were the products more closely linked to the second industrial revolution's association with the application of chemical processes to production, and the pivotal place of the automobile industry, than rubber.[28] Eventually dominated by a quartet of corporate giants—Goodyear, Goodrich-Diamond, Buckeye, and Firestone—Akron grew explosively in the period from 1900 to 1920, its population expanding fivefold, from 43,000 to 208,000. Established as the world capital of rubber making, Akron's key industry employed 23,000 workers on the eve of World War I, many of them drawn from an Appalachian hinterland. With an annual product valued at $100 million and a capitalization of $50 million, rubber was big business. Dividend payments were said to run 700 to 800 percent annually, sometimes topping out at 100 percent in a lucrative month. But no working-class organization from the time of the Knights of Labor had been able to make a serious breakthrough in Akron's greasy factories.[29]

The Ohio rubber town was overripe for industrial unionism. A beading machine introduced in 1908 led to layoffs and skill dilution among tire builders, while a Tayloresque speed-up trimmed piece rates according to the output of pacesetter "company men," thereby dropping the wage rate to anywhere from $2.25 to $4.00 a day. Unskilled "girls" employed in nontire industries were fortunate to get off a ten- to thirteen-hour shift with $2.00; some cleared only 45 cents. Unorganized, the workers nevertheless protested with a short-lived strike early in 1912. "The speeding up system is wearing out men and girls while they are yet young," one irate reverend observed. "It is borrowing from the future, and is creating a social condition which no person who knows of it can view without fear for the future." The Wobblies, characteristically less restrained and more colorful, spoke a different language, one of earthy bluntness: "You don't have to die to get to hell. Just come to Akron, Ohio and get a pass to enter any one of the many rubber shops."[30]

IWW agitation in Akron began in the summer of 1912, led by Cleveland Fellow Worker Walter Glover.[31] Little was achieved, however, until early 1913. At this point there were fewer than sixty actual IWW members in the Ohio center,[32] but the organization was on the ground, mounting meetings and leafleting in English, Serbian, German, Slovak, Italian, and Hungarian. A walkout of 25 tire finishers at Firestone, on February 12, precipitated by a draconian cut in piece rates, escalated within a day to a crippling strike of 600. The IWW was quick to link arms with local Socialist Party reds, such as Frank and Marguerite Prevey and C.E. Ruthenberg, securing and sharing a well-known socialist hall and other venues for mass meetings, setting up a strike headquarters, and orchestrating the establishment of a 100-strong strike committee that included representatives from all the major rubber factories. Within three days the number of strikers had soared to 4,000, and Wobbly claims were that by the middle of the month 14,000 to 20,000 had left work in protest, with anywhere from 6,000 to 12,000 of them signing IWW cards. Six secretaries were working overtime inducting laborers into the "one big union." Mass picketing closed the plants, Akron stores sold out of red ribbon (the symbol of support for the strike), and revolutionary songs echoed in the streets.[33]

St. John dispatched a flood of agitators[34]—George H. Swasey, George Speed, Jack Whyte, William Trautmann, Arturo Giovannitti, Haywood, William "Red" Bessemer, Carl Bailey, Matilda Rabinowitz, Paul Sebestyen, and others—to Akron. Mass pickets and parades, mobilizing meetings, daily walkouts of workers joining the strikers and affiliating with the IWW, and spontaneous street-corner propagandizing transformed the rubber city in mid-February 1913. The "pageantry" of the mass strike was on public display: "20,000 workers were walking the streets of Akron, laughing, singing, giggling, jollying the police . . . treat[ing] the whole business as a holiday."[35] Everyday life became infused with the cause of the strikers. As rubber workers entered into "holy matrimony" proudly sporting their treasured pieces of crimson cloth, or appeared in court to face nonwork-related criminal charges wearing red ribbon, all was not normal in Akron.[36] Disciplined organizers knew it would not last, and Cannon's traveling hobo companion, George Leppert, found his way to the rubber worker action, setting up a commissary tent and lending an experienced organizational hand in an effort to bolster the material sustenance of the strike.[37]

Authority could not easily countenance such a seismic shift in the state of routine affairs. Within weeks local employers were toughening their stand, drawing on the police to break through the weaker picket lines and arrest prominent radicals and strike supporters, such as the editor of the *Youngstown Socialist,* Frank Midney, whom Cannon remembered as a "spellbinder and agitator."[38] Press, pulpit, and mainstream American Federation of Labor (AFL) organizers (John L. Lewis among them), denounced the alien rebels and decried the threat of anarchy. It would later be revealed that the rubber barons had been recruiting agents among the workers for years, their infiltration of the uprising beginning almost immediately and penetrating the upper reaches of the General Strike Committee.[39]

Most menacing was the formation of the Akronesquely named Citizens' Welfare League, known among the IWW ranks as the Cut-Throats' Warfare League, which graduated from pious pronouncements of seeming impartiality to overtly ideological anti-strike warfare, in which calls for the rubber labor force to come back to Work, God, and Country coincided with threats and intimidations directed at prominent pro-strike figures. Their lapels adorned with yellow ribbons, forty of these citizen vigilantes formed a "reception committee" to welcome Haywood, who was scheduled to speak one evening, at the train station. From their wrists dangled long hickory sticks. The sight of a prominent preacher parading the streets with a club drew predictable guffaws from the godless Wobblies. As the strike wore on, though, the vigilante citizen's league became anything but a laughing matter, and it played a pivotal role, supplementary to the police, in breaking the rubber workers' picket lines and demoralizing the ranks of the strikers.[40]

A March 7–8 set of Akron riots pitted armed police and "deputies" against defenseless strikers, many of whom suffered clubbings and serious injuries, including a life-threatening fractured skull; after these affairs ended in a street melee, countless arrests, and fisticuffs between strikers and scabs, the writing was on the class-war wall.[41] Street battles continued for a week, but the agitators and the rubber workers got the worst of it. Over the next three weeks, employers, newspapers, police, vigilantes, AFL bureaucrats, and small businesses denounced the strike and did what they could to turn back the tide of class conflict. "We are not ready for anarchy yet!" was the rallying cry of reaction. Immigrant workers began drifting out of the strike, often opting to return to their European homelands. Protest rallies of thousands dwindled to hundreds; picket lines sagged and evaporated into nothing; a late March flood further dampened spirits and closed at least one major tire plant. Arbitration initiatives and a state inquiry into conditions in the rubber plants, orchestrated by the Democratic Party senator, United Mine Workers figurehead, and future AFL leader, William Green, spelled a sedate end to the struggle. The strike petered out, IWW organizers started to drift out of town during the third week of March, and the rubber workers' walkout was declared off on 31 March 1913.[42]

Cannon arrived on the Akron scene during the last week of February, directed there by St. John. "That was the first action I saw," Cannon recalled. The instructions were few: "See what you can do," the Saint told him. "Just like that," Cannon exclaimed in astonishment thirty-five years later. What impressed Cannon as he immersed himself in the struggle was the insurgent quality of the rubber worker uprising and the pivotal place of revolutionary soapboxing and mass agitation in sustaining class battle. "It was a remarkable demonstration of how easily a cadre of agitators can take over a popular movement," he recalled, explaining further: "The AFL routine organizers didn't know what was happening. We had the crowd in our hands before they knew what was going on." The art, seemingly contradictory, but central to the Wobbly experience, of "organizing a spontaneous revolt," was what Cannon assimilated from the Akron events. "That was the first demonstration of it I had seen."[43]

Cannon immediately dashed off an enthusiastic report on the rubber workers' confrontation to his recent co-worker, Solidarity's Ben Williams, on 23 February 1913. At that point, mass picketing had the plants tied up, every hall in the town was engaged for the nightly "monster meetings," and the revolt was almost daily on parade, with marchers 7,000 strong hoisting high banners in large red letters, "WE ARE THE I.W.W." and "ONE BIG UNION." For the twenty-three-year-old Cannon, it was "an inspiring spectacle." When the mayor tried to outlaw such processions, he was, according to Cannon's first report, persuaded to back down, the "gentle reminders of Spokane and San Diego" reestablishing "free speech and free assembly." Cannon took particular note that the foreign-speaking workers were solidly in line with the great bulk of the strikers, who were native-born Americans. He praised the support of the American Federation of Labor ranks, but decried the divisive role of AFL organizer Cal Wyatt, "a notorious labor fakir of Lawrence and Little Falls infamy." Convinced that the Akron fight was "undoubtedly the most important yet conducted by the

I.W.W.," Cannon stressed the significance of a mass strike in which "the great majority of the strikers are Americans," and predicted "a glorious victory." Working with the guidance of veteran organizers George Speed and William Trautmann, Cannon urged "every social rebel" to get behind the strikers.[44]

In the critical days that followed, Cannon became one of the central IWW figures writing for the rebel press, appealing for funds, and taking the struggle of Akron's workers beyond the boundaries of Ohio.[45] In an early March dispatch, he succinctly summarized the forces arrayed against the strikers: the Citizen's Welfare League, the state arbitration board, the Senate probe into the "unrest," the police attacks on picketers, a press servile to the interests of large capital, ideological appeals to "God and Country," and provocative efforts to foment riot and violence.[46] Though Cannon was not in the front ranks of IWW orators, in his first days in Akron, with the momentum of the strike carried forward by impromptu soapboxing and huge hall addresses, the young rebel found himself addressing boisterous throngs. "I was up there speaking to four and five thousand just like a veteran." Cannon shared a platform with George Speed at a Socialist Hall afternoon rally addressing female strikers on 6 March 1913. The following weekend Cannon was one of a corps of IWW/Socialist Party speakers scheduled to address strikers at mass meetings, sharing the spotlight with Whyte, Speed, Trautmann, Rabinowitz, M. A. Druso, and the "Joan of Arc" of the "girl strikers," Marguerite Prevey.[47] When Haywood was met at the Akron train station on March 13 by police and vigilantes, Cannon was one of the large crowd of agitators and strikers who marched with the famous Wobbly to Reindeer Hall. Cannon recalled speaking at the event, and decades later could quote from memory Haywood's "rip-roaring speech," an enthralling, "revival-like" delivery in which the impassioned revolutionary traced the bloody trail of exploitation involved in the production of rubber from the jungles of the Congo to the streets of America.[48] The Kansas hobo rebel also journeyed to St. Mary's, Ohio, where he spoke at a meeting chaired by the town's "red socialist" mayor, Scott Wilkins; helped in the organization of a female rubber workers' tag day that collected funds in Newcastle; and likely kept in touch with his former Kansas City, Missouri, comrades who formed a Strike Maintenance League for the Akron rubber workers.[49] Jim Cannon's first stint as an IWW organizer saw him "preaching an eight-hour day and working eighteen."[50]

Overshadowed by the pageantry and drama of the Paterson, New Jersey, silk weavers' uprising of the same time period, which featured a gala reenactment of the Wobbly-led mass strike in Madison Square Garden and the agitational presence of Haywood, Elizabeth Gurley Flynn, Carlo Tresca, John Reed, and others, the Akron rubber workers' strike has been downplayed in the historiography.[51] Nevertheless, it was a critically important contest, and one marked by unique features, such as a volatile mix of native Americans, foreign-born workers, and "girl" operatives, as well as an innovative array of organizational tactics, including support for saloon closings and rebel prayers that appealed for strength to "the fine spirit of revolt."[52] Often depicted as a decisive defeat, the strike staved off the threatened wage cut, and served notice to the rubber barons that their workforce was capable of resistance.[53] In the end, though, the overwhelming power of local capital and municipal authority coalesced to stamp out the rubber workers' revolt. IWW postmortems were critical of both the strikers and of the Wobblies themselves, acknowledging that the spontaneity of the masses was, in and of itself, insufficient to carry the workers to either a short-term victory or long-term organizational strength.[54]

Frank Dawson, a revolutionary socialist and IWW agitator linked to Cannon confidantes and friends, George Leppert and Scott Wilkins, was a perceptive commentator on the Akron struggle, and one whose early vision of the strike's significance dovetailed with, or at least influenced, that of the apprentice agitator. In an unsigned contribution to the *Industrial Worker,* Dawson placed the same emphasis on the crucial character of the native-born American workers in the Akron battle as had Cannon, arguing that the rubber workers' strike outstripped in significance seemingly more noteworthy uprisings such as those in Lawrence and Paterson. The latter were strikes of "aliens tasting capitalist law and order at the point of the bayonet and club." In contrast,

> Akron is a strike of Americans whose ideals about constitutional rights, American freedoms and other bourgeois abstractions have been rudely and crudely shattered by the crash of the club and the zipp of bullets. . . . Clubbings were the order of the day. Shots were fired. The trust in despair organized the Citizens' Welfare League. Local citizens housing out of town agitators and organizers have been told to quit or be tarred and feathered. The local press spoke as though the foundations of government were tottering. Despite this, the strikers stand firm. It is being demonstrated that when the American gets the veneer and myth of American working-class rights knocked out of his head he will fight as no other race.

A week later, with the strike on its last legs, Dawson remained optimistic, noting that "the strikers are taking the necessary steps to perfect their organization," assimilating the lessons of industrial unionism and establishing shop committees. "Loosening the chains of slavery," the rubber workers were hastening the day when "a new social class—the antithesis of the Capitalist class," would prove capable of inspiring a revolutionary transformation. "All hail the modern proletariat," Dawson declared with finality.

Days later, Dawson's revolutionary optimism had been acutely tempered with the hard edge of a socialist intellect's pessimism. In defeat, Akron was called a "fiasco." Betraying the racial underside of his analytic privileging of the native-born American, Dawson found the strikers insufficiently rigorous in their appreciation of what was at stake in the momentous clash with the rubber barons, likening their cavalier combativeness to the "carefree" attitude "of the proverbial negro on the southern plantation." For four weeks the rebellious masses marched and met in gigantic assemblies, enjoying the sociability of their strike. IWW organizers tried to establish strike and shop committees, but the casual combatants paid them little heed, and in the end they were unwieldy and lacking in "executive authority." When the massive array of capitalist power was finally and decisively brought to bear on the strikers, symbolized by the "Citizen's Hellfare League" and their seventy-five armed automobiles, things began to fall apart. Organizers, fearful that their ranks were poorly equipped to face an onslaught of armed antagonists, balked at leading the masses to a slaughter, and the strikers, once cheerfully willing to follow the agitational lead of outsiders, began "to lose heart." Drifting back to the shops because "there was nothing doing," the rubber workers' revolt ended not with a bang, but with a whimper. Promising a project of perfecting organization in the months to come, the IWW Strike Committee declared the revolt over before the defeated workers had to face an April Fool's Day on pathetically small picket lines. "The Akron strike has taught us one thing," concluded Dawson: "A spontaneous strike is a spontaneous tragedy unless there is a strong local organization on the spot or unless a strong force of outside experienced men are thrown into the town immediately."[55]

There is no indication that Cannon pondered such perspectives seriously in the aftermath of the Akron strike. He had been baptized in the front-line fires of class struggle, and it was this experiential moment that he savored for the rest of his life. The strike introduced him to the dynamism of the agitator's art, as well as to the power of mass action. Cannon rubbed shoulders with major figures in the advance guard of the "red ranks" of the pre-World War I socialist and syndicalist milieus, such as C.E. Ruthenberg[56] and Haywood; future notables in the bureaucratized wing of the labor movement (William Green and John L. Lewis) came into his critical sights. Jim Cannon's commitments were now a proven part of the historical record. It would be difficult not to discern in the unfolding of the rubber workers' struggle the raw power of capital's brutalizing authority. Nevertheless, the more lasting impression Cannon seemed to take from his March sojourn in America's leading tire-producing town was the revolutionary ferment of working-class life, and the critical importance of a steeled cadre of agitators, whose role it was to instill in strikers what Elizabeth Gurley Flynn called "a class feeling, a trust in themselves and a distrust for everybody else." Now seasoned as an organizer, Cannon had no desire to return to the editorial offices of *Solidarity*. He struck out for Cleveland, an IWW stronghold in this period, and a city always welcoming to itinerant soapboxers.[57]

Fast-Train Hoboing and Hell Popping in Peoria

Cannon's new traveling companion was Tom Moore, alias "Overland Spike," a Wobbly hobo known not for his speaking or organizing abilities, but for appearing whenever there was "an action." His stature as "a very high class hobo" renowned in IWW circles, Moore was a member of the traveling elite. Disdaining the slow freights, skilled trainsmen like Moore caught their rides with passenger trains, a mode of travel Jim had not managed to master. With Spike he furthered his education in the fraternity of hobo rebels: "He was an expert. It was from him I got my first experience of a fast-train hobo." From Cleveland, Jim and Spike moved on to Chicago, catching a passenger train by "hiding the blind," a hobo method of evading the railroad bulls' detection by utilizing the obscured door of the mail car at the front of the train to pass unnoticed as the train pulled out of the yard. They then climbed to the top of the train and rode into Chicago, another first for Cannon, who found the elevated spring journey "very chilly." Hanging about the Wobbly offices, Cannon grew restless. "I didn't know what the hell we were doing in Chicago. Just like a good many Wobblies, you get tired of one place and jump to another."[58]

A strike of 500 workers at the Rock Island Sash and Door Works provided Cannon with his exit. Commencing 18 April 1913, the western Illinois walkout was led by the IWW and involved a series of typical demands, from a wage hike of 25 percent, the eight-hour day, and sanitary and working-condition improvements, including provision of iced water for drinking purposes. Dispatched by St. John as an IWW organizer, Cannon carried his credentials proudly and earned the privilege of a paid rail ticket to Rock Island. As he got off the train, he found that Spike Moore was waiting for him at the back of the platform. He had ridden the same passenger train, but as a hobo. "It seemed to me that he knew every track of the railroad," marveled Cannon. But the duo arrived late; the strike had "sagged and petered out—that was the common strike then." Cannon met and befriended some militants, trumpeting the cause of "one big union." He was learning that even out of defeat, organizers could reap small victories, winning "fellow workers" to the politics of struggle, and possibly to a long-standing commitment to the IWW: "We always got a few—some who became militants and some full-fledged Wobblies. They would show up someplace else."[59]

In the spring of 1913, this was Peoria, Illinois. Peoria's industrial slaves were said by Wobbly organizers to be "the most responsive of any we have tackled this side of the Rocky Mountains." Trouble had been brewing, particularly among the millwrights and machinists associated with the IWW's local at the Avery Implements Works, but St. John was originally far more concerned with a volatile situation that turned less on labor-capital antagonism and more on sexual politics—a "squabble" that would give the IWW "a black eye." Cannon and Moore were thus ironically sent to Peoria, not to wage class war, but to displace "a couple of free-wheeling women" who held the IWW charter, and the right to speak in the name of the organization, but were tearing "things to pieces" by "hustling . . . [and] fooling around . . . with married men." Advised to use their authority as national organizers to get rid of such "disrupters," Cannon and Moore went in, suspended the charter, and straightened out "the problem." Local agitators continued to champion the right of the workers to run the shops, but as of mid-April the working-class scene was relatively quiet.[60]

Cannon and Moore made sure that this soon changed. They connected with Peoria SP activists and, in the possibly exaggerated words of one IWW authority, Cannon's talents as an agitator turned "a socialist meeting into a local of workers at Avery Implement." Peoria radicals convinced Cannon and Moore to stay on the ground, putting them up in a rooming house and providing them with meal tickets. Cannon soapboxed, made contacts, and recruited a discontented core of Avery employees. Three to four weeks of organizational effort came to a head on 15 May 1913. A strike was precipitated prematurely as four IWW members working in the plant were fired, the dismissals ostensibly orchestrated by the Mercantile and Manufacturers' Association. Cannon and other Wobbly leaders were forced to pull "the whistle without any preparation for [a] strike or getting many organized." The issues included the standard Wobbly strike fare: an eight-hour day with a half-Saturday at full pay; a 20 percent wage hike, with a minimum wage of $2.00 a day, and established overtime; no dismissals or reprisals; with slack work, no layoffs and hours shortened for all.

At first there was barely a baker's dozen of picketers walking outside a plant whose total workforce approached 1,000—and then the strike took off. A retired real estate agent/lawyer/banker, Rudolph Pfeiffer, described in the local press as a "theoretical socialist, but practical capitalist," took a shine to Cannon, offering him some cash and an office and earning the enmity of the local authorities for his trouble. Organizational and agitational meetings were held at noon outside the plant gates. The ranks of rebels swelled as Wobblies from as far away as Los Angeles began to arrive in Peoria. Pickets expanded from the tens to the hundreds in the course of a week. As Cannon reported in a late May dispatch to Solidarity: "Morning, noon and night we were always on the job—arguing, persuading, and marching. Women and children were there with us and their presence had a telling effect." Years later he stated simply, "We had the thing sizzling."[61]

For the first five or six days of the conflict, no disorder was evident, but as the strike gained momentum, with hundreds of Avery employees leaving their workplace, things got ugly. On May 21, police and "deputies," on duty since the beginning of the strike, seized the offensive and arrested Cannon, Moore, and approximately twenty-four strikers. "The game of the other side," wrote Cannon, "is to throttle us at the start by grabbing all the experienced rebels." In the next days, Frank Little, Jack Law, and other roving IWWs arrived in town, only to be promptly arrested as the struggle took on the usual trappings of a Wobbly free-speech fight. The prosecuting attorney pledged himself to "stamp out the IWW," and it was apparent to Cannon that the Wobbly brand of unionism itself was on trial. Under the title "Hell Popping in Peoria," Cannon appealed to all "footloose rebels." One hundred men apparently left Salt Lake City in early June, willing to "spread the spirit of revolt" in Peoria, while in nearby Galesburg, Illinois, a Wobbly local promoted a "Jungle to Jail" movement.[62]

Arrested agitators faced a hostile press, zealous prosecutors, judges blinded by prejudice, and juries packed with advocates of the open shop and members of the "Commercial Club." Convictions were certainties. Spike Moore, the seasoned hobo rebel, was first up in the docket, netting a summary conviction ostensibly for the crime of picketing the Avery plant. His cause was perhaps not helped by Cannon, whom Moore allowed to speak on his behalf. The youthful revolutionary offered the judge a blistering class-war defense. Acknowledging that there could be no justice in a bourgeois court, Cannon waved the red-flag cover of the May Day issue of the *Industrial Worker* defiantly in the face of the jury. The perturbed magistrate, none too impressed with Cannon's performance, was quick to find Moore guilty, fining him a hefty $200 or, alternatively, imposing six months in the workhouse. "Fellow worker," Spike drawled laconically as he headed off to the rock pile, "that was a fine agitational speech you made, but it struck me that you were mighty generous with my time." A few days later, after a pliant jury was secured, Cannon received the same sentence.

He then shared cells with Moore, Frank Little, and other class-struggle veterans. There he benefited from the calming influence of the one-eyed Little, who, at thirty-five years of age, was an elder statesman of the IWW. Part Native American and a kind of father figure to "traveling men" who spread the word of one big union, Little was a revolutionary who would later be murdered in a Butte, Montana, vigilante midnight execution in August 1917. Though he chafed under the restriction of his liberties, hating the cages of the jails he so often found himself locked up in, Little counseled wisely, mulling over the situation in Peoria and reining in the impulsive Jim.[63]

The class-war prisoners were behind bars for a week and more, pondering whether they were going to do hard time in Joliet, a nearby prison. Arrested agitators, pilloried for preaching "the gospel of treason to the flag," were described in the press as felons, wanted in distant cities for "peddling dope," or as "of the unspeakable class of men who live by the slavery of women." Beatings were common, both during arrests and after, when the men were in police custody. Those in the pens waged a hunger strike. St. John decided to call things off in Illinois, sending a Wobbly lawyer to negotiate the release of Cannon, Moore, Little, and others. Cannon and his comrades apparently were for "staying and fighting it out," but that was not the final result. By 12 June 1913 it was all but over, and it ended badly. The hobo rebels withdrew from town, Peoria's ruling fathers reneged on an agreement that promised the strikers freedoms of organization and agitation, and the Avery militants were released only to find themselves blacklisted and any semblance of free speech or job protections throttled. Cannon conceded that the mass arrests had broken the strike and, in Wobbly-like resignation, turned the page on yet another momentous conflict: "After that they dropped the thing and there was nothing more for us there. The action was over and we pulled out."[64]

Peoria was pretty much Cannon's show, and it seasoned him: "I was like a person transformed, as though you grow to maturity within the space of a year. . . . I could walk in and take hold of it like that." By the end of the summer Cannon was one of only sixteen Wobbly agitators who were recognized by the General Executive Board of the IWW as having "voluntary credentials" as itinerant organizers. It was a distinguished crew of soapbox militants that included Haywood; a leader of the Spokane free speech fight, John Pancer; the notable Jack Whyte, famous for his San Diego courtroom declaration, "To hell with your courts. I know what justice is"; the colorful agricultural workers' organizer, E. F. Doree, who had struggled in 1912 to build an IWW-Brotherhood of Timber Workers alliance in the solidly anti-union American southwest; and one of Cannon's early teachers, George Leppert. Directed by the General Organizer, George Speed, and orchestrated by the General Secretary-Treasurer, Vincent St. John (who held the only full-time paid positions in the IWW), this contingent was but a step removed from the handful of national organizers and General Executive Board members that included Matilda Rabinowitz, Frank Little, and Joe Ettor. "We formed sort of a fraternity," Cannon reminisced years later. "We used to call it the Soapboxers Union as a sort of a joke."[65]

A Solidarity of the Jail Cell: Marriage

Jail time is conducive to solidarities of many sorts. In Cannon's case, confinement in Peoria and the prospects of a longer sentence at Joliet brought Lista Makimson back into his life. When he left Rosedale in 1912, en route to the

IWW national convention, Jim and Lista had parted company as affectionate lovers, but it was unclear at best if their relationship had a future. Lista had refused Jim's marriage proposal and the couple faced a series of seemingly insurmountable hurdles, their problems compounded by Cannon's commitment to the revolutionary movement, especially a section like the IWW that placed such an emphasis on the footloose rebel agitator. With Cannon's departure for Chicago imminent, Jim and Lista had a final "farewell," going to the secluded section of a large park "where you had absolute privacy."[66]

Cannon and Makimson nevertheless corresponded throughout the fall of 1912 and into the winter and spring of 1913. As things heated up in Peoria, Lista came to the embattled town to "see what was going and to be with [Jim] in the action." According to Cannon, "She was quite game too." Two girlfriends accompanied Makimson to Chicago, perhaps for companionship, perhaps as a cover to deflect parental or wider social suspicions about a woman traveling alone. By the time Lista arrived, Cannon had already been jailed, but was out on bail. Because it looked like he would be "sent up," Jim and Lista began to discuss the practicalities of marriage, as a legal union was the only safeguard that would secure Lista visiting privileges were Jim to end up in Joliet. The couple were married "during all the action" before a justice in Pekin, Illinois, the sanctified union taking place on 5 June 1913. Lista misstated her age as twenty-four to Jim's twenty-three. Cannon was entering a new phase in his life as a revolutionary, although he was perhaps not immediately aware of how much his circumstances would soon alter. The newlyweds clearly had not thought through the mechanics of how they would be living and sustaining themselves. Their "honeymoon" was spent in the last gasps of the Peoria battle, Cannon working with the Free Speech Committee and discussing the pros and cons of withdrawing with the impending collapse of the strike. Jim and Lista had a meager $14 between them.[67]

Duluth and the Testing of Class-War Leadership: Gunmen, Kidnappings, and Beatings

Perhaps that pocket of small bills treated the newlyweds to a few days in Chicago, but before long, Lista was back in Kansas and Jim was heading west, to Omaha and Minneapolis. He was in the latter locale when the largely immigrant dock labor workforce[68] servicing Duluth, Minnesota, and Superior, Wisconsin, handling the ore deposits being transferred from ships to railroad cars, erupted in a revolt against deadly working conditions. Two workers had been killed on the last day of July 1913, another gruesomely maimed. Reputed to be the result of a feud between the train crews (almost certainly English-speaking, native-born American workers associated with the skilled running trades) and the ethnic laborers, the tragic loss of life brought work to a stop at the Allouez docks of West Superior. Lacking a union since shortly after a 1907 strike, the laborers were soon the beneficiaries of IWW intervention as organizers were instantly on the spot to sustain the struggle, encouraging the workers to stick to their demands for increased safety measures, the right to discharge checkers or foremen judged by the laborers to be objectionable, and wage hikes. Within a week, approximately 1,000 Duluth laborers had walked off the job, and large meetings were held at a local Finnish Socialist Hall. The railroads began importing strikebreakers and laid off 500 trainmen, as local boosters wrung their hands in worry that the flow of iron ore to the steel magnates would be shut down, thus imperiling the economy of the region, where a new steel mill was under construction. The battle lines were drawn in blood: class against class.[69]

Cannon was one of the first IWW organizers to appear in Duluth, arriving just after the dockers' walkout. He benefited from a partnership with the local "red" Finnish leader, Leo Laukki, the flamboyant and theoretically inclined director of the Work People's College. Once a Finnish theological seminary, the Duluth college had been taken over by radical Finns in 1907; they quickly transformed the institution, dropping religious studies to place the accent on science and evolution, political economy, and the history of socialism. At its height at the time of the 1913 dock workers' struggle, the college employed 8 teachers and taught 150 students. A veteran of the Finnish general strike of 1905, Laukki had practiced radical journalism in the old country and was adept at threading the needle of left sectarian difference, advocating industrial unionism *and* the politics of socialist revolution, embracing the IWW but refusing to discount the AFL.

Laukki and Cannon built up strike sentiment in the first days of the laborers' job action, supplementing previous efforts of the main Wobbly figure on the ground, Frank Little. Little had a broad vision of what needed doing. An integrated Wobbly organization of all workers, from the Mesabe mining range in the north through the transportation arteries of the Great Lakes and the railroads into the producing plants of Minnesota, Wisconsin, and Illinois, promised to strike a serious blow at capital's hegemony, providing a model for future regional agitations across the country. As Little wrote in an appeal— "Rebels Wanted in Duluth"—sent out two days before the dock laborers struck, the aim was "to build up the organization so as to enable the workers to capture the industries." The initial foray was envisioned as a campaign to draw the workers in the new steel plant into the IWW and to link them to other economic sectors where the Wobblies had some established support. Ironically, the dockers threw the weathered Wobbly advocate of the spontaneous strike a somewhat spontaneous curve: the carnage of July 31 precipitated a mass protest that Little, Laukki, and Cannon were forced to address.[70]

By the second week of the strike, the lines of battle had hardened and it was apparent that there would be a turn for the worse. The mayor of Superior indicated his willingness to petition the governor for troops to patrol the docks. Parades and large open-air demonstrations were banned. The Duluth, Mesabe & Northern Railway Company issued an ultimatum to the strikers and men began drifting back to work. Late on the Wednesday evening of 6 August 1913, Frank Little was reported missing by the strikers. Abducted by five men, he was spirited away to Holyoke, thirty-five miles from Duluth, where he was incarcerated in an abandoned farmhouse under armed guard by "special detectives." In his absence, and without knowledge of where Little was or what had happened to him, Cannon assumed the decisive leadership of the strike.

Cannon addressed a mass meeting on 7 August 1913, shocking some prominent businessmen and professionals by refusing their offerings, ostensibly labeling them and their wives as parasites. "It was an awful speech, inciting people to violence," moaned one noteworthy, "I never heard anything like it." Expecting to be "boarding at the city jail by tomorrow," Cannon closed his brief report to a Wobbly newspaper with a resounding, "Long live the revolution!"

The next day Cannon and Laukki were pummeled by "special deputies," and the chief of police denied their right to hold a large strikers' meeting. Concern ran high at the IWW's hall over the escalation of physical intimidation and the missing Frank Little. One Wobbly nevertheless offered an unambiguous warning that violence would not deter the revolutionists: "The IWW has a thousand Littles. When one falls, another stands ready to step into the breach." E. F. Doree was brought in from Minneapolis to add some flames to the agitational fire, his soapboxing style said to "guarantee to make any worker dissatisfied with his work and with the condition of society in general."

On 10 August 1913, the IWW secured knowledge of Little's whereabouts, and Cannon dispatched a midnight party of twenty men who successfully rescued the agitator from his abductors. After a daybreak skirmish at an isolated farmhouse, in which gunplay ensued, newspaper reports treated the matter jocularly, poking fun at a Wobbly army routed by a general of the special deputies; no mention was ever made of pressing charges. The kidnapped Little was returned triumphantly to Duluth where, haggard and unshaven, he made a dramatic appearance before 3,000 strikers and their supporters who were protesting police brutality.[71]

Little promptly took Cannon for a morning stroll around the docks, his hand always on a revolver resting in his pocket. The seasoned Wobbly rebel calmly passed through "places swarming with gunmen . . . crossing and recrossing company property many times." It was a dangerous trip, Cannon acknowledged, but Little was insistent on demonstrating that the leaders of the struggle would not be intimidated, a public display directed at both company thugs and striking workers. It was also meant to show the young organizer that he too could be fearless in the face of the coercions of armed intimidation.[72]

At about this time, Little and Cannon were summoned to Chicago. St. John, known as a centralizer committed to preserving the governing authority of the General Executive Board, undoubtedly had received word of his opponents' organizational orientation at the September convention, and he assembled his cadre from the field to discuss how to respond to the impending attack. This confab did indeed pave the way for an initial St. John victory, but it would prove rather pyrrhic: the forces of decentralization, beaten back at the 1913 convention, would, in the end, set much of the future course of the Industrial Workers of the World. St. John, Cannon, and others were put on unambiguous notice that the western ranks of the Wobblies had an agenda quite different from their own.[73]

Because he was afflicted with arthritis, bearing the scars of many beatings and the physical ailments of an older hobo, Little was treated to a special dispensation on the occasion of the St. John factional assembly. He rode the passenger cushions from Duluth to Chicago, courtesy of IWW headquarters. Cannon wanted desperately to demonstrate to Little the acumen he had acquired as a traveling man, so he caught night express trains, riding on top of the car right behind the locomotive. Railroad security police never imagined that hoboes would be so reckless as to ride in this manner, where they battled fatigue, cold, and blinding cinders. Arriving in Chicago after his grueling ordeal, Cannon cleaned himself up and sauntered over to the convention headquarters, taking a seat fifteen minutes before Little's entrance. Appreciative of what his young protégé had accomplished, Little walked over to Jim, put a hand on his shoulder, grinned, and said, "You damned hobo." Cannon thought it "one of the greatest accolades that he ever got in his life."[74]

Cannon and Little returned to the Duluth strike to face a worsening situation. Meetings were routinely broken up; police and "detectives" ran roughshod over strikers; and the banning of parades, as well as other acts of official repression and vigilante violence, took their toll. Each passing day saw signs that the workers were facing defeat, even if some of their original demands for safety improvements had been quietly implemented. On 14 August 1913 Cannon had to admit that "[m]ost of the old men are back at the ore docks and judging from present indications will remain there." Although Little was reluctant to call it quits, insisting as late as 18 August 1913 that the strike was still on and that money should be directed to Cannon, now ensconced as secretary of Duluth's

Local 68, this particular chapter in the "guerilla attack" on capital had run its local course.[75] Indeed, there was another battle brewing among the harvest hands of North Dakota, and Cannon, though not destined to participate directly, did send some Minneapolis-based organizers to the trouble spot of Minot. A number of the Duluth strikers, having had their fill, struck out for the work in the west.[76]

The Home Front: Cannon Back in Kansas

Throughout the dock workers' battle, Lista was setting up a household in Kansas City, Missouri. As a high school teacher, Lista's income had probably been no more than $70 a year in 1912, and her marriage ended the prospects of employment at Rosedale High School. For a time, in 1913, Lista took up a position as investigator for the Board of Public Welfare, but she would soon be pregnant, and convention dictated an end to her paid employment.[77] Cannon was thus well aware that he would have to return to Kansas.

Moreover, he could not have been oblivious to the momentous conflict unfolding in the Kansas City building trades, where Max Dezettel, his old soapboxing inspiration, was agitating among 6,000 locked-out AFL trades-men and continuing to promote the struggle of the 38,000 amalgamated shop craftsmen of the Illinois Central and Harriman Lines and their embattled machinist leader, Carl E. Person. In the process, the free-speech gains of 1911 were being threatened as the Chicago-based, Jay Fox-edited paper, *The Syndicalist,* was banned from the streets, and utterances of sabotage or general strike drew police repression during open-air meetings.[78] It was in this context that Cannon made his way back to the Greater Kansas City region, setting up a Missouri home with Lista on East Ninth Street before moving back to Rosedale sometime in 1914–1915, where the new Cannon family shared accommodations with John Cannon. Jim listed his occupation as real estate agent, but his real work was with Dezettel's paper, *The Toiler,* a unique blend of syndicalism, industrial unionism, opposition to capitalist war, and advocacy of all manner of freedoms, from speech to women's rights. In this capacity, Cannon crossed paths with Earl Browder.[79] When Dezettel and Browder hardened their advocacy of William Z. Foster's position, calling for promoting syndicalism by "boring from within" AFL unions into a break with the IWW, Cannon remained firmly in the Wobbly dual-unionist camp, albeit in ways that opened out into future united-front campaigns around specific issues.[80]

This was the background to the revival of the free-speech movement in Kansas City in the late fall of 1913 and early winter of 1914. The first arrests were made in December 1913, as Wobbly soapboxers appealed for funds to support their comrades imprisoned in the aftermath of California's notorious Wheat-land riots, in which 2,000 migratory hop pickers erupted in a mass revolt pre-cipitated by the threatening intimidations of the sheriff's posse. When the dust settled, four were dead, including a district attorney, a deputy, and two agricul-tural workers; countless others, on both sides, were wounded and beaten. In the repression that followed, the IWW was targeted the length and breadth of Cal-ifornia, and two Wobbly figures were imprisoned.[81] Five soapboxing Kansas Wobblies, originally arrested on December 4, were sentenced to 200 days in the workhouse; 20 more were hauled off on Christmas Eve. Soon the number of those jailed climbed to eighty-five, with Frank Little leading a contingent of IWW rebels into holding tanks the conditions of which plunged to depths few Wobblies had before experienced. The Wobbly hall was raided repeatedly and eventually closed. Nevertheless, the industrial rebels offered not a cent to lawyers, deplored the apparent lawlessness of Kansas City—where the IWW claimed that "hold-up men" and "white slavers" received more leniency from the police than they did—and refused to give in. The number of Wobblies arriving in town to support the protest dwindled, but those on the ground held firm, and on 8 March 1914 the Free Speech Committee declared the action over. City authorities conceded the right to agitate to the IWW, which promptly mobilized a contingent of women soapboxers and refused to retreat in the face of continued beatings and police repression.[82]

Kansas City was one of the IWW's last free-speech stands. However much free-speech confrontations had focused the IWW in the public eye during the period 1909 to 1912, and whatever the Wobbly commitment to freedom of assembly and the right to address its migratory constituency, a turn was being made by the time of the Kansas City agitation. The IWW was increasingly committing itself to organization of the fields and factories, rather than bat-tling for the streets and the somewhat threadbare principle of free speech.[83]

Cannon reflected this process. At first, he penned appeals and served as the secretary and fund raiser for Local 61's free-speech fight. In an initial call for support Cannon declared, "To meekly surrender the right to carry on agitation and education means to abandon the idea of the abolition of wage slavery." In contrast, a 2 January 1914 communication, signed "Press Committee" but des-ignating that correspondence be sent to Cannon, closed, "On to a speedy vic-tory. Then to the industries."[84] Like many in the IWW army, Cannon had come to regard industrial organizing as pivotal. After mid-January 1914, no communication would bear his name. A soapboxer of note, Cannon was not jailed in December 1913, nor at any point subsequently in the Kansas City free-speech campaign. He was clearly being shielded from the solidarities of the cell. No longer a footloose hobo rebel, Cannon was now a member of what some Wobblies rather condescendingly referred to as "the homeguard."

Defined as "a town worker who does not move around from job to job," the term *homeguard* reflected a tension that ran through the history of the IWW: "The hobo is the migratory worker; the homeguard is the non-migratory worker. The former is footloose, homeless, uncouth; the latter may have a home and family, and is perhaps not so much accustomed to hardship and rude living. In the IWW the hobo and the homeguard psychology never fused." Cannon would later fictionalize this opposition in "Trails of Glory," outlining a debate at the "dingy hall" of the Kansas City IWW:

> "But what the hell," said Frank Anderson in one of the discussions of the respective advantage of the "homeguard'" and the "floater," "It[']s a question of choosing, of selection. The rebel, especially the migratory rebel, gives up a so-called home, a regular job, and other things which the scissor-bill has and thinks worth something. But the hobo has leisure. That is worth something more than all the money in the world if the hobo knows it and knows how to enjoy it. . . . The scissor-bill workingman, slaving over a machine all day, knows nothing of the value of leisure and is even educated to think that there is something wrong about it.

As he became a homeguard, Cannon had to address how to live and make ends meet in ways that went well beyond a ride on the rails and being treated to his dinner for an admirable speech. In the process, he reevaluated the Wobbly creed.[85]

Cannon's son Carl was born in the latter half of 1914. Lista and Jim were likely new parents by the time of the Ninth IWW Convention, held in Chicago in September 1914. Cannon allowed his name to stand for editor of the Wobbly newspaper, *Solidarity*, an indication of his willingness to take on the settled role of publishing propagandist. He did not secure the post, as he faced stiff competition from the other two nominees, long-time editor and former Newcastle co-worker, Ben Williams, and the IWW theorist, Justus Ebert. Although Cannon was no doubt active in local Wobbly events, he was less and less of a leading figure. He recalled speaking in the IWW hall at a memorial meeting for the martyred Wobbly songster, Joe Hill (executed by the state of Utah on 19 November 1915), and worked closely with Browder on the Kansas City campaign to free Tom Mooney, who had been unjustly sentenced to death as a result of the bombing of the 22 July 1916 San Francisco "Preparedness Day" parade. Still, Cannon's renditions of such time-honored agitational song favorites as "The Tramp," were now delivered in a homeguard voice. "That was the windup in the evening, singing," Cannon recalled of his early years as a father. "We'd have some songs," and Carl would "finally say, 'Daddy, sing about the tramp.' So I'd take him on my back, tramp him down":

> If you all will shut your trap,
> I will tell you 'bout a chap,
> That was broke and up against it and thread-bare,
> He was not the kind that shirk,
> He was looking hard for work,
> But he heard the same old story everywhere.
> Tramp, tramp, tramp, keep on a-tramping,
> Nothing doing here for you,
> If I catch you 'round again,
> You will wear the ball and chain,
> Keep on tramping, that's the best thing you can do.[86]

With the infant prepared for sleep, what did Jim and Lista talk about? What did Cannon, barely removed from battles such as Akron and Duluth, where he had witnessed class struggle at its most raw, think about his future and the prospects of the revolutionary working class? It is impossible to know, but a series of developments were marking these years as ones of difficult transition for Cannon. They were undoubtedly trying and fearful ones for Lista, now into her thirties, as well: motherhood having removed her from the teacher's salary that sustained her for years, she faced the confinements of childrearing in an ugly atmosphere of local hostility and a domestic economy always stalked by basic need. The conversations around the kitchen table were likely full of foreboding, depressing in their seeming lack of options.

World War I and Revolutionary Doubt

The outbreak of war in 1914 exposed limitations in the IWW's brand of industrial unionism, as well as the failure of the broader socialist/anarchist movement to develop a coherent approach and explanatory framework within which to situate capitalist war. Positions ranged from an isolationist, hands-off stand through resistance to the draft to varied strains of conscientious objection. The Wobblies, Cannon among them, had an instinctual aversion to fighting what they knew was a war in which the working-class had no interest, but they never quite developed an appropriate internationalist stance. As Cannon later stressed, "the American movement was quite primitive, quite provincial [.].. [T]he IWW never took an official position on the war [.].. [T]he prevailing decision was 'ignore it.' More concerned here with industrial unionism, organizing the workers on the job." Avoiding being drafted, Cannon paid a price, facing ostracism and material hardship. For Jim, Lista, Carl, and a new addition, Ruth, born in 1917, circumstances were anything but good. "I was a pariah in my own home town," Cannon remembered with bitterness, "[t]he whole world seemed against us." It was a time of "desperate poverty."[87]

To make matters worse, the later years of the war, and the immediate post-World War I period, would witness an unprecedented reign of vigilante violence and state legal terror directed against the Wobblies. Although it was not clear to Cannon and others what the full nature of the assault would entail until it had run its course through 1917–1919, it was apparent that a threatening persecution had descended on the IWW. Three major trials—in Chicago, Sacramento, and Wichita—placed hundreds of Wobblies under arrest and had as their purpose "putting the IWW out of business." There were also difficulties within the IWW itself. At the Ninth Convention in 1914, Vincent St. John declined to remain as general secretary-treasurer; Cannon's revolutionary godfather left the organization he had directed, and the young organizers he had so skillfully hand-picked, to take up prospecting in New Mexico in 1915. In Kansas City, meanwhile, all indications were that the Wobbly organizational drives would focus on harvest hands, as the IWW increasingly placed most of its agitational eggs in the basket of agricultural workers. Cannon's own predilections had always been to focus on the more industrialized proletariat of eastern factories. Thus, in a later assessment of the IWW he would write:

> The IWW program of revolution was designed above all to express the implicit tendency of the main mass of the basic proletariat of the trustified industries of the East. . . . If the logic of the class struggle had worked out formally—as it always does in due time—those workers in the industrial centers east of the Mississippi should have been the most class conscious and the most receptive to the IWW appeal. . . . On the contrary, its predominant activity expanded along the lines of least resistance on the peripheral western fringes of the country, which at that time were still under construction. . . . [D]efeated and repulsed in the industrialized East, where the workers were not ready for organization and the corporations were more than ready to prevent it, the IWW found its best response and concentrated its main activity in the West. It scored some successes and built up its organization primarily among the seasonal and migratory workers there.[88]

Cannon's year in the Wobbly trenches had been the last gasp of the eastern organizing efforts, and upon his return to Kansas City he faced the hard recognition that the IWW's future lay, for worse rather than for better, with the harvest hands. It was not an acknowledgment he would have been comfortable making.

This combination of forces left Cannon somewhat directionless. Still, as a revolutionary he struggled to find a way out of what he grasped, conceptually and politically, as the "terrible insulation" of the radical movement in the Midwest. Cognizant of his material responsibilities, he was deeply troubled by a stifling lack of economic prospects. Eventually this would register in Cannon's "alienation" from the IWW; while he remained a member, he became less and less active.[89] In a context of political confusion, debilitating impoverishment, and rabid ideologically charged marginalization, Cannon kept a foot in the revolutionary movement, to be sure, but he also began to devote three evenings a week to the study of law, which he undoubtedly saw as a profession open to his talents, not necessarily uncongenial to his politics, and capable of providing for his family. By day he earned what he could in an office.[90] The homeguard had come a long way from his days as a hobo rebel, but his resting place in 1916–1917 was anything but comfortable.

The Personal Is Political: Radical Manhood

His homeguard years as a disillusioned Wobbly, then, were among the worst of Cannon's life, whereas his year as a hobo rebel, immersed in the rough-and-tumble class struggles of his time, was a period of his fondest memories and most prideful accomplishments. One part of this dichotomy was the gendered radicalism of the pre-World War I revolutionary movement. Cannon's background as a Rosedalian native son allowed his development as a radical, up to certain points. Opposition to the war, which he consciously chose, was beyond the pale, as were advanced views on the "woman question," which he put forward in his theoretical defenses of woman suffrage and in his life choice of a female partner older than himself, albeit one drawn to his attraction for working-class insurrection. Later in life Cannon was open in his acknowledgment that women in the revolutionary movement of this period were prominent only if they were speakers, and only as speakers. Elizabeth Gurley Flynn, Emma Goldman, Ella Reeve Bloor, Kate Richards O'Hare, Luella Twining, and Matilda Rabinowitz were figures of this sort. "They were speakers, but they were not leaders of the movement in the sense that they are now," Cannon told Harry Ring in 1973.[91] This meant that the early revolutionary movement was both far to the left of mainstream American gender relations—as evidenced in the IWW's willingness to endorse Emma Goldman and her politics of "free love"—and caught in the web of gender conventions and their everyday reproduction. When Lena Morrow Lewis, an outstanding female agitational speaker in the Socialist Party, actually seemed to be living out some of the theory espoused by the party's leading male advocate of free love, J. Mahlon Barnes, leaving the office with him in the afternoons to drink whiskey and engage in perhaps other more salacious encounters, she was subjected to a thoroughgoing scandal-mongering in SP bulletins and was eventually virtually exiled to an "organizer's post" in Alaska.[92]

A resolutely masculine body such as the IWW could ironically be both rebellious and conformist around issues of gender, and there was something of this in the early making of Cannon, who seemed to embody an odd fusion of traditionalist, Victorian notions of gender relations and sexuality and a bohemian, avant-garde disdain for material acquisitions and the trappings of money. It was a somewhat incongruent pairing in the resolutely radical circles that Cannon would always inhabit, both prior to and after World War I, but it shared, without knowledge, a common ground with positions put forward by Russian revolutionaries such as Lenin.[93] "When I became a revolutionist, I threw off my early training, both in money and sex," Cannon once told Reba Hansen: "Since I became a revolutionist, I haven't had a bank account." Thus, although Cannon enjoyed the *class* spectacle of Goldman's free-love advocacy being tossed in the face of pious power, he never really engaged with the potentially transformative *gender* politics of a militantly feminist approach to the personal realm.[94] As a revolutionary, he propounded some of the abstract theory of free love—especially its assault on the sanctity of marriages blessed and authoritatively constituted by church and state—but he practiced a conventional monogamy, albeit one in which his family would never be secure in the comforts of acquisitions and financial stability. Love was to be cultivated, not spent loosely like cash, which was, in any case, the symbolic *and* substantive currency of bourgeois order, to be shunned as the entrapment it inevitably led into. The politics of this personal/political crossover were destined to remain obscure, precisely because it was not, for the most part, the stuff of open debate in the movement or explicit discussion in the workers' press.[95] Cannon's and the IWW's public views would always be to the left when the "woman question" was raised, and these were genuinely held radical principles. However, beneath the surface relations of advocacy lay more difficult negotiations, in which a latent conventional gender prejudice perhaps survived.[96] A hint of this appeared in Vincent St. John's decision to send Cannon and Spike Moore to Peoria to reestablish stability in a local supposedly rocked by the acts of "unruly women," or in the Kansas City Wobbly willingness to contribute to the "moral panic" surrounding the exaggerated presence of an alleged "white slavery" ring during the 1913–1914 free speech fight. "One girl a day is reported missing in Kansas City," claimed a statement by IWW rebels, "Why We Go To Jail." "It is a well-known fact that a gang of White Slavers are operating here, yet one of these despicable criminals, caught red-handed, was fined only $100 by Judge Burney. The same honorable judge fined a workingman $500 for speaking on the street corner."[97]

This problem of gender construction was perhaps most evident, however, in Cannon's fictional account of the downfall of his old Wobbly mentor, Max Dezettel. In "The Renegade," Cannon portrayed Dezettel as a tragically flawed figure, a larger-than-life expression of revolutionary potential brought to traitorous repudiation of his politics of class resistance by a dual weakness: attraction to women and money. Originally an exponent of "casual free love on a purely physical basis without obligation or permanence," Dezettel managed to stay "shy of the women who flocked around him, although he was not indifferent to their admiration." On the one hand, he longed to be a footloose rebel again; on the other, his lack of domestic entanglement meant that he could devote himself to the movement, where his "tireless energy . . . [and] saint-like devotion to the cause" secured him considerable prestige. Comrades predicted that Dezettel would strike out on an agitational tour. "[N]ever born to be a home guard," the rebel was not expected to stay in Kansas City long. "'Mark my words,' said one time expired hobo whose roving days were over, 'he'll be on his way before any of us knows it.'"

According to Cannon's fiction, Dezettel's days as a transient rebel, as well as his theory of free love, "went to smash on the rock of infatuation." The object of his affections was a clerk in the office of the company where Dezettel worked. Cannon's depiction of the female enticer betrays a conception of women that must have been common both in general masculine working-class circles and among Wobbly agitators: "A simpering man-hunter, light-headed and with no uncommon graces or beauty but physically alive and attractive with the first bloom of womanhood. She flaunted her swelling young breasts at [Dezettel] and landed him, dazed, in the marriage net before he knew what he was doing." Dezettel brought his new bride, rather sheepishly, to the IWW hall one night, introducing her as "Maudie" "to the womanless hoboes." They sized her up as a "fourflusher 'on the make,'" convinced that Dezettel would soon "get wise to himself." Belief was strong that the "snap marriage" would not last, for Dezettel understood, as did all true rebels, that "holy matrimony" was "a bourgeois fraud."

Somewhat surprisingly, the marriage did prevail, and it was Dezettel's contact with and ties to his rebel comrades that seemed to be fading. The adored agitator eventually became his opposite: "The soul of the revolutionary died, and the soul of the apostate was born, by inches." Cannon acknowledged that "[t]he springs of this metamorphosis were coiled within his own character, of course," but he insisted that the woman temptress "set them off." His authorial language is brutal in its angry, sexualized reduction of "Maudie" to the class-enemy, gendered female:

An ignorant, selfish bourgeois-minded slut she was, but strong, with the strength of those subnormal types who concentrate their whole life's energies on small designs. She—with her single-mindedness and her woman's body— had no intellectual spiritual kinship with [Max]—was too strong for [him] and for all his ideals, his philosophy, his vagrant yearnings for the days of footloose freedom. She kept him and, in the end, made a traitor out of him.

The manuscript breaks off prematurely, before Cannon can take us through the full fall of Dezettel, but it is apparent that the congealing of gender and class, in which woman is a metaphor for bourgeois temptations, takes place within boundaries of money and social advancement, which Maudie craves and induces her once-revolutionary husband to pursue. As a final statement of degeneration, she breaks the staunchly atheistic revolutionary will of her apparently now defenseless captive by accommodating him to spiritualism.

Cannon's presentation of Dezettel's incorporation into the world of bourgeois practice and ideology is clearly a preface to Max's Judas-like repudiation of IWW comrades, compromises with the state, wartime chauvinism, and incorporation into corrupt labor officialdom. The unpublished manuscript ends before the story can travel to these sorry pages. Even so, in his presentation of revolutionary apostasy, Cannon embraces a language of radical manhood implicitly distrustful of women, who are seen as competitors alienating the affections of revolutionaries:

> The moral disintegration of the man was a long and complicated process. The firm substance of his rebel manhood crumbled slowly, almost imperceptibly; discovered in weakness, irresolution, cross-purpose, even cowardice. . . . It began, of course, of the conflict between the two powers that had taken hold of him, the two powers that pulled him in opposite directions with the strength and fury of wild horses. There was the mad infatuation for the woman, the woman who wanted the whole of his personality, his allegiance, his affection, his energy; and there was the revolutionary movement, alluring him like a dream, the movement which is not unlike a woman, with its insatiable and jealous demands, its unappreciation, its unceasing cry for more! more! Dan McGlynn [Max Dezettel] was a fool, a madman trying to serve two mistresses, two unreasoning and all-demanding rivals mutually excluding one another. That contradiction was the starting point of his fearful deterioration as a revolutionary, as a man.

Cannon felt that Dezettel had been destined for a major place on the IWW's General Executive Board. His movement into the upper ranks of the revolutionary movement was now finished, however, done in by "the unfortunate marriage, which hung on like a drawn-out cold." In the end, Max/Dan reneged on every principle he had once held dear, leaving him an object of "red hot hate" among those who had revered him. Bourgeois values, toward which he was pushed by a woman, negated his revolutionary manhood and its aspirations of proletarian purity and virtue.[98]

What are we to make of this plodding, cryptic, and unfinished manuscript, in which a kind of revolutionary brotherhood is allowed to articulate, in a way that no public document of the IWW ever would, the fears that hobo rebels harbored of women's challenge to the fraternity of the soapbox agitators?[99] Much less benign than the language of differentiation separating bindle-stiff organizers and homeguards, this fiction speaks, as did Cannon's attempts to narrate his Rosedale youth, about the facts of a specific period of his life in a way that no political statement ever did. It reaches into characterizations and resentments destined to remain suppressed; it is a lid lifted off unconscious antagonisms and contradictory impulses, boiled down to their simplified, hence fictionalized, essence. We must read this document not as truth, but as suggestion; not as a statement complete in its development of gendered meanings, but as a fragmentary underside, such as is harbored by most human beings, that has to be placed alongside other, often counterposed, pieces of a past that can never be recovered in its totality. To ignore it would be no less distorting than to elevate its ten pages to a place of absolute analytic prominence.

Cannon did not marginalize women, although he was a product of an era that allowed females little latitude either in mainstream society or on the revolutionary Left. He recognized women's critical role in the mass strikes of his time, noting their significance on picket lines in Peoria and addressing huge meetings of women strikers at Akron. He admired women agitators as he respected male soapboxers, and he appreciated Lista's support for his politics and willingness to sacrifice to participate, in her way, in the making of a better world. But when he looked at Dezettel's fall he must have seen, reflected through the dirty mirror of corruption, something of his own predicament as a homeguard. Drawn into a "snap marriage," attracted to the love he felt for Lista and the possibility of a shared union, he found his life as a mythical Wobbly largely over. His days of addressing thousands of strikers or walking defiantly through the very battles of class struggle, his comrades "giants" of proletarian authority such as Frank Little, seemed far distant, a world away from the familial routines of Cannon's life in Kansas City's World War I Left milieu. Cannon, like Dezettel, might have been a candidate for high office in the IWW, but honors of this sort did not go to homeguards. There must have been moments during World War I when Cannon wondered what he had sacrificed for love and marriage; other doubts, equally central to her identity but quite different, were almost certainly troubling Lista as well. These were, it must be stressed, moments counterposed to other moments, thoughts troublingly dark always balanced by other sentiments. The couple loved one another, and cherished their young children. If the revolutionary Left faced a clearly uphill fight, there was still the fight to wage. Jim and Lista hung on, through an unimaginably difficult few years.

The IWW: The Great Anticipation

Cannon was later able to engage somewhat critically with the *political* shortcomings of the Wobbly reification of the footloose rebel, defiant of social norms and shunning home, family, and female companionship for the endless pursuit of revolutionary agitation. He certainly recognized that there were those, like Frank Little, who could sustain a migratory rebelliousness for a decade and more, devoting the entirety of their lives to building the movement and its youthful cadres, never settling in a single locale or sustaining structures and institutions of transformative authority. Yet, Cannon was also able to grasp that such lifelong organizers were few and far between, that they were themselves usually worn old before their time or sacrificed to a grisly martyrdom.

No movement could survive historically on the basis of this kind of burning intensity, which inevitably left the cinders of revolutionary human material smoking in the ashes of proletarian defeat. As "a revolutionary organization proclaiming an all-out fight against the capitalist system," the IWW "led many strikes which swelled the membership momentarily. But after the strikes were over, whether won or lost, stable union organization was not maintained." This deficiency, in the heat of the agitational moment, seemed an understandable shortcoming, precisely because there was so much to value in the rebel spirit that lived in the Wobbly struggle. The "non-conformists, the stiff-necked irreconcilables, at war with capitalist society," would always be, to Jim Cannon, "big men, and they all grew taller when they stood together." Distinguished from those who adapted to inequality, the "radicals, rebels, and revolutionists" who founded, led, and supported the IWW were characterized by "the immensity of their ambition which transcended personal concerns, by their far-reaching vision of a world to be remade by the power of organized workers, and by their total commitment to the endeavor." To the downtrodden, the IWW *was* this visionary anticipation, and it became "their union and their party; their social center; their home; their family; their school; and in a manner of speaking their religion, without the supernatural trimmings." As "a genuinely indigenous product of the American environment," then, the IWW took sectors of the American working class to places where they needed to go, *anticipating* the possibility of revolution in an epoch when the actual mechanisms of producing a proletarian order were barely conceivable. It was a heroic part of a whole yet to be grasped, a fitting way station for a revolutionary native son and, as such, the dramatic conclusion of Cannon's apprenticeship as a Rosedale radical.[100]

In 1920, Jim Cannon and his old Wobbly pal, the illustrator-poet Ralph Chaplin, paid a visit to William Z. Foster at Foster's spartan Chicago apartment, during which Cannon attempted to recruit Foster to the underground communist movement. Foster would have nothing to do with the offer, deprecating the Soviet Union, replying with pejoratively dismissive barbs about the political leaders of the world's first proletarian state. Cannon was disappointed and, as he and Chaplin awaited a streetcar, Foster's words, "I'm sorry, nothing doing," echoing in his ears, he snorted with disgust, "Once a Wobbly, always a Wobbly." The words carried contempt, a derogatory blow struck against the characteristic IWW failure to engage adequately in politics, and to isolate the struggle of American workers in the narrowest understanding of workplace battle and street confrontation.

Cannon's curt characterization also resonated in his life's experience positively. Those who were once Wobblies, as he had been, if they remained true to the revolutionary heritage of the IWW, were always rebel workers, and that was a legacy to cherish. As a future comrade, Arne Swabeck, recalled in an unpublished tribute penned on Cannon's death: "[T]hroughout his life, Jim retained the Wobbly imprint; that is, in the good, the highly dedicated, and wholly uncompromising sense of the term. He drew strength from the indomitable courage of the Wobblies, the resolute militancy and inspiring audacity." In one of the last interviews of his life, Cannon closed his commentary with a Wobbly-like statement. "The thing that inspires life and makes one's life worth living in the face of all the calamitous danger everywhere, uncertainties and insecurities," he concluded, "is at least to have committed one's ownself to an effort to change it." As part of Vincent St. John's Wobbly agitational cadre, Cannon would never relinquish the project of "making" workers militantly class conscious. This was the foundation upon which all IWW action rested. But the question of the hour, in the later years of World War I, was how to change life as it was lived within capitalism, how to deepen the trenches of class consciousness and raise higher the organization of the revolutionary Left. Cannon would come to refer to himself and others in the communist and Trotskyist movements as "Wobblies who had learned something." The learning, and his salvation in the midst of depressing personal circumstances—economic, psychological, and political—in 1917, came from examination of Russia's Bolshevik Revolution and its implications for the American working class and its movements.[101]

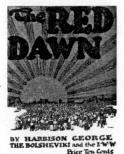

BY HARRISON GEORGE
THE BOLSHEVIKI and the I·W·W
Price Ten Cents

4

Red Dawn

1917: Revolution in the East; Repression in the West

Harrison George sat in a Cook County, Illinois, jail cell in December 1917, awaiting the trial that would net him a $30,000 fine and a total of seventeen years on four criminal counts. He heard much of new developments in the East, where workers had turfed out their feudal-like ruler, the czar, and supposedly established a society governed by "soviets," an "industrial parliament." Cook County's incarcerated Russians were elated; others, however, were skeptical. George was an enthusiast. He penned a twenty-six-page tract, the first pro-Bolshevik pamphlet published in the United States. The imprisoned IWW litterateur, who would soon issue a stream of booklets on the killing of freedom in America, as well as a 205-page account of the Chicago trial, put forward the view that the Bolsheviks had changed their society, creating the world's first workers' state. The IWW, he suggested, should follow suit. War and revolution brought George to a new consciousness. As George's title suggested, 1917 was a *Red Dawn*. Jim Cannon would be one of those Wobblies who, like Harrison George, experienced this momentous historical transformation as something of a new political day.[1]

A few days before President Wilson signed Congress's declaration of hostilities against Imperial Germany, state militiamen and "off-duty" Marines raided the Kansas City IWW hall, ransacking the headquarters, destroying papers, and smashing office furnishings before departing under the agreeable eye of local police. The illicit spring 1917 raid was a sign of things to come: a blurring of officially sanctioned state repression and informal, "citizen's committee" actions that created a climate of lynch-mob coercion directed against all forces of the Left, particularly the scapegoated Wobblies. In the months that followed, vigilante reprisals against the proponents of "one big unionism" culminated in the terrorism of Butte, Montana, where Frank Little was murdered; an infamous, violent, and transparently illegal deportation of 1,200 suspected Wobblies from the town of Bisbee, Arizona; and the September 1917 Justice Department offensive, in which Harrison George and 165 other IWW members were indicted in Chicago on various counts of conspiracy and hindrance of the war effort.[2] The Socialist Party of America faced a legal assault, including prosecution of five of its leaders—Victor L. Berger, Adolph Germer, William F. Krause, Irwin St. John Tucker, and J. Louis Engdahl—for conspiracy to violate the Espionage Law of 1917, and the Post Office's refusal to circulate socialist newspapers, pamphlets, and other material that contained anti-war and other ostensibly offensive statements.[3] A repressive "red scare" as vicious as anything seen up to that point in American history was unleashed, surpassing even the Haymarket "hysteria" of 1886 and leading inexorably to the anti-communist pogrom of 1919–1920.[4]

His objection to the war stated quasi-publicly in registration as a conscientious objector, Cannon was a figure of bewildering disappointment to the Rosedale patriotic elite. Elder statesmen counseled him to offer no resistance, and when he failed to comply were astounded at his statement, "I don't believe in the war." Ostracism resulted: "People [he] had known all [his] life," Cannon later stated, treated him as an outcast, a process of vilification that had economic ramifications. Living in rented Kansas City, Missouri, and Rosedale houses with one and then two young children and his wife, Lista, Cannon was barely able to eke out a subsistence existence. The domestic economy seemed to have bottomed out. There was apparently no food for the table and no money for creditors, who supposedly repossessed furniture and other items in the Cannon home. Eventually, sometime in 1917 Cannon secured a job, which he held into 1920, at the "bottom rung" of a "big office," the Loose-Wiles Company. His parochial school training in penmanship and arithmetic paid off in his ledger clerk work, but the atmosphere was stifling in its pro-war patriotism. The job was a tedious grind, of value only because of the wage: "the whole routine and everything else was of no interest to me whatever. . . . A job like that, I'd come home Saturday afternoon and I'd never think of the job till I got there Monday morning." But at least Cannon had time for movement work and avoided incarceration, a fate that befell Earl Browder, his brother William, a future Browder-brother-in-law, Thomas Sullivan, and other Kansas City revolutionaries who refused to register for the draft.[5]

At loose ends politically, Cannon at times slipped into despair.[6] As we have seen, war's repression was a breakpoint for Jim's relationship with the IWW:

the "political state," which the industrial union movement had done its best to ignore, "was revealed as the centralized power of the ruling class. . . . The 'political action' of the capitalist state broke the back of the IWW as a union." Compelled to "protect the political and civil rights of its members against the depredations of the capitalist state power," the Wobbly fetish of decentralization returned during the political trials of 1918. Cannon was, in retrospect, shocked at the lack of a coordinated revolutionary defense campaign: in Sacramento, the vast majority of the indicted Wobblies refused to provide any concessions to a bourgeois court, offering a "silent defense" that ensured stiff sentences and eliminated possibilities of appeal; in Chicago, the strategy was diametrically different, with the accused opting for a "legal defense" that shied away from a series of political challenges, including propagandizing against the class nature of capitalist war.[7]

Socialist Revival

Cannon had no illusions about the Socialist Party of America (SP) at this point. By the time the Victor Berger-led wing of the Socialist Party expelled Haywood in 1912, ostensibly for advocating sabotage in violation of the recently passed Article 2, Section 6 of the SP Constitution, Cannon and most other left-wing socialists had grown weary of what they regarded as the "slippery, desperate crew" at the helm of the party's National Executive Committee. These "yellows," as they were derisively known, were thought to have repudiated Marxism and the possibility of workers' revolution (Trotsky characterized them as "Babbitts . . . ideal socialist leader[s] for successful dentists"), although there remained "reds" in the Socialist Party, from Debs at the upper echelons of symbolic authority to many in the trenches of locals spread across the country.[8] There were obvious political differentiations at almost every level of SP activity, including around the pivotal question of war, where gradations of left, right, and center articulated positions that could clash. Even the reddest of revered socialists, Eugene Debs, could falter, having offered support for Haywood's expulsion in 1912–1913, albeit in ways that he would later come to regret. Other more conservative socialists, such as Berger and Morris Hillquit, while routinely compromised in their opposition to war (Hillquit declared in 1914, to Debs's chagrin, that "The workingman has a country as well as a class"), could also tilt against the most bellicose of American socialists, who harbored pro-war sentiments to the point of urging military preparedness, as did elements of Milwaukee's socialist municipal administration in the summer of 1916. If support for the war was weak in SP circles, the patriotic chauvinism of the hour led to resignations of some leading SP members. Among those departing by publicly supporting United States involvement in the hostilities were William English Walling, J. Phelps Stokes, Charles Edward Russell, and Algie M. Simons.[9] All of this came to a head in 1917, with the formal entry of the United States into the war exposing the contradictory character of the Socialist Party. The SP's right-leaning leadership's rationale for opposition to World War I was in part an ethnic identification that translated into a position of "Hands Off Germany," but it nevertheless often seemed to parallel the revolutionary opposition to capitalist war that galvanized the militants of the socialist movement.[10]

When Morris Hillquit ran a successful anti-war campaign for the mayoralty of New York City in 1917, Cannon sat up and took notice. As 20,000 jammed Madison Square Garden, Hillquit thundered a cry for peace and the defense of civil liberties. With thousands of anti-war dissidents surging through the streets of immigrant neighborhoods in protest, Hillquit and the Socialist Party gained new ground, even in the face of much repression. News coverage of the peace project, its rallies and propaganda, swept the nation. Hillquit secured an eventual 145,000 votes (at 22 percent, this increased the previous socialist tally fivefold), and Cannon confessed to being "shaken up on my anti-political wobblyism." Realizing that "if an opportunist like Hillquit could wage a campaign and get nationwide publicity about it while the IWW couldn't conduct any strikes because of the tremendous repression, couldn't do anything," then "how much better [could] be done by genuine revolutionaries if they [got] this crazy ultraleftism out of their system?" This was the beginning of James P. Cannon's "evolution away from syndicalism and in the direction of leftwing socialism."[11]

The positive alternative was provided by the Bolshevik Revolution of 7 November 1917. As Cannon remarked in his commemorative pamphlet, "The IWW: The Great Anticipation":

> It took the First World War and the Russian Revolution to reveal in full scope the incompleteness of the governing thought of the IWW.... The turning point came with the entrance of the United States into the First World War in the spring of 1917, and the Russian Revolution in the same year. Then "politics," which the IWW had disavowed and cast out, came back and broke down the door. From one side, this was shown when the Federal Government of the United States intervened directly to break up the concentration points of the IWW by wholesale arrests of its activists.... From the other side, the same determining role of political action was demonstrated positively by the Russian Revolution. The Russian workers took the state power into their own hands and used that power to expropriate the capitalists and suppress all attempts at counter-revolution.

Cannon's central recognition in 1917, moreover, was that "the organizing and directing center of the victorious Revolution had turned out to be, not an all-inclusive union, but a party of selected revolutionaries united by a program and bound by discipline." At first it appeared that this would be grasped by industrial unionists and acted upon, and this lengthened the transitional stage in Cannon's conversion to Bolshevism, delaying his formal exit from the Wobblies. Many leading or former "one big unionists," including John Reed, Louis Fraina, and Haywood, did gravitate to the cause of the Russian Revolution. However, it was soon apparent that there was as much opposition to Bolshevism among the IWW ranks as there was support: a large number of the "bummery brigade" looked with suspicion on the notion of a disciplined vanguard that was rumored to ride roughshod over unions and workers alike. In failing to come to grips with the lessons of war and revolution, Cannon concluded, the majority of the IWW had sealed the fate of their once-heroic organization, condemning its post-1917 history to an "anticlimax" of "defeat and decay."[12]

Wobblies such as Cannon dipped lightly into anything that would have allowed them to understand continental Marxism or the nature of Bolshevism. What little European influence there was in the indigenous American Left was as likely to be Dutch as it was Russian, its socialism always cut with a dose of syndicalism. William English Walling's rare pre-World War I references to Lenin hardly made the Bolshevik leader a recognizable name in the United States industrial union milieu.[13] "Maybe there was a little more internationalist consciousness on the East Coast, in New York," Cannon stressed, "but in the West we never heard of Lenin, Trotsky, or anybody else." The Russian Revolution "awakened and reeducated" the Left. "You see, the revelation that this had been led by a party was a great blow to a simplistic Wobbly. They thought you didn't need any party. They thought all you needed was direct action. But [the Bolsheviks] had direct action plus an organized party plus theory . . . . I had enough sense to realise that this was something different from ours and I had better study it a little bit." Cannon thus confronted political theory for the first time in 1917, rupturing the rigid action-versus-theory dichotomy that had separated sections of the revolutionary ranks. This realization was in effect Cannon's introduction to *internationalism* as something more than "an abstraction to which you paid lip service." The Russian Revolution remained forever embedded in his consciousness as an event that awakened awareness of the need to situate and develop the American Revolution within its global context, a direct political *action* that lived in its concrete accomplishments as well as in its wide-reaching implications for the *theory* of the revolutionary movement.[14]

This qualitative change registered first with midwestern revolutionaries such as Cannon through the coverage of the capitalist press, where the accomplishments of 1917 could not be totally eradicated in the luridly slanted journalistic accounts of the Bolshevik victory. Trotsky's brief stay in New York early in 1917, where he met with Russian revolutionary exiles and American-based comrades, convinced him of the need for the Left to sustain a theoretical propaganda organ. Instrumental in this effort would be Louis Fraina, editor of a four-page militant sheet, *The New International*. Fraina, who had immersed himself in the classic writings of Lenin and Trotsky, was first influenced in his Marxism by Daniel DeLeon. Joining with Louis Boudin, author of perhaps the most theoretically acute work of the pre-World War I socialist movement, *The Theoretical System of Karl Marx* (1907), and the literate, German émigré socialist editor, Ludwig Lore, Trotsky's most intimate American acquaintance, Fraina and his colleagues put out the bimonthly *Class Struggle*.[15] It provided United States socialists with the views of European Marxists such as Kautsky, Bukharin, Lenin, Trotsky, and Mehring, and the Japanese revolutionary Sen Katayama, as well as an outpouring of articles from the editors themselves—Fraina was the most prolific[16]—and the odd piece from old practitioners of mainstream socialist agitation, such as Austin Lewis and James Oneal. Late in 1918, Fraina launched *The Revolutionary Age*, subtitled *A Chronicle and Interpretation of Events in Europe*, a virtual "party" organ of the now-coalescing forces in the left wing of the Socialist Party. Its message resounded throughout the country in locales such as Kansas City, where militants moved increasingly into a nascent underground communist movement. Lenin's "Letter to American Workers" originally appeared in this early United States revolutionary press. In a pivotal text published in 1918, *The Proletarian Revolution in Russia*, Fraina offered a wide-ranging introduction to some central writings of Lenin and Trotsky, the first serious documentation available to English-speaking Americans on the Bolshevik triumph. In all of this editorial work and writing, Fraina bridged the class struggle of the IWW and the revolutionary vanguardism of the Russian Revolution, making common cause with emerging American communists such as Reed, as well as stalwarts of the Marxist foreign-language milieu, including contributing editor N. I. Hourwich.[17] To be sure, Fraina presented a more volatile and syndicalist Leninism than would mesh easily with later orthodoxy, but the essential point for Cannon and many others was that he opened the American movement to questions of revolutionary theory for the first time.[18]

At the more popular level, Max Eastman's graphically creative *Liberator* brilliantly combined the avant garde and the political, with John Reed writing a series of articles on Russia that would later form the core of his immensely influential journalistic tour de force, *Ten Days That Shook the World* (1919). Eventually reaching a national audience of 60,000, the *Liberator's* first number appeared in March 1918, proclaiming the Russian Revolution "the most momentous event in the history of peoples." John Reed, writing from the world's first workers' state, provided a rousing call to action: "Lenin and Trotsky send through me to the revolutionary proletariat of the world the following message: 'Comrades! Greetings from the first proletariat republic of the world. We call you to arms for the international Socialist revolution.'"

This concentrated body of work, produced by Fraina, Eastman, and others, constituted a new word of revolution, simultaneously theoretical and practical, the impact of which rocked Cannon's settled midwestern syndicalist-socialist-populist world: "I was out in Kansas City living there. That's like living in the North Pole. . . . And hell's fire the whole world changed in our movement."[19]

A Revived Class Struggle

The Russian Revolution and its stimulus to the left wing within the Socialist Party thus altered the nature of revolutionary thought in the United States. Moreover, a new balance of class forces appeared simultaneously to be in the making. The tumultuous working-class upheavals of the next two years saw strikers as a percentage of all workers soar from 3.7 in 1915 to 22.5 in 1919. Annual work stoppages per year in the quarter-century reaching from 1881–1906 had averaged just under 1,500; between 1916–1921 this figure skyrocketed to 3,343. Organizing drives and strikes in Chicago's meatpacking industry and the great steel strike of 1918–1919; Boston's unique work stoppages among police and telephone operators; a wave of streetcar struggles that clogged city thoroughfares in Chicago, Denver, Knoxville, and Kansas City; as well as highly important general strikes in Seattle, Winnipeg, and elsewhere, reconfigured the relations of labor and capital. As David Montgomery has suggested, widespread use of the strike to extend workers' control of industry by the skilled, and increasing use of wage walkouts by the unskilled and machine tenders, if not necessarily orchestrated by revolutionaries, nevertheless expanded the nature and meaning of class conflict in the United States in the period from 1916 to 1920. The mix was even more volatile, with a congealing of immigrant nationalisms and class militancy. "One big unionism" was rampant, then, even when it was not paced by the IWW.[20]

Future Communist Party theoretician, Alexander Bittelman, recalled the heady atmosphere of the times. From an old-world Jewish socialist background, Bittelman had joined the Bund at the age of thirteen, grappling with Bolshevism and Menshevism from the time of the first Russian revolutionary agitations of 1905. Settling into America and adapting to its culture during the war years, he joined the Socialist Party, part of a wave of revitalized revolutionaries riding a new tide of consciousness rooted in understanding the need to harness the American Left and its future struggles to the experience of Russian Bolshevism:

> The feeling of an approaching storm was especially aroused in us—I felt it very strongly—by the widespread strike struggles and sharp industrial conflicts in the years when the left wing was taking shape—1917, 1918, 1919. The so-called "open shop" offensive of the large corporations and the resistance of the unions in many industries had much to do to stimulate left wing thought and action in those days. In this connection, the Seattle General Strike in February 1919 had been especially effective. We talked a lot about Seattle at that time; also about the General Strike in Winnipeg, Canada in May of the same year. These events were in my eyes—in our eyes—eloquent indications that things were coming to a showdown of some kind. This meant that the socialist party must prepare itself properly to take the lead and the left wing were the force to bring this about.[21]

Recruits like Bittelman swelled the ranks of the Socialist Party in 1918–1919, membership rising from roughly 81,000 to 108,000. This influx galvanized broad socialist activity, and registered in the rising percentage of the popular vote captured by the SP in various electoral campaigns. As the left wing strengthened, it produced a February 1919 manifesto that criticized old-guard socialists for not having turned "an imperialist war into a civil war—a proletarian revolution." All of this consolidated an alliance between the two major Kansas City revolutionary activists of this period, men destined to play significant roles, in divergent ways, in the future history of American communism.[22]

Browder and Cannon

Earl Browder and Jim Cannon had coexisted in the Kansas City revolutionary Left for a number of years, despite their differences regarding the American Federation of Labor and the Industrial Workers of the World. A Wichita-born son of a Kansas socialist, Browder gravitated easily to the pre-World War I Left, where, after a stint in the Socialist Party, he found himself aligned with William Z. Foster's syndicalist forces. Browder broke from the Chicago-based Foster when the latter refused to come out against the war, but he nevertheless maintained strong ties to AFL unions through his presidency of the Kansas City local of the Bookkeepers, Stenographers, and Accountants; involvement in the Central Labor Council; and activity in the "Labor Forward Movement." Still, Browder largely lacked the authority of Cannon's agitational history in the IWW front lines of epic class struggles, and as a former small businessman he tended to embrace cooperation as ardently as strike activity. Destined to bear the burden of his chosen occupation of accountant, for much of his life Browder clearly bridled at his denigration in Left circles. A nonpolitical prisoner once sneered to Ralph Chaplin as he saw Browder walking through the yard with another inmate, "Look at those little girls. What a swell example of the sort of men who are going to lead the American revolution!" Later, with Browder a communist functionary dispatched to China, a party limerick found its way into the federal prison where a core of IWWs remained incarcerated. The "Wobbly shed" rocked with laughter: "Hats off to our comrade, Earl Browder,/Who works with hot air and gun-powder./Believe me, he said, I will make China red,/Though I don't know chop-suey from chowder."[23]

This was unfair, a product of masculine bravado, antagonism to learned debate, and an unfortunate reductionism, in which revolutionary commitment was boiled down to its point-of-production essence. As Cannon, whose competitive placement in Kansas City radical circles, in Browder's eyes, grated on the Wichita native, was later to stress, "Browder's background and my own were almost identical," and while they diverged in the paths their syndicalism followed in the years 1912–1916, "partings of the ways organizationally never brought . . . a sharp break in cooperation and in personal relations." The two revolutionaries worked through the war years in tandem, and engaged in a wide range of "united front" work (although it was not so named at the time), especially around defense of political prisoners. Both strong opponents of the war, Browder and Cannon were "drawn together more closely" after these views became decidedly unpopular and increasingly dangerous in the latter half of 1917. If Cannon's later characterization of Browder as "an intelligent, industrious and dependable chief clerk by nature" carries more than a whiff of condescension, it was nevertheless the case that he valued Browder's anti-war, pro-Bolshevik stand in 1917–1918, and the two men soon forged a working relationship. "We saw the leftwing developing in the Socialist Party and we decided to make an entry . . . in 1918."[24]

Browder clearly felt "bested" by Cannon in some ways, and he used his later unpublished memoirs to right the wrongs he perceived, reconstructing a historical relationship that was quite close and supportive in dark strokes of a righteous, principled radical (himself) manipulated by a devious intriguer (Cannon). In actuality, the two midwestern radicals collaborated in the local "Free Tom Mooney" campaign[25] that drew in the entire labor movement and reconstituted the Socialist Party of Kansas, Missouri, and Nebraska on a thoroughgoing revolutionary basis. This and other political work laid the foundations for the establishment of a Browder-Cannon revolutionary press, *Workers' World*, the first issue of which appeared 4 April 1919, and marked the region as an early bastion of the proletarianized left wing.

To be sure, Cannon credits himself with bringing Browder into the fold of the developing revolutionary ranks, linking the lessons of the Russian Revolution to the possibilities inherent in the new political alignments evident in the Socialist Party. As Browder was finishing his first anti-war stint in a Missouri jail, Cannon, A. A. "Shorty" Buehler, and a number of other Kansas City militants, stimulated by talk of the Russian Revolution and, later, materials in Fraina's *The Revolutionary Age,* struck on the idea of starting up a weekly paper expressing their political views. Early in the resulting discussions, Browder and his brother were released from prison and Cannon "immediately took up the new program with them." It took some long talks to win the Browders away from syndicalism and cooperationism, Cannon claimed, noting that they were "rather disdainful of the left wing," and distrustful "of the foreign language federation movement" in the SP, which was thought to be rather isolated from workers, unions, and labor struggles, all the more so in the Midwest. Like himself, though, Cannon explained, Earl Browder "was a pronounced anticapitalist revolutionist to start with, and I found him receptive and sympathetic to the new idea." Agreement struck, Cannon, Browder, and a group of "live-wire militants . . .—former IWWs, AFL syndicalists, socialists, and quite a few independent radicals who had previously dropped out of the SP"— revived and transformed the old pre–World War I Workers Educational League of William Z. Foster. They made it into something of a Kansas City regional forum for radicalism (Cannon would be listed as its secretary as late as 1920): testing the waters of the local Socialist Party, talking with sympathizers, securing a majority support, applying for membership, and being admitted. Simultaneously agitating, organizing, and building for the launching of their new paper, Browder, Cannon, and others soon "took over the local" and promoted positions "in favor of the national leftwing which was forming around the country." It was something of a coup.[26]

A Revolutionary Press

Building the left wing in the tri-state area of Kansas, Missouri, and Nebraska required a propaganda organ dedicated to socialist education. The *Workers' World* aimed to be just that. It was one of a handful of early pro-Bolshevik newspapers in the United States, and one of only a select few under the editorial control of native-born revolutionaries outside of New York, Boston, and Chicago. Appearing under the auspices of the Workers' Educational League, the weekly *Workers' World* published thirty-five times over the course of eight months. It was edited by Browder from 4 April 1919 through mid-July 1919 (although he only appeared on the masthead as managing editor from the issue of 20 June

1919); thereafter, with Browder incarcerated for a second time at Leavenworth, the editorial duties fell to Cannon, from 18 July 1919 to the last issue of the paper on 28 November 1919.[27] Browder and Cannon drew on a dozen or so local contributors, including Ralph Cheyney, son of a University of Pennsylvania professor who contributed regular columns on "the cultural front"; and Ella Reeve "Mother" Bloor, whose writings supplemented coverage of her agitational speeches for Kansas City socialists. In addition, the editors reached outside of their immediate circles, soliciting columns and previously published matter from Seattle's Anna Louise Strong, Butte's William F. Dunne, Alanson Sessions of the Arkansas Llano Cooperative Colony, the anti-war radical Scott Nearing, and England's noted syndicalist, Tom Mann, who had spoken in Kansas City in 1913 and knew Browder through his previous contact with Max Dezettel's *The Toiler*. The Browder-Cannon paper was a judicious blend of the local, national, and international events of concern to class-struggle socialists.[28]

Workers' World devoted its first-issue pages to the four-month-old Kansas City strike of street railway workers, who pioneered mass action in the face of militia repression, fines, and jailings only to find themselves defeated, as well as to the repression of local Wobblies charged under the vagrancy laws. Alongside articles on the jobless of Detroit and accounts of the Chicago Mooney Convention ran commentary deploring United States intervention in revolutionary Russia, applause for the "Spartacans" of Germany, and brief notes of enthusiasm for the writings of John Reed. Spliced between lines of radical verse and accounts of the efforts to raise funds for a Kansas City "labor lyceum," short declarations of support for the European Revolution appeared. Dedicated to "The Incarcerated," the initial editorial, "Why the 'Workers' World'?," proclaimed:

> Capitalist society is destroying itself with the forces generated within its own body.... Today, in spite of the frantic endeavors of "statesmen" and "captains of industry," the whole economic and social structure is crumbling. We are too liable to look upon events in Europe as due to conditions peculiar to the Old World, and to congratulate ourselves upon the assumed fact that America is immune from such developments. America is just beginning to experience a rude awakening....
>
> Socialism offers the only way out. But Socialism, to be effective, must be organized and must become vocal. This is the "Why" of the Workers' World, to demand the abolition of the exploited workers; ... to show the inevitable breakdown of the capitalist system, and assist in developing the practical program by which the workers will take over industry for society as a whole.

It was a message aimed to unite immigrant revolutionaries and native sons of the United States left-wing proletariat in a revived socialism.[29]

Twenty-four numbers later, with Cannon at the helm and a subscription list of 1,200, the *Workers' World* mourned the passing of Horace Traubel, heir of Walt Whitman's nineteenth-century radicalism; publicized a Kansas City stop on the speaking tour of Bob Minor, recently returned from Russia and Germany where he had interviewed Lenin and Trotsky and witnessed the German uprising; upped the pace of criticism directed at the bureaucratized leadership of the AFL craft unions; detailed the role of strikebreaking college youth in the Boston police strike; and provided brief notice of both a local SP picnic and the last open-air socialist agitational meeting of the season. Now endorsed by the Omaha Socialist Party, the Kansas City organ was clearly the focus of a tri-state effort to bring the socialist ranks into line with the Bolshevik Revolution. "We Look to the East," proclaimed former Wobbly, Albert B. Prashner, recently released on bond from Leavenworth: "[A]n industrial autocracy has arisen in the Western Hemisphere more crushing as it is more efficient than the ruling class of Europe. . . . And now our eyes turn East—to Russia and the rising Industrial Democracies of Europe for inspiration that we may not grow faint and weary in the struggle for freedom." In the West, concluded Prashner, "night cloaks the land. In the East is the Red Dawn of the rising sun coming with the new day."[30]

A Fractious Left Wing

Newcastle, Pennsylvania, was as far east as James P. Cannon had ever been. He took leave of the Kansas scene late in the spring of 1919, making his way to New York City to attend the three-day National Left-Wing Conference at the Manhattan Lyceum, commencing 21 June 1919. "This was my first introduction to the national movement and international flavor and so on," Cannon later recalled. "That's where I met a lot of big prominent people." Among those James Cannon came into contact with, either as delegates or because they were in New York at the time, were Charles E. Ruthenberg (whose path crossed Cannon's briefly during the Akron strike of 1913) and Alfred Wagenknecht, from Ohio; the Irish revolutionary Jim Larkin; and the New York-Boston English-speaking core of emerging communism: John Reed, Benjamin Gitlow, Bertram D. Wolfe, Jay Lovestone (an alternative delegate), and Louis Fraina, who was assigned the task of opening the convention and acting as the first, temporary chair. Cannon was one of ninety-four delegates from twenty states, all deeply committed "reds," but divided irreparably over the strategic question of what was to be done to develop American Bolshevism.[31]

Those who gathered in the convention of the left wing were in agreement that what the United States revolutionary movement needed was a communist party. They disagreed, however, over the means to get to this desirable end. Cannon stood with the eventual majority, headed by the native-born American contingent from New York, Fraina, and the Ohio duo of Wangenknecht and Ruthenberg. The latter stressed that if revolutionaries were indeed seeking new methods of agitating as socialists, looking to the Russian Revolution, they were doing so possibly because conditions in the United States necessitated a new course. Against them stood a theorist blessed with Lenin's authority, Nicholas I. Hourwich of the Russian federations, Dennis Blatt and others from Michigan's recently expelled branch of the SP, and a loose ultraleft body of foreign-language delegates who spoke for the vast bulk of immigrant revolutionaries. This latter alliance of the self-proclaimed "Extreme Left" tended to dismiss allusions to the particularities of American experience as little more than centrist evasion of revolutionary commitment. "Here as everywhere in Europe," wrote Alexander Stoklitsky of the Russian Federation, the center "has learned nothing." In the face of revolution's call, continued Stoklitsky, too many were "irresolute, [prone to] vacillate, temporize, and remain stupid."[32]

The opposing groups at the fractious June gathering of revolutionaries battled over whether to transform the meeting into a full-fledged Bolshevik organization, on the spot, or, more judiciously, organize to capture "the Socialist party for revolutionary socialism" at the forthcoming Chicago "emergency convention," called for 30 August 1919 by the stolid executive of the mainstream Socialist Party, which was obviously terrified of the challenge posed by the left wing. Defeated decisively on the floor, the Russian Federation's leading spokesman, Hourwich, marched thirty-one delegates out of the convention, vowing to meet separately from the mainstream SP later in the summer and form a United States Communist Party. The remaining majority committed itself to winning the Socialist Party to revolutionary socialism at the end of August, or to break decisively from it. A manifesto, drafted by Fraina, drank deeply from the well of the IWW, challenging the SP's "petty bourgeois socialism," deploring the elevation of electoral politics to a programmatic orientation, extolling the virtue of the "mass strike," and marking out the AFL for special derision. Obviously highly influenced by Russian and German developments, the Left-wing convention nevertheless insisted that in the United States "revolutionary socialism" was "invigorated by the experience of the proletarian revolutions in Europe," but that it remained, "in a fundamental sense, the product of the experience of the American movement." None of this would have been alien to Cannon, who lined up behind the elected National Council, headed by Fraina, Ruthenberg, Larkin, Benjamin Gitlow, and Bertram D. Wolfe. His participation in the conference was low-key: Cannon, who lacked the experience and confidence to criticize those with whom he was obviously in disagreement, was drawn to those revolutionaries who professed concern with the "industrial labor movement." Most of the relatively raw Kansas recruit's direct association with conference participants likely involved Reed, Gitlow, and Larkin, key players in the "trade union commission." With them he consolidated "an informal alliance" that would carry forward into the next months.[33]

Foreign-Language Federations and the Dialectic of Revolutionary Mobilization

Indeed, the critically important contingent of European immigrant communists was a difficult body for Cannon to fathom, and to draw necessary lines of distinction within. The delegates representing the foreign-language federations at the New York conference of Socialist Party left-wingers in June 1919, headed by a vociferous Russian contingent, were hardly comparable to the foreign-speaking Wobbly agitators or the Kansas City socialistic Jews with whom Cannon had had much experience. Pushing relentlessly their right to lead the left wing, they maneuvered to secure absolute control, seemingly unconcerned about the costs to the movement they sought to dominate. To separate the actions, dogmatism, and arrogance of such delegate leaders from both their own theoretical sophistications and immense contribution to the United States revolutionary Left, and from the masses of immigrant radicals for whom they confidently spoke, in a vocabulary they understood to be unadulterated Leninism, has proven a considerable historiographic difficulty, complicated by the language of sources and the tendency of historians of the Left to essentialize the experience of "alien" revolutionaries. Too much commentary on the foreign-language federations homogenizes the personalities, politics, and practice of Old World revolutionaries, steeped in the richness of classical Marxism and often deeply respected within the ranks of immigrant communists. Some, especially those within the Russian Socialist Workers' Federation and the "physical force" wing of the Yugoslav Socialist Federation, were undoubtedly hard-hit by the disruptions, repressions, censorship restrictions, and infiltrations mounted by the state in 1917–1920. Their base of immigrant leftists, much broader than this leadership layer itself, proved pivotal in the creation of revolutionary communism in the United States, and would remain central to the Left throughout the 1920s and beyond, when the leaders of a few years before were long dispersed.

Between 1907 and 1915, fourteen foreign-language federations affiliated with the SP, and by the time of the 1919 Left-wing conference their ranks formed an absolute majority of the party, at 53 percent. Among the ultraleft federations, headed by the Russian contingent and, in general, buttressed by the South

Slavic, Latvian, and Lithuanian sections, significant expansion occurred, especially in the brief period from December 1918 to April 1919. On the eve of the
Chicago conventions, the numbers in these bodies approached 22,500, the
Russian Federation alone mushrooming from 600 to 12,000 in the space of
two years. This troubled mainstream socialist leaders, and conditioned a climate in which "shedding" the "extremists" was judged to be not only acceptable but a preferred option, especially among the more conservative-leaning
"old guard," such as National Executive Secretary Adolph Germer. It was evident that the struggles, revolutionary agitations, European understandings of
radicalism, and rich institutional life (embracing mutual benefit societies, fraternal orders, cooperatives, choirs, churches, and the ethnic press) of the
socialist immigrant milieus were increasingly difficult forces to harness and
control in ways acceptable to reform-minded SP leaders. There was resentment, as well, that the foreign-language federations exercised considerable
independence in their relations with the Chicago National Office, controlling
their own (often quite extensive) resources. The Finnish socialists, not generally known for their leftism, were astute managers of an extensive property
network. They owned some sixty-five to seventy halls valued at $600,000 in
1913, ran a printing plant and a Workers' College, were extensively involved in
cooperative businesses, and published a radical daily, *Tyomies*. If this foreign-
language federation complexity was difficult for mainstream SP officials to
negotiate, and for historians to grapple with subsequently, it proved no less
contentious, in 1919, for the emerging revolutionary left wing. Jim Cannon was
as perplexed as any.[34]

With the Left-Wing conference completed, Cannon took the opportunity to
kick around New York a bit, hanging out with Max Eastman and other writ-
ers/artists/poets associated with the recently repressed radical journal, the
Masses. "The *Masses* had a profound affect [sic] on the radical movement in the
West as well as in the East," Cannon noted. "Our movement had been a very
poor provincial and perhaps ultra proletarian movement. Its press was rather
limited by the circumstances of its membership and the knowledge of its leaders. And the *Masses*, I can't tell you how great was the influence it lighted up the
movement. Here, all of a sudden, a great array of artists, writers and poets
championing the cause of the revolution." Cannon basked in the limelight of
Eastman and his associates, enjoying the bohemian sociability. What was left of
the *Masses* crowd shared an office building on East 13th Street with the civil libertarian Roger Baldwin, and it became Jim's New York haunt.[35]

Cannon clearly enjoyed his first taste of New York, but home and comrades
were in the Midwest, and he returned to Kansas City in mid-July 1919. He had
to wrestle with a series of dilemmas, in which his emerging theoretical insights

into the needs of the American revolution—how to form its organizational center, a Bolshevik party—ran headlong into his understanding of the practicalities confronting his day-to-day work as a leading figure in the Kansas left wing and his appreciation of what that movement (and, more widely, the United States working class) was ready to accept and assimilate. Committed to the loose alliance of the Reed-Gitlow-Fraina-Ruthenberg coalition of the SP left wing as it emerged during the June National Conference, Cannon nevertheless found himself awkwardly uncertain of the immediate tactical orientation, which demanded alignment, or at least a statement of position, as to which leadership to follow. These dilemmas and their negotiation consumed Cannon's thought and time for the next six months, especially as he struggled to keep the *Workers' World* afloat.

For Cannon, one contingent was ruled out. He had absolutely no faith in what he perceived to be the ultraleftism of the Hourwich-led foreign-language dissident SP leaders, concentrated among the Russians. Ironically, the Russian Federation, the strongest foreign-language group in terms of its *ideological* capacity to claim the revolutionary heritage as its own, was the weakest in many other ways. With its origins in a small, New York-based Russian intellectual corps that concentrated energies on writing for the sophisticated Marxist Russian-language newspaper, *Novy Mir,* and lecturing on questions surrounding the European revolution, the founding fathers of the Russian-American revolutionary Left bothered themselves too little with the U.S. scene, relying on sectarianism to establish their rhetorical superiority. Unlike the Jews, the Germans, or the Finns, the Russian Federation exhibited "little sense of building and guiding stable cultural and political institutions." As Paul Buhle concluded, "Probably in no other group did the leaders hold themselves so seldom accountable."[36]

Cannon acknowledged readily that the theoreticians of the foreign-language sections, especially the Russian leaders, brought much of value to the American Left. "Earnest communists," they "helped inculcate the doctrines of Bolshevism." In many locales, especially eastern seaboard cities where the foreign born were particularly prominent, Latvians, Ukrainians, Russians, Hungarians, and Poles established "red" circles of revolutionary cadre that proved the beginning of United States communism, the bone and sinew of a post-1917 American left wing. The chauvinism of mainstream unionism, centered in the nativist hierarchy of the American Federation of Labor, was reproduced in the SP. When seven of the most left-wing foreign-language federations were expelled by the Hillquit-Berger-Germer SP triumvirate in May 1919, a mere three months before the Chicago "emergency" gatherings, Hourwich and Stoklitsky promptly parlayed their banishment into proof that the left wing's revolutionary credentials were unquestionable. Their opponents in the movements of SP dissidence were now bludgeoned with charges of centrism and worse. This, however, did little to convince Cannon that such repressed leaders could successfully mobilize the forces of American revolutionaries and extend their reach into the wider working class. Instead, Cannon saw their major impact as an unfortunate tendency to color the early communist movement with "excesses of unrealism" and a "tinge of romanticism," isolating the left wing forces from the activities and thoughts of workers. It was an old story. Engels confronted the problem as early as 1893, writing to Friedrich Sorge about the kind of sectarian Marxist who ignored "the necessity of learning the language of the country or getting to know American conditions properly."

Just how much these foreign-language federation theorists and leaders spoke for the masses of immigrant communists was also open to debate. The immigrant revolutionary ranks were in fact far more politically differentiated than the Marxist proclamations and intransigence of a few federation spokesmen suggested. Anarchists, communists, social democrats, Marxists, radical republicans, and those drawn to the cultural life of the immigrant neighborhood jostled in this ethnic Left. It would be these complicated rank-and-file forces that would provide critical material support, intense internationalism, diverse propaganda organs, and other varied contributions to the consolidating organization of revolutionary communism. If Cannon, like many others, appreciated this complexity incompletely, he could nevertheless not support the Hourwich-Stoklitsky Russian leadership. "They were not living in this country and I was dead set against the idea that they could lead the American movement," Cannon later recalled. Moreover, their sectarianism was excessive: "They wanted to show that they were one hundred percent Bolshevik . . . hell bent on a split."

Attracted to the Reed-Gitlow group, which placed a far greater accent on trade union questions than either the foreign-language federations or the longer-established English-speaking SP left-wingers in the Ruthenberg group, Cannon was nevertheless not entirely enamored of this contingent either, judging it too hasty in its precipitate rush to irrevocably divide the Socialist Party, insufficiently appreciative of the extent to which "the rank and file of the party were not ready." His wariness must have increased in the aftermath of the New York convention, as a series of Byzantine maneuvers, secret negotiations across factional lines, and arguments by Russian left-wingers hived Fraina and Ruthenberg off from Reed and Gitlow, drawing them into the foreign-language federation cause. This ensured that the forthcoming Chicago conferences at the end of August 1919 would be a complicated and polarizing clash. National Executive Committee (of the SP left wing) member Isaac Ferguson, a lawyer, exemplified the critical problem of nonproletarian socialist elements, distanced from the labor movement and the character of class struggle, subordinating themselves to the Russian leaders on the ground that they were the true heirs of Bolshevik successes. Although Ferguson pledged himself publicly at the 1919 June convention to the Reed-Gitlow faction, he and others then engineered clandestine negotiations with the Russian foreign-language federation leaders, abandoning the supposed left-wing majority from the June conference. "Comrades, the Russians made the Revolution, we did not," he pontificated. "They know how; we do not. I for one trust the Russians and will follow them."

In the end, the Windy City gatherings of the Socialist Party and its now split left wings were a volatile cross-current, in which the reformist forces of the Berger-Hillquit Party turned renegade, drew on their considerable knowledge of procedural obfuscation, and eventually called on the police to preserve their understanding of order. Reed and Gitlow, rebuffed from the SP convention, walked out to form the Communist Labor Party, and Ruthenberg, hovering about as many tendencies as he could manage to locate, eventually joined Hourwich, Fraina, Ferguson, and those foreign-language federations exiled from the Socialist Party to establish the Communist Party. Both newly declared parties issued their respective manifestoes/constitutions, as well as contradictory statements as to their memberships. When all was said and done, the United States revolutionary movement was forever changed by the Chicago events of late August/early September 1919: the two communist parties might realistically draw on ranks that numbered 40,000, but of these the foreign-language federations provided fully 90 percent of all ultraleft membership, a process of ethnic polarization that deepened as the Communist Party expelled its English-speaking Michigan branch (which then formed the Proletarian Party) mere weeks after the Chicago conference confusion and chaotic party formations.

Many revolutionaries, especially those from the American heartland, simply melted away from the movement, and the Socialist Party was left holding the shell of its former substantive body. From 108,000 early in 1919, the SP ranks thinned markedly by the end of the year, and dwindled to 12,000 by 1923. Yet a left wing, however fractured, was no longer on the leash of the "yellows." A red dawn, to some, was now more than a distant horizon.

It was most emphatically a foreign-federation phenomenon, at least for the immediate moment. Things leaned decidedly in the direction of the Russian and other East European sections, which constituted at least 75 percent of the entire left wing. Yet, significantly, the pivotal Jewish Federation—including leaders such as Alexander Trachtenberg, J. B. Salutsky, Benjamin Glassberg, Moissaye J. Olgin, and Melech Epstein—could not yet break decisively from the SP, although Alexander Bittelman and Noah London, a future labor editor

of the *Freiheit* (established in 1922), did make the move to the original communist underground, albeit associating themselves with contending camps.
Indeed, the Jewish socialist/communist forces of 1919 reveal how foreign-
language federations were riven with political differentiation. Thus, the Jewish
Socialist Federation contained a number of currents as the left wing emerged.
On the one hand, there remained a "right" element that would broach no
break from the Socialist Party. Well ensconced in the needle trades, this group
was often tied to established union officialdoms that were the preserve of
males whose background lay in the artisanal trades of a garment sector
increasingly dominated by female workers, and in which a gendered radicalism would emerge as increasingly salient in labor politics. There was, as well, a
more radical contingent that, whatever its hesitancy in opting for an early
embrace of communism, advocated workers' council and shop delegates'
movements within the powerful New York-based International Ladies Garment Workers Union, especially the pivotal Local 25, composed of waist and
dressmakers. London, for instance, promoted the council movement, and
moved into the same underground tendency as Cannon in 1919–1920. In contrast, the former Bundist, Bittelman, less sanguine about councilism and
increasingly critical of the undertone of syndicalist sympathy so pronounced
in revolutionary circles at the time, led the original exodus from the Jewish
Socialist Federation. As John Holmes has suggested, it was this evolving Bittelman politics, critical of syndicalism, that would perhaps eventually align the
Jewish theorist with William Z. Foster, a hardened antagonist of "dual unionism" in the 1920s. Bittelman headed the formation of a Jewish Communist
Federation in September 1919, a body that affiliated itself with the Hourwich,
foreign-language-federation group of the left wing. The Finnish Socialist Federation, the first such body admitted to the SP in 1907, and arguably the largest
and most united federation in socialist circles in the years 1917–1921, displayed
similar differentiations and also delayed its movement into the communist
ranks. In the future, it would ironically be with these foreign-language federations and their leaders, some of whom consciously held back from the sectarian and dogmatic excesses of the "Extreme Left" in 1919, with whom Cannon
and other native-born "industrial union" revolutionaries would align most
comfortably and effectively. These later alliances would exhibit considerable
strength, but they would never quite liberate themselves from the problematic
politics of "rightist" tendencies and factions, always present in the Finnish and
Jewish sections of early communism. In contrast to these groups' exemplary
staying power, the ultraleft Russian Federation leadership soon faded, repression in part forcing it to the margins. Some of its ideas would nevertheless survive in segments of the communist movement throughout the 1920s.[37]

Cannon and the Communist Labor Party

Cannon did not attend the Chicago conventions. Reasons both prosaic and principled kept him from being there. On the one hand, he had no funds, and delegates to Leftist assemblies always paid a considerable portion of their own expenses in this period. In addition, he was responsible for putting out *Workers' World,* and there was apparently a shortage of alternative editorial personnel. On the other hand, Cannon was a Socialist Party left-winger comfortable in neither contending faction—Russian-led "Extreme Left" nor eastern-seaboard New York cosmopolitan—and he was disturbed that the revolutionary ranks were being stampeded "into [a] premature and costly split." Cannon passed on being nominated to the convention, citing as his reason the need to pay strict attention to SP constitutional rulings in what was clearly an openly factional situation. He felt that a more respectful approach to party legalism and a more carefully delayed final reckoning with "the yellows" would have realized important gains. Because he had not been a party member in good standing for the requisite number of years, joining only after the Russian Revolution in 1917, Cannon was technically ineligible to attend the mainstream SP convention in 1919, and he would abide by this definition of eligibility. (John Reed had the same problem, but chose to attend and defend his right to be seated physically.) Another Kansas City left-winger was therefore sent.

The Chicago Socialist Party emergency convention debacle, in which Germer relied on tight security measures to bar entry to left-wing delegates and culminated in cops clearing a socialist hall and a series of secessionist walkouts, left Cannon few options. "The precipitate split cut the left wing off from thousands of radical socialists who were revolutionary in their sentiments but not yet ready to follow the left wing in a split," Cannon later concluded, noting as well that with the breach birth of the communist forces in Chicago resulting in two rival party factions, American Bolshevism appeared in 1919 "as a result of an unnecessary, or at any rate a premature, Caesarian operation, which weakened and nearly killed the child at birth." Such a development was quite antithetical to the desires of the Kansas City left wing. The choices of (1) working with the Russian leadership that had drawn Fraina, Ruthenberg, and a few other left-wing luminaries into its sphere of influence; (2) sticking with the staid socialists of the Germer-Hillquit-Berger ilk; or (3) opting for continuing relations with the one contingent that had some grounding in the actualities of American conditions and the labor Left, were, for Cannon, very close to no choice at all. He worked on winning Browder (still imprisoned) and others over to an alignment with the Communist Labor Party (CLP). The mid-September 1919 issue of *Workers' World* carried the platform and program of the Reed-Gitlow group, as well as an editorial denouncing the "black infamy" of the SP henchmen on the right. Only through "packed delegations and with the aid of the capitalist police" did SP stalwarts secure control of the emergency convention. This the *Workers' World* would not sanction, and as manager of that left-wing organ Cannon no doubt penned the concluding lines of the editorial statement, drawing Browder into the cause: "For the paper to take a coward's position for the sake of temporary expediency would make it unworthy of the further support of the many comrades who have put forth such tremendous effort to start it and keep it going. It would be unfaithful to the trust of the boys in Leavenworth and they would be the first to repudiate it."[38]

Cannon and the Kansas City comrades thus affiliated immediately with the CLP, which continued to publish Fraina's and Lore's journal, *Class Struggle*. At a 21 September 1919 set of tri-state meetings of left-wing supporters from across Nebraska, Missouri, and Kansas, held in Kansas City, Missouri, and Kansas City, Kansas, the Communist Labor Party was organized in the region. Cannon served on the Temporary State Executive Committee of the new revolutionary body, signing its original statement along with two women and four men; he was elected state secretary of the Missouri branch, and acted as district organizer of the party in Nebraska, Missouri, and Kansas. He was now a major figure in the initial communist movement in the Midwest, and his days as a wage-earning clerk were over.[39]

The Agitator's Return: Kansas Coal Fields, 1919

Cannon's links to the Reed-Gitlow group had been rooted in that group's interest in industrial unionism, and this concern—the old Wobbly fixation on direct action in the sphere of productive relations—remained central to Cannon's understanding of himself as a revolutionary socialist in this period. *Workers' World* proclaimed in its first issue:

> [W]hile this paper will unceasingly exert its efforts to broaden the scope of the labor movement in Kansas City, by making trade unionism, so far as possible, an expression of the will of the working class to entirely control industry, at the same time, its voice and power will be thrown into every labor struggle on the side of the oppressed, without regard to the politics of leaders, defects in organization, or blindness of the rank-and-file to the larger meaning of the fight.[40]

In the fall of 1919, Kansas revolutionaries, Cannon among them, could not but be aware that a critical flashpoint in the class struggle was unfolding in the state's coal mining sector. An incipient proletarian revolt pitted miners against the operatives, the state, and their international union bureaucracy.

The coal fields of southeastern Kansas, organized as District 14 of the United Mine Workers of America (UMWA), seemed a perpetual anarchy of labor conflict in the period 1916–1919. Roughly 10,000–12,000 largely foreign-born miners toiled in almost 300 mines, managed through 70 operatives but owned by a small number of companies, whose strength was sustained by the Southwestern Interstate Coal Operators' Association. The mine owners moaned of a strike count in the coal fields that reached well past the official four-year tally of 150, claiming a figure closer to 750. At the union headquarters of the United Mine Workers of America, discontent with the district was also rife: the region was regarded as in a state of "continuous turmoil," a "loose cannon" of "irresponsible . . . contract breakers." Leading the miners was a hard-drinking and hard-fighting coal digger who, according to Cannon, had "not yet learned the profession of labor leadership," in spite of having held union office since 1912. Indefatigable and volatile, Alexander Howat, born in the coal district seat of Pittsburg, Kansas, would head the smallest UMWA district into the largest conflicts, and not only with the bosses.

By 1920, in an effort to stabilize the coal districts, Kansas inaugurated draconian legislation that effectively outlawed strikes and dictated compulsory arbitration: all strikes had to be settled by three Industrial Court judges appointed by the state governor. Howat threw down the gauntlet, securing passage of provisions in the district union's constitution forbidding members from having any dealings with the court; defying the governor-appointed judges by endorsing strikes; occasionally breaking contracts; hauling the international union and its rising bureaucratic star, John L. Lewis, into endless litigation; and even serving time in prison. It earned Howat the enmity of all officialdoms—union, municipal, state, and federal—and loyalty and high regard with miners and militants, Cannon foremost among them. "The workers can't go too far until they have gained complete mastery of their own lives," Howat told Cannon in 1923. "Every strike is a step toward that goal."[41]

The immediate background to the Kansas Industrial Law Court was a 1 November 1919 national walkout of the miners, but that conflict itself was conditioned by wartime legislation, the Washington Agreement of October 1917. Through this pact, orchestrated by the War Fuel Administration, the UMWA and the mine owners agreed to a contract, to run from 1 April 1918 through 1 April 1920, or until the war was declared officially over, whichever came first. The miners won wage increases in exchange for their contractual commitment not to strike. Wartime and postwar inflation rapidly ate into the pay hike, however, and miners fell further and further behind in their struggle for a living wage. Meanwhile, an armistice was signed in November 1918, but into the fall of 1919 no formally ratified peace had been secured. As the miners watched workers in other sectors mobilize to secure economic redress, their hands appeared to be tied by a disingenuous technicality, and many were vociferous in their demands for betterment or strike action. The push from the rank-and-file was not to be denied, and a strike date was set for 1 November 1919: the miners wanted a whopping 60 percent monetary increase, changing shift practices, and a six-hour day. Attorney General A. Mitchell Palmer secured an injunction prohibiting union officials from abetting the walkout; troops were placed on alert in some coal districts; and Labor Secretary William B. Wilson, declaring the UMWA demands to be "impossible," offered a 30 percent raise, which the coal barons promptly refused to pay. Lewis and most UMWA officials complied with the court order, but almost 400,000 miners, ostensibly "leaderless," downed their tools and defied the government. Howat was among their early backers and he stood extraordinarily combative ground in the Kansas fields. Tightening the noose, the federal government slapped Lewis and eighty-three other UMWA officials with contempt citations and promised that 100,000 troops would be sent into the coal communities to reopen the mines. Bowing to "the inevitable," Lewis and his UMWA associates called it quits. The strike was beaten, and even the resolute Howat agreed, belatedly and reluctantly, with the capitulation. Nevertheless, Howat refused to order two Kansas locals, technically out on strikes unrelated to the general walkout, back into the pits. For his recalcitrance he was charged with violation of the wartime Lever Act, a statute not intended to be enforced against unionists but prohibiting conspiracies by two or more individuals to restrict the distribution or production of fuel or food.[42]

Caught in the Anti-Red Dragnet

Along with Charles Baker, national organizer of the Communist Labor Party, and a well-known figure in the Ohio left wing, Cannon championed the miners' rebellion with an autumn agitational tour. The pages of the *Workers' World* were soon promoting the coal strikes, and Cannon traveled to see Howat in Pittsburg, Kansas, witnessing the mine leader's courtroom defiance of judicial authority. As the climate of repression lowered in early December, with Cannon back in Kansas City and attending the mass trial of former Wobbly comrades (the Wichita case), he was arrested in the courtroom. Baker and Cannon, charged under the Lever Act, had allegedly "conspired to obstruct, hinder and delay the production of bituminous coal," by speeches and the publication of articles in the *Workers' World* calculated to "inflame the minds of the miners against their officials" and encouraged a disorderly defiance of a return to work order until such time as the miners' demands were met. Bail was set for each agitator at $15,000, an immense sum at the time, and $5,000 more than was levied against Howat. Cannon cooled his heels in jail for sixty days. Not until early May 1920 did a federal grand jury, convened in Kansas City, eventually return indictments for Baker and Cannon. Hanging over Cannon's head for two years, the charges were routinely postponed until they were finally dropped in 1922.[43] In the interval, Howat and District 14 led a vigorous opposition to the Industrial Court Law, resulting in unauthorized strikes; jail sentences for the insurgent leaders; and a Lewis-led assault that suspended Howat, revoked the charters of eighty-one Kansas locals, and installed a compliant officialdom instructed to tame the rank-and-file.[44]

Sitting in jail at the end of 1919 and the beginning of 1920, the red dawn that Jim Cannon had heralded in 1917 seemed to have passed into a night of dark repression:

> Seek you rotten politics?
> Go to Kansas!
> There's where legislative sticks,
> Turn to lances;
> That belittled and betrayed,
> And put labor in the shade
> To dim its chances.[45]

The "rotten politics" of state terror was not, however, a local, Kansas-only problem. Cannon had been indicted under the Lever Act as part of a generalized "red scare" that, in its 1918–1920 assault on the Left, has come to be known as the Palmer Raids. Attorney General Palmer's injunction efforts in the coal strikes of 1919 were but the industrial tip of an iceberg of political repression aimed at the new bodies of revolutionary communists that first surfaced out of the turmoil of the Chicago conventions. In a relentless purge, affecting scores of cities, thousands were rounded up, many of them beaten and abused; countless halls and headquarters were broken into and literature and other items destroyed and confiscated; public meetings were rudely attacked; "alien" deportations abounded; a servile press fanned the flames of an anti-Bolshevik "hysteria." An initial wave of arrests and seizures in November 1919 was followed by a wider assault on the notorious night of 2 January 1920. Across dozens of states, a dragnet indiscriminately herded dissidents into the arms of a less than welcoming state.[46]

In Cannon's Communist Labor Party, the red hunt left the organization, barely four months old, shell-shocked. As Cannon recalled, "Almost every local organization from coast to coast was raided, practically every leader of the movement, national or local, put under arrest, indicted for one thing or another." The CLP was literally wiped out in the American heartland, home to much of its native-born working-class constituency, while in the large urban centers its foreign-born members were terror-driven into retreat. Leaders lived with indictments hanging over their heads, trials to prepare for, defense committees to mobilize, lawyers to meet with, and a seemingly endless round of criminal charges, sentences, convictions, and appeals. In Kansas City, the nascent communist movement was decimated, with more than 100 comrades arrested and 35 held over for trial. The regional organ of the left wing, *Workers' World,* collapsed with Cannon's arrest; the last issue appeared on 28 November 1919, and Ella Reeve Bloor recalled with understatement that the paper "was raided" and "one of the editors arrested."[47]

Cannon's prospects were thus anything but bright in the cold winter months of 1920. Awaiting bail, the jailed revolutionary must have pondered what he had sacrificed for the movement. Low-paid office work that was of no interest to him, weekends with his Wobbly "boys," and poring over type for the next issue of *Workers' World* had left scant hours for Lista and the children. Tensions must have been developing. If Lista had been "pretty game" in 1913, she may well have lost some of her enthusiasms for the revolutionary Left by 1920. There is no indication, for instance, that she embraced Cannon's leftward-moving Bolshevik commitments. And yet Jim and Lista stayed together, a bond of love and affection existing that was not easily broken.

A part of that process of continuity was forged around young Carl and Ruth. Cannon sensed, in later life, that he had inevitably shortchanged his children. "There's a double problem with parents and children in the movement," he suggested. "Having children and being active . . . is like taking two jobs. One of them has to suffer a little bit. And I think my children resented the fact that the movement took so much of my time and energy." But in 1920, even this problem might have been in the future. Cannon recalled coming home to nights of play and joyous father-child interactions, ones that Lista would have relished as much as her husband: "Yai, yai, yai, here's Daddy home! Then the kids would run and jump all over me . . . [a]nd for the rest of the evening when I'd be with them there was nothing but laughter and fun and stories and games and all of a sudden you realize they think I'm the greatest guy that ever came down the pike. It's a wonderful thing for one's own moral[e] to have even children think that."[48]

Did James P. Cannon, separated from his wife and children by jail bars, reflect on these relations and their meanings in 1920? We will never know. It is almost certain, though, that he invested some of his thought in worry about the state of the communist forces. Cannon still had criticisms of his chosen left-wing milieu, which retained, even in the face of the Palmer Raids, unrealistic and romantic notions.[49] As the climate of coercion worsened with convictions, prison sentences, deportations, and further harassment, the assailed Bolshevik ranks of the United States retreated further into the illusory world of sect-like isolationism.[50] With prominent spokesmen such as Max Bedacht facing arrest four times in a five-week period, the Communist Labor Party used its beleaguered official organ, *Communist Labor,* to admonish capitalism in bold headlines: "Caesar—Beware the Ides of March" and "Capitalism Your Days Are Numbered." "It may be midnight in the United States," declared the revolutionary newspaper, "[b]ut dawn in the east tinges the world with crimson."

Driven underground, communists embraced their class enemy's caricatured, fantasied understanding of the clandestine "red," living an otherworldly, "illegal" political life. Active agitational work was replaced by an atmosphere of conspiratorial intrigue, increasingly distanced from the material circumstances of the United States. Proclaiming that "the sun of communism was rising in the East," the red advance guard of the CLP called on workers to down tools on 1 May 1920. Its entire leadership jailed or under surveillance, hundreds of its rank-and-file and supporters facing sentences or deportation, the CLP "vanguard" had barely a half-dozen organizers in the field, and they were but steps ahead of the police. A general strike was the last thing the Communist Labor Party could have organized.[51] "The elements in the leadership who tended toward unrealism gained strength," Cannon suggested, "inasmuch as the movement was then completely isolated from public life and from the labor organizations of the country." Cannon was underground at this point, and from where he was "down below" it was difficult to see the red dawn that had originally attracted him to communist ideas and Leninist party practices, however much he might see allusions to it in the revolutionary press. Nonetheless, he remained committed to trying to get back to a higher ground of political life, where he could once again envision an American revolution on the skyline.[52]

Russian Revolution Anniversary Number

The

COMMUNIST

No. 9   *All Power to the Workers!*   1an Cents

OFFICIAL ORGAN OF THE UNITED COMMUNIST PARTY OF AMERICA

Boycott the Election!

5

Underground

A Suit of Clothes

Cannon was often pressed by comrades to write an autobiography. Those who knew his character, especially, as he would have put it, "the merit of his defects," could have predicted that it would never come to pass.[1] But had he managed to pen his life's story, Cannon once claimed that he would have entitled one of the chapters, "A Suit of Clothes." The anecdote central to the chapter was set in 1919, with Cannon languishing in jail. It took the comrades two months to scrape together $30,000 in property/cash that could be put up as bail needed to secure Jim his freedom. Cannon's benefactors were not his Rosedale chums, the old-style Irish patriots. "I was sick and fed up with the Irish by then. . . . [W]hen I looked around and saw all the god-damned Irishmen were either cops or politicians or grafters and contractors and prosecuting attorneys, I said to hell with it. I disaffiliated." Rescuing him from jail were Kansas City's "radical socialistic Jews," one component of the mass base of the foreign-language federation's left wing.[2]

Released from his cell, Cannon surveyed the revolutionary Left and saw the carnage of the state's campaign of terror and suppression. Alexander Bittelman later characterized 1920 as "the worst year in the history of our movement."[3] As he brooded in the office one day, his clothes a seedy match for his mood, Cannon was suddenly and unexpectedly confronted by three determined Jewish comrades. They hustled him down to a Jewish merchant's clothing store, where he was introduced as a distinguished revolutionary. "The Irish community had thought that I was a damn ne'er-do-well," Cannon recalled, "[b]ut there it was a great honor—editor of the paper and a speaker for socialism." Outfitted with a new suit of clothes, the socialists demanded that the merchant cut the price down to wholesale, and kick in an extra five-dollar reduction as his own contribution. It was all for "Comrade Cannon," and it slashed $30 worth of apparel to a mere $15, which the hard-bargaining radicals handed over to the haberdasher. "I walked out of the store with a brand new suit of clothes and an uplifted spirit that kept me going for a long time," Cannon remembered with fondness. "Now, how could I quit on people like that?"[4] A revolutionary native son thus sealed a pact with immigrant left-wingers.

The Divided Communist Underground

As one of the few Communist Labor Party figures who had a long-standing connection to the American radical movement, reaching beyond that of propaganda work into the leadership of class struggles, Cannon was quite unusual among native-born American revolutionaries in 1919–1920. C.E. Ruthenberg confessed in 1923 that among the delegates who attended the founding conventions of the two communist parties in 1919, there were barely a half-dozen "who knew anything about the trade union movement." Most of the communists of 1919 were indicted, tried, and sentenced under various criminal anarchy/syndicalist or sedition laws; among them were many who were further targeted for potential deportation as "aliens." They were the victims of overtly *political* repression, and it was their ideas that were being put on trial or shipped into exile. Cannon's indictment, in contrast, grew out of his *industrial* activity among the beleaguered coal miners, and he was one of the few communists alleged to have transgressed the law of class relations on the basis of his advocacy of striking workers. That the indictment was weak, resting on supposed violation of legislation drafted during a war emergency that had actually ended with the termination of hostilities, was perhaps one reason that the charges against Cannon were never pressed, allowing him relative freedom to pursue organizational and agitational work for the embattled communist cause.[5]

The central issue, aside from weathering the storm of repression, was that of bringing together the warring factions of the communist forces, bridging the gaps that separated foreign-language federation leaders in the Communist Party (CP), and the more native-born, English-speaking heads of the Communist Labor Party (CLP)—which still, of course, contained many immigrant revolutionaries. From the moment of their separate births, the larger Communist Party adhered to a conception of itself as the anointed vanguard of American communism, rebuffing attempts on the part of its rivals to foster unity. Bittelman later acknowledged that the "wise men" of the federations feared the dilution of the Marxist program that they felt was inevitable if the more vocal

English-language "federation eaters" ever gained entirely the upper hand. These "theorists" and "philosophers" were willing to concede that native-born American and English-speaking comrades should lead any united communist party publicly, but they actually demanded that such figureheads be subordinate to the behind-the-scenes programmatic guidance and recognized authority of the old-guard, European Marxists. This was not separable from certain communists' "underground philosophy," in which "illegality as a principle" was often strongly embraced. There were some such communists, including elements in the Lettish group, for whom he had much regard, who Cannon saw as "professional undergrounders." All of this conditioned the CLP/CP divide. When the CLP proposed that its Executive Committee meet with that of the CP to search out a basis for unification of the two revolutionary bodies, it was responded to, for the most part, with standoffish disdain. Of the two bodies, the CP was undeniably more isolationist, clandestine, and sectarian. Trade unionism was assailed as "the arch enemy of the militant proletariat," and all forms of laborism, "moderate petty bourgeois socialism," and illusory electoralism were considered not far behind in their pernicious political effects. Communists of all stripes tended in this direction,[6] but because the CLP was less strident in its calls for attack and abstention than the CP, the latter could tar the former with the brush of reformism, and root itself in a kind of revolutionary purity that ensured the continuity of acrimonious separation. Particularly on the question of trade unionism, CLP figures such as Arne Swabeck and Charles Krumbein, whose experiences touched down on events such as the Seattle General Strike and labor organizing in Chicago, found the ultraleft, undergroundist positions of some foreign-language federation leaders in the CP difficult to swallow.[7]

It was also beginning to take its toll within the CP itself. Charles Emil Ruthenberg, the old-time Socialist Party left-winger and electoral campaigner from Cleveland who had aligned with N. I. Hourwich and other foreign-language federation leaders in the original founding of the Communist Party, secured his position of national secretary on the basis of past prominence in the revolutionary Left and familiarity with the American terrain. A man drawn to the revolutionary movement as a substitute for the ministry, and known to appreciate being referred to in the initialed nomenclature of corporate executives as C.E., Ruthenberg quickly wearied of the ultraleft posturing indulged in by some left-wing Russians, whose "federated" numerical dominance assured them the capacity to overrule Ruthenberg and also licensed internal maneuverings and machinations that offended his businesslike sensibilities and moralistic haughtiness. Along with supporters such as Jay Lovestone, Ruthenberg no doubt looked longingly at the English-speaking leaders and ranks of the Communist Labor Party. The Ruthenberg group's discontents heightened in February 1920,

when the Russian ultraleft insisted on issuing a leaflet to striking railroad workers calling for armed struggle as the precondition for proletarian victory.
Ruthenberg questioned the tactical advisability of advocating violence, given
that such a rhetorical stand could elicit a new round of state repression or
buttress the ongoing court claims against communism's seditious intent. He
was severely chastised for his "menshevism" by the "great theoreticians" of
the foreign-language majority. Eventually, Ruthenberg tired of the charade. He
took a rump of the Executive Committee with him in a split occasioned by an
acrimonious and somewhat abstract battle over how the Communist Party
should approach the masses: to Ruthenberg and his supporters, the "crying
need" was for communist propaganda to be brought into "the everyday
working-class fight in the United States." Opponents in the Russian-dominated
CP were content to make little impression on the American working class until
"the disintegration of world capitalism" compelled the masses "to listen to our
message." By such straws the back of the Communist Party camel was broken.
For a month the Ruthenberg group, consisting of a majority of English-
speakers and a small contingent from the foreign-language federations, existed
as a separate party, one that refused to give up the name, the newspaper, the
funds, or the organizational records of the original CP. Both wings of the now
divided Communist Party began to court the Reed-Gitlow CLP, but the
Ruthenberg group made more of the need for unity, and engineered a late May
1920 set of meetings in Bridgman, Michigan, where it was hoped that parallel
conventions of the two bodies would culminate in a Unity Conference.[8]

All wings of the fractious communist milieu were now deeply underground.
Party leaders wrote under pseudonyms. Membership cards and charters were
discarded and destroyed, and communists were told not to divulge their political affiliations unnecessarily. Connections among groups separated by huge
geographic expanses were difficult, public meetings were exercises in guarded
caution, and recruitment work was next to impossible. Max Shachtman
recalled going to communist street meetings in what was then commonly
called Trotsky Square, at the end of New York's Central Park, 110th Street and
Fifth Avenue. Determined to approach speakers to voice his support and link
up with the communists, Shachtman could not buy his way into the movement: "They were exceedingly cagey, and here is a young fellow who talks
English without any foreign accent, who may be a spy trying to permeate our
ranks. And I was getting cold treatment everywhere."[9]

The climate was possibly even more severe in Kansas City, where Cannon
must have kept his head low. He read the communist press, no doubt with a
keen eye on its distillation of theoretical questions, reporting of various party
developments, and coverage of the state of the trade unions and class-struggle

mobilizations.[10] Undoubtedly his main source of non-Kansas City information appeared in the publications of his own tendency, *Communist Labor,* the
official organ of the Communist Labor Party, and the CLP's *The Voice of Labor.*
Dominated by accounts of developments in revolutionary Europe, reports on
the trials and imprisonment of CLP leaders, polemics against socialist adversaries in the United States, and a stream of educational articles on the canon of
revolutionary Marxism (Liebknecht, Lenin, and others), *Communist Labor*
devoted most of its space to agitational political writing. Front-page headlines
generally proclaimed the arrival of the revolution, and when workers specifi-
cally were addressed, it was to call them to urgent tasks: "Down Tools May
First, 1920" or "A Call to the Workers of All Countries to Help Save Soviet Russia." *The Voice of Labor* was probably more to Cannon's liking, its articles providing accounts of the workers' movement in other lands, its theoretical
discussions focusing on matters of strategic direction for the trade unions, and
its propaganda directed to striking railroad workers or the meaning of IWW
repression at Centralia, where a murderous vigilante attack on the lumber
town's radical hall, on Armistice Day, 1919, ended in the lynching of Wesley
Everett. A subsequent trial revealed the complicity of the courts in papering
over an Employers' Association killing spree.[11]

Isolated revolutionaries such as Cannon craved the words of revolutionary
propaganda that came their way through pages of journals such as *Communist
Labor* and *Voice of Labor.* Ultimately, though, it was the deed they wanted: Revolution was in the doing, which is precisely why the communists of 1919 had
such high regard for Lenin, Trotsky, and the Bolsheviks. As the CLP and CP
engaged in public discussions concerning the possibility of unity in the winter
and spring of 1920, communists such as Cannon glimpsed the possibility of
working themselves out of the trap of underground marginalization. From
their deportation pens on Ellis Island, the "Lettish Group of Communists"
issued a stirring unity appeal, an indication that within the ranks of the foreign-
language federations there were indeed revolutionaries who had grown tired of
sectarian divisions. When Ruthenberg and his supporters split from Hourwich
and the Russian majority of the Communist Party in May 1920, the door was
opened much wider to the likelihood of a regrouping of the United States revolutionary Left.[12]

Bridgman Brokering: The Emergence of Cannon
as a Potential Communist Leader

Cannon was no more than a regional figure in the pre-May 1920 communist
ranks. To some, like the German Marxist theorist Max Bedacht, a proper and

straitlaced man, Cannon's proletarian demeanor was a disappointment not easily forgiven: Bedacht never managed to get over the revulsion he experienced
upon meeting a tobacco-chewing Cannon for the first time.[13] Foreign-language
federation figures were likely to see Cannon as one of the "new people" linked
to, but not quite of, the trade union forces associated with William Z. Foster's
later entry into communist circles.[14] Benjamin Gitlow recalled dismissively: "I
remembered him merely as a colorless individual of medium height and com-
plexion, who spoke with a nasal twang and in sentimental monotone. He was
not then very talkative . . . [but] joined the Communist Labor Party [and] soon
rose to prominent leadership."[15]

The path to that prominence ran through the unlikely outpost of Bridgman,
Michigan. For the last week in May, thirty-two delegates associated with the
Ruthenberg wing of the Communist Party, twenty-five from the CLP, one fraternal delegate, and a Comintern representative battled over old differences in
an effort to form a United Communist Party. Most of the communists in
attendance sported the words "AT LAST" pinned to their breasts, that being
the large proclamation of a circular distributed among their ranks; it would be
the first headline of *The Communist,* a special convention number of the official organ of the United Communist Party of America (UCP) that appeared 12
June 1920. The delegates succeeded in their unification purpose, but only
barely, securing compromises over the language of a program, the name of the
organization, and the composition of the Central Executive Committee (CEC)
after six days of often-acrimonious jockeying for position.[16]

Cannon went to the conference, which was convened in part in a clearing in
the woods, as the Kansas City Communist Labor Party delegate. The tenor of
the gathering was set by the climate of brutal repression. A once-promising
revolutionary vanguard had been railroaded into jails and pressed to adopt a
fugitive stance, branded as an outlaw force. Defeated in their division, those
who came to Bridgman aimed to unite the revolutionary Left. Still, the scars of
repression were evident in the almost ritualized attachment to revolutionary
purity that galvanized the delegates.[17] Cannon recalled that the underground
ideology of the movement manifested itself in wildly sectarian flights of fantasy.[18] Its program honored Marx and Engels as well as Lenin, commencing
with a quote from the *Communist Manifesto* and ending with a ringing declar-
ative endorsement of the dictatorship of the proletariat. In an age of collapsing
capitalism, imperialist war, and democratic illusion, the United Communist
Party embraced mass action, industrial unionism (albeit with criticisms of the
IWW), and electoral boycotts, all of which were assimilated to the general
direction of class struggle. As a "bulwark of capitalism," the American Federation of Labor was perceived as a reactionary job trust for the privileged skilled

workers, and communists were expected to oppose its leadership's betrayals and the program of craft disunity that it inevitably espoused.[19]

Cannon intervened in the debate over industrial unionism. Coverage of the convention acknowledges that, under the pseudonym "Dawson" (all delegates were provided with or adopted new "identities"), he convinced the united communists to moderate what must have been highly sectarian positions.[20] Speaking two or three times, Cannon argued on the basis of his experience in the IWW, and his contact with AFL unionists, for a more flexible policy on the labor front. The struggle in his view was for "a double": new organizational breakthroughs among workers abandoned by craft sectionalism, coupled with "boring from within" established trade union bodies, where the ranks were undoubtedly open to a more revolutionary perspective than their suffocating bureaucracies allowed. In the words of *The Communist,* "Dawson" was the leading spokesman of the CLP current that wanted "neither direct endorsement of the IWW nor absolute condemnation of the AFL." He insisted "that the AFL must be considered from the angle of the local unions, not from the side of the Gompers officialdom; that industrial unionism was having a development in many fields aside from the IWW; that the need was for a call to a new general central theme of . . . a new One Big Union." Proud of his contribution, Cannon later acknowledged that it was a large advance over his previous IWW perspectives. Although he did not secure a majority on behalf of his positions (on the contrary, he recognized that he was in a distinct minority), Cannon clearly took the convention by storm, establishing himself as an authority on industrial unionism and labor questions.[21]

As a representative of a minority (the CP delegates probably clung more rigidly to sectarian positions on trade union work, but Cannon's views would not have been accepted by all CLPers either, especially those influenced by John Reed's strong tilt toward the IWW), Cannon/Dawson was elected to the CEC, polling an impressive thirty-two votes that trailed narrowly another candidate's leading tally of thirty-three. At the CEC meeting immediately following the convention, Cannon was elected as one of three associate editors, with assignments to a party press to follow, and as one of two auditing committee members. He was immediately dispatched to St. Louis, Missouri, with particular charge of the Belleville district of the southern Illinois coalfields; the district organizer's post came as a consequence of his past work among the Kansas miners. Southern Illinois's coal diggers had thrown down the gauntlet of radicalism in 1919, forming a Belleville District Miners' Defense League, using the pages of the *United Mine Workers' Journal* to issue a nationwide appeal to organized labor for funds in support of their cause. Belleville's Subdistrict 7 insurgents were led by a young miner militant, Luke Coffey, and they challenged the coal barons' use of the Lever Act to dock paychecks in August 1919. Their wildcat strikes drew the ire of Illinois District President Frank Farrington who, funded by UMWA President John L. Lewis, launched an anticommunist crusade in the coalfields, tarring the rank-and-file rebels with a brush of Socialist Labor Party domination.[22] The UCP no doubt thought it could capitalize on the obvious discontent in the region.[23] Cannon possibly felt that the pace of his integration into the life of the professional revolutionary was moving too fast for his liking, and he later claimed that he fought against his nomination and election to the Central Committee, knowing full well that it would involve relocations that he resisted "quite vociferously" on the ground that he was needed in the "Kansas City movement." Overruled by his comrades, Cannon had become one of the United Communist Party's leading organizers and ranking executives.[24]

Cannon was now playing in an entirely different league.[25] We have no way of knowing what Lista, Carl, and Ruth thought of Jim's 1919–1920 move into the underground communist milieu, but there is little doubt that as a husband/companion and a father he was largely an absent figure in these years. The children were too young to grasp fully their father's commitment to the cause of revolution, but Lista must by then have come to understand that the hobo rebel she had married in 1913 was indeed in the movement for the long haul, and that in the shifting politics of the post-1917 years Jim's commitment was deepening in ways that encompassed increasingly dangerous and distancing assignments. There is no hint of any marital breakdown at this time, but neither is there much in the way of allusion to the importance of loved ones in Cannon's life. Lista's relationship with her family was reasonably close, and the Makimsons showed little fondness for Jim, whom they must have regarded as, at best, little more than an "irresponsible red." The extended Rosedale family of John Cannon would have been a source of aid and comfort, but its material resources were never expansive, and, aside from Jim's father, no one from that quarter had any real grasp of what the communist underground was truly about. Kansas City comrades—the socialistic Jews and others to whom Jim felt so indebted—likely saw Cannon's rise to prominence in the United Communist Party as a powerful promotion, and one that confirmed their judgment of Jim as a revolutionary of weight and substance. They undoubtedly wished him well as he departed to take a place on the national stage. In 1920, for the first time in his life, Cannon's ties to Rosedale-Kansas City were decisively broken. He would be back, but only out of obligations to the movement first; secondarily, in the case of his father's death in 1947, for personal reasons that were not without their political content.[26]

Cannon's UCP posting to St. Louis, Missouri/Belleville, Illinois could hardly even have allowed for much in the way of a trip back to Kansas City. His reception among the miners, whatever his talents, was not likely all that warm. The UCP's programmatic reification of "uncompromising class struggle under all circumstances" and staunch refusal to "cooperate with groups or parties" not of the same mind, including formations such as a Labor Party, isolated it from most workplace conflicts and political developments. Its strident advocacy of soviets, proletarian dictatorship, and armed opposition to American capital and the state too often fell on deaf, uncomprehending ears.[27] In the late spring and early summer of 1920, the practical context of the coalfields militated against Cannon being able to promote this kind of politics, however deftly they were pitched.

The miners were already impaled on the horns of a struggle that hardly allowed much voice to the kinds of positions espoused by the UCP. The Illinois counterpart of Cannon's contact among the militant miners of Kansas, Alexander Howat, was the left-leaning Scots radical, John H. Walker, a member of the pre–World War I Socialist Party and a leading figure in the 1919–1920 push to establish a National Farmer-Labor Party. Never as radical as Howat, Walker was more integrated into trade union and mainstream socialist circles, and his opposition to World War I was less than resolute. Nonetheless, with a long history in the United Mine Workers of America, where he was president of District 12 from 1906–1913, and a distinguished place in the influential Illinois State Federation of Labor, over which he presided from 1915 into the 1920s, Walker was a presence to be reckoned with in what remained of socialist circles, among the miners, and in the ranks of left-leaning labor in general. Within the miners' union, Walker crossed swords with John L. Lewis, then perfecting his bureaucratic machine in the UMWA. The sides for the radical miners in 1920 must have seemed clear enough, then, and there was too little space for the likes of Cannon and the UCP. With the Right (the Lewis machine) and a seeming Left alternative (Walker and the movement for a Labor Party) firmly established in the southern Illinois coalfields in 1920, Cannon would have found communist propagandizing and the organization of UCP branches a tough row to hoe. Making little headway, Cannon was sent to Cleveland after the second Central Executive Committee meeting of the UCP. There he took up the editorship of the *Toiler*, successor to the original left-wing organ, the *Ohio Socialist*.[28]

A Cleveland Sojourn: Challenging Ultraleftism

Arriving in Cleveland late in the summer of 1920, his family now in tow[29] and the presidential election campaign underway, Cannon might well have pondered his time in St. Louis and the coalfields of Illinois. He must surely have confronted arguments that Walker as a labor candidate deserved socialist support, and while they could be deflected with reasons, other difficulties were posed for the UCP position as well. Debs, for instance, was running for president from his jail cell in Atlanta, and many revolutionaries grasped intuitively that a vote for the old socialist warhorse, victimized by the capitalist state, stood for something other than endorsement of the now distrusted Socialist Party.[30] Yet, in October 1920 the UCP issued a proclamation, "Boycott the Election!", which allowed no support, however critical, to be extended to any compromised candidate, which amounted to all of those running for office on whatever basis, whatever ticket. The UCP, in effect, articulated a syndicalist-like elevation of the industrial struggle at the point of production as *the* strategic orientation of political transformation, calling for armed working-class uprisings, general strikes, and the formation of workers' councils/soviets. This was little more than the mechanical application of a caricatured Bolshevik model. It lacked appreciation that workers' soviets appeared in Russia as the economic parallel of the political development of Lenin's leadership and the Bolsheviks' increasing presence as a factor in state power, and, after 1917, as the governing party.[31]

Beginning to appreciate the problematic "unrealism of the ultraleft," Cannon was gaining awareness of the extent to which the repression of 1919–1920 had distorted the program and practice of the revolutionary vanguard: "We didn't have public meetings; we didn't have to talk to workers or see what their reactions were to our slogans. So the loudest shouters at the shut-in meetings became more and more dominant in the leadership of the movement. Phrase-mongering 'radicalism' had a field day. The early years of the Communist movement in this country were pretty much consecrated in ultraleftism." The Kansas revolutionary was also increasingly uncomfortable with the conception "that it [was] a revolutionary principle to remain underground."[32]

Few industrial centers had revolutionary pedigrees more illustrious than Cleveland. Ruthenberg hailed from there, and manifestoes of the early communist movement had appeared routinely in the *Ohio Socialist*. The paper gravitated almost immediately to the Communist Labor Party and pushed the cause of unity among communists rigorously.[33] With the *Workers' World* ceasing publication at about the same time, the *Ohio Socialist* became the voice of midwestern revolutionaries in the CLP.[34] A long-time leader of the Philadelphia Communist Party, Herbert Benjamin, first crossed paths with Cannon in Ohio in this period, when the Rosedale radical impressed him with an impassioned speech defending the leaders of the Russian Revolution as "guiding stars" of the international proletariat. Benjamin described the editor of the *Toiler* as "a very eloquent orator, with a lot of emotion, a lot of feeling, and even some poetry in his eloquence, . . . a true revolutionary, one that a person could model himself after."[35]

Edited by Elmer T. Allison, a future CEC member of the Workers' Party, the *Toiler* first appeared at the end of November 1919, informing radical readers of the state's ongoing anti-communist repression and the mobilizations of workers and reds; class-war prisoners were the subject of much treatment.[36] The *Toiler*'s pages were a judicious blend of labor reporting,[37] revolutionary agitation, and theoretical education, mixing national and international coverage. A serialized course in "Proletarian Science History" outlined some of the basic materialist themes that older, pre-World War I socialists had cut their teeth on, including the doctrine of evolution.[38] Very much resembling the *Workers' World*, the *Toiler* received an early, enthusiastic response among Cannon's Kansas City, Missouri, comrades.[39]

Cannon probably took over editorship of the *Toiler* in August 1920, although the underground practice of leaving names off the masthead makes it impossible to date his Cleveland arrival precisely. Only three articles signed by Cannon appeared in the *Toiler* between 27 August 1920 and 7 May 1921, the first two dealing directly with communist criticism of the IWW, the last a polemic aimed at those who would have non-trade union forces revive the labor movement.[40] There is, however, no mistaking Cannon's touch on the pages of this Cleveland-based communist newspaper, which was not above reprinting articles from the IWW's *Solidarity* or running pieces such as "Facts of Hobo Life."

The youthful Mollie Steimer of the anarchist Federated Commune Soviets, convicted of sedition during World War I and a voice of education and armed resistance to "white terror," demanded freedom for radicals who had suffered the repression of the state. Throughout the fall and winter of 1920–1921, the *Toiler* sustained a series of particularly Cannonesque commitments: to class-war prisoners, such as jailed Wobblies, Tom Mooney, and Sacco and Vanzetti, not to mention incarcerated communists such as C.E. Ruthenberg, I. E. Ferguson, and Benjamin Gitlow; to "outlaw" strikers and their insurgent leaders, among them the railroad switchmen, Illinois miners, and Alexander Howat; to industrial unionism and the mobilizing power of organizing all workers and amalgamating those hampered by sectionalism; and to the powerful significance of the Communist International. An emerging radical avant garde of labor journalists and communist artists were recruited to the pages of the paper. Much of the direct work and writing was no doubt done by staff and associates, including the original editor, Elmer T. Allison, who remained with the paper in some capacity until its eventual departure for New York, where it would later become *The Daily Worker*. Cannon acknowledged just before his death that although he enjoyed the editorial work at the *Toiler*, "the trouble was that I got drawn into political work of the Party so deeply that I didn't have time much for the technical work. They had another fellow taking care of that." Still, responses to letters by the editor often exhibit Cannon's sensibilities, conveying the extent to which he was grappling with the ultraleftism of the underground.[41]

A dialogue thus developed within the pages of the *Toiler*. The accent of a native son of the American working class could be heard, as the struggle to elaborate a revolutionary program grew out of the specific conditions of the United States in 1920–1921 and the guidance of the Communist International.[42] The latter had, at its Second Congress in the summer of 1920, adopted twenty-one points or conditions of admission, by which adherents of the revolutionary Left could join its ranks and unite in opposition to all temporizers. As much as the twenty-one points, with their explicit call to engage in illegal work and keep all reformists at bay, appeared to lend Comintern authority to the positions of the American "Extreme Left" and undergroundism, their impact would prove limited, especially in the trade union realm. In fact, CI rigidity eased somewhat in the following months, giving way to more united-front orientations. Much of the trade union content of the twenty-one conditions was softened, if not jettisoned directly, through a June 1921 Communist International declaration calling on communists in all countries to "bore from within" mainstream unions. In the United States, this brought William Z. Foster's Trade Union Educational League decisively into the communist camp. Cannon's attempt to negotiate positions that advanced a revolutionary program within the working class in ways that accorded with the actualities of life in the United States thus proved prescient.[43]

At first glance, Cannon's *Toiler* views on communist work in the unions could embrace almost rudimentary positions, not all that far removed from those he espoused as a Wobbly.[44] This was the substance, for instance, of Cannon's last signed *Toiler* article, a 7 May 1921 statement, "Who Can Save the Unions?" that appeared first in the Duluth communist paper, *Truth*, under the title "Open Shop Fight a Conflict of Classes." Cannon assailed the Central Trades and Labor Council of Greater New York for adopting a series of recommendations about how best to combat capital's open-shop drive. Advocating reliance upon closer relations with the Interworld Church Movement, suggesting the need for a speaker's bureau that could coordinate forums with religious and civic bodies supposedly sympathetic to labor's cause, and urging constitutional amendments to the council's governing procedures that would allow the seating of fraternal delegates from nonlabor bodies, the mainstream New York trade union movement was shifting the focus of the struggle from a class-against-class perspective, arguing instead for the need for cross-class alliances, coalitions, and activities to combat the bosses' war against the unions. Cannon's response was predictably critical. In elaborating a more orthodox class-struggle position, though, Cannon was nevertheless not yet capable of putting forward a resolutely Leninist program, and he retreated into a syndicalist-like assertion that the unions could prove the sole engine of revolutionary transformation: "No, the labor unions can get no help in their struggle outside the working class. More than that, they need no other support. The working class has the power not only to defeat the effort to destroy the unions, but to end the system of exploitation altogether." The residue of Cannon's IWW past remained in a slighting of the role of revolutionary political organization, largely because the sectarian ultraleftism of the underground milieu provided a kind of insular insurance against it being shed decisively.[45]

Nevertheless, Cannon was clearly developing an almost intuitive understanding of how to apply Leninism to the American scene. This was evident in the *Toiler*'s response to a Scott Nearing lecture in Cleveland on "The Labor Crisis in America," where Nearing was reported as balking at the need for a revolutionary leadership of the working class that was prepared to seize power from the ruling class when the opportunity presented itself.[46] More significantly, Cannon was developing a quiet challenge to the reification of soviets so pervasive in underground circles, where the unthinking, routinized call to form workers' councils had taken on, in the aftermath of 1917, an almost ritualized character. "When the idea of soviets became popular in this country there were widespread efforts to organize local councils," Cannon wrote in reply to one of a series of letters to the editor. "But because there was no need for them they withered away one after another. The organization of soviets must be preceded by certain definite conditions or they will amount to less than nothing. There must be a period of national turmoil, with a spirit of revolutionary aggressiveness developed on the part of the working class, before soviets can be effectively organized."[47]

As Cannon later confessed, his perspective at the time "came close to being a Leninist position. I didn't know it at the time."[48] Given what was appearing in other communist publications, and acknowledging the programmatic ultraleftism of the United Communist Party, formulated barely six months before the *Toiler* published the first of these exchanges, Cannon's editorship of the Cleveland paper was on the edge of heresy. Yet precisely because such unorthodox positions were clearly making the *Toiler* as much of a mass organ as the underground communist movement was capable of producing[49]—a paper with obvious links to workers, their unions, and their everyday lives that other, more theoretical organs came nowhere near developing—Cannon was not only given a relatively free hand in his Cleveland work, but he was also drawn increasingly into the upper echelons of the UCP. There he pressed consistently for mass work, especially around issues with which he had voiced longstanding concern: dissident unionism and the defense of political prisoners.[50] It had been a long step from Rosedale to Cleveland, and one that Cannon took with some misgivings and trepidation; it would be a shorter, quicker, and perhaps less conflicted jump to New York.

New York: Bohemians and Clandestine Communists

The *Toiler* was moved to New York in September-October 1921; Allison wrote an editorial on September 17 announcing the decision to relocate.[51] Jim went with the paper, although he had probably stepped down as editor some time earlier. Cannon had in fact been spending much time in New York while formally based in Cleveland, dispatched to the "party center" to address the evolving politics of the revolutionary vanguard. At this time, the leading cadre of the UCP and other communist bodies consisted of extremely young men. The "veterans" were approaching forty, and among them many—Ruthenberg, Bedacht, Isaac E. Ferguson, L. E. Katterfeld—were serving sentences in 1920–1921. Cannon and Gitlow (also jailed), not yet aged thirty, were among the leaders of another lot that included Earl Browder, Bill Dunne, and Arne Swabeck. An even more junior contingent, of which Jay Lovestone, William W. Weinstone, and Bertram D. Wolfe were the best known, was barely out of its teens, fresh from college.[52] John Reed, a mercurial figure with little capacity to contribute to organizational stability, but a personage of immense moral authority on the communist Left, died in Moscow on 17 October 1920, after his last writings on the Second Congress of the Communist International were dispatched to his UCP comrades.[53] The most tragic figure of all, the theoretical light of post-1917 American Marxism, Louis C. Fraina (whose abilities managed to antagonize those, such as Reed and Ruthenberg, who imagined themselves at the head of the revolutionary forces), disappeared from the movement. Almost exactly Cannon's age, he was the victim of ludicrous allegations of being a spy as well as some of his own mistakes of judgment, which left a cloud of Comintern suspicion relating to the misappropriation of funds earmarked for revolutionary work in North America hanging over his head.[54] The balance sheet of any leadership review undertaken by the UCP in 1920–1921, then, was unambiguous: the movement was somewhat headless. Cannon was a logical candidate to fill the void, "one of the few available communist leaders who had the English-language ability and office skills necessary for party administration."[55]

Cannon's closest New York comrades were not the leading party theoreticians, but its Greenwich Village bohemians. He renewed acquaintances with the old *Masses* crowd and Roger Baldwin of the Civil Liberties Bureau, a forerunner of the Civil Liberties Union. It was at the Bureau that a young Louis Francis Budenz found himself approached by "the secretive Cannon" and his old Kansas City comrade, "Mother" Ella Reeve Bloor. "Repulsed" by the underground character of the communist movement, Budenz was unmoved by the pair's enticements to come into the revolutionary underground and change its condition from clandestine to open.[56] The Left of this avant garde was gathering around Max Eastman's new project, *The Liberator* (the *Masses* having been snuffed out by the Post Office in 1917), and included the writer Joseph Freeman; Robert Minor, at that time a highly respected commercial cartoonist who had moved through anarchism into being a staunch advocate of Lenin and the Russian Revolution; and Mary Heaton Vorse, a radical journalist cultivating a commitment to labor's cause. The latter were a couple, and they "invited [Cannon] to stay with them while waiting" for his family to arrive from Cleveland. "We got along beautifully," Cannon recalled in 1974 with some nostalgia for a friendship forged in the moment of comradeship, but destined, like many others, to turn sour in the factional ugliness of coming years. Jim picked up some pointers from Mary on how to "organize material for speeches and articles," developing a "patching" technique, which involved cutting up a manuscript and shifting sections of it around, that he would use for the remainder of his life. He became especially close with Eastman who, though not a Bolshevik, grasped intuitively the significance of Jim's efforts "to break out of this ironbound undergroundism," and offered the professional revolutionary "great sympathy and understanding." For a midwestern native son, the path of revolution was cosmopolitan indeed, and Cannon's circles were widening appreciably.[57]

The underground, however, remained a closed shop. So clandestine was activity that it was difficult for major figures to connect up with anyone outside of the small collective of ten that defined a captain-headed communist group in this period. Such captains were then one of a further ten whose single representative belonged to a still more elevated "decemvirate," with further gradations leading eventually to the Central Committee. Communists never knew who else was in the ten-member phalanxes outside of their own small group, and they were discouraged from socializing with other known revolutionaries. Meeting places changed from week to week. Organizers collected dues, distributed literature to their designated comrades, and kept in touch with the wider party apparatus, but few communists actually knew where to locate the party in the event that there was some need to do so.[58]

Earl Browder was a case in point. After his release from Leavenworth early in November 1920, Browder concluded that he had been blacklisted from employment in Kansas and struck out for New York, leaving his wife (who had no desire to relocate) and a young son. His only party connection was Cannon, but the

underground was so impenetrably dense that Browder, who had no idea of Cannon's whereabouts, knocked about New York and secured a bookkeeper's position at a Broadway wholesale import-export company before making any
political contact with the revolutionary Left. "It took me longer to find the party
than to get a job," he later quipped. Browder was eventually steered in the direction of the United Communist Party, and he and Cannon reconnected surreptitiously at a restaurant on 125th Street. The meeting ended with Cannon stressing
that Browder's approach to revolutionary work in the American Federation of
Labor put him in "a very favorable spot right now," there being "a big swing in
favor of a new trade union policy" along the lines of Earl's past work in Kansas
City. With that, Jim pressed a copy of Lenin's *Left-Wing Communism: An Infantile Disorder*, into Earl's hands and, begging off to go to an "urgent appointment,"
left his old comrade to ponder the conversation and the pamphlet.

Cannon was quick to trumpet Browder's credentials as a revolutionary
familiar with midwestern labor leaders, a militant known for his honorable
activism in the AFL. He claimed to have helped orchestrate Browder's appointment to a large American delegation to the first Congress of the Red International of Labor Unions (RILU), although Browder later painted an entirely
different view of how the two Kansas revolutionaries related to one another.
Whatever actually happened, the Kansas clerk now had a foot in the offices of
international communism. From there he convinced William Z. Foster to
accompany him to Moscow as an "observer." Out of happenstance such as this
were future leaders of the Communist Party put on their roads to success.[59]

Cannon, Consolidation, and an Above-Ground Party:
Kansas Charm and the Politics of Revolutionary Regroupment

Cannon, "a curiosity in [this] stifling underground atmosphere," was at this
time "in the thick of party politics."[60] The issues were threefold, and not unrelated: (1) the need to further extend the regrouping of the revolutionary forces,
uniting *all* revolutionaries under the banner of the Communist International in
a single, decisive American party; (2) a reformulation of communist program
and practice, in which the sectarian ultraleftism of the past would be replaced
with an orientation that would allow communists to intersect with the labor
movement and American public life; (3) a break from the shadowy stagnation
of "the underground blind alley."[61] Two developments, emanating from the
Communist International, spurred Cannon and others to actively fight for a
new kind of communism. The translation and publication of Lenin's *Left-Wing
Communism: An Infantile Disorder* began to register with the revolutionary
ranks of the United States in January 1921. Its sober justification of "legal,"

above-ground parties and unambiguous call to penetrate mainstream unions, as opposed to isolating the militant minority of trade union reds in dual unions, was complemented by Comintern directives from Zinoviev that specified the need for unity in the American communist movement.[62] Coinciding with a softening of the climate of repression that had characterized the Lusk Committee and Palmer Raids years of 1919–1920,[63] this Soviet prod pushed the communist underground in new directions. In January–February 1921, the UCP newspaper, *The Communist,* was dominated by discussions of unity and tactical reorientation,[64] and Cannon was central in a number of ongoing negotiations that, over the course of 1921, would bring the remaining holdouts of the foreign-language federations into line with their English-speaking communist counterparts and assimilate the "belatedly" dissident collection of Socialist Party leftists, who formed a Workers' Council group in April.

Cannon also participated in the Comintern-ordered "shotgun marriage" of the old foreign-language-federations-dominated Communist Party and the UCP atop Mount Overlook, at Woodstock, New York, in May. He was called away to Kansas City on the closing day to appear in court for the final time in relation to his Lever Act indictment, but before he departed the convention Cannon left his mark on the politics of the period. He also met two communist cadre who would figure centrally in his life as a Left Oppositionist. One, the Danish-born, Seattle-Chicago-based trade unionist and editor of the left-wing Scandinavian organ, *Socialdemokraten,* Arne Swabeck [pseudonym, "Max Everhart"], recalled that Cannon was achieving a particular prominence in underground circles, advocating policy and practice that would later crystallize into a general position of party legalization: "At the 1921 underground convention it was Cannon who led the way and explained the reason for orienting toward active party work in the trade unions. He also most consistently took the lead in the complex process of getting the party out of the underground straightjacket to work openly for its great communist ideals." Swabeck also recalled "a gentle, beautiful, and very capable young woman," Rose Karsner, a committed revolutionary militant who had been recruited to the National Office of the underground communist movement by an old friend from the Socialist Party left wing, Ludwig Katterfeld. Rose was the recording secretary at Woodstock, and as she took notes her dark eyes must have crossed the bright blue counterparts of Jim Cannon, as he punctuated a speech with a flashing smile or an oratorical gesture. Later in the year, Cannon was appointed to the newly formed Communist Party's negotiating committee, and instructed to ease the Workers' Council group into the revolutionary fold.[65]

A seventeen-year-old Max Shachtman was associated with this current, and he began to hear tales of Jim Cannon, a thirty-year-old senior communist, at this time. Cannon's reputation preceded him, Shachtman recalling that "[h]e was known as an excellent orator, a very smooth writer, an exceedingly intelligent and shrewd politician, who had what comparatively few of the then leaders of the Communist party had: namely, he had a living, personal connection with the pre-Bolshevik revolutionary radical movement in this country."[66] Less in awe, but more mature in his appreciations, which grew out of proximity to inner-party life, was the Jewish revolutionary Alexander Bittelman, whose judgment of Cannon in this period was full of praise:

> As I became better acquainted with Jim, I began to notice and appreciate his skills in internal party politics . . . [bringing] unity into the warring groups of the Jewish Communist and Left-Wing movements. He managed, by his political skill as well as his charming personality, when he chose to be charming, to win the respect and also confidence of our group—the Jewish section of the Communist Party—as well as of the Olgin-Salutsky group—formerly the Jewish part of the Workers' Council. . . . I remember a certain image of him that I acquired after a while. It was the image of a caretaker of a large experimental institution or laboratory, moving about various machines, tools, gadgets, testing tubes, etc., making sure they operate properly, oiling, fixing, changing, improving, and adjusting. . . . His humor and his wit played no small part in all of that.

To opponents and personal adversaries, this might smack of the ward heeler, and Gitlow, whose treatment of Cannon can be counted on to be nothing if not unduly harsh, noted in later years, "When he spoke, I thought I was listening to a miniature Boss Murphy of Tammany Hall." Bittelman saw things differently: Cannon's skills were "a source of strength" to those attempting to build a communist party, and in 1921 "for the particular phase in its development," Rosedale's native son made "a very important contribution."[67]

By the summer of 1921, Cannon's fight to unite the communist cadre on a different, less ultraleft, program appeared to be gaining impressive ground. Following on the heels of the Woodstock amalgamation in May and paralleling the proceedings of rapprochement with the Workers' Council leftists, Cannon aligned with Ruthenberg's junior lieutenants Lovestone and Weinstone (C.E. was still in prison), and the Jewish federation theoretician, Bittelman, forming something of an interim leadership. It was committed first and foremost to overcoming "undergroundism" by the creation of a legal, aboveground communist party. In the underground vanguard, a decided lack of party discipline—in which meetings were sporadic, so-called mass work uncoordinated and attended to unenthusiastically, and internal educational work cavalier and unfocused—coupled with the general absence of an English-language press and the imprisonment or marginalization of potential

leaders such as Ruthenberg or Alfred Wagenknecht (whose resolute commitment to undergroundism ran him afoul of the Comintern and cost him reelec-
tion to the national secretary's post in 1921), ceded a certain space to the
Cannon-led cohort on the Central Executive Committee.

As a preliminary, tentative step in this group's march away from ultraleftism, the American Labor Alliance was launched, "a legal instrument of the
Communist party in the field of mass propaganda and agitation" with a Provi-
sional Executive Committee, and an ostensible National Office at 201 West 13th
Street, New York. A federation of communist foreign-language bodies and
labor/educational/defense groups, many of them little more than paper organizations under the secretaryship of Cannon's old Cleveland co-worker, Elmer
T. Allison, the Labor Alliance appealed for an organizational fund of $25,000;
sponsored an original foray into electoral activity, running Gitlow for mayor
of New York; conducted forums and lectures; and launched a coast-to-coast
speaking tour by Ella Reeve Bloor. Its significance was not great, and it was
soon undercut by Comintern directive, the Soviets feeling that it was inadequate and that a more far-reaching stretch into above-ground activity was
required. Nevertheless, it was a beginning, and it had served as an organizational umbrella under which Cannon, Lovestone, and Bittelman sat down
with their counterparts in the Workers' Council group—J. Louis Engdahl,
Alexander Trachtenberg, and J. B. Salutsky—to hammer out terms of unity.[68]

There remained resistance to abandoning the underground; certain forces
appeared implacable. On the CEC Cannon now worked with a fragile majority. His main ally was Bittelman, both men agreeing that the stakes were high
precisely because the communist forces had faded from significance to the
point, in Bittelman's words, that "the Communist Party of America practically does not exist as a factor in the class struggle." Writing under a pseudonym, "J. P. Collins" stated bluntly that "[w]e have virtually disappeared from
the public scene."[69]

Cannon may well have been "more determined" on the question of the
complete legalization of the communist party than anyone within his immediate circle, but he appreciated the need to proceed judiciously. He recognized
that dispensing entirely with the underground party would never curry sufficient favor with the ranks or a majority within the leadership, but there was,
given the Comintern's orientation, sufficient support on the CEC to move in a
dual direction, creating a legal party while preserving an underground apparatus. The numbers of rank-and-file communists plummeted from the exaggerated claims of 90,000 (CP and CLP combined) in 1919 to 11,000 (UCP) in
1920, to possibly as low as 10,000 (some estimates put the actual figure at
6,000) in 1921, as repression and schism took their toll. The foreign-language

federations, never "eaten," remained numerically all-powerful, controlling as much as 90 percent of the membership.[70] Well into 1921, 10 such federations claimed dues-paying members of just under 11,000, enrolled in some 410 branches, controlling 6 daily newspapers (including Finnish publications in Worcester, Massachusetts; Superior, Wisconsin; and Astoria, Oregon, as well as the German *Volkszeitung* and the Hungarian *Elore*), a smattering of weeklies, biweeklies, monthlies, women's, and comic publications, and an extensive leaflet and pamphlet press. This was the mass base of "undergroundism." If its membership numbers were on occasion inflated, there is no question that communism's ongoing presence in the class struggle of the United States was kept financially afloat by the material contributions of this foreign-language federation milieu.[71]

Cannon's interim coalition leadership was backed implicitly by the Third International, as well as by various pressuring forces still outside the party, among them the Workers' Council group. Yet, it was only tolerated by other CECers, such as Robert Minor, whose position on the underground was consolidating. As preparations began for the launch of a legal party, opponents started to clamor for a full gathering of the underground party to discuss the nature of the shift into above-ground activity. A so-called Left Opposition coalesced in the CEC, a trio of hard-nosed extremists composed of Massachusetts' John J. Ballam [Moore]; the Minnesota Lettish communist, Charles Dirba [Dobin]; and George Ashkenudzie [Henry], a Russian who eventually found his way back to the Soviet Union. They claimed the endorsement of 4,000 communists, an absolute majority of the party membership. The crisis finally came to a head on 2 November 1921, when the dissenting threesome was suspended from the Central Committee. With the way cleared for various negotiations, the formation of a new legal party was announced, its convention to take place at the end of December 1921. The suspended oppositionists, further chastised by a Comintern document brought to America by Minor, refused to accept the Moscow decision and threatened to launch a rival communist party.[72]

The critical document swaying the Comintern was a nine-page, single-spaced typescript, authored by seven members of the Central Executive Committee of the Communist Party of America, headed by Cannon [Cook] and including Lovestone [Nelson], Bedacht [Marshall], and almost certainly Bittelman and Weinstone. An amazing appeal "For a Party of the Masses," it developed a decisive case against the three "minority members" of the CEC. Detailing the minority's breaches of discipline and relentless opposition to all efforts "for the extension of legal work," Cannon and his co-authors stressed that the ultraleft "resisted every plan to co-ordinate and centralize the already existing communist organizations, to say nothing of creating a new one on a broad, national scale. Party nuclei feverishly 'controlling' a local lodge or fraternal order here, a singing society there, a debating club yonder—such was their conception of 'utilizing all legal possibilities.'" "Nimble acrobats on the trapeze of 'sacred principles,'" the minority stood convicted of sabotaging the work of reaching out to the masses.

Acknowledging that an underground party had a place in the struggle to build communism in the United States, Cannon and the CEC majority stressed that it was nevertheless likely that in different times and different places the relationship of the underground and legal parties would shift: "underground organization is no doctrine and no panacea. It is a revolutionary expedient to be used according to needs." Emphasizing the successful beginnings of open, communist work among the independent unions, for the unemployed, and in defense of class-war prisoners, the CEC majority document made a strong case that communism could grow in the United States only if it was liberated from its underground confinements. Finally, it signed off with adherence to the leadership of the Comintern: "Forward to a communist party of the masses, a worthy section of the Communist International—the inspirer, organizer and leader of the world's proletariat!"[73]

Cannon and his comrades of the CEC majority would win this skirmish against the most intransigent elements of the underground: a legal party was clearly about to be formed. The point of friction would later prove to be around the way it would come into being, exactly what its role was to be, and in particular how its relation to the underground Communist Party of America was to be defined. As Ludwig E. Katterfeld, appearing as "Carr" before the American Commission of the Fourth Congress of the Communist International, 27 November 1922, would later report, "A legal party was decided upon, a legal party not to take the place of the old existing Communist Party, but a legal party to serve as instrument of the Communist Party for its work—the work of rallying the workers to the political struggle." The underground leadership accepted this as the basis for founding the new legal party, but warned that "in building up this legal organization" it was imperative to guard against "the idea that the regular party might be liquidated without any trouble." Katterfeld then identified the divisions in the early communist movement, placing Cannon in the forefront of the "right" liquidationists.[74]

Cannon was thus destined to spend little time with Lista, Carl, and Ruth over the holiday season, the family's first in New York City, but he no doubt had cause to feel elated about what he had accomplished over the last year. The forces of the revolutionary Left were indeed small, but they had been united, albeit weakly, and were apparently in the process of consolidation. Cannon's role in the making of this reconstructed Bolshevism was second to none, and

around him was gathering a promising cadre, disciplined in the inner workings of the party and talented in their varied abilities.[75] Above all, the confin-
ing ultraleft undergroundism seemed finally, after almost four years of
slugging through its sectarianism, to be a thing of the past, a millstone no
longer encircling the neck of revolutionary agitation. This had never been, as
it would appear to so many "side-line philistines," a tragicomedy of P.T. Bar-
numesque proportions; Cannon refused to regard the struggle to excavate the
party from its underground ultraleftism as a "circus" event.[76] The ultraleft of
the 1919–1920 years erred, but it did so out of courage and conviction, learning
lessons, habits of work, and depths of commitment that ensured it a place in
the history of world revolution.[77]

Cannon stood for a new kind of communism in 1920–1921, one that had a
chance to lead an American revolution. To the extent that this native son of the
United States heartland had contributed to a realignment of communist forces
in the most powerful capitalist nation on earth, struggling to translate the
vocabulary of Bolshevism into an American idiom, he had reason to be proud
of his accomplishment. In the months to come, however, whatever satisfac-
tions of 1921 remained were tainted by new realizations of just how much of an
uphill battle the struggle against undergroundism had become. Cannon could
not have fathomed, as he sat down to some kind of abbreviated (and perhaps
postponed) Christmas dinner with Lista, Carl, and Ruth in December 1921,
that in the period ahead he would be dining, not on mass action and revolutionary recruitment, but on peppered goose.

PREPARING
FOR OCTOBER

The Historic Sixth Congress of the Bolshevik Party
(August 1917)
Illustrated   TWENTY CENTS

6

Geese in Flight

Founding the Workers' Party

Manhattan's New Star Casino was the site of the founding of the Workers' Party, 23–26 December 1921. The casino convention summoned a diversity of early bodies, many of them overlapping in their constituencies, and some less integrated than others into the consolidated communist underground: the Communist Party, the United Communist Party, the American Labor Alliance (which by then encompassed a number of foreign-language federations), the Workers' Council (largely Jewish Left remnants in the SP, but also containing some midwestern revolutionaries who had not affiliated with the movement for revolutionary unity), and the Arbeiter Bildungs-Vereine, or Workers' Educational Association, composed of German socialists.

In all, slightly more than 108 delegates filed into the historic meeting: 94 from the agreeing bodies, and fraternal representatives (at least 14, but not likely more than 20) from organizations such as the Michigan-based Proletarian Party, headed by the holdout from the left-wing schisms of 1919, Dennis E. Batt; the African Blood Brotherhood;[1] the IWW Committee for the Red Trade Union International; and various unions, clubs, and foreign-language federations. A representative from the Marx-Engels Institute of New York attended uninvited.[2] The balance of delegate power rested decidedly with the American Labor Alliance. Its forty-seven votes overshadowed all other organizations, including the critical contingent from the Workers' Council—thirteen delegates who, in the eyes of many in the communist movement, represented the last revolutionary gasp of the Socialist Party. These council communists were the most outright opponents of *all* aspects of undergroundism, including some of its attachment to the revolutionary theories and organizational principles of Leninism.

Borrowing from the language of native American radicalism's favored author, Jack London, the revolutionary assembly convened under the declaration that "American capitalists are using the present economic crisis to increase their power of exploitation and oppression. The whole working class is being crushed under the iron heel of a brutal capitalist dictatorship." Assuming unity of the revolutionary Left to be "already a living reality," the petition to form a new above-ground communist party fed off of obvious Leninist and Comintern prodding, and was indeed a statement that the first round against undergroundism had been won. However, this left largely unresolved the residual ideological weight of secretive sectarianism. Its entrenchment in the apparatus of the revolutionary Left, so routinely assimilated to the clandestine character of an "illegal" body, had to be shed, or at least rethought in terms of its role once a legal party was established. This was a more protracted process, clearly not resolved by a mere statement of programmatic change. The tensions, debates, and clashes of the early 1920s thus reflected a growing native American movement, associated with Cannon and others, to legalize a component of revolutionary political activity in order to make inroads into mass work in the electoral arena, within the trade unions, and in the propaganda sphere. Party activities and an open party press, it was increasingly thought, could "unmask the fraudulent capitalist democracy and help mobilize the workers for the final struggle against their common enemy."

To this end, the segments of the communist milieu that were approached to come together in 1921 were required to approve five specific principles before they were allowed to participate in the proposed convention: (1) the necessity of the working class governing through the creation of a workers' republic; (2) the need for communists to participate in political campaigns, including on the electoral front, in order to carry the anti-capitalist message to the workers; (3) acknowledgement of the central place of the trade unions as sites of battle in which militant struggle, education, and exposure of the reactionary labor bureaucracy could take place; (4) the vital need for a party of class-conscious workers, bound by the discipline of a democratic-centralist body; and (5) the pivotal role of a party-owned and controlled press. Absent in the organizational preliminaries associated with bringing a new Left body into being were the sectarian exhortations so common in the brief history of the United States underground. Not a word, in this initial call for communist organization, was said of dictatorships of the proletariat, armed insurrection, the reformist cancer of competing socialist bodies, or the necessity of soviets.

Given the contradictory essence of the American political scene at the time, simultaneously one of actual repression and ongoing containment of the Left *and* a culture of reification of individual "rights" and freedoms of speech and association, Cannon and many other early communists came to an appropriate conclusion. An underground apparatus was superfluous, incapable of ultimately shielding revolutionaries from the state's assaults, at the same time that it isolated them from the masses of U.S. workers and failed to fully exploit the possibilities of propaganda available in the contradictory climate of "bourgeois democracy."[3]

A decisive 50 percent bloc of delegates adhered strongly to this view, but it was in fact a fragile coalition, pieced together by the interim leadership of Cannon, Bittelman, Weinstone, Lovestone, and Allison. Seemingly led by English-speaking advocates of mass work and the creation of a legal party apparatus, the American Labor Alliance base was a fusion of ethnic federationists—Finnish, Jewish, Hungarian, Greek, South Slavic, Spanish, Ukrainian, Armenian, Italian, and Russian—some of whom certainly harbored attachments to the isolations and insularities of the recent past. Although they voted with Comrade Cannon, it was apparent to many that much of the bridge to an above-ground, *American,* communist party remained to be built, whatever the formal, constitutional consequences of the Star Casino convention. J. B. Salutsky, for one, led a brief assault on what he termed "the subway party," caucusing with Moissaye J. Olgin, future editor of the Jewish daily *Freiheit (Freedom)*, and a couple of other Workers' Council delegates. After the first day of deliberations, Salutsky was convinced that the established underground party would never cede enough political control to the emerging legal body to actually allow it to function, and he tried to convince others to bolt the Star Casino with him. His arguments went unheeded.[4]

One reason they were ignored was Cannon. He had, along with Bittelman, played a decisive role in bringing divergent communists/socialists together. Cannon's keen eye of awareness, trained on political differences as well as personal frictions and incompatibilities, forged a measure of commonality in a way that, aside from Salutsky, stuck. The architect of "legalism" later explained why it was that New York's intellectual, literary, Jewish socialists found common cause with him as a midwestern proletarian in the shared project of building an above-ground party led by native-born Americans:

> The Jewish communists were, by far, more assimilated in American life than the other foreign language groups; they had a more realistic appreciation of the decisive significance of a party leadership that would appear to be a genuine American product. They wanted to be a part of a larger American movement,

and not merely the leaders of a futile sect of New Yorkers and foreign-born communists. I think this was their main motivation in allying themselves with us, and it was a politically sound motivation.

This Jewish-native American alliance was the first, and foundational, bolt in holding together the communist elements that gathered at the Star Casino.[5] It had the backing of the Comintern, which promised $10,000 to fund a Jewish-language daily, and a further $50,000 for a similar English-language newspaper if the American revolutionary forces could come up with $10,000 on their own.[6]

As chairman of the convention, Cannon opened with a warmly received speech, accenting the extent to which some in the communist movement were committed to making a break with the practices and attitudes of the under-ground years. His remarks regularly interrupted with applause, Cannon focused on the achievement of unity, laying particular stress on the extent to which, guided by the Communist International, an array of revolutionary forces in America had managed to come to common programmatic agreement in spite of the varied paths that had brought them to this powerfully impor-tant new beginning. He was not without appreciation of the difficulties the communist movement faced. In addressing these, Cannon placed central importance on the need to build a class-struggle leadership in the demoralized trade unions. Cannon also deplored the failure of the revolutionary Left to mount an adequate amnesty campaign to free the many class-war prisoners who had been languishing in jail since the Palmer Raids. He promised that the Workers' Party would fight on every front, holding high the banner of revolu-tionary transformation, to be sure, but also addressing the range of day-to-day issues, from housing to wages, that agitated workers. Concluding with strong advocacy of a disciplined, centralized party, Cannon ended forcefully, "We have come together to face the future."[7]

Convention documents were developed and passed with remarkable ease. In the critically important trade union realm, the conference adopted policies that implicitly embraced the developing perspective of William Z. Foster, head of the Chicago-based Trade Union Educational League (TUEL). Although he did not attend the New Star Casino gathering, Foster, won over to communism through his observational involvement in the Browder-orchestrated trade union delegation to the Red International of Labor Unions (Profintern/RILU), was by late summer 1921 a secret member of the communist underground. In a sense, Foster had been parachuted into a position of trade union prominence within the consolidating revolutionary Left from the moment that RILU head Solomon Lozovsky took him under his wing and endorsed, materially as well as programmatically, Foster's TUEL as the American constituent of the Com-intern's labor organization. Although the TUEL would not be officially recognized as the sole American section of the Profintern until 1923, Foster's importance in communist trade union circles in the United States was now secure. The Workers' Party's new labor program condemned dual unionism, and pushed strongly the "amalgamation" of union bodies into powerful industrial combinations—ideas about to become central with the launching of the Foster-edited TUEL publication, the *Labor Herald,* in March 1922. Sustained in part by funds from Lozovsky and the RILU, the *Herald* was an impressive agitational organ, innovative in its use of graphics and bold in the presentation of revolutionary ideas, that acted as a link between the militant minority and widening circles of American radicalism, as well as a connection to European developments for U.S. trade unionists and leftists.[8]

The Workers' Party also hammered out short statements on blacks and women, as well as a position on labor defense work. Perhaps the most striking departure was the first explicit commitment to a communist youth organization, which would be consummated in the creation of legal and underground bodies early in 1922. From this quarter Martin Abern, a future Cannon ally, would emerge, writing regularly for *The Young Worker,* and assuming the position of national secretary of the National Executive Committee of the Young Workers League of America by May of 1922.[9]

The new party did not affiliate directly with the Communist International, although it acknowledged the CI as "the citadel and hope of the workers of every country." Between conventions, actual decisionmaking was concentrated in the Central Executive Committee, a seven-member body of supreme authority. This party cadre was to be elected by delegates, chosen by a process twice removed from the rank-and-file. Branches elected representatives to district conventions, which then elected delegates to national conventions. All district organizers were to be appointed by the CEC, and all press and propaganda activity was to be undertaken with its directive. Moreover, this central body was to choose an executive secretary, a chairman, and "all other officers." Because many of the leading figures in the above-ground party were members of the older "illegal" Communist Party of America, this ensured that the legal organization would remain somewhat tied to the underground's authority.

Much of the new party's orientation, programmatically, was not to the old ultraleft's liking. The twenty-one points of affiliation stipulated by the Communist International,[10] on which all bodies were to agree before they could directly connect with the Moscow-led forces of world revolution, were simply not discussed. Instead, the program of the Workers' Party emphasized issues rooted in the conditions of the United States: protection of unions, African Americans, and the unemployed, and defense of their respective rights and entitlements; and the cessation of war preparations and withdrawal of the U.S.

military and governing forces from imperialist enclaves in the Caribbean and the Philippines.

Advocates of the underground undoubtedly found this orientation inadequate in its revolutionary resolve. They were also chagrined at the seeming structure of the apparatus of the new party. When seventeen members of the newly formed Workers' Party were nominated for the Central Executive Committee, a body ostensibly limited to seven, the convention simply overrode its constitutional guidelines and, in what was clearly a spirit of "unity" meant to appease all quarters, acclaimed all nominated individuals to the central ruling body. This left certain leaders of the entrenched underground, adamant in their opposition to what they regarded as menshevism and Workers' Council liquidationism, to nurse what they surely perceived to be some political wounds. The legal party's CEC now contained five Workers' Council representatives, including the much-maligned Ludwig Lore, as well as midwestern labor and former SP left-wingers such as Cannon (Kansas); Elmer T. Allison (Ohio); Debs's Ohio comrade, Marguerite Prevey; Arne Swabeck (Illinois); and Caleb Harrison, a rare recruit from the denigrated Socialist Labor Party, a situation that did not augur well for the ultralefts still committed to undergroundism. The inclusion of young New York figures aligned with the still-imprisoned C.E. Ruthenberg, Jay Lovestone, and W. W. Weinstone, as well as the Jewish "liquidationist" Alexander Bittelman, all of whom had worked with Cannon in the transitory leadership that pieced together the formation of the Workers' Party, was further cause for concern in some quarters. When consideration was also given to those elected as alternatives to the CEC (a group of seven that included Cannon's old Lever Act co-conspirator from the agitations among miners in 1919, Ohio's Charles Baker; the newcomer from Kansas, Earl Browder; and a hard-drinking Irish rebel with a literary flare, Thomas O'Flaherty), the leading elements of the new legal party, to be headquartered in New York City, looked very much to lean in Cannon's direction. Caleb Harrison was elected to the pivotal administrative post of national secretary, but it was Cannon who served as the Workers' Party's national chairman, a position that placed him foremost in the ranks of public representatives of the newly born legal communist movement.[11]

There were, of course, rumblings of discontent.[12] The push to unity raised the hackles of the uninvited representative of the Marx-Engels Institute, who ended a conference-floor harangue with the denunciatory exclamation: "Go to hell, you damned skunks."[13] The most forceful challenge, albeit one that had little impact, came from the Proletarian Party's delegates. Leading this dissident charge was the Detroit Labor Council's Dennis E. Batt, a former machinist recently returned from the American trade union body that had traveled to Europe to attend the first congress of the Red International of Labor Unions;

John Keracher, a theoretician, writer, and owner of a shoe store; and the ultra-left Harry M. Wicks, who would later gain notoriety as a suspected spy in the ranks of the communist milieu. Long a separate strand in the communist weave, this trio carried the pre-World War I impossibilist legacy of the Social-ist Parties of Great Britain and Canada into the American underground, where they trumpeted the projects of education and political agitation from their Proletarian Party pedestal in Detroit, downplaying the significance of trade unions as nurseries of class combat and revolutionary mass work. They con-sidered the Proletarian Party to be the above-ground expression of commu-nism, and saw no need to affiliate to a new body, Comintern-backed or not. Cannon had long regarded the Proletarian Party leadership as "hair-splitting scholastics" and "pompous wiseacres," agreeing with Bittelman's characteriza-tion that they "completely missed the everyday fighting nature of Leninism and communism." Keracher, Wicks, and Batt were obviously odd men out at the Star Casino in late December 1921, marginalized and responded to with condescension and even sarcasm. The way seemed cleared for a legal party.[14]

Undergroundism Unreconstructed

The ink was barely dry on the Workers' Party constitution when the advocates of illegality waged a campaign directed at the Cannon-headed communist forces, raising a hue and cry about the need to return to the old sectarian iso-lations. Ballam, Dirba, and Ashkenudzie were suspended in November by a majority of the Central Executive Committee of the Communist Party of America because they refused to abide by the decision to call a conference endorsing the formation of a new legal party without first convening the entire underground membership; this act of discipline was appealed to the Com-intern. From the international comrades came unambiguous instructions to proceed with the creation of the Workers' Party; on the suspension of the lead-ers of the so-called Left Opposition, the Comintern later approved the actions of the CEC, confirming that the trio, now dubbed subway revolutionaries, had committed "a serious and intolerable breach of discipline." The door remained open for reinstatement, however, if the opponents of legalization agreed to embrace the new developments and the political principles that underlay them. Unsurprisingly, the suspended central committee members refused such a course, and instead defied the Comintern, organizing their ranks into a national caucus and continuing the publication of an underground journal with the same name as the official organ of the majority of the CEC, *The Com-munist*. Out of this confusing maelstrom, the underground, foreign-language-federation-based ultraleft assailed the formation of the legal party, and in the process signaled that the second stage of communist battle against what would come to be known as the Goose Caucus would be a more difficult and sustained endeavor than the first programmatic blows struck against illegality by Lenin's *Left-Wing Communism,* Comintern resolutions, and the formation of the Workers' Party (WP).[15]

A relatively moderate wing of this ultraleft tendency was still represented on the CEC of the underground Communist Party of America, had delegates at the WP's founding convention, and opted for a positive assessment of the new party. Its opening statement was one of cautious endorsement: this layer of leftists found that the program of the WP contained sufficient elements of revolutionary combativity to warrant support. With respect to the constituency of the new party, though, elements of the ultraleft refused to bury the sectarian hatchet, most particularly concerning the Workers' Council leadership, which in some quarters was regarded as "violently antagonistic to our [underground] party." Quick to constitute themselves "the revolutionary vanguard of the American Working class," the still-in-existence Communist Party of America adopted a stand of "watchful waiting," hoping that the Workers' Party would further the "development of a political mass-movement of fighting workers."[16]

Less benign was the extreme underground position, associated with the suspended ostensible Left Oppositionists of November 1921, the leading English-speaking figure of which was John J. Ballam. These die-hard forces of the ultraleft underground responded to the formation of the Workers' Party by refusing to compromise the revolutionary isolation of entrenched elements of the foreign-language federations. When they met in a 7–11 January 1922 "Emergency Convention," their 38 delegates claimed to represent 4,361 convention-assessment paying members—a figure which, if accurate, certainly constituted close to a majority of the United States communist ranks. The blunt reality, however, was that there was no way of knowing how many of the immigrant ranks actually supported the "Extreme Left" politics of the modest number of delegates who presumed to speak for them. Approximately 95 percent of the revolutionary mass supposedly represented at the Emergency Convention of opposition came from the foreign-language federations, headed by the large Ukrainian, Lithuanian, and Russian contingents, whose respective memberships were between 900 and 1,100. The delegates speaking for these ranks were depicted as "men fresh from the grime and smoke of the factories; men who are at grips with the every day struggle of the workers." Bourgeois intellectuals and professional leaders had deserted them, the careerists and "machine politicians" absconding to the Workers' Party. To a person, the delegates of the Emergency Convention realized that "out of the body and bone and blood of the proletariat must come the future leadership of the Communist Party in America." They would countenance no "liquidation."[17] The convention admitted Robert Minor, who read a "secret" communication from the Executive Committee of the Communist International that was interpreted, in spite of its upholding of the CEC suspensions and seeming advocacy of the Workers' Party, as "bearing out the position" of the Emergency Convention delegates. Ending their convention with the slogan, "Down with the traitors and betrayers of the communist movement," the thirty-eight oppositional delegates vowed to remember "those who have deserted and gone over to the enemy for their personal advantage."[18]

In diatribes entitled "The 'Workers' Party'" and "Fooling the Workers into Communism," as well as in a manifesto concerning the WP that took the form of an open letter "To the Workers of America," the underground assault continued over the next months, its language hinting at the generalized condemnation that most likely was in part directed at Cannon himself.[19] Judging the revolutionary core of the WP to be "mainly misled Russians and Lithuanians," the oppositionists took aim at a second group consisting of "former C.P. and C.L.P. leaders, calling themselves Communists," but in reality "bastardized caricatures . . . utterly devoid of ability to accomplish anything except play the game of peanut politics in true Tammany style." Regarding the WP as the product of a "machine steam-rolling" convention, the dissident communists of the Emergency Convention expressed outrage at the reformist illusions cultivated in the process, and at the failure to provide the tried-and-true advocacy of proletarian dictatorship, soviets, the Comintern's twenty-one points, and the world hegemony of the Third International. A menshevik "menace," "this aggregation of Compromisers, opportunists and centrists" was called a mask blinding the American working-class from seeing its class-struggle destiny.[20]

Those embracing these views convened in mid-February 1922 to establish a legal party of the underground communist vanguard, the United Toilers of America, quickly dubbed the "United Toilets" by the irascible Jay Lovestone. Ballam and his largely foreign-language-federation followers appointed the Proletarian Party delegate to the WP convention, Harry M. Wicks, editor of the United Toiler press, the *Workers' Challenge*. The publication soon gained a reputation as one of the most violently polemical sheets in the history of early communism. The Toilers, when not engaged in factional assaults, made ready to plead their case in Moscow, where they were certain that, as representative of a "majority" of U.S. communists, they would receive Soviet endorsement at a March 1922 adjudication hearing. They were sadly mistaken.

Ballam was bested by Katterfeld and Bedacht of the officially sanctioned communist movement; the Comintern-appointed commission gave the upstart Left Oppositionists a stern rebuke, insisting that all communists "must obey the discipline first." Ballam and the underground ultraleft had opposed the Workers' Party on the ground that it was insufficiently Marxist and Leninist in its program and practice, constituted as it was out of what they regarded as the flotsam and jetsam of the left-wing Socialist Party milieu. They lived, as did Cannon and the emerging movement to legalize party activity, by the sword of Comintern authority. Majorities and minorities actually meant little, not the least because their advocates could never be "counted" with any precision. The original sin of the die-hard underground had been to defy the Communist International, which by November 1921 had quite correctly perceived the need to move into a more open political engagement with American conditions if communism were ever to push past the boundaries of clandestine cells. Ballam swallowed hard, admitted defeat, and returned to the United States, where he toured the country promoting the Workers' Party. His comrades in the ultraleft underground, for the most part, regarded him as having failed to properly explain what was at stake to the Comintern representatives. Some carried their commitment to clandestine, underground organization throughout the 1920s, refusing to affiliate with any revolutionary current that insisted on basing its program in open political work. A number simply faded away.[21]

Illustrative of the truly convoluted politics of this United Toiler milieu was an eight-day convention likely held in September 1922. An ultraleft contingent was led by George Ashkenudzie, the staunch undergroundist who had earlier been suspended by the Comintern for his failure to abide by directives to unify all communists in the United States. The United Toilers passed a resolution accepting "the ruling of the EC of the CI . . . to unite on the basis of the decision of the CI"—only to also add amendments naming prominent liquidators (Cannon, Ruthenberg, Bedacht, and Lovestone), calling for their removal from the CEC and expulsion, demanding that no United Toilers be required to join the Legal Political Party (LPP, or Workers' Party), advocating control of the Jewish press and other open party publications by the underground party, and insisting on revising the Communist Party's constitution to emphasize "Democratic Centralization." A Special Representative of the Comintern, the Pole H. Valetski/Walecki ("Wilkes"), stated that the resolution violated the instructions and decisions of the Comintern, and threatened the underground dissidents themselves with expulsion. Ashkenudzie and others walked out in protest, a move that was followed by a demand from the United Toiler majority that they turn over all "funds, documents, and party property" to the convention. The hard-liners eventually returned, preferring to give up their demands and remain aligned with the CI; the Comintern representative was implored to assure the delegates that there would be no recriminations or retaliations against them; Ashkenudzie faced grievance charges on another matter; and the proceedings turned into what Valetski derided as "a joke." A final motion to adjourn passed by the merest of majorities, twelve to ten.[22]

Cannon and the Struggle for an Activist Communist Party, 1922

Rounds one and two—the battle to create a legal party and beating back the challenge of Ballam and the United Toilers—appeared to have gone to Cannon and his supporters. In fact, these were only opening skirmishes in what would prove an ongoing war to take American communism out of the labyrinth of undergroundism.[23] From the moment he arrived in New York, Cannon had been forced to look the existing leadership of the underground squarely in its political eye. What he saw, he found disturbing. The leadership available in 1921–1922 was not capable, in Cannon's view, of actually leading. "I knew then," he later said, "that I had to fight for the leadership." Cannon claimed to have "overcome [his] own 'anti-intellectualism' to a considerable extent," but he grasped that communism would never make inroads into the mass workers' movement if it was led by "a purely 'intellectualistic' leadership." Only in his early thirties, Cannon acknowledged that he "didn't know much," but never found himself "overawed by the others," whom he recognized as "one-sided products of a primitive movement." All of the potential leaders, Cannon rightly saw, "needed each other and complemented each other in various ways."[24]

Much of what Cannon did, as a consequence, was highly internalist, consolidating within the upper echelons of the communist movement an interim leadership that was based on foundational political principles relating to the twinned strategic issues of trade union policy and legalization of the communist forces through the creation of an above-ground party capable of intervening in actual working-class struggle. The cornerstone of this project of creating a new leadership was an odd alliance, the "Lovestone-Cannon combination." Others played key supporting roles, including Cannon's allies, Alexander Bittelman, and the staid German, Max Bedacht, or Lovestone's City College of New York chum, William W. Weinstone. Nonetheless, the Lovestone-Cannon connection was pivotal, indicating that Cannon was able to transcend clashes of personality to address organizational and political necessity. If the alliances Cannon constructed in 1921–1922 were transitory and impermanent, they nevertheless were vitally important in overcoming the blockages that threatened to forever mire American communism in a cocoon-like ineffectiveness.[25]

This making of a leadership orientation was also forged administratively. The orchestration of the day-to-day tasks associated with running the Workers' Party should have fallen to the old DeLeonite, Caleb Harrison, elected as secretary of the WP at the Star Casino convention. Unfortunately, Harrison, who would soon drift out of the communist movement as he faced personal difficulties, proved an inept administrator, and for the first four months of 1922 much of the mundane work in the party's New York offices at 799 Broadway (corner of Eleventh Street) fell to Cannon. The routine correspondence in March and April 1922, for instance, included letters to comrades that addressed the inadequacy of dues collection, explaining how the Central Executive Committee could now not meet weekly because of "lack of funds"; reminders to all district organizers to commemorate the Paris Commune (March 19); offers to district organizers of 40 percent commissions on subscription sales of the party press, *The Worker;* extensive writing promoting forthcoming May Day events, stressing their united-front character and urging alliances with other labor groups; many letters to editors of party newspapers, especially the foreign-language press; and an array of other communications, addressing branches on such issues as the Trade Union Educational League or more mundane concerns associated with the granting of charters.[26]

Cannon was thus one of the few communist leaders who, even with his limited education, proved able to muster the organizational skills that could keep a nascent party afloat, thanks in part to his Wobbly apprenticeship in the Newcastle, Pennsylvania, shop of Ben Williams's *Solidarity,* and later stint as a Kansas City clerk. He understandably regarded it as a "godsend" when C.E. Ruthenberg was able to assume the national secretary's post upon his release from Sing Sing in April 1922. Although Jim thought C.E. cagey and egotistical, "concerned with problems of self," he recognized, again, that different individuals had particular complementary roles to play in the successful development of a revolutionary movement. Of Ruthenberg, Cannon stated unequivocally: "He was a devoted communist, fully committed to the cause—I don't think anyone ever doubted that. Moreover, he was a man of responsibility, concerned about the progress of party work in all departments." Cannon thus proposed that Ruthenberg take over the office of executive secretary. "Ruthenberg, with his great prestige and special aptitude for executive work," Cannon stressed, "was the indicated man . . . [and this] was undoubtedly the general opinion of the party ranks."[27]

An early public face of the Workers' Party, Cannon spoke regularly, both inside and outside of New York, and was prominent in issuing party proclamations. He traveled, for instance, to his old stomping grounds, Kansas City, Missouri, promoting the cause of the new Workers' Party among his former comrades by addressing a gathering of 300 at the Mercantile Hall on 29 January 1922. The trip was likely occasioned by the need for Cannon to consult with his lawyer: federal authorities had finally decided to lift the threat of his 1919–1920 Lever Act indictment, and all charges against Cannon and Charles

Baker were being dismissed. With a postwar economic recovery under way and the prospects for the decade seeming to promise unbridled prosperity, capital and the state loosened the reins of repression somewhat, although never, of course, completely. Ironically enough for revolutionaries, defeats on the class front thus relaxed the grip of coercion; a confident ruling class could give freer play to the rights of dissenters.

The context of 1922 was thus the mirror image of that of 1916. In the latter year, a strike upsurge had been waged with great hopes and militant enthusiasms, the so-called "full employment" of the war years and the powerful appeal of revolution abroad and international class solidarities sustaining a radical confidence that, tragically, unleashed a period of vicious state assault on the Left and the workers' movement. Winning or losing—and they won a goodly number of fights—the militants of 1916 were ready to fight again, and they did so in 1917.

A half-decade later, the terms seemed reversed. More than 1.6 million men and women struck work in 1922, with major battles erupting in the mines, in textile mills, and among railway workers. However, these brutal conflicts were almost uniformly suppressed by recalcitrant employers, aided by a servile state. Largely defensive campaigns aimed at preserving wages, hours, and union rights on which capital and governing authority had declared war, the strikes of 1922 were doomed from the outset: the streets teemed with unemployed workers, the reserve army of labor supplemented by the actual armed forces of state militias and federal troops, whose job it was to patrol neighborhoods and escort "scabs" through faltering picket lines. The courts provided injunctions, presidential decrees a useful ideology of "law and order." As railway shop workers carried the first national strike in the industry since 1894 into the summer of 1922, they faced a vicious and concerted opposition, one that drove a wedge between them and train crews, trackmen, and switchyard workers, who refused to join the militant march off the job. The strike defeated, and communist railroad workers threatened and blacklisted, the door was opened to a new climate, less rigidly coercive, of which the Workers' Party was one beneficiary; Cannon, in particular, was given a reprieve from the charges long held over his head. "I guess I got the benefit of the general republican climate, which my friend, Warren Harding, called, 'Back to normalcy,'" Cannon later quipped.[28] Nevertheless, advocates of the underground could still point to the possibility of state repression, and as Cannon spoke in Kansas City and elsewhere his talks were always monitored by Department of Justice agents looking for fresh grounds for an indictment.[29]

In the realm of class struggle, it was evident that the broad labor movement was downshifting into a more conservative, less combative, stand.[30] Opposing an early 1922 Conference for Progressive Political Action (CPPA) that convened in Chicago, prompted by Socialist Party activity among the railway unions, Harrison and Cannon issued a call on March 19 for united-front labor actions to challenge the use of sweeping injunctions to stifle strikes of railway shopmen. Critical of the rising tendency of trade unionists to rely on conferences of "progressives" when the sole way forward was through the program of the class-struggle Workers' Party, Harrison and Cannon hailed labor's triumph in creating a workers' republic in Russia and called for sustained resistance against the capitalist offensive, in which Chambers of Commerce, Employers' Associations, and the courts had launched a wage-cutting initiative and an open-shop drive, introducing as well the scourge of unemployment. "Workless, hopeless, and ignored," the jobless needed defending, just as the railway shopmen required a leadership that would stand firm for their right to strike. Cannon and Harrison ended their open letter by calling on the conference to reconvene on a firmer proletarian foundation, "to move for a general Labor Conference to be elected by the rank and file."[31] Such outspoken refusal to accept the rightward drift of labor politics brought the left wing into particular sights. When the largest national coal strike in United States history erupted in April 1922, Cannon was rumored to be the "paymaster" of the communists in the coalfields; the Lewis machine in the United Mine Workers of America named him as part of the "Attempt by Communists to Seize the American Labor Movement."[32] Anarchist assault on the Soviet Union by Emma Goldman necessitated response, and Cannon urged editors of party newspapers to use their pages to reply to the "counter-revolutionary" articles syndicated in the capitalist press in March 1922.[33]

The best response to this varied attack was open, public, communist initiative. In mid-April, Cannon was issuing appeals to labor bodies across the United States to endorse the Sacco-Vanzetti Defense Committee. The freedom of the accused anarchists was a cause he had promoted at the Toiler, where he had commissioned an article by Mary Heaton Vorse.[34] This effort was followed by another jointly signed (Cannon and Harrison) "Proclamation of the Workers Party for International May Day, 1922," in which the plight of the jobless was stressed, alongside attacks on the pliant capitalist courts, apathetic mainstream unions, the prisons teeming with class-war victims, and a kept press always ready to do the bidding of business. "Capitalism and Chains, or Social Revolution and Freedom!" thundered the May Day manifesto.[35]

Cannon and Robert Minor were the featured speakers at New York's First of May Festival and Ball at the New Star Casino, proceeds from the Sunday-evening dance going to the Russian daily, Iskra. Edgar Owens of the Workers' Party's National Defense Committee accompanied Cannon to Massachusetts immediately after the Casino soiree, as the New York duo were featured at May Day events in the seaboard state.[36] At approximately the same time, Cannon spoke to "rousing applause" at a Workers' Party luncheon commemorating the release of Ruthenberg and Ferguson from prison. He called attention to the new tenor of communist times: "We are building the Workers Party to become the centralized party of the rebel, dauntless workers of the United States." Subsequently, the WP sponsored a gala coming-out celebration, with Cannon and William F. Dunne listed among the many speakers, at the Central Opera House, 205 East 67th Street; there the trio of Ruthenberg, Ferguson, and Gitlow received a hero's welcome when freed from Sing Sing and Auburn. With Ruthenberg now a proponent of legalization, Cannon, Lovestone, Bittelman, and others seemed to have their "liquidationist" hand strengthened considerably.[37]

For Cannon, it was nevertheless rather lonely at the top. He had few political soul mates among the heterogeneous layer of revolutionary leadership, and his close ties to William F. Dunne and other more proletarian elements in the party were not yet fully cultivated. Lovestone, ostensibly his major ally, "had graduated from City College into party leadership without any detours." Perhaps Cannon's most loyal and genuinely sympathetic comrade at this time, Bittelman, was "a student and critic, hardly more than that." His talents were essential to the Workers' Party in its formative years, so fundamental was the need to appreciate the errors and defects of the underground period of communism's United States birth. As a politician, though, Bittelman lacked "originality," and his thinking was somewhat formulaic and "sterile"—traits that may well also have characterized another advocate of legality, the German master of Marxist doctrine, Max Bedacht. Cannon thus stood somewhat alone, and was always on the lookout for recruits who might provide "a proletarian counterbalance" to New York's "Second Avenue intellectuals," responsible for the party center's deprecated reputation as an exemplary site of sectarianism.[38]

Cannon's 1920–1922 work in bringing American revolutionary advocates of the Soviet Union out of their subterranean lair, which included his pioneering role in charting the formation of the legal Workers' Party, propagandizing and recruiting for the Left cause, and sustaining newspapers and organizational stability, was undoubtedly critical in the formative years of United States communism. The upside of this activity registered in the successes that seemed so unambiguous in early 1922. It must also be recognized that Cannon had been elevated almost overnight to a figure of national importance. It was understandable that a young recruit such as Cannon, thrust into perhaps the leading role in the campaign to create a legal communist party at a time when he was barely thirty years of age, would suffer some deformations.[39]

Elements of the "Extreme Left," for instance, bemoaned the Workers' Party assimilation of a language of American individualism, which some undoubtedly attributed to Cannon's limited theoretical background in what would have been considered populism, small-town midwestern Socialist Party circles, and the IWW.[40] Others, such as those seeking WP endorsement for Project Kuzbas, an early western Siberian industrial colony set up by émigré workers keen to sustain the revolutionary Soviet economy in 1921, perhaps found Cannon unhelpful, prone to postures of bureaucratism. Appealed to for support, Cannon, as well as Ludwig Lore and Ruthenberg, were standoffish from the start. Cannon attended a January 1922 meeting, but kept his distance. He doubted the wisdom of sending men and women to Russia and identifying them with the IWW, which was now on record as opposing the Soviet Union. Cannon further stipulated that the communist press would decline to publicize the Kuzbas endeavor. The project's advocates found this slight to internationalism disappointing, suggesting that at the very least the Workers' Party should give "moral support to other revolutionists who were willing to go ahead with the job." Cannon stated that "his time was taken up with other work," which was no doubt as true as it was likely to ring rather hollow.[41]

The critical question for the revolutionary Left in 1922 remained whether or not the Workers' Party and the drive to develop a public, as opposed to clandestine, communist presence was to go forward or stall. A confusing array of parties, factions, and splinter groups constituted the communist ranks at this time, notwithstanding the formation of the WP. The Proletarian Party continued to exist as an above-ground organization, separate from the official communist parties, while within the latter the United Toilers served as a legal arm of the more extreme underground. Within the officially recognized, Comintern-supported communist milieu, there were actually three designated organizations: the official Communist Party was known as Number One, and remained an underground body; the Workers' Party, or LPP (Legal Political Party), was Number Two; and the Trade Union Educational League, the labor wing of communism, was designated X. All members of the underground CP supposedly joined the above-ground WP, their leaderships were largely interchangeable, and parties Number One and Two held their meetings on alternative weeks. Care was, of course, taken not to reveal in documents and public pronouncements the overlap and connection of the two organizations, but the fundamental issue turned on control. Though all decisions were formally arrived at by the underground leadership of the CP, they were carried out publicly by the WP. Personalities chafed under the frictions that resulted, but the ultimate factional formations and political differences arose over decisive questions. Was America in the early 1920s different from the repressive anti-communist context of 1917–1920? Could an above-ground party function without being subjected to state repression of the sort that had decimated the communist ranks during the red scare of the not-so-distant past? Over the course of 1922, signs of a change in the political climate appeared, and the WP published its press and pamphlets, had no difficulty in putting on forums and agitating publicly, and was not barred from elections or subject to wholesale arrests.[42]

Upon securing his freedom from jail, Ruthenberg judged the climate sufficiently open and, along with Cannon, Lovestone, Bedacht, and others, he began to up the ante around the issue of "liquidationism," arguing that the underground party should be disbanded, although he intimated that an illegal apparatus could be kept ready, able to conduct such rare political work as could not be carried out in the public arena. Such a position downgraded the advocacy of armed insurrection as an ultraleft irrelevancy, a hangover from the sectarianism of a past time, and Ruthenberg suggested excising altogether from the party program any reference to the workers seizing state power through violence. This general position was strengthened as the activities of the Workers' Party expanded and, perhaps more importantly, as Foster's work in the TUEL grew in stature and, for the first time, a trade union communist leadership of significance emerged in the United States and showed itself as unambiguously aligned with the liquidationist position.[43]

From April into the summer of 1922, a debate raged within the CEC of the underground Communist Party, spilling out into the ranks of the two parties. It pitted the liquidators against a determined contingent of undergroundists, led by Israel Amter[44] and Abraham Jakira, who remained the voice of the remnants of the old Russian, Lettish, Lithuanian, and Polish foreign-language federations. Around them they consolidated those who, to one degree or another, sought the preservation of the illegal, underground party: Ludwig E. Katterfeld, Alfred Wagenknecht, Benjamin Gitlow, and Robert Minor.[45]

The Birth of the Goose Caucus and the Turn to Moscow

Subtleties of slight difference aside, this latter faction was soon dubbed "the Goose Caucus." Again, it was the sharp tongue of Lovestone, described in one source as a "bench jockey for the [liquidationist] faction," that cut this christening into the historical record of American communism. Amidst stormy debate, in which Jakira's interventions were characterized by what Gitlow dubbed his "unceasing and persistent stuttering," an irate Bill Dunne interjected, "Jakira, you make me sick; you cackle like a goose." Amter was quick to defend his comrade. Alluding to the mythologies of ancient history, he noted that cackling geese had once saved Rome, and "we shall yet save the party." Lovestone was quick to retort: "All right, then; from now on you're the Goose Caucus!"[46] The wrangling spilled out into the upper echelons of the Workers'

Party, affecting routine party activity in various sectors of mass work.[47] Bedacht put the case for the necessity of a legal party bluntly, arguing:

1. That three fourths of the sections of the Comintern are open parties.
2. That the CPA was formed as an open party and went underground not as a matter of revolutionary virtue, but as a matter of necessity.
3. That only as long as that necessity exists must it continue such exclusive underground existence.
4. That the CPA cannot accomplish its task in America thru the underground organization and for that reason creates open instruments.
5. That through such instruments the Party must consistently and diligently work its way back out in the open again.

He challenged the "whole congregation of the chorus to prove—not to me, but to the Communist International—that it is 'liquidation' and 'centrist' to operate on such principles."[48]

The communist forces thus stalemated in the spring of 1922, all eyes, and all paths trod, turned to Moscow. Cannon, as a founder of the Workers' Party, and a major figure in the fight to legalize and Americanize communism in the United States, led the way. On 10 May 1922 he sailed for the Soviet Union on board the SS *Lativa*, his purpose stated to the authorities as being associated with his supposed membership in the very Kuzbas colony that he had declined to support only a few months earlier. The Bureau of Investigation was not fooled, but did nothing to thwart the trip, and the Rosedale native arrived in Moscow on 1 June 1922. It wasn't Kansas. Cannon would be gone the better part of eight months, returning in January 1923.

During this time Cannon attended various Comintern gatherings, observing and sometimes meeting and talking with the Russian and Comintern leadership (Zinoviev, Radek, Bukharin, Kuusinen, Trotsky), and working as well with the executive body of the Red International of Labor Unions, acquainting himself with Lozovsky and others. Cannon had been appointed a "special representative" of the Profintern, supposedly with sole supervisory authority over U.S. implementation of the decisions of the RILU's First Congress. In actuality, Cannon was almost certainly a figurehead in this realm, for while he undertook tasks associated with trade union work in the United States, aided by Browder and Foster, it would be the latter who was poised, late in 1921, to assume direction of this field. Cannon's RILU "appointment" was likely a reflection of Foster's newcomer status in Profintern circles, and the need for an established WP/CP CEC representative to oversee developments, at least for a minimal few months. It would, however, be only a matter of time before the "instructions" and "special representative" status granted to Cannon by the

RILU would be turned over to Foster. Cannon undoubtedly left his mark on the trade union politics of this period, however, pressing Profintern activities that cultivated "a united front with the syndicalists and anarchists against the [labor] bureaucracy."[49]

In various meetings of the Anglo-American Colonial Group of the Comintern, from 29 June 1922 through 7 September 1922, "Cook/Cooke" (Cannon) figured prominently. His predictable interventions turned largely on two related issues. First, in discussions relating to the Australian Question, he advocated a general position on questions of party disunity and their elaboration within the Anglo-American Colonial Group, arguing that a lack of decisiveness was obviously hobbling specific communist work and that such matters should be ruled on by the Comintern, which for too long "had acted somewhat indefinitely, as in the American case." Second, Cannon/Cook gained significant stature as a leading authority on the U.S. situation, offering lengthy and balanced commentary on the strengths and weaknesses of communism in the world's leading capitalist nation.

Cannon was clearly no mere mouthpiece of "Russian authority," nor did he readily spout Comintern slogans. For instance, Cannon pushed for a certain autonomy within the group, arguing that its secretary should be elected directly by the body rather than appointed by the executive committee of the Communist International. He also dismissed "Moscow's idea of working all the separate unions into one large federated union[—]an impossibility at present for the unions are so entirely different in every respect." In his account of conditions in the United States, Cannon reported that although government persecution was in general weakening, there remained a fierce struggle between the communists and the socialists for hegemony in the labor movement. Cannon nevertheless remained optimistic about recent developments in America, recounting the role of communists in promoting "the idea of the national agreement" in various unionized industries, and suggesting that the formation of the Workers' Party and the Trade Union Educational League constituted important breakthroughs in overcoming the isolation of communists from the mass workers' movement. On the critical relationship of the illegal and legal parties, Cannon struck a note of realistic acknowledgment of the separate but complementary contributions of each, in effect displacing a critique that turned on the inherent opportunism of a liquidationist position, while making his own advocacy of developing the legal party unambiguous.[50]

It was exhilarating for Cannon, barely thirty-two years of age, to witness the living Revolution, and he drank it all in, considering his membership in the Presidium a schooling: "my attitude was that of a listener, to learn what I could." He found the Russian revolutionaries "the most enlightened cosmopolitan thinkers and doers," his time spent in the birthplace of the proletarian state "a priceless experience." Innocent of "the rumbling struggle inside the Russian leadership," then only beginning with Lenin sidelined by illness, Cannon was clearly captivated by the atmosphere of internationalism and the ways in which the Bolshevik leadership seemed to master the issues of the hour. Cannon found himself immersed in the problems of the European communist parties, especially those relating to application of the united front. Staying at the relatively posh Lux Hotel, he chummed around with the British contingent and, for the most part, kept his eyes and ears open. In touch with Browder, Cannon concentrated on trade union issues as they related to the Workers' Party's need to secure proper influence in the Profintern. This was his apprenticeship in revolutionary internationalism.[51]

Cannon's priority was to win the Russian leadership to the policy of legalization in the United States. He soon found himself discouraged. The Comintern representatives, from Zinoviev on down, though friendly and patient, were routinely noncommittal. Convinced that the Soviet leaders were prejudiced against the notion of legality by their own past struggle against Menshevik liquidationist tendencies, Cannon felt "somewhat of a pariah." As late as 12 August 1922, on the eve of the second United States Bridgman Convention, Cannon wrote, "for two-and-a-half months I have been in Moscow trying to interest the Executive Committee in the affairs of the American Party; trying to get advice and direction as to what we should do—but without the slightest success. Our party is being allowed to drift into a most serious crisis, without one word of advice from Moscow." Finally, Cannon got a boost with the summer arrival in Moscow of Alexander Bittelman. The Jewish communist had been seconded to Russia to develop ties between Soviet and American Jews and to raise money for the *Freiheit,* but he also threw himself headlong into the effort to win over the Comintern leaders to embrace formally the need for party legalization in the United States. Now part of a team, with a U.S. representative fluent in Russian at his side, Cannon made gains. Bittelman assured his Kansas comrade that Zinoviev and Radek "were really not arguing against us." Though endorsing the legalization of the United States Party, the Comintern leaders were not, however, ready to see the current behind this development achieve a dominance over other revolutionary forces, some of which they regarded quite positively. Nonetheless, as Bittelman prepared to depart from the Soviet Union in late September or early October 1922, he felt that "our side was going to win."[52]

Back in the United States, the Goose-versus-Liquidator conflict had erupted into virtual party warfare, "raging furiously." According to Cannon ally and confidant Max Bedacht, Katterfeld ("Carr") was pushing the cause of undergroundism in particularly anti-Cannon ways, aligning with the discredited former Left Oppositionist Ballam, appealing to the sectarian and isolationist prejudices of the rank-and-file with unbridled accusations of the majority CEC's "menshevism" and "centrism," and preparing the way for a coup at the mid- to late August convention, scheduled by Katterfeld for Bridgman, Michigan. The revolutionary air was "thick with recriminations and feuds, with charges and countercharges." To cool the brew, in July 1922 the Executive Committee of the Communist International (ECCI) sent three official representatives to participate in the party debates and the Bridgman proceedings. The leading figure was H. Valetski (Walecki), a Polish professor of mathematics with a checkered revolutionary past among the old-guard Bolsheviks whose memories reached back far enough to appreciate his origins in Pilsudski nationalism and idealist mysticism. None of this, however, was known in America, where, as the Comintern representative, Valetski was soon the object of much political and social attention, all of it fawning. Robert Minor, according to Cannon and others, distinguished himself in his sycophancy, which was paralleled by his transformation into the nastiest of Goose factionalists, while Rose Pastor Stokes, another underground advocate, cultivated the charming, if unkempt and almost caricatured-looking, foreign Bolshevik. The "Geese" appeared to have the upper hand. When the convention, a charade by most accounts, and one characterized by bad judgment (it was held in a state that still had criminal syndicalist legislation on its books, and thus subjected those with past records to the possibility of truly draconian sentences), was infiltrated and eventually raided by four Department of Justice agents, a local sheriff, and a score of patriotic townspeople, it seemed to confirm the very thesis the advocates of illegality had long been pushing: the United States was simply too repressive a society for communists ever to fall victim to the illusion that they could operate above ground in an open revolutionary party. Katterfeld had been warned by his own caucus members that the convention location, past site of an underground gathering, was a poor choice; amidst rumors that the government had a bead on the convention and planned a bust, Bill Dunne asked Gitlow, a moderate in the Goose caucus, to intercede with Katterfeld to change the venue and timing of the proceedings. It was all for naught. Katterfeld, in the grip of a deep sense of factional intrigue, was convinced that such cautionary advice was merely a ploy of the liquidators to buy time to strengthen their hand, widely perceived to be endorsed by only a minority of the party. To Cannon, continuing to plead the case of legalization and Americanization before the Comintern leadership, and beset by a series of communication breakdowns, it was all little more than a blur, and he "never could get a clear account of what happened there." In the immediate, short run, however, it was certainly, in Draper's words, "sauce for the geese."[53]

This sauce seemed to scald Ruthenberg. Tipped off that agents were ready to make a move against them, the comrades beat an orderly retreat from Bridgman and the idyllic rural site where they had convened. The national secretary stayed behind with a few others, claiming it was his responsibility to bury incriminating documents and correspondence. He was one of seventeen arrested, although charges would later be levied against others, primarily William Z. Foster, the evidence being easily recovered. Facing a prison term, Ruthenberg threatened, for a brief period, to reverse his position on party legalization, retreating into undergroundism, as the prospects of yet another prolonged period behind bars apparently convinced him of the sagacity of the Goose faction's position. The Geese registered other victories. Now representing barely 6,000 members, the Communist and Workers' Party delegates (Numbers One and Two) who gathered at Bridgman spoke for an overwhelmingly immigrant constituency: 500 at most were "American comrades," and a mere 5 percent were active trade unionists. The Geese elected the temporary chairman of the convention by a vote of twenty-two to eighteen, but a later vote of undetermined significance went to the underground caucus by the narrowest of margins, twenty-three to twenty-two, and a spy cast the deciding ballot. In the pivotal construction of the CEC, the Goose Caucus demanded a clear majority, and Valetski sided with them: of the reconstructed body of twelve, two came from relatively neutral quarters, proposed by both factions; six were Geese; three were Liquidators; and one was from the ostensibly unaffiliated Young Communist League.[54] In the end, however, all was not lost, and Cannon likely sensed that the ultimate line of defense of the Workers' Party, and the project of legalization and Americanization, lay in wielding influence with the ECCI.[55]

The liquidationist view that Harding's America was not as repressive a political climate as that of the Palmer Raids was in fact ironically borne out by the trials of the Bridgman communists. William Z. Foster, for instance, managed to secure a hung jury, and the Workers' Party's Labor Defense Council raised large sums and propagandized for the revolutionary cause, developing a united-front campaign that drew on the support of the American Civil Liberties Union and major Chicago-based, noncommunist, labor figures. In another case, stemming from Foster's kidnapping by Colorado Rangers during a 1922 speaking tour amidst the strike of 400,000 railway shopmen, the publicity and political impact was similar, a reflection of the extent to which the vigilante actions of the World War I and 1919–1920 years were no longer palatable. As spies testified in ways that made clear their role as *agents provocateurs* (one notorious figure who had infiltrated the communist ranks indicating that he had adopted the most ultraleft "Goose" positions), the United States public indicated that it had little stomach for a new round of witch hunts. Benjamin

Gitlow, who would do a second jail term as a consequence of the ill-fated Bridgman convention, grasped the contradictory meaning of the repression of 1922: "The raid upon the Bridgeman [sic] Convention," he later wrote, "instead of whipping up Red hysteria, had the opposite effect. On the one hand, it put us in a ridiculous position; while, on the other hand, public opinion turned definitely against the raiders. The trade unions rallied to our defense, as did the liberal forces of the country." Out of Bridgman, then, came a new sensibility about the possibilities of legal, above-ground communist agitation, in which mass work might lead to converts and a widening of the revolutionary cause in the United States.[56]

Cannon thus faced the final, decisive test of his so-called liquidationist position, which was in actuality a call for both legalization and Americanization, at the Fourth Congress of the Communist International, 5 November–5 December 1922. Zinoviev eventually established an American Commission, chaired by the Finn Ottomar V. Kuusinen, and including Lozovsky, Radek, Bukharin, Valetski,[57] and eight others, by which the legality/underground opposition would be resolved. By this time, apparently, the leading figures of the Comintern had, through the efforts of Cannon and others, slowly come around to accept the necessity of legalization, with Zinoviev and Bukharin the most reluctant. But this was unknown to the United States delegation, which included Cannon, Bedacht, and Arne Swabeck from the camp now dubbed the Liquidators; Katterfeld, Rose Pastor Stokes, the Surinam-born black West Indian, Otto Huiswoud, and possibly Israel Amter as representatives of the Goose Caucus; trade union and youth delegates (Jack Johnstone, Rose Wortis, and Martin Abern, all in favor of legalization); and a range of other unofficial figures, including *Liberator* editor Max Eastman and the African American poet Claude McKay. McKay, whose rich experience already included involvement in Cyril V. Briggs's African Blood Brotherhood, Sylvia Pankhurst's London-based *Workers' Dreadnaught,* and editorial and contributory writing with radical magazines in New York, had been in the Soviet Union for some time, growing close to Cannon. A member of the Workers' Party not prone to proclaim himself a communist in America, McKay, like a number of other black radicals of the time, had not so much linked arms with immigrant and native-born leftists in the United States as he had "joined the Comintern," which looked to him to be a revolutionary body attuned to the global significance of race.[58]

Things did not appear all that good for the forces of legalization until the eleventh hour. A critical turn was taken with a late November 1922 meeting that Eastman arranged for Cannon and Bedacht to have with Trotsky. Strictly limited to one hour, the conference (which Bedacht suggested was far less important than Cannon indicated) won Trotsky over to the legalization side.

Cannon did most of the talking, his commentary supplemented by Bedacht's observations. The WP leader stressed four points:

1. The lack of class consciousness of the American workers, and as a result, the elementary tasks of propaganda imposed on the Communist Party.
2. The actual political climate in the country which made possible and necessitated a legal political party.
3. Our proposal to support the formation of a labor party based on the trade unions.
4. The necessity of Americanizing the party, of breaking the control of the foreign-language federations and assuring an indigenous national leadership.

Trotsky expressed amusement at the ultraleft view that an underground party must be upheld as a matter of revolutionary principle, suggesting that if the foreign-language federation heads persisted in this wrong-headed "theory" they could be invited back to Russia. He told Bedacht and Cannon that he endorsed their position; indicated that he would convey this opinion to the ailing Lenin, whom he thought would be in agreement; and asked the Americans to provide him with a one-page written statement so that he could pass it on to the Bolshevik leaders. They did so—the document would be two pages, not one—and secured the support of seven other American delegates.[59] When Lenin was shown a copy of the underground press, *The Communist*, he ostensibly scrawled in its margins, "Stop this nonsense."[60]

The American Commission formally convened on the evening of 27 November 1922. Katterfeld attempted to limit attendance to Communist Party of America members and the single comrade, Cannon, who had been designated to attend as the voice of the Workers' Party. This would have restricted admission to the proceedings greatly, banishing not only minority members Bedacht and Swabeck, but also Alexander Trachtenberg of the old Workers' Council group and McKay—an unofficial observer, to be sure, but one whose symbolic importance as an African American was striking. Words were exchanged between Katterfeld and Cannon, the former claiming that he was opposed to the minority's formation of a "subcommittee" to push for more open hearings. "Can't we have a conspiratorial subcommittee?" Cannon joked, in reference to the underground's preferred methods. "Yes, you have quite a few of them," huffed the old warrior of the Socialist Party left wing. Katterfeld's move to close the doors to McKay and others was quickly rebuffed, the Japanese Marxist Sen Katayama declaring bluntly, "This is a well known case, and there is no need of limiting admission to Communist Party members."[61]

Katterfeld, whom Cannon always regarded as a hard-bitten sectarian who was nevertheless "a sincere communist of incorruptible integrity" with a long-standing history of contribution to the revolutionary movement, was then given the floor.[62] His speech was a restrained argument about the necessity for the continuity of Comintern policy, in which the vital and respective roles of the underground and legal parties would remain acknowledged. The bulk of the underground party's membership, he claimed, supported the tasks of the legal party, when they were adequately explained to them, but too often they were assailed with the need "to get rid of the underground party, to abolish the Communist Party." For this reason, many opposed the legal party, which was growing slowly, and Katterfeld betrayed his hand somewhat when he explained why: "There is no way of building a legal party in the United States except thru our membership. There may be some good writers, literateurs, poets, even some labor leaders here and there, but the only real driving force, the only real revolutionary elements that can be got for this work are within the ranks of the workers and the successful work with outside elements alone is impossible." He could have been pointing to Eastman, McKay, and Cannon. To be sure, Katterfeld conceded, the underground ranks were "sectarian" and "narrow," "sometimes cursed because they are foreigners and cannot speak the English language." But they were, in his opinion, the bone and sinew of revolutionary communism in the United States and, at bottom, they were not to be displaced by the creation of a new legal party with its slogan "to the masses." Katterfeld made an impassioned plea for the status quo: a legal party, to be sure, but one always under the discipline and direction of the tried-and-true underground Communist Party.[63]

As reasonable as Katterfeld's arguments may have seemed, they masked the fundamental question. Who controlled what and why? Many Bolshevik leaders were, as Bittelman astutely grasped, reluctant to dispense entirely with underground parties. Their pasts and their instinctual appreciations of "white terror," which many of them had experienced directly, solidified their understanding of the absolute necessity of keeping in reserve the protections illegality could, in dire circumstances, offer the revolutionary ranks. The undergroundist conception of America as a brutalizing environment of capitalist coercion and state repression, in which open work as a communist was next to impossible, was not entirely discredited, even if its mirror-image—a sense that the revolution was around the corner, the masses seething, the "illegal party" preparing the way for a violent seizure of proletarian power—was no longer tenable. As restrained as Katterfeld's plea for Comintern continuity was, many ECCI officials and Bolshevik Party leaders had their fill of more extreme presentations in informal discussions; the Goose Caucus delegates, in Claude McKay's words, buoyed "up the Russians with false pictures of the American situation." He heard plenty of "tall rhetoric" and "purple phrases," all of it putting out a distorted message of impending revolutionary upheavals.

Against this caricatured optimism, Cannon, Bittelman, Bedacht, and Swabeck presented a more sober judgment. This was reinforced by the talks of nondelegates such as Eastman (who had a strong connection to Trotsky) and McKay, whose prestige among the Russian ranks and leaders was truly awe-inspiring, and helped bring forth the first serious Comintern discussions of "the Negro Question." Katterfeld may have sensed that although he would have some support among the appointed figures on the American Commission—Valetski being a prime example—he would have to tone down the underground pitch if it were going to have any resonance with Zinoviev and other leading Bolsheviks. For that reason, he made no hard-line assault on the Workers' Party as a legal body, nor was there much in the way of debate on older questions, such as the necessity of promoting armed insurrection. Finally, and perhaps decisively, the crucial point of departure for almost all discussions at the Fourth Congress was the implementation of the united front. If one was able to get past the coded language of Katterfeld's presentation, it was not difficult to discern positions that would make joint actions of communists and other workers' movement organizations, even on the basis of principled Leninist notions of single-issue campaigns, highly unlikely.[64]

Cannon, blasting for the Liquidators,[65] refused to join in "the general love feast of comrades Valetski and Carr." Denying that anything approximating a revolutionary situation prevailed in America, Cannon stated forthrightly that the working class in the United States was not class conscious: the majority thought and acted as citizens in a democratic republic, rather than as workers; in general workers voted for capitalist parties; and their unions were "reactionary and numerically weak." Agreeing that there was movement to the left in labor's ranks, Cannon nevertheless stressed that the way for communists to capitalize on this development was to agitate openly among the masses of workers for a variety of shifts in practice and politics that would revolutionize the toiling classes. The Workers' Party and the TUEL were doing just this, but they were handicapped in their struggle, and this was the fundamental issue before the Commission:

> We have the disadvantage of being a new party. We have not tested our leaders in open struggle. Our party was underground the first year of its existence and it has very little confidence of the working masses. The working class in America have democratic illusions. They do not understand why we are underground as a party, and they do not yet have the sympathy for us that it is necessary for them to have for our party to be a factor in the life of the workers.

I say it with great regret, that our underground party instead of having the sympathy and attraction of the workers is regarded by the masses as a good deal of
a joke. They think it is illegal because we want to be illegal, and I must say that
that is true of a large majority of the illegal party.

Persecutions, Cannon understood, were ongoing under capitalism, but they
could be opposed and beaten back, and much could be gained in the educational and political realms as a consequence of such fights. "There is not a
strike in America where men are not shot down and beaten and jailed, yet the
trade unions have not been driven underground," he argued. Nor had the
IWW succumbed to repression; rather, it had fought, time and time again—
and not without success—for the freedoms of speech and association. White
terror, as it existed in the United States, was not of the same repressive order as
it had been in czarist Russia or Europe of the recent past, and there were openings in the political and economic spheres that demanded attention. In what
would prove to be a theme of his intervention, Cannon asserted, "These comrades have changed their position, but not their mind." In principle, he argued,
Katterfeld and the Geese were "still illegal." Katterfeld's argument for continuity was thus a recipe for future implosions. Many in the communist milieu
were embittered, Cannon complained, and they had a right to be: "After three
years of fighting to get a chance to do our work we have still to come to
Moscow to fight it out. Not one split, Comrade Valetski, but four splits have
been forced upon us."

Cannon thus pleaded with the Comintern American Commission to end
the split, and the prospects of future splits. Why, Cannon asked, had this condition of immobilizing controversy continued? "It is time for us to be honest
and frank," he declared. The inability to do "the simple things" was, in Cannon's view, attributable to the sociodemographic makeup of the majority of
the communist ranks in the United States:

The large majority of our membership is a foreign born membership, mainly
Russian, Ukrainian, Lettish, etc. that has not assimilated itself. They live for the
most part in separate colonies and there life is entirely a Russian life. And the
peculiarity of the situation is that our party is not troubled with an American
nationalism but with an anti-American nationalism. It is troubled with prejudice on the part of these comrades against the American workers. There is a
. decided anti-American sentiment.

These were brave words to utter before a determining Comintern body composed of Russians, Finns, Poles, and other non-American revolutionary inter-
nationalists, but this was also a formulation easily misinterpreted, or, worse,
disingenuously manipulated. Cannon pressed the American Commission for

"real political leadership" rather than the accustomed "diplomacy." Laying the two-page statement he, Bedacht, and Swabeck had prepared for Trotsky before the commission, Cannon concluded on a revolutionary loyalist note: "What the Comintern says is the light we go by."[66]

Following Katterfeld and Cannon, the Lettish underground Boston ultra-leftist "Sullivan" spoke, deriding liquidationism and promoting the politics of 1917, transposed to the United States in the early 1920s. He claimed that world revolution was around the corner, an intensification of the class struggle imminent. "Only fools or agents of the bourgeoisie" advocated legalization of the underground in this context. There was little in the trade union section that occasioned support from Sullivan: "The breaking out of syndicalist anti-communist boils on the body of revolutionary labor organizations is to a large extent but a sign and result of an opportunistic blood-poisoning in the communist organization." Often put down as a faction of one (except by Cannon, who saw him as representative of larger, if more diffuse, tendencies within the underground milieu), Sullivan spoke forcefully if futilely. He was followed by another speaker from the ultraleft. According to this source, not only Cannon and Company in the minority were "infected" by liquidationism, but also significant sectors of the majority, indicating that the foreign-language federations did not give quite the homogenous mass support to undergroundism that some suggested.[67]

After the presentation of these opening statements, the American Commission broke and reconvened a few days later, meeting over the course of the morning and evening of 30 November 1922. The U.S. delegates skirmished over minor matters and then turned their sights on the larger issue. More combative, the tone of exchanges now had an edge. With the realization that a fight was actually on, and that the Comintern might be pressed to break from its fence-sitting on the illegal-legal controversy, the polemical temperature was raised a few degrees. Cannon was heckled by the Goose Caucus delegate Otto Huiswoud ("Billings"), aside from McKay the only black in attendance at the commission: "When comrade Cook speaks of democrats he should look in the mirror, he is one of the worst we have."[68]

Katterfeld, almost on cue, took up Cannon's explanation that the resistance to a legal party developed out of the isolating sectarianism of the foreign-language federations, rebuking the native-born Midwesterner in ways that catered to a Russian lowest common denominator:

> It is not an easy task to take a legal mass organization and take out of it the good conscious Communist elements, the best elements that formed the nucleus of the underground party. I don't want to lose them. They may be ignorant foreigners, it is true, they may not be able to speak the English language as elo-

quently as Comrade Cooke, but know that these men are Communists and that
their whole lives are devoted to the cause; and no one can insult them or min-
imise them in my presence. That is one of the real troubles in the American
party, too much of this prejudice against the foreigner, too much hatred of
Rooshians, as Comrade Cooke calls them.

The United States was now in the grip of bourgeois repression, Katterfeld
closed, and it was no time to shut down the underground party. Cannon, he
suggested, should be back in the United States making revolution, rather than
forcing issues in the Comintern.[69]

When the body reassembled on 1 December 1922, the discussion by the main
protagonists had largely run its course. International delegates took the floor,
followed by some final warnings. Zinoviev was brusque in his embrace of
legalization. The central Bolshevik figures on the commission had tipped their
hand, although Valetski remained something of a holdout, trying unsuccessfully to get the members of the Cannon minority to agree to a compromise.
Katterfeld took a last stand, committing himself to following whatever decisions the Comintern arrived at, but insisting that it would be his responsibility
as a communist to argue for and fight against policies that he thought detrimental to the revolutionary movement. Cannon, watching the last-ditch
stands of resistance, continued to press for "decisive directions" that would
make "sabotage" of the American Commission's "instructions" impossible.[70]

He got just that. The succinct Comintern document (ten short paragraphs
on two pages), which seemingly ended the long-standing factional battles
within United States communism over legality and Americanization, gave
Cannon everything he had come to Moscow, and toiled over the course of six
months, to achieve. The opening paragraph dispelled any notion that an
underground party could ever again claim pride of place in the Comintern's
eyes: "the center of all Communist activity in America lies not in the underground or illegal but in the open and legal work." Whatever repression might
befall the revolutionary movement, any underground organization that
proved necessary must be adapted to the needs of the open work of communists, "a driving force" for the legal struggle. Such secret activity, if demanded
by specific conditions, was to "remain for a time," rather than be adhered to as
a principle. The open party was "under no circumstances to be an appendix or
a passive instrument of the illegal party," but was instead to be an active and
leading element in all class-struggle work. "Illegalist prejudices" of a "super-
radical" sort were to be combated, and the foreign-language federations were
to see as their primary responsibility the "revolutionary development of the
American working class." All tendencies were encouraged to put their injuri-
ous factionalism aside, to reach out to the broad masses through the Workers'

Party, which was now recognized as a sympathizing component of the Communist International, "with the right to participate in all International gatherings with consultative vote." For Cannon, the Comintern decision was a mandate for "new work," "opening up the possibility of a new era for the American movement." The Geese were cooked.[71]

As to Cannon himself, he was further steeled by the experience of charting the seas of revolutionary activity in which programmatic direction, and hammering out a Leninist orientation, were of decisive importance. If he came away from Moscow with an abiding antagonism to the functionaries of bureaucratic regimes, he nonetheless cultivated a genuine appreciation of the Bolshevik leaders from whom he learned. His brief encounter with Trotsky, for instance, would linger in his political subconscious for some time. With Zinoviev, Lozovsky, and Radek, he had more sustained and deeper relations, and it was perhaps the former who left the longest-lasting impression. Zinoviev's shifting stature in the politics of world revolution had not, in 1922, so sullied his reputation that his close collaboration with Lenin during World War I, and his strong role in Bolshevik propagandizing against both imperialist war and the abdication of the social-democratic Second International, was forgotten. Cannon retained a "soft spot" for the Zinoviev of the early Comintern years, even though he had vacillated in 1917 and, along with Kamenev, published his objections to the Bolsheviks leading an insurrection. Later, of course, Zinoviev would lead the Communist International in the direction of bureaucratization, and he would then succumb to the Stalinist counterrevolution, but this was not evident in 1922. In Cannon's eyes (and Trotsky's as well), Zinoviev was in this period a pillar of revolutionary commitment, chairman of the Petrograd Soviet, the founding chairman of the Communist International in 1919, and a rousing orator unrivalled in the Bolshevik ranks. Like Bukharin and other Russian leaders of the early 1920s, Zinoviev disdained privilege and lived for the advance of world revolution. In 1922, these revolutionary Russians taught Cannon what Leninism looked like as a living process, and he never forgot that.[72]

As Cannon was preparing to leave the Soviet Union, the second annual convention of the Workers' Party opened on 24 December 1922: the underground party's functions were "retired," folded into the legal party, which took on more of the public trappings of a communist vanguard, calling for the creation of a Soviet "dictatorship of the Workers" and accepting the leadership of the Communist International. If the old Number One remained in existence for a time, it was but a shell of its former self. Cannon, *in absentia,* was elected to the Workers' Party's ruling bodies, the twenty-four-member Central Executive Committee and the eleven-member Executive Council.[73] All in all, 1923 was shaping up as a good year for the young revolutionary, who was about to turn thirty-three while getting reacquainted with the United States. Returning to his homeland in seeming triumph, Cannon, now one of the leading native sons of the United States revolutionary movement, was thoroughly unprepared for his next ordeal, in which, as in Marx's famous maxim, events and personages would appear twice in history, the first time as tragedy, the second as farce.[74] If the Geese and their politics of undergroundism were a deformative tragedy in the making of the United States revolutionary Left—one that contributed much of positive note—American communism's indefatigable farce would go by the name of John Pepper.

"UNDERGROUND
RADICALISM"

An Open Letter to
EUGENE V. DEBS
and to All Honest Workers
Within the Socialist Party

By
JOHN PEPPER

PRICE TEN CENTS

PUBLISHED BY
WORKERS PARTY of AMERICA
799 BROADWAY   NEW YORK CITY

7

Pepper Spray

The Americanizer's Return to America

Cannon returned to the United States late in January 1923.[1] The Workers' Party
(WP) that he chaired was now the undisputed center of American communism, and a few months later, in April 1923, the underground Communist
Party of America finally dissolved itself. Reported membership in the WP at
that time was 16,421, although the number of actual adherents to the above-
ground communist milieu more likely hovered around 10,000 to 12,000. New
York alone comprised almost 25 percent of the communist ranks, and Chicago
contributed a further 15 percent; Boston, Minneapolis, Cleveland, and Detroit
were home to a remaining bloc of 40 percent; while the Pacific Coast added
another 5 percent. The Workers' Party was, fundamentally, urban and north-
eastern, although the discerning detective might well find a communist presence in far-flung places such as Plentywood, Montana, and even unlikely
outposts in the Deep South. Its class composition was strongly proletarian,
roughly three-quarters of all members coming from the working class. Metal
and machinery workers, building tradesmen and laborers, miners, and men
and women from the needle trades represented the most important occupational sectors within the communist Left. Unskilled workers may well have
predominated, for barely one-third of the communist ranks also belonged to
unions, traditionally the preserve of the skilled and the English-speaking.
Superficially, the rise of the Workers' Party and the demise of the underground
Communist Party of America would seem to have pushed the balance of constituencies away from the foreign-language federations, long the dominant
force in the revolutionary underground. But while the Lettish and Russian fed-

erations faded, their memberships demolished and disorganized in the aftermath of state attack and a mass return of their ranks to Russia, the powerful majority of the communist movement remained ensconced in Finnish (now 45 percent of the entire Workers' Party membership), South Slavic, Lithuanian, Jewish, Scandinavian, and German sections. As in 1922, the party could likely point to not much more than 2,000 of its ranks who were not members of foreign-language federations, and many of those were also first-generation immigrants. Indeed, in the latter half of 1922 the WP had been able to overcome a crisis of fiscal solvency (a $10,200 deficit and the national office's unpaid tab of $2,200) by securing the dues of branches of the United Toilers, now united with the legal party, in November and December, setting them aside as an ironically designated liquidation fund to clear the party books of debt. The foreign-language federations thus funded communism's Americanization. In central locales, the dominance of non-English-speaking elements remained undeniable. Of Chicago's fifty-two WP branches in 1923, for instance, fully forty-seven were non-English-speaking. Unlike the older Russian and Lettish federations, though, the numerically powerful Finns never pushed to run the entire revolutionary show. Things had certainly changed— yet there were suggestions of stasis as well.[2]

For Cannon, the moment was one of optimism, albeit tempered with the sober assessment of reality. This emerged in Cannon's response to the socialist militant Scott Nearing. Nearing toured the Midwest as the communists were prodded by the Comintern to come out of their underground lairs, and then spoke at New York's Rand School. The well-known radical claimed, inaccurately, that the Socialist Party was now dead, concluding that the Workers' Party had "fallen heir to the present radical situation in the United States." Cannon found this a nice welcome home. He immediately defended Nearing's analysis and, moreover, emphasized the significance of his movement toward communism. Like many in the IWW or the trade unions, Nearing was thirsting for revolutionary leadership, and these people constituted a base of recruitment that, for Cannon, was "the living material out of which we must build our party." Nearing, however, was not yet ready for the WP. He expressed concerns about what he called Moscow's "system of dictation," about foreign control. Cannon turned the tables, arguing that communists never "put the question on the vulgar basis of birth place," stressing that while American communism was now rightly going to be led by native-born revolutionaries, no foreign-born worker would be shunned. The Workers' Party, he insisted, rejected narrow nationalism and was engaged in building a fraternity of the native-born and the immigrant. In moving communism in this direction, and in pushing to have an open party of the sort that could engage directly in the day-to-day political issues of the United States, a struggle had to be waged, Cannon confessed, and many costly splits had handicapped the revolutionary Left in its underground period. But those days of the "subway" party were over, Cannon claimed. And who had used their authority to turn American communism in the direction of openness, legality, and an orientation to United States conditions? "The 'Moscow Dictators!'" he snorted in derision. Far from fearing Russian dictatorial control, Cannon concluded, "We who have fought for a realistic party have found our best friend in 'Moscow.'"[3]

Cannon on the Road Again: The Push and Pull of Party Assignment

Cannon's reappearance on the United States scene was marked by an odd decision. Barely unpacked, he departed for a five-month cross-country speaking tour. A series of factors perhaps explains this choice to take one of the Workers' Party's leading figures, absent in Moscow for almost eight months, away from the party center at a pivotal period in its transition to a new kind of political organization. The first two of these factors, combining the personal and the political, were most definitely products of Cannon's own decisions.

First was the entirely personal realm of Cannon's private, family life. No evidence survives of the nature of Jim's relationship with Lista and their children, Carl and Ruth, during this period. The children were of school age, and their father's absence could not have failed to register with them. Lista had moved from Kansas to Ohio to New York, setting up a household in a Greenwich Village apartment at West 11th Street and 9th Avenue, but no sooner was she settled than Jim left for Moscow.[4] Cannon's willingness to touch down in New York and then happily depart on party assignment after his long separation from Lista, Carl, and Ruth in 1922–1923, spending barely a month at home in the interim, spoke legions about what was obviously a deteriorating domestic scene.

Second, this complex of forces, simultaneously pushing Cannon out of New York and pulling him into the role of propagandist, meshed personal desires and needs with political conviction. Cannon, after all, was strongly advocating that the new legal Workers' Party be an agitational body, appealing to the broad ranks of American labor and the Left. Speaking to mass audiences across the country, Cannon was revived politically, shaking the cobwebs of officialdom and bureaucratism off his person in the refreshing work of the rebel propagandist.[5]

The necessary but somewhat stifling and tedious work of consolidating leadership alliances and strategic positions *within* the party was something Cannon may well have wanted a brief respite from as he reintegrated himself in the world of United States communism. Later in the year, he wrote to a close friend, the former Roxbury, Massachusetts, Lettish revolutionary, Charles Scott (formerly Carl Jansen or Charles Johnson), posted in Moscow on Comintern business. Jim enthused to Charley how much he enjoyed the tour, where he connected with old friends such as the miner militant, Alex Howat, still at the center of the class-struggle storm in the UMWA.[6] Now riding the cushions, the former hobo rebel rekindled some of his attachment to the Industrial Workers of the World, writing a futile two-part article in the midst of his tour that urged the Wobblies to embrace the united front of world revolution and affiliate with the Red International of Labor Unions.[7] Cannon relished crossing polemical swords with the likes of Vancouver's remnants of the Socialist Party of Canada. "I make a speciality of dealing with these 'Scientific Socialists,'" Cannon wrote, obviously enjoying getting back into the open fray of public debate. All of this, however, necessarily limited his involvement in the officialdom of the party: "In fact," Cannon added, "I have had very little to do with CEC activities since I returned from Russia as my whole time and energy has been taken up with propaganda." The speaking tour confirmed, for Cannon, a politics of "going to the masses," as did an editorial appointment to the *Liberator*. Cannon was, in this context, somewhat nonchalant in immersing himself in the industrial committee of the Central Executive Committee, where he worked with Gitlow, Harry M. Wicks, and William Z. Foster (clandestinely referred to as "A"), ceding places on the powerful political committee to others. His voting behavior in CEC meetings carried a tone of conciliation, and when given the opportunity to settle old scores with prominent Goose Caucus members, Cannon took the high road and avoided any hint of petty, personalized politics.[8]

With this personal/political background as part of the context of February–March 1923, it is possible to grasp more fully Cannon's distanced relation to an emerging inner-party struggle for factional authority. Had Cannon's ear been fully pressed to the rumbling ground of Workers' Party leadership regrouping, he would have heard the ominous sounds of trouble on the way, but it is likely that he was not really listening, needing a separation from New York.

For instance, Cannon was aware, as he returned to New York early in 1923, that there were new problems in the fragile unity among the Jewish sections of the Workers' Party that he had helped knit together in 1921. As Cannon was arguing against the Goose Caucus before the American Commission late in November 1922, Ruthenberg sent a telegram to the Comintern outlining splits among New York City's Jewish communists.[9] Apparently, it was Cannon who patched things together within the Jewish leadership ranks, bringing Moissaye Olgin, Alexander Trachtenberg, and Alexander Bittelman together, although he did not accomplish this until late in 1923 or early 1924.[10] It is possible that Cannon at first wanted to isolate himself from the Jewish Federation battle, because in acting as a conciliator he would necessarily have to make concessions to the Olgin faction, which contained ex-Socialist Party figures such as J. B. Salutsky ("Hardman"). Advocates of "an open communist party," these former members of the Workers' Council group were generally regarded as only weakly committed to Leninist understandings of Bolshevik discipline. To have them perceived as allies in his ongoing battle with the Goose Caucus would have cost Cannon credibility.[11] In any case, in absenting himself for the five-month period of his speaking tour, Cannon allowed the Jewish crisis to simmer. More importantly, he seemed unable to recognize the pivotal role of a recently arrived element in the upper echelons of the WP, a figure who was a key ingredient in the volatile mix of leadership realignment that was taking place over the course of 1923, and a major player in the disruptions of the Jewish section.

Upon Bittelman's return to the United States from Russia in the fall of 1922, he found "a new comrade in our midst, in the leading circles of the party. His name here was John Pepper. . . . I found that he was functioning, among other things, as the representative of the party in the leading body of the Jewish section." Indeed, Pepper emerged out of the 1922–1923 crisis in the Jewish section with something of a factional base, thereby catapulting himself into a leadership role in the nascent Workers' Party.[12] Bittelman, who did not warm personally to Pepper, also resented "this stranger" in the Jewish Bureau of the party. He "never could find out whose idea it was" to place Pepper so strategically in the communist hierarchy. Cannon was similarly perplexed. What *was* clear, although how it happened had something of the air of the fantastic about it, was that Pepper, appearing on the scene in the summer of 1922, had managed, by February 1923, to put himself "in full charge of everything, deciding everything, including the positions and the fate of individuals who pleased or displeased him."[13] Albert Glotzer, a fifteen-year-old recruit to the communist movement, first met Pepper in 1923, and remembered him as "a communist carpetbagger on a world scale."[14]

Cannon's speaking tour undoubtedly figured into Pepper's capacity to ingratiate himself further into the upper echelons of the Workers' Party, precisely because he did not have to maneuver around the national chairman. It was in this period that the Cannon-Lovestone combination came unhinged, although it may well have been disintegrating for lack of attention over the course of Cannon's months in Moscow. Central to this was Pepper's role in "building up a leading group in the party, a new leadership, with himself, Ruthenberg, and Lovestone at its core." It was critically important for Pepper to isolate Cannon and Foster as working-class leaders, and to break Bittelman's authority in the Jewish section, casting this linked trio in the role of secondary players in the politics of the new legal party. Unwittingly, Cannon's willingness to concentrate his energies in the industrial committee of the CEC fed into this Pepper plot, as did the national chairman's lackadaisical response to the political committee being constructed around Pepper (its four other members being Gitlow, Bedacht, Ludwig Lore, and Lovestone). When a new deciding body, the Secretariat, was established in mid-February 1923, composed of Pepper, Ruthenberg, and the former Goose leader, Abraham Jakira, Cannon offered not so much as a whisper of opposition; the motion to ensconce the Pepper-led triumvirate passed unanimously.[15]

Pepper embraced unequivocally the Soviet-supported push into open party work, and he broke the political back of those Goose Caucus advocates, such as Ludwig Katterfeld and Alfred Wagenknecht, who could not be cajoled into embracing his climb up the United States revolutionary ladder. Former undergrounders who adapted to Pepper's bid for power, such as Jakira, were rehabilitated and integrated into his personal faction. To the more illustrious of these went prestigious party posts, the most egregious example being Gitlow who, in spite of difficulties in functioning at a high literary level in Yiddish, was parachuted into the political monitoring of the Jewish press, which only further antagonized the cultured element usually responsible for handling the *Freiheit*'s affairs.

Lovestone, however, was Pepper's star recruit. With Cannon out of the country for the latter half of 1922, the Lovestone-Cannon combination, always an expedient alliance of dissimilar party types held together only by agreement on the central issues of legalization and Americanization, and forged in Ruthenberg's absence, faded away. Lovestone assumed more and more of the administrative tasks of the communist headquarters, describing himself as Ruthenberg's "maid of all work" while chafing under the long hours and bristling with indignation at the party secretary's shortcomings, personal and political. Known as a Workers' Party workhorse and the young man behind the Ruthenberg administration, Lovestone's presence was increasingly visible in the party press, in its educational and agitational apparatus, and in the everyday administration of much communist activity. However, Lovestone's ambitions were always struggling to break out into the open, and when he and Ruthenberg competed for the affections of a female comrade, Clarissa Ware, in the summer of 1923[16] (C.E. being something of a womanizer), the younger Lovestone was more than ready to see in Pepper a possible factional ally with whom to unite in combination with the prestigious, but superior and aloof, party secretary. Any notion of loyalty to Ruthenberg was easily dispensed with by Lovestone. Ruthenberg's personal inclinations, in which distance from the trade unions, jealousy toward those—such as Foster and Cannon[17]—who had different bases of authority and power in the revolutionary movement that made them more attractive to mass constituencies, and a sense of himself as an educated Marxist in the European mold, undoubtedly pushed him in the direction of Pepper, at the same time as his distance and superiority ensured that he would leave the heavy-handed power pushes or unseemly factional intrigue to others "below" him. As Cannon recalled of Ruthenberg, "he appeared to stand above the dirty little vices, such as outright lying, double-dealing, betrayal of confidence. He would have considered such things, if he thought about them at all, as not simply wrong but, more important, beneath his dignity." This was the ideal situation for Pepper, who could be truly relentless in his suppression of opponents, and for Lovestone, bent on consolidating party power and soon to stand alone in WP circles as someone none of the leaders trusted.[18]

With Cannon back in the United States in February 1923, then, Pepper was "the real boss of the party behind the scenes, [with] Lovestone as his first lieutenant." Ruthenberg found himself holding the public reins of leadership, but he guided things from the backroom shadows of the Pepper-Lovestone combination. This reconfiguration of party leadership, which had ironically grown out of the attempt to Americanize the party only to place its first period of legal work in the hands of a figure who had lived in the United States less than a year, largely passed Cannon by: "I was outside these developments during my long stay in Moscow, and again for many months on my tour after my return." Pepper and Lovestone found this fortuitous. Indeed, there is some suggestion that through the CEC they made sure that Cannon was absent from the party center at a period of critical decision making.[19]

Cannon's tour commenced the first week of March 1923. Its initial jaunt took him throughout New England and adjoining states, where he delivered more than a score of speeches to audiences assembled in public auditoriums and trade union halls throughout cities, large and small, in Massachusetts, New Hampshire, Pennsylvania, Connecticut, and New York. In a second phase, beginning in mid-April, Cannon whistle-stopped amidst the industrial districts of Ohio and Pennsylvania, touching down in his old stomping grounds of New Castle, Cleveland, and Akron as well as in Pittsburgh, Youngstown, and elsewhere. Working his way west, he was in Grand Rapids, Michigan, on 9 May 1923, appearing at the Trades and Labor Council Hall, and in Minneapolis shortly thereafter. In mid-June he returned to Kansas, speaking at a number of locales. His popularity in Alexander Howat's coal district remained high: at a Sunday-afternoon talk in the small mining community of Franklin, whose entire population was little more than 1,700, Cannon drew an audience of 800. Five days later, on 19 June 1923, he addressed a crowd in Denver, Colorado. Cannon closed out his speaking with West Coast stops in Los Angeles, Oakland, San

Francisco, Seattle, Tacoma, Spokane, Portland, and Vancouver, Canada; on his return home he appeared at select locales, such as Butte and Duluth, to deliver more agitational lectures. In all, it was an ambitious itinerary, encompassing many weeks of travel and talk and more than 100 meetings.[20]

Drawing on his seven months in Russia, Cannon presented a sobering assessment of the difficulties facing the revolution, and acknowledged the extent to which workers' standards of living were anything but high. Nonetheless, the national chairman also used his podium time to strike a blow against worker passivity and demoralization, presenting the Bolshevik victory in 1917 as a historic accomplishment, proof that the workers could seize power and establish a state in their interests. In the end, Cannon stressed, the Soviet regime could not stand alone, and its leaders, such as Lenin and Trotsky, were counting on "revolutions taking place in the European countries such as Germany and France." Cannon also emphasized that the workers of the United States had their role to play, urging organization to "help the Communist Government of Russia," but also to "organize powerfully" at home, the better to "be in a position to establish an international working and ruling class to cooperate with Soviet Russia." In the published version of his talk, a Workers' Party pamphlet entitled *The Fifth Year of the Russian Revolution,* Cannon concluded: "For after all, Soviet Russia is not a 'country.' Soviet Russia is part of the world labor movement. Soviet Russia is a strike—the greatest strike in all history. When the working class of America and Europe join that strike it will be the end of capitalism."[21]

In contrast to the ultraleft rhetoric of the immediate post-World War I underground, Cannon's presentations of revolutionary program relied on a realistic assessment of American actualities and possibilities balanced by a truthful commentary on Soviet conditions. To be sure, Cannon never wavered in his accent on the imperative of international proletarian revolt and workers' control of the means of production and the levers of state power as preconditions of humanity's betterment, but his speeches provided little that played into the hands of the forces of repression, still alert to any opportunity to silence revolutionaries with an array of criminal charges.

This no doubt left some in the audience disappointed. Government spies were often troubled by the lack of red flags and incendiary rhetoric, this being the stuff of their remuneration.[22] The file from Minneapolis expressed incredulity at Cannon's forthright descriptions of Russian conditions.[23] Lacking evidence of criminal speech, some informers resorted to garbled editorializing: "Agent's opinion of this meeting is that he believes this man CANNON is trying to get the different members of the Reds to try and over throw our Govt." Occasionally, Cannon thumbed his nose at the spies he knew were present: "I don't want to say that the workers of this country will revolt," he commented mischievously in Pittsburgh, "but it is coming. No one can say what's in the air. You know we can't say what we like to say in this country, and I want to obey the laws."[24] Cannon's care paid off. Unbeknownst to the WP chairman, a 23 March 1923 petition was filed with the attorney general requesting the prosecution of Cannon under a section of the Criminal Code of 1910 targeting subversive organizations. It came to naught.[25]

In general, Cannon spoke to audiences of 55 to 300, as reported by Department of Justice agents, with attendance usually 150 or more. Spy reports paid particular attention to the composition of the crowds, but there was no uniform constituency, either in terms of demography, politics, or level of enthusiasm. The Butte assembly was considered a bust, the turnout of 50 people at the Carpenters' Hall generating barely $15, but in Portland a large crowd of approximately 300 materialized. "The audience was almost 100 per cent foreign," reported the Department of Justice agent, and "outside of the speaker, not a word of pure English was spoken in the hall during the entire evening." Worse, "a small sprinkling of negroes" also attended. The Minneapolis agent identified only 48 of the lecture audience of 250 whom he thought "American born citizens," and these he pigeonholed as "past forty years of age, poorly dressed and with all the appearance of the person who has made an effort at life and failed, and is disgusted and bitter with mankind." From people such as these, the Workers' Party garnered support. In Spokane, Washington, Cannon's talk resulted in the recruitment of fifty new members.[26]

A mixed success that brought the message of communism to the masses and supposedly secured many new subscribers for the revolutionary press,[27] Cannon's cross-country tour impressed upon him the potential of the Workers' Party, as well as the fragility of the revolutionary ranks, who were spread thin and had insufficient roots in the organizations of the working class: "I knew how unrealistic it was to imagine that we could lead . . . by ourselves."[28] Cannon thus wanted to win new rank-and-file members to the Workers' Party, solidify old relations with revolutionaries in the foreign-language sections, and sustain the momentum of organizations such as the Trade Union Educational League; he also desired to draw the Upton Sinclairs, Scott Nearings, and Eugene Debses into the WP, where they would march under the red flag of American communism and the Communist International.[29]

One topic that Cannon raised quite regularly in his mid-1923 lectures was the Labor Party. A Portland agent reported that Cannon had stated: "The present program of the Communist Party is to unite all radical elements in the United States in the proposed 'Farmer-Labor' Party and make an effort to gain political attention in this manner."[30] On the one hand, there is no question that Cannon gravitated almost instinctively to the idea of communist involvement in the creation of a labor party, as part of his project of expanding the appeal of the Workers' Party and pushing communists into more open engagement with American conditions. Lovestone, he suggested, had broached the matter indirectly in 1922, and from there the liquidationist wing of the party, Cannon included, was sympathetic to almost all efforts to move communism in "an outward direction, even at the risk of opportunist errors," to which few in his circle were "very sensitive at that time."[31] On the other hand, by the time Cannon reached the WP's proletarian stronghold of Chicago, around May Day 1923, there were strong indications that the communist forces were about to embark on an ill-fated adventure. Arriving in Chicago, Cannon listened to the complaints of Swabeck and others and gave a speech urging every trade unionist to line up behind Foster's leadership.[32] Here for the first time Cannon had to face Pepper's impact in the Workers' Party. A confrontation was not long in the making. Out of it would come an entirely new set of factional alignments, consolidating the trade union contingent of the Workers' Party as a discernible *political* grouping.

Pogany/Pepper

Born Joseph Pogany, Pepper was characterized, as Trotsky later noted, by his infinite adaptability. Undistinguished by service to the revolutionary cause *before* the Bolshevik seizure of power, Pogany's World War I years were spent as an orthodox social democratic journalist. As the war ended, he had sufficient charisma and political *chutzpa* to organize a soldiers' council with himself at the head; a brief political stint in support of the bourgeois liberal, Count Michael Karolyi, followed, with Pogany gaining notoriety for his suppression of communists. Yet he must have had a sense of the impending collapse of the Karolyi regime, for he crossed sides in 1919, signing a unity pact with the communists and ingratiating himself sufficiently to attain the status of Commissar of War, a post he held for only a matter of weeks. His shift to the Left consummated, Pogany promoted himself as a major figure in revolutionary circles, basking in the glow of those who dubbed him the "Hungarian Trotsky" and forging a close relationship with Bela Kun. The revolution in Hungary proving short-lived, Pogany gravitated toward the Comintern, where he was a pronounced ultraleftist, clamoring at the 1921 Third Congress of the Communist International for policies of a decidedly adventurist turn. Over the years 1921 to 1929, Pepper was the kind of communist functionary who destroyed Bolshevism, internationally as well as in its home base of Soviet Russia, having a hand in the failed German uprising of 1921. In Trotsky's words, "[T]he Peppers

... and their sort are so useful and irreplaceable [because] [a]daptation is their native element. In seeking to obtain the obedience of the International, they realize their highest destiny. For many of these parasites, the maximum of bureaucracy has become the preliminary condition for their maximum personal 'freedom.' They are ready to make any kind of right-about-face, on the condition that they have the apparatus behind them." The best that could be done with the Peppers, Trotsky concluded, was "to keep them a good long distance away from the institutions where the destinies of the revolution are decided."[33] The Workers' Party was not to be so fortunate.[34]

By mid-1922, factional cliques in the Hungarian émigré leadership had so disrupted the Communist International that Zinoviev looked for ways to disperse the personnel of two contending camps. Pogany was one of the central figures who had to be shuffled off somewhere, and he apparently considered the United States a more congenial place to be put out to pasture than most, talking himself into an overseas assignment. Sent as one of three representatives from the Comintern to the Bridgman, Michigan, convention, and clearly a junior voice meant to be heard very much after Valetski, Pogany's ongoing assignment was to work with the U.S. Hungarian Federation and its newspaper, Uj Elore.[35] Thus was born "John Pepper," whose first month in America was spent in nondescript attentiveness, lulling his party prey into unconscious underestimation.[36]

Clearly, the thirty-six-year-old Hungarian was biding his time, assessing the situation, and getting a feel for the new surroundings in which he found himself. With the historical experience of revolutions made and unmade behind him, able to name-drop with alacrity, and offering up a seemingly endless stock of stories confirming his personal connections with Lenin, Trotsky, Zinoviev, and others, Pepper seemed to all who encountered him the very personification of the experienced, all-knowing central European Bolshevik. Who knew otherwise? Charmingly self-confident, apparently well versed in Marxist theory and adept at the elaboration of arcane theses, Pepper also carried himself as the official voice of the Comintern, an exaggerated pose that gained credibility with each week of his stay. He played to the conspiratorial sensibilities of the former Geese, and buttressed this by appealing regularly to the Goose Caucus/United Toiler commitment to undergroundism as a necessary adjunct to the legal party. Obviously accomplished in languages, he conversed at first only in German (with Ruthenberg as his translator), but within a matter of months he was able to mount rostrums and deliver fast-paced harangues of hours' duration in dazzlingly effective English. Soon he was not only writing in various party presses and organs, but also producing the major propaganda pamphlets for the Workers' Party; the powerful Political Committee appointed him to the decisive position of secretary.[37]

Even his party opponents had to grant this particular devil his due: "This room shakes when that man talks," Foster once said in awe. "That man worked fast," Cannon acknowledged. "He was a European to his finger tips, dripping with the sophistication and facility of continental journalism. But when it came to getting things done in a hurry and getting around natural obstacles, he was more American than any hustler or corner-cutter that I ever knew, and that covers a lot of territory." In the end, however, the Workers' Party was not quite as vulnerable to Pepper's domination as the Hungarian exile would have liked. Having come, by mid-1923, "to regulate party affairs with the arbitrary authority of a receiver appointed by the court to take over a bankrupt concern," Pepper's "only trouble," in Cannon's words, was that the Workers' Party "was by no means bankrupt, and the receiver's operations met with challenge and opposition which limited his tenure to a rather short term." In the meantime, however, the Pepper years proved "a real merry go-round which left everybody dizzy . . . a humdinger while it lasted."[38]

A complex swirl of issues associated with Pepper undoubtedly came to a head in mid-1923. Certainly the ways in which Pepper exercised his increasingly tyrannical power within the Workers' Party was an issue, as were fundamental disagreements separating the now-divided leadership cadre (Ruthenberg, Lovestone, and Pepper versus Foster, Cannon, and Bittelman with Browder, Dunne, Swabeck, and others as supporters) on the question of trade unionism and communism's relation to it. Nevertheless, the decisive and ultimately telling fault line that ran through the leadership of the WP in the summer of 1923 was widening difference around the so-called Farmer-Labor Party.

Communists Outmaneuver Themselves: Farmer-Labor Party Illusions and Intrigues, 1923

The significance of a Labor Party in the United States was an issue that reached back to the first Workingmen's Parties of the Jacksonian period. In its more modern history, however, the Labor Party came to the fore in 1919 as the head of the Chicago Federation of Labor (CFL), John Fitzpatrick, and his chief aide, Edward Nockels, spearheaded a drive to form a national labor party that spread from Cook County, throughout Illinois, and into Minnesota, New York, Michigan, Utah, Indiana, Washington, South Dakota, and elsewhere. Fitzpatrick and Nockels were hard-line "laborites," unaffiliated with the communists, to be sure, but staunch opponents of business unionism's staid Samuel Gompers, and dubious about schemes to fast-track the labor party to public prominence on the back of "progressive" non-working-class elements. They had stood strongly in support of William Z. Foster's 1919 organizing drive in the steel industry. Buttressed by the old-guard Ohio socialist Max Hayes; endorsed by the United Mine Workers of America in 1921; and promoted in the pages of the Chicago-based newspaper, *New Majority,* the drive to promote a labor party was well under way by 1922–1923, although it never registered all that forcefully in the electoral arena.

The Conference for Progressive Political Action (CPPA), founded in 1922 by the machinist and railway union labor tops as a nonpartisan body that could throw working-class political weight to Democrats or Republicans according to the perceived needs of the moment, intersected such developments ambiguously. It had an ambivalent, but unmistakable, connection to the labor party movement, albeit one that worked against the class content that Fitzpatrick and others wanted to maintain in its push to incorporate religious, intellectual, and other progressive-minded figures, as well as in its challenge to truly independent working-class political action. So too did attempts to broaden the populist appeal of the third-party formation by including farmers in its designation, a decision taken at a 1920 Convention. Fitzpatrick fought to retain the preeminence of workers, but to no avail.[39] The problematic politics of hitching the working-class electoral horse to the progressive/populist bandwagon in the early to mid-1920s would prove a minefield communists could not negotiate without blowing a part of themselves up.[40]

Buoyed by the drift of certain labor-party developments to the Left, and enthused by the Fitzpatrick-Nockels receptiveness to a more radical orientation in the formation of a third party, the WP leadership in New York began charting an ever-more-aggressive approach to the Farmer-Labor Party in the winter of 1922 and spring of 1923. This included an unsuccessful attempt to seat WP and Young Workers' League delegates at the 11–12 December Cleveland convention of the CPPA.[41] Fitzpatrick, who by this time had tired of the CPPA's reluctance to embrace a laborist politics of class, grew impatient with the endless skirting of what he thought the formation of a third party required, and he soon moved, against some pleas of moderation from the Chicago Federation of Labor communists, for a decisive break. "We can't fiddle around with these liberals and their mushy third party," editorialized the Fitzpatrick forces' newspaper, the *New Majority,* in late December 1922. Now a hurried advocate of the immediate formation of a labor party, Fitzpatrick argued for a 3 July 1923 convention in Chicago to inaugurate such a political body. He pressed communists around the Trade Union Educational League (TUEL) and the CFL (Arne Swabeck, Charles Krumbein, Jack Johnstone, and Earl Browder as the primary cadre, with ethnic communists Nels Kjar, Steve Rubicki, and Dora Lifshutz playing critical roles as well) to make common cause in this venture into labor politics.[42]

Undoubtedly the strongest state center of farmer-labor electoral activity, however, was Minnesota, where a party had been organized in 1918, founded by unionists in the Twin Cities of Minneapolis-St. Paul. It proved dormant until the 1922 revival kick-started a third-party impetus backed by spokesmen associated with the State Federation of Labor's newspaper, the *Minnesota Union Advocate*, and dissidents in the Non-Partisan League movement. Between November 1922 and July 1923, the Minnesota Farmer-Labor Party secured both the state's seats in the Senate. Reluctant, until then, to make a move into the national electoral arena, Minnesota's farmer-laborites were shored up by their early 1920s victories and readied themselves for entry onto the national stage.[43]

In its formative, pre-Workers' Party underground years in 1919–1920, the communist movement's sectarian ultraleftism kept it isolated from such labor-party developments. As the internal differentiation between Geese and Liquidators proceeded, fueled by the Comintern's directives to attempt more open work and to put in place united-front practices, the issue of the labor party gradually surfaced as a pivotal question. At the American Commission held before the Comintern in 1922, Cannon and others promoted their project of so-called liquidationism through an appeal to Trotsky, Lenin, and others of the necessity of recognizing the latent desire for a labor party among the more militant of American workers. For Cannon and like-minded comrades, the key task was to make the Workers' Party "an integral component of the labor party when it is founded," by crystallizing and organizing the impulse of American workers for an independent, class expression in the political arena. Katterfeld, the key spokesperson for the Goose Caucus, approached the question of the labor party with a slightly different, and almost certainly more defensive (given the obvious need to placate a Comintern bent on pushing united-front activity), perspective. Rightly insisting that in 1919 the Labor Party had "no masses back of them," Katterfeld defended the underground's isolation from the nascent movement. By 1921, however, the leading figure in the Geese acknowledged (at least seemingly) that enthusiasm for the formation of a labor party had grown significantly, and it was thus crucial to "support this idea," albeit not by placing communists in the lead. In short, there was not a great deal of difference between Cannon and Katterfeld in their basic approaches, as oppositional factional leaders, to how communists should function in relation to the tactics and strategy of work in labor-party situations—at least not late in 1922. The fundamental issue was what the Workers' Party would actually do.[44] When Fitzpatrick called for the formation of a new Farmer-Labor Party in March 1923, and invited the Workers' Party to participate, a new stage in the history of communist/labor party relations in the United States was unfolding. However, simultaneous developments were working at cross-purposes.

First, within the New York Central Executive Committee, where Pepper now held almost unopposed sway, there was increasing skepticism about the supposedly reformist integration of the Chicago Federation of Labor Workers' Party members, whose ostensible trade union opportunism was suspect. Second, Pepper actually outed Foster in the pages of the *Worker*, in a 14 April 1923 article, "William Z. Foster—Revolutionary Leader," that laid on the praise of the Chicago-based trade union figure and proclaimed him "the American face of Communism." This laudatory notice buried any possibility that Foster could remain a force in mainstream labor circles and not declare his Workers' Party affiliation, which may have been precisely Pepper's purpose. Third, in a climate of rightward-moving labor politics, and the increasingly anti-radical retrenchment of the American Federation of Labor (AFL) bureaucracy, this public identification of Foster as a communist could possibly have conditioned an adverse reaction on the part of Fitzpatrick and Nockels, whose willingness to separate themselves from the reactionary officialdom of mainstream trade unionism had its limits. Content to support militant action and promote the cause of industrial amalgamation in the labor movement, such radicals remained wary of "foreign domination" by Moscow. They preferred their relations with the Workers' Party to take place at various steps removed from direct Workers' Party contact, and Swabeck and others had cultivated just this kind of practical relationship in their everyday work in the Chicago Federation of Labor, where Foster himself, though a major figure, was also kept somewhat out of the front lines of direct WP-CFL negotiations.[45]

With rumors flying that Gompers was about to launch his "long-expected war" on the CFL, with some labor militants still rankling from Ruthenberg's aggressive performance in attempting to seat himself as a WP delegate at the December 1922 Cleveland convention of the CPPA, and with Socialist Party and other progressive sources complaining to the Chicago Federation of Labor that the worrisome communists were planning to "seize control" of the July proceedings, Fitzpatrick issued a veiled warning. He declined an invitation to address a Workers' Party May Day meeting in Michigan, adding as explanation: "The vast majority of American workers, both native and foreign born, resent what they regard as imported programs and they subscribe to the home-grown variety." As the AFL executive slapped the Seattle Central Labor Council on its political wrist for calling for recognition of Soviet Russia, Fitzpatrick was clearly taking his cues from the signs of the times.

Meanwhile, in New York, Pepper was loading up the May 1923 pages of the *Worker* with articles that retreated into the rhetorical excesses of the older underground. In a Workers' Party-published pamphlet, *Underground Radicalism*, Pepper claimed that "[t]he capitalist government of the United States has become just as centralized and as sinister as the former monarchy of the Czars." This hyperbole may have appealed to former Goose Caucus members, but Fitzpatrick and Nockels were not amused. Given that Pepper was now the Workers' Party's major proponent of the Farmer-Labor Party, they must have found less than edifying his public reminders to all communists that the dictatorship of the proletariat, the role of force in history, the necessity of soviets, and the undying devotion to democratic centralist notions of the party distinguished the revolutionary vanguard from all variants of "Tammany Hall Socialism." All of this threatened to derail the national farmer-labor mobilization, in which non-Workers' Party trade unionists and Non-Partisan Leaguers in Minnesota figured prominently. It was not long before Swabeck, Browder, and Jack Johnstone were being raked over the coals by the CFL leadership. "Let's get the record straight," Fitzpatrick supposedly stated bluntly with respect to the Workers' Party role in the formation of a new Farmer-Labor Party: "we are willing to go along, but we think you Communists should occupy a back seat in this affair."[46]

The situation, as spring blossomed into summer in 1923, was thus quite delicate. Much hung in the balance. Chicago was the central communist locale of trade union work, and the TUEL had its core strength there, sustained in part by the goodwill of the CFL hierarchy. The pivotal plank in the trade union program—amalgamation—was dependent upon the relations built up in the radical wing of the labor movement, a militant program spreading the gospel of industrial unionism and trade union reconstruction, like concentric circles, from a Chicago base throughout the industrial urban cores and mining enclaves of a regionalized U.S. capitalism.[47] It was apparent that it could all be jeopardized, if not squandered, by the wrong Workers' Party moves.

With Pepper increasingly influential, the Workers' Party abandoned the cautious distance of its underground origins, and opted instead for a more positive assessment about the prospects for the formation of a labor party. Yet, not until May 1922 did communists actually develop a formal statement in support of the *idea* of a labor party.[48] However, those at the helm of the Workers' Party agreed that when and if such a third party was actually formed, the WP's propaganda and its involvement should contribute to the new political formation without orchestrating it from its inception as a communist undertaking.

Pepper pushed the envelope, and by 1923 the WP was committed to much more than endorsement; communists began to maneuver "*to bring about the actual formation of a Farmer-Labor Party.*" As early as January 1923, after the CPPA rebuffed the Workers' Party by refusing to credential communist delegates, Ruthenberg called for an offensive "campaign to build a mass political party of workers and farmers in the United States." As Fitzpatrick and Nockels championed the labor party, and progressives in the CPPA called instead for "non-partisanship," communists and the CFL hierarchy were forced closer and closer together. The resulting small, but central, united front was clearly a fulcrum on which any third-party breakthrough balanced precariously.

Agreement was reached by the WP and the Fitzpatrick-Nockels Farmer-Labor Party advocates that the July convention could inaugurate a new party if half a million workers were represented. Costs of promoting such a convention were to be shared by the two groups; consensus was achieved on who to invite (all trade unions, local and state farmer and labor parties, and various socialist bodies); and procedures of representation, construction of key committees, and a list of resolutions to be presented were mutually decided. Under Foster's guidance, the TUEL launched a nationwide referendum among all trade unions, designed to secure the founding of a labor party; 7,000 labor organizations replied, something of a slap in the face to AFL officialdom and the CPPA. In spite of limited delegate attendance and even more disappointing voter turnout at various labor-party-related confabs and elections in 1922, the Workers' Party was editorializing in June of 1923 that the coming Labor Party was a certainty, predicting that 1,500 to 2,000 delegates would flood Chicago in the first week of July to found a new and potent political movement. Such starry-eyed optimism fit well with Pepper's emerging thesis, articulated in a July 1923 article, "The Declaration of Independence of the American Working Class," that the United States was ripe for revolution: "Capital, the great revolutionist, has laid the foundation for a Labor Party," thundered Pepper in the *Liberator*. "The duty of the Workers' Party of America as the class conscious revolutionary party of the working class," was thus, as Pepper wrote, "to be in Chicago on July 3, with all the power and militancy, to give an impetus to the Convention, so that it shall really mean a step towards the Declaration of Independence of the American working class."[49] Communists had traveled, in three short years, from sectarian dismissal of 1919 labor-party initiatives, to 1922 support in principle for formation of a labor party, to a 1923 push to form a third party in which its own WP forces would be a leading element.[50]

The 1923 full-out labor-party advocacy undertaken by American communists also took place, however, at the very point when both the Comintern and noncommunist labor-left elements were backtracking on the *class* nature of the labor party. Within the Comintern, the 1922 Fourth Congress had rearticulated older united-front tactics on the basis of a specific set of failures: of the defeat of proletarian revolution in Europe; of the inability of the working class to sustain the economics of revolutionary production in a Russia constrained by capitalist containment and the social dominance of the peasantry. As Zinoviev explained in 1922, "The Russian proletarian party was compelled to make extensive concessions to the peasantry, and in part also to the bourgeoisie."

Comintern confusions about "worker and peasant governments" in this period muddied the waters of class politics within the international communist movement. Over the next two years and more, Zinoviev, seemingly Lenin's heir apparent, led the Communist International along an increasingly opportunistic course, plunging the forces of world revolution into organizational bureaucratism and adventurist twists and turns. Trotsky would eventually turn back the tide, but not until much damage had been done, some of it in the United States communist milieu where no issue was more important than the politics of farmer-laborism. It was perhaps Pepper in America, a weather vane of political adaptability, who would tilt the labor party in the direction of working farmers, defined loosely as tenant and *mortgaged* farmers. To be sure, Pepper's early formulations of the class relations within the Farmer-Labor Party asserted the primacy and leading role of the working class, but he defined *working farmer* so diffusely (what farmer was not mortgaged, in the 1920s?) that he hardly escaped the problematic populism of early, pre-Bolshevik mobilizations, such as the Greenback and Populist Parties of the nineteenth century. Moreover, he compounded the difficulties of characterization by providing an opening salvo in the descent into "American exceptionalism" that Lovestone would champion more vociferously and widely in the later 1920s, declaring in his *For a Labor Party* (1923) pamphlet, "One of the most important conditions for the victory of a Labor Party is that it develop the cooperation of the farmers and workers, which has become traditional in America. America is a favorable exception in this respect. Of European countries such collaboration takes place only in the Soviet Union." Fitzpatrick and Nockels, in earlier concessions to the program of the CPPA, had already thrown in a similar towel. Their Farmer-Labor Party proposal, and the 3 July 1923 conference that would constitute it, was premised on abdication of an earlier 1919–1920 commitment to independent working-class political action.[51]

What worried the Chicago trade union comrades in the summer of 1923 was that the judicious caution of historic farmer-labor party policy, which insisted on any third-party formation being deeply planted in the soil of broad working-class conditions, had been dumped by Pepper, and possibly by Ruthenberg as well. The Workers' Party writing appeared on the wall of Labor Party formation over the late spring, it becoming increasingly apparent that Ruthenberg and Pepper planned to stack the 3 July 1923 convention with delegates from a plethora of front groups to make it a WP event. Cannon pointed out that if the forthcoming Chicago convention were overtaken and manipulated by communists, "Gompers will feel free to attack the conference as a red proposition. . . . If we flood the conference with Workers Party delegates, we simply lay the conference open to such a successful attack and thereby defeat ourselves by defeating the conference." Insisting that the significance of the conference lay in stimulating "the organized drive towards a labor party and our party cooperating in it as an integral unity from the start," Cannon underscored his concern that any attempt by the Workers' Party to overzealously dominate the gathering would produce an ugly backlash. Urging the immediate formation of a subcommittee composed of Browder, Swabeck, and Krumbein to monitor events and keep daily contact with the Political Committee of the Workers' Party, Cannon complained that he had received "absolutely no information about the discussions." He suggested that Ruthenberg would benefit from talking to Swabeck, and asked to be kept apprised of future developments.[52]

It is impossible to ascertain with certainty what happened next, and what related movements of factional alignment were made on the New York Central Executive Committee, with significant liaisons to Chicago provided by Foster and Browder. Too much weight has been placed on a later 11 April 1924 (possibly self-serving) letter from Ruthenberg to the Executive Committee of the Communist International, explaining the evolution of the factional crisis in the American section.[53] What is indisputable, however, is Pepper's role. He had dazzled Foster, who at this time was quite new to the inner, executive workings of the communist milieu, and was in the earliest stages of his evolving adaptation to the party bureaucracy. It is entirely possible that, as Jack Johnstone, a former Wobbly and chief Foster lieutenant in the Chicago-based TUEL, attempted to convince Browder in 1923, Pepper and Foster had worked out an agreement in which the former would push the necessity of the Workers' Party breaking from Fitzpatrick and the CFL progressives if it proved necessary, while the latter would go along with this strategy as long as he did not have to carry it out with a great deal of public fanfare. In the New York CEC machinations of April, May, and June 1923, Pepper clearly used Foster. His acquiescence was taken as good coin with which to purchase roughly the silence of the old Left remnant of the Goose Caucus, Katterfeld, whose all-out opposition to a Farmer-Labor Party of any sort betrayed the two-faced nature of his performance at the American Commission of the Comintern late in 1922. That quarter quashed, Pepper then beat back Ruthenberg. The latter had consulted with the trade union cadre in May, reaching with Browder what was thought to be a "peace proposal," but was now somehow enticed to carry "the Comintern rep's" heavy-handed instructions to the Chicago comrades, Foster among them. Ruthenberg wrote a peremptory letter to the communists in the CFL. It chastised Cannon, instructing Browder, Swabeck, and Krumbein to stay out of the dealings with the Fitzpatrick-Nockels forces, which would now be handled by Ruthenberg and Pepper, en route to Chicago.[54] As such controversy heightened, it blurred into competitive, although often unstated, rivalries. Foster and Ruthenberg, and possibly Cannon, seemed claimants for leadership posts in a restructured Workers' Party hierarchy.[55] Behind the scenes, however, as nearly everyone in the CEC recognized, was Pepper. The 3 July Farmer-Labor Party Convention debacle brought Pepper out of the shadows and into the direct line of oppositional fire.

The run-up to the July gathering was truly ironic. Fitzpatrick's forces finally grasped the veracity of earlier Workers' Party warnings that going it alone to establish a farmer-labor party was premature and "a lost hope." They begged for time, wanting a postponement of the convention. Pepper, however, had a taste of the "get rich quick" gamble that the Farmer-Labor Party conference now entailed. The pleas of Fitzpatrick and Nockels, not to mention those of the Chicago comrades, fell on deaf ears. Ruthenberg first, then Foster, were whipped into line; the CFL trade union core of Workers' Party activists notwithstanding, the process of packing and orchestrating the conference was put into motion. In all likelihood, Fitzpatrick and his supporters did not know what was hitting them until they entered the Ashland Auditorium Convention twenty-four hours before Independence Day. Of the total of approximately 600 delegates, the Workers' Party was entitled to 10. In reality, the communists organized some 190 representatives; most major figures in the Workers' Party were there, representing various unions, death and benefit societies, and other dubious bodies, including the Lithuanian Workers' Literature Society, the United Workingmen Singers, the Workmen's Gymnastic Association, and an array of alphabet-soup organizations from locales as unlikely as Bartlesville, Oklahoma. The exceptions were those very forces that should have been in attendance: Browder, for instance, who had done so much to cement the CFL-TUEL united front, was banned from being a delegate by a Pepper dictate "which both Ruthenberg and Foster accepted in silence."

With Pepper sitting in the gallery, his "floor leader" (and Foster's son-in-law), Joe Manley, pulling the strings, the communists—their block vote of 190 constituted anywhere from one-quarter to one-third of the total delegates—outmaneuvered the now disconsolate Fitzpatrick forces, which found themselves steam-rollered by a superior organization. Those at the conference who wanted radical leadership and were not already aligned with the Workers' Party no doubt found themselves voting with the Pepper machine almost by default. Fitzpatrick and others argued to delay the call for an immediate formation of a Farmer-Labor Party; failing in that, they took the floor to point out that the United States working class would never follow the lead of communists. Foster and then Ruthenberg rose to mock indecision and demand leadership rights for the Workers' Party. Eventually, Fitzpatrick walked out in humiliation.

It was the end of the old Irish American Chicago blacksmith's days as a radical. He wasted no time in denouncing communism as "a man being invited into your house as a guest and then once in the house seizing you by the throat and kicking you out the door." Such whining did not endear the CFL leader to Pepper. Fitzpatrick was merely one more "well-intentioned leader" whose "political corpse" now paved the road to revolution. The vote to adopt the constitution of the old Fitzpatrick Farmer-Labor Party was a mild, and meaningless, concession. In the newly formed Federated Farmer-Labor Party, so designated because affiliation was by organization rather than individual membership, communists were in the driver's seat. Joe Manley was appointed national secretary.[56]

Pepper now had his Federated Farmer-Labor Party. He was all smiles walking through the Ashland Auditorium as the convention wound down on 5 July 1923, shaking hands with comrades, beaming in his victory. Soon Pepper would be filling the communist press with pontification on the historic breakthrough of the Federated Farmer-Labor Party convention, which he likened in significance to 1776. Claiming the adherence of 600,000 workers, Pepper was quick to adapt the Federated Farmer-Labor Party to the Comintern's confused articulations of the need for workers' and farmers' governments, claiming that United States communists were the first to apply the new approach.[57] Immediately following the July convention, Pepper beat back an irate challenge from Browder and Dunne, condescendingly berating "inexperienced comrades" who lacked what he called direct involvement in revolutionary situations and the courage to face inevitable splits from ossified bureaucracies such as that of Fitzpatrick and Nockels. Praising the newly formed Federated Farmer-Labor Party's acceptance of steeled communist leadership, Pepper predicted a bright future for the revolutionary cause.[58]

Nothing of the sort was in the cards. The supposed mass base of the Federated Farmer-Labor Party never materialized, not even as paper phantoms; 155,000 (not 600,000) was the most the Ruthenberg-Pepper forces could ever claim, and this too was a highly inflated figure.[59] As one communist eventually conceded in the pages of an international publication, the Federated Farmer-Labor Party was an incestuous creation, consisting of "ourselves and our nearest relatives." Even the efforts of the Minnesota farmer-laborites, their willingness to accept Workers' Party candidates campaigning openly as communists in electoral mobilizations brokered in the face of a grim necessity to keep the chimera of a national third party alive, did little good.[60]

Cannon heard about the events of July 3–5 as he was touring the West Coast, speaking at Portland. Publicly he pushed the Farmer-Labor Party initiative, but obviously he had his inner doubts. En route back to New York, Cannon and Foster hooked up in Duluth, where both were lecturing. They spent an afternoon at a trade union picnic, talking under the shade of a tree. Foster let his worries about the disastrous implications of the split from the Chicago Federation of Labor forces out of their Pepper containment. As Cannon pushed for an explanation of how all of this could have happened, Foster offered a commonsensical construction of the events:

> In the party caucus at the convention, so many of our people, carried away by the enthusiasm of the moment, spoke so emphatically about our strength here, there, and everywhere, including the Chicago Federation of Labor, that I got carried away myself and was convinced against my will and better judgment. . . . The trouble is, we've got the hangover, but the others in New York are still living in a fool's paradise. Something has got to be done to change this course, or we will soon fritter away all the gains of our trade-union work up to now.

Such a comment was true enough, as far as it went. But it betrayed Foster's weakness, even though at that point he had ostensibly not yet become corrupted by the lure of office and party status. A trade union organizer without peer, Foster had Cannon's deep respect—even reverence—up to a point. Cannon looked upon Foster's accomplishments in the Great Steel strike of 1919 and in getting the Trade Union Educational League off the ground as monumental achievements, earning him a place of prominence alongside Ruthenberg as one of the two deservedly leading public officials in the Workers' Party. Symbolizing "the proletarian-American orientation," Foster was the single outstanding "mass" leader the Workers' Party could put into the field, and his popularity was unrivaled. However, over the years, according to Cannon, he had "learned too much in the school of the labor fakers, who got what they wanted one way or another, without regard to any governing theory or principle." In his understanding of what had unfolded at the Farmer-Labor convention, Foster neglected to reach beyond the "crude American pragmatism, which 'gets things done' in simple situations," a tradition in which he had been schooled in the United States labor movement.[61]

Cannon, unlike Foster, was quicker to see past the particularities of the July convention into the Workers' Party regime, and from there into a generalized critique of communist leadership and policy in 1923. He later recalled: "It took the shock of the July 3 Convention to convince me that Pepper's politics was all of one piece; that the fantastic unrealism of his internal party policy had its counterpart in external adventurism." As factional lines hardened in the summer and fall of 1923, Foster and Cannon eventually came to share a similar perspective, but they had arrived at it from different routes. For Cannon, "Pepper's labor policy was only one item in the catalogue. . . . I was not content to rest on that single issue." Cannon, then, had a sense of where the factional battle was heading. It was not unrelated to his long-standing struggle to Americanize the communist movement: "The party had to recognize realities, and adjust itself to them." Pepper stood in the way.[62]

Cannon, Foster, and Trade Union Combination, 1923

A Cannon-Foster combination had been sealed, informally, at the Duluth picnic. It did not require elaborate discussions, and Foster came into the pact unsteadily and slowly, but it was inevitable that Pepper would eventually force his hand. A hard pull was provided by the labor movement's leading anti-communist ranks, which now included not only Gompers and his ilk, but also Fitzpatrick and Company. The former pressured the latter, who responded by ostracizing Foster and the Workers' Party. At the Illinois Federation of Labor's September 1923 annual convention, Foster found himself painted into an unenviable corner. Resolutions and positions previously promoted by the WP and supported by Fitzpatrick and Nockels were now given the cold shoulder. The cherished TUEL plank of amalgamation, narrowly voted down in 1922 by 148–119, lost by a landslide count a year later, 313–80; a resolution on the labor party, which would have passed easily a year before, now crashed in ignominious defeat. The *New Majority* headlines told it all: "State Movement Disavows Foster—Illinois Federation Repudiates Every Issue Communist Leader Advocates." As Eugene Staley noted in 1930, "There was little room for a 'progressive' trade unionist to advocate a Labor party; either he must come into the fold of the American Federation of Labor and its 'age-old non-partisan political policy,' or he must betake himself into outer darkness with the fanatical Communists."[63]

As went Illinois, so went the nation. The TUEL program was taking a beating. In the International Ladies Garment Workers Union (ILGWU), Socialist Party activists led an assault on communists that began in the summer of 1923 and reached into 1924. Encompassing expulsions, refusals to seat delegates at union conventions, trials of noted "Lefts" before special committees of local unions or joint boards, and the breaking up and rechartering of locals to secure noncommunist control, the ILGWU battle generated a 2,000-strong protest meeting among needle-trades workers in Chicago. The low point was an ostensible assassination attempt on Foster's life; the TUEL leader was shot at while addressing the throng of dissident garment workers expelled from their union. The situation was complicated deeply by gender divisions in the garment industry. Moreover, dissension weakened working-class capacities to resist capital. At the same time that the ILGWU was banishing "reds" from the WP and the TUEL in New York, Boston, Philadelphia, and Chicago, the embroidery trades and various cloak, dress, and raincoat makers were striking for higher wages and the forty-hour work week, putting themselves in the front lines of a battle against the employers' open-shop offensive. Trade union cadres in the Workers' Party were learning the price to be paid for Pepperism.

At the AFL convention in Portland late in 1923, Bill Dunne was unseated as a delegate, his legitimate credentials from the Silver Bow Trades and Labor Council revoked. Dunne's eviction was a rough dismissal of the sole sitting member of the Workers' Party; conservative AFL boss, William Hutcheson, of the Carpenters, demanded a roll call, insisting that all delegates stand and have their votes recorded. As historian David Montgomery suggests, the resulting 27,837 to 108 drumming indicated the lynch-mob atmosphere of late 1923 labor anti-communism. Dunne and others publicly directed their animus at the "labor fakirs" and "Gompersite skates," but privately they lambasted the New York CEC of the Workers' Party, whose "demagogy" had squandered so much. "We have alienated a lot of support to which we were entitled, and are now completely isolated," Dunne wrote bitterly to Browder.[64]

Cannon, for all his public presentation of the Workers' Party's official positions, found such setbacks deeply disturbing, and with his return to the party center eased into the coming battle with Pepper. Considerable opposition to the approach taken in Chicago at the Federated Farmer-Labor Party convention was emerging in New York, where the needle trades were a stronghold of the TUEL. It coalesced around pivotal figures in the garment unions, such as Rose Wortis, and a group of young communist intellectuals formerly associated with Harry Waton's Marx Institute. As Cannon noted in a private communication, this group was at times characterized by a "strong strain of pessimism and skepticism," perhaps a consequence of Socialist Party influence and hostility to the Workers' Party. Nevertheless, whenever the "Federated" was on the agenda of the Political Committee of the Workers' Party, sparks flew.[65]

To be sure, Cannon was a loyal Workers' Party advocate, appearing with Ruthenberg at an 8 August 1923 Webster Hall postmortem assessment of the Socialist Party's Albany Conference for Progressive Action that excluded five communist delegates and continued the moderate socialist movement's overt hostility to the Federated Farmer-Labor Party; he wrote a scathing indictment of supposed radicals whose politics routinely tailed the "Gompers-like labor fakirs."[66] As late as mid-August, Cannon continued writing articles in the party press claiming success for the labor party campaign: the accent remained one of differentiation, separating revolutionaries and progressives from enemies within the House of Labor, such as John L. Lewis and other elements of a labor officialdom that was nothing more than a "formidable section of the fighting forces of the bosses." In a veiled critique of Pepper, however, Cannon took aim at the underground years of American communism, when the tendency to collapse politics into talk and theory proved little more than a cloak for windbags and quibblers.[67]

Cannon had increasingly less and less stomach for Pepper's diatribes against the trade union core of the Workers' Party in Chicago, whatever the TUEL shortcomings, which were becoming apparent in both the needle trades and mining sectors. Cognizant of the need to develop a "fighting policy," Cannon was also conscious of the limitations within which the young WP operated, aware of what could be squandered by ill-advised misadventures. Cannon did not feel that such "dissenting opinions" marked him out as an "oppositionist." He felt "closer to the main body of the party, ideologically, than ever before," and acknowledged that, "The party is on the right road, its general line of tactics is correct, and it is beginning to crystallize a stable leadership." Yet, within this positive constellation of developments lay some persistent problems, many of which were associated with Pepper. His distance from and hostility toward the trade union cadre and complication of the leadership question had manifested themselves in forcing the revolutionary ranks "to do too much with the forces at our disposal." The Federated Farmer-Labor policy was but the most visible reflection of this disturbing tendency, and it was prodding Cannon to a widening critique of Pepper and his allies on the Central Executive Committee, none of whom, coincidentally, were embedded in the actual struggles of the labor movement.[68]

Indeed, the Foster-Cannon challenge to "intellectuals" in the Workers' Party at this time was a complicated orchestration of antagonism to Pepper that had less to do with actual resistance to theory—they were, after all, drawing Bittelman into their oppositional faction, and clearly recognized his importance—than a tactical choice that appeared to suit well a downplaying of the likes of Pepper and Lovestone, and their contributions to the movement. "[O]ur objections to a party leadership dominated by intellectuals did not extend to 'anti-intellectualism' and the lunacy of imagining that intellectuals should not be included in the leading staff," explained Cannon.

This all meshed perfectly with a forceful demand to physically shift the Workers' Party center. Cannon and Foster pushed for the party headquarters to be moved to Chicago, a stable proletarian core that they insisted was more appropriate as the Workers' Party base of operations. The Windy City was closer to the mine fields, more geographically favorable in terms of the United States labor movement, less dominated by "petty bourgeois intellectuals" than New York, and, ultimately, in the eyes of many, more quintessentially American. At issue then, was no mere debate over locale, and the relocation of the party headquarters, which took place in September 1923, was one of a number of opening shots in what would become the hot war against Pepper, signaling the crystallization of the Cannon-Foster-Bittelman faction in the Workers' Party and an ongoing resistance to the Pepper-Ruthenberg-Lovestone forces. Cannon could never figure out why the Pepper group yielded so easily to the proposal to establish Chicago as the unambiguous capital of American communism, but the lack of resistance from Pepper may have originated in his sense that the dissidents in the powerful trade union section could be better controlled if they were close at hand rather than half a continent away. Ruthenberg, by now disenchanted with Lovestone's intrigues, may have seen the move as something of a peace offering to the Cannon-Foster forces.[69]

Before and during the relocation to Chicago Cannon moved on four overlapping fronts, consolidating forces and taking the lead in putting the fight against Pepperism into a more open and political arena. First, he began the process of mending fences in the warring Jewish sections led, respectively, by Olgin and Bittelman, neither of whom had any liking for Pepper, whose relations with them had merely exacerbated tensions. This necessitated political discussions with figures such as Noah London, a former CLP member, as well as contact with Ludwig Lore, around whom a number of needle-trades communists coalesced.[70] Second, he cultivated relations with Bittelman, whose place in the leadership of the party he defended, shoring up Foster when the latter was prepared to succumb to various factional demands to dump the Jewish "wise man." Cannon also handled Foster with judicious care, allowing the somewhat politically inexperienced trade union leader to find his way in the Central Executive Committee without pressuring him unduly to come on side immediately. Over the course of a few months, Foster moved from mild indications of discontent stemming from the Farmer-Labor Party convention into overt alliance with Cannon in a factional opposition to the entirety of the Pepper regime.[71]

Third, and most decisively, Cannon penned a five-part series of articles in the *Worker,* "The Workers Party—Today and Tomorrow," which ran from 25 August through 23 September 1923. In these articles, drawing on his experience in the underground, his 200 days in Moscow, and his country-wide 1923 lecture tour, Cannon defended the necessity of the Workers' Party involvement in the labor party, but he took cautionary note of the errors of Pepperism. "The united front against the capitalists is still a propaganda slogan; but the united front against the Communists is a reality," he declared in his opening installment. "We seem to be organizing our enemies faster than we are organizing our friends." Stressing the immaturity of American working-class consciousness, Cannon simultaneously argued for the necessity of realizing the limitations of the so-called progressives and blocking with them for a temporary

advance of labor political action. His articles constituted a realistic conceptualization of united-front work in the early to mid-1920s. The immediate
impact of these articles, however, registered less in the realm of mass action
than in the emergence of party recognition that there was a problem of program—with its attendant tactics and ultimate strategy—to grapple with. Cannon later noted that everybody within the Workers' Party understood these
writings to be "an indirect criticism of the prevailing party policy, and they
encouraged a lot of other people to express themselves along the same lines."[72]

Fourth, and finally, Cannon supported an expanded and reorganized CEC
composed of three committees—political, organizational, and editorial—that
eliminated Pepper's capacity to contain party leaders such as himself and Foster in trade union/industrial isolation. Having constituted enlarged seven-
member political and organizational committees, Cannon then successfully
had himself moved to the political committee, where he joined Foster. In
pique, Pepper requested resignation as secretary of the political committee,
but the vote refused this appeal, Cannon abstaining. Never one to give in to
defeat easily, Pepper then moved to transfer Engdahl and Minor onto the
political committee, a motion that was passed unanimously save for Cannon's
abstention.[73]

Pepperism Rampant

Pepper responded aggressively, dressing Cannon down in the Central Executive Committee and demanding that his published articles be cleared through
the political committee. Cannon stuck to his guns and beat back the Hungarian's attack. Pepper also failed in a bid to have Cannon's ally, Arne Swabeck,
removed as district organizer for the industrial region encompassing Illinois,
Indiana, and Minnesota.[74]

Dueling theses on the Federated Farmer-Labor Party appeared over the course
of August–November 1923, consolidating the factional positions of opposition.
Ruthenberg and Pepper put forward their August theses, bluffing through the
debacle of the post-July-convention isolation of the Workers' Party, claiming that
a third party of 300,000 was in the offing and blasting the trade union opportunists for being insufficiently committed to the struggle to build a mass Federated Farmer-Labor Party. Pepper responded to Cannon's *Worker* articles with
flights of arcane fantasy, insisting on the imminence of world revolution, theo-
rizing wildly about the "LaFollette revolution of the well-to-do and exploited
farmers, small businessmen, and workers." He promoted a first them/then us
understanding of the initial stage of the unfolding American revolution, one that
Pepper prophesied would contain "elements of the great French Revolution, and

the Russian Kerensky Revolution. In its ideology it will have elements of Jefferso-
nianism, Danish cooperatives, Ku Klux Klan and Bolshevism. The Proletariat *as
a class* will not play an independent role in this revolution." After its victory, however, "there will begin the *independent* role of workers and exploited farmers, and
there will begin then, the period of the *fourth* American revolution—the period
of the proletarian revolution."[75]

This was perhaps too much for many to take. Among the cooperatively-
minded Finns of the Midwest, Cannon's and Foster's practical turn of mind, as
opposed to the Pepper spray of almost mystical proportions and the seemingly
infinite invective and incivility emanating from the party executive, won the
emerging opposition over to them. Pepper had adapted to Comintern injunctions that the Workers' Party was not sufficiently Americanized, as a 26 May 1923
article in the *Worker* suggested: "If we were to read the nine dailies and twenty-
one weeklies of the Workers' Party carefully," he wrote, "one would get the complete picture of all European countries, but a very incomplete picture of the
political life in America."[76] This insight, however, with which many could agree,
became translated into assaults on the foreign-speaking elements of the party,
who were increasingly admonished to shed their cultures and linguistic isolations, much as Pepper had himself managed to do, while keeping very much
alive the huge dividends of his "revolutionary" past. As the largest contingent of
the Workers' Party in 1923, numbering approximately 6,600, the Finnish federation and its Swedish secretary, Fahle Burman, was a touchstone of discontent
relating to this treatment, and proved a feather in the cap of the Cannon-Foster
combination. They likely appreciated Foster's efforts to steer a nonsectarian and
practical course in support of the one seeming bright spot in the 1922–1924
farmer-labor imbroglio, the successful Minnesota Farmer-Labor movement,
which drew on a range of native-born and ethnic radical constituencies.[77]

The Cannon-Foster-Bittelman hand was strengthened accordingly, and
they drafted their own program of policy opposition in November 1923, a
forty-thesis document entitled, "Statement on Our Labor Policy." An unambiguous repudiation of the "false policy of the CEC" and the failure of the
"Federated" to achieve the grandiose claims made on its behalf by the Pepper
group, as well as a warning not to elevate the farmer over the worker in terms
of leadership, the central plank in this internal document was to drop the pre-
tense of the Federated Farmer-Labor Party and try to restore a balance of pro-
gressive-communist united-front work of the sort that existed in the spring of
1923. From that reconstituted foundation, Cannon and Foster suggested, some
headway might be made in a reinvigorated farmer-labor movement.[78] Pepper,
perhaps finally sensing the reality of his predicament, and undoubtedly influenced by Ruthenberg, offered concessionary countering "November theses," in

which the Workers' Party front Federated Farmer-Labor Party would be kept as an instrument of propaganda that might feed into third-party formations in 1924 (which was precisely the formulation advocated as the first of a six-point programmatic conclusion in the Cannon-Foster statement). Expecting a bonanza out of the LaFollette "revolution," Pepper and Ruthenberg flipped from their summer 1923 position that the communists could lead the labor party, to a liquidationist flop that embraced any electoral campaigns of 1924 (Socialist, farmer-labor, third party) save those of their own party, on the grounds that they offered promise of a break from the established capitalist electoral machines. Worn down by months of left sectarianism, Cannon and his allies found the right opportunist concession of Pepper and Ruthenberg suffi- ciently placatory to induce them to table their own agenda in order to avoid a direct, and possibly debilitating, clash at the Workers' Party's Third Conven- tion, scheduled for Chicago from 30 December 1923 to 4 January 1924.[79]

In the meantime, Cannon courted independent oppositional voices within the leadership, such as that of Ludwig Lore, whose record of programmatic attachment was unstable, but who seemed resentful of Pepper's dictations (which he perhaps equated with those of Zinoviev), and the ultraleft former Goose, Alfred Wagenknecht, a lone figure of isolation. Such disaffected Work- ers' Party advocates found the "LaFollette alliance" of Pepper-Ruthenberg something to rail against.[80] Cannon also worked the hinterland and the mar- gins, translating the politics of his campaign against Pepper to audiences of workers and communists in which he did not so much address party faction- alism as offer his own accent on mass activity. He spoke at meetings in Ohio, stressing the importance of the trade unions in party work, a cause he also promoted through defense of class-war prisoners at the second TUEL conven- tion in September 1923. Articles that appealed to an old personal constituency, the beleaguered miners, appeared under Cannon's name.[81] By late in the fall of 1923, Cannon had managed to patch together a wide-ranging coalition, reach- ing across the political spectrum of the Workers' Party. It was a monument to the Kansas native son's abilities as well as to the Pepper regime's capacity to generate grievance: the Cannon-Foster faction was as much organized by the Comintern adventurer as it was built by its leaders. Even Pepper's "magnificent performances" in facing down hostile crowds, and his willingness to risk arrest and physical harm by appearing in public to debate his detractors, could not stem the tide of growing challenge.[82]

Nor were maneuvers that commenced in October 1923, bearing the signature of Pepper, to prove very effective: in the political and organizational commit- tees, Cannon was singled out for party assignment in work that would take him directly away from the factional struggle inside the Workers' Party.[83] At the organization and political committee meetings of October–November 1923, much time was taken up discussing Cannon's assignments, possibly including a Mexico posting, an organizational sweep through the Indiana coal fields, and a lecture series on the Workers' Party's educational circuit. Begging off on the grounds of "his health" did Cannon little good. Somebody wanted the national chairman out of the way, but little came of these disingenuous efforts to bury Cannon in an impossible workload, although they continued into 1924.[84]

Jim in fact had his hands full, politically and personally. Having moved to Chicago in the fall of 1923, Cannon made more than a political statement. His private life was obviously in the throes of upheaval. Lista and the children did not accompany him in the relocation from New York to Chicago; indeed, it would be difficult to place him very much in their lives for the entire period reaching from June 1922 through December 1923. Jim and Lista had clearly drifted apart. Their marriage, for all intents and purposes, was over. No doubt Jim loved his children, and possibly even Lista, but the demands of being a professional revolutionary meant that he saw little of his family; for this form-ative period of Carl's and Ruth's childhood he was simply not much in the pic-ture as a father, and he could not possibly have been much better as a husband.

The Romance of Politics

The move to Chicago was not an easy one for Cannon. Pepper was an adver-sary who did not know how to quit. He and his factional allies were, in Can-non's later words, "the toughest bastards you ever ran up against in your life." Whatever spare money he had—and it would not have been a lot—probably went to Lista and the children. Cannon's life was the Workers' Party, and its struggles. His paths kept crossing, however, with a vivacious, slender, thirty-five-year-old brunette, Rose Greenberg Karsner. Rose was a "small, frail-look-ing woman, with a mobile, very expressive, very handsome thin face. In it, set deeply, were mischievous dark eyes that most often sparkled, sometimes with good humor, sometimes teasingly, and on rarer occasions with blazing fury." Her hair jet black, the petite Rose "was always interesting to watch." Jim, a month-and-a-half Rose's junior, was distinguished by his firm jaw, sharp blue eyes, full head of blonde-brown hair, and an attractive smile. Much sought after in Chicago circles—there were stories that she had been pursued by Jay Lovestone—Rose paired up nicely with Cannon, whose dashing physicality and reputation as the Workers' Party's finest speaker no doubt made him a sought-after companion.[85]

Jim knew Rose from New York, but clearly not well; the two communists had a passing acquaintance with one another that had developed through sporadic contact, conventions, and the hit-and-miss of routine administrative and political work. With the move to Chicago in September 1923, though, the two left-wing veterans found themselves in a new city, their social and political networks far more constricted than they had been in the larger, more cosmopolitan New York. As Cannon jocularly put it at a speech delivered on his seventieth birthday:

> I don't know how it happened, but it seemed like every place I'd go, a party affair, a meeting or a social, always—accidentally—she'd bump into me and say, "Fancy meeting you here." So, first thing you know, in order to quit bumping into each other, we said, "Well, let's go and live together." And we went to live in a furnished room with a daybed, if you know what that is, a daybed that folds up into a cot—and kitchen privileges—and we lived that way for three years and we never thought we were sacrificing at all. We thought we were in clover. As a matter of fact, we were.[86]

A classic male mythology of feminine pursuit, the story would likely have had a slightly different twist were it told by the independent-minded Rose, a militant woman who cut her teeth on the pre–World War I socialist movement and cast her lot with the revolutionary ultraleft in the years of Palmer Raid repression. Nevertheless, it dates the beginning of a lifelong comradeship, a love relationship sealed in political collaboration, that overcame the superficialities of very different identities. An Irish-American native son with the touch of the ward heeler about him hooked up with an Old-World "Roumanian materialist," might be one construction. Cannon had another: "Now Rose, here, claims that she's a hippie," he joked in the 1960s, "and I believe her. But as for me, I know that I am a Digger to the end."[87]

Rose Greenberg, born into a relatively well-off Jewish mercantile family in a small Romanian village on 22 December 1889, was the sixth of nine children. The father was of orthodox religious belief, and after years in business decided that he wanted to study the Talmud full-time, and expected his wife to take over the store. Instead, this rebellious woman emigrated to the United States, settling in New York in the 1890s. Originally Rose was left behind, being the youngest daughter, along with two school-aged brothers and two older, married sisters. Her mother set up a household based on the waged work of three daughters employed in the garment trades, and then sent for Rose and her brothers. The family had fared relatively well in the old country, although the premature death of Rose's father in 1896 left them somewhat insecure. Socialist obituaries would portray Rose as one of "the poor and oppressed," but her upbringing, as the last-born daughter, was relatively sheltered and she never had to work in the sweatshops where siblings earned their livings. Rose's brothers, indulged in their American educations, became, respectively, a doctor and a dentist, and Rose, privileged to finish high school and then train secretarially, secured employment in the offices of various Left publications and organizations.

It was at the Rand School of Social Science, where Rose attended socialist lectures given by Algernon Lee and W. H. Ghent, and befriended the school's secretary, Bertha Mailey, that she met her first husband, David Fulton Karsner, the future editor of the socialist daily, the *New York Call*, and Eugene Debs's friend and first biographer. After joining the Socialist Party in 1908, Rose became the first secretary of the radical cooperative magazine, *The Masses;* she sold the publication at socialist gatherings in the New York-New Jersey area, and later worked with Max Eastman, John Sloan, Art Young, and Boardman Robinson in moving the journal decidedly to the left. Rose married Karsner in 1911, and found her life revolving around the politics of working-class revolution as they moved to Chicago to work in the national office of the Socialist Party. Later Rose was employed as the business manager of the *Minnesota Socialist,* edited by her husband. For a time she and Karsner shared a home with Horace Traubel, editor of the radical Philadelphia/Camden-based *The Conservator,* and known to contemporaries on the left as "the socialist Walt Whitman." Rose's and David's daughter, Walta, was born on the eve of World War I, and was named after Whitman, for whom the young Traubel had served as secretary and, after the nineteenth-century poet's death, as his literary executor. The Karsners knew Whitman in his last, dying days, and Walta remembered into her eighties, with fondness and pride, a prized, signed picture of the famous white-bearded poet, dedicated to her parents. Among the prominent socialists of these years whom Rose counted as friends and comrades were George R. Kirkpatrick, author of the much-republished left-wing classic, *War—What For?* (1910), a tract dedicated to the victims of "civil war in industry" that sold 40,000 copies during its first 16 months in print; and the Christian Socialist, Rufus Weeks.[88]

Like many who came to political maturity in the years of the opening decades of the twentieth century, Rose was captivated by Eugene Debs. From the age of eighteen Rose saw Debs as the personification of socialism, "loved by the great mass of workers, some of whom were even opposed to his ideas of socialism. But Debs exuded love for humanity and conveyed a sincerity and passion about his convictions for a better world for everyone, regardless of race, color or religion." For the remainder of her life Rose regarded Debs as "an idea—a cause, a something you agree or disagree with, intensely human at the same time, loving and being loved by the masses of people."[89] In 1921 Rose turned to Debs during the difficult time when her relationship with David Karsner was ending. Karsner had left Rose for one of her closest friends, Esther

Eberson, and the papers for divorce that were filed in June 1921 were finalized in December of that same year. In her sorrow Rose wrote to

> Dear Gene—OUR GENE: Were I in a position to know the exact day when you are going to be released, I should move heaven and earth to be at your side. I shall do all I can to find out, but in the event that I dont succeed, know that I am with you in the spirit—right there every step of the way. Oh Gene, you can never know what you have meant to me these past few months. What inspiration I have drawn from you, when others have failed me![90]

At this moment Rose felt herself a woman alone, "thinking and feeling things she never dared to think or feel before."[91] It must have been a desperate time, but it was also one in which she was in political motion. The Russian Revolution had galvanized the American Left. It also forced political difference into the public spaces of the socialist cause. It no doubt fractured the private realm as well. In the Karsner household, David remained in the camp of the Socialist Party and he would eventually leave even its ranks to pursue a career in mainstream journalism. Rose, in contrast, gravitated to the communists. Elected to the post of national secretary of the New York-based Friends of Soviet Russia (FSR), Karsner raised funds for the purchase of food and machinery for the new workers' state. In 1923 she accepted transfer to Chicago with the move of the Workers' Party headquarters, and worked for the International Workers Relief/International Workers Aid, especially in its efforts to alleviate the distress of German workers. A year later she was the energetic mainstay of the now highly successful FSR. It proved a phenomenal fund raiser for Willi Munzenberg's Berlin-based aid operations, and funneled more than $100,000 worth of food and clothing to Germans and Russians in need. Karsner's exemplary efficiency stood her in good stead with Munzenberg and other Comintern figures, who valued the propaganda role of the FSR as well as the steady cash flow it generated. Boarding out her daughter to a somewhat rigid woman in Wilton, Connecticut (one later comrade referred to this caregiver as a Nazi, although that was certainly an exaggeration), or having her live with uncles and aunts, so that she could do this communist work, Rose maintained a loving relationship with her child, but one that was not allowed to overwhelm her work for revolutionary change. When nine-year-old Walta published a four-line poem, "Exmas Time," in the *Liberator*, expressing her loneliness at the separation from her mother—"A little lonly girl/Went calmly off to bed/And all the Xmas that she had/Was in her little head"—a progressive reader thought the child must be poor, and sent her $10. Rose made Walta donate it to communist international relief work.[92] Jim had clearly found a woman of firm convictions and deep commitments.

The Third National Convention of the Workers' Party, 1923–1924

Walta missed her mother that Christmas of 1923. For Jim and Rose, their first "Xmas Time" was consumed in preparations for the Third Convention of the Workers' Party, opening the day before New Year's Eve.[93] It was shaping up as a final showdown between the Cannon-Foster group and the Pepper-Ruthenberg-Lovestone combination. Things did not begin auspiciously for Cannon and his confreres, as the Comintern wrote its greetings to the gathering in a language of praise for the formation of the Federated Farmer-Labor Party, assuring the Americans that differentiating themselves from labor bureaucrats, social democrats, and "a few so-called 'progressive' trade union leaders from the Middle West" was a solid foundation upon which to build "the United Front of all proletarian and farmers' parties and organizations." Browder thought it "the final crushing blow," but it was difficult to predict how the fifty-two delegates, supposedly representing a membership of 15,000, were going to cast their votes on various resolutions, or even how those resolutions might be framed. What was clear was that something was going to come out of the convention that would reconfigure the leadership of the Workers' Party.[94]

The key player turned out, ironically, to be Ludwig Lore, who held a sort of balance of power, influencing some fifteen delegates while the Foster-Cannon and Ruthenberg-Pepper coalitions split the remainder, roughly nineteen apiece.[95] Ruthenberg unleashed Pepper and Lovestone on Lore as he debarked from the "Twentieth Century" train from New York to Chicago. They cajoled the strong-willed radical, hustling him into a private conference where they pressed him to support their positions. As Gitlow tells it, the efforts were futile, and largely for one reason: "Lore hated Pepper."[96] At the actual convention, Pepper tried unsuccessfully to lure Lore into his camp. The long-time socialist editor refused the bait, and in the subsequent crucial reconstruction of the party leadership, he aligned himself with the Cannon-Foster group. Key votes saw this latter faction in dominant control of the proceedings, the final tallies going in their favor by a thirty-seven to fifteen margin.[97]

Ruthenberg's aloofness meant that he managed to keep Pepper somewhat at a distance, and he continued to command the respect of all quarters. He would thus remain as secretary in the aftermath of the convention. Foster, increasingly recognized as the most visible proletarian element in the Workers' Party and, now, by broadening his involvement beyond trade union questions into the political realm, a force to reckon with in the upper echelons of broad decision-making, came out of the year-end conference with a much higher profile. He was eventually elevated to the national chairmanship at a Central Executive Committee meeting in mid-February 1924; Cannon resigned that post to make way for Foster and take up the newly created position of assistant secretary. Pepper attempted a motion abolishing the post of national chairman, but failed on procedural grounds. The Foster-Cannon-Lore combination thus controlled the Central Executive Committee, on which Lore now sat, and in due course the Foster-Cannon loyalist, Bittelman, replaced Pepper on the political bureau, where four of the seven voting members were Foster-Cannon supporters. Cannon, Foster, Dunne, and Browder were initially on both ranking bodies. In the crucial districts of New York and Chicago, the Foster-Cannon combination now also ruled supreme, Swabeck retaining the midwestern district organizer post as Krumbein relocated to assume the same position in New York. The Young Workers' League was now a bastion of Cannon strength, with his personal follower Max Shachtman editing the semi-monthly organ, the *Young Worker;* Jim's 1922 Comintern protégé, Martin Abern, functioning as national secretary; and the teenage Albert Glotzer a leading youth recruit. Such precocious communists were drawn primarily to Cannon's oratory, renowned in party circles, his reputation as an outstanding political figure with a history of involvement in the class struggle, and a vigorous platform presence and congenial sociability that perhaps set him apart from the stodgier Ruthenberg-Pepper-Lovestone crowd.[98] Foster was capable of recruiting trade union militants to the revolutionary ranks, but once there they needed Cannon desperately, for Foster himself was no match for factional opponents such as Ruthenberg and Lovestone, who baited him mercilessly. "Jim Cannon was then only 35, but he was the old man of the faction," Glotzer remembered, adding in explanation, "In Cannon the faction had a strong leader, wise in the ways of political struggle and a match for the Pepper-Ruthenberg-Lovestone leadership, the only one in the Party who could seriously challenge them."[99]

If Jim appeared to have been demoted from his leading role as national chairman, he gave few indications of any regrets; he resigned with goodwill and voted for Foster. "Pepperism" appeared to have gone down to a decisive defeat, and Cannon's base of authority in the Workers' Party was now wider than ever before. Although other commentators, especially Browder, would interpret Cannon's being replaced as chairman as "a bitter pill . . . to swallow," a price that had to be paid for a pact with the "ruthless" Foster, Cannon had an entirely different explanation:

> As far as Foster and I were concerned . . . our maximum program at that time was simply to end Pepper's domination. . . . We still hoped . . . to come to an eventual accommodation with Ruthenberg, and in general to share party responsibilities with the others, within that framework. . . . Once Foster had become fully identified with the party, it was perfectly obvious to me that he,

with his greater prominence and public prestige, should succeed to the office of Chairman. The only question was whether Foster was ready to identify himself publicly with the party. I believe the change met with general approval, but I am equally certain that it would not have taken place at that time and under the conditions of the time if I had not myself proposed it.[100]

As 1922 had ended, then, with the seeming success of Cannon's oppositional struggle against the Geese, and the Comintern validation of liquidation/Americanization, so 1923 concluded with an ostensible rout of Pepper.

The mercurial politics of oscillation, in which Pepper's swings from mechanical undergroundist extremism to flights of adaptation to the seeming fluidities of American politics, had been wrestled back to ground. Cannon and Foster looked forward to building the Workers' Party into a presence on the United States labor and Left scenes. There were signs of dangerous concessions to opportunism in their politics, to be sure, but they were difficult to discern given the general ultraleft fantasy world Pepper had perpetrated throughout 1923. With Rose as a new love in his life, a base among the trade union "industrialists" concentrated in Chicago and Minneapolis, and a renewed lease on the political life of the Workers' Party he had helped to form, Cannon must have approached 1924 with optimism. He remained a soldier of the International, having in part lived by almost unquestioning loyalty to Comintern decision. Unaware of the nascent Stalinist degeneration of the Russian Revolution orchestrated by the internal clash of preserving "socialism in one country" and ousting the dreaded Trotskyist notion of "permanent revolution," and equally innocent of knowledge of Zinoviev's bureaucratization of the Communist International, Cannon had no idea of what was in store for him over the next years. Ignorance may, in this case, have induced a kind of bliss. On the immediate home front, Cannon would soon have to come to grips with his underestimation of the respective rancors of Pepper, Ruthenberg, and Lovestone, and the limitations of his combination with Foster.

8

Stalinist Suspensions

Of Factions and Foreign Domination

The years from 1924 to late 1928 appear to most historians of the United States revolutionary Left to be a communist wasteland, a landscape scarred by incessant party wrangling and bizarre reconfigurations of leadership. First-person recollections, such as those of Benjamin Gitlow and Peggy Dennis, as well as commentaries by historians as different in their positionings as the 1940s social democratic duo James Oneal and G. A. Werner or the New Left spokesperson Paul Buhle, have tended to place analytic accent on the psychosis of a factional "gang warfare" that reduces communist history in these years to screaming matches, conniving caucuses, Keystone Kop-type scenarios, and even physical gangsterism.[1] One Central Committee meeting submitted documents to a handwriting expert to try to ascertain who had been circulating specific factional caucus material.[2] This fractious internal party life was debilitating and, as James P. Cannon later testified, it deformed the revolutionary movement and its cadre. It would take generations to right the wrongs of this debasement, framed within the political degeneration of the Communist International.[3]

These conventional wisdoms, however, take us in the wrong direction. Buhle, for instance, refers to a "sickness" at the core of communist being and stresses the incomprehensibility of factionalism, a conceptual choice that strips the men and women of the communist movement of responsibility and avoids a *political* reading of tactics and strategies that is the only way of truly appreciating what was done in this period and why:

> It is difficult now, for the ordinary participants in these melees, to understand what the argument was all about. They recall finding themselves lined up on

one side or the other . . . glad to see the trouble end through Russian-commanded bureaucratic fiat. . . . [They] made their own low-profile adaptations to the stubborn phantasmagorias of the Party leadership on the one side and the stubborn realities of American working-class life on the other.[4]

Cannon, in contrast, explained the outbreak of factionalism as a contest rooted in large socioeconomic forces. American capitalism consolidated its most sustained victories in the aftermath of world revolution's first partial successes. The loud economic boom of an aggressively expansive United States economy, and the low level of class struggle in capitalism's increasingly conservative pacesetter nation-state, demonstrably obvious by 1923, reverberated around the world. In conjunction with stabilizing European class relations, this produced a climate hardly conducive to the revolutionary Left. Felt deeply in the Soviet Union, this aftershock underlay a series of mistakes, concessions, and political retreats that would eventually combine to produce Stalinism. As Cannon stressed, "the deadening conservatism of American life, induced by the unprecedented boom of post-war American capitalism, coinciding with the reactionary swing in Russia, caught the infant movement of American communism from two sides, as in a vise from which it could not escape. . . . As the wave of labor radicalism was pushed back into ascending prosperity, the party began to run into difficulties on all fronts."[5] Leadership of the young communist movement was then constantly tested and reconfigured. Precisely because the U.S. party, like the working class from which it emerged, was itself not homogenous, but was composed of various groupings—ethnic, social, and political—the executive ranks of the revolutionary movement were also heterogeneous. "Instead of a unified leadership with authority and influence over the party as a whole," Cannon noted, "the outstanding leaders were leaders of factions which reflected the contradictions in the party. . . . Many who appeared to have leadership ability one year, and were elected accordingly, would be swept aside the second year and replaced by previously unknown men."[6]

There is no question that in the consolidation of factional groups in the 1920s, a perceived difference of style divided Cannon and his varied allies from Pepper, Ruthenberg, and Lovestone. The hedonistic Pepper, known for his fondness for cognac, foppish clothes, and "revelling in the luscious bourgeois life of America"; the vain Ruthenberg, conservative in dress and romantic in spirit (a kind of Thoreau in Leninist vanguard cap), outwardly expressing propriety at the same time as he was inwardly driven by what Gitlow characterized "a Messianic complex," which demanded his public presence as the undisputed figurehead of United Communism; the "City College" schemer, Jay Lovestone, "a veritable Tammany chieftan [sic]" among communists, feared for the "files" he kept on all prominent party figures and genuinely despised by most of his opponents as well as a few of his followers—such leaders were distanced from "trade unionists" in character, and their day-to-day activity included little involvement in mass, agitational work.[7]

Cannon's forces carried themselves differently. The tone of faction was set by a proletarian sensibility and carried through in his relations with both his equals in the movement—William Z. Foster, Arne Swabeck, and Bill Dunne, for instance—and with those who aligned with him on the basis of an often shifting, but fused, relationship of political agreement (including, at various times, Jack Johnstone, Alexander Bittelman, William Weinstone, and Earl Browder). These relations were sometimes sealed in a youth-mentor pact (Max Shachtman, Martin Abern, Albert Glotzer), or, as in the case of Rose Karsner, cemented in personal intimacy. Bittelman commented on the style that stamped those around Cannon:

> Most of the Cannon-Foster circle were a rather rough-and-ready group of individuals. There was among them much camaraderie, plain-spoken talk and few niceties in mutual relations. In group discussions they would use what they chose to call "trade union language," in which variations on "damn it" were of the more innocent expressions. And candor compels me also to say this: in our own circle four-letter exclamations were a dime a dozen and sometimes cheaper. Whereas Ruthenberg, in circumstances which tempt one to some such exclamation, would merely say: "Goodness gracious." I can never forget the expression on the faces of some of my comrades in the Cannon-Foster circle on such occasions.[8]

Secured environmentally in New York establishments such as McSorley's saloon (on Seventh Street near Third Avenue), or the popular Italian cafe, John's (located at 302 East Twelfth Street), and buttressed with a Chicago circle of sociable comrades, this revolutionary trade-union-leadership contingent consolidated throughout the 1920s. Yet, it also experienced complications and, particularly with respect to Cannon and Foster, an acute differentiation. If Foster, for instance, was a trade union leader in the Workers' Party, Cannon was, in contrast, always a party leader concerned with trade union issues. Moreover, as identifiable as was the Cannon-Foster combination as a "trade union" grouping, the mass base of their bloc was the numerically large Finnish cooperative movement.[9]

By the end of the decade, the salty language of proletarian factional style—which also, interestingly enough, crossed over into corners of avant-garde cultural radicalism quite separate from the clique of Pepper, Ruthenberg, and Lovestone, and linked to the old *Liberator* crowd that Cannon and Dunne, if not Foster and Browder, sustained connections to—eased toward a more political consciousness. It seeped instinctually but gradually into a nascent critique of bureaucratism and unease with proto-Stalinism.[10] Thus, Joseph Freeman wrote to Mike Gold sometime in 1925–1927, bemoaning the "petty ambitions" of the American leadership of the communist movement, longing for a revolutionary breakthrough that would force the party officialdom off its smallish pedestals of apparent careerist concern. He added, as an endnote of emphasis, "Jim Cannon, who has just returned from Moscow, said as much at a booze-party given in honor of Tim Tippet at John's. He contrasted the unselfishness of the Russian leaders with the pie-card psychology of the Native Napoleans in a way that must have made them squirm in their B.V.D.'s."[11]

A few years later, in the fall of 1928, on the verge of his public declaration of Trotskyism, Cannon sat in John's with Alexander Bittelman. The two old comrades shared drinks and memories, their political paths now ones of divergent factions for some time, Bittelman having secured the stature of being the theoretician of the Foster group. Drawn together for a brief period in 1928 because of a convergence of views around trade union policy that separated them from Foster, Bittelman and Cannon were close enough to talk frankly, but they were now political opposites. The former was a Cominternist to the core. "He was first, last and all the time a Moscow man," Cannon later recalled of Bittelman, "and the line from Moscow was law to him." The latter, as Bittel-man later stressed, was, by the summer of 1928, increasingly disillusioned with the Comintern leadership. "Stalin makes shit out of leaders," Bittelman remembered Cannon declaring many times, a judgment that possibly alluded directly to Foster and concluded on a note that likely targeted Pepper, "and leaders out of shit."[12]

It was a Rosedaleian formulation, quintessentially Cannonesque, but even the succinctness of this earthy summation had taken years to germinate. The politics behind this pithy statement did not happen overnight; they were formed over years of intense maneuvering and clarification, in which unseemly acts and principled stands coexisted. Gradually, a recognition of political degeneration and a grasp of what was truly at stake in the seemingly endless rounds of factional recrimination and oscillating programmatic adventures took root, but Cannon and many others were slow to appreciate that their project of revolutionary party building had been, by the mid- to late 1920s, stunted if not strangled.

These, then, were years that gave rise to an original joke that would later become the interpretive core of Cold War historiography, in which United States communism was understood to be little more than a Moscow-dominated movement, ever dependent on Stalinism's Comintern directives, conveyed to the party hierarchy in coded "cables" (telegrams). "Why is the Communist Party of the

United States like the Brooklyn Bridge?" revolutionaries asked, their answer speaking of something more than mirth. "Because it is suspended on cables."[13] Communist International cables/Stalinist suspensions.

Labor Organization, Communist Education, and Sustaining Collective Leadership

By 1924 Cannon thought he could put an end to "unprincipled factionalism." He fought, eventually, to overcome the concept of "hereditary" leadership, which he associated with Ruthenberg and which produced endless wrangles and combinations that sustained the machinations of first Pepper and then Lovestone. Cannon's answer was the consolidation of a "collective leadership." A loyal Comintern soldier, Cannon was, throughout much of this period, largely blind to the bureaucratization of the Communist International under Zinoviev, the subsequent Stalinization of the Soviet Communist Party, and the faltering of the Russian Revolution. His project of building an executive corps of communist leaders was insightful, even visionary, but his understanding of the larger context within which such American steps could be taken was, until late in 1928, partial and limited.[14]

Fresh from the Chicago Workers' Party 1923 convention, Cannon took up some unfinished business that grew out of his attendance at the annual meeting of the Industrial Workers of the World, held in Chicago in mid-November, and penned an article on the IWW's Fifteenth General Convention. This was a tense period in IWW-AFL relations. Strongholds of Wobbly "closed shop" authority, such as Philadelphia's Marine Transport Workers' International Union, imploded as employers, the state, and mainstream labor officialdoms undermined what had been, since 1913, an irksome bastion of working-class power on the waterfront. Effectively led by Ben Fletcher, the only African American IWW figure swept up in the mass 1918 Chicago trial (he had quipped to Haywood: "If it wasn't for me, there'd be no color in this trial at all"), Philadelphia's longshoremen battled intransigent bosses and an IWW General Executive Board that resented their $25 initiation fees, which contravened the anti-craft unionism provisions of the one big unionist constitution. Upon his release from Leavenworth, the talented and popular Fletcher marched the transport union stevedores through a defeated strike and out of the IWW into the AFL. At about the same time, New York's Bakery Workers Industrial Union, Local 146, was suspended by the IWW's executive board under similar circumstances.[15]

The Wobblies were now almost exclusively a body of migratory workers, two-thirds of their members being concentrated in agriculture, lumbering, and general construction. Many leading figures were hard-line opponents of the communists and their Russian Revolution. Cannon focused his coverage of the 1923 gathering, at which he and Robert Minor were given the floor to invite the IWW to send delegates to a world congress of the Red International of Labor Unions (RILU), on the small trends toward united-front work that he felt would draw the IWW inevitably into the world communist movement. In developing a brief statement on the dominance of the IWW in the field of migratory agricultural labor, where the Wobblies constituted the only active trade union in the field, Cannon put forward a more supple and subtle orientation to the question of "dual unionism" than was the norm in Workers' Party circles. He suggested that communists needed to work within the AFL where the AFL was established and powerful. But where another, more revolutionary, body, such as the IWW, was on the ground in an abandoned sector of the economy, as was the case with migratory agricultural laborers and perhaps even Fletcher's stevedores, then revolutionaries could quite usefully work in seemingly "dual" organizations. Lecturing on "The IWW and Communists" in Chicago and prodded by Lozovsky to write a pamphlet on the Industrial Workers of the World for the Comintern, Cannon was constantly grappling with the legacy of revolutionary industrial unionism in its pre-Leninist United States form. When Cannon debated old-time Wobbly Forrest Edwards at Chicago's North Side Turner Hall on 13 April 1924, 1,600 thronged to the afternoon political fireworks. His remarks were a judicious mixture of tribute to the IWW's class courage and insistence that the programmatic direction of the Workers' Party, especially as it related to leadership and the need to confront state power, was the only way forward for all opponents of capitalism. Cannon thus did what he could to forge the possibility of IWW-WP united-front activity, taking the tenets of the Trade Union Educational League (TUEL)—amalgamation and boring from within—but applying them in ways that Foster, with his perhaps overly mechanical rejection of the IWW, would not have had the political creativity to develop.[16]

If fissures that would widen into a Cannon-Foster set of stark differences around the TUEL appeared in this journalistic commentary on the IWW convention, Cannon's political priorities in early 1924 were undoubtedly elsewhere. He continued to adhere to the old, agitational path, applauding the militant miners of Williamson County, in the southern Illinois coal fields. The United Mine Workers of America local was situated in Herrin, Illinois, site of an armed union resistance to strikebreakers during a 1922 confrontation that culminated in a massacre of scabs and left nineteen dead (an act labor czar John L. Lewis, as well as many pro-capitalist voices, attributed to the communists). This UMW local took a strong stand against the invasion of their county by the Ku Klux Klan in 1923–1924. As violence escalated and the miners struck their bosses, Herrin was placed under martial law; Cannon entered the fray to urge the anti-vigilante forces on, linking the causes of capital and the Klan in general condemnation of the Williamson County climate of hostility to immigrants, unions, and workers.[17] Later in the summer, Cannon again addressed midwestern miners, his 27 July 1924 speech before a party conference of coal miners in St. Louis, Missouri, focusing on "Our Aims and Tactics in the Trade Unions." This talk was reproduced in the Saturday magazine section of the *Daily Worker*.[18]

As the assistant executive secretary of the Workers' Party, Cannon dealt with day-to-day administrative party work,[19] communicated with fractious comrades, and was a sounding board for complaint about factional matters of all kinds.[20] He was also often the public face of the Workers' Party. Typical of his routine were the summer months of 1924. A much-sought-after speaker, Cannon was often seen and heard on the soapbox and party podium. He taught comrades the arts of public speaking and the techniques of agitational oratory, initiated a twelve- to fourteen-week course in the history of the American communist movement, and orchestrated campaigns such as the anti-capitalist war week.[21] Over the course of these same months, Cannon also corresponded around a wide range of issues, among them two that dovetailed with the specific interests of his new companion, Rose Karsner: women's work and international aid. In both, the issue of factionalism and how to overcome it was never far from the surface.

Blind Spot: "Women's Work"

Throughout the spring and summer of 1924, Cannon carried on a correspondence with Rose Pastor Stokes, Jeanette D. Pearl, and Benjamin Gitlow's mother, Kate (two of these leading women were linked directly or by family connection to the former Goose Caucus, and aligned with the New York-based triumvirate of Pepper-Lovestone-Ruthenberg), about the issue of "women's work" and the future of an organization to further communist activity in this realm. The Workers' Party created a Women's Commission/Bureau in 1922, composed of Mary Heaton Vorse, Margaret Undjus, Jeanette D. Pearl and Elmer T. Allison. As a body that grew directly out of Comintern directive and pronouncements by Lenin, reproduced in the U.S. revolutionary press, the Women's Commission was largely a figurehead organization. It appears, however, that it stimulated particular regionally rooted bodies and, along with others in New York, Stokes played a pivotal role in establishing the locally based United Council of Working Class Women/Wives in December 1923. Counterparts of this women's affiliate existed in Boston (Mothers League), Detroit

(Proletarian Women), and elsewhere. Like many of the women who joined the communist movement in this early period, Stokes had little sympathy for bourgeois feminism, and was known to deny flatly that there was any such thing as "a separate women's problem."[22]

This did not, however, mean that she was not an advocate of women's organization, albeit of an auxiliary sort, intended to draw proletarian women, as workers *and* as housewives, into the revolutionary ranks. Nor did it suggest to Stokes and others that there was not a need for work among women. There was pride in the ways in which such work exposed the bourgeois underside of the economics of housing and further advanced the project of recruitment. Yet Stokes, Pearl, and Gitlow could not induce Cannon and other male party leaders to endorse the work of the United Council to the point of legitimizing the new body by sanctioning its right to membership cards and dues collection.

There was apparently a split in the Central Executive Committee over whether the United Council was stepping on the toes of the larger Workers' Party, usurping its *political* authority by engaging in work that reached beyond mere economic agitation. In addition, elements in the New York-based Jewish Federation sought to draw this women's work under their control. The Foster-Cannon-led "trade union" majority was more prone to call for the integration of the United Council into the Workers' Party, where as an auxiliary body it would be subject to committee discipline from "higher" (and male) authority. The Ruthenberg minority on the CEC was less resistant to letting the women's work proceed under its own steam, and both Ruthenberg and Benjamin Gitlow introduced unsuccessful motions in the Central Executive Committee and the Executive Council that would have endorsed the United Council of Working Class Women and sanctioned the development of its work "on a national scale."[23]

Cannon, despite remaining locked into certain conceptions of what communist work entailed, and however much he could not relinquish control over publications and organizational matters to the women directly involved in the struggle, did not lapse into overt condescension, as a letter to Pearl of 22 September 1924 indicated:

> I have to confess that the women's work is very complicated and I am far from being able to qualify as an "expert" on the question. However, its importance is self-evident. I wish we could devise some means of getting hold of part of the energy and spirit which seems to animate many of these women's movements and harness it to the general political activity of the Party. A great deal of propaganda is necessary and we must lay a firm foundation of correct theory. I have no doubt you could assist greatly in this respect. It seems to me that you could render a good service to the Party by contributing a series of articles to the *Worker* on the question, explaining the various phases of the "women's movement" and

criticizing their activities from the standpoint of the class struggle—then follow up by laying out a general line of activity for the Party, calculated to draw the working class women into the political and economic struggles.

A month later, after receiving a number of articles from Pearl, Cannon wrote that he had turned the writing over to Bittelman for publication in the magazine supplement to the *Daily Worker,* although he was unsure of some of the points developed. He closed with a suggestion that if Pearl was amenable to "some editing if we find it necessary," the party press would continue to welcome further contributions on the subject of the women's movement and a communist approach toward it.

This did not resolve the fundamental issue. Stokes resisted integrating the United Council into the Workers' Party, arguing that although it should eventually become a direct auxiliary of the WP, to demand this of the women's organization prematurely would squander an opportunity to win recruits to the party: "We have control and are leading the work well, I feel. Several of the very active women have joined the party. Several more will join before long. This will pave the way for the action the CEC desires. But I hope the party will not try to force it." Stokes also apparently requested party assignment, where she clearly felt her speaking talents could be put to good use, in a national lecture tour associated with the 1924 Workers' Party election campaign, in which Foster and Gitlow were running for president and vice president.[24]

Cannon's responses to these admonitions were a blend of tact and evasion, mixed with a mindfulness of the necessity of not making the issue of women's work a cause for further factionalism. As one of a committee of three looking into the issue of women's work, he originally pleaded "unfamiliarity of the field," asking for the indulgence of studying the question more thoroughly "from the standpoint of the lines laid down by the Comintern." Alluding to "a time which we all remember when we could not work in our own name at all," and when "camouflage organisations" were a vehicle of underground communist work, Cannon's final letter to Stokes carried something of a sting in its referential tail: the old Goose Caucus member could not have appreciated being reminded by Cannon that the Workers' Party now worked openly in the American political and cultural milieus. Cannon offered a personal, but perhaps rather empty, gesture of accommodation in a suggestion that he was in favor of sending Stokes on a national speaking campaign. When nothing came of this placation, Stokes replied with resigned resentment: "So I'll plan to pitch into the New York campaign tho I feel I could be more useful thru the country."[25]

Given Cannon's response to the issues raised by Stokes and Gitlow, it is little wonder that women's work in the 1920s did not register strong gains.[26] This disappointing reality was in part attributable to the general communist shortcomings on "the women's question," of course, but it also fed directly into the rancorous atmosphere of the factionalized WP in 1924. Cannon, in this sense, was both warden and prisoner of a particular edifice of incarceration. Asked in 1973 if the early Communist Party had "any conscious attitude toward the whole question of the status of women," Cannon replied: "If it did, it didn't show it very much. . . . it was at most a formal recognition. We had only one woman member of the National Committee of the CP during the time I was in there. That was Juliet Stuart Poyntz who was a high school teacher who became head of the educational department of the New York local. . . . I knew Rose Pastor Stokes quite well but she was never a member of the National Committee although she deserved to be."[27]

Closely aligned with the discussion of women's work, both in terms of parallel personnel, the attitude of the entirely male Central Executive Committee of the Workers' Party, and the implications of factionalism, was the shifting nature of defense and international aid work. The Friends of Soviet Russia (FSR) was first established in August 1921 to aid the Soviet people then suffering through a severe famine. Though the FSR became the first mass-appeal communist united-front organization, pushing figures like Alfred Wagenknecht into the public eye and securing him a lasting reputation as the Workers' Party's most skilled fund raiser, it was women such as Rose Karsner and Rose Pastor Stokes, occupying prominent positions in the Friends of Soviet Russia, who kept this international defense work moving. Karsner was the effective administrative officer of the cause, as its national secretary, and Stokes played the same role in the Women's Division of the FSR, as well as organizing a children's contingent of Famine Scouts, aged eight to sixteen. Their efforts paid huge economic and political dividends. FSR committees mushroomed across the United States, raising tens of thousands of dollars, almost all of it from small, individual donations or contributions from immigrant, left-wing groups. This material support sustained Willi Munzenberg's aid efforts in Europe. Defense work at this time in the communist movement was often regarded disparagingly by key factional leaders as the kind of benevolent activity best left in the hands of "lesser" communists, especially women. As Cannon, who was not given to such condescension, recalled with disdain decades later, "It was supposed to be an avocation," something that professional revolutionaries need not take up their serious time with.[28]

In April 1924, the Friends of Soviet Russia having given way partially to the International Red Aid (1922), Friends of Soviet Russia and Workers Germany (1923), and later the Workers International Relief (1924), Cannon offered his support to broad international relief and defense work in ways that cultivated a new, collective leadership, liberated from unprincipled factionalism. What was needed was not the continuity of old acrimonies, but "merging and amalgamating the various elements who are going in the same general direction and establishing the leadership, *in fact,* of the CEC."[29]

Race and Revolution

Outside of women's and defense/relief work, a major arena of activity in which communists endeavored to make breakthroughs in the 1920s was in the sphere of anti-racist activism: "the Negro Question" was of concern to all factions. A central progressive historiographic conventional wisdom is that the revolutionary Left in the United States never grappled seriously with the difficult, but pivotal, issue of race until 1928 and the elaboration of the Black Belt nation thesis.[30] This is an especially attractive argument, given the legacy of the Socialist Party's record on race, which veered too often toward an indifference bred of a mechanical privileging of class *exploitation* over the *oppression* of "color." Moreover, there is some validity to this view, inasmuch as the Comintern-influenced programmatic support of African American self-determination necessarily addressed race more directly than had been the norm within radical circles. Nevertheless, in placing undue emphasis on the 1928 self-determination thesis, there is a danger of understating other communist initiatives in the 1920s and overplaying the significance of a problematic programmatic direction taken with the development of the idea of a Black Belt nation. Moreover, in skirting the Workers' Party attempts to address race and revolution in the mid-1920s, the complications of this period are invariably slighted.[31]

From the establishment of the Workers' Party in 1922, the particular oppression of African Americans was, if not a priority on the revolutionary Left, nevertheless very much on the agenda of United States communists. Yet, the capacity of white revolutionaries to attend to the significance of race in the project of socialist reconstruction, as well as the possibility of black comrades figuring forcefully in the struggle to build a proletarian vanguard and a politics of class struggle, was always compromised. Central to understanding why this was so is an appreciation of the complexities of party factionalism in the mid- to late 1920s.

Cannon himself had established cordial relations with Claude McKay in Moscow in 1922, but this did not translate into gains for the "trade union" grouping, and next to no African American recruits were won to the Cannon-Foster bloc. Cannon's energies during his Moscow sojourn had been very much concentrated on the issues of legalization and Americanization, and he contributed only marginally and indirectly to the historic discussion of "the Negro Question" in the Fourth Congress of the Communist International,[32] where McKay jousted with the Goose Caucus's black delegate, Otto Huiswoud ("Billing/s"), and in which Rose Pastor Stokes participated. McKay's remarks acknowledged the centrality of racial oppression in the United States and detailed the coercions of the color caste in the American South, insisting that "[t]he situation in American today is terrible and fraught with grave dangers." Claiming that socialists and communists were not immune from racial prejudice, McKay argued forcefully that "the Communists of America have got to overcome the fact that they first have got to emancipate themselves from the ideas they entertained towards the negroes before they can be able to reach the negroes with any kind of radical propaganda." Harking back to the writings of Marx on the Civil War, McKay emblazoned the necessity of emancipation from chattel slavery on the banner of revolutionary struggle against wage slavery, urging the Comintern to convene "a Negro Congress and the Third International will be amazed at the fine material for Communist work there is in the Negro race."[33]

This perspective gradually infused revolutionary ranks in the Workers' Party, and communists participated in the unsuccessful and bourgeois-dominated "All-Race Negro Congress" in Chicago in February 1924.[34] A year and a half later, the American Negro Labor Congress (ANLC) was founded.[35] Its core group consisted of 33 black communist delegates and their close sympathizers; its first flush of curious enthusiasm generated a wider, if somewhat loose, constituency embracing crowds of 500 overflowing a hall in the midst of Chicago's black ghetto. The leading figure behind the congress was a Moscow-trained Bolshevik, Lovett Fort-Whiteman. A graduate of Tuskegee University, and a former drama critic on Cyril Briggs's *The Crusader* and A. Philip Randolph's *The Messenger*, Fort-Whiteman cut a dashing figure on Chicago's south side. Affecting Russia-style dress, he often wore a *robochka* (a man's long belted shirt) draped to his knees, ornamental belt, Cossack boots, and fur hat, his panache of personal presentation complemented by a general flamboyance gained through his training as an actor. Self-centered and somewhat sectarian, determined to allow no competition to threaten his dominance of early communist activity linking labor and African Americans, Fort-Whiteman adapted easily to the factional milieu of the mid-1920s Workers' Party, where established black communists from the African Blood Brotherhood (ABB) referred to him as aligned with the Ruthenberg-Lovestone-Robert Minor forces by a derogatory designation, "Minor's Man Friday." When the Cannon group attempted to cultivate relations with perhaps the leading black trade unionist on the East Coast, longshoreman organizer Ben Fletcher, Fort-Whiteman wanted little to do with the highly successful Philadelphia unionist. Robert Minor and the Ruthenberg faction pandered to this antipathy to Fletcher, perhaps costing the WP an opportunity to build a foundational plank in any black-labor alliance. Fort-Whiteman's impact on the United States scene was cut short, however, by his return to Moscow where, ironically, he was able to indulge his need to be somewhat larger than life, if only for a few years, before he almost certainly and tragically disappeared in the purges of the 1930s.[36]

The American Negro Labor Congress lasted barely five years; its significance lay less in what it did than in what it attempted, which was a revolutionary milestone in the history of race and radicalism. A militant challenge to William Green and the American Federation of Labor, whose craft affiliates often clung to racist exclusion of blacks from union membership, the ANLC was a ringing declaration of African American demand for equality in all spheres of life, including the labor movement. It provided a rare forum for black women to call for the abolition of wide-ranging economic and social discrimination, and linked domestic cries for freedom to the message of anti-imperialism, a cause embraced by C. T. Chin of the Chinese Students' Alliance, who addressed the ANLC on capitalism and colonialism at a well-attended evening session of the first "Negro Workers' Congress" in 1925. And, of course, the ANLC proved a relentless voice against all forms of racist lynch-law terror directed against the masses of blacks in both the North and the South.

In Chicago, the ANLC had a substantial, if limited, core membership, but elsewhere in the country it proved difficult to generate support, in part because the organization was repeatedly scapegoated as a "communist" body. By the end of the 1920s, the ANLC boasted only 5 active chapters and 180 members.[37] Indeed, the pioneering labor-black alliance was an almost wholly owned sub-sidiary of the Workers' Party, and within that framework it belonged largely to the Ruthenberg-Lovestone faction, where Robert Minor was a central player in "Negro work," assigned by the CEC to oversee issues relating to race. Minor and his wife, Lydia Gibson, turned their Chicago apartment into an interracial salon, were active in tenants' struggles that brought them in contact with black militants, and supported trade union work in which African Americans were centrally involved in various struggles. Personal endeavors greased the wheels of the African Blood Brotherhood machinery, easing Cyril Briggs, Otto Huis-woud, Fort-Whiteman, H. V. Phillips, Richard B. Moore, the brothers Otto Hall and Harry Haywood, and others into leading posts in "Negro work" in the 1920s. There they placed their mark on struggles for housing, lower hours, pan-Africanism, and anti-imperialism, stimulating campaigns and touching class uprisings with the color of race awareness. If recruits were few, there were those, such as George Padmore (Malcolm Meredith Nurse), destined to occupy piv-otal ground in the making of black Marxism.[38]

A critical problem thus plagued the black-communist relation in the mid-1920s. As Winston James has suggested, and Harry Haywood long ago noted, blacks entered the Workers' Party in an odd way. Locals of the Workers' Party

often contained members who had difficulty shedding the deeply and historically embedded white skin of racial prejudice/privilege, and even leaders of the
contending party factions were not immune from shortcomings in their grasp
of the significance of race in labor and Left circles, where a residue of the Socialist Party's inadequacies on appreciation of the place of African Americans in
the struggle for socioeconomic transformation remained. Nonetheless, the
advanced cadre of black revolutionaries who made their way into the communist movement, most often in the early years from the African Blood Brotherhood, started this journey of 1919–1925 affiliation with the strong belief that the
Bolshevik Revolution and the Comintern were the vanguard of an anti-colonial
multinational army, struggling to rid the world of class *and* race exploitation.
Black recruits to the Workers' Party thus joined less to enter the ranks of American communism than to affiliate with the party of the Communist International and world revolution. This impetus behind black recruitment meant that
African Americans never fully engaged in the political struggle to realign the
WP in the 1920s. Their loyalties were to Moscow. No doubt the factionalism of
this period left many black communists cold, but it could not be escaped, and
was put to particular use. There is no question that the initial personal connections, and a genuine willingness to address material matters of relevance to
African Americans, sealed an early relationship of blacks and the Ruthenberg
wing of the WP, in which Otto Huiswoud, Robert Minor, and Lydia Gibson figured prominently. Max Bedacht, a Ruthenberg lieutenant who used the pseudonym "Marshall," forged a 1923 entree of the ABB into the communist ranks,
easing the Brotherhood's financial problems with payments to fund an office
and forums run jointly by the WP and the militant black organization. It was
not long before the independent voice of the ABB was gone, its leadership
incorporated into the communist movement. Perceived from without as an
appendage to the Ruthenberg group, and from within as committed to the
cause of the Communist International, the possibilities of the development of
African American communists as a Marxist cadre *within* the United States were
thus overshadowed by a race question that was never accorded the serious consideration it merited. In later years, some black recruits extended this process to
direct (and long-standing) loyalty to Stalin, whom they perceived as the leading
Comintern figure responsible for pressing the United States revolutionary Left
to address the "Negro Question."[39]

As a consequence, black membership in the Workers (Communist) Party
throughout the 1920s never tipped the scales at much over fifty, to take a figure
often thrown about by party insiders.[40] This poor showing appeared all the
more dismal given the mass base for "race pride" evident in the Universal
Negro Improvement Association of Marcus Garvey and the effervescence of

African American culture associated with the "New Negro" and literary movements such as the Harlem Renaissance. A black contingent of communist
leaders, well versed in *all* aspects of Marxist theory and practice and active in
party leadership (broadly conceived), never cohered and, indeed, seemed distant from the concerns of any WP or Communist Party faction. In 1924, a Central Executive Committee vote to raise a mere $100 to send a black delegate to
the Congress of the Communist International—it being understood that the
remainder of the funds would be raised by the comrade himself—lost by a six-
to-five margin. As with women's work, the Workers' Party was resistant to
acknowledging the "special oppression" afflicting the black working class, and
even the African Blood Brotherhood, a central recruiting ground for the WP
during this period, was regarded rather cavalierly by the Central Executive
Committee; in 1924 it was decided "we should not make it a major factor in
our work among the Negroes but carry on the work as at present thru Workers party channels."[41] The Ruthenberg group's attraction to African Americans
registered factionally less through a principled development of programmatic
understandings than through a prejudicial construction of the Cannon-Foster
group as "opportunist, narrow-minded trade unionists lacking in Marxist theory and hence in the ability to lead a Marxist Party." Few black communists
could discern much difference between the contending factions as policy
issues were actually debated.[42]

Not until 1928, when James Ford, a future Foster ally, stood aloof from the
factional groupings, and the Stalinized Comintern veered into the theoretically problematic but perhaps ideologically attractive posture of the national-
istic right of self-determination of American Negroes in the southern Black
Belt, did "the Negro Question" actually appear to be manifestly on the agenda
of United States communists.[43] By that point, however, the waters of class and
race had been muddied by African American suspicions of Lovestone.[44] Disappointment at the ANLC's failure to secure advances for labor and black
organization, Stalinist informal influence prodding black communists in the
direction of the Black Belt nation "theory," and the Cannon group's inability to
move beyond Bill Dunne's compromised characterizations of Negro oppression as little more than a subset of the generally poor lot of the United States
working class,[45] kept the race question politically cornered in a factionalized
communist milieu.

Dunne, the Cannon group's expert on race, had a mixed record of accomplishment in this regard, not unlike an entire generation of trade union militants whose formative engagement with the "Negro Question" took place
within the Socialist Party. Connected closely with emerging black communist
leaders such as Harry Haywood,[46] Dunne was nevertheless regarded, as was

Foster, as too limited in his critique of the craft-led American Federation of Labor unions, many of which had racist, lily-white membership clauses. Heckled on occasion as a racist,[47] Dunne simply could not acknowledge that there was much to struggle against in terms of a communist program for black equality, and tended to bury the race question in a mechanical opposition to dual unionism: "If we are opposed to dual unionism in general, then we can not be in favor of parallel Negro unions. Certainly racial antagonism exists, but the best way to fight it will be by accepting white and black workers into one organization, not by mobilizing the Negroes on one side of the barrier and whites on the other." Citing the example of the United Mine Workers of America and, rather fantastically, the building trades unions, Dunne claimed that, "In those industries where Negroes work, they are admitted into the unions as members with equal rights," a position that could only have been put forward with a straight face in Comintern meetings, far from the actualities of American conditions.[48] No black communist would have swallowed silently this cover-up of racial animosity in trade union circles. Although Dunne did author a series of important articles on African American oppression in the *Workers Monthly* and elsewhere, his orientation tucked the race card into the large deck of working-class exploitation, where it was lost to the Cannon group in the factional hands of the 1920s.[49]

Indeed, by the late 1920s Workers (Communist) Party initiatives around race were far more likely to come from the likes of Pepper who, under the pseudonym "J. Swift," submitted a statement, "Policies on Negro Work," to the Political Committee at the end of May 1928. Pepper would later figure in the development of American communism's rapprochement with black nationalist aspirations, contributing to the exploration of African American self-determination in articles that appeared after discussions at the Negro Commission of the Sixth World Congress of the Comintern in the summer of 1928. Pepper's formulation of the need for "the establishment of a Negro Soviet Republic" represented a repudiation of his earlier stands on the prospects of black self-determination in the United States. The consummate opportunist, Pepper quickly adapted to Comintern directive and the influential arguments of Harry Haywood. While overreaching himself in ways that would finally help to seal his fate within the CI, he nevertheless set part of the stage on which many American communists accommodated themselves to the idea of a Black Belt Negro nation, premised on the population density of blacks in sectors of the American South and the special oppression that was the daily lot of African Americans.[50] Cannon, Dunne, and their faction were left unmistakably behind in the rush to draft "innovative" programmatic statements on the black question. Not until 1933 would Cannon and his allies clarify their ambivalences with respect to the Black

Belt nation thesis and the issue of self-determination for African Americans.[51] That Lovestone and Wolfe, the Cannon faction's resolute opponents in the late 1920s, regarded the self-determination bandwagon as something of a deviation from Marxist analytic principles—a reverse "Jim Crowism" that flew directly in the face of the aspirations of American blacks—perhaps facilitated the acceptance of the thesis in certain quarters. Ironically, the original African Blood Brotherhood cadre found little to its liking in the Black Belt Nation proposition, the exception being Harry Haywood. Otto Huiswoud opposed the program of self-determination forcefully, and there is no doubt that it registered weakly, if at all, with noncommunist blacks.[52]

Small wonder, then, that with this configuration of forces and the stunted programmatic development of "the Negro Question" within the Cannon circle, Dunne and others adapted so readily to the programmatic confusions of the Black Belt thesis in 1928.[53] As Cannon would later concede, the Workers' Party approach to race, which it was pushed to address by the early Comintern, was a revolutionary advance, a breakaway from past decades of socialist abstentionism, that was nevertheless unable to translate into concrete gains in the arenas of either theory or mass work:

> The American communists in the early days, under the influence and pressure of the Russians in the Comintern, were slowly and painfully learning to change their *attitude;* to assimilate the new theory of the Negro question as a *special* question of doubly-exploited second-class citizens, requiring a program of special demands as part of the over-all program—and to start doing something about it. ... Everybody knew that the Negro was getting the worst of it at every turn, but hardly anybody cared about it or wanted to do anything to try to moderate or change it. The 90 percent white majority of American society, including its working class sector, North as well as South, was saturated with prejudice against the Negro; and the socialist movement reflected this prejudice to a considerable extent—even though, in deference to the ideal of human brotherhood, the socialist attitude was muted and took the form of evasion. The old theory of American radicalism turned out in practice to be a formula for inaction on the Negro front, and—incidentally—a convenient shield for the dominant racial prejudices of the white radicals themselves ... But the Russians followed up year after year, piling up the arguments and increasing the pressure on the American communists until they finally learned and changed, and went to work in earnest. And the change in attitude of the American communists, gradually effected in the Twenties, was to exert a profound influence *in far wider circles* in the later years.[54]

Just how much factionalism in the communist movement contributed to this slow development is impossible to calculate with precision, but it was undoubtedly a factor. The "Negro Question," by 1928 stalled in a series of routinized gestures, of which the Black Belt Nation thesis was perhaps the most extreme, would not be revived until a wave of anti-racist agitations through-out the early 1930s—anti-lynching campaigns, Scottsboro Boys mobilizations, and unemployment agitations—actively established that communists were committed to African American liberation.[55]

Pepper, Bureaucratism, and Permanent Factionalism

As Cannon constructed a bloc with Foster throughout the first months of 1924, there were those in the Workers' Party leadership who saw him as the engine of factional intrigue. Lovestone, for instance, later wrote to the Com-intern complaining that "[t]he seeds of the present factional struggle were sown when Comrade Cannon returned from the Fourth Congress of the Comintern and stubbornly pursued . . . opposition to a policy of unity and assimilation, as it was being presented and put through by Comrade Pepper," explaining that the one group in the party that could not be integrated was the liquidationist trade unionists.[56] Others, however, turned to Cannon; one fig-ure in a foreign-language federation wrote, "Our party functions badly. The membership is sick at heart. A healing hand is necessary to reform our ranks, inspire confidence and instill some activity. . . . The sores will expose them-selves later. A good eye can discern them now."[57] Within leading Workers' Party committees, it was all too evident that the acrimonious alignments that had preceded the December-January Chicago convention continued well into 1924.[58] The factional rigidities of the period expressed themselves in pro forma votes in the highest of WP bodies, and the crossfire of competing motions and amendments was transparently partisan. Ruthenberg declared a war that all knew could only be settled abroad, as he announced in the CEC of 15–16 February 1924 that to avoid further debilitating "factional struggle . . . a repre-sentative delegation [would] be sent to Moscow immediately to present the matter to the Executive Committee of the Communist International."[59]

Cannon tended to see these bloc rigidities in either/or formulations rooted in nebulous understandings of class *character*,[60] entirely restricted to the dif-ferentiated layers of American communist leadership. This was a limited perspective that allowed him, and others with whom he was aligned, to per-sonalize the programmatic crisis of the party in a view of John Pepper's prob-lematic influence on revolutionary leadership. There was something to this visceral opposition to Pepper, of course, precisely because the irrepressible Pogany was producing some truly bizarre political formulations. On a deeper level, however, Pepper was the archetype of the machinations that were begin-ning to characterize the Comintern in this period.

Indeed, the leading Comintern figure, Gregory Zinoviev, had an appetite for bureaucratic centralism, as well as a personal connection to its emerging human face in America, John Pepper. Zinoviev was close to a coterie of exiled Hungarians around the Moscow-ensconced Bela Kun, of whom Pepper was one, and these forces were animated in the post-1919 defeat of the central European Revolution by what a young Georg Lukacs described as "messianic sectarianism." Kun sought to establish an ultra-centralized Hungarian Communist Party built up among those around him who had been forced to flee right-wing repression. This party, which Kun contended could function in the Hungary of the early to mid-1920s only in conditions of underground illegality, was purposively "a movement from above, directly from Moscow." Eventually this orientation was challenged and repudiated by another Hungarian communist faction (also in exile), led by Eugen/Jeno Landler and Lukacs. Like Cannon, they argued forcefully for the need to break out of bureaucratic utopianism; connect with the mass struggles of the workers; and intersect other noncommunist, socialist forces. Their orientation, in the particularly repressive aftermath of the Hungarian Revolution's 1919 defeat and the consolidation of the dictatorship of Admiral Horthy, was a judicious blend of underground work and legal agitation.

All of this fed into the "official Marxist" repudiation of Lukacs's *History and Class Consciousness,* a compilation of previously-written but extensively revised essays first published in 1923. The text was welcomed in certain literary and philosophical circles of the European Left, but generated blunt hostility in Comintern quarters, including a short, dismissive review by Bela Kun. The orchestrated assault on Lukacs's essays, which wrongly associated their thought with Trotsky's Left Opposition, provided something of an aesthetic preface to a mid-1920s hardening bureaucratism in the Communist International, culminating in an intellectual mugging of the Hungarian critical theorist by Zinoviev at the Fifth Congress of the CI in 1924. A recently unearthed lost manuscript, Lukacs's *Tailism and the Dialectic,* written in 1925–1926, and penned in opposition to this rough repudiation, indicates that Lukacs's later embrace of Stalinism was not a foregone conclusion. It provides a theoretical parallel to the organizational positions embraced by Landler and Lukacs, arguing strongly that the class consciousness that develops within the proletariat is not inevitable. Rather, the making of class consciousness is a dialectical process in which the relations of objective material conditions, the subjective activity of the working class, *and* the interventions of a revolutionary party are *the* critical conjuncture. This was, of course, exactly the practical premise of Cannon's positions. Eventually the Landler-Lukacs group prevailed in the rebuilding of the Hungarian Party, but this localized programmatic consolidation was soon overshadowed by developments in the larger and ultimately more determining Communist International. Zinoviev's direction of the Comintern in this period was influenced by the Kun circle, and, in the United States, Pepper's place of significance was undoubtedly buttressed.

In any case, led by Zinoviev, after 1924 the CI embarked on a series of bureaucratically orchestrated adventures that initiated the shift of the Comintern from a Leninist body of world revolution to an unduly centralizing force that too often suffocated national initiatives and increasingly subordinated sections of the CI to the perceived needs of a program of "socialism in one country." Pepper's rise within the ranks of the Communist International was thus emblematic of this larger problem. Knowledge of these Hungarian developments within the Comintern, and Zinoviev's connections, would have helped Cannon and others situate Pepper and appreciate the bureaucratism developing at the pinnacle of the Communist International. "I was preoccupied with 'our own' American questions at that time," Cannon later confessed, "and did not know, or even suspect, that the fate of our party was so directly involved in the Russian party struggle." A living articulation of the nascent degeneration of the Russian Revolution, Pepper appropriated class politics to the cause of his particular personal power, and actually anticipated Stalin in his willingness to adapt the programmatic orientation of the revolutionary movement to cynical, if often cleverly formulated, "theoretical" pronouncements, which could oscillate wildly given their foundation in a willingness to subordinate principle and position to the needs of the moment. Cannon could not possibly have grasped the totality of Pepper's meaning as early as 1924, and during this period (and for a few years thereafter) he "fumbled and stumbled in the dark like all the others."[61]

Fresh from the convention victory of late 1923, Cannon reacted with resentment when Pepper refused to take seriously the vote of thirty-seven to fifteen against his political positions; the implacable "Comintern rep" treated the defeat as an expression of mere impudence on the part of the Cannon forces.[62] On the ground in Moscow, Foster wrote a detailed letter to Zinoviev, outlining Pepper's destructive impact on the American Party.[63] Securing the support of the Central Executive Committee majority, Cannon and Foster led the move to purge Pepper in the winter of 1924, issuing a 27 March declaration to the ECCI that Pepper be recalled, "the welfare of the American Party imperatively" demanding such a course.[64]

A loyal Cominternist, Cannon ironically fought the tendency toward bureaucratic opportunism that was manifesting itself in the Comintern and within the Workers' Party through Pepper within the Central Executive Committee. He built a faction in opposition to unduly "theoretical" poseurs such as Pepper, yet appealed to Zinoviev's Comintern for guidance, relied on its judgment, and became one of American communism's most ardent advocates of what would come to be the position of the Fifth Congress of the Communist International on Bolshevization.[65] Addressing a Sunday evening gathering at the New York Workers' School in early October 1924, Cannon presented the case for a "monolithic party hewn of one piece," endorsing the Comintern directive that its sections must be "centralized" and prohibit "factions, tendencies, and groups." Explaining the failures of the Workers' Party to do just this, Cannon laid the blame of deformation at the feet of an incomplete assimilation of "Marxism and Leninism."[66]

It was an odd mix, to be sure, but it contained a certain logic. "The influence of Moscow" Cannon regarded as "a perfectly natural thing." Trotsky, Radek, Zinoviev, and Lenin had tilted the scales against the underground ultraleft in 1922, and Cannon and other U.S. revolutionaries were understandably willing to trust in the "influence and authority of the Russian party." Max Eastman's *Since Lenin Died* (1925) had not yet been published, and until its appearance (the meaning of which was muddied by Trotsky's repudiation, undertaken so as to be able to continue the Left Opposition's work within the Soviet Union), there was little indication of the degeneration of the Communist International in the United States.[67] And so Cannon clung to the record of a revolutionary past, and the Comintern within which it was embodied; he had seen these forces pull the American movement back from its sectarian tendency to self-immolate in 1922, and he thought all wrongs would be righted, ultimately, in this same manner.

Farmer-Laborism, Again

During the spring of 1924, however, the layering of developments and complexity of politics associated with the bureaucratization of the Comintern, the incoherence of the Workers' Party program, and the relationship of Russian authority and American activity—all of which congealed in the crisis of revolutionary leadership and a state of permanent factionalism—began to take discernible shape. A precipitating factor was the long-simmering issue of the communist orientation to the Farmer-Labor Party. Farmer-laborism would prove the weak link in a chain that secured Moscow, New York, and Chicago in ways that revealed the initial irreconcilability of Stalin and Trotsky in the aftermath of Lenin's death on 21 January 1924.[68] Moreover, the issues associated with farmer-labor politics would expose the most fragile component of the Cannon-Foster bloc's secure control of the CEC, Ludwig Lore.

Something of a factional truce had been worked out by the Foster-Cannon and Ruthenberg-Pepper groups around the question of the Farmer-Labor Party in the aftermath of the disastrous break with the Chicago Federation of Labor Fitzpatrick-Nockels leadership and the fiasco at the July 1923 Federated Farmer-Labor Party convention.[69] With the aging reform maverick Robert M. LaFollette's 1924 campaign for the United States presidency endorsed by the Conference for Progressive Political Action (CPPA) and giving rise to a third-party movement joined by socialists, farm groups, the American Federation of Labor, and individuals such as W. E. B. DuBois and Margaret Sanger,[70] the Workers' Party's divided leadership rallied to the seeming possibilities present in the newly charged political arena. Between January and April of 1924, Pepper elaborated further his convoluted 1923 conception of the meaning of the LaFollette "revolution," and constructed a rationale for what the communists would characterize as a "Third Party alliance." The arcane analytic justification for this opaque politics was one of Pepper's usual interpretive leaps, the theory of "the two splits." Thus, for a revolution to develop in America it was necessary to split the petty bourgeoisie from the bourgeoisie (the LaFollette movement) and then to further split the working class from the petty bourgeoisie (through the creation of the *class* Farmer-Labor Party). This conception managed to unite the leading figures in the Workers' Party in 1923–1924. Worn down by the "factional gang warfare" of party committees, many were searching for common ground rather than looking for points of difference.

The Foster-Cannon group, in particular, found the two-split notion to their liking, interpreting it in light of demarcations that would emerge between leaders and led in the American Federation of Labor, opening windows of opportunity for militants in the trade unions, and shoring up the flagging fortunes of the Trade Union Educational League, which was taking a beating with the downturn in class struggle. To this end Cannon and Foster helped in orchestrating the WP's involvement in two 1923–1924 conventions, held in St. Paul, Minnesota, in November 1923 and June 1924, awkwardly developing a united front of communists and left farmers in a Farmer-Labor Federation.[71] The WP also looked forward with anticipation to the LaFollette nomination convention, scheduled symbolically to take place in Cleveland on Independence Day, 1924. Plagued by many of the same difficulties that had torn apart the Federated Farmer-Labor Party orchestrations of the year before, the delicate and difficult WP balance of both strongly criticizing and supporting LaFollette at the same time was something of a political tightrope, drawn more taut by LaFollette's refusal to endorse a "labor party." This he judged "class," not "independent politics." In the end, as we will see in more detail later, this tightly-stretched WP orientation would snap.[72]

Factionalism's Enigmatic Fulcrum: Ludwig Lore

The holdout over this embrace of "a Third Party alliance" and further entanglement in farmer-labor adventures was Lore, who headed a complicated mix
of Jewish trade union communists and long-established German American
socialists embedded in the International Ladies Garment Workers Union that
included Juliet Stuart Poyntz, Charles Zimmerman, and Moissaye J. Olgin.
Lore, whose revolutionary history in the United States embraced time as a
Wobbly; close connection with Trotsky in 1917, when the two collaborated
around the newspaper *Novy Mir;* an early editorial alliance with Fraina and
Boudin; and governance of the daily voice of German leftism, the *New Yorker
Volkszeitung,* was known for his independent-mindedness. As Paul Buhle has
indicated, Lore's literary and cultural contribution to the continuities of German American socialism was, by the 1920s, prodigious. However, Lore was at
root a Left social democrat and, like many of the first-wave supporters of the
Russian Left Oppositionists (such as Boris Souvarine in France and Paul Levi
in Germany), was resistant to Leninism and democratic centralism. In time,
his defense of Trotsky would be a personal and democratic one, distanced
from the fusion of Bolshevik organizational understandings and Marxist programmatic direction that animated Trotsky. Over the first few months of 1924,
Lore used the pages of the *Volkszeitung* to offer up a volatile cocktail of inflam-
matory characterization. If it lacked a clear-cut political direction, it nevertheless added vociferously to the factional stew of the Workers' Party.[73]

Originally Lore championed the Foster-Cannon bloc and its coup at the
Third Convention of the WP in 1923 as a victory for Trotsky, whose nascent
oppositional voice early in 1924 was not yet widely perceived to be pitted decisively against Stalin. A direct opponent of Comintern head Zinoviev, whose
stature in international communist circles eclipsed that of all other Bolshevik
leaders, Lore's rather scattered articulations of dissent praised Trotsky's inclinations without grasping fully or assimilating with sophistication his programmatic conceptualizations and critiques of rightward movements within
European communist circles.[74] He soon graduated to a March 1924 assault on
the "opportunistic" lack of "guiding principles" within the Comintern.[75] Lore
thus fell into almost immediate disfavor among all factions of the communist
leadership in the United States, for whom criticism of the Russian comrades
was tantamount to heresy. The enmity of Zinoviev, Radek, and others in the CI
hierarchy was, of course, quick to develop.[76]

Paralleling these developments was the Cannon-Foster bloc's struggle to
have Pepper recalled. Given that Lore was a pivotal support for the Chicago
assemblage of trade unionists that now, along with Cannon, formed a precar-

ious majority on the Central Executive Committee, he was soon targeted by Pepper.[77] Pepper and Trotsky had crossed polemical swords at the 1921 Third Congress of the Communist International, the former parroting Bukharin's ultraleft position that the revolutionary Left must continue to exploit openings arising as a consequence of civil war and widespread social crises, fomenting class struggle at every possible opportunity. This "offensive" orientation was embraced by Zinoviev, but its most ardent advocate was Bela Kun, Pepper's former Hungarian comrade. Lenin and Trotsky had a more sober assessment of the realities of the period, accepting that in the aftermath of World War I, and with the disciplining of revolutionaries and a militant international workers' movement during 1919–1921, the bourgeoisie had successfully purchased for itself a "breathing space" in which to consolidate power. Trotsky gave Pepper a tongue-lashing, offering a harsh indictment of the central European adventurer, and the Hungarian exile never forgot or forgave the humiliation. Quick to appreciate the way the winds were beginning to blow in the early 1924 Comintern, the adaptable Pepper was characteristically fast out of the polemical gate with the initial hint of official condemnation of Trotsky, being one of the first to mouth Zinoviev's deprecation of the formerly exalted leader of the Red Army. When Cannon scotched Pepper's efforts to publish a *Liberator* article on "the old Guard Bolsheviks" (Zinoviev, Kamenev, and Stalin), the grounds being that not enough was known about "some" of these people, Pepper began to "raise the issue" more widely in the party, "calling for condemnation of Trotsky and his views." In March 1924, with Lore's anti-Comintern journalism now a matter of public record, Pepper upped the ante, demanding a full airing of the contentious issues in the Executive Council and in the Central Executive Committee, putting forward motions that demanded all loyalties consolidate around Zinoviev and the Russian party and calling for censure of Lore. Protected for a time by Cannon and Foster, Lore was now on the defensive; his days as a leading figure in the Workers' Party hierarchy were clearly numbered; and the Cannon-Foster bloc had been dealt a serious blow, both in terms of a potential weakening of its majority and in a Comintern "guilt by association" that would stick with both leaders for years to come.[78]

Comintern Changes

The Foster-Cannon group still had sufficient credibility in Moscow, especially with the head of the RILU, Lozovsky, to secure Pepper's recall, and the disappointed émigré prepared in April 1924 to depart the United States. He did not go empty-handed. Having organized the Ruthenberg faction to close ranks, he had Gitlow and others write to Zinoviev to shore up their leadership credentials, attack Foster, and extol the virtues of Pepper. Along with Pepper, Foster and Olgin traveled to Moscow to plead the case of the majority. It was a wasted trip. The entire political program of the Workers' Party as it related to the "Third Party alliance" was soon jettisoned.[79] To be sure, Pepper was exiled from the United States, but he readily ensconced himself in Moscow, delivering key addresses at the Fifth Congress of the Comintern, where he enjoyed showboating as a ranking American delegate, and secured for himself the administrative post of head of the International's new Information Department. Nevertheless, the Workers' Party found itself on the short end of the political stick with respect to the farmer-labor issue, with which it had been preoccupied for many months. Trotsky's critique of the American party's position on LaFollette had just been aired and accepted in the Comintern, and he singled out the Pepper-orchestrated but widely accepted "Third Party alliance" orientation of the United States communists as a glaring example of opportunistic adaptation to petty bourgeois elements.[80]

The better to bury the depth of the German revolutionary debacle of 1923, Zinoviev and other leading Cominternists veered to the left, conveniently using the American communists' deviations to cover their own sins. The United States section, slapped on the wrist for its misguided LaFollette orientation, was called to order. This Comintern embrace of Trotsky's Workers' Party critique was in fact used, ironically, to deflate the significance of a Left Opposition whose positions were usefully incorporated the better to marginalize their leading exponents. The American comrades were expected to offer their support in the emerging anti-Trotskyist campaign. Cannon's old friend Charlie Scott called on Ruthenberg to greet the Thirteenth Congress of the Russian Communist Party with a telegram supporting "the old Bolsheviks," which at the time was a coded embrace of Stalin's superiority over Trotsky. At the Fifth Congress, the task of presenting the resolution denouncing Trotsky fell to the Americans. Foster followed the prudent course. He backtracked on LaFollette, abandoning not only any notion of an alliance but dropping, as well, the seemingly "hot-potato" support for the emergence of a farmer-labor party. Upon his return to the United States in June 1924, resolutions in praise of the "old Bolsheviks" were passed in the Central Executive Committee by a vote of twelve to one, Lore being the singular dissenter.

Lore stood alone in more ways than one. Ironically enough, he had anticipated the Comintern's repudiation of the LaFollette Third Party alliance and should, logically, have been elevated in the estimation of his comrades, with whom he had engaged in an ongoing debate over the wisdom of dancing on the head of a "splitting" thesis that left the Workers' Party prone to incorporation into campaigns of the "progressive" bourgeoisie. In April 1924, for instance, Cannon and Bittelman had publicly put themselves at odds with Lore and Olgin, defending the communist orientation toward the third-party movement and stressing the possibilities that political developments in 1924 presented for differentiating the bourgeoisie/petty bourgeoisie/workers. Their position was no different from that of anyone on the CEC, but Cannon's remarks before a meeting of the South Slavic Federation generated specific Comintern comment, bordering on censure. Cannon was forewarned that he now skated on thin ice as far as Russian officialdom was concerned.[81]

Still, it was Lore who committed the sin not only of espousing Trotsky, but of defying the authority of the Communist International. That high crime was sufficient to condemn him to oblivion in Comintern circles. Radek, at the time aligned with Trotsky, denounced Lore's ostensible social patriotism, and called for his removal from the Central Executive Committee, urging as well that a campaign of vilification be directed against him. Lore was now a casualty of his own mercurial politics and a heavy-handed Zinovievist appreciation of the coercive potential of Bolshevization. "As regards Lore," stated Zinoviev, "I really do not know whether he belongs in the CEC."[82]

In Cannon's eyes, Lore was never assimilated thoroughly to a politics of communism, the German-language leader being ensconced in his own editorial principality and given to the indiscipline of the "free lance." He thus barely blinked at the rough treatment meted out to the long-established editor. With Pepper gone and the Comintern having zeroed in on Lore, Cannon had some space, for the first time in years, to try to Leninize and professionalize the Workers' Party apparatus. He had heard Lenin's address to the 1922 Fourth Congress of the Communist International, the second part of which concerned itself with the need for western comrades to transform the organization of their parties. Strictures to Bolshevize, in the aftermath of this speech, were taken in communist circles as admonitions to follow Lenin's guidelines, and Cannon had long embraced the need for such tightening up of party procedure. He moved into an ardent embrace of the Fifth Congress's injunction to Bolshevize the American section, promoting the registration of all industrial comrades in shop nuclei. Cannon dedicated himself to "strive by all means to weld the forces of our party into a single piece of metal that becomes harder in the struggle." He pursued this end, as well, in addressing coal miner members of the Workers' Party in St. Louis, Missouri, and in his work as chairman of the party's Education Committee. He promoted the Bolshevization of the Workers' School, insisting that party instructors be closely supervised by the Central Executive Committee and see their primary task as educating the WP membership in "the doctrine and spirit of Leninism." Not content to view the Workers' School as a "neutral academy standing between various tendencies,"

Cannon insisted that educational work be "a fighting instrument for the Bolshevization of the Party . . . [,] a weapon . . . in the struggle against all deviations from the line of the Communist International."[83]

Cannon, interestingly enough, thus embraced the two-edged sword of early Bolshevization. On the one hand, he eagerly tried to implement those measures of the policy that would strengthen communist capacity to create a disciplined Leninist vanguard, a party that would register all the more effectively in the class struggle of the United States. Much of Bolshevization was thus necessary and a valuable corrective to a certain looseness in revolutionary practice that had been common in the United States (and elsewhere) since the underground period. On the other hand, there can be no doubt that, in the climate of Comintern bureaucratization and nascent Stalinization, Bolshevization also contributed to the forceful push into slavish adherence to "Moscow authority."

Not surprisingly, then, Cannon shifted gears on the LaFollette "Third Party alliance" orientation as soon as the word came down in late May 1924 from the Fifth Congress of the Communist International that support of a progressive bourgeois politician was nothing more than a misadventure of the American Workers' Party. In March 1924, Cannon reviewed a February 1924 gathering of the Conference of Progressive Political Action. Highly critical of its labor-aristocratic leadership, Cannon nevertheless espoused the position of the Central Executive Committee that there remained some possibility that the CPPA, now a cabal of trade union tops constituting a virtual LaFollette nominating machine, might be pressured into joining forces with the Farmer-Labor Party of the exploited agrarians and rank-and-file working-class militants if only the forthcoming St. Paul convention could galvanize a *class* alternative.[84] His May 1924 article in the *Labor Herald*, "St. Paul—June 17th," signaled the changing perspective, preparing the way for a decisive break from LaFollette and the CPPA that would not have been apparent in pre-April pronouncements of the Workers' Party. Declaring "St. Paul Means Class Struggle," Cannon argued that it was the duty of all communists to "press the labor traitors [of the CPPA] to the wall, and organize a fight against their treachery." The forthcoming June 17 gathering at St. Paul was dedicated to "one point": concentrating "the whole struggle of the rank and file of exploited labor against the capitalists, the capitalist government and the agents of the capitalists in the labor movement."[85] Cannon thus adapted rather easily and uncritically to Comintern directives, paying little attention to the price that would be paid in an intensified labor anti-communism. The pressures and shifting nature of 1924 factionalism no doubt blinded him to what he had been able to see more clearly in the 1923 farmer-labor entanglements.

Bolshevization and Electoral Campaigns

If the leadership factions within the Workers' Party assimilated the new position rather effortlessly, problems soon emerged in whipping more distant
comrades and allies into shape. Cannon had to travel to Minnesota to meet
with those spearheading the Farmer-Labor Party movement in the Midwest,
and the fallout was almost immediate. The standard-bearer of the mobilization was a staunch farmer-laborite editor, William Mahoney, whose relationship with communists grew increasingly precarious as the Workers' Party
shifted gears. The farmer-labor forces convening in St. Paul, Minnesota, in
mid-June 1924, nominated Duncan MacDonald, a mine union official, for
president, and William Bouck of the Washington state Farmer-Labor Party
Federation for vice president, whereupon Mahoney threw in the towel and
urged that all progressives gravitate to LaFollette.

The farmer-labor "united front" was now irreparably divided, and the CEC
of the Workers' Party opted, on 8 July 1924, to run its own candidates in the
1924 election, Foster and Gitlow. Cannon stood for Governor of New York. He
announced the turn to fielding candidates under the banner of communism,
and withdrawing all Workers' Party support for farmer-labor party federations, at an early July "national conference" to nominate presidential and vice
presidential candidates, as well as in a 29 July 1924 article in the *Daily Worker*.
Communists who balked at the abrupt "turn" away from farmer-laborism
were told to follow discipline and get behind the party.[86]

As events unfolded in the fall of 1924, the Foster-Cannon group drifted
increasingly away from anything approaching support for the labor party, and
Cannon later conceded that "we did bend the stick backward in the course of
the conflict and . . . began to show a decided sectarian trend." In his propaganda campaign in New York, initiated in a September push to secure representation on the ballot, Cannon hammered away at supposed Socialist Party
willingness to do LaFollette's bidding. Communist accounts in the *Daily
Worker* alluded to the political struggle against a "motley army of enemies of
the workers, against the exploiters, the LaFollette-Tammany alliance, and the
latter's socialist fig leaf."

The campaign for governor began with three mass meetings in the first
week of October. Adopting an increasingly critical stand toward all third-party
activity, Cannon pilloried the Socialist Party leader, Norman Thomas (also
running for governor), as taking his orders from LaFollette, and LaFollette as
taking his orders from the bourgeoisie. The Workers' Party candidate also
attacked the "Tammany" candidate, Democrat Al Smith, as a "labor foe," and
conducted an end-of-October "Red Nights" blitz of speeches at various New

York City halls, capped by a "Monster Rally" of all communist candidates in the Lower East Side's Rutgers Square, on Second Street at the corner of Avenue B. Politics, in 1924, was a case of Tweedledum and Tweedledee. When the final electoral count was in, Calvin Coolidge had outpaced all rivals, amassing 15,720,000 votes—almost double those of his opponent who, in turn, outdistanced LaFollette by a margin of about 2:1. Foster's 33,000 presidential votes were 0.68 percent of his third-party rival's and 0.2 percent of Coolidge's tally. The Foster-Cannon majority now considered "the labor party a dead issue," and by the end of the year had moved into an aggressive opposition to what it labeled "farmer-laborism."[87]

At the 5 November 1924 meeting of the Political Committee, Browder submitted a lengthy statement dissecting the meanings of the recent "Coolidge or Chaos" political campaign. Cannon, Foster, Bittelman, and Browder saw the election as indicative of just how cowed the American working class really was, but their document struck hardest in its repudiation of the very possibility of now building a "Mass Farmer-Labor Party." As Cannon would later stress in internal party documents, the task of the hour was to create a new psychology among the Workers' Party ranks. Ringing declarations of the imminent appearance of a "mass labor party" and a "mass Communist Party" had taken their toll, Cannon suggested, because advances of this magnitude had not occurred, leaving the ranks of the Workers' Party demoralized. If the 1924 election confirmed, in the Cannon-Foster group's eyes, the validity of the Communist International's directives to abandon the LaFollette ship, there was now the need to come back decisively to the shore of actual political conditions: "The demonstrated weakness of the LaFollette movement, compared to the pre-election estimates of all sides, not only seriously retards the development of the third party movement, but also completely eliminates the immediate possibility of the growth of a mass farmer-labor party of industrial workers and poor farmers, distinct from the Workers Party." This the Ruthenberg-Lovestone minority could not abide, and they protested vigorously the attempt to reformulate party policy "in the form of five or six sentences in a manifesto."[88] As Browder wrote to Lozovsky, "We told them to go to hell. We are going to have a Bolshevik Party, not a goddamned job trust or priesthood."[89]

Neither faction adequately addressed the costly fallout from the Workers' Party flip-flop on farmer-laborism.[90] Communist relations with progressive elements, such as Minnesota's William Mahoney, were now soured forever. Mahoney had bucked the rising tide of labor anti-communism and AFL redbaiting in 1923, insisting that the Workers' Party was a persecuted minority, extreme in its views but a legitimate component of any third-party coalition. He welcomed communists and the Federated-Farmer Labor Party into the

1924 Minnesota campaign. By the time of the June 1924 St. Paul convention, though, it was apparent to Mahoney that the WP had changed its stance on the LaFollette movement, whose leader wanted no support from the communists anyway. Relations between the Minnesota progressives and the WP cooled noticeably. A year later, Mahoney, ever the committed farmer-laborite, offered a bitter postmortem on the 1924 Minnesota election mobilizations, characterizing the Workers' Party efforts as a "vilification of LaFollette and the leaders of the Farmer-Labor Party." Now a vitriolic anti-communist, Mahoney deplored the tactics of the WP, which he saw as "calculated to destroy the progressive movement of the state and nation." In 1925 Mahoney supported an amendment to the Constitution of the Minnesota Federation of Labor barring communists from sitting as delegates to its meetings.[91] It was the Fitzpatrick-Nockels fiasco all over again. The problem was not so much that the Comintern critique of the Workers' Party adaptations to LaFolletism was wrong, for Trotsky's scathing commentary was very much on the Bolshevik mark. Rather, the mechanical reversal of communist policy spoke to the ways in which the WP was now subject to a Communist International bureaucratism that had no sensitivity to international realities and little flexibility in its local renegotiation of programmatic error.

All of this seemed lost on WP leaders, however, as animosities on the CEC diminished perceptibly over the course of mid-1924. The assault on Lore drew somewhat together both the Foster-Cannon and Ruthenberg-Lovestone groups, deflecting attention away from long-standing differences, substantive reflection, and serious consideration of the problematic relations of the United States Workers' Party and the Communist International.

Lore, Escalating Anti-Trotskyism, and Factional Stalemate, 1924

Outed as a dangerously undisciplined dissident by the Comintern in May 1924, Lore operated within the CEC on borrowed time thereafter. When the *Volkszeitung* published a 1 August 1924 advertisement offering for sale at discounted rates bonds being floated by the counterrevolutionary Horthy regime in Hungary, notorious for the slaughter of communists, the CEC moved decisively and unanimously to censure Lore. The ad was published without Lore's consent, and he had immediately written an editorial, "For Horthy Hungary Not One Cent," that appeared the day after the offensive solicitation. The Cannon-Foster forces, while by no means sympathetic to Lore, were nevertheless the moderates, Lovestone especially calling for measures that would have meant Lore's head.[92]

As anti-Trotskyism began to filter into the Workers' Party via Moscow and the Comintern directed its American affiliate to abstain from its annual conference until the two factions with opposing views on the Farmer-Labor Party had had an opportunity to attend the Enlarged Executive Committee of the Communist International and present their positions, the question of Lore festered. In late November, the CEC directed Lore and the *Volkszeitung* to cease publication of Trotsky material and to feature prominently a recent *Pravda* repudiation of the former head of the Red Army. Browder and Cannon joined the fray, banning Trotsky articles from the *Workers Monthly*.[93] Lore's tendency toward indiscipline, and his movement into more and more blatant social democratic formulations, prompted a full-blown critique of his ostensible advocacy of a "Two-and-a-Half" International, a designation the Comintern appropriated from Kautsky's 1921–1923 efforts both to separate himself from the reformist Second International and to reconcile with it. Cannon, Krumbein, and Gitlow were dispatched to investigate claims of the Lore group's disloyalty.[94] The wheels of political assassination were put in motion, with Olgin penning a three-part attack on his old factional leader in the *Daily Worker* magazine supplement, Ruthenberg reinforcing the climate of antagonism, and the entire CEC joining in the anti-Lore fray; the Jewish Federation was thus left deeply divided.[95]

Cannon ended the year disappointed with the ongoing leadership stalemate. He accented the need to struggle, in albeit seemingly worsening objective conditions, to forge communism into a mass party. With legalization now established and the push to stay underground defeated, Cannon thought that efforts should be made "to speak the language that [workers] understand." This was not unrelated to the biggest danger facing the Workers' Party, "the disregard for objective facts and reality, dangerous self-conceit as to the strength and abilities of our party, the worship of empty phrases, and a grave lack of realism, practicability and Leninist objectivity." Inflationist self-presentation Cannon, Foster, and Bittelman identified as "the spirit of the minority." In a public CEC majority statement, this core of the "trade union communists" claimed that they had placed the illusory and impossible task of creating a united farmer-labor party on a class basis capable of defeating LaFollettism behind them, the CEC developing an appropriate strategy toward its electoral campaign over the course of June and July 1924. "Everyone in our ranks, except the incorrigible farmer-laborites, are convinced that our party made an excellent showing in the election campaign and greatly increased its prestige among the toiling masses."

Behind the scenes, Cannon was less sanguine about the lessons of the November election. He nevertheless took some solace in the patient evolution and propagandizing of the party position on the struggle against unemployment, developed within the TUEL; in the emergence of a functioning Industrial Department in the Workers' Party that sustained the left wing in the unions in the face of relentless attack by the labor bureaucracy; in ongoing educational work; in the consolidation and centralization of the *Daily Worker* and the party press; and in the organizational project of Bolshevization—all of which, according to the public statement of the CEC majority, strengthened communist morale and deepened the membership's Leninist convictions. Acknowledging shortcomings, Cannon and those with whom he was aligned in 1924 nevertheless thought the Workers' Party was on the right track.[96]

If the Cannon-Foster group constituted a majority on the CEC, however, it was never, in spite of the positive outcome of sheer vote counts, entirely secure, and though Foster had managed to have Pepper recalled, the Hungarian's first Moscow appearance at an American Commission had resulted in programmatic reversals for the Workers' Party. Nor was the factional differentiation producing unambiguous programmatic clarity. Cannon had yet to show any signs that he could see the forest of bureaucratizing Comintern opportunism for the trees of Workers' Party factional infighting.[97] Complicating matters was the workload of a party functionary. Cannon was often overwhelmed with the routine speaking engagements, lecture tours, and regular party work that found him one month in Chicago, another in the coal fields of Indiana or the bustling streets of New York.[98] These often brought rival factionalists together in common cause.[99]

Uncertainties of this political work, in which the activist routine seldom managed to rise above the factional din, were, moreover, exacerbated by the complications of Cannon's private affairs. Obviously in the throes of reconstitution, these remained unsettled toward the end of 1924. No one in the inner circles of the Workers' Party could possibly have been unaware that Cannon was now romantically involved with Rose Karsner, but officially he remained married to Lista. Both Cannon and Karsner had children in New York—Carl and Ruth, and Walta—and this undoubtedly posed acute problems for the couple, now based in the midwest and immersed in the maelstrom of party activity. Cannon actually solicited Jay Lovestone's help in accompanying Walta to Chicago around this time (possibly for Christmas, 1924) and the factional opponent was obliging enough to bring the ten-year-old girl with him on the "Twentieth Century" New York-to-Chicago railway run. The precocious Walta remembered Lovestone fondly to the last days of her life, proud of the inscribed volume of *The Government-Strikebreaker* that Jay presented her with as a remembrance of their journey together. It was then that Walta recalled accompanying Rose and Jim to a restaurant, getting acquainted, and Jim excusing himself to go to the washroom. Rose asked Walta what she thought of the new man in her life. Walta, understandably, was somewhat diffident, and her mother explained that Jim had asked her to "marry him" (there would be no official marriage). Surprised by all of this, Walta thought the whole thing "somewhat strange," but accepted it: "adults did these things."[100]

Rose and Jim had obviously been discussing seriously their life together, and struggling to juggle political commitments and domestic desires. In September 1924, for instance, they had both asked to be relieved of specific party assignments, Cannon requesting that he be allowed to step down from his position as assistant secretary of the Workers' Party and Karsner submitting her resignation as secretary of the International Workers' Relief. Little came of these petitions.[101] In early October, while on party assignment in New York to run for governor, Cannon asked that funds be directed to "Mrs. Cannon," stating that she needed them "on account of expenses connected with moving," a suggestion that he was separating from Lista and the children.[102] It may well have been at this time that he finally conveyed to Lista the sorry news about his involvement with Rose, a confession/break that he ostensibly judged extremely difficult, choosing between the two women he loved being one of the "hardest things" he had to do in his life. When Jim finally let Lista know about Rose, his wife supposedly reacted with calm understanding, saying, "Jim, let's go to bed." But the relationship was doomed, and had Jim been willing to maintain—sexually and emotionally—his ties to both Rose and Lista, the latter's pride "wouldn't let her take it."[103]

Two months later, the opening for an eventual Cannon-Karsner relocation to New York[104] was created by Cannon's long-standing work in the educational department of the Workers' Party and Juliet Stuart Poyntz's resignation as director of the Workers' School, ostensibly on the grounds of poor health but undoubtedly related to her association with the Lore faction, now very much on the defensive.[105] But if factionalism thus seemingly eased Cannon's and Karsner's move back to New York, it would also delay it: the growing rift between the Cannon-Foster and Ruthenberg-Lovestone forces demanded redress, and settlements of such magnitude could only be fashioned in Moscow. Another American Commission was scheduled for the Fifth Plenum of the Executive Committee of the Communist International, convened for 21 March 1925, displacing a Workers' Party convention slotted to take place at the end of 1924. The central issue, yet again, would be the Farmer-Labor Party. As Draper noted sardonically, "The Farmer-Labor movement's revenge was ironic. Dead, the movement disturbed the communists more than it had disturbed them alive. After having done more than their share to kill the Farmer-Labor movement, the communists could not bury it in their own minds."[106]

Return to Moscow and Comintern Degeneration, 1925

Cannon's credentials as a delegate to the ECCI were secured on 14 January 1925,[107] but he had in fact been preparing for the pilgrimage to Moscow much earlier. He applied for and secured a passport in his own name the last week of October 1924. A month earlier, Cannon had requested that his wife Lista M., whom he stated had been born in Romania on 22 December 1889, be included on his passport. Bureau of Investigation agents later reported with interest that the photograph Cannon supplied of "Lista M." bore a striking resemblance to a woman identified as "Rose Karsner, alias Karlsov alias Red Rose," but their suggestion to investigate Cannon's actual marital status stalled in inaction.[108] Arriving in the Soviet Union sometime in early February, weeks before the Fifth Plenum convened in late March 1925, Cannon, Foster, Karsner, and their youth section allies, John Williamson and Max Shachtman, settled into a routine of endless meetings with various Comintern figures, their purpose being to win those figures over to the majority's perspective. There were also day-and-night discussions, out of which came stacks of position papers. Cannon and Karsner no doubt managed to steal some time for themselves for what was in effect a working political honeymoon, and they made sure their paths crossed with the likes of Big Bill Haywood, whom they saw two or three times every day during their stay. Walking the streets of revolutionary Moscow, the red couple felt they belonged to an international movement, as well, perhaps, as to one another.[109]

The American communists arrived in Moscow unaware of the shifting programmatic foundations of the Russian Communist Party and the Communist International. Less than a year before, Zinoviev had been insistent on what Trotsky called the "pseudo-'Left' policy of 1924," in which peasant mobilizations were championed as the opening shots in a "united front" war leading inexorably toward "workers' and peasants' governments." Instead, what happened was disastrous defeat, as outbursts of despair culminated in terrorist adventures that were brutally suppressed (Bulgaria and Estonia being two locales of particularly bloody denouement). Given the unambiguous consequences of this period of "Left mistakes and putschist experiments," Zinoviev clutched at the inflated ghosts of revolutionary possibility, endorsing the Croatian Peasant Party leader Radic and the chimera of LaFollettism in the United States. His hand coming up empty, the Comintern moved to dispel its left illusions with a right turn. If, indeed, capitalist stabilization on a world scale had been the defining feature of the early to mid-1920s, as Lenin and Trotsky had attempted to convey, then the long-standing commitment of Bolshevik principle to world revolution had to be forthrightly abandoned, in

Stalin's view, in favor of sustaining "socialism in one country." The theoretical chasm separating Stalin and Trotsky, from December 1924 on, was visibly widening, and this analytic gulf developed with Trotsky and the reemerging Left Opposition concentrating their firepower on the programmatic degeneration of the Russian Revolution. Stalin utilized internal party power to consolidate his regime, which resorted to increasingly autocratic methods and nefarious innuendo (descending even to anti-Semitism) to isolate and marginalize all opponents. Trotsky's demotion from the powerful position of Commissar of War and Defense in January 1925, barely noticed at the time, was the initial move of isolation and exclusion that would end, within a few years, in banishment to Siberia and eventual exile to "a planet without a visa." When Zinoviev and Kamenev had a falling-out with Stalin, the latter joined with the increasingly right-leaning Bukharin, a party favorite, in advancing an emerging ideology of "socialism in one country." The Fifth Plenum of the ECCI was a venue for the dissemination of muddled programmatic concoctions that grew out of this juxtaposition of "Left illusions" arising and feeding into "the Right leaven"; the preferred formulation was that "partial stabilization" had to be met with tactics balanced on this material indecision, a hair-splitting orientation that of course fed directly into the demonstrable talents of Pepper. As Trotsky would later suggest, "everywhere the communists had to drag the heavy ball and chain of the false position of the Fifth Congress."[110] The U.S. delegation, not unlike Bolshevik forces around the world, did not quite know what they were getting into, although the eyes and ears of the Ruthenberg-Lovestone faction in Moscow, John Pepper, likely had an inkling of which way various ill winds were blowing.

Factional skirmishes began almost immediately within the American delegation, a jockeying for accredited status that reintroduced the irksome presence of Pepper. Since his recall to the Soviet Union, Pepper had played the same game in Moscow that he had perpetrated in New York and Chicago: once the Comintern representative in the United States, he was now United States communism's authoritative voice in the Soviet Union, champion of the oppressed immigrant masses. Small wonder, then, that when the four delegates—Foster and Cannon from the majority and Ruthenberg and Lovestone from the minority—appointed by the CEC to attend the plenum touched down in Moscow, the minority moved to secure official delegate status for Pepper. Foster and Cannon were rightly incensed, not only seeing in the move a factional attempt to secure an extra representative for the minority, but also pointing out that Pepper was an unscrupulous agent, constantly sowing seeds of dissension. For his part, Pepper went for the jugular, berating Foster, whom no one disputed as a legitimate delegate, as the Gompers of the revolutionary

Left. In a 13 February 1925 address to the American Commission, Cannon was unequivocal: "Pepper does not represent the American party, cannot, and never will by our consent." When the Comintern ruled to expand the delegations of both factions to three, adding the youth delegate, John Williamson, to the majority and Pepper to the minority, Cannon recognized the inequity of the supposed "balance" mandated by the ruling.[111]

Cannon and Foster produced a lengthy statement of their positions in "Controversial Questions in the Workers Party of America," a document that appeared in German- and Russian-language editions of the *Communist International* in March–April 1925. This published account was clearly edited by Comintern officials (who accentuated the anti-Trotskyist activity of the majority). The English draft, never published in Cannon's time, was particularly directed against Pepper. Prefaced by a discussion of the political and economic context of the United States in the early 1920s, the article staked out the differences of the minority and majority over the Farmer-Labor Party question. Pepper's extravagances and overestimations of the revolutionary forces and their potential were singled out for derision, with the damage done in 1923 through the split of the Chicago communists from Fitzpatrick-Nockels, the chasing after the illusory mass communist party, the opportunistic drift to LaFollettism, and the cultivation of nonproletarian, farmer elements by the Workers' Party all being castigated as consequences of theoretical Pepperism. Chided for their opportunism, the minority was presented as minimizing the role of the Workers' Party, and stifling its natural development as a proletarian vanguard, a problematic liquidationism surfacing in the half-hearted electoral campaigning in November 1924 and in the downplaying of the actual votes received by communists. Insistent that the Workers' Party had to "penetrate deeply into the labor movement and draw the workers around it," Cannon and Foster decried the grasping after straws that the imagined "class" farmer-labor party always entailed.[112]

From mid-February into early March of 1925, Foster and Cannon battled in the American Commission. The minority was castigated as "encouraging the anti-trade union tendency in the party," its "indifference and passivity and objection to go into the trade unions" scorned. The contentions were perhaps ugliest around Lore, with the minority claiming that Cannon and Foster were "solidly united" with the "renegade" forces of incipient Trotskyism. As the American Commission proceeded, claimed Ruthenberg, Pepper, and Lovestone, the "Foster-Lore" forces, fearful of facing a Comintern ruling against them, were "carrying on a ruthless campaign to exterminate the Ruthenberg supporters before the C.I. decision can reach the United States." Clearly standing the ground of Bolshevization, Cannon and Foster detailed their group's struggle against the so-called revisionist tendencies associated with Lore and Trotsky.[113]

It was not enough. Cannon was not long in Moscow before he judged that the "eventual decision was pretty clearly intimated." He came to "the chilling impression" that the Foster-Cannon group, strongest on its home turf of the United States, was weaker in Moscow: "With Pepper as an active representative, busy in the apparatus of the Comintern, the Ruthenberg faction seemed to have the inside track." Of the key Russian officials to whom they had access—Trotsky was no longer available—Bukharin was "particularly outspoken in favor of the Ruthenberg faction." Only Zinoviev seemed to have much time for the "trade union" group, and he conceded much to the minority, pressuring Foster and Cannon not to constrain the rights of their opponents and urging them to "slow down the factional struggle."[114]

The final American Commission decisions were less than clear-cut, altogether too vague and general, and certainly much less forthright than the Cannon-Foster forces would have liked. They were characterized by what could later be identified as Stalinist manipulation and subordination. On the key organizational question, Zinoviev's original proposal that the forthcoming Fourth Congress of the Workers' Party elect a CEC in which the Foster group was conceded a majority, with the Ruthenberg faction having a proportion of members not less than one-third, pleased Foster, for whom party control was paramount. However, such a provision worried Cannon, who was put off by the notion that Moscow was calling the shots over the composition of the American section's leading body so arbitrarily. Things got worse, however, when the Ruthenberg-Pepper forces rallied opposition to this suggestion and instead secured the Comintern's endorsement of a Parity Commission, to be constituted at the upcoming party convention and chaired by a "neutral comrade"—who could only, of course, be a CI appointee. In effect, any notion of United States party autonomy was now patently gone. Foster played into this process. In 1924, Zinoviev had suggested sending a Comintern representative to the United States to stem the tide of factionalism. The Foster-Cannon majority requested that this not be done, but in March 1925 Foster asked that the Soviets dispatch someone to America to aid in the struggle to achieve party unity, thus legitimizing whomever Zinoviev seconded to the United States.[115] This miscue would come back to haunt Foster.

Finally, on the key political question of the Farmer-Labor Party, the Ruthenberg forces received something of a concession. The Comintern decreed that the Workers' Party should agitate for the creation of an independent political voice, in order to break workers and poor farmers away from the LaFollette movement. This, in effect, constituted a call for continued orientation to the remnants of farmer-laborism. As a sop to Foster and Cannon, the Comintern eventually insisted that such an orientation be premised on mass trade union support (defined as 500,000 organized workers),[116] and advocated designating all future work in such areas as building the *Labor* Party, dropping the troublesome hyphenation of farmer-labor struggle. Foster and Cannon had to eat a little crow, but in the process they took their last stand. Cannon's remarks before a 5 April 1925 session of the American Commission ceded the Foster-Cannon group's support to the new orientation, but insisted that "we must have a clear understanding, and it must be put in the decision that it will be a real labor party, and not a fake caricature organization." Though Foster's general approach to trade union questions was accepted, he had to swallow a bitter pill in the accolades heaped on his old nemesis, Pepper, and it was left to Cannon to draft a placatory amendment praising the Hungarian. It all added an understated show-trial dimension to the proceedings, one that could not have sat well with Cannon, however loyal a Cominternist he remained. Cannon's and Foster's attempts to politicize rather than personalize the attack on "Two and a Half Internationalism," in contrast, came to naught as the Comintern fixed its sights on Lore, targeting him for expulsion.[117]

Months of preparation and anguish, and many solid weeks of discussion and preparation, thus produced some backtracking on the third-party question and a large question-mark guillotine hanging over the heads of the two CEC factions. As Cannon and Karsner, accompanied by the youth delegates Williamson and Shachtman, made their way back to the United States, passing through Great Britain on 19 April 1925, they were undoubtedly unsettled.[118] Who knew, however, how it would all work out? There were likely just as many conversations about the exhilarations of actually seeing firsthand the home of the Russian Revolution, of experiencing the accomplishments of the first workers' state. Shachtman, for instance, recalled the USSR of this period as "a brilliant red light in the darkness of capitalist gloom." Years later, it was not so much the heavy-handed retreats dictated by the American Commission that the young revolutionary remembered of his 1925 adventure, but the feeling of pride as he crossed the border into the Soviet Union, passing under arches that proclaimed: "Proletarians of the world unite!" The legacy of 1917 had a long reach, although one that, by 1925, was beginning to cover much.[119]

"Tearing Each Other to Pieces": Factional Gang War

Having returned to the United States while assimilating the final Comintern decision, which appeared in the *Daily Worker* on 19 May 1924, Cannon and his factional allies had to deal with tensions that had been building since their departure. Some of the leading cadre, put on hold by Moscow's delays, and guarding the gates in Chicago with Cannon and Foster away, were clearly spoiling for a fight.[120] There were, moreover, obvious strains developing within the bloc, and Foster, more so than Cannon, was having difficulty adapting to the new situation. Reports were that he was constantly fuming about Pepper and railing against "that bastard Lovestone."[121] The need for a final, decisive break with Lore threatened Foster far more than Cannon, for the former's stature in trade union circles, with the German editor and his supporters of central importance in the New York needle trades, was at stake.[122] Also, the two leading figures in the majority had slightly different responses to the Comintern directive on farmer-laborism. Its endorsement of labor-party work, conditioned as it was on there being mass acceptance within the trade unions, again proved easier for Cannon to accept than it was for Foster. On the one hand, Bittelman and Browder, controlling the American party while Cannon and Foster were abroad, were inclined in this period to a sectarian abstentionism, having been burned by so much of Pepper's labor-party firepower.[123] Foster may have come under their sway, although this was never decisive. On the other hand, Foster always harbored doubts about the efficacy of labor-party involvement, knowing it was an inevitably fractious issue in the American Federation of Labor circles where he saw his political work concentrated, and perhaps carrying with him into the 1920s the residue of syndicalist suspicion of political entanglements.[124]

All of this boiled over at a large Central Executive Committee meeting, convened for 12–15 May 1925, and chaired by Foster. It encompassed all members of the CEC, CEC alternatives, members of the National Executive Committee of the Young Workers League, district organizers, eight language-section representatives, three invited guests (Robert Minor, Juliet Stuart Poyntz, and Charles Zimmerman), Rose Karsner from the International Red Aid, and assorted others.[125] Lore delivered a long speech deploring the altar of factionalism on which his sacrificial offering was being made to the Comintern gods. The unrepentant "free lance" challenged the foundation of much of the CEC's attack. Weakest in his defense of positions he had adopted toward early Comintern outcasts Giacinto Menatti Serrati (Italy) and Paul Levi (Germany), Lore was much stronger in refuting allegations about his violation of communist positions with respect to publishing material in or through the *Volkszeitung*, noting with some enjoyment that charges about what he had in fact placed in print were garbled and often incorrect. Moreover, Lore was defiant in defending his attacks on farmer-laborism. The Comintern had confirmed his 1923 critique of wasting scarce human and material resources on chasing after "fake farmer-labor parties" and adopted, for a time, the "Loreist" position of not giving "so much attention to the farmers." This, of course, was also Trotsky's view. The decisive nail in Lore's coffin was thus his statement on Trotsky: "All the enemies are now branded as Trotskyites. I never made bones of the fact that I am sympathetic with Trotsky." Lore closed his defense with strong words of commitment to revolutionary communism, refused to "quit the Party," and claimed he would attempt to abide by decisions arrived at by the Central Executive Committee. He must have known, though, that his case was a foregone conclusion, for he protected his followers: "If Lore is to be condemned then I want it to be understood that it is Lore to be condemned and no one else. To fasten it upon a group is to create a bug-a-boo that does not exist."[126]

That set the stage for Juliet Stuart Poyntz's entry, a Judas-like performance that was orchestrated by the Ruthenberg faction to do the most damage to Foster and Cannon, who, after all, were in the process of dumping Lore. This allowed the adaptable Poyntz to break from the German editor, associate her disillusioned past with the "trade union" majority, and declare her loyalty to the Comintern in such a way as to fling yet another arrow in Trotsky's direction.[127] The first day of the CEC meeting was turning into a pressure cooker of payback. It ended predictably, with Foster, Lovestone, and Bill Dunne at each others' throats.[128]

The next day saw the majority take charge more authoritatively, with Cannon submitting a statement that rehashed the labor-party issue in such a way as to repudiate the wrong turns of Ruthenberg and Pepper. Bittelman presented a preamble on the Lore case as an introduction to a long resolution on the crisis of communist leadership in the needle trades, where Poyntz, Zimmerman, and Rose Wortis were said to be combating the CEC's authority with the help of the Ruthenberg faction's operative, Benjamin Gitlow. At issue for the Foster-Cannon group was the opportunistic tendency of the Ruthenberg-Lovestone forces to collapse "the central aim of the Communists in the trade unions . . . [into the] capture and hold[ing of] office at all costs and by all means." According to Bittelman, Zimmerman's and Wortis's reduction of left-wing tactics to mere maneuvers for bureaucratic influence sacrificed the program of the Trade Union Educational League.[129] The final day of the three-day CEC meeting tidied up the mess with a series of resolutions, the majority, of course, carrying the day with their votes.[130]

All now turned on the delayed Fourth Convention, which could not take place until the arrival of a "neutral" Comintern representative to oversee the Parity Commission. As the American communists stewed in their factional juices over the late spring and early summer of 1925, the Workers' Party was effectively immobilized. "We are doing nothing in the field of political and industrial work," Lovestone wrote to his friend Bertram Wolfe. "We are simply tearing each other to pieces."[131]

Of Cables and Comintern Men: American Communism's Decisive Subordination

The Comintern eventually dispatched Sergei Ivanovich Gusev to North America, his task as much to ensure that the CEC factions were themselves drawn into a properly disciplined appreciation of bureaucratic governance as it was to calm the troubled atmosphere of gang warfare that ensured communist ineffectiveness in the United States. Gusev was an old Bolshevik, one who had stood with Lenin from 1903 to 1904, earned impressive military credentials during the revolutionary seizure of power in Petrograd in 1917, and thereafter in the civil war, where he was a member of the Supreme Revolutionary Military Council headed by Trotsky. His hatred of the Red Army commander, whose involvement in a number of clashes over military policy he had always resented and sided against, dated from this period. Gusev claimed to have been one of a number of officers saved by Stalin's intervention when Trotsky ostensibly threatened to have them shot for insubordination—a probable fabrication. Thus indebted to Stalin for his life and his rehabilitation as a military commander, and later a Bolshevik functionary (or so he told the story), Gusev was one of an early group quite loyal to the new head of the Soviet state. As Stalin moved to weaken Zinoviev's long-standing dominance of the Comintern, Gusev was quite possibly a natural agent, and was transferred to the International where he functioned actively at the Fifth Plenum of the ECCI before departing early in the spring of 1925 for the United States, via Mexico. Once established there, and looked after and tutored in English by Ella and Bertram Wolfe, old Lovestone friends from City College and the underground communist movement, Gusev prepared himself for his immersion in the majority-minority fight. He was also being prepared to enter the United States: the Ruthenberg-Lovestone minority made arrangements to slip the short, rotund, bespectacled Gusev past American immigration authorities at the Laredo, Texas, border crossing without suspicion. As the Foster-Cannon group cabled the Comintern, wringing its hands over the whereabouts of the "neutral" governor, Lovestone was welcoming Gusev to Chicago, indulging his wants and stroking his ego. This "nursing" work was of a sort that Lovestone excelled in, whereas the Foster group "lacked the finesse and technique for this kind of activity." The Ruthenberg faction christened Gusev, in the United States illegally, as "P. Green," Wolfe having secured fake documents in Mexico under this name. In Foster-Cannon circles a wariness was soon apparent. "We got rid of Pepper," some faction members complained, "only to get a dose of Paris Green."[132]

Gusev arrived in Chicago during the first week of July 1925, and the Parity Commission was established shortly thereafter: Foster, Bittelman, and Cannon for the majority, and Ruthenberg, Lovestone, and Bedacht for the minority.

This now became the ruling body of the Workers' Party, and the leading elected committees virtually ceased to exist. Disliking Foster, whom Gusev regarded as little more than a trade union figurehead, the CI representative tired easily of Bittelman's "theoretical" meandering, and judged Browder less of a communist than a missionary. On Cannon Gusev was more mixed: appreciating his "political" smarts, he nonetheless thought Cannon vain, easily led by Comintern authority, and possible to split away from Foster. Nothing as sophisticated as Pepper, Gusev was a plodding, if authoritative, functionary whose only attribute was his decisive finality. A series of "unanimous" resolutions to be presented to the upcoming Workers' Party convention, now set to open 21 August 1925, were soon drafted.[133]

If Green/Gusev now effectively decided all issues within the Parity Commission, he could not *govern* the communist ranks, from which fifty-four delegates had to be chosen for the August convention. The contending factions, their Communist International-ordered liquidation aside, barred no holds in their efforts to secure representation: foreign-language-federation heads were wined and dined; dues-stamp payment records, the basis of district delegate apportionment, were padded to enhance the membership lists in favor of one group or the other; individuals were cajoled and maneuvered. When the powerful New York district, with its eleven delegates up for grabs, convened under the chairmanship of the Ruthenberg loyalist Benjamin Gitlow, the air was thick with combative tension. The Ruthenberg forces, according to Gitlow, were "heavily armed," its leadership "well guarded and protected." Foster had traveled to New York to lead his forces, who awaited the *líder máximo*'s arrival, staged to occur so as to make the most forceful impact: "Five minutes before the convention was to be opened, the door in the rear of the hall opened and Foster marched in, leading the Finnish delegates, who marched in twos behind him. It was a real military display." As Gitlow rose to open the meeting, a Foster lieutenant from the Amalgamated Clothing Workers jumped the platform and attempted to introduce the convention himself. The Ruthenberg defense guard circled the podium. Shouts and angry jostlings rippled through the hall; the bedlam was soon so overpowering that nothing could be heard. The two camps eventually struck a wary, and ineffective, compromise in which two conventions proceeded at the same time, the Ruthenberg and Foster groups electing their slates and proceeding with two secretaries, two credential committees, and two sets of motions, up to and including a dual adjournment. The Parity Commission, in the end, would rule on whose election, or what combination of the two, would actually be recognized. Gusev reprimanded both factions, appealed for the avoidance of a split, and, on the basis of recognizing the numerically dominant, if somewhat loose and even "fake," 7,000-strong Finnish Federation, awarded the Foster-Cannon forces a preconvention majority of 60 percent of the Central Executive Committee. A CEC made by Comintern decree, however, could also be unmade by it.[134]

As Cannon and Bittelman later acknowledged, Gusev's supposed neutrality was a balancing act, in which the majority's claims at least had to be recognized, but the minority was given the best of it whenever the Comintern representative could do so "neatly and plausibly." In the fury of the organizational war that preceded the actual convention, the Foster-Cannon forces managed to line up an even stronger majority than Gusev's CEC ruling of a 60/40 split mandated, by adding seven delegates of their own from highly contested districts. "It was clear to everyone in the Party," Gitlow recalled, "that the national convention would be the most violent one ever held." When, on 21 August 1925, Foster was elected chairman over Gitlow by a margin of almost two to one (forty to twenty-one), the stage was set for a battle. The Workers' Party program was not at stake, and Cannon featured prominently in the proceedings, offering conciliatory responses to challenges from Ruthenberg and representing the CEC's endorsement of Bolshevization. Although the convention was something of a marathon, there were almost no policy issue disagreements. Lore was given the bounce, and little seemed at stake. What kept the rancor alive?[135]

At issue, ultimately, was the meaning of the convention in deciding the regime question: who ruled the party? In fact, as events would soon establish, this was not going to be decided by a gathering of delegates, although neither faction understood this clearly at the time, in spite of some pretty clear signals from "the old Bolshevik" among them. The Communist International, through its agent, Gusev, and the sanctified Parity Commission, was where all power truly lay. Foster thought differently. From the outset of his convention victory, Foster indicated that he was prepared to dump Ruthenberg from the secretaryship, refuse the despised Lovestone a seat on the CEC, secure undisputed control over the party press, and disperse the leaders of the opposition to districts distant from the Chicago center. Lovestone supposedly rallied the Ruthenberg forces to within one vote of agreeing to stage a walkout in protest, and at the Fifth Session, 24 August 1925, Foster, Cannon and the majority delegates waited more than two and a half hours for the minority delegates to grace the proceedings with their presence. Name calling and finger pointing became "political acts." The tone of the convention was perhaps captured most succinctly as Lovestone, target of continual abuse on the part of majority delegates, came to the floor to defend himself:

> Lovestone—(Applause, cheers, singing of "Internationale" by minority supporters while majority delegates and supporters remained stolidly in their seats) . . . Comrades, I was one of the most active working for the creation of the

Communist Party, fighting against the law while many of your supporters were fighting against the soul of the Russian revolution. . . . Comrades, these political virgins with Wagenknecht's wings who are coming around here in the person of Comrade Cannon, protesting against being provoked. The innocent Comrade Cannon! (Interjection by Comrade Sullivan) Nonsense, nonsense. Comrade Sullivan—keep your mouth shut when you are not called upon to speak (Sullivan—You can't shut me up) The chairman will shut you up. . . . Why does Abern yell so much against me? Comrade Abern has been chosen as the goat, has been the unfortunate one to spill the worst bucket of filth and do the best that the CEC of the majority can do. . . . If you want unity in the Party you will have to work with us and discuss with us the questions before this convention—the ways and means of building a mass Communist Party and not the ways and means of disfranchising miners and steel workers from Ohio. If you want to disfranchise the Ohio miners don't hide behind agreements. Don't pose as angels while you are working overtime to destroy this Party. . . . Dunne—I demand that Comrade Lovestone detract that statement.

And so it went. Comrades brawled in the aisles and threatened each other in the corners. Reference to majority and minority groups faded as the Ruthenberg group branded the Foster-Cannon faction the Right-Wing, appropriating for themselves the designation Left-Wing. Both cohorts had defense units ready to protect their leaders, and rumors of concealed arms being brought onto the convention floor floated about the hall. For their part, a contingent of the Foster-Cannon forces, led by Bill Dunne and including a young Max Shachtman, armed themselves with "a few pistols," seized the West Washington Boulevard Chicago offices of the *Daily Worker,* barred the doors to the Ruthenberg co-editor, Louis Engdahl, and held the fortress, day and night, for forty-eight hours. Convinced that their majority entitled them, morally and politically, to the "property of the party," Dunne, Shachtman, and others relinquished the building only after Lovestone made as much of "the scandal" as he possibly could. Pro forma resolutions aside, the end-of-August meeting was taking on the character of a Wild West show.[136]

Gusev had had enough. On the eighth day of the proceedings, 28 August 1925, he summoned the Parity Commission to a five o'clock meeting at the "hideout" the Ruthenberg faction had found for him. Once the principals were gathered together, Gusev calmly handed Ruthenberg a Moscow cable, arranged for previously by "Paris Green" and almost certainly after consultation with Lovestone, instructing him to read it aloud. Nebulously signed "Michael," the telegram was addressed to Lydia Gibson, Bob Minor's wife, and was directed to Green. It laid out an elaborate set of ultimatums, justified by a preamble declaring that the executive of the Comintern had determined that under no circumstances should be allowed that majority suppresses Ruth-group. Because firstly it has been finally become clear that the Ruthgroup is more loyal to decisions of CI and stands closer to its views. Secondly because it has received in most important districts the majority or an important minority. Thirdly because Foster group employes excessively mechanical and ultrafactional methods.

Green/Gusev was instructed to demand, as a minimum set of concessions:

> Firstly, Ruthgroup must get not less than forty percent of CEC Secondly demand as ultimatum from majority that Ruth retains post of secretary Thirdly categorically insist upon Lovestones CEC membership Fourthly demand as ultimatum from majority refraining removals, displacing, dispercions against factional opponents Fifth demand retention by Ruthgroup of coeditorship of central organ Sixth Demand maximum application of parity on all executive organs of Party.

The Comintern document made it clear that little store was placed in the convention election results. It was "unclear who has real majority." But the "methods of majority raise danger of split and therefore [the Executive] proposes that now only a temporary parity CEC be elected with neutral chairman to call new convention after passions have died down." Those who refused to submit to the dictate were warned that they "will be expelled."[137]

This bombshell left the Ruthenberg forces, now obviously orchestrated by Lovestone, elated. They clearly knew, before the actual staged delivery of the Comintern's cabled orders, what was going to happen, as the telegram had been delivered to the Gibson-Minor household. For Foster, Cannon, and Bittelman, however, this was, to put it mildly, fairly catastrophic news. Moreover, they clearly had not seen the penny dropping. Outside the room where the major figures were gathered, Ella and Bertram Wolfe awaited the outcome. As the defeated majority departed in dejection, Ella danced in to congratulate her comrades. Gusev, nonchalant throughout the proceedings, smiled and welcomed his English teacher wittily: "Why are you dancing? Do you think this is a love affair? This is a Lovestone affair."[138]

Foster said as much with a curse, declaring as he withdrew that he knew "who [was] responsible." The Cannon-Foster group was now split down the middle. Bittelman, forlorn and unable to appreciate where this blow was coming from, was at a theoretical loss to explain the situation. It was not to be Foster's finest hour either. He was livid. In August 1925, Foster stood on the brink of Workers' Party control, and he simply could not condone any trifling with his obvious victory. Having seemingly won all of the battles for his rightful place at the head of the party, he could not fathom that he had indeed lost the

war for position. He thus resisted compliance, refused in a bluster to participate in the Comintern-ordered watering down of his coveted dominance of
the party apparatus, and threatened to resign and leave the Ruthenberg group
in absolute control, as opposed to the suggested 40 percent of the CEC that the
cable had stipulated. Gusev declined to accept such an abdication of communist responsibility, and Foster, "flushed with anger," agreed to formally accept
the Comintern decision, knowing that he would take his discontents directly
to Moscow.[139]

Cannon's response to this "sudden blow for which we were in no way prepared, a blow calculated to put one's confidence in the Comintern to a rather
severe test," was very different, although what motivated him is open to contrasting interpretations. Gitlow and Wolfe, from their vantage point inside the
Ruthenberg faction, and drawing on Gusev's boastings of how he was playing
Cannon, plying him with flattery and empty promises of leadership positions,
suggest that Cannon was drawn to support the Communist International's directions and break from Foster out of careerist aspiration, an interpretation reiterated somewhat in an unpublished attack on Cannon by Foster.[140] Another
Ruthenberg faction member, Vera Buch Weisbord, recalls the Gusev-Cannon
relationship in a less jaundiced way, noting that the Comintern representative
"used diplomacy in the situation, working on James P. Cannon, who was with the
Foster group but showed signs of independence, which [Gusev] encouraged."[141]

For his part, Cannon might well concede that the Comintern's "Green" had
manipulated him in specific ways (he later referred to the Machiavellian Gusev
making contributions to "The Education of a Young Man" in the ways of the
post-Lenin Communist International), but his understanding of what had
happened turned little on the bribe of office. Rather, he would have seen Gusev
playing on his commitment to the Comintern:

> I was then a convinced "Cominternist." I had faith in the wisdom and also in the
> fairness of the Russian leaders. I thought they had made a mistake through false
> information and that the mistake could later be rectified. I did not even suspect
> that this monstrous violation of the democratic rights of our party was one of the
> moves in the Moscow chess game, in which our party, like all the other parties in
> the Comintern, was to be a mere pawn. I thought Foster's attitude was *disloyal;*
> that his ostensible willingness to hand over the majority to the Ruthenbergites,
> and to withdraw from the Central Committee himself, was in reality designed to
> provoke a revolt of our faction against the Comintern. Foster made the dispute
> between us a question of confidence in himself personally, as the leader of the fac-
> tion. This hurt him more than it helped him, for the communist militants in
> those days were not the regimented lackeys of a later day. There was outspoken
> resentment at Foster's attempt to invoke the "follow the leader" principle.

Cannon, Foster, and Bittelman left the Parity Commission disaster and headed to a full caucus meeting; Cannon and Foster, now irreconcilable, did not talk before putting their positions to the ranks. The caucus debate was a long, drawn-out affair, supposedly thirty-four trying hours in duration, and comrades were worn down by the length and intensity of the debate. In the end, Cannon's coolness prevailed, but it tolled the death knell for the old Chicago-based trade union caucus. Cannon opted for a fifty-fifty split between the Foster-Cannon/Ruthenberg-Lovestone forces on the newly appointed CEC, thinking that such a proposal for equal balance would "stalemate the factional struggle, make each faction equally responsible for the leadership, and compel them to work together." With programmatic issues largely settled, it seemed a solution that might work, although it had to go into effect quickly and demonstrate its utility immediately. Cannon drew to his support the young leaders Shachtman and Abern, as well as Arne Swabeck and the influential Bill Dunne. The latter was suffering through a personal crisis—his son had been killed in an automobile accident and been buried only days before—and was both a respected leader with the trade union ranks and a highly sympathetic figure at that particular moment. Foster retained the support of Bittelman, Jack Johnstone, and Charles Krumbein. In the end, Cannon and Dunne won the day; they solidified their relations with a circle of revolutionary Minneapolis unionists, including Dunne's brothers, that was originally created in the struggle against Pepper in 1923. The vote was secured to abide by the obnoxious conditions of the Comintern cable and, indeed, to split the CEC down the middle. As a concession to the losing side, Foster and Bittelman were proposed as candidates to the Political Committee.[142]

When the Parity Commission reconvened, late in the evening on 29 August 1925, Gusev perhaps sensed the beaten and broken nature of the majority. Bittelman shriveled up in a corner, his face dark with depletion. The disheveled and unkempt Foster appeared shipwrecked on the shoals of helplessness. Cannon, according to Gitlow, "was a nervous mass" of "weary and exhausted flesh," his eyes bleary and bloodshot, hands pressed to his forehead in depression. The victorious Ruthenberg group found nothing to quarrel with in the notion of a "parity" committee structure, and a procedural document, in which both camps named ten members to the CEC and equal numbers of representatives to other party bodies, was unanimously agreed to and later implemented at the close of the convention.[143] In line with CEC agreements reaching back months, and initiated by Ruthenberg, the communists took as a new name the Workers (Communist) Party.[144]

The Moscow representative had one more covert card up his bureaucratic sleeve. At the first meeting of the CEC, a few days after the August convention folded up its embattled tents, he informed the assembled leaders that because the Ruthenberg group was favored by the Comintern, he intended to oversee its relations by voting with those in whom the voice of proletarian revolution invested the greatest authority. A "parity" Central Executive Committee was thus thwarted, in effect turning Foster's caucus proposal to hand the majority to Ruthenberg into a reality, albeit one presented by fiat after Foster and Cannon had been split and the former's credibility with the Communist International called into serious question. Bittelman was refused a seat on the Political Committee, Gusev turning to Cannon instead, claiming that he would not see Cannon punished in this way by the Foster forces. Cannon would later write: "If I admit that I went along with this treacherous double-play and still refused to have any part in any revolt against the Comintern, it is not to claim any credit for myself. . . . [D]evotion to the Comintern, which had originally been one of the greatest merits of the pioneer communists, was being turned into a sickness which called for a radical cure."[145]

Cannon now walked the minefield of varying contentions gingerly, blocking with Foster on certain votes in the Political Committee throughout September 1925. On the crucial Foster initiative to take his resentments over the August cable to Moscow for discussion within the Comintern, at the same time as party membership meetings were made open forums of opposition to the Gusev-elicited cable, he drew the line. In alliance with Dunne, Cannon refused his support on the ground that the former majority, with whose political program he continued to.agree, had no intention of opposing the Communist International's guidance. He did what he could to squash the rumblings of discontent in the Foster ranks, which contained significant rightist elements in New York's needle trades (where Lore's supporters remained in the party following their leader's expulsion) and among the core group of older Cannon-Foster allies, the Finns. The Cannon-Dunne faction was in the process reduced to the smallest, numerically, in the party, and two of its key organizers were quickly dumped by the Ruthenberg-Lovestone leadership, now the only united faction of prominence in the communist milieu: Shachtman was taken off the editorial masthead of the *Young Worker* and Abern was bumped out of his Chicago posts. The possibility of the old political coherence of the Foster-Cannon bloc—materially rooted in trade union work, connected with Jewish comrades in the garment industry, and tied to the largest cohort of ethnic radicalism, the Finnish section—had been effectively vanquished, although Cannon and Dunne continued to press for the importance of labor movement work, albeit in ways that often differentiated them from Foster.[146]

Cannon and his supporters grasped intuitively the conundrum they were now in if they appeased Foster in certain anti-CI ways and broke emphatically with Ruthenberg. As Shachtman recalled:

The kind of support we would necessarily rally, the kind of support that would come to us whether we rallied it deliberately or not, would be of a kind that first would mobilize all of the right-wing elements of the party against the Comintern, and in mobilizing them behind the appeal, we would be placed increasingly at the mercy of these right-wing elements. They would constitute more and more of our troops. And, willy-nilly . . . a split would ensue. Why willy-nilly? Because nobody really felt the Comintern would reverse its decision.[147]

This judgment was largely confirmed throughout the fall of 1925, in two ways. First, pro-Foster membership meetings drew out an increasingly problematic politics of opposition to the Comintern, with such noted former majority members as Joseph Zack, Charles Krumbein, and Philip Aronberg in New York openly attacking the cable of 27 August 1925. Second, George Kraska in Boston upped the level of resistance by condemning Zinoviev and the Communist International. When Foster and Bittelman traveled to the Soviet Union to get a hearing, they came back largely empty-handed.[148]

If Cannon was lenient in how he originally reacted to the Foster-led membership rebellion in the inner circles of the Political Committee, he was nevertheless staunchly opposed to his former ally's decision to simultaneously appeal to the party and to the Communist International, making public a leadership opposition to Comintern directive. Cannon called for a break from past traditions of "diplomatizing" with the Communist International, of regarding it as something outside of the party; he urged instead the necessity of developing an understanding that the party and the Comintern were an inseparable whole.[149] "Unify the Party" was the slogan adopted by Cannon and Dunne, who offered a six-point path to the reconstitution of CEC leadership that combined with the Ruthenberg forces in an embrace of Bolshevization and fealty to the Communist International. For his sins, perhaps, Cannon was linked with Lovestone in a "unity tour" across the country in early December 1925, and possibly with the latter's New York lieutenant, Jack Stachel, there being some consternation that Foster would hive himself off in the Trade Union Educational League, splitting the party into industrial and political fiefdoms.[150]

As the Cannon-Dunne group took shape in this period, many in the communist ranks now held Jim Cannon in exceedingly low regard. A satirical "meditation," penned by someone in the Foster group, pilloried Cannon as indecisive and self-interested:

For twenty months I thought that Bill was wrong,
But then—who knows—he might be right.
So I pondered, pondered, pondered. . . . ?
I wooed the Finns, I charmed the Lorelei,

I knocked C.E., I slandered Jay,
And I waited, waited, waited. . . .
For to build a Cannon group,
For to build a Cannon group.[151]

Whatever its merits or demerits, this denigration of Cannon's political activity in the communist movement did have one thing right. By the end of 1925, Cannon was intent on building a group. More precisely, such a group needed rebuilding, but the task was not to be an easy one, and there were few principled guidelines available for Cannon to follow.

On 16 December 1925, Cannon wrote to Rose Karsner in Chicago from New York, outlining some considerations on their emerging party battle. Brooding and soaking up the not always exhilarating news from the party ranks, Cannon worried about those around him and their resolve, realizing that although they had "the best group in the party," there were many barriers in the path of the project of reforging a collective leadership on the basis of a communist program. It was vital to deal with all questions, not on the basis of caucus convenience, but "as they arise according to our main political line, regardless of who is for or against." He urged that Dunne be encouraged to attend the ECCI's Sixth Plenum in February 1926, where Foster was still, through his connections to Lozovsky, "strongly entrenched in *what should be his weakest position* (the trade union question)." Cannon, en route to Moscow, thought that he and Dunne might be able to make some headway on reorienting the party's important work in the labor movement, which seemed threatened during the fall of 1925 by a dual danger: on the one hand, lapsing into opportunistic alignment with union bureaucracies (which Gitlow, as the main figure in the Lovestone-Ruthenberg group active in the unions, seemed prone to embrace); or, on the other, continuing in the constricted sectarianism that allowed the Foster-led TUEL to become increasingly identified as a restricted assembly of isolated and small communist factions rather than a true united front of the left wing in the unions. Cannon's greatest misgivings, however, were of a more ominous sort. He confessed to being deeply troubled about organizing a fight in Moscow, and was pessimistic about what could be accomplished at the plenum. Under no circumstances, he thought, was it possible to get "what we want and what is really necessary for the party."[152]

If the Workers (Communist) Party of the mid-1920s was indeed suspended by Stalinist cables from Moscow, then Cannon was on the verge of appreciating just how frayed those lines actually were, even if he could not discern their make. Nevertheless, he was still astride the communist bridge, relying on the security of Comintern authority in spite of a growing sense of unease.

9

Labor Defender

Bolshevization and Leninist Mass Work

As Cannon embarked upon yet another transatlantic crossing, his sense of the politics of revolutionary communism was anything but settled. A public advocate of Bolshevization, he could not have helped but be aware of the human costs that were being exacted, month by grueling month, with the hard turn against the cultural softness and political indeterminacy of a language-federations-based cadre. Party membership had begun to inch back after a low point in 1922 and, all complications associated with the dual-stamp system that allowed husbands and wives to purchase a single stamp and record themselves as two, often fictitious, members (eventually abolished in 1925) aside, the dues figures for the months of January through April 1924 constituted a high water mark of 1920s communist membership: January, 16,875; February, 18,323; March, 19,471; April, 17,401.

On the eve of Bolshevization, the Workers' Party seemed to be growing, or at least holding its own in terms of a stable membership. Bolshevization, implemented gingerly in 1924, but in a more thoroughgoing fashion by 1925, seemingly stifled this growth; party rolls dipped dramatically, falling to roughly 14,000 in September 1925 and declining precipitously to 7,200 a month later. Comments in the *Daily Worker* acknowledged that Bolshevization had contributed to a loss of members. Party insiders generally agreed that membership over the course of the 1920s never really exceeded 10,000, and although the Workers (Communist) Party ranks would expand slowly in 1927–1929, climbing to perhaps as many as 9,500, the combination of Bolshevization and factional battle that coincided with the breakup of the Foster-Cannon group in 1925, in conjunction with a generalized political economy shift detrimental to radicalism, resulted in at least two years of membership stagnation at the rather low number of roughly 7,500. Factoring in the routine fluctuations in membership, by which it has been estimated that of the 23,000 new members who joined the communist movement between 1923 and 1927, fully 18,000 subsequently dropped out, it is obvious that the mass communist party that Cannon had been struggling to build was a long way from realization. The party ranks remained dominated by the immigrant Finns, East Europeans, and Jews who, together with a smattering of Central and Southern Europeans, continued to constitute approximately 90 percent of the communist membership. Heavily proletarianized, the party rolls were 75 percent waged working class, 15 percent housewives, and 10 percent petty bourgeois, but the small shop nuclei that Bolshevization staked out as the central unit of Workers (Communist) Party organization never really "took" among the communist rank-and-file. This was at least in part because such nuclei were always relatively tiny and inconsequential within any given industry. They were particularly weak in the primary economic sectors of metal production and mining, where large workplaces were the norm, but only 25 percent of all working-class communists could be found. With more than half of its proletarian ranks concentrated in the relatively small-scale productive enterprises of the needle trades and foodstuffs distribution, the communist project of making shop nuclei the foundation of a revolutionary penetration of the working class was doomed to failure because of the marginality and isolation of the nuclei themselves, a problem further compounded by the geographical concentration of communists in New York and Chicago. After two years of pushing them to the fore, party organizers had to confess that no more than 15 percent of American communists belonged to the much-promoted shop nuclei, a number of which contained only two or three comrades. Fewer than one in three wage-working communists actually belonged to unions in 1924–1925. Bolshevization appeared as something of a dark cloud hanging over the project of communist recruitment; its only silver linings were that it appeared to increase union affiliation among the party ranks, which climbed to almost 50 percent by 1927, and those recruited to communism under Bolshevization were more likely to remain affiliated with the Workers (Communist) Party than those who came into the party at other times.[1]

Had this sorry record, combined with the ongoing factional gang warfare that, by 1925, had fractured the party leadership into at least three discernible groupings, been the sum total of communist practice in this period, Cannon's perspective and prospects would have been glum indeed. In the mid-1920s, though, Cannon's experience as a communist leader was steeled in a Leninist duality complicated by a particularly complex context. On the one hand, to be

sure, Cannon the loyal Cominternist was assimilating the Leninist organizational orientations that he struggled to comprehend, a project by no means as
simple as it might appear. This political program as it applied to party formation, after all, was being filtered through a growingly bureaucratized Comintern, whose degeneration few communists inside or outside the Soviet Union
(Cannon among them) actually grasped decisively. Moreover, it had to be
applied creatively in the nonrevolutionary situation of the 1920s United States,
where a highly heterogeneous working class had largely accommodated to the
roller-coaster ride of a rather unstable, but strikingly dynamic, capitalist economy whose state forms and political culture were draped in the appealingly
illusory trappings of the world's most vaunted "democratic order." On the other
hand, it was precisely his understanding and grasp of this "American" political
economy and culture that separated Cannon, now one of revolutionary communism's leading native sons, from other Workers (Communist) Party leaders,
marking him *as a Leninist* attempting to develop a Bolshevik program within
the inhospitable climate of the United States in the post-World War I epoch. To
compare Cannon's record and programmatic stance in these years, balanced as
they were between the potential bureaucratizing pitfalls of Cominternism and,
later, the worsening malaise of Stalinism, and the always seductive appeal of
varied opportunisms organically associated with the peculiarities of "the American condition," is to appreciate the extent to which this difficult period was a
singular moment of political maturation. It was one that encompassed politics
and principles decidedly different from those crystallizing in the theoretical
pyrotechnics of Pepper; the administrative aloofness of Ruthenberg; the
Machiavellian machinations of Lovestone; or the quintessentially "American"
pragmatic adaptations, however reluctantly they were originally undertaken, of
Browder or Foster. The duality of Cannon's Leninism in these years of the mid-
1920s lay precisely in his negotiation of how to build a communist vanguard in
a climate—political, economic, social, and cultural—unwelcoming and challenging to revolution and its advocates.

Labor Defense and the Shifting Nature
of Communist Trade Union Work, 1923–1926

At the core of this party-mass dialectic was labor defense, work that was, in
Cannon's words, "organized on a scope and basis never known before."[2] It was
a project that Cannon carried out through old connections to the Industrial
Workers of the World and a politicized understanding of the class struggle.
Cannon was now differentiated from Foster, whose Trade Union Educational
League's (TUEL's) opposition to dual unionism increasingly took on the trap-

pings of a wooden reaction and inevitably separated communists and the masses of mainstream workers, while at times bowing to the authority of the labor bureaucracy in the American Federation of Labor. Cannon increasingly gravitated toward labor strategies, and particular tactics within specific class struggles, that would broaden the Workers (Communist) Party approach to trade unionism and working-class organization, rather than narrow it.[3]

This alteration in trade union perspective was most clearly articulated after Cannon and Dunne assimilated the lessons of a shift in the terms of trade between conservatism and radicalism in the labor movement, evident in the reactionary tide of 1923. Foster's TUEL had in fact peaked prematurely, its record of accomplishment of 1921–1922 largely in arrears by 1923. Eleven short months told the tale of demise: a December 1922 TUEL conference of railroad workers attracted 425 delegates, whereas a national gathering of the same body in October 1923 could draw a mere 143.[4] No sooner had the TUEL's programmatic counter to craft unionism's sectionalism, amalgamation, been given its most concise statement in Jay Fox's 1923 TUEL pamphlet of the same name than this strategy of regroupment within the unions, which had many noncommunist advocates in the 1921–1922 years, began to unravel in the face of rising AFL hostility.[5] This was the "trade union" face of the Cannon-Foster differentiation, a countenance conditioned by changed circumstances, and one put forward in party committees, to be sure, but also on display in forums largely external to the Workers (Communist) Party apparatus.

Inside this party machine, Cannon's uncompromising advocacy of Bolshevization seemed to tilt against the foreign-language federations and ethnic cultures within the Workers (Communist) Party, and it apparently did little to attract African American workers, but his outside campaigns to free various victims of capitalist oppression took up the banner of the coerced immigrant masses, so often the direct targets of state-orchestrated frame-ups, jailings, and deportations, or fought overtly the racist rule of Judge Lynch. As a labor defender, then, Cannon in the mid- to late 1920s sustained his presence as a figure of leadership stature in the Workers (Communist) Party, and developed a Leninist understanding of the relationship of party work to mass struggle.

Perhaps the major strike that best illustrates the trajectory of developments in these areas was the Passaic, New Jersey, textile mills battle of 1926, a struggle that unfolded, for the most part, while Cannon attended the Sixth Plenum of the Executive Committee of the Communist International in February 1926. An ideological climate associated with "Coolidge prosperity" dampened enthusiasm not only for radicalism, but also for labor activity of any kind. As union memberships declined from 1920 to 1923, the number of strikes eased off precipitously: one index established that if the annual rate of industrial work stoppages were pegged at 100 for the years 1916–1921, it would drop to 34 between 1922–1925, bottoming out at a mere 18 during the closing years of the decade, 1926–1930. Adding particular punch to this generalized beating, New England textile manufactures were one of a number of industries experiencing the unbalanced economic growth of the 1920s adversely. Judged "sick," and plagued by so-called overproduction, with plants closing in the unionized and now declining mill towns of the northeast to reestablish in the open-shop centers of the "new South," the long-established textile industry of New Jersey, Massachusetts, and elsewhere was in a serious depression by 1926. Wage cuts were the norm, and the workforce, largely immigrant and female, was increasingly without union protection.[6]

Passaic's textile mills were typical of this embattled milieu, and were hardly a site anyone, including the Workers (Communist) Party, expected to erupt in class warfare in the mid-1920s. The city's workers had a reputation for wariness toward "outsiders." Earning less than $15 a week, Passaic's female immigrant workforce lacked traditions of conventional organization and radicalism. There was no established union on the ground, although the IWW had tried unsuccessfully to unionize workers in 1912 and the Amalgamated Textile Workers had repeated, with no further gain, the exercise in 1919–1920. The United Textile Workers, the American Federation of Labor affiliate, did not even attempt to sign these workers into its ranks. Some communist shop nuclei were in place, with a few party members enrolled in various foreign-language federations. Nonetheless, Passaic was hardly a hotbed of militancy.

Into this milieu, fresh from the silk mills of Paterson, New Jersey, and leadership of a 1925 West New York textile strike, came an idealistic, mercurial, and willful bespectacled youth, a twenty-five-year-old graduate of the Socialist Party and the Young People's Socialist League, as well as City College and a few years of Harvard Law School. Converted to communism by reading Lenin in his last year at Harvard, Albert Weisbord dropped his legal training, joined the Workers (Communist) Party, and aligned himself with the Ruthenberg group. In September 1925, when Passaic's Botany Mills cut the wages of its operatives by 10 percent, Weisbord—whether he went on party orders or under his own steam is still open to debate—wasted no time in establishing himself in the New Jersey mill town, a national center of the woolen and worsted industry known for its appalling domestic and working conditions: the 63,000 immigrant workers and their families, constituting one-half of the city's entire population, lived in congested conditions and occupied barely one-sixth of Passaic's area; the illiteracy rate was the third highest in the nation; tuberculosis was a dreaded killer, the local death rate from this disease being twelve times the national average; infant mortality was an astounding 116 per 1,000 live births. A mere half an hour by train from the metropolitan radicalism of New York City, Passaic was sized up by the indefatigable Weisbord as having the makings to rival the Paterson mill strike of 1913, when William D. Haywood, John Reed, and others turned a mass strike of silk workers into a pageant of revolt that galvanized the urban intelligentsia.[7]

Weisbord established a united-front committee and issued dues stamps and membership books to the embattled workers. In effect defying Foster's established resistance to dual unionism, Weisbord appealed to the unorganized mill workers, tapping into their resentment. The Ruthenberg camp was now willing to give lip service to a more straightforward program of communist leadership in labor politics and working-class organizing, especially among those without union protections. Buttressed by the differentiation of the Cannon-Dunne group from the Chicago-based Foster-Jack Johnstone contingent of TUEL advocates, the Ruthenberg shift on trade union policy was not secured until a December 1925 Plenum of the Workers (Communist) Party, where Cannon backed the move away from Foster's "AFL fetishism." In a summary of the Plenum Trade Union resolution, Cannon was adamant in his opposition to the Foster group, posing the issue of "dual unionism" and left leadership in ways that drew upon his past experience, as well as offering words that would soon seem eerily prophetic in terms of Weisbord: "You put the question—who shall enter the left wing? We answer, whoever is prepared to fight the bureaucracy . . . if in drawing the workers on that program into the left wing some unreliable leaders come either push them to the left or win the workers away from them." "Dual unionism," Cannon noted, came into Leninist usage for particular reasons, but as a political designation it had now taken on new connotations: "The revolutionists of the world," Cannon insisted, "speak of secession movements, of independent unions, but never with the unsympathetic attitude [to] workers" that had become all too common among the Foster-led, Chicago-based trade unionists. A phobia of "dual unionism" had been used to "terrorize" communists and poison their relations with the IWW, Cannon insisted, adding that, "I consciously refrained all these years of my life in the party from using the term 'dual unionism' because I hate the damned bureaucrats' word, because it is not the phraseology of trade unionists." As Cannon later recalled, "a one-sided policy of working in existing unions" was, if imposed as "an absolute," a dead-end.[8]

The "cyclonic activities of Weisbord" thus pushed Cannon, and the Workers (Communist) Party, in specific ways. Parlaying the discontent in Passaic into a 25 January 1926 walkout that precipitated 16,000 mill workers into the streets without the sanction of an AFL union, Weisbord held a mirror before the eyes of communist trade union policy. Clearly an instance of working-class militancy being harnessed by revolutionaries, the Passaic struggle gained immediate recognition in public awareness as "the outstanding conflict of the Coolidge era," placing the small Workers (Communist) Party very much in the eye of the storm over labor-capital relations in the mid-1920s. Upon his return from Moscow in April 1926, Cannon saw firsthand what Weisbord had accomplished.

With the talented radical journalist, Mary Heaton Vorse, directing the publication of a brilliant agitational organ, the *Textile Strike Bulletin,* Weisbord and the Passaic upheaval gained increasing attention in national newspaper coverage. Picket-line violence, in which mounted police clubbed women strikers who coughed up tear gas and firemen turned their hoses on the protesting workers, outraged commentators. Countless "outside agitators" were tossed into jail, Weisbord among them. Refusing to succumb, the textile workers' united-front committee orchestrated powerfully provocative mass pickets and marches, one of which was led by a Slavic woman wheeling a baby carriage. Strikers donned gas masks and World War I army helmets, taunting the mounted police with gestures and words of derision. Dragging on for thirteen months, the strike eventually saw the incarceration of hundreds of workers and their supporters, including college students, Greenwich Village bohemians, and various radicals. Weisbord maintained a disciplined control of the walkout for an extraordinary three months, but the recalcitrance of the mill owners, the treacherous sabotage of the AFL textile union, and the relentlessness of civic officials and police finally produced the inevitable dampening of enthusiasm, notwithstanding the extent to which Passaic had become something of a "national scandal."[9]

The denouement was not unrelated to the initial shifting of Stalinist gears within the Comintern, where the danger of ultrarightism was replaced at the Sixth Plenum of the ECCI by an oppositional turn against ultraleftism. (Stalin had an axe to grind against the "left" elements around the Maslow-Fischer leadership in Germany and the Bordiga group within the Italian party.[10]) Foster fortuitously translated this new "political line" into an attack on Weisbord's ostensibly adventurist practice of dual unionism; his stock raised in the Comintern, Foster was ceded control of the trade union committee, where the failing fortunes of Weisbord led the charismatic strike leader to become a Workers (Communist) Party sacrificial lamb. To wind the strike down, Foster and his supporters placated both the employers, who refused to meet with a communist leadership, and the trade union bureaucracy of the United Textile Workers, which agreed to take on the governance of the strike only if Weisbord was displaced from its leadership. The militant struggle was thus turned over to the American Federation of Labor union in August–September of 1926. Weisbord railed against the decision, but the die was now cast. All of Passaic, and many in the wider world of labor reform, appreciated the sinister role that the United Textile Workers had played in gutting resistance and denouncing communist leadership. In the first week of August, for instance, a less-than-revolutionary organ, *The Christian Century,* had declared, "if the strike is broken, the AFL will have been a conspicuous part in breaking it." With a former strikebreaking labor officialdom now in charge of the Passaic confrontation, the heart was clearly gone from the battle; "some kind of ragged settlement . . . wound it up," and after four months of negotiations that secured the beaten workers very little, the Passaic standoff was over.[11]

Its future lay in its rewriting, Foster in particular dressing it up in various accounts according to the needs of the moment.[12] Cannon and Dunne were later chastised by Vera Buch Weisbord for having been cowed by employer statements that they would never negotiate with communists, and Cannon and his group did indeed offer too little in the way of direct support to the embattled Weisbord. In an 11 August 1926 Political Committee meeting attended by Ruthenberg, Bedacht, Engdahl, Dunne, Cannon, Foster, and Bittelman, a series of motions that in effect abandoned Weisbord were passed unanimously.[13]

In retrospect, though, there were those who understood the price that had been paid for sacrificing the irksome if talented Weisbord. "We deserve censure," Cannon recalled in a 1955 letter to Theodore Draper, "not for giving conditional support to the organizing work of Weisbord, but for failing to go all-out in such support and to make the issue of AFL fetishism clear-cut."[14] Within the Comintern, Foster's ally Lozovsky later came to the same conclusion, bluntly criticizing his American protégé: "Your sacrifice of Weisbord in fullfilment of the demands of the employers and the Trade Union Bureaucrats was the beginning of the end."[15] Cannon put the larger consequences of the Passaic imbroglio in political perspective, appreciating in the years to come that Stalinist accommodations leaning to the right were invariably followed by wildly oscillating policies that lurched to the ultraleft.[16]

Before the final demise of the mass struggle and Weisbord's fall, Cannon lent his political weight to the battle, participating in the formation of a joint committee that included representatives from Workers (Communist) Party groups, the League for Industrial Democracy, the Federated Press, and civil liberties organizations. Throughout April, May, and June, he proposed extending the struggle, proclaiming the "czaristic actions of the Passaic officials" an affront to the entire United States working class. Praising the energetic Weisbord and the resolute strikers in *Daily Worker* appeals, Cannon called on the forces of the workers' movement to "build a wall of defense around them." As late as June 1926, Cannon was helping to orchestrate the legal campaign and the funding that was necessary to free strikers and their leaders, involving himself in a New York City conference of bodies that stood behind the mill workers. "They crammed the doctrine into deed," he enthused, urging the defense of Weis-bord, other leaders, and the mill strikers as a matter of class duty.[17] Such appeals were not posed abstractly, but were made through the structured apparatus and in the name of a new Cannon-led organization, the Interna-tional Labor Defense (ILD).

"Professionalizing" Nonsectarian Labor Defense

Few communists entered the 1920s with Cannon's direct experience in and commitment to the politics of labor defense. His socialism had been forged on a foundation of specific campaigns and repressive incarcerations: Moyer-Haywood, Mooney-Billings, Wobbly jailings, and Palmer Raid indictments. "I came from the background of the old movement when the one thing that was absolutely sacred was unity on behalf of the victims of capitalist justice," Can-non told Harry Ring in 1973. "And I carried that over with me."[18] A part of his belief in the need for a legal, above-ground communist party lay in his appre-ciation that bourgeois America in the mid-1920s afforded unique opportuni-ties for the Left, which could exploit the contradictions of democracy the better to bring a revolutionary program to the masses.

One measure of this, and one that brought labor defense campaigns to the potential forefront, was the extent to which repressive currents continued to flow through the political culture of the United States, even in the face of radi-calism's retreats and reaction's seemingly stabilizing hegemony. They did so, however, in ways that contradicted claims of bourgeois order. The Palmer Raids, following on the heels of the Russian Revolution of 1917 and the explosive erup-tion of the revolutionary left wing within the United States, could be legitimized far more easily than the actions of the municipal "Red Squads" of the mid-1920s, but this did not lessen their impact, felt in cities such as Los Angeles, which was regarded as "the open shop citadel of the country, blatantly and cruelly anti-labor, racist, and unorganized." It was no better in the steel town of Pittsburgh, which Steve Nelson remembered as "strictly open shop; any union men were fired and blacklisted." In Gastonia, North Carolina, which would be torn asun-der by a strike involving communists in 1929, Liston Pope uncovered a 1920s cul-ture in which "God and good roads and cotton mills and contented labor and legal justice were all closely connected." Disrupters were most unwelcome, and in the trial that grew out of the labor-capital confrontation at the end of the decade union organizers were convicted less for civil offenses than for "heresy."[19] If the vigilante terror of 1917–1919 was ugly enough, there were those who could justify it as "Americanism's" last stand against the revolutionary alien, riding the wave of Bolshevism's powerful international conspiracy. The brutal ransacking of a San Pedro IWW hall in January 1924, in which children attending an evening dance were scalded with boiling coffee and disfigured for life, seemed to have descended to new depths of reactionary depravity. There was little in the political economy of the mid-1920s that could justify such barbarity, even to the most steeled of evangelical counterrevolutionaries. One account titled the outrage "Atavism at San Pedro."[20] The Ku Klux Klan, riding to the sway of a widespread racist populism in the aftermath of a Civil War that ostensibly freed the slaves, had a mass appeal in the plantation south during the late 1860s that was much harder to sustain in the 1920s, when "hooded Americanism" marched against the religions of the immigrants and the marginal. In Carnegie, Pennsylvania, a 1923 parade, headed by the Imperial Wizard and followed by thousands of robed Klansmen, was routed by an enraged phalanx of workers, who used stones, clubs, and guns to disperse the KKK invasion.[21]

These same immigrant workers, however, often bore the brunt of a nativist state and legal assault, being subject to a widening net of deportation procedure developed by the Department of Labor and its Bureau of Immigration. Over the course of the 1920s, such federal bodies steadily eroded the legal protections afforded "alien" workers, the standards by which warrants were served, arrests undertaken, and the foreign born charged, convicted, sentenced, and/or deported regressing until two officers were eventually processing 20,000 warrant applications a year.[22] If immigrant workers could not be moved out of America, their need to be footloose to secure a living could easily be criminalized: Los Angeles police made more than 12,000 arrests in 1927–1928 alone on vagrancy charges.[23] It was precisely because the 1920s was such a decade of legal attack on immigrant labor in the United States that the unsuccessful defense of two Italian anarchists, Nicola Sacco and Bartolomeo Vanzetti, respectively a shoe worker and a fish peddler, proved perhaps the most dramatic and ongoing progressive campaign of these difficult years, congealing sectors of a fractured and beleaguered revolutionary Left and translating the sentiments of this political milieu to a mass—and sympathetic—working-class audience.[24] Labor defense, as Cannon would come to grasp more decisively than his counterparts among the factional heads of the Workers (Communist) Party, was perhaps the quintessential Leninist united-front activity in a 1920s United States that was increasingly and obviously distanced from the realization of revolutionary transformation.

The ILD was a combination of Comintern inspiration and homegrown adaptations. Cannon had been toying with the idea as early as April 1924. He wrote to Noah London of plans to amalgamate all labor defense work—international, national, and local—into a new body that Cannon suggested be called the International Workers Defense Committee.[25] At its most specific, the idea to form a United States Workers (Communist) Party body for the defense of class-war prisoners was first kicked around in Moscow in March 1925, as William D. Haywood, Jim Cannon, and Rose Karsner discussed the political situation in the United States and its relation to the Communist International's evolving organization of relief and defense work. On the one hand, Haywood and Cannon knew well the old pre-World War I practice of the American Left, in which ad hoc defense committees quite often gave rise to concerted campaigns that mobilized tens of thousands. Karsner, on the other, had been a pivotal figure in the Workers' Party efforts to drum up support in the United States for various Comintern projects of aid and defense.[26] First initiated in 1919 by Ludwig C. A. K. Martens, head of the Russian Soviet Government Bureau, the original official Soviet agency in the United States, these endeavors reached from The Society for Technical Aid to Soviet Russia, through the more locally focused National Defense Committee and Labor Defense Council, both of which were organized out of the need to defend arrested communists in 1920 and 1922; to the highly successful, Alfred Wagenknecht-led Friends of Soviet Russia (which underwent a series of name changes and shifts in focus to become, in 1924–1926, the Workers International Relief/International Workers Aid); into, finally, the Comintern's International Red Aid, or, in the nomenclature of the Russian acronym, MOPR.[27]

By 1925, with the failure of various revolutionary movements in Europe, the latter body was the subject of considerable discussion. Comintern sources identified more than 85,000 political deaths throughout Southern, Central, and Eastern Europe between 1925 and 1927, attributing these executions to a wave of reactionary violence that engulfed territories in which revolutionaries had succumbed to defeat in the post-1919 years. As a white terror unleashed its repression in the aftermath of communist failure, at times seizing state power and consolidating regimes dedicated to the brutal suppression, jailing, and worse of revolutionary forces, the Comintern rightly saw the need to widen the International Red Aid into a series of national sections, expanding MOPR's function of raising money to assist communists under attack into a broader program of international protest and defense of political prisoners. Cannon approved of the project, but in conversations with Haywood and Karsner the trio struck on the notion of "Americanizing" the plan, making "our chief appeal for the hundred class-war prisoners in the United States while at the same time adding our voice to the protest in behalf of the victims of white terror in Eastern Europe." If the cause of labor defense was to be properly promoted and made a living part of the United States political scene, however, Haywood, Cannon, and Karsner agreed that it must have a "broader characterization" than past Workers' Party efforts. Making it "really non-partisan" was the primary consideration.[28] The ILD was close to being born.

When Cannon and Karsner returned to Chicago in April 1925, the International Red Aid was already in the process of organizing an American branch. They rightly saw that by its very name such a body "signified a communist outfit." Determined to create and build something other than "an auxiliary group of the Communist Party," Cannon took the matter into various Workers (Communist) Party committees and got a reasonably warm reception, in which factional considerations, though present, seemed confined within relatively nonpartisan bounds: "I met the representative [of MOPR] at the meeting of the Political Bureau and we came in with this broader concept of the Americanizing of it and giving it a title which would not push away the non-Communist elements. We hit on the idea of the International Labor Defense. Everybody understood that. That's American language. We discussed it in the Political Committee and got their approval to go ahead."[29]

Cannon spent much of the spring of 1925 setting the stage on which the ILD would soon make its appearance. He and Haywood had identified an initial 106 class-war prisoners still in United States jails on various criminal syndicalist and other related charges. Over the months of April and May, this tally climbed to 128. Many of these were convicted as members of the Industrial Workers of the World, whereas others, such as the well-known Sacco and Vanzetti, Mooney and Billings, or McNamara and Schmidt, were believed to have been incarcerated because of their union activism or revolutionary politics. None of the originally named prisoners was actually a member of the Workers (Communist) Party, although some of Cannon's comrades, such as Benjamin Gitlow, were under indictment or out on bail. Cannon's contact with former Wobblies, such as Ralph Chaplin, was thus crucial in the first stages of setting up the ILD. Still radical and sympathetic to the IWW, these individuals had dropped out of organized political life on the Left, but remained dedicated to those who, like themselves, had lost their freedom in the fight for some variant of a proletarian order.

The new labor defense cause also attracted the immediate interest of the Department of Justice: agents attended ILD branch meetings and offered confusing commentary, not being able to figure out whether this was a communist, American Civil Liberties Union, or IWW body. A part of the state's difficulty was that the nascent ILD incorporated local defense committees in places such as Pittsburgh; used Workers' Party defense networks, especially the Labor Defense Council, that had been established to propagandize around the ongoing legal cases of Ruthenberg, Foster, and others facing charges arising out of the 1922 Bridgman, Michigan raid; and attracted the support of a number of noncommunist notables. Among the latter were Andrew T. McNamara from the Machinists' District Council of Pittsburgh (often confused with brothers John and James of the same surname, imprisoned for the bombing of the *Los Angeles Times* building in 1910), who was elected the original chairman of the ILD at the first national conference in 1925; others included the seasoned defense campaigner from the Chicago Carpenters' Union, Anton Johannsen; Eugene V. Debs; Upton Sinclair; Scott Nearing; Clarence Darrow; Lucy Parsons, widow of the Haymarket martyr Albert Parsons; and Cannon's old friend from the Kansas coal fields, Alexander Howat. The fiery "rebel girl," Elizabeth Gurley Flynn, once a Wobbly and now in motion toward the Workers (Communist) Party and its united-front work in the 1920s, was targeted by Cannon, who eventually secured her involvement in the defense body as its second national chairman.

Promoting the new ILD brought out the best in Cannon, who enjoyed traveling to meet potential supporters, talking up the mobilization, extending old contacts, and establishing new ones. It was perhaps all the more exhilarating for Cannon to spend at least a part of his time on what he considered "honest work and solid achievement for solidarity in the old IWW spirit [using his] . . . influence for simple honesty and good will . . . toward all the prisoners of the class war," given the factional ugliness in which he was constantly embroiled. Half of Cannon's energy remained "devoted to keeping the Party faction together," and as he would later note in exasperation, "that was really defense." Generating funds was always a difficult, ongoing concern. There is no doubt, though, that the first surge of organizational effort associated with getting the ILD off the ground pumped up Cannon's political adrenalin.[30]

To be sure, factional jockeying was a part of the early history of the ILD. Cannon originally proposed a slate of twenty-nine candidates for the national committee of the new organization, thirteen of whom he listed as "non-party" and sixteen being "party" figures; and a smaller Executive Committee of seven, eventually expanded to nine. Lovestone battled unsuccessfully to strengthen the Ruthenberg group's representation, but later took some solace when Rose Karsner resigned from the International Workers Aid, allowing, in Cannon's words, "one of their hacks" to be put in the vacated post.[31] Ruthenberg, Lovestone, and Bedacht attempted to water down the ILD's potential growth by constitutionally eliminating the possibility of specific branches being formed outside of existing unions, fraternal organizations, and benefit societies, thereby ensuring that the new organization would be harnessed to the established structure of the Workers (Communist) Party; this move would have greatly handicapped individual affiliation and lessened considerably the likelihood of nonpartisan mass action. In this they were defeated by the combined votes of the Cannon and Foster groups (Bittelman, Cannon, Dunne, and Burman). The same voting alignment defeated Ruthenberg's effort to torpedo Cannon's being designated the chairman of the first national conference of the new defense group until a full-time national chairman could be elected and the executive secretary of the ILD named upon its formation.[32]

Karsner later found dealings with Ruthenberg somewhat strained, and in particular had difficulty even getting to see him, not to mention extracting commitments and funds from the de facto party leader. "Must we always go through such ceremony before getting to see you?" she wrote sharply, one year after the formation of the ILD. "I phoned you twice and finally came to your office only to have to go away without speaking with you."[33] As early as January 1926, Cannon faced charges of factionally stacking the ILD headquarters with his supporters, and an irate George Maurer, who had headed Workers (Communist) Party defense work in Chicago and seemed poised to assume the leadership of the ILD upon its creation, produced a four-page statement of pique and a three-page series of resolutions on what was wrong with the united-front work on behalf of class-war prisoners.[34] Cannon and Karsner nevertheless managed to weather the storm, with Rose in particular producing an impressive defense of early ILD procedures, explaining financial expenditures of the organization clearly, and establishing strict accounting methods that would successfully keep even the most carping critics at bay.[35]

Benjamin Gitlow, whose animus to Cannon was unmistakable, later alleged that the launching of the ILD was a "political plum for any ambitious leader." Cannon, whom he regarded as "unsuited" to head the defense mobilization, utilized the organization "for his personal prestige" and factional interests. "I am not surprised that [Cannon's] political vision did not extend beyond his caucus," Gitlow stated with obvious rancor. He failed conveniently to mention that Gitlow was himself on a steering committee of three, joining Cannon and Dunne, appointed by the Workers (Communist) Party's powerful Executive Council (Political Committee), to oversee the first national conference of the ILD, and that the new defense center's publications featured his case from the very beginning of the organization's history (Gitlow's and Anita Whitney's convictions and potential jailing under criminal syndicalist legislation were made a prominent part of ILD protests and meetings throughout 1925).[36] Even Theodore Draper, his ear to Cannon usually schooled in sympathetic respect given the credibility he had come to expect from Cannon as an informant on the communist experience in the 1920s, judged the relationship of personality, faction, and party front somewhat harshly: "In a faction-ridden party," he wrote in 1960, "party control assumed the form of factional control. Cannon converted the ILD into his personal political fortress."[37]

Appearances are easily mistaken for intentions. Cannon's "take-over" of the ILD "plum" might well be a case in point. Draper, Cannon contended, had missed the main issue:

> I am somewhat disturbed that the bulk of your questions refer to possible fac-
> tional implications and maneuvers in setting up and operating the ILD. All that
> was secondary. The real story of the ILD is the story of the work it did. . . . Our
> faction served the ILD as a border guard to keep factional disruption out of the
> ILD, or, in any case, to reduce it to a minimum.

Factionalism, which was devouring the party in those years, affected the ILD
less than any other field.[38]

To begin with, Cannon was later quite insistent that he had not sought out
the leadership of the new defense body; indeed, he had imagined that George
Maurer would head the ILD. However, the pivotally important noncommunist
elements in the ex-IWW grouping ostensibly pressured Cannon in what he
perhaps exaggeratedly claimed was "the surprise of my life." Refusing to consider anyone else as the secretary of the ILD, these Chicago-based former Wobblies balked at Cannon's suggestion that another Workers (Communist) Party
figure head the defense work. "Nothing doing," they said, "you're going to be the
secretary. You got us involved in this, and we trust you to keep it nonpartisan."[39]

Maurer, who would later nurse resentments, supposedly agreed,[40] ostensibly
because he grasped that without the enthusiastic support of noncommunist
elements the united defense front was doomed. In this scenario, Cannon did
not seize the "political plum" of the ILD. Rather, he planted the seed, nurtured
its early growth, and then had control of its future entrusted to his care; there
was no plum for the picking. If the Ruthenberg-Lovestone forces balked at the
way things were going, their hearts were clearly not in an all-out fight, and in a
sense they also handed the reins of the new body over to Cannon and those
around him, as did Foster's faction. "I think Lovestone and Foster and Ruthenberg were kind of glad," Cannon remembered. "They thought they'd get me out
of the way in the party, out of the faction fight." An almost pro forma factional
opposition to Cannon's ILD proposals and leadership stature soon gave way to
what Cannon perceived as indifference: "I must say that the other leaders of the
Communist Party paid no attention. . . . A lot of them had the idea that this was
'women's work,' a little charity. They didn't have that deep, gripping feeling that
a rebel has for one of the movement who has fallen into the clutches of the
enemy. I don't think they felt it at all." As Cannon would later acknowledge,
"Each faction gained elbow room to work in certain fields with practically
unlimited authority and a minimum of control. . . . We organized the International Labor Defense and ran it virtually as we pleased."[41]

The ILD, over time, certainly came to be a bastion of the Cannon faction,
although the podiums it organized and the pages of its press were never closed
to other Workers (Communist) Party members or noncommunist advocates
of labor defense. Cannon conducted most of the organization's significant

correspondence and visited both notables in the public arena and political prisoners; when the ILD had a national conference or a local gathering, Jim was usually the chair. "I spent a great deal of time on the road organizing conferences and speaking, visiting prisoners, keeping in contact with people who were interested in the ILD work but who were not in the Party," he reminisced in 1973. In June 1926, Cannon even returned to his old Kansas City haunts, reliving his student debating society days as he appeared at the Open Forum of the Midwest Student Conference, where he spoke on "Justice and the Wage Worker," clashing with judicial and military scions of the conservative cause.[42]

Rose Karsner handled fund raising and the routine administration of "the office, watched the finances and did the bookkeeping," producing, as well, a regular column for the ILD press, the Labor Defender, the first number of which appeared in January 1926. In her "Building the I.L.D.," Karsner wrote of the defense body's work throughout the country, or assembled notes written by local figures, so that the column served as a monthly update on campaigns and activities. She likely had a hand, as well, in putting together the "Voices from Prison" section. It contained letters from class-war prisoners, and was followed by the publication of meticulous accounts of donations, numbered sequentially, that took up two pages of small print in each Labor Defender issue and that were summarized and accounted for in terms of expenditure in a year-end published financial statement scrutinized by a certified public accountant.

Cannon insisted on such careful and public procedures because he knew that the ILD's reputation depended on fiscal responsibility. But if Jim laid down the administrative laws of ILD procedure, it was likely Rose who had to carry them out. It was not an easy task, and the times were difficult enough without other complications, of which there were two. Plagued by ill health since the inception of the ILD, Rose battled fatigue and at first worked full time for half wages (although she was soon put on full pay), conscious that her relationship with Jim opened the defense body to charges of nepotism, but aware that the interests of the new cause justified her presence in the office, however it might be misconstrued for factional purposes. She was perhaps too accepting of playing second fiddle to a male dominant in the party hierarchy, but she no doubt rationalized the respective roles she and Jim could play on the basis of a realistic assessment of their different talents. Also she probably understood the unfortunate truth that a man would command greater authority in radical circles than she as a woman could muster. Rose no doubt breathed a sigh of relief as the ILD got off the ground in 1926 and part of her office responsibilities were taken over by Martin Abern, a long-standing Cannon loyalist who had honed his administrative skills in the leadership of the Young Workers League (1922–1924) and a district organizer's posting in Chicago (1924–1926).

Abern played a prominent role in managing the growing responsibilities of the ILD, especially as it came by 1927 to organize mammoth annual fund-raising bazaars, four days in duration, and orchestrate national speaking tours by Elizabeth Gurley Flynn, Bishop Brown, and Cannon. One of the more abrasive of Cannon factionalists, Abern had, of his own accord, opted to be a point man in the Cannon-Foster group's attacks on Lovestone at the raucous August 1925 Workers (Communist) Party convention. The Ruthenberg group, ascendant after Gusev's rulings as head of the Parity Commission, repaid the favor by doing what it could to drive him out of the key post of Chicago district organizer. Cannon kept such retribution in check; nevertheless, the marked youth leader eventually found his way to the assistant national secretaryship of the ILD, making for more congenial party relations all around. Even if the roads of factionalism's inner-party hell were not always paved with good intentions, they sometimes ended up producing results that worked in everyone's best interests.[43]

Press and Propaganda

There was no better barometer of the ILD's developing success than its magazine, *Labor Defender*.[44] The monthly publication was the vehicle through which the ILD's work was translated to a diffuse membership, and it too was firmly in the hands of Cannon supporters. At first, the hard-drinking, jocular Irish communist journalist and Cannon confidant, Tom O'Flaherty, brother of the literary limelight Liam O'Flaherty, was seconded from the *Daily Worker,* where he was an experienced columnist, and placed in editorial control of the monthly magazine, which Cannon recalled was originally O'Flaherty's idea. From its beginning numbers, *Labor Defender* was an imaginatively put-together propaganda organ, its pages alive with photos and article titles presented with graphic boldness and unconventionally disparate print type and size. Covers were, like the then-defunct *Labor Herald,* usually adorned with pen-and-ink sketches by the cartoonist Fred Ellis, whose signature form was one of brutal frankness. Under O'Flaherty's editorship, communist convention was, for the most part, followed; his guiding strengths lay in making the *Labor Defender*'s articles powerful evocations of the need to defend class-war victims.[45]

Helping out was a young Max Shachtman, another Cannon recruit, barely twenty-one years of age. Soon, however, pressure was put on the ILD to have O'Flaherty return to the *Daily Worker,* and he was replaced as editor of the *Labor Defender* in July 1926 by the precocious Shachtman. "One of Cannon's right hand men" in the struggle against Pepper, Max had obvious talents as a journalist. More creatively, his aesthetic modernism and venturesomeness with the relatively untried medium of photography were immediately appreciated by

Cannon, who, though his own abilities in this area were undeveloped, had a strong attraction to innovation and avant-garde presentation of radical ideas from his first contact with Max Eastman and the *Masses* in the aftermath of World War I. The ILD leader thought the editorship of *Labor Defender* was "made to order" for the irrepressible Shachtman, who soon adapted the innovative styles of revolutionary European publications to the monthly magazine, making it a pioneer of modernist journalistic presentation in the rather staid circles of left-wing United States propaganda. A powerful influence, no doubt, was that of Willi Munzenberg, a founder of the communist youth international (1919–1922), and a figure known to Cannon and Karsner through his 1921 coordination of hunger relief for the Soviet Union and his extensive and imaginative revolutionary media empire in Weimar, Germany, which included publishing houses, a film company, a library, several newspapers, and journals that routinely featured avant-garde use of photography. Shachtman took it all in until some thought it had taken him over. Comrades worried that the party favorite "Maxie" was becoming too much of a camera hound, prone to neglect political duties by spending his days "shmoozing" with photography store clerks. Jokingly they would ask when he was going to open his camera store, to which the sharp-tongued Shachtman replied that he already had: "it's right above Cannon's saloon." *Labor Defender*'s circulation soon grew to 22,000, outstripping that of the *Daily Worker* by at least two to one.[46]

If the ILD never quite managed to become the truly mass organization that Cannon and others wanted it to be, its impact was nevertheless considerable. The ILD grew from 59 to 128 locals in 8 months; 13 September 1925 was declared Labor Defense Day and 34 cities held local conferences. Well over 200,000 pamphlets, leaflets, collection lists, and posters were distributed, and a Paris Commune commemorative week was planned for March 1926.[47] After its founding convention at Chicago's Ashland Auditorium on 28 June 1925, attended by more than 100 delegates and addressed by Bishop William Montgomery Brown, Ralph Chaplin, Andrew T. McNamara, Gitlow, and Cannon, the ILD was well under way in establishing itself as a major presence in American left-wing circles. At the end of 1926, the defense organization claimed 156 branches with 20,000 individual members and fully 75,000 affiliates associated with it by belonging to bodies that offered their collective endorsement. Dues were a modest ten cents a month, raised to fifteen cents by 1927.

Dedicated to leading protests aimed at freeing all class-war prisoners, the ILD also challenged anti-labor legislation and the arbitrary use of court injunctions against workers; provided legal aid to those facing trial and sentencing; educated the labor movement and the wider public about the extent of class persecution in the United States; was committed to united-front cooperation and building solidarity of all defense forces, national and international; struck repeated blows against racist brutality and lynching; and continued the Comintern-inspired project of exposing the nature of white terror in other capitalist countries. Especially important was the organization's commitment to relieving the misery of class-war prisoners by sending them $5 monthly, with a Christmas gift of $25, and supporting the wives and children of such victims of capitalist justice with monthly stipends and holiday donations ($20 per month for dependent families and $50 at Christmas, as well as smaller gift amounts for children). Birthdays of class-war prisoners were published monthly in the *Labor Defender*, their jail addresses provided along with a reminder of how much they would appreciate a letter of support; when prisoners were released, that too was noted. The relief-effort undertaking was a large task, unprecedented in the history of United States left-wing movements, and it highlighted a particular set of politics.[48]

First, in its striving to be nonpartisan the ILD relief mobilization integrated itself into existing defense committees, such as those already set up by the IWW. "We sent $5.00 a month to I guess 70 or 80 IWW prisoners but we didn't send it over the head of their committee," Cannon later recalled. "We sent it in a lump sum to their committee and they forwarded it. There was no question of invading jurisdiction or pushing others out of the way." Second, relief work was provided as an act of revolutionary solidarity, dispensed without expectation of the return of any kind of political capital, and there was never thought of restricting defense donations and ILD activity to struggles in which the particular causes of the Workers (Communist) Party would be highlighted (as would later be the case). Cannon stressed that this was important to the prisoners, who greatly appreciated the small latitude a monthly stipend made in their lives of boredom, in which a commissary purchase could well prove the highlight of their day, and, as well, that it broadened the movement's sense of its accomplishments. Third, developing defense work in this new and extensive way required organization, and Cannon made it a priority to move the ILD out of the "volunteer framework" that had beguiled so many past relief efforts, consigning them to a "lower" place on the hierarchy of revolutionary activity and ensuring that, after the initial agitation around specific trials and cases had subsided, the material support for class-war prisoners would fade. "We had full time organizers in Los Angeles, in Frisco, Seattle, Chicago, New York, Boston and Philadelphia," Cannon explained, "and that was something entirely new in defense work." Fourth, and finally, if the ILD was plagued with the usual gendered assumptions about the class struggle, in which the ranks of the revolutionary forces were too easily constructed as male, with females being wives and mothers reliant on the male wage, it nevertheless broke from past practice with explicit recognition: "It must be recorded to the shame of the labor movement that poverty, hardship and neglect have too often been the fate of dependent families and the consciousness of it eats into the very hearts of those in prison. . . . The International Labor Defense feels it a first duty of the labor movement to provide regular material and financial aid to the dependents of class war prisoners." Whatever its limitations, the politics animating the ILD were expressive of "genuine solidarity on a non-partisan basis for all class-war prisoners."[49] As an antidote to years of sectarianism, undergroundism, and factionalism, the ILD was Cannon's, and potentially the party's, bridge back to a politics of mass activity.

One of the first cases Cannon and the ILD took up was the international campaign of protest waged against the Horthy government in Hungary, especially its efforts to send Mathias Rakosi, the former People's Commissar of the short-lived Soviet Hungary, to the gallows. Mass meetings were held across the country; a continuous ILD picket was maintained outside the Hungarian consulate in New York City (drawing more than fifty arrests); Cannon petitioned Secretary of State Frank Kellogg and successfully enlisted the support of William C. Bullitt. Bullitt, who had married Louise Bryant after John Reed's death, was an aristocratic liberal well connected in foreign-relations circles even after his repudiated mission to Moscow in 1919. *Labor Defender* kept members abreast of developments abroad in regular columns entitled "In Other Lands" and through feature presentations of specific defense work. On rare occasions, the journal highlighted anti-imperialist struggles, as in July 1927, when the cover proclaimed "Hands Off China" and Shachtman contributed a major article, "American Imperialism Shall Not Throttle the Chinese Revolution." The drift to fascism in continental Europe, covered especially in treatment of Italy, was a regular component of ILD propaganda. Cannon penned a *Daily Worker* article calling for an end to deportations of Italian American dissidents, who faced execution at Mussolini's hands, and decried the extent to which the United States Department of Labor was colluding with fascist spies who were infiltrating the immigrant milieu to track down exiles and opponents of the right-wing regime in the Old World. Major European events, such as the British General Strike, were often the subject of treatment, and Shachtman's innovative use of visual material was deployed to highlight international campaigns, the *Labor Defender* regularly and effectively presenting full-page photomontages of contemporary struggles that brought events in France, Italy, Hungary, and elsewhere into American view. Still, the priorities of the ILD were inevitably more focused on homegrown cases.[50]

Class-War Prisoners

One of the earliest and most prominent of these cases involved midwestern miners, among whom Cannon was often a speaker. In Ziegler, Illinois, a mining community in the south of the state that saw a progressive local of the United Mine Workers of America confront the Ku Klux Klan and intransigent employers, twenty miners faced "frame-up" charges of conspiracy to murder, a case promoted avidly in the pages of the *Labor Defender*. Eight defendants were eventually sentenced to prison terms of one to fourteen years.[51] The Weisbord-led Passaic strike of 1926, and the trials and prison terms that grew out of it, was a major ILD cause; the *Labor Defender* provided almost constant coverage of the struggle for two years, with Cannon contributing many statements. The ILD claimed in June 1927 that the Passaic battle had resulted in hundreds of arrests; 185 strikers fined more than $4,000; bail bonds that had soared in excess of $600,000; 11 prisoners serving sentences ranging from 1 to 21 years; and a final count of "almost 1000 cases" defended. Weisbord faced a possible prison term of fifteen years. (All of the imprisoned strikers were immigrant workers, and they included two Italian women with five children.) The veteran African American journalist, Cyril Briggs, wrote a 1927 article acknowledging the end of the strike but insisting on the need to continue supporting the Passaic prisoners and their families. Children of the incarcerated New Jersey textile workers were featured guests at the third annual National Conference of the ILD, held in New York City, 11–13 November 1927. As the Workers (Communist) Party appeared to abandon the strike and its impetuous "dual unionist" leadership, the ILD kept something of the memory, and a little of the communist commitment, to Passaic alive.[52]

Among the many cases pursued by the ILD in its early years were "the Haverhill frame-up," in which a Massachusetts shoe worker and active unionist, John Merrick, was charged with placing a bomb outside of a factory; the joint IWW Defense Committee-ILD support of Richard Ford and Herman Suhr, railroaded to prison for the ostensible murder of a California district attorney and deputy sheriff, in which the charges grew out of their involvement in the Wheatfield riots of 1913 and, upon Ford's eventual parole in 1925, his immediate arrest on another murder allegation; a stand in support of Boston taxi drivers who, during a strike they waged while essentially unorganized, were charged with "robbery with intent to maim and kill" when they endeavored to induce a strikebreaker to stop working; the Alcatraz imprisonment of two Hawaii-based soldiers, Walter Trumball and Paul Crouch, for their efforts to form a Communist League at the Schofield Barracks; the arrest and trial of three Portuguese anarchists in the textile town of Fall River, targeted by state prosecutors, the Catholic hierarchy, and the Portuguese consul for their "blasphemous" irreverence; and various Pittsburgh, Wheeling, West Virginia, Brockton, Massachusetts, New York, and Bridgman, Michigan, criminal syndicalist, conspiracy, sedition, and "Red Flag" cases involving prominent and rank-and-file members of the Workers (Communist) Party, some of whom faced imprisonment for the crime of being in possession of revolutionary literature such as *The Liberator*. Much more than a propaganda vehicle, the ILD funneled funds and directed lawyers to specific individuals and groups, providing a front line of defense against the forces of state prosecution.[53]

With an increasing reputation as a militant defender of labor's interests, the ILD was drawn inevitably into the fray of labor-capital relations. Like the Wobblies of old, it championed free speech, defended the communist *Daily Worker* from the censorship of the "pay-patriots," and found its meetings broken up by police and agents of the business trusts.[54] When class struggle managed to erupt out of the trade union containments of the 1920s, be it among the New York furriers; Perth Amboy, New Jersey, copper workers; or the Colorado miners, the Cannon-led defense body was almost certainly to be heard.[55] Given the pivotal place of immigrant workers, and the nefarious role of the state and deportation in coercing accommodation in this potentially disruptive quarter of the United States working class, Cannon and the ILD provided a forceful voice defending the civil rights of those too often stripped of democratic entitlements.[56]

A critical ILD case, and one in which Cannon took a particular interest, was that of the communist Italian exile, Enea Sormenti, editor of the Workers (Communist) Party newspaper, *Il Lavoratore*, an organizer of the Anti-Fascist Alliance of North America, and a powerfully fearless speaker before Italian American crowds hostile to Mussolini. Seized early in October 1926 as an "illegal alien" by order of the Department of Labor's John M. Davis, Sormenti's proposed deportation to Italy, after he had been imprisoned and tortured in fascist jails in his homeland and hounded throughout Europe and northern Africa by fascist agents, was tantamount to a death sentence. The campaign to free Sormenti, whose real name was Vittorio Vidale/Vidali, and who would later be known as Carlos Contreras or "Commandante Carlos," was not without its tragic ironies. Vidale would eventually escape Mussolini's clutches by removing himself to the Soviet Union in July 1927, where he was soon posted to Mexico by the Comintern. Subsequently, he would come back to his adopted Russia, be involved in the Spanish Civil War, and return to Mexico in its aftermath. Rumored to have been implicated in the assassinations of both Leon Trotsky and the Italian American anarchist, Carlo Tresca (as well as an attack on a Mexican memorial meeting for Tresca), Sormenti/Vidale/Contreras was a shadowy figure in the degenerative international politics of Stalinist terrorism. A lover of the beautiful and talented Tina Modotti, whose renown as a photographer reached from Mexico to Russia, and who died mysteriously in a Mexico City taxicab after a 1942 dinner party, Vidale, by this late date, was vilified by anarchists and dissident communists alike. In the mid-1920s, though, Sormenti was a victim of capitalist America's assault on the "alien" other, and he brought Cannon into a closer working relationship with Tresca, with whom Jim had a warm, personal relationship, and other noncommunist immigrant revolutionaries.[57] The centerpiece of such evolving alliances of the 1920s was the defense campaign built around Sacco and Vanzetti.

Sacco and Vanzetti

Few cases in American legal history, save that of Julius and Ethel Rosenberg, still evoke the passions aroused by the chain of events that commenced in South Braintree, Massachusetts, on 15 April 1920, in which a paymaster at a shoe factory was shot to death during an armed robbery. Three weeks later, in the aftermath of a red scare that had seen the net of repression and deportation lowered over the Italian American anarchist community, Nicola Sacco and Bartolomeo Vanzetti were arrested and charged with participation in the crime. Their trial, following on the heels of a September 1920 bombing of Wall Street that was a retaliation for the arrest, took place from 31 May through 14 July 1921. It failed to establish the guilt of the two immigrant workers, but the poisoned political climate of the times, in conjunction with nativist antagonism toward foreigners, atheists, and anarchists, as well as circumstantial evidence of Sacco's and Vanzetti's being armed on the night of the robbery, produced the state's desired guilty verdict. From the outset, the defense campaign was a fractured affair, in which communists, anarchists, and liberals carved out their particular stances. The tempestuous political alignments of the Italian Defense Committee, split along oppositional lines since a 1915 separation of the *anti-organizzatori* (Luigi Galleani) and anarcho-syndicalist (Carlo Tresca) wings of Italian American anarchism, further complicated matters. So, too, did the seldom spoken, but always subterranean suppressed conscience of the Sacco-Vanzetti movement, in which there was thought—all the more common within mainstream trade union and public circles—that, unlike other frame-ups (Mooney and Billings were the striking example), guilt indeed might rest with one of the convicted, Sacco, who was thought among the *Galleanisti* to have participated in other robberies, even if he had not been guilty of the Braintree shooting and theft.

Despite all such divisions and problems, Sacco and Vanzetti stirred the soul of America in the 1920s. As the legal process appeared impenetrable to rational appeal, as new evidence of the two anarchists' innocence was rejected time and time again, as mass protests and political strikes and mounting police repression of the growing movement highlighted the closed-shop character of politicized justice, a truly heterogeneous united front was forged. It grew outward from America to encompass the world. The Uruguayan Congress, Swiss town councils, British unionists and Labor Party figures, and the municipal authorities in Rio de Janeiro, not to mention various Soviet bodies, petitioned on behalf of Sacco and Vanzetti; the ILD claimed that millions had gathered in protest meetings and huge demonstrations from East to West, North to South, in London, Paris, Brussels, and elsewhere. As the date of execution of the condemned men neared, the frustrations of those committed to the cause, especially some on the direct-action wing of the anarchist milieu, boiled over into bombings, which rocked New York, Philadelphia, and Baltimore on 5 August 1927. The house of one of the original trial jurors was later dynamited. Workplace walkouts developed spontaneously. In Colorado 6,000 IWW miners struck in protest on 21 August 1927, staying out three days to ensure that there would be no reprisals. At a Scranton, Pennsylvania, lace mill, the workers were more circumspect: bands on the large machines were sliced apart, the act of sabotage bringing production to a halt. Chalked into the limp leather were the words "Sacco-Vanzetti." The Workers (Communist) Party called for a general strike on the day preceding the execution, armed guards patrolled the nation's capital, and Mother Bloor was arrested as she tried to harangue a crowd to action from the second-story headquarters of the Boston Hod Carriers Union near the Charlestown prison where Sacco and Vanzetti awaited their fate. None of it did any good. On 23 August 1927, shortly after midnight, Sacco and Vanzetti were strapped into the electric chair, the current switch was thrown, and the jolt of state-directed volts burned them alive. Sacco went to his death with the shout, "Long live anarchy!" Vanzetti with a more subdued assertion of his innocence and a benevolent last bequest: "I now wish to forgive some people for what they are doing to me."[58]

The campaign to free Sacco and Vanzetti became the ILD's most significant case, and Cannon himself was at the center of the defense body's journalistic and agitational propaganda. Having promoted the protest against the frame-up of the anarchists since the beginning, Cannon stepped easily into the growing public agitation.[59] In a trio of communist publications, leading with the *Labor Defender*, but including as well the *Daily Worker* and the Chicago-based *Labor Unity*, Cannon authored or had a hand in approximately twenty articles and lengthy statements associated with Sacco and Vanzetti between May 1926 and November 1927. Many were the basis of public speeches, ILD talks, and agitational leaflets. "We splashed the . . . . case all over the magazine," Cannon would later comment, referring to the *Labor Defender*.[60]

Cannon and the ILD organized meetings, participated in mass rallies tens of thousands strong in cities across the United States, and pushed a steady stream of pamphlets, press releases, flyers, leaflets, buttons, posters (a powerful 22-by-32 black-and-white ILD image was distributed free), stickers, and other propagandistic ephemera into trade union, fraternal society, ethnic community, and left-wing circles. Eugene V. Debs was enlisted to write a Sacco and Vanzetti "Appeal to American Labor," which the ILD featured in the *Labor Defender* and circulated by the thousands as a leaflet. Such propaganda called for a national conference; promoted numerous local Sacco and Vanzetti united-front assemblies; raised money; and refuted slanders that, as communists, they were corralling the movement for narrow, sectarian purposes and siphoning off funds directed to Sacco and Vanzetti. Through bodies like the Sacco-Vanzetti Emergency Committee, organized in New York, the ILD sponsored mass rallies of 15,000 to 25,000 at Madison Square Garden and Union Square, demonstrations that were paralleled in size and enthusiasm by gatherings in Milwaukee, San Jose, Boston, Denver, Seattle, Chicago, and other major metropolitan centers; smaller outposts, such as Avella, Pennsylvania, saw lesser numbers drawn to the cause in picnics and meetings, but commitment to the freedom of the Italian anarchists was no less resolute. The New England district ILD was understandably centrally involved in the Sacco-Vanzetti defense campaign, and at its second annual conference, 28 November 1926, the cause of the imprisoned anarchists was of pivotal concern to the 138 delegates representing some 20,000 workers. When the Boston Defense Committee issued a nationwide call to mount protests for 30 July, 31 July, and 1 August 1927, Rose Karsner contacted ILD secretaries throughout the United States. Its agitators often physically intimidated and occasionally beaten by local "Red Squads," the ILD also extended the Sacco-Vanzetti defense campaign into the realms of free speech and workplace protest, encouraging political strikes throughout the spring and summer of 1927.[61]

Grateful for the widespread opposition to their "bloated judicial murder," the two anarchists strongly supported the call for the widest possible class unity in their defense.[62] It was not an easy task. United-front committees of defense brought together socialists, anarchists, communists, and liberals, and there were sometimes tensions. At a 7 July 1927 New York Union Square meeting, socialists and communists clashed, and after Ben Gold of the Workers (Communist) Party was kicked in the chest to prevent him from addressing the Sacco-Vanzetti crowd, the police were apparently called in by Socialist Party leaders to quiet the ranks and subdue the meeting.[63] Some quarters in the Sacco-Vanzetti mobilizations were quick to condemn "irresponsible elements," coded language for "anarchist bomb throwers." Cannon's speech before a Chicago Sacco-Vanzetti mass meeting, on 13 May 1927, in which he was preceded by the now anti-communist head of the Chicago Federation of Labor, John Fitzpatrick, indicates how the ILD refused the easy condemnation of some of its anarchist allies:

> The cause of Sacco and Vanzetti demands of us, of the entire labor movement, militant, unhesitating and united support. We may have different opinions on many problems; but there is one thing we have become sure of in these seven years in which we have said our word for Sacco and Vanzetti. . . . We have become convinced that Sacco and Vanzetti are not only innocent of this specific crime which they are charged with, but that they are innocent of any crime except that of being rebels against capitalist exploitation of the masses. . . . While I agree with the statements of Fitzpatrick that our meeting should disso-ciate itself from irresponsible people, let us not forget the year 1915 . . . [:] when the wave of working-class protest began to rise in protection of Joe Hill, gangs of detectives began to fake threatening letters. After the heart of Joe Hill had been pierced by the bullets of the death squad, it was exposed that frame-up let-ters had been used. . . . The protection of Sacco and Vanzetti is the job of the working class of the world, which is knocking on the door, not with the hands of irresponsible individuals, but with the titanic fist of the workers of the wide world because they believe . . . that the real aim is not only to burn Sacco and Vanzetti in the electric chair but to burn the labor movement in America.[64]

Such words took on added meaning as the summer of 1927 wound down, leav-ing fewer and fewer days for effective action.

The last days of July and first three weeks of August saw Cannon pull out all the stops. He shared podiums with figures from the labor Left, sent telegrams to a wide array of potentially influential public figures and politicians, coordi-nated large demonstrations, and put in motion a call for an August 22 general strike, with instructions going out to 200 ILD locals. By August 19, cablegrams from Boston contained the dispiriting news that "Sacco Vanzetti returned to death house die Monday," adding with a note of desperation, "use every effort strike." On the evening of 22 August 1927, it was apparent that the mobiliza-tions had failed to arrest the grisly proceedings. Cannon stood the "Death Watch" along with hundreds of thousands of other defenders of Sacco and Vanzetti in the United States and around the globe. ILD headquarters was draped in black and red, preparations in place to hold memorial meetings around the country. When, on 23 August 1927, Sacco and Vanzetti were finally executed, Cannon called for "a living monument" of class struggle to be erected to the memory of the fallen anarchists, heroic labor defenders who refused to succumb to the demands of the capitalist class and its legal and political spokesmen. At the Boston funeral of the executed rebels, a massive crowd of 100,000 wound its way through the narrow streets and drizzling rain,

40 abreast, responding to police provocation with a solemn linking of arms and refusal to be routed; across the nation similar, if smaller, "marches of sorrow" expressed an outpouring of grief and a resolute refusal to be cowed into submission. Seeing Sacco and Vanzetti as part of a continuity of repression reaching back to the Haymarket martyrs of the late 1880s, Cannon eschewed any notion that their trial, conviction, and execution was at all a "legal" or local "Massachusetts" case; instead, he regarded it as "a class frame-up" exposing a "vengeful, cruel, and murderous" elite. The ILD, Cannon asserted with pride, had done what it could to see that "the crucifixion of Sacco and Vanzetti was not prepared and carried out in a quiet and 'orderly' way in whispered consultations behind closed doors." Rather, the immense international opposition that crystallized around the demand to free the two immigrant workingmen developed a "sweeping vision [that] painted the whole monstrous frame-up on a canvas big enough for the workers of the world to see." Sacco's and Vanzetti's heritage, Cannon proclaimed, was "deathless" and it would live in the International Labor Defense campaigns of the future.[65]

The ILD attempted to make good on this promise by suggesting the burial of Sacco and Vanzetti next to the Haymarket martyrs in Chicago's Waldheim Cemetery, and by organizing a countrywide wave of Sacco and Vanzetti memorial meetings on the first anniversary of the state-ordered executions, 22 August 1928. It continued to agitate, as well, around the judicial murder, especially in volatile Massachusetts mill towns.[66] This appreciation of the past struggles of a heroic working class registered routinely in ILD work in the mid- to late 1920s, and the *Labor Defender* was commonly given over to theme issues, to which Cannon contributed, memorializing the Paris Commune, Frank Little, Eugene V. Debs, and C.E. Ruthenberg. The deaths of the latter two figures, on 20 October 1926 and 2 March 1927 respectively, took from the American revolutionary Left a beloved figure of almost unrivalled authority and one of the founding pioneers of communism in the United States. Responding with memorial meetings and commemorative issues of the *Labor Defender*, the ILD championed the legacies of these spokesmen of the oppressed, both of whom had been strong advocates of united-front defense work and had themselves been class-war prisoners. Over the course of one month, between 30 October and 28 November 1926, Cannon alone spoke at nine Debs memorial meetings from Boston in the east to Minneapolis-St. Paul in the west.[67] He promoted the historical "cause of the martyrs," connecting Haymarket and the 1927 Sacco-Vanzetti tragedy in Dedham throughout his life, and most especially in his late 1920s ILD work, notably at the third national conference of the defense organization in November 1927, a gathering that honored the memory of Albert Parsons and his comrades with a special guest appearance by his widow Lucy.[68] In a four-page folder dated 21 October 1927 and circulated throughout the United States, Cannon linked 1887 and 1927, appealing to workers to become better organized in defense of their class. "We must learn the lessons of the past forty years," he admonished. "Remember the Haymarket Martyrs. Remember Sacco and Vanzetti." Listing forty currently incarcerated class-war victims, and picturing seventeen children of imprisoned Passaic strikers, Cannon appealed for cards, funds, and packages to be sent to the jailed workers or their family members as an expression of "class solidarity for Christmas." "Join the Ranks of the Labor Defenders," he urged, explaining the necessity of "labor defense without conditions—without discriminations."[69] This message was continued at the Third Annual Conference of the International Labor Defense, convened at New York's Irving Plaza Hotel, 12–13 November 1927, with Cannon as the chair.[70]

A few months later, Cannon undertook a March–April 1928 lecture tour of the west, encompassing thirty-five cities and fifty meetings, which offered him a unique vantage point from which to view the communists' electoral campaign in the ongoing presidential contest. The prospects for a labor party, in the midst of Coolidge prosperity, were dismal indeed, and Cannon stressed the need for a communist party to unfurl the banner of revolution. He dropped in on the embattled Colorado miners, once again forced to the wall by the armed operatives of the Rockefeller corporate empire, reliving the repressive days of the Ludlow Massacre of 1914. At the struck Columbine mine, state troopers tear-gassed a crowd of men, women, and children, and then fired into a march of miners and their families, killing five and injuring a score more, including women and those attempting to aid the fallen. Other mine sites were scenes of lesser brutality, and the coal fields were said to be a battlefield, littered with arrests and wounded, the armed might of the state escorting student scabs from California into thug-protected, fenced mining compounds. Cannon soapboxed on "the frame-up system" and rekindled the passions of ILD work around some of its incarcerated victims, traveling from Colorado to the West Coast, visiting Mooney and Billings in the California prisons of San Quentin and Folsom, and talking with the seven Centralia prisoners who were serving twenty-five- to forty-year sentences in the Washington State penitentiary at Walla Walla. The incarcerated men's hearts warmed to the message that militant western miners stood behind them, and Mooney urged Cannon to continue the ILD struggle to make class-war prisoners a central cause for the labor movement. "I have been fortified all through these years of prison," he reported, "by my faith in the movement which I serve and by the consciousness that, even though confined here, I am an instrument of the workers' cause and a symbol of their struggle."[71]

Factionalism's Toll, 1927–1928

A whirlwind of agitational activity, the Sacco-Vanzetti-dominated years of 1926 to 1928 were ones that saw Cannon at his organizational and journalistic best, a communist committed to mass work and clearly energized by the day-to-day immersion in the battle for freedom and justice—a struggle he situated historically in an effort to cultivate the class memory of the labor movement. Shachtman judged the ILD of this period "by far the best of the non-party organizations created by the CP," stressing that its relations with noncommunists were on the whole quite cordial and productive, largely because, aside from some criticisms of money expended during the Sacco-Vanzetti campaign, there was little to grumble about. Cannon made sure that the defense body met its commitments to class-war prisoners and their families, allies in the left movement, and attorneys. "Say anything you want about Cannon," Shachtman later insisted, "he was absolutely, you might say, religious about seeing to it that those obligations were met and that the good name of the ILD was not open to any attack." Funded by itself, not beholden to the Workers (Communist) Party apparatus or the Comintern, but equally insistent that its own treasury should not be raided, headed by a strong factionalist who nevertheless refused to allow defense work to descend into "narrow factional purpose," the ILD was "close to [Cannon's] heart." "It is one of the purest and cleanest memories of my time in the Communist Party of the Twenties," Cannon told Draper in 1958.[72]

Cannon struggled to keep the pace of accomplishment quick throughout 1928, but in hindsight it appears that the ILD momentum, and especially Cannon's personal contribution to it, slowed. The defense campaign to exonerate Calogero Greco and Donato Carillo, anti-Mussolini activists in New York defended by the ILD and Clarence Darrow against charges of killing two fascists, was judged a repetition of the Sacco-Vanzetti "frame-up." The acquittal of the targeted Italian-American dissidents early in 1928, though a blow struck against reaction and its embrace of legal lynching, ended ILD mobilizations, and the cause of Greco-Carillo never came close to achieving the public prominence of the Sacco-Vanzetti agitations.[73] After this, and the publication of some articles resulting from his western speaking engagements and dialogue with Mooney, Billings, and the Centralia Seven, Cannon's writing for *Labor Defender* dried up. Having produced seventeen articles for the ILD paper in 1927 and the first two months of 1928, as well as a significant number of defense-related pieces for other communist publications, Cannon's journalistic count dropped precipitously, and included only two items associated with his interviews of class-war prisoners on the West Coast, both appearing in the June 1928 *Labor Defender.*[74]

Increasingly, Cannon's byline appeared in the *Daily Worker,* or other non-ILD party publications, and his writing was now less agitational. It had the eclectic quality of a leader being assigned (or choosing) an array of writing that kept him both off the central ground of party control and oddly distanced from his own chosen medium of labor defense. He took a stab at cultural criticism, penning a critique of Mike Gold's *Hoboken Blues,* a play that attempted comment on black-white relations and the development of a culture of hedonistic recalcitrance. Put on by the New Playwrights, a cooperative venture formed by Gold, John Dos Passos, and Howard Lawson in the aftermath of their arrest during the Sacco-Vanzetti protests, *Hoboken Blues* was one of the first efforts to sustain a new revolutionary theater. Cannon, however, found too little "fighting faith in any of the characters." He could appreciate Gold's desire to "see people happy and living in 'Hoboken' where folks don't work too hard, where there's plenty of food and beer and music, where both black and white are free and equal and all men are brothers," but "the note of struggle for the conquest of the machine [was] entirely lacking." Booze and blues, not the inevitable battle of the classes, seemed the answer in Gold's Hoboken, and it was not one that Cannon found entirely to his liking.[75]

Drawing on his old Rosedale days, Cannon suggested in one *Daily Worker* contribution that the mixed message of the fraternal order might be drawn upon by the Left.[76] In his election journalism he struck hard at the reformism of the Socialist Party, the impending collapse of the 1920s "economic boom," and the need to begin a concerted attack on American imperialism and its designs on global hegemony.[77] The mechanics of party building Cannon addressed with his characteristic attention to detail and responsibility, publishing a statement in a manual for communist organizers as well as in the party press.[78] When Cannon echoed Lozovsky's criticisms from the Comintern of the Workers (Communist) Party's trade union policies, his efforts to place the article in the widely circulated pages of the *Daily Worker* were rebuffed, his arguments buried between the covers of a communist theoretical organ.[79] Ironically, upon the death of his long-time friend and admired workers' leader, Bill Haywood, Cannon's obituaries were published, not in the logical magazine, *Labor Defender,* of which Haywood had been something of an original inspiration, but in the pages of other party forums.[80] Something was awry.

Cannon's 1928 tour was no doubt a means to spread the ILD message to the west, and revive concern with those languishing in California and Washington penal institutions. It was also possibly an indication of Cannon's desire to escape certain party/personal difficulties, the agitational road being, for him, not only a responsibility, but a chance to breathe new air outside the stale atmosphere of factionalism. Indeed, as will be apparent in the next chapter, a series of developments dating from 1926, including the fallout over a Ruthenberg-Lovestone-initiated move to transfer the Workers (Communist) Party headquarters from Chicago to New York, and Ruthenberg's unexpected death early in 1927, which elevated Lovestone to a dangerous, and increasingly fractious, prominence, added heat to the factional fires that had simmered as Cannon built the ILD into a public force on the revolutionary Left. This worsened as Sacco and Vanzetti faced execution. The ILD executive secretary found himself stymied in the Lovestone-controlled Political Committee. It refused, in August 1927, to accede to a number of Cannon's reasonable requests that the defense campaign be made an urgent priority. When Cannon's efforts to call a national conference of labor protest against the Sacco and Vanzetti "frame-up" were thwarted by Lovestone, Cannon pleaded in the Political Committee and in an Arrangements Committee to delay a Workers (Communist) Party convention, scheduled for 31 August 1927. The factional intensity of the moment, in which Lovestone was making a concerted bid for party power, made the membership meetings, held to select delegates in ten major cities of communist strength over the course of the first week of August, of critical importance. Cannon realized that the ensuing organizational fray would leave both the party and the ILD handcuffed in their capacities to be a forceful part of the last-minute agitations against the execution of Sacco and Vanzetti. Protesting the *Daily Worker*'s understated coverage of the ILD's significant role in the Sacco-Vanzetti mobilizations, Cannon's pleas fell on deaf Lovestone ears. Even Foster, embroiled in differences with Cannon around trade union questions but aligned with him in opposition to Lovestone, conducted an official ILD correspondence around the events of the summer of 1927, and would later charge that the Politburo majority had been following a "systematic, persistent, determined effort . . . to isolate the Cannon group, to get them in a corner." In the immediate aftermath of the execution, the Workers (Communist) Party produced a public statement condemning the capitalist murder of the two Italian anarchists, but within the still fractious Political Committee Cannon argued unsuccessfully against a strong majority that the national conference called by the liberal defense forces in Boston not be "packed" by ILD and communist trade union forces. In advocating that only a WP delegation be sent and sufficient ILD representatives attend to give communists "a good base at the Conference," Cannon was trying to preserve the principled practices of the International Labor Defense body as a united-front organization. Such a stand was wasted on Lovestone and, to a lesser extent, Foster, both of whom had their reasons for rejecting Cannon's advice. The future did not bode well for the ILD under such circumstances.[81]

Throughout 1928, the ILD continued to keep the issue of class-war prisoners and labor defense campaigns alive. The threatened deportation of European revolutionary leader Bela Kun to Hungary brought an immediate response from the United States, and Shachtman was promoting the defense of the Chinese Revolution with a twenty-eight-city tour and a riveting illustrated lecture. Much work coordinated the efforts of the Anti-Imperialist League and the ILD, as a former Foster-Cannon caucus figure, Manuel Gomez (Charles Shipman), promoted the prospects of revolution in Nicaragua under an "Enlist with Sandino" campaign. Circulation of the *Labor Defender* was rising, to the point that it outstripped that of the *Daily Worker, Labor Unity,* and *The Communist* combined. Pamphlet distribution was widespread in English, Italian, and Yiddish, and one four-page leaflet, "What Is International Labor Defense" had circulated massively (150,000 copies in English). Miners were the subject of defense campaigns in Colorado, Pennsylvania, Ohio, West Virginia, and Illinois, as were textile workers in New Bedford, Massachusetts, and Cannon's commitment to revive the older Mooney-Billings and Centralia agitations remained firm. Finances were low, but the ILD could account for its expenditures in a range of deportation, anti-injunction, anti-militarist, and strike-arrest cases.

Still it was not enough. Elements of the ILD were subjected to Lovestone's ridicule. Upon hearing the internationalist slogan, "Stop the Flow of Nicaraguan Blood," the caustic communist dubbed the pro-Sandino mobilization, "Gomez's Kotex Campaign." More dauntingly, Lovestone's lieutenant, Benjamin Gitlow, launched an attack on the ILD in the Political Committee, citing "complaints" from the ranks and demanding a report. Martin Abern, with a thorough and impressive accounting of the work of the International Labor Defense, was able to beat back this assault, but it was all too apparent that the factional gloves, which Ruthenberg's leadership had kept on during the heyday of the ILD, were now off as far as any Cannon-led party initiatives were concerned.[82]

It was clearly getting Cannon down, and it was likely affecting his personal life with Rose. The couple had forged an intense love relationship and principled political comradeship over the course of building the International Labor Defense, but the tensions associated with their being based in Chicago, while all of their children were largely located in the New York metropolitan area with other parents, had no doubt taken its toll. Moreover, Karsner, somewhat frail, had never quite been able to recover from a series of health problems, and her heavy workload with the ILD could not have helped matters. For his part, as the earthy and occasionally hard-drinking "trade union factionalist" with allies such as Bill Dunne and Tom O'Flaherty, Cannon was now exhibiting signs of the professional revolutionary's lifestyle, in which the days were short, the nights long, and the masculinist penchant for the sociability of the bar alluring. Amidst the revived ugliness of the gang warfare of party factionalism, Jim and Rose began to face private problems in 1927.

En route to yet another American Commission convened in Moscow in June 1927, with Cannon no doubt perturbed that he could not be on the ground as the Sacco-Vanzetti mobilization went into high gear, Jim wrote to Rose. After a restful night in Berlin, he felt revived after "the tiredness of the past weeks." Obviously attempting something of a reconciliation, he reminded Rose that a close comrade had once said of him that, "I always do things when it is *almost* but not *quite* too late!" Yearning for old times, Jim offered Rose the promise of better things to come:

> I was up early this morning (5:30) and took a walk about town before breakfast feeling like a lark. I enjoyed myself looking in store windows which displayed nice things for women and thinking of the prospect of going on a real shopping spree someday all for you. The dear thought of you was beside me at the breakfast table in memory of our first breakfasts together and the contemplation of a recreation of the old atmosphere when our breakfasts were a love rite, in the good times coming. Be of good heart, my own. The best is yet to be. Your own, Lover-husband[83]

What Cannon wanted, and what he would get, however, would be very different kettles of political fish. Though the ILD had been something of an interlude of peaceful coexistence in the factional gang warfare of Workers (Communist) Party internal struggle in the mid- to late 1920s, Cannon was inevitably forced back into the debilitating wrangling. Indeed, the years 1926 to 1928 would see the situation deteriorate. For Rose and Jim, matters would get a lot worse, and stay that way for years, before they took a turn for the better.

Rosedale Society of Debate, Rosedale High School, 1910, with Lista Makimson, back row, second from right; James P. Cannon, second row, second from right. Kansas Collection, University of Kansas Libraries.

James P. Cannon, 1928. *Labor Defender.*

Rose Karsner, 1925. Walta Ross/Prometheus Research Library.

English-speaking delegates at Comintern's Fourth Congress, 1922: front, floor, Otto Huiswoud and Rose Pastor Stokes; second row, Arne Swabeck (far left), Anna Louise Strong (second from right), Alexander Trachtenberg (far right); back row, Martin Abern (second from left), James P. Cannon (fourth from left). Ed Swabeck/Prometheus Research Library.

William F. Dunne, Tom O'Flaherty, William D. Haywood, James P. Cannon, Moscow, 1925. *Workers Monthly.*

Workers' Party, Paris Commune Memorial Meeting, Madison Square Gardens, 1925. *Workers Monthly.*

Fur Worker Arrested During New York Strike, 1926. *Labor Defender.*

Group of delegates, American Negro Labor Congress, 1925. *Workers Monthly.*

Fifteen Thousand Passaic Workers Give Albert Weisbord Vote of Confidence, 1926. *Workers Monthly.*

International Labor Defense Sacco-Vanzetti Poster, 1926. *Labor Defender*.

Carlo Tresca Addressing International Labor Defense Sacco-Vanzetti Meeting, 1927. *Labor Defender*.

James P. Cannon (arm on daughter Ruth's shoulder) and International Labor Defense National Office Staff, Chicago, 1928 (Martin Abern and Max Shachtman to left of Cannon; Rose Karsner front right). *Labor Defender.*

Youth Support of Cannon Faction, 1927: from left, Gil Green, Carl Cowl, Max Shachtman, and Albert Glotzer, with Foster supporter Nathan Schaffner in background. Albert Glotzer/Prometheus Research Library.

10

Living with Lovestone

A Cannon Faction to End Factionalism, 1926

The International Labor Defense (ILD) mobilizations of the 1920s gave Jim Cannon a respite from the factional intrigues that had become a ubiquitous feature of the social and political relations within a divided Workers (Communist) Party of America leadership. As we have seen, though, such united-front labor defense work was never thoroughly insulated from the cold and hot drafts of factionalism's changing seasonal climate. The intense factionalism of 1920–1923, dominated by a struggle to transcend undergroundism, gave way to the first forays into a factionalism colored by the bureaucratic degeneration of Zinoviev's Comintern, of which Pepper and his theoretical adventurism were striking examples in the 1923–1924 period of farmer-laborist maneuvering, and which continued into 1925, given Pepper's physical displacement, but adept adaptation, to Moscow. The founding of the ILD in 1925 was in some senses a symbolic interlude, in which the growing factionalism of the mid-1920s was asked to content itself with a partition of political territories. This was never more than an unstable and transparently incomplete containment, in which Ruthenberg's authority as an overseer was acknowledged grudgingly, if only for a time, and the consequent balance destined eventually to implode:

> Something went wrong, and the party began to gyrate crazily, like a mechanism out of control. The purposeful and self-explanatory internal struggles of temporary factions in the earlier periods, by which the party was propelled forward in spite of all mistakes and inadequacies of the participants gave place to a "power fight" of permanent factions struggling blindly for supremacy or survival in a form of political gang warfare. People who had started out to fight for

communism began to lose sight of their goal. Factionalism, which in earlier times had been a means to an end, became an end in itself. Allegiance to communism and to the party gave way, gradually and imperceptibly, to allegiance to the faction-gang. There could be no winners in this crazy game, which—unknown to the participants at the time—was destined to find its eventual solution in a three-way split and a new beginning.[1]

No figure looms larger in this unfolding history of new beginnings born of sorry deteriorations than Jacob Liebstein, a European Jew born in 1897 or 1898 who settled with his family in New York a decade later and who, in 1927, though not yet thirty years of age, was poised to assume the outright leadership of the Workers (Communist) Party. Jay Lovestone, as he was known in the United States, "set a pace and a pattern in party factionalism, the like of which the faction-ridden party had never seen before."[2]

Lovestone's significance was always an exchange relation with the Comintern, where decisions were, especially in the post-1924 years of hardening Stalinism, ultimately brokered. Cannon would come to acknowledge his failures in this milieu. He wrote to Draper in 1955:

> I never was worth a damn on a mission to Moscow after my first trip in 1922. Then everything was open and aboveboard. A clearcut political issue was presented by both sides in open debate and it was settled straightforwardly, on a political basis, without discrimination or favoritism to the factions involved, and without undisclosed tensions, arising from internal Russian questions, motivating the decisions and determining the attitude toward the leaders of the contending factions. That was the Lenin-Trotsky Comintern, and I did all right there. But after 1924 everything was different. . . . [and] by the time the Commission meetings got under way they were mere formalities. Everything had been settled behind the scenes; the word had been passed and all the secondary leaders and functionaries in the Comintern were falling in line.

The Rosedale communist came to detest "groping in the dark without knowing what was going to be decided by others without our participation."[3]

Arriving in Moscow in late January 1926, Cannon had a vague sense of the Stalinist climate of targeting a Trotsky-Zinoviev-Kamenev opposition, the consequences of which were a generalized drift to the right and the elevation of Bukharin, with whom Lovestone had close personal connections. Foster and Bittelman had preceded Cannon and others, working their way to Moscow in the fall of 1925, petitioning Stalin directly to overturn the Gusev-orchestrated coup of the previous summer. In this endeavor they made no headway. The Foster-Bittelman efforts nevertheless redounded to some effect: the Foster group was clearly held in low *political* regard by Stalin, but as a reserve body it could be conceded the trade union terrain, and kept in background readiness as an antidote to Bukharin and his U.S. advocates in the Ruthenberg-Lovestone camp, whom Lozovsky, as head of the Red International of Labor Unions, regarded as mere "dabblers" in labor movement work. This juggling of the American party's leadership contenders would continue throughout the 1920s, but as a tactic in the strategic emasculation of revolutionary leadership, conceived with the obvious intention of balancing Stalin's convoluted options in the struggle to secure unimpeded dominance of the Russian and Comintern apparatus, it probably jelled most coherently in 1925–1927. In the immediate context of February–March 1926 and the ECCI, this ensured that the American Commission was largely concerned with trade union questions, Foster's preeminence in this field, and the strategic orientation of his flagging Trade Union Educational League (TUEL), all brought to the fore by the Passaic textile strike.[4]

The American Commission that convened in the Kremlin, on 16 February 1926, was something of a brawl, pitting Foster and his allies (represented by Bittelman and Browder) against a fragile Workers (Communist) Party Central Executive Committee majority, headed by Ruthenberg and including the Cannon caucus. Ironically, Cannon found himself "nearer to the Ruthenberg-Lovestone" forces, but as a group he found them "too intellectualistic," and by themselves incapable of leading the party and building it as "a genuine workers' organization."[5] But Foster, whatever his proletarian credentials, was no better. Bill Dunne, who was the most vociferous in his opposition to Foster's control of trade union work, and who leaned more heavily in the direction of liquidating the TUEL as opposed to Cannon's attraction to broadening it into open communist work in the labor movement, declared Foster's presentations of labor issues in the United States nothing but "lies." Foster probably convinced no one in the Comintern of the rightness of his positions, but a combination of Bukharin's favoring of the Ruthenberg group, Lozovsky's appreciation that this contingent would never truly command the heights of trade union work and that Foster was still a better bet to conduct communist activity related to labor, general Comintern suspicions of Cannon's "softness" on Trotskyism, and Stalin's powerful need to stalemate potential (and future) oppositions, dictated a balkanization of the American leadership. A weakened Central Executive Committee majority, in which Ruthenberg's political authority was counterposed to the hegemony of Foster in trade union work, with Cannon's role shunted off as something of an appendage to each (by which his labor defense field was necessarily related to these bifurcated wings, but somewhat subordinate to both), undoubtedly satisfied competing sectors of the Comintern and suited Stalin's agenda adroitly.[6]

At the American Commission Soviet Union meetings in February–March 1926, Cannon thus tried to stake out ground different from that on which either Ruthenberg or Foster walked. His interventions were both less defensive (Ruthenberg) and less aggressively condemnatory (Foster) than those of his counterparts, and he scaffolded his positions on an appreciation of a dual necessity: the imperative of communists' developing connections with the masses; and the need for a systematic set of mechanisms by which this could be done in the trade unions. In this Moscow dueling, Cannon stood on the Central Executive Committee's December 1925 plenum vote to reorder the trade union work, in effect reconfiguring the TUEL.[7] Ironically, the TUEL's isolations and marginalizations had allowed Foster and his trade union lieutenants to orient toward dissident factions *within* the trade union hierarchy, a practice Cannon, Dunne, Swabeck, and the communist trade union militant Tom Bell challenged decisively in party committee meetings in December 1925 meetings. Foster had come under particular attack, and TUEL work in the furriers' union was sharply criticized for aligning with elements of labor officialdom; the implications of such an approach for other unions were also aired, but within the CEC Cannon's perspective was rejected aggressively.[8] To be sure, the Cannon caucus understood that the capitalist boom of the mid- to late 1920s and the weakened capacities of both the unions and the revolutionary Left had reduced the receptiveness to the TUEL greatly. This was not, then, simply a case of wrong-headed policies, but a situation in which objective conditions reinforced subjective error.

Cannon's orientation to the TUEL, which he continued to press in Moscow, thus stressed the need for serious changes in communist trade union policy. All too "amorphous" in its constituted lack of apparatus, the TUEL needed a thorough overhaul that entailed "at least a semi-form of organization" that would put it on an independent financial footing distinct from the Workers (Communist) Party—materially sustained, if not through dues, then by registration, journal subscriptions, voluntary contributions, or fund drives. Second, the League had to be broadened, and an elementary beginning was to "legalize" it before the masses of trade union members, who had to be able to recognize its standard and rally to it. This meant overcoming the most hostile elements of the union bureaucracy, some of whom had waged successful campaigns to "outlaw" the TUEL in their industrial sectors, thereby ensuring that the League could not conduct its work in the unions openly. Foster's TUEL had given the union bosses all the ammunition they needed to attack the League as communist and to expel left-wingers on the ground that they owed their allegiance, not to the union, but to a body whose first plank in its published program called for "the dictatorship of the proletariat"; whose administrative office had been amalgamated with that of the party; whose personnel, from its leading figures down to its rank-and-file activists, were almost to a person known Workers (Communist) Party members; and whose press, the *Labor Herald,* had, in 1925, been liquidated and, along with the *Liberator,* folded into the communist propaganda organ, the *Workers Monthly.*[9]

Obviously drawing on his conception of the International Labor Defense organization, Cannon was calling for the party's trade union work to be reconstituted as a united front, paced by communist cadre and leadership, but not ultimately controlled by or rigidly associated with the Workers (Communist) Party: "[W]e must have an absolute end to this chaotic condition in which Party and TUEL are practically the same body. We are under the illusion that we have a Left Wing and under the illusion that [since] we have a Left Wing we do not create a red mass organization."[10]

As central as the trade union issues were to Cannon and Dunne, Cannon also stressed the extent to which there was a need to unify the Workers (Communist) Party and put it on a footing that could break loose from the factional logjams that were now a permanent feature of poisoned leadership relations. He saw in Foster's American Commission interventions nothing "except the trade union question and the factional differences in the Central Executive Committee." Appealing to all factions to "let the past be dead," Cannon pointed out that although Foster had had a majority before the 1925 August Workers (Communist) Party convention, he did not have that same majority now. Distrustful of any settlement that would enshrine Foster and his allies in a position of trade union control within the party, Cannon called for programmatic clarity—"the important thing now is a clear line in the trade unions"—which he saw as a prerogative of the Comintern. That done, the defining body within the party must be a unified CEC, and Cannon appealed to Foster to work with the other groups for a party without factionalism.[11]

It was an impassioned ECCI intervention, but it had little effect. The Comintern decision was already made, and it would largely cede the trade union field to Foster and essentially maintain the TUEL, a concession that infuriated Dunne.[12] Cannon who, ironically given future developments, always played the good cop in the Cannon-Dunne appearances before the Comintern, tried to calm the troubled waters at the closing session of the American Commission, conceding to Bukharin "the present CEC remaining the majority, retaining the leadership of the Party and we agree upon Foster having the leadership of the trade union work and of Comrade Foster's close friends and collaborators devoting themselves primarily to the trade union work." Cannon nevertheless warned against allowing Foster entire control over appointment to the party's Trade Union Committee, and balked at the claim that the Comintern representative should be the arbiter of all decisions were contentious differences to arise. To be sure, Cannon agreed, the Comintern had the final say in all large matters of policy, but, he suggested, no communist party could function if its Central Committee and Political Committee were stripped entirely of their executive authority on small matters.[13]

The American delegation, Cannon among them, made its way back to the United States in late March 1926. Ruthenberg and Cannon, at least, were at their posts, attending Political Committee meetings in Chicago by early to mid-April. Factional warfare showed no signs of abating. Roughly speaking, the twenty-two-member CEC divided into eleven Ruthenberg votes and eleven votes split between Cannon and Foster; the Swedish-born representative of the Finnish communists, Fahle Burman, shifted his support from Cannon to Foster depending on the issue. Outside the confines of leading party committees, the factionalism was often of a rougher sort, with one extreme Ruthenberg supporter insisting on the necessity of paying "Foster with the head of Cannon." Cannon's quest for unity was not going to be an easy one.[14]

Asserting that Cannon suspended hostilities with Ruthenberg after breaking with Foster in 1925, only to come to nurse "feelings of being neglected," Theodore Draper claims that when he was "unable to win by the factional system, Cannon declared war on it." There is, however, virtually no evidence for such cynical claims. The independent voting record of Cannon on the seven-member Political Committee throughout 1926 and early 1927, in which he blocked at times with Foster-Bittelman and in other instances with Ruthenberg-Lovestone (on rare occasions reserving judgment by abstaining), all the while campaigning within the party against blind factionalism, is understandable less as a consequence of personal pique and more as a principled commitment to premise all political activity on a "main political line, regardless of who is for or against." It was inevitable that Cannon would find himself differentiated from particular leaders and tendencies at some point. At the root of such shifts was an insistence that *politics*, rather than instinctual factionalism, should determine votes. The break from Ruthenberg, at its most decisive in the summer of 1926, had nothing to do with Cannon's subjective sense that his importance was being neglected. It emerged, instead, out of a clear-cut opposition to a Ruthenberg-Lovestone attempt to reconfigure the Workers (Communist) Party regime in ways that Cannon and many others opposed by virtue of a politics of class affiliation.[15] Among the seemingly minor points of contention that pitted Cannon (and Foster) against Ruthenberg and Lovestone in this period, and that reflected larger issues, were the latter's management of the *Daily Worker*[16] and a push to relocate it, and the party offices, from Chicago to New York.[17]

Ongoing Stalinization

Internationally, the ongoing Stalinization of the Comintern was heating up as the aftermath of the British General Strike hardened a rightist opposition to the Left criticisms of a reconfigured bloc of Trotsky-Zinoviev-Kamenev.[18] Cannon group supporter Clarence Hathaway linked the turmoil in the Soviet Party with the less consequential contentions in Chicago, writing to Jim from Moscow at the beginning of July 1926.[19] A detailed lament came from Bill Dunne at the beginning of August 1926. No unity was emerging, Dunne contended, and Foster exhibited a by now tiresome penchant for oscillation. Work on the labor movement front was being squandered daily. The Passaic imbroglio having largely run its course, the New York needle trades fraction drifted from the party as both Ruthenberg and Foster offered it concessions that "may bring about a debacle." Unions in Chicago sidled up to the right wing of the bureaucracy in a "disgraceful united front" that sacrificed labor defense prisoners who had defied injunctions, and the organized left wing in the United Mine Workers of America had virtually collapsed. Demoralization was sweeping the ranks. Anti-leadership sentiment was growing and Ruthenberg's public addresses, in which the party was likened to an employment office where unity was to be brokered by patronage appointments, were only worsening an already poor situation. "The power behind the throne" was none other than Lovestone, Dunne asserted, and how long the contradictions in the Ruthenberg-Lovestone group could be "submerged" he was "unable to say but the cleavage is obvious to a blind man."[20]

How blind were the Soviet functionaries? They saw enough of what they wanted, and eventually ruled on the *Daily Worker* shift to New York, instructing Ruthenberg to make the move. Cannon's and Foster's opposition was crushed by the unassailable cable, and any further appeal to the party ranks or an expanded Central Executive Committee was decisively undercut. At the 13 October 1926 Political Committee meeting, Ruthenberg forced a motion on the move, his camp (Ruthenberg, Lovestone, Bedacht, and Gitlow) outvoting Cannon, Foster, and Bittelman by the narrowest of margins. A month later, at the Central Executive Committee plenum, the same outcome was secured, the majority predominating by a vote of thirteen to nine.[21]

All of this occurred at precisely the time that anti-Trotskyism in the Stalinizing Comintern went into overdrive, eventually pressuring a weak Zinoviev into capitulation and deposing him from his position of dominance in the Communist International. With the publication of Max Eastman's 1925 book, *Since Lenin Died,* in England, the United States, France, and Prague, the increasingly bureaucratized Comintern certainly had an eye on things American. Cannon, known to have once been extremely close to Eastman (Maurice Spector would later describe their relationship as one of "love"), inevitably came under a certain scrutiny. Denunciations of Eastman, most notably by Trotsky and Lenin's wife, Krupskya, appeared in the international communist press, either orchestrated by the Soviet apparatus or pressured by the political situation facing the Left Opposition in Russia. In October 1926, reports reached the Workers (Communist) Party Political Committee that Eastman was negotiating with the *New York Times* and the United Press to publish segments of "Lenin's Last Testament' and "Zinoviev's Confession," placing Cannon in an awkwardly defensive position. Like most agitational speakers in the communist milieu, Cannon's public speeches of the earlier 1920s had sometimes alluded positively to Trotsky. Cannon had apparently seen some of Trotsky's dissident writings critical of the role of the Anglo-Russian Trade Union Unity Committee in the scuttling of the British General Strike, and he harbored sympathies for positions that were increasingly represented as anathema in Stalin's demonization of Trotsky. The climate was one in which nary a leading figure dared to take a stand in favor of Trotsky, although many, as Shachtman later reported, held rather conflicted views on the leader of the Left Opposition: revering his role in the Russian Revolution, honoring his memory as second only to Lenin, but going along, if often quietly, with the political condemnations current in the mid- to late 1920s.

Consistent with his overall policy of refusing to further factionalism at every opportunity, Cannon distinguished himself in the general Central Executive Committee factional rush to condemn Trotsky by refusing to jump on the bandwagon of political invective, but he did go along for the ride. In the Political Committee statements lining up with the Stalinist attacks on Trotsky and Zinoviev that came out of the October 1926 meetings, Cannon offered no overt opposition to the general Workers (Communist) Party drift, in which Trotsky was characterized as guilty of "unLeninist deviations" and Stalin and Bukharin as upholders of the revolutionary legacy of the Communist Party of the Soviet Union. When the Political Committee addressed who should be sent to the Seventh Plenum of the ECCI, scheduled for mid-November 1926, both Ruthenberg and Foster declined to make the trip, neither apparently placing much of a priority on understanding the inner-party struggle within the Soviet Union. Cannon, in contrast, stated that "he didn't want to go personally but felt obliged to go from the standpoint of the MOPR and also in view of the Comintern situation." Obviously interested in being present as Stalin and Trotsky crossed swords over the nature of revolutionary program, Cannon was nevertheless shut down by the Ruthenberg machine. Named as one of three possible fraternal delegates, none of whom would eventually make the trip, Cannon responded to what was obviously a patently empty gesture by refusing to vote for his own ritualized displacement. The Ruthenberg majority sent Lovestone in his stead.[22]

Regrouping a Collective Leadership

As Lovestone departed for the Soviet Union, Cannon, whose time was also devoted to ILD matters,[23] launched a Political Committee challenge to Foster's de facto attempt to undermine the Workers (Communist) Party commitment to broaden trade union work. A series of crises in various unions erupted in this period.

Most critical was the bastion of TUEL strength throughout the 1920s, the New York needle trades unions. Having continuously run up against the non-communist but socialist leadership of the International Ladies Garment Workers Union, headed by President Morris Sigman, Workers (Communist) Party activists waged an uphill fight in the three largest New York locals, winning majorities on the executive boards of these bodies by the end of 1924. Sizeable gains were also registered by party supporters in Boston, Chicago, and Philadelphia. As the Cannon-Dunne critique suggested, Foster was, in the period 1923–1925, most likely to emphasize issues of "shop, of trade, and union," or, in the words of one organizer, "cautious by nature and not given to revolutionary phrases." This led to some consolidation of left-wing position, but it also impaled Foster on a dual dilemma. On the one hand, he was subject to critique from elements of his own party that he was insufficiently Left in his approach to trade union work, brokering too many accommodations with the trade union bureaucracy, especially the Sidney Hillman administration of the Amalgamated Clothing Workers in the men's industry. On the other, rightist elements within the unions, and particularly top layers of the leadership in the American Federation of Labor unions, were not even fair-weather friends, and many clearly waited for an opportune moment to drive Foster and the left wing into the ground.[24]

In the needle trades, this latter scenario unfolded with particular bitterness early in 1925, as Sigman moved to crush the TUEL opposition. Communist-dominated locals were suspended and raided, and charges were brought against left-wing leaders for having violated the union constitution. Revolutionaries in the garment trades responded by organizing a joint action committee (JAC) that directed the TUEL work in the industry, functioning in effect as an alternative union, collecting dues, servicing grievances, and negotiating with employers. But because "dual unionism" remained a heresy in communist circles, and one particularly abhorred by Foster, the JAC stressed that this program was merely the "fullest reinstatement" of the left-wing locals.

It commanded the support of a clear majority of ILGWU members who, if they were not committed communists, resented Sigman's heavy-handed, undemocratic repression. A mass demonstration of 40,000 dress- and cloak-makers rallied to the JAC cause. The suspended left wing successfully mobilized 30,000 needle-trades workers to strike.[25]

The ensconced ILGWU leadership, which maintained a stranglehold over top union offices by controlling voting procedures in ways that favored the many small locals that it held firmly in its political grip, was forced to retreat and make concessions to the TUEL. Nevertheless, something of a civil war took place in the unionized garment trades. Led by Charles Zimmerman and Louis Hyman, the left wing battled the Sigman leadership at a 30 November 1925 Philadelphia convention, but was outflanked by emerging ILGWU boss David Dubinsky. An impetuous left-wing walkout, pressed spontaneously by Hyman, was muzzled back into line by party figures Gitlow and Dunne. A year later the TUEL led a long, violent, and much-publicized strike of New York cloakmakers, a battle generally depicted in historical writing as a disastrous defeat; and a more successful work stoppage among the furriers. To be sure, the cloakmakers' walkout dragged on interminably, and neither the Foster nor the Ruthenberg-Lovestone factions appeared overly willing to sanction a settlement that did not proclaim "revolutionary" victory.[26]

Factionalism thus stalemated the communist leadership, and led to a destructive balkanization of authority. A Ruthenberg-Lovestone-created Needle Trades Committee within the CEC, chaired by Benjamin Gitlow, competed with Foster's longstanding CEC Trade Union Committee, which was largely frozen out of the garment trades picture by 1926. On the ground of the clothing industry struggle, Zimmerman, Rose Wortis, and Joseph Zack headed the TUEL Needle Trades Committee. This latter body, which actually led the strike, was apparently split between Lovestoneites and Fosterites. For their part, Cannon and Dunne struggled to transcend the impasse with a two-pronged, but interrelated, critique. On the one hand, they suggested that the left wing in the needle trades was guilty of provincialism and inflated understanding of "union control," which pushed Foster as well as the Lovestone forces into unwholesome relations with entrenched labor bureaucracies. They urged, in contrast, a wider grasp of the project of the left wing in larger workers' movement circles, their position premised on a principled resistance to brokered arrangements with the trade union tops in the garment trades. On the other hand, inside the party, Cannon and Dunne pushed for a complementary programmatic shift. Reminding the Political Committee of "the wrong path into which we are drifting in handling trade union work," they called for an end to the deliberate marginalization of Foster's trade union department, insisting that the Political Committee keep Foster apprised of all labor movement matters. Demanding that the Trade Union Committee meet regularly and formulate recommendations for the Political Committee, Cannon and Dunne were pressing the Ruthenberg-Lovestone majority to integrate the leading cadre in the trade union field into CEC decisionmaking.

The party leadership's inability to present a coherent face in the 1925–1926 needle-trades events compromised the capacity of the Workers (Communist) Party to chart an effective course in the unfolding garment-sector clash. To be sure, in contrast to the ideologically hostile account of the strike in Benjamin Stolberg's anti-left-wing tirade, *Tailor's Progress* (1944), unpublished work by David Gurowsky and John Holmes notes that the strike was militant, effectively organized, and generated overwhelming support that included mass pickets and rallies of 20,000 workers, as well as successful defiance of a New York Supreme Court injunction. It possibly played a role in securing the forty-hour work week in the industry and raising wages by as much as 10 percent. All of this was no mean feat in the harsh anti-labor climate of 1926. But the protracted struggle had also taken its toll, exposing the left wing to rank-and-file discontents, exacerbated by Sigman-Dubinsky attacks and manipulations, and paving the way for the future demise of the left wing and the ILGWU. In the years 1927 to 1929, the bureaucracy rode roughshod over once-powerful communists in the union, and the garment trades as a whole were precipitated into an unsavory period of sweetheart deals with manufacturers, police, corrupt politicians, and organized crime. A proud chapter in the history of labor and the Left was coming to a sorry close.[27]

Foster and the TUEL had thus succumbed, in the years 1923–1926, to the same oscillating practices in the trade union realm that had pulverized communist political work in the rancorous minefield of farmer-laborism, lurching from problematic accommodations to sectarian isolations. The trade union question in communist circles had become a quagmire of divergences and convergences within the factional camps, with Browder and Foster promoting the view that American imperialism was shoring up capitalism's capacity to "petty bourgeoisify" the working class, and Dunne and Swabeck placing the accent on the unfavorable circumstances confronting the left wing. These Cannon supporters insisted that those who misread the changing circumstances of American political economy as potentially favorable for revolutionary breakthroughs, as they suggested was typical of the Ruthenberg group, were bound to miscalculate and lead the party astray. Foster could lean in this direction as well, but he was also too often capable of standing pat on the old adherence to formulaic AFL fetishisms and opportunistic cultivation of trade union office. Such practice inevitably left its advocates mired in a rut of ossification. Cannon, no doubt influenced by Dunne and Swabeck, nevertheless worked to chart a more accommodating relationship with the Ruthenberg group, especially now that Lovestone's Moscow sojourn had opened doors to other party personnel in New York.[28]

This question of trade union work was also addressed centrally at the Seventh Plenum of the ECCI, where both Lovestone and Bittelman offered reports. The slowness of reconstructing the TUEL along the lines advocated at the 1926 American Commission, as well as the ongoing factionalism among U.S. communists, were the main concerns of Lozovsky, Bukharin, and Stalin. Notes and other documents from that encounter confirm the continuing deterioration of relations between the Ruthenberg and Foster groups (Lovestone had produced a long list of quotes entitled "Fakes of Fosterism"), as well as Stalin's cynicism with respect to Ruthenberg and his willingness to order the cessation of factionalism even as he was prepared to do nothing to fundamentally alter the balance of forces within the Workers (Communist) Party leadership.[29]

In this atmosphere Cannon continued to promote the idea of a collective leadership, premised on agreement around political line, that could finally supersede the factional gang warfare now seemingly lessening in the Workers (Communist) Party. If Cannon was often forced to butt heads with the Ruthenberg group in the Political Committee in January–February 1927 (C.E. and his allies appearing insistent, at times, in ramming their majority down the throats of a Cannon-Foster-Bittelman minority), he was still encouraging rapprochement on two fronts.[30] On the one hand, Cannon participated in a 7 February 1927 conference with Ruthenberg, Lovestone, and Bedacht with the express purpose of moderating inner-party tensions, and authored a late February statement with Ruthenberg designed to stop factional contests in the party's work within the cooperative movement.[31] On the other hand, cognizant of the reality of the move of party headquarters and daily press to New York in January 1927, Cannon used the absence of Lovestone in the late fall of 1926 to approach two of the leading eastern Ruthenberg-Lovestone field marshals, William W. Weinstone and Jack Stachel. The latter had already rubbed shoulders with Cannon a year previously as the two addressed audiences in tandem, countering Foster's factionalism in their promotion of party unity. Stachel had enthused about Cannon's "masterly job," and was deeply impressed with "the earnestness of Jim for unity."[32] This original foray into common work thus paved the way for a late 1926–early 1927 alliance, one that solidified with Cannon's recruitment of Weinstone, a Lovestone lieutenant with high popularity in New York, where he was the district secretary, and followings among the youth and in the South Slavic Federation. Apparently sickened, for the time being at least (for he would eventually return to the Lovestone fold), by the cynicism, corruption, and opportunism of the Ruthenberg group, Weinstone blocked with Cannon in a "faction to end factionalism," and aligned with Foster's supporters in New York where a principled combination around specific political questions was reasonable. Strides forward were made in strengthening ties to needle-trades militants and reconnecting with remnants of the Jewish Federation.[33] Cannon thus appeared to be making great headway.[34]

Ruthenberg's Death and the Lovestone Coup

Circumstances were not to pave this thoroughfare of good intentions in ways that would smooth the journey against factionalism. Rather, they led quickly to a Lovestone hell. On 1 March 1927, Ruthenberg was rushed to the hospital, where he was operated on for a burst appendix. The party leader never recovered, succumbing to peritonitis the next day. The veteran socialist campaigner, one of a handful of founding figures of American communism, was not yet forty-five years of age. Anna David, Ruthenberg's secretary as well as his lover, and a confidant of Lovestone, issued a "Lenin's Last Testament"-like report to a 4 March 1927 memorial meeting in Chicago, claiming that her comrade's dying words were: "Of course the Party will have to move to New York immediately. Comrade Lovestone, Jay, will have to be Secretary. . . . Tell them to preserve their unity." It was a timely declaration.

Between 2–4 March 1927, Cannon, Foster, and Weinstone came together in a bloc aiming to thwart Lovestone and install Weinstone as general secretary. They controlled the Central Executive Committee, which was constitutionally empowered to elect the secretary. At a 5 March 1927 Chicago meeting of the Political Committee, in which the Lovestone forces predominated, Gitlow headed off the Foster-Cannon-Weinstone triumvirate with a motion that Lovestone be installed as acting secretary. The next day Lovestone, Bedacht, Gitlow, Foster, Bittelman, and Cannon, along with two Young Workers League representatives, served as pallbearers at Ruthenberg's funeral, an event Cannon recalled as "obscenely manipulated" by Lovestone to "start off the factional campaign on the appropriate note." "The corpse of Comrade Ruthenberg is not a lifeless corpse," Lovestone proclaimed loudly, "but a source of inspiration. A very fortunate heritage to me," he continued with some hyperbole, "has been my almost twelve years of close association with Comrade Ruthenberg."

The dead had their uses. Throughout March the Lovestone forces bombarded the Comintern with communications; worked over former factional allies such as Weinstone; repaired some broken fences, drawing Stachel more decisively back into their ranks; and thwarted the "opposition" demands by insisting that a plenum of the CEC had to be "carefully prepared" and that a full convention of the Workers (Communist) Party of America had to be called so that "the present leadership [which] has directed the Party for the last eighteen months" could place its record before the membership. In the meantime, Lovestone was the acting secretary, and once ensconced in this position of power he would prove difficult to dislodge.[35]

With his commitment to the Sacco-Vanzetti campaign drawing Cannon away from the internal struggle for much of April 1927, his time devoted to the potential building of a national conference and organizing limited general strikes,[36] the Lovestone coup that both Cannon and Foster had no doubt regarded as an impossibility in early March began to take on discernible shape later in the month. At every turn, the Cannon-Foster-Weinstone bloc was tied up in procedural/factional knots by the Lovestone-controlled Political Committee. Eventually, a plenum of the Central Executive Committee of the Workers (Communist) Party of America was scheduled for Chicago on 4 May 1927, to be followed by a late August convention. All sides had appealed to the Comintern to intervene in the deteriorating factional war, in which theft of files and demands for investigations were now routine. An early April cable from Moscow exhorted the United States comrades to lay aside the factional battle, "categorically insist[ing that] there be no changes in the Political Bureau or other leading positions of the Party until the Party Convention." The Comintern vetoed an American delegation to the Soviet Union, asking instead for written statements. Lovestone seemingly had all that he wanted, yet the cable also called for a "Plenum of the Central" to be convened as quickly as possible to consider pressing political questions, and thus lent a certain authority to the upcoming Chicago gathering of the CEC.

Moreover, under separate cover, word came of the Eighth Plenum of the ECCI, to take place in the middle of May 1927, at which three obligatory American delegates (Lovestone, Gitlow, and Foster) were expected and two (Cannon and Weinstone) could appear at the discretion of the Political Committee. It was thought that the plenum of the Central Committee would take place before the departure of the delegation. Lovestone and his faction, predictably, nixed Cannon's and Weinstone's attendance, but the excluded CEC members appealed vociferously and persistently to the Comintern and finally secured Moscow's permission to make the trip. As the May plenum of the CEC approached, Foster, Cannon, and Weinstone sensed the possibility of reversing the factional tide with their majority in the Central Executive Committee, and Arne Swabeck, general secretary of the Chicago District, orchestrated a meeting of "Cannon group" supporters to consolidate the growing opposition.

Lovestone was forced to share the chairmanship of the plenum with Foster and Weinstone. Chastised, but well aware that the plenum was essentially meaningless and that all decisions were to be made in Moscow, Lovestone simply snubbed his nose at the CEC and, technically, defied Comintern directive. He and Gitlow packed their bags and departed for the determining plenum of the ECCI before the American CEC meeting had run its course. Cannon later commented:

> The meeting of the sovereign Plenum of the Communist Party of the United States, forbidden in advance to make any binding decisions, was made even more farcical by the failure of Lovestone to show up for the second session. He and Gitlow had abruptly departed for Moscow, where the decisions were to be made, without so much as a by-your-leave or goodbye to the elected leading body of the party, to which they, like all other party members, were presumably—or so it said in the constitution—subordinate. In a moderately healthy, self-governing party, involved in the class struggle and functioning under its own power, such reckless contempt for its own leading body would no doubt be sufficient to discredit its author and bring prompt condemnation from the party ranks. Nothing like that happened in reaction to the hooligan conduct of Lovestone on this occasion. . . . Since 1925 the party had gradually been acquiescing in the blotting out of its normal rights as a self-governing organization until it had already lost sight of these rights.

In May of 1927, however, Cannon was somewhat blind to the dynamics of Lovestone's initiatives, his judgment skewed by Weinstone's impressive political condemnation of factionalism, the rightward drift of the party under the direction of Lovestone and Bertram Wolfe,[37] and the shift to Cannon of a long-standing opponent, John J. Ballam.[38] Few in the party leadership could apparently fathom the likes of Lovestone and Wolfe holding a communist organization together. Cannon and Weinstone thus set out for the Soviet Union full of confidence.[39] The fly in the ointment was the usual coupled relationship of international and national matters: the predictably compromised response of the Stalinized Comintern, and Lovestone, who was about to *become* Lovestone.

Stalinism and Lovestone *Becoming Lovestone,* 1927

Cannon, Foster, and Weinstone arrived in Moscow on the last day of the Eighth Plenum of the Executive Committee of the Communist International, 30 May 1927.[40] The American Commission, appointed toward the end of the plenum, convened in June, and for it Cannon and Weinstone provided a detailed set of theses outlining the necessity of Bolshevizing, centralizing, and Americanizing the Workers (Communist) Party, reconstituting the party press and communist work in various foreign-language, women's, youth, African American, agitprop, and other sectors. Especially significant was the imperative to orient to the actual struggles of the United States working class, to "take into account the traditions and psychology of the American workers." A mid-June 1927 letter to the Comintern served as the statement of a newly forged bloc of the Cannon-Weinstone and Foster forces.[41]

Of paramount concern was the Lovestone group's factionalization of inner-party life, with Cannon and Weinstone having earlier claimed that the acting secretary had routinely thwarted unity and kept burningly alive a set of artificial party crises in the Finnish, South Slavic, Jewish, and needle-trades sections. Additionally, they accused him of exploiting the death of Ruthenberg by propagandizing, memorializing, and caucusing in such a way as to present the former party leader as a *factional* head, properly eulogized only by his allies, who routinely excluded other group leaders from participating in the prejudicial canonization. One party member wrote to the *Daily Worker,* sickened by what he termed "the continual glorification" and "slop" about Ruthenberg: "It would be all right for sob-sisters, a religious sect, Messiah-peddlers and the like, but for non-hero worshipping revolutionaries it is absolute bunk."[42]

The Cannon-Foster-Weinstone coalition found the early Soviet response to the crisis in the American section heartening, and after hearing that the Comintern seemed "in principle" to support most of their positions throughout a series of late June 1927 meetings, they cabled supporters in the United States on June 28 that their forces were prevailing on all questions. It seemed that the Comintern had endorsed the minority positions on imperialism and the danger of war; on the ideological campaign to "bourgeoisify" United States workers and the labor movement (where the opposition bloc was more subtle in its appreciation of the tensions inherent in this process than Lovestone, who was tending toward his later developed "American exceptionalist" argument that an expansive capitalism was capable of stifling class struggle); on trade union work and the TUEL (where Dunne's underestimation of the latter's potential was criticized[43]); and, most importantly, on the internal party situation, where unity was required and the Cannon and Foster groups were committed to the need to work with and win to agreement all party elements, including the Lovestone group.[44]

But for all the political agreement that seemed to grace the proceedings of the American Commission, it is likely that behind the scenes in the Stalinist Comintern, where the decisive assault on Trotsky had just taken place, issues of dire concern to the United States communists were little more than a foundation on which Stalin's maneuvers could more effectively take place. Stalin had, for instance, granted the Lovestone delegation an unprecedented meeting, in which he supposedly pontificated on the need to better the conditions of the American working class and forego the struggle for power, incapable of being won in the short term—a position that resonated well with the politics of "socialism in one country" and coincided with the Comintern's disastrous China policy, which would lead to the bloody defeat of the Chinese Revolution in 1927. Cannon and those with whom he was aligned waged a forceful opposition to the Lovestone group's tendency to regard American imperialism in the Far East as somehow subordinate to the lead of the British empire—the party slogan "America is the cat's paw of England" reflected this—and the debate over China also heightened an appreciation of the political differences within the American section, where the Cannon-Weinstone-Foster grouping adopted the position that it was mandatory to "Fight your own imperialism first and foremost."[45]

Lecturing Lovestone that "the proletarian revolution in the United States could wait, that it was a long way off," Stalin pushed the majority faction of the CEC to follow in fact the basic orientation of the Cannon and Foster groups: "to build up a good and powerful press, enter the trade unions and gain influence in them, develop our party methodically, especially attempting to draw into it leaders in organizations which exerted influence over the masses." Stalin moreover apparently told Lovestone that "anybody who thinks American imperialism can buy the whole working class is a *durak* [a fool, one of the worst of Russian insults]." The irony was that as Stalin advised this course he did so in such a way—a personal interview with a select faction—that bestowed authority on Lovestone and his followers, a group far less practiced in such an orientation than were either of the Foster or Cannon tendencies. However, Stalin trusted neither of these components of the Workers (Communist) Party, and he preferred to cast his lot with Lovestone, who had Bukharin's backing, a fact that no doubt encouraged Stalin to hedge his bets somewhat. Otto Kuusinen, a Stalin loyalist often prominent in Comintern American Commissions, apparently told Foster a week before the final resolutions that "Lovestone cannot take the place of Ruthenberg and collective leadership must now be established."[46]

The Cannon-Foster-Weinstone bloc promoted this reconfiguration of the internal party regime vigorously. To be sure, the Cannon forces were not unaware of the Foster group's continued adherence to a problematic politics of trade union work. In Cannon's opinion, though, the needs of the hour called for the concentration of "our blows upon the Lovestone regime while drawing, at the same time, a clear line between our position and that of the Foster group." Hammering away at the CEC majority mercilessly in his appearances before the American Commission in late June 1927, Cannon pilloried Lovestone for leaving the plenum of the Central Committee of the Workers (Communist) Party "without an explanation"; insisted that the majority had cultivated relations and obligations with "right wing philistines" in the party, on whom they relied to "do their work"; castigated the continuing influence of Pepper as a large factor in the ongoing factionalism of the party and a problematic barrier to unity; and, overall, demanded that the attitude of the Lovestone group— that it was "the party" and that all other groups were interlopers—had to end if unity was to emerge out of factional gang warfare.[47]

It was thus not terribly surprising that when the debates and hearings of June 1927 had run their course, the "Resolution of the Comintern on the American Question" offered a programmatic politics highly congruent with the Cannon-Foster-Weinstone positions. America as an imperialist power was identified as an aggressive danger to world peace and the forces of the international proletariat. The material and ideological "bourgeoisification" of United States labor was flagged as an objective consideration, and one that would undoubtedly slow the progress of revolutionary advance. Trade union work was to be structured in ways that built up the possibility of TUEL activity, but did not restrict it, as was Foster's tendency, to working only within the mainstream AFL unions; this embraced Cannon's appreciation of the need to build new unions in fields where none existed or where craft sectionalism had conditioned a long-standing lack of activism. Politically, the Comintern had all but wholly endorsed the Cannon-Foster-Weinstone program.[48]

On the regime question, though—ironically and somewhat tragically, now *the* paramount issue—there was a twist. To be sure, yet again, the Comintern deplored the ongoing factionalism, and "in principle" seemed to embrace the unity platform and a sense of shared leadership. It distributed blame for the factional imbroglio across all leadership groupings, and in proposing procedures for the preparation of the Workers (Communist) Party convention at the end of August, the Comintern gave the appearance of cultivating a broad authority spread across the established tendencies, endorsing a collective secretariat of three that was to include Lovestone and Foster. However, it also rejected as "inexpedient" any changes in the top leadership, which certainly gave Lovestone the upper hand. The central question was how all of this was to play out in the organization of the end-of-August 1927 Fifth Party convention, when, it appeared, either unity would be consolidated, or a factional power play by one or more of the groups would be mounted. Cannon had addressed precisely this question, insisting before the American Commission hearings that the Comintern provide sufficient "organizational guarantees" for "free discussion, free elections, etc." An elaborate document, signed by representatives of the Lovestone majority and the Cannon-Foster-Weinstone bloc, and overseen by the German Bolshevik, Arthur Ewert ("A. Braun"), though never published in any public party press, laid out guidelines in which proportional representation was stressed, but also contained some disturbing indications of how much the Comintern was in fact tilting toward Lovestone and seeking, in particular, to isolate Cannon.

First, Pepper, identifiable as a Lovestone factionalist and a signatory of the document on the Lovestone side, was designated the "representative of the party to the CI in the Presidium until the newly elected central committee" could send a replacement in the aftermath of the convention. This in effect ensured that in any future disagreements among the groups prior to the convention, where appeal for resolution to the Comintern had to be undertaken, Lovestone could count on the decision going in his favor. Second, the Cannon-Weinstone group, which had been named directly in the original "Resolution on the American Question," was isolated and marginalized as somehow outside of what the Comintern designated "the two main historical streams in the Party . . . the majority of the Pol[it]buro and the group of Comrade Foster." Ewert had apparently told Cannon and Weinstone during the American Commission meetings that he felt their group had a large role to play in the development of the Workers (Communist) Party, but only if they were *Bolshevik enough to establish a clear line and stick to it.* "A middle group is either buffer or Bolshevik!," he exclaimed; "Buffer groups do not cut much ice here." At the end of the American Commission hearings, the Cannon-Weinstone group appeared to have been reduced to such a buffer status. Cannon must have sensed at the time the maneuvering that was going on, and the results it was designed to produce, because he pushed to produce a "Declaration" that tried to deflect the political meaning of the Comintern's construction of the "historical streams" that had fed the making of American communism:

> Generally speaking it can be said that there are "two main historical streams" in the party, but it is incorrect to say or imply that these streams are represented exclusively by the majority of the Pol Bureau and the group of Comrade Foster. The Weinstone-Cannon group has its share of all the history and traditions of the party and contains elements from both the "main historical streams." Under no circumstances will we allow our signatures to the agreement to be construed as an admission that the Lovestone group is the only bearer of the "party traditions" because such a claim would be false.

In this defense of historical tradition, Cannon would, however, find himself increasingly bested as Lovestone became Lovestone.[49] Lovestone, in Cannon's later characterization, was a Stalinist "before Stalin's own method was fully disclosed to the Americans."[50] In this Lovestone had undoubtedly been schooled by Pepper.

The Cannon-Weinstone-Foster forces also played unwittingly into Lovestone's hands. An overly optimistic and premature judgment of the American

Commission's favorable disposition to those antagonistic to Lovestone possibly prompted Alexander Bittelman, a key figure in the Cannon-Weinstone-Foster coalition who had remained in the United States, to commit a fatal blunder by constituting what he called a National Committee Opposition Bloc, under whose auspices documents were issued to the dissident caucus's supporters. The name conjured up for the Comintern bureaucracy shades of the Trotsky-Zinoviev United Opposition Bloc, and in issuing a July 1 circular promoting the opposition *before* the final "Resolution on the American Question" was actually made public, Bittelman tipped the balance of forces badly. The flyer alerted the Lovestoneites to the need to secure a more unambiguous statement of endorsement from the Comintern, and it also flagged the Stalinist watchdogs that a potentially troubling opposition threatened to emerge decisively out of the chaos of American factionalism. No sooner had the American dissidents declared themselves an opposition than the Comintern Presidium pounced, issuing yet another authoritative cablegram, an ultimatum that solidified the notion of "two historical streams" by repeating its endorsement of the Ruthenberg group's superiority politically and the Foster group's legitimacy as a voice on American trade union issues. More tellingly, it struck out at Foster and those aligned with him, now claiming that all political and trade union differences had been disposed of, and condemning "most categorically every attempt towards sharpening the [factional] situation in the party, especially in the present objective situation as exemplified by the formation of a National Committee of the Opposition Bloc. The Comintern considers factionalism without political differences as the worst offense against the Party." Stung by this directive, which the Lovestoneites, who controlled the party press, made sure appeared boldly on the front page of the *Daily Worker*, 8 July 1927, the Cannon-Weinstone-Foster bloc was decidedly stillborn, forced to drop an unfortunate name and inhibited from presenting its politics before the party membership. Lovestone and his allies waged a relentless campaign to establish themselves as "the basic element," governing all aspects of party life. Foster in particular faced public denunciation. Bittelman would later acknowledge that although both Lovestone and Cannon aspired to build machines within the Workers (Communist) Party, there was a fundamental difference in their methods: "Lovestone's way was ruthless, unscrupulous and iron-fisted. Cannon's . . . was principled, comradely, personally warm, and diplomatically-clever."[51]

The Lovestone Regime: A Right Lurch, 1927–1928

Upon their return to the United States in July 1927, Cannon and Weinstone, as well as Foster, would thus find themselves almost entirely displaced, but they maintained their right to combine as groups to bring about the unification of the Workers (Communist) Party. Foster, who had been somewhat assured of an interim sharing of the party secretaryship with Lovestone by Comintern officials, and who was also forced to relinquish his personal control of the Trade Union Committee, splitting it with the Lovestone ranks when Gitlow was made a co-secretary of that section, found that Lovestone now claimed that he had been named "First Secretary" through a private meeting of top Comintern officials to which Foster had not been invited. The Lovestone group, which in turn named Foster "First Secretary" of the Trade Union Committee, interpreted this as placing their head in the powerful position of general secretary. Refusing to allow Foster to function as Lovestone's equal, the majority went so far as to deny him a desk in the national office. Foster and Cannon battled these arbitrary decisions in a 28 July 1927 Political Committee meeting, but were repeatedly outvoted by the stalwart, and dominant, Lovestone faction. Cannon's project of collective leadership was now further from realization than ever, and within the party hierarchy his personal authority and capacity to influence others had dipped noticeably.[52]

At the Workers (Communist) Party convention, held 31 August–7 September 1927, in New York's Irving Plaza Hotel, Cannon delivered a powerful address appealing for a consistently left-wing line in the party press around the questions of American imperialism and labor defense campaigns (such as that conducted by the ILD in support of Sacco and Vanzetti). The party had to begin the process of appealing to native-born American workers, Cannon insisted, pointing out that this all-too-often suppressed commitment had been central to the Communist International's instructions. He warned against the danger of allowing the fight against the right wing to "degenerate into a sport," and targeted forcefully the Lovestone "policy of patronizing the Foster group and attempting to isolate and struggle against [the Cannon group]." Cannon pleaded with the Lovestone winners to refrain from "the policy of which we have become familiar, of always selecting members of one faction to represent the Party." Standing on the Communist International's earlier resolution, Cannon insisted, "We are also leaders of the Party. We are also members of the Party. . . . [T]here has got to be conscious efforts to break down the faction walls, to break down the old divisions and to really merge the active elements of the Party into a single whole."

Lovestone disagreed. He attacked Cannon for allowing too many of his convention remarks to "degenerate into a spirit of quarrels and insults," in which "veiled, implied, and inferred" threats predominated. Against Cannon's charge that the party majority was "smothering" differences, Lovestone claimed that such political disagreements had been "magnified." Responding to the programmatic issues that had been articulated around the questions of United

States imperialism and the Chinese Revolution, Lovestone slipped into a dem-agogic defensiveness. "Comrades, you can go all around the world to find obstacles to unity," he pontificated, "but you will not stop unity," closing with threatening thunder: "[Y]ou will not interfere with the unification of our Party, because the basic obstacles have been removed, first by our Party devel-opment, second by the CI decision, thirdly by this Convention, and whatever is left, all of us can get together and we will remove the rest." It was all rhetor-ical rabble-rousing for a done deal.

Although the Central Executive Committee elections supposedly produced a Lovestone majority of twenty-five to thirteen, this was nothing more than putting into place the Comintern directive of 1 July 1927, which had stipulated a CEC to be composed of thirteen members of the minority opposition (the Cannon group took six places, the Foster forces seven) and twenty-two from the Lovestone majority. The slight wrinkle of some additional majority mem-bers was undoubtedly a consequence of the abandonment by William A. Weinstone and John J. Ballam, part of the bloc of oppositionists during the convention, of what they perceived to be a sinking dissident ship. In Draper's words, they "crept back into the Lovestone majority" after the proceedings were completed. A wrangle over the inclusion of John Pepper in the majority, strongly opposed by Cannon and Foster, was likely resolved by allowing Pep-per to be seated on the CEC and the fleeing Weinstone and Ballam to be replaced by minority figures as they crossed the floor to the majority, thus reconfiguring the original Comintern division of membership from twenty-two to thirteen to twenty-five to thirteen. Little came out of the August–September 1927 Workers (Communist) Party convention that had not already been determined in Moscow two months before.[53]

Lovestone was now virtually unstoppable. The opposition bloc was obvi-ously unraveling, and in a symbolic vote over the move of the party headquar-ters to New York, the Cannon-Weinstone-Foster forces were unable to agree.[54] By mid-September, Weinstone had cut his deal with Lovestone, and was allowed to continue to head the New York District, albeit with a slightly dressed-down title. Lovestone was crowned with a new office, executive secre-tary. The majority wasted no time in showing its colors: Bertram Wolfe was appointed head of the agitprop department and took over the editorship of a new monthly magazine, with *Workers Monthly* ceasing publication and *The Communist* taking its place; Jack Stachel, having been brought back into the Lovestone fold, was placed in charge of the organizational department, where he would grow into a truly devious and vicious factionalist; Max Bedacht, admittedly demoted from his previous stature as key counsel to Ruthenberg, was used to oust the Cannon advocate, Arne Swabeck, as district organizer in the powerful trade union stronghold of Chicago; of the twelve district organizers throughout the country, all but two were now affiliated with the majority; and William F. Dunne, arguably Cannon's closest ally, and formerly co-editor of the *Daily Worker*, was demoted to assistant editor (one of the nastiest of Lovestone's henchmen, Robert Minor, was given the sole editorial responsibility for the party's major propaganda organ). The powerful Political Committee was a bastion of Lovestone strength, with the isolated trio of Cannon, Foster, and Bittelman running into a solid brick wall of eight factional opponents.[55] A majority that had only just recently buried its leading comrade was now as hegemonic as any faction had ever been within the Workers (Communist) Party. Lovestone managed to do in less than a year what Ruthenberg, Cannon, and Foster had been unable to accomplish over the course of half a decade. Heads were shaking.

Programmatically, the period was one of contradictory impulses, with Lovestone and Wolfe pushing the United States communist forces decidedly to the right, but Stalin tacking left to eliminate his final potential Soviet challenger, Bukharin, whose rightist inclinations had greased the wheels of Lovestone's rise to power. Shorn of Ruthenberg, whose sensibilities leaned left, Lovestone and Wolfe began to develop their conservative "American exceptionalist" perspective on the expansive United States capitalism of the late 1920s. Within this framework, the Lovestone group ironically *assimilated* much of Cannon's positionings on Bolshevization, Americanization, bourgeoisification, and a realistic appraisal of the objective conditions of class struggle, adopting the language of the opposition but in effect emasculating it programmatically. Cannon's and Dunne's insistence on Americanization began as a call to address native-born workers and engage with their experiences, worldview, and potential, cultivating an appreciation of the revolutionary traditions of the not-so-distant past, from Haymarket to the Industrial Workers of the World. It was transformed into a Lovestone-Wolfe accent on adapting the revolutionary workers' movement in the United States to the heritage of 1776, eulogizing Jefferson and even Washington as heroic leaders of a "bourgeois national liberation struggle" from which communists had much to learn. Dunne's editorship of the *Daily Worker* had pursued a different trajectory, following in the tradition of early socialist critics of the "Founding Fathers" such as James Oneal, whose *The Workers in American History* (1911) assailed the propertied leaders of the American Revolution as gravediggers of the Revolution from below. Wolfe took a different approach. In a lengthy *Workers Monthly* article, "Whose Revolution Is It?" he shifted the terms of discussion to insist that it was time for the working class to embrace the heritage of the American Revolution. It was but a short step to take this newfound appreciation of the unique legacy of the United States, combine it with the downplaying of the significance of American imperialism, reconfigure Workers (Communist) Party discussions of the ideological and material tendencies of bourgeoisification, and extend the arguments to a theory of capitalist stabilization that actually precluded the possibility of revolutionary advance.

If such shifts in theory seem, in retrospect, abstract and distanced from actual communist activity, they were not unrelated to local, sectional struggles that pitted Cannon, Dunne, and Swabeck, as well as Foster, against Lovestone, Wolfe, and Weinstone. Thus, Cannon, Foster, and Bittelman opposed the support Weinstone's New York apparatus extended to a Socialist Party candidate for judge, Jacob Panken, whose ties, not surprisingly, were to the needle-trades unions where the Lovestone group sidled up to right-wing elements in the aftermath of the TUEL's 1926 strike. (The Comintern would later somewhat confirm the oppositionists' critique of the support for Panken.) Cannon also pushed aggressively against the Lovestone forces in arguing for a forceful communist role in the developing opposition to John L. Lewis in the United Mine Workers of America. Dunne demanded that attention be paid to the mining struggles in Colorado, where the Industrial Workers of the World was leading a militant miners' movement in contrast to the bureaucratized abstentionism of the Lewis officialdom, going so far as to call for censure of the *Daily Worker's* inadequacies in addressing the situation. These calls for critical intervention in the UMWA paralleled dissatisfaction with what many perceived to be Foster's timidity in the dissident miners' "Save the Union" movement. Cannon also opposed a Lovestone initiative engineered by Jack Stachel, in which Workers (Communist) Party members were to be sent into the Socialist Party to "get definite information as to the internal situation . . . and carry out any other tasks the Party finds necessary."

Such particular differences were the concrete articulation of a fundamental divide, primarily political but also encompassing methods of party work, that separated the now entirely dominant Lovestone majority and the Cannon-Foster forces. The latter, especially Cannon, simply could not accept the implications of Lovestone's "American exceptionalist" arguments, perhaps laid out most clearly in a two-part May–June 1927 article in the *Communist,* in which the CEC head developed the notion that the rightward drift of American politics, coupled with the continuing ascent of United States capitalism, meant that the advocates of revolution must concede most united-front work to an "outward leadership" of noncommunist workers. This decisively contradicted Cannon's practice in the International Labor Defense work of the mid- to late 1920s, where the Sacco-Vanzetti mobilizations stood as strong reminders of the gains that could be registered if a nonsectarian and politically sophisticated communist leadership worked well with noncommunist progressives in the labor and Left milieus. Within the Workers (Communist) Party itself, Dunne and Swabeck voiced strong resentments at the Lovestone-Wolfe machine's ugly means of combating factionalism and "building" unity by suppressing specific proletarian sectors. Dunne took particular exception at the February 1928 CEC plenum to talk of "pus" and "infection" within the ranks. "One cannot carry out a unity action," the labor warhorse thundered, "against loyal and active proletarian members of this Party under the slogan of 'squeeze out the pus.'" On every level, from the general understanding of capitalism's and imperialism's specific United States content, to the particularities of local political practice and the means and meanings of creating unity in the Workers (Communist) Party, a divide now separated the Lovestone and Cannon forces.[56]

Lovestone's drift to the right continued Comintern policies of the 1925–1927 years, in which Bukharin had risen, Zinoviev had fallen, and Stalin had consolidated his hold on a bureaucratic caste that now sat atop the revolutionary state. With Trotsky and other Left Oppositionists banished from influence by the end of 1927, Stalin's only rival for undisputed dominance as a leader of the world revolutionary forces was Bukharin. Within the Workers (Communist) Party, discussions of Trotsky and the Left Opposition invariably produced pro-Stalin pronouncements and repudiations of the dissidents. Cannon voted with the majority, and endorsed documents expressing the American Party's antagonism to the Left Opposition, although he claimed, in retrospect, that "[i]t was Zinoviev's bloc with Trotsky and his expulsion, along with Trotsky, that first really shook me up and started the doubts and discontents which eventually led me to Trotskyism." The best that could be said of Cannon in this period, however, was that he may well have been part of a Political Committee discussion that derailed Robert Minor's motion to have Dr. Antoinette Konikow, a Boston dissident, expelled. Apparently his only direct involvement in constructing motions stressed the need to circulate Comintern documentation to "all members of the Central Executive Committee for study." Cannon clung to the reasonable position that it was necessary to develop "educational and propagandistic work . . . strengthening the revolutionary morale and ideology of the members," being systematic both in winning proletarian and legitimately communist figures within the dissident Russian ranks to the party and in "unifying and consolidating the party and eliminating remnants of factionalism." Such honest admonitions were of course irrelevant. Stalin no longer needed to embrace the right tilt of Bukharin's orientation toward capitalist stabilization, of which Lovestone's United States was the prime example. Having exorcised the devil of Trotsky, exiling his more theoretically brilliant and politically acute rival to Alma Ata in Central Asia, he could now latch on to some of Trotsky's programmatic critique, the better to show up Bukharin as a right deviationist.

As early as late 1927, there were rumblings out of the Soviet Union of the need for united fronts from below and a "left turn." Bukharin's pessimistic assessment of the prospects for revolution in the United States were sniped at during the Fifteenth Congress of the Communist Party of the Soviet Union in December 1927. When, at the Ninth Plenum of the ECCI in February 1928, Lozovsky picked up on the Stalinist vibes and pushed for a left revision of Profintern and international communist trade union policy, the Workers (Communist) Party came in for a political spanking: it had waited in the wings rather than forming new unions in areas where the AFL had refused to venture; and it had placated the labor bureaucracy, refusing to offer sufficient resistance to old-guard bastions of craft union power. Lovestone's duo in Moscow, Pepper and Louis Engdahl, resisted the assault, which was a direct repudiation of Foster's TUEL trade union policies, and seemed to echo at least some of the critiques long associated with Cannon. At the Profintern's Fourth Congress in March 1928, attended by a large contingent of secondary leaders from the American section, among whom Dunne was the chief Cannon spokesman, Lozovsky upped the ante and characterized the Foster-led trade union sector of the party as suffering from the illness of excessive fear of "dual unionism"—a charge Cannon had leveled previously. Dunne, chosen by the American delegation to be placed on the firing line, responded to Lozovsky's battering with the charge that abandoning AFL workers to the reactionary bureaucracy, through a risky toss of the dice in favor of building entirely new unions, was dangerously one-sided. Others, such as Gitlow and Foster's chief trade union strategist Jack W. Johnstone, were also skeptical of Lozovsky's demanding directives, but Albert Weisbord, still smarting from his abandonment in Passaic, greatly enjoyed the Profintern head's denunciation of the Workers (Communist) Party's sordid surrendering of the mill workers to the corrupt AFL textile union bosses. Ten days of Profintern discussion quieted the American delegation somewhat, and in the end a subtle breakthrough was heralded in communist trade union policy when the door was opened to dual unionism. Lovestone suppressed the news, the various organs of the Workers (Communist) Party managing to avoid coverage of the new turn. Eventually, though, a Lozovsky article in a March 1928 issue of *The Communist International,* written before the Profintern convened, made its way to the United States. Its harsh denunciation of the American communists' "overevaluation of the importance of the Fascist A.F. of L." threw the trade union ranks of the party into turmoil and ironically complicated the "Save the Union" movement in which American communists had aligned with John Brophy's Progressives to thwart John L. Lewis's stranglehold over the UMWA. Cannon penned an article entirely sympathetic to the Lozovsky position, pressing to publish it in the *Daily Worker,* but Lovestone buried the piece in the party's theoretical organ, *The Communist.*[57] Ironically enough, in the Stalinist left turn, Cannon's stock appeared to be rising, Lovestone's falling.

This, of course, is easier seen in retrospect. At the time, Lovestone's lock on the party apparatus was decidedly tight, and though it was apparent to Cannon and others that the Comintern's new left tilt had caught Lovestone off guard, too much could not be made of a shift in trade union policy, which the major- ity had little principled commitment to and all recognized as a subordinate area long reduced by Stalin and others to a factional reserve. Cannon conceded that at the time it was "all a mystery" to him.[58] Moreover, with Lovestone's victory at the 1927 American Party Congress, Cannon stepped back from the factional fray, catching his political breath and rejuvenating his communist principles by immersing himself in International Labor Defense work.

Immediately following the Fifth Congress, there were preparations to be made for the Third Annual Conference of the ILD, a gathering that Cannon chaired at New York's Irving Plaza Hotel on 12–13 November 1927. With 306 delegates from 30 cities convening mere months after the execution of Sacco and Vanzetti, and Lucy Parsons attending and addressing the conference on "The Message of the Haymarket Martyrs," the event brought Cannon back into the mindset of the agitator, impressing on him the need to take commu- nist work into mass arenas and break out of the straightjacket of factional- ism.[59] For much of January and February 1928, the Political Committee danced around the factional question. Lovestone attempted to weaken the Cannon group by proposing that the recently demoted Chicago trade union leader, Arne Swabeck, be marginalized by removing him to California to take up a district organizer's post. He also drafted a highly rhetorical document, "Against Factionalism," that aimed to silence all criticism of his regime. More ominously, Lovestone submitted an "Open Letter of the Comintern to the American Party" that closed the door on debate and reemphasized "the great danger of Trotskyism" and the need for U.S. communists to address this "species of Menshevism." Cannon occasionally absented himself from Politi- cal Committee meetings on the ground of illness and, along with Dunne, he took leave of leadership contentions in late February to agitate among the beleaguered coal miners, a group central to communist labor work, but one clearly slipping away from the Workers (Communist) Party. A disastrous strike/lockout had dragged on in Ohio and Pennsylvania, the United Mine Workers of America's District 2, where John Brophy and Powers Hapgood had spearheaded the dissident, anti-Lewis "Save the Union" movement, and the miners had been without paychecks since April 1927. There was much talk of the need for a new union in the coal fields, but Foster, pushed toward dual unionism by radicalism among rank-and-file miners and nudges toward such an orientation from the Comintern that eventually culminated in a hard authoritative push, was slow to take the final steps. No doubt Cannon and Dunne wanted to get something of the lay of the land in the mining enclaves, but in the process they also distanced themselves from Lovestone's hold over the party center. Nevertheless, the damage had been done: when the National Miners' Union was finally formed in September 1928, the old "Save the Union" leadership found itself distrusted among many secessionist miner militants. Cannon also committed himself to a national ILD tour that took him away from the party headquarters for much of March and April 1928. He attended both the Workers (Communist) Party Central Executive Committee plenums in February and May 1928, and chaired the Resolutions Committee at the 25–27 May nominating convention that put forward Foster and Gitlow as running mates in the upcoming presidential election.[60]

All indications are that Cannon now knew that his efforts to sustain a collective leadership had been thwarted: Lovestone governed the party apparatus with an iron hand and, with Wolfe, had orchestrated a programmatic shift to the right; Foster, rebuked by Lozovsky for "dancing a quadrille the whole time around the AFL and its various unions" in his trade union policy, gave little sign of assimilating the like labor critique Cannon had been voicing. Uncomfortable with the increasingly shrill denunciations of the Left Opposition within the Soviet Party,[61] and discontented about the expulsion of Trotsky and Zinoviev, Cannon commiserated with the Canadian dissident Maurice Spector at the American Party's February plenum. He refused a push from Bill Dunne to speak out on the Russian issues, his factional ally demanding a distancing from Trotsky for the sake of the Cannon group's future. Sitting in the back of the hall, "disgruntled, bitter and confused," Cannon sensed there was something contrived about the Lovestone-Wolfe denunciation of Trotsky and other oppositionists, but aside from a surface acquaintance with some Russian documents critical of the Stalinist Anglo-Russian Committee's quashing of independent communist activity in Britain during the 1926 General Strike, Cannon had no fundamental grasp of what was at stake, programmatically, in the 1927–1928 battle inside the Soviet Communist Party. Rather than address the Russian issues, therefore, Cannon concentrated his fire elsewhere.

In his February 1928 plenum remarks, Cannon emphasized the need to shed the phobia about dual unionism, while remaining steadfast in the party's commitment to work in those mainstream unions where much of organized labor in the United States was inevitably to be found. He pointed to the ongoing crisis of factionalism, and its debilitating effect in the American party, arguing for the necessity of doing the hard slugging of independent communist political work in the electoral arena, which gave few signs of harboring the possibility of a genuine labor party of the kind communists could support in the immediate months to come. (Lovestone, true to his origins as a protégé of Pepper, was at the time oscillating between grasping for a labor-party straw[62] and conducting a thoroughly opportunistic canvassing campaign that suppressed communist politics in the interests of securing liberal support for Workers (Communist) Party candidates.) Cannon would return to this theme of labor politics by penning a *Daily Worker* article on the presidential election campaign in the aftermath of the May 1928 CEC plenum, where the issue of the Russian Left Opposition was largely ignored and the proceedings given over to discussions of trade union issues.[63] Cannon also devoted writing time to the relatively safe political terrain of tightening up party work in terms of committee reports and conducting propaganda.[64] If there were some signs that the factional logjam was breaking up in positive ways, there was little in the overall configuration of internal party politics to warm Cannon's heart. It was in this period, according to Alexander Bittelman, that Cannon began to routinely refer to Stalin disparagingly, and to attribute the crises of both the Russian and American sections to his degenerating leadership.[65]

This depressing political scene complicated Cannon's personal and family life. Jim and Rose Karsner had now been lovers for almost four years, and their relationship was clearly rooted in personal attractions and common political views, but the two committed communists had sacrificed much to build a party they now nurtured reservations about. Rose contributed significantly to the 1927 communist project of relief for the miners of Pennsylvania and Ohio, organized under the auspices of what the Workers (Communist) Party called "The Helper." Committed to raising funds and maintaining food distribution for the embattled miners, the Pennsylvania and Ohio Relief Committee and "The Helper" conducted tag days, film showings, and other entertainments that had as their purpose the raising of funds to support miners' children, the organization of African American miners, and the bringing of nonunion miners into the ranks of the strikers. So successful were communist efforts that, by early 1928, they had displaced the UMWA as dispensers of coal-field relief in some thirty towns in western Pennsylvania. Along with Bittelman, Bedacht, and others, Karsner drafted a policy report on "The Helper," but by April 1928 Rose was no longer associated with the mining relief endeavors. In the months that followed, the miners' welfare became a communist political football, kicked around by Alfred Wagenknecht, who considered relief work his particular bailiwick, and the implacable Juliet Poyntz, Director of Work and Women, who insisted on her right to orchestrate the activities of women organizers. It was a situation that, in conjunction with the downward-spiraling fortunes of the militant miners' movement and the factional logjam in the upper echelons of the Workers (Communist) Party, straightjacketed the work Rose had begun, and it must have caused Karsner and Cannon considerable consternation. All of this could not help but have taken a toll on the Cannon-Karsner relationship, introducing tensions and disillusionments.[66]

Jim's attraction for alcohol, reinforced by his increasingly close connection in this period with Dunne and Tom O'Flaherty, a duo known as the hard-drinking faction of the party, undoubtedly had an impact on Karsner's and Cannon's relationship as well.[67] However, the decisive issue that Jim and Rose struggled to resolve, and that must have taken on added salience as they grew more distanced from the Workers (Communist) Party, was the geographical removal from their children—Carl and Ruth for Jim, and Walta for Rose.

Cannon's and Makimson's separation had, for all its original ambiguities and ambivalences, hardened into an irreversible breakup over the course of the 1920s. The relocation to Chicago in this period, as well as regular trips to the Soviet Union and a rigorous schedule of public speaking, political campaigning, and other party work, alongside Jim's genuine attraction to Rose, necessarily wrote *finis* to Cannon's first marriage. It also distanced him from Carl and Ruth as the youngsters grew from infants into their adolescence. To support herself and the children (although Cannon helped when he could, his material capacity to "provide" for the family was constrained severely), Lista moved to Long Island, New York, and reestablished herself as a teacher. Rose, too, was parted from her daughter, who lived more with her father and step-mother, Esther Eberson Karsner. Despite the obvious tensions associated with these reconfigured families, relationships among the Karsner-Cannon, Karsner-Eberson, and Makimson-Cannon domestic units were, for a part of this time at least, quite cordial and cooperative. Walta recalled her mother and father, with their new spouses, sitting around apartment kitchen tables in New York and conversing amicably. A few years later, Esther Karsner and Rose would establish a progressive "Playday House" crèche together, in which Rose was the "kindergartener," Esther the sculptor instructor, and another friend the Montessori school teacher. After trips to the Soviet Union, Rose and Jim would meet the children in New York, and there were always toys for them from the far-off lands that had been recently visited. Lista, for her part, was remarkably generous, looking after Walta as Rose departed for Moscow late in 1924 or early in 1925, and inviting her to spend time with Carl and Ruth at their Long Island home. All of the children went to see Rose and Jim off at the docks. Such admirable relations, however, grew somewhat strained as the

1920s wore on. After Lista forged a relationship with another teacher, Tilden Collar, new tensions understandably came into the picture. It was perhaps not surprising, then, that Rose and Jim, who had originally expressed a desire to return to New York, but found themselves politically resistant to the later factional push from the Ruthenberg-Lovestone quarter to relocate the party press and headquarters from Chicago back to the eastern seaboard metropolis, eventually gave in to the pressures and took the opportunity to establish a home in the city where their children were permanently located. Setting up an apartment with their close friends, Bill and Margaret Dunne, Rose and Jim perhaps retreated somewhat from the leadership factionalism of the Workers (Communist) Party in late 1927 and early 1928, trying to rebuild relations with their children and place their private lives on a more satisfactory footing.[68]

Cannon's state of mind in mid-1928 was thus fairly clearly one of resignation. Living with Lovestone had almost certainly shattered his hopes of building a collective leadership within an American party liberated from factionalism. Uncomfortable with merely holding his tongue, he nevertheless had no words with which to speak.[69] A man who valued reserve, and who refused to pander to inconsequential complaint or directionless doubt, Cannon "did not communicate [his] inner thoughts" to his associates, and it is quite possible that even Bill Dunne and Rose Karsner were never fully aware of Jim's deeply troubled state of mind at this time. Pressured by his factional allies to attend the Sixth Congress, Cannon at first begged off accepting a party nomination, citing the importance of the ongoing struggles in the United Mine Workers of America and the textile sector,[70] as well as the communist campaign in the presidential election.[71] With the large delegation about to depart, he explained, a minimal few of the Workers (Communist) Party national leaders should remain on the ground to oversee various activities.[72]

In the end, though, Cannon succumbed. At a mid-June Political Committee meeting, he reluctantly accepted the nomination to the forthcoming congress of the Communist International. Cannon was off to Moscow yet again. "Not much interested," the dissident was "a more or less sullen participant in the business."[73] What could come of such despairing diffidence?

11

Expulsion

Cannon and the Corridor Congress, 1928

The Sixth World Congress of the Communist International convened in Moscow from 17 July through 1 September 1928. It was the first time the Congress had assembled in four years. The internal situation in the Soviet Union was largely hidden from the revolutionary ranks who descended on the first workers' state from all corners of the globe. Had they seen conditions as they actually were, it could not have been reassuring to the some 515 visiting delegates, who represented 58 national sections of the international communist movement. Unemployment was now a recognized reality in the workers' republic. A bread crisis threatened urban centers with famine.

Politically, the turmoil obscured in the mid-1920s was now apparent, although the outcome was anything but easily perceived. Trotsky had been banished from power, Zinoviev had been driven from Moscow, the Left Opposition had been expelled from the Communist Party of the Soviet Union, and the arrests of its advocates, such as Victor Serge, had begun. Even the rising star, Nikolai Bukharin, had recently fallen out of favor with the ruling apparatus.

Historically, the World Congress of 1928 proved a major step toward subordinating the *world* communist movement, with its diversity of struggles and needs, to the dominance of the Soviet Union, and, in hindsight, to the consolidation of Stalin's unquestioned rule and elevation to a theoretical maxim of the contradictory notion of "socialism in one country." The communist climate seemed barely recognizable when compared to the early 1920s. Passionate debate and committed revolutionary leadership had then, it was generally agreed, characterized Comintern meetings. A few years later, international figures shook their heads in despair at the arrogance of the Russian leaders, who obviously demanded and received "dull and sad parades of loyalty." It made the Italian Marxist Togliatti feel like "hanging oneself," while the French communist, Thorez, thought the mood of the congress one of "uneasiness, discontent and skepticism."[1]

To the twenty-nine American delegates—twenty voting and nine advisory—who were already settled in the Soviet Union through appointments to the Lenin School and other secondments, or who arrived in Moscow in July 1928 (Cannon among them), the crisis of communism in the Soviet Union weighed lightly on their minds. "I am sorry to say," Cannon would later report, "all of us [were] more or less preoccupied primarily with our own little fight in the American party." Of all the leaders, Cannon was probably in the least preferable situation. There could have been an element of truth in Max Shachtman's later claim that Cannon approached the Comintern meetings knowing that his faction was the smallest, and that it could never play an ultimately determining role, only that of an auxiliary body.[2]

Undoubtedly depressed by the poor prospects of securing any "real clarification of the Russian question," and apparently "bothered" by the routing of the Left Opposition, Cannon claimed that he did what he could to familiarize himself with the situation upon his arrival in the Soviet Union. He pumped an old friend, Minnesota trade unionist Clarence Hathaway,[3] a recent graduate of the Lenin School, on the happenings, and was given something of an insider's track on the official line against a nebulously identified "right wing" associated loosely with the powerful Bukharin, whom it was nevertheless not yet "safe" to attack directly. Conducting himself at first in familiar ways, Cannon's original acts were perfectly consistent with that of a factional leader struggling to secure advantage, although, to be sure, one somewhat disaffected even to the point of being displaced in decisionmaking by others. Soon, however, it was apparent that Cannon was less than committed to the traditional infighting.[4]

Without doubt, the Lovestone group was in control of the Workers (Communist) Party, and its forces were the undisputed majority in the critical voting-rights delegation.[5] However, the combined Cannon-Foster opposition was well represented at the Sixth Congress, and even appeared to have consolidated its somewhat fragmented ranks.

First, the Cannon and Foster forces, for all of their differences over trade union and other questions at the May 1928 CEC plenum, had a specific informal agreement about their joint discontents with the Lovestone-Bertram Wolfe leadership. Subsequently, this general, if constrained, solidarity was consolidated in the opening rounds of factional activity that took place in the Soviet Union, where Cannon's leading labor militant counterpart, Bill Dunne, and one of his factional lieutenants in anti-imperialist work, Manuel Gomez (Charles Shipman), strengthened the Cannon-Foster alliance. Dunne had arrived in Moscow well before the larger delegation, assigned by the Comintern to carry out some pre-Congress arrangements. He later claimed to have quickly grasped that there was a new lay of the political land, and his sense that although the Lovestone-Pepper majority might receive "formal support" from the Comintern, "its days were numbered" no doubt steeled his determination. Cannon's arriving later than Dunne and Gomez, who caucused immediately, meant that he was not on the ground for important preliminary discussions that set a Congress agenda for the Cannon-Dunne faction and the Cannon-Foster group as a whole. Especially important was the piecing together of the Cannon forces' close working relationship with Alexander Bittelman, Foster's theoretical senior statesman, and the logical ties that were forged with Jack W. Johnstone, an old Wobbly and chief Chicago-based Foster organizer who had significant Comintern experience in the mid-1920s, and was beginning to chafe under Foster's often tyrannical character.

Second, in addition to the coalescing of this singularly anti-Lovestone bloc, Cannon and his closest supporters had intimate ties to individuals who were already on the ground in Soviet Russia, including nonvoting Lenin School students such as Hathaway (with whom Dunne and Gomez met immediately and staked out an orientation), Charles Krumbein, and the first African American to study in the Moscow experiment in Marxist education, Harry Haywood. Haywood, whose organic ties through his brother Otto Hall were to the old Ruthenberg group, owed his tenure at the Lenin School to Lovestone, but never warmed to his patron's penchant for dirty factional infighting. Attracted to Bill Dunne, Haywood was soon proposed by the Cannon-Foster forces as a counterpart to Lovestone's choice of a black comrade to address the World Congress, Lovett Fort-Whiteman. All told, the Cannon caucus alone could well have accounted for close to ten of the twenty-nine-member American delegation—a remarkably strong showing for a group that was numerically far weaker in the Workers (Communist) Party than either the Lovestone or the Foster factions. Combined with the Foster supporters in Moscow, this group was a numerical majority of the American contingent, even if it could never take on that role in official circles, where many of the representatives lacked voting rights. The fact that Earl Browder, in 1928 in the middle of a two-year stint as a Comintern representative in the Far East's Pan-Pacific Secretariat, had now sensed that Stalin was the bureaucratic horse to back in the Soviet power struggle, further fed into the Foster-Cannon bloc's authority. If the cagey Browder would not publicly endorse any faction, he clearly aligned with the politics of those who placed themselves against the Bukharin-endorsed

Lovestone. This positioning of delegate personnel thus fed into the third, and critically important, area where the Cannon-Foster combination seemed to occupy strong ground in its campaign against Lovestone: the shifting fortunes of "right" and "left" labels within the upper echelons of Soviet leadership.

A right wing, headed by trade union top Mikhail P. Tomsky, and chair of the Council of People's Commissars, Alexis I. Rykov, was rumored to be on the Stalin chopping block; this enhanced the possibilities for a Cannon-Foster assault on the "right danger" of Lovestone's emerging program of American exceptionalism. The implications of this doctrine, apparent to Stalin and his many hand-raisers, flew directly in the face of the orchestrated programmatic directives that would emerge from the Sixth Congress, especially the claims that in a new "Third Period," capitalism everywhere, including the United States, was on an edge where only a steeled revolutionary vanguard could ensure that it toppled into communism. If Bukharin's place in this war of left against right remained something of a guess, there were still enough signs of which way the political Comintern winds were blowing. With Bittelman a rare Russian speaker among the United States delegates, the Foster-Cannon forces had a translator's ear in the "Corridor Congress." It was there that Stalin's agents supposedly buttonholed foreign delegates to let them know, albeit informally and possibly as much by innuendo as by unambiguous statement, that Bukharin was on the outs and that a left turn was in the making against the right deviations of various renegades.[6]

The initial meeting of the American Bureau, composed of ten leading U.S. delegates, determined election of members to the Comintern's three major bodies: the Presidium, the Senioren Konvent, and the Program Commission. This electoral body was heavily weighted in favor of the Lovestone group, which had a seven-to-three dominance. Foster, Bittelman, and Cannon were a decided minority that could exercise influence only where their opponents willingly ceded them an opening. Ironically enough, the preoccupation of the entire American delegation with the internal factional situation in the Workers (Communist) Party, in addition, perhaps, to the growing realization that all major decisions taken by Comintern bodies were already predetermined by the Soviet leadership, ensured that Lovestone and Company cared little about who ended up as the United States representatives on the major Comintern Program Commission, an unwieldy sixty-person council with representatives from forty countries charged with the important task of drafting a finished programmatic statement of the forces of world revolution.

Instead, Lovestone concentrated on securing his election to the leading Presidium, a kind of Politburo, the central executive body of the Comintern, and the Senioren Konvent (or Council of Elders), a prestigious subcommittee chaired by Bukharin and on which Stalin routinely sat. The latter council's Budget Committee held the purse strings of revolutionary largesse, ruling on requests for Comintern funds from affiliated national sections. Lovestone and Foster, as the ranking factional leaders of the American section, were elected to both the Presidium and the Senioren Konvent, although Foster clearly wanted to apportion his time elsewhere, quite possibly to the Trade Union Commission. Lovestone, in turn, certainly had his eye on the Anglo-American Secretariat, where the internal situation of the Workers (Communist) Party would be discussed fully and critically, with Foster pressing a continuous challenge against Lovestone's leadership. Thus it came about, ironically, that Cannon, along with Lovestone lieutenant William Weinstone, was elected to the Program Commission, "shoved on to [it] as a sort of honor without substance. And to tell you the truth, I was not much interested in it either."[7]

The Foster-Cannon bloc wasted no time in launching an attack on the Lovestone leadership.[8] Late in July 1928, a Bittelman-authored document entitled "The Right Danger in the American Party" was submitted to the American Commission of the Sixth Congress, signed by Foster, Cannon, Bittelman, Dunne, Johnstone, Gomez, and George Siskind. A long forced march of retreat of the United States working class had ostensibly been halted, and a new stage of class struggle inaugurated. According to "The Right Danger," Lovestone and his ruling faction overestimated the reserve powers of U.S. imperialism, failing to appreciate that the mood of laboring people had shifted, the break from passivity signaled by rising militancy, revived antagonism to the threat of war, and initiatives to counter conservative union officialdoms in sectors such as mining. The Workers (Communist) Party, claimed the opposition document, had taken insufficient steps to build a communist vanguard and instead was letting key party work, the party press, and central campaigns falter. United-front policy was being applied opportunistically, especially in the 1928 presidential election campaign, and in ways that understated potential communist strengths among African Americans, industrialized women, and anti-imperialist strongholds. Lovestone's faction supposedly reduced communism to a left-wing tail of established and reformist trade union bureaucracies or farmer-labor party initiatives and, true to its "petty bourgeois" and "dilettante" character, pandered to pacifism and conservative elements in the cooperative movement.[9]

A forceful, if at times strained, indictment of Lovestone (strongest in its critique of party work, the document was weaker in depicting trends in U.S. capitalism and class struggle), "The Right Danger in the American Party" seemed, on the surface, to run with the Comintern political pack, although it refrained from any direct reference to "right" elements in the Communist Party of the Soviet Union or the Communist International. Yet it also let loose the hounds within the Foster camp, where personal resentments had been festering for some time.

The Temporary Eclipse of Foster

At a joint Moscow caucus meeting of the Cannon and Foster forces, the latter lost control of his faction, the baton of leadership passing to the unlikely Alexander Bittelman, who almost certainly nurtured no leadership aspirations. The consummate "inner" party man, Bittelman had few skills as an orator and none as a mass leader; he was no match for either Foster or Cannon, whatever contributions he had to make to the communist movement, and he knew it. Nevertheless, he had perhaps seen too much of Foster's capacity to bludgeon his dependent factional allies into sycophantic followers incapable of critical reflection, and Bittelman, a social being who enjoyed the conviviality of the Cannon-Dunne circle, had experienced enough of Foster's longstanding aloofness. Perhaps feeling his political oats after drafting "The Right Danger," Bittelman was also enthralled by his first appearance at a World Congress of the Communist International. He took pride in speaking at plenary sessions and before the Presidium, and would later be privileged with a semiprivate hearing with high-ranking Stalinist officials, for whom he had an undue regard. Moreover, unlike Foster, Bittelman and his factional allies had nothing to lose by insisting that the Workers (Communist) Party trade union policy, with its routinized fear of dual unionism, coddling of social democratic and mainstream union bureaucracies in the New York needle trades, and pandering to the conservative American Federation of Labor, was a Lovestone accommodation to capitalist class relations in the United States. Foster, of course, had followed exactly the same trajectory. However, his pride, and inability to offer sufficient *mea culpas* to the Comintern leaders on his past labor movement orientation, seemed to compromise the oppositional force of those endorsing "The Right Danger in the American Party" document.

This all came to a head as the Foster-Cannon forces caucused after submitting their dissenting theses to the Comintern. Cannon thought the unexpected explosion was triggered by Bittelman, Browder, and Johnstone drawing courage from finding themselves on the same side as the prestigious Lozovsky, but grasped intuitively that more was at stake than a dispute over trade union policy. Foster's usual methods of intimidation and his theoretical bluntness were now met with contemptuous, even ruthless, repudiation from his leading supporters, many of whom clearly bristled with grievances against their leader. Even if this anti-Foster uprising was never conceived as an attempt to displace Foster, his prestige and public prominence in the movement being too great for his faction to sacrifice, the fallout from the caucus rebellion was not inconsiderable. It would take Foster the better part of a year to regain ultimate authority within his group and piece his faction back together. His return to the United States in September 1928 was an embittered and somewhat uncertain one.[10]

Foster's seeming fall from grace placed Cannon in an awkward position. The Foster forces' being on the outs with their leader created a political vacuum at the head of the combined opposition. Cannon's ranks thought he should move more forcefully to the front and fill the gap. A meeting was called of the Cannon group and Cannon was told in no uncertain terms to stop dragging his feet and "go all out in the factional struggle."[11] Cannon gave no answer. By this time a startling development had shifted his thinking dramatically.

Cannon and a Canadian: Maurice Spector

As a member of the Program Commission, Cannon crossed paths with a Canadian delegate, Maurice Spector. Spector, Canadian communism's leading theoretical light, and the first revolutionary of the country to be elected to the ECCI, was a prolific writer (one student has located fifty-three signed articles by Spector in the Canadian communist organ which he edited between 1922 and 1928, *The Worker*) and a sensitive judge of revolutionary program. In the mid-1920s, though, the Ukrainian-born Jewish Spector, not much older than twenty-five, and fresh from student days as a radical at the University of Toronto, was learning his way in the vocation of professional revolutionary. Little better than a mediocre public speaker in his youth (Royal Canadian Mounted Police agents repeatedly described Spector as "the poorest paid agitator I have ever met," prone to being "rattled" by hostile questions or heckling, "a little green at the tub-thumping game," and so on), the inside party critique of Spector was that he was somewhat lazy. Few, however, could match his incisive intelligence and his cosmopolitan reach, which Spector cultivated with a keen interest in the European revolutionary movement, especially relating to Germany and the failed revolution of 1918–1919, a topic on which he often spoke in public meetings. He not surprisingly distinguished himself with an acute analysis of the German defeat of 1923, having been in Europe at the time, thereby parting company, partially at least, with Zinoviev's rationalizations and obfuscations in the Comintern apparatus. The seeds of a sympathetic approach to Trotskyism lay in that encounter, although Spector did not embrace a Left Opposition analysis on his own, and indeed somewhat downplayed early dissident positions on the German Communist Party's responsibility for the tragic failure of the 1923 revolution. At best, Spector's political reading of the German events of 1923 could be described as incorporating features of the mainstream Comintern position, but backtracking into areas of critique that would later be developed by Trotsky. Upon his return to Canada, Spector became chairman of the Canadian party, and did what he could to deflect Moscow's demands for obeisance to official discontent with the Trotsky-led dissidents. A mere twelve months before the Sixth Congress, Spector was the most supported of the Canadian Central Executive Committee leaders, more ballots being cast for him than for any one of the other eight nominees.[12]

Spector was thus anything but an unambiguous advocate of Trotsky, and he and Cannon, separated by geography and other factors, had never explicitly discussed or corresponded about the question until early 1928. Openness to Trotskyism most often was quite muted, and took the form of requests that decisions within Central Committees and other bodies not be taken until more information was secured. Cannon had heard talk of Spector's reluctance to condemn Trotsky, of course, reaching back to 1925, but the two North American party leaders knew one another largely by reputation when their paths crossed at a February 1928 U.S. party meeting. Confronted with escalating anti-Trotskyism, doubt and dissatisfaction were as far as Cannon and Spector managed to go together during that single winter evening of frank discussion in New York. Nonetheless, this sharing of dangerous political ambivalences and confidences paved the way for a discreet Moscow alliance at the Sixth Congress.[13]

Trotsky's Draft Program Surfaces

Had things worked on the Program Commission the way they were supposed to, it is possible that Cannon and Spector would have had little to do, the decisions about Comintern program having already been predetermined by the established Stalinist functionaries. But, in this period of the late 1920s, the bureaucratic machineries of the Soviet state and the Comintern were perhaps not as forcefully mechanical and as repressively efficient as they would be in later decades. Alternatively, they may have been in perfectly Machiavellian order.

Trotsky and the Left Opposition, largely driven into exile, faced a series of awkward dilemmas as they found themselves maneuvered into various political cul-de-sacs by Stalin's left lurch and anti-rightist move against Bukharin. They nevertheless appealed to the Sixth Congress with a number of short documents detailing the theoretical degeneration of the Soviet Union's revolutionary leadership and outlining the repression that had been visited upon the heads of communist dissidents.[14] However, *the* critical statement was Trotsky's *The Draft Program of the Communist International: A Criticism of Fundamentals.* The document, a withering assault on the draft of a Comintern program pieced together by Bukharin, Stalin, and his various hangers-on, was submitted to the Sixth Congress and found its way—in error, according to Cannon—into the translation department, where a dozen or so stenographers and language experts had little enough to do that they put two of the three sections of the document into readable form for foreign delegates and distributed a limited number of poorly translated copies to heads of the convening communist sections and members of the Program Committee. "[S]o, lo and behold, it was laid in my lap," Cannon later exclaimed, "translated into English!"[15] Claiming that the *Draft Program* was in fact buried in a special committee, where its closely monitored and numbered/labeled copies were leaked surreptitiously to various quarters, Manuel Gomez perhaps adds substance to the apparently common Comintern rumors that Stalin may well have allowed the Trotskyist document some circulation, the better to best Bukharin from the left. William Z. Foster supposedly saw the document and considered it a masterful critique of Comintern practice.[16]

Cannon and Spector rightly grasped that serious scrutiny of Trotsky's *Draft Program* demanded the close quarters of individual attention among those who could be trusted to bide their time and work for the creation of a Left Opposition in North America. Laying bare the deficiencies in the Bukharin-Stalin draft, Trotsky pointed out that prior to 1925, all theoretical traditions in the Communist International adhered to basic Leninist premises. It had long been understood that capitalism's uneven, sporadic development determined the episodic nature of the socialist revolution, and that, moreover, the interdevelopment of national political economies in the epoch of global capital and imperialism structured not only the political but also the economic impossibility of building socialism in one country. Abandoning such premises led to programmatic error, evident in the official draft program of the Sixth Congress. Among the mistakes Trotsky singled out four: the exaggeration of the level of productive forces in the Soviet Union; blindness to the uneven development of various branches of industry; a basic ignorance of the international division of labor; and a critical slighting in the imperialist epoch of the contradiction inherent in the expanding productive forces and the boundaries of nation-states. In what registered immediately with Cannon and Spector, Trotsky also laid great emphasis on the hegemony of North American capital, arguing that its inevitable forthcoming crisis would seek resolution at the expense of Europe.

At issue, of course, in all such comment, was the need to prepare for and oppose the imperialist war drive (a point Spector raised in his Congress speeches), as well as the extension of revolutionary class struggle internationally. This Trotsky saw as fundamentally compromised by Stalin's notion of socialism in one country, rooted in the thoroughly mistaken view that the internal contradictions of the Soviet workers' state could be overcome within Russia, rather than through world proletarian revolution. Programmatically, this reduced the Communist International to a merely auxiliary body, a guardian of Soviet well-being rather than an arm of revolutionary internationalism.

National reformism was born at the interface of such theory and its programmatic logics. This was the seedbed of various Comintern blunders, such as the disastrous orientation to the Chinese Revolution of 1926–1927, when a bureaucratic conservatism pressured Chinese communists into an ill-fated alliance with their own bourgeoisie, on the grounds that the "national" revolt against imperialism led by Chiang Kai-Shek was the critical cutting edge of social transformation. As the Chinese revolutionary forces discovered in bloody defeat, Lenin's grasp of the necessity to wage bourgeois revolution in the East depended on the proletariat's capacity to open the eyes of the oppressed people to the treachery of the bourgeoisie, and to wage its own struggle for power. When, under Stalin and Bukharin, the Comintern failed to do this, it severely compromised the World Revolution—in China, to be sure, but also in Russia, Europe, Africa, and the Americas.[17]

For Spector and Cannon, this critique was a bolt out of the blue, explaining their doubts and reengaging them with what they considered Marxist truth. It was anything but easy for Cannon, and it forced some difficult personal reassessment:

> The foot-loose Wobbly rebel that I used to be had imperceptibly begun to fit comfortably into a swivel chair, protecting himself in his seat by small maneuvers and evasions, and even permitting himself a certain conceit about his adroit accommodation to this shabby game. I saw myself for the first time as another person, as a revolutionist who was on the road to becoming a *bureaucrat*. The image was hideous, and I turned away from it in disgust.

The question remained of what to do. In the end, Cannon and Spector decided to take the high, if quiet, road. They kept relatively to themselves, and talked to very few comrades about the unsettling programmatic meaning of Trotsky's criticism of Comintern fundamentals. The two nascent Left Oppositionists saw their main responsibility as organizing support for Trotsky's positions within their own parties, and to do that they had to return to North America and make contact with potential supporters before they were isolated and mobilized against by the wide array of Stalinist Comintern forces. Cannon apparently pushed for biding their time until the two dissidents could take their stand on the full articulation of the politics of Trotsky's *Draft Program*. Therefore, in Cannon's words, he and Spector "let the caucus meetings and the

Congress sessions go to the devil while we read and studied this document."[18] Such recollections feed the view that Cannon was an almost nonpresence during the 1928 July–August Comintern meetings.[19] This is not entirely correct.[20]

Keeping his political cards rather close to his chest, Cannon nevertheless undoubtedly engaged in discussions with his most trusted factional allies, trying to feel them out on the questions he now knew were central. Cannon almost certainly mishandled what must have been some kind of attempt to open a dialogue on Trotsky with Bill Dunne, and it would have been surprising if he did not have discussions, however veiled, with Clarence Hathaway. The latter would have been a perfect conduit through which information about Cannon's "wavering" on Trotskyism could have been passed to Stalinist authorities. In any case, the Russian secret police (GPU) were sufficiently aware of Cannon's "monkeying" with Trotskyism that they supposedly compiled a file on the American delegate during his Comintern stay in Moscow.

As for Spector, the adaptable German communist, Heinz Neumann, warned the Canadian of "rumors that he was meeting with the wrong people." Whether acting on his own or as an agent of other forces, Neumann clearly had a bead on something. The gregarious, affable, and well-liked German, who traveled in the Bukharin circle for a time only to abandon it as Stalin threw a noose around its collective neck, would later be executed in one of the purges of the 1930s. In 1928, he was playing a particular game, and offered to arrange a Stalin interview for Spector. (Similar consultations would be orchestrated for Foster and Lovestone—separately, of course—with Stalin, and for Bittelman and Gomez with Stalin's alter ego, V. M. Molotov.) When the Toronto Marxist turned down the visitation, he found himself interrogated by the GPU. One Lovestone supporter, the persistently demagogic Harry M. Wicks, attacked Cannon openly for using Trotsky's document as unattributed ammunition in his polemical shots against the notorious John Pepper. Ironically, Wicks would end his days denouncing "the eclipse of October," insisting that a "Kremlin tyranny arose that was able to obliterate the achievements of the Russian Bolshevik revolution of October, 1917, and to turn to its own designs the various parties in other countries that comprised the Communist International." As circumspect as they thought they were, Cannon and Spector were indeed putting out signals.[21]

Nor was Cannon entirely silent in the public discussions of the Comintern. He spoke decisively, for instance, in a major speech before the Comintern on 28 July 1928, pillorying the record of the Lovestone leadership and extending the minority opposition's attack through discussion of various opportunistic errors of the Workers (Communist) Party, particularly as they related to the Socialist Party, the trade unions, women's work, and the cooperative sector.[22] In the enlarged Anglo-American Secretariat, he locked horns in August with the presiding Soviet official, the former Ukrainian Menshevik turned die-hard Stalinist, G. Petrovsky, demanding the floor to air some differences that he had with Bittelman, who had spoken for the minority. Cannon was unequivocal in his support of the platform of "The Right Danger in the American Party," but he continued to press the task of forming a "collective leadership." This drew on Cannon's growing separation from many in the combined opposition (especially Bittelman), including those of his own faction, who had been too easily swept up in Stalinist maneuvering that cavalierly labeled specific tendencies and positions. Cannon insisted on correcting the mechanical characterization, stressing that the combined Cannon-Foster group had developed "along a zig-zag line." Lovestone, Cannon claimed, had historically harbored ultraleft tendencies, but upon assuming the leadership of the American Party he had invariably tacked right. Such positions, couched in language that betrayed no hint of Cannon's emerging Trotskyism, must have seemed rather beside the point to many in the opposition group, but they meshed well with a reading of Trotsky's *Draft Program* and separated Cannon from the cynical and opportunistic adoption of "left/right" phraseology that, by August, had overtaken the Sixth Congress vocabulary.[23]

A contingent of the opposition against the "Right Danger" and its Lovestone orchestration, including Cannon faction members Dunne, Hathaway, and Gomez, would later claim that Cannon signed the Bittelman minority document only "after the greatest pressure had been exerted by us." Frustrated in his attempts to garner support for his new positions, this contingent later claimed, Cannon apparently withdrew from group and delegation meetings, and when he did attend he was largely silent in discussion, abstaining from a number of important votes. Dunne, Hathaway, and Gomez characterized Cannon's theoretical position as one of a retreat into "ILDism as opposed to a line of political struggle," repeating a charge that Max Shachtman and Martin Abern had leveled in the United States as early as February 1928.[24]

The Cannon-Dunne Split

Whatever the veracity of this account—and the documentary record provides some partial confirmation as well as serious suggestion of repudiation—there is no denying that as the Comintern's Sixth Congress wound to a close, a tempestuous breach separated Bill Dunne and Cannon. Cannon's abstentionism was probably most pronounced at the very end of the proceedings, and he almost certainly had some kind of hand in the initial drafting of Bittelman's "Right Danger" opposition document.[25] In the last days of the Congress, with the minority opposition bloc formulating a series of disagreeing statements on

Bukharin's Congress theses as they related to Paragraph 49, pertaining to the United States, Cannon was a nonsigner of the group's unprecedented eight-point document of dissent. He also played no role in a Bittelman-drafted motion on the "Russian Question," which applauded "the defeat of the Trotsky opposition in the CPSU."[26]

Dunne, who had perhaps been Cannon's closest political ally, and almost certainly his most intimate friend within the Workers (Communist) Party, did not look kindly on his Kansas counterpart's seeming retreat from the fray. An acrimonious wall of difference now stood between the two old comrades. They shared much that Cannon simply could not reproduce in other circles, however tight such alliances were. As late as the summer of 1929, Cannon continued to harbor hopes that Dunne could be won away from the bureaucratized officialdom of Stalinist communism. "We hardly believe his heart is in it," Cannon wrote to one confidant in August 1929. There was, however, no denying that Cannon had somehow lost Dunne's trust during the Sixth Congress creation of a Cannon-Foster opposition, and there is some suggestion that at this time Dunne gravitated willingly to Stalin.[27]

A Clandestine Cannon

The American delegation departed the Sixth Congress in September 1928. They left more divided, and more precariously perched, vis-à-vis the Communist International, than when they arrived. Lovestone and Company remained at the helm, but this faction had overreached itself in siding with Bukharin, not so much out of principle as, in Cannon's words, by "guessing wrong." When it came time, later in 1929, to call for Bukharin's head in order to placate Stalin and retain its hold on the American communist apparatus, the Lovestone group was quick to jump on the bandwagon of denunciation. But such mending of fences was not enough. Lovestone, in particular, had transgressed the bounds of Stalinist subservience at the Sixth Conference in rudely censorious dismissals of Lozovsky, then much favored by Stalin, and through demanding a measure of financial independence from the Comintern. More ominously, he had brazenly challenged Stalin directly in the Senioren Konvent, asking for clarification of the undercover Stalin-Bukharin fight, suggesting that the Russian Party's dirty linen be aired before a Comintern subcommittee. Lovestone, and by implication his entire faction, was thus marked by Stalin for future demise.

Pepper, to be sure, a political cat with more than nine lives, was finally finished (although he would remain as a Lovestone factionalist, useful in future anti-Cannon exercises). He had been the whipping boy of the entire Congress, with the minority opposition, including Cannon, flailing away at him whenever the opportunity presented itself, which was quite often. More to the point, a wide array of Russian, German, and other Comintern officials took their swipes at Pepper, chastising his "petty intrigues and quarrelsomeness." Dismissed on the basis of his "unprincipled manner," and dubbed a rare "muddler of two hemispheres," Pepper was routinely attacked as "a petty bourgeois adventurer." This Hungarian with so many names was now referred to as "Der Tripper" or The Gonorrhea. Christening himself, appropriately, Swift, Pepper responded in kind, using his glib tongue to good and fast effect, but anyone could see that his cover as a much-vaunted "Comintern rep" was now blown.

The Foster-Cannon group was, of course, torn asunder, its forces dispersed by Comintern appointment (Dunne and Browder were in the Far East), its key factional leaders isolated from their former followers, and its ranks tarnished by their final refusal to accept entirely the official Congress theses. Stalin, through interviews with both Lovestone and Foster, managed to keep both figures off their political balance, feeding them sweet nothings as to what was coming next. He danced them into political corners out of which they would never truly reappear, or in which they remained, wallflower-like, for years. Only the opportunistic Browder left the Sixth Congress in good graces, his strategic plague on all houses and orchestrated oscillations of outburst and occlusion an astutely calculated gamble on future dividends to be garnered in the quest for power within the now renamed Communist Party, USA (CPUSA).

Over the course of the summer, most of its leaders embroiled in the Sixth Congress factional fisticuffs, the American Party had itself been the site of increasing domestic hostilities, with Cannon-group figures such as Tom O'Flaherty and Manuel Gomez facing disciplinary charges for financial and other improprieties. Leading the attack was the Lovestone hatchet man, Jack Stachel; point man on the Cannon defense team was Martin Abern. These crudely factional assaults rankled because, while they faced such denigration within major party committees, Cannon supporters had been carrying the bulk of communist mass work throughout the summer of 1928. Labor defense campaigns continued in the International Labor Defense, as did anti-imperialist work, and Arne Swabeck and others had been promoting a new and militant unionism among Illinois miners and textile workers. Coming home was clearly going to be no political picnic.[28]

Having decided not to fight the battle for a Trotskyist program within the Sixth Congress itself, but to return to their native United States and Canada to build up the ranks of an effective Left Opposition, Cannon and Spector faced a difficult situation. They both knew that it was mandatory to "smuggle" Trotsky's *Draft Program* out of the Soviet Union so that they could use the document to propagate the ideas of the Left Opposition among potential United

States and Canadian converts. Cannon and Spector had no way of knowing how rigorous a tally of the Trotskyist critique of Comintern fundamentals was being kept, but they had reason to suspect that leaving the Soviet Union without returning the official document to the secretariat was going to be difficult. Both men, in the end, spirited Trotsky's *Draft Program* out of Russia in September 1928, Spector carrying it with him to Europe as he attempted to build bridges to opposition groups in France and Germany before returning to Toronto in the second week of October. For his part, Cannon apparently relied on the aid of George Weston, a Trotskyist-leaning British delegate known as the "Mad Irishman" for his free talk of Left Opposition ideas at the Sixth Congress, in "liberating" the *Draft Program* from its Stalinist incarceration. Rumor later had it that Weston, whose base of operations within the Comintern was labor defense work in the International Red Aid (making him a logical candidate for collaboration with Cannon), managed to get hold of another numbered document, possibly pilfered from an Australian delegate, thus allowing Cannon to return his copy. Weston's wife, Mary Morris, then removed the insides of her son's teddy bear, placed Trotsky's writings within the restuffed animal, and passed the pamphlet back to Cannon at a prearranged meeting in Berlin, from which Cannon departed for the United States, arriving home on 23 September 1928. There would later be anguished cries from Comintern quarters of the "illegal means" undertaken to circulate Trotsky's draft, "thereby endangering the proletarian dictatorship."[29]

Cannon first shared Trotsky's *Draft Program* with his lover and closest comrade, Rose Karsner. To her it was as if "at last light [had] been thrown on the troubles" the American section had lived through with the Comintern. With only a solitary copy of the document, no way of duplicating it, and conscious of the dangers of exposing themselves prematurely to a full-scale party attack, Cannon and Karsner proceeded cautiously. The red couple's quarters at this time, a flat on New York's Lower East Side in the Second Avenue and 19th Street district, were modest to the point of spartan; one by one, a few trusted comrades from the Cannon faction were brought to the apartment and sat down with Trotsky's *Draft Program*. The first were Cannon's closest co-workers in the International Labor Defense, the youthful but seasoned communist factionalists, Shachtman and Martin Abern. This duo was later expanded to include the long-time Cannon ally and former editor of the *Daily Worker* and the *Labor Defender,* Chicago-based (and increasingly disaffected) Tom O'Flaherty. Discussions ensued. Within three or four days after his arrival in New York from the Soviet Union, Cannon, Karsner, Shachtman, and Abern had agreed to "start the fight" for a Left Opposition within the Communist Party. That fight was not destined to go more than a round or two.[30]

American Trotskyism Underground

Unbeknownst to Cannon and his small cohort of allies, there had been others in the United States who were struggling, in an underground way, to forge some kind of a Trotskyist nucleus. Spearheading one clandestine operation that began months before the Sixth Congress, in the winter of 1927–1928, was a young Russian named Eleazer B. Solntsev, employed by the official Soviet trade corporation, Amtorg, in New York City. Solntsev hooked up with the expelled dissident Ludwig Lore, who contacted the bohemian Max Eastman and his Russian wife, Eliena.

At this time, Eastman was perhaps the most knowledgeable individual in the United States about Trotsky's Left Opposition, and although his past efforts on behalf of Trotsky had met with a tactical repudiation from the leader of the Russian dissidents (to be rescinded in September 1928), the former editor of the *Masses* remained remarkably open-minded. His efforts to explain the ideas of the Left Opposition, through articles submitted to communist magazines such as the *New Masses*, had been futile. Solntsev approached Eastman at a New York tête-à-tête, in which five potential Trotskyist sympathizers met in Lore's apartment to discuss the dim prospects for organizing the forces of revolutionary Trotskyism in America. Eastman had no taste, at this time, for organizational engagements, and his unwillingness to throw his attractive hat into the obviously rough-and-tumble ring of active communist politics slammed the lid shut on the possibility that a Solntsev-Lore-Eastman alliance would come to anything substantive.

Eventually, though, Eastman, a man of literary rather than political productions, was guilt-persuaded that a Solntsev-suggested book, to be composed of Trotsky's assessment about the situation in the Soviet Union, should be published in the United States. The Russian, like Cannon, had smuggled documents out of his homeland, and he had copies of pre-Sixth Congress material, including Trotsky's last speech in Russian, the "platform" of the Left Opposition, and one of Trotsky's long letters on Stalinist falsifications of the history of the Russian Revolution, written to the Bureau of Party History of the Central Committee of the Russian Communist Party. Along with some supplementary material, including Lenin's "Testament," previously published by Eastman, an account of Trotsky's deportation, and the appeal of the Left Opposition to the Sixth Congress of the Communist International for restoration of the Communist Party memberships of its advocates, this writing formed the bulk of a book Eastman pitched to Alfred Harcourt and Donald Brace sometime in the late winter or early spring of 1928. He molded the articles, speeches, and letters into *The Real Situation in Russia*, which appeared in June 1928, coincident with the rumblings of the Comintern's Sixth Congress.

Solntsev, in a selfless act of heroism, returned to the Soviet Union, where he faced certain brutal repression. Over the course of the next years, the economist turned dissident communist suffered through three years of jail, a like period of detention by "administrative order," exile to Siberia, separate deportations to other locales for his family, and a final sentence, without trial, of five years' imprisonment. As a last resort, he offered his body in an eighteen-day hunger strike. Emaciated and afflicted with a serious infection of the inner ear, one of the few remaining Left Oppositionists was released by the GPU and "allowed" to make his way to his wife. He died before he managed to get to the village to which she had been "transported."[31]

Antoinette Konikow: Boston's Red Birth-Control Advocate and Pioneer Left Oppositionist

The fifth person to meet with Solntsev, Lore, and Max and Eliena Eastman was Dr. Antoinette Konikow. She was perhaps the most crucial participant in this meeting, because she was a founder of the socialist and communist movements in the United States, and still affiliated with the Workers (Communist) Party. Long known to Ludwig Lore, Konikow, approaching age sixty at the end of 1928, was born Antoinette Buchholz in Russia. Coming from a family of revolutionaries, she became a socialist at the age of nineteen, joining Plekhanov's original Emancipation of Labor group in 1888. Enrolled in medical school in Switzerland sometime in the late 1880s, Buchholz came to the attention of czarist authorities when her boardinghouse, obviously something of a magnet drawing radicals, was the site of an accident involving explosives being handled by an advocate of revolutionary terrorism. This forced the leftist aspiring doctor into permanent exile. In defiance of czarist proscriptions against "intermarriage" of Jews and Christians, which were observed by Swiss authorities in the case of residents subject to Russian law, Antoinette feigned pregnancy in order to pressure a minister to marry her and her Jewish lover, William Konikow. The couple emigrated to the United States in 1893. Adept at languages (she spoke at least five), Konikow picked up Yiddish in order to organize unemployed Jewish workers during the bleak downturn of the mid-1890s, and gravitated to the Socialist Labor Party of Daniel DeLeon. Her stay in that body was brief: a delegate to the 1896 convention, she was expelled in 1897 for her opposition to the bureaucratic tone of SLP life. She soon aligned with Eugene Debs and helped to found the Socialist Party of America, where Konikow earned a reputation as a forceful orator and a defender of women's rights, sitting on the SP's five-member Women's Commission. A mother of two children, Konikow eventually graduated from Tufts College and set up a medical practice in the Boston area.

She catered to a female immigrant clientele, and was especially committed to putting women in touch with their bodies, educating the poor about the possibilities of birth control, which she regarded as an essential prerequisite of female emancipation. Well aware of the legal prohibitions on disseminating birth-control information and practicing abortion, Konikow kept all of her medical records in code so as to protect both her clients and herself from feared raids upon her office. Targeted by the notorious "Watch and Ward Society" of Boston, as well as that city's intolerant Catholic hierarchy, Konikow was relentless in disseminating information on birth control and in pushing socialists to "get off the fence" and deal with women's oppression in the realm of procreation immediately, rather than awaiting a socialist revolution that would supposedly deal, finally, with the problem. Divorced from her husband in 1910, she remained active in birth-control and socialist causes, linking the struggles for women's and workers' emancipation in the pages of the Socialist Party's major organ, the *New York Call.*

With the outbreak of war in 1914, Konikow toured the United States on behalf of the radical movement, inspired by Karl Liebknecht's example of opposition and defiant of the spies that lurked at the back of immigrant halls, ready to report on dissidents whose utterances marked them as dangerous offenders to the status quo. Quick to assimilate the lessons of the Russian Revolution, she joined the emerging communist underground and cast her lot with the Workers (Communist) Party throughout the 1920s. Konikow continued her crusade for birth control, publishing a powerful pamphlet in 1923, *Voluntary Motherhood* (it went through three editions and 10,000 copies), and offered an annual course of five lectures on sex hygiene and sex problems that was open to women only at Boston's Boylston Street Social Hall. Opposed to the professionalization of birth control, which restricted knowledge to the medical community, she was an early advocate of the Birth Control League of Massachusetts when no doctors other than herself supported its policy of radical openness. Later, as the organization adapted to medicalization, Konikow resisted the trend strongly.

A keen observer of the Comintern, Konikow opposed Zinoviev's bureaucratism, and made an unsanctioned trip to the Soviet Union in 1926. Hoping to promote an anti-spermicidal birth-control jelly, whose chemical formula Konikow filed with a Soviet government office, the revolutionary doctor was escorted from Berlin to Moscow by the notable African American radical, W. E. B. DuBois. This 1926 visit confirmed Konikow's worst fears about the degeneration of the Russian Revolution, and her talks with both factory women and leading Bolsheviks did little to curtail a growing pessimism.

Konikow returned to the United States depressed at the prospects of world revolution abroad and at home. Her immediate reaction in 1926 was, like most

Left Oppositionists inside the Soviet Union, to remain a loyal opponent rather than break explicitly from the Communist International. She judged the Soviet Union still a "transition state," and appreciated that she had to learn about the debates that were then dividing Trotsky, Stalin, and others. Also, not unlike Cannon and Spector two years later, she appreciated the need to proceed cautiously: "I kept officially quiet, and tried to find more facts and explanations to strengthen myself for the final break." At *precisely* the historical moment that she was reaching this point, in February 1928, she was arrested in Boston for her public advocacy of birth control. A long-standing socialist pioneer, an outspoken and courageous feminist crusader, an independent-minded internationalist —Konikow was ripe for Trotskyist ideas and the perfect candidate to gravitate to the program of the Left Opposition. But Cannon and his small New York circle had little knowledge of her potential openness.[32]

Piecing Together Possibilities of an American Left Opposition

The climate of constraint—isolations and enforced hushed recruitment of allies already within a circle of trust—inhibited Cannon's activities for three weeks to a month after his arrival in New York late in September 1928. He was actually happy with the headway he was making. Besides consolidating a small cell of adherents, and reaching out with feelers to comrades in other locales, such as Chicago, where it was thought he could count on support, Cannon also utilized his authority within the International Labor Defense to secure party mailing lists of 10,000 names, a vital prerequisite to actually intervening effectively within the Communist Party when the time to open discussion was forced. Moreover, he tapped into some funds, especially significant given that the publishing costs of Left Opposition material were going to reach well beyond the resources of Cannon, Karsner, Shachtman, and Abern, all of whom were professional revolutionaries entirely dependent on their paid party positions. Sometime in September or October, Cannon picked up the phone and made a call to his old friend Max Eastman, who had a house in Croton-on-Hudson, sixty miles or so from New York. Cannon informed Eastman that "things were happening" and that he wanted to come up to see him and have a private conversation. Cannon knew too much of Eastman's character to expect the old radical to join with him organizationally, but he suspected, rightly, that Eastman retained enough interest in the principles of Trotskyism's platform to want them to have wider dissemination. Thus, he asked no more of Eastman than the literary figure could be expected to give. In Eastman's words, he "godfathered" the new revolutionary movement, dedicating his royalties of Trotsky's *The Real Situation in Russia* to the publishing needs of the new American oppositionists. The $200 to $300 at stake proved a veritable windfall fortune to the impoverished Trotskyists.[33]

In Canada, meanwhile, Spector faced a similar uphill battle upon his return to Toronto on 9 October 1928, but one that was clearly heading quickly toward a point of crisis for the underground Left Oppositionists. Spector arrived home to find a letter from Cannon detailing the minor successes of September 1928. He was steeled by reading Eastman's translation of the correspondence between Trotsky and the CPSU, published as "Stalin Falsifies History," which suggested the importance of republishing the documents appearing in *The Real Situation in Russia* in cheap and popular editions, as had been done in France and Germany. Translation into Yiddish and other languages, he thought, "would be very effective in rallying support to us." Full of "cheerful surprise" that Cannon had managed to win four critical comrades to the cause, Spector promised to "send a complete list of the literature" he had obtained in Europe, and to begin the job of translating material from the French and German. The Canadian Marxist had obviously grabbed whatever he could, indiscriminately, in what was a quick canvassing of the situation. Assimilation of the lessons of this cache of literature would come later.

Spector's brief sojourn in Europe also allowed him a cursory introduction to Hugo Urbahns, a leader of the German Left along with Arkadi Maslow and Ruth Fisher. The Canadian also spent a day in Paris, scouting out a highly fractured set of oppositional forces. All of this reinforced Spector's appreciation of "the crisis in the International." The pivotal German Party he thought split into four factions, corrupt and spent: "Anybody who dares discuss or criticize except in the official channels, is driven out of the Party." Spector was now more convinced than ever that Cannon's "decision to come out with the fundamental program is, I believe, correct." Having thought the matter over in Europe, the Canadian Left Oppositionist could not "see any reality in a fight on a limited program." But, as would become apparent in the next weeks, Spector was unable to move past these critical beginnings to reproduce Cannon's modest organizational achievements in New York. Unlike Cannon, Spector had, after a few weeks back in Canada, failed to win pivotal recruits, and could not manage to pry from the Communist Party of Canada any mailing lists of significance, they being "kept under lock and key all the time I have been in the city." The slightly more than two weeks by which Cannon preceded Spector in his return to North America seemed a pivotal breathing space for activity that allowed Cannon to take steps that Spector simply could not, or perhaps neglected to treat with the proper regard. In the interval, the forces resistant to the Left Opposition were beginning to appreciate that a revolt needed to be nipped in the bud, for by the first week of October Cannon's

Trotskyism was more than a matter of conjecture among the leading forces of the Foster and Lovestone groups.[34]

Flushing the Trotskyists Out

Foster, somewhat demoralized, and seemingly originally overwhelmed by his antipathy for the Lovestone leadership, had little appetite for an anti-Trotskyist witch hunt upon his return to the United States in September 1928. Schooled in the old ways of factional alliances, Foster staked much on bonding with Cannon, the better to best Lovestone and, once and for all, secure his coveted leadership of the Communist Party. Moreover, although Foster returned to the United States before any of the other delegates attending the Sixth Congress, he was immediately immersed in the go-arounds of his mass work: upheavals in the mining and textile trade unions took up his time, as did campaigning as the Communist Party's candidate in the 1928 presidential election. As long as Cannon did not come out openly as a Trotskyist, Foster could maintain the alliance and the possibility of defeating Lovestone. However, he then faced the danger of his position: that Lovestone would make factional hay out of the discovery that the Foster caucus had "borne in their loins a Trotskyist group," nursing it "in their bosom." Such revelations could never be lived down in the Comintern and, indeed, Foster would soon face Stalin's condemnation for having made common cause with "hidden Trotskyists."

Nevertheless, Cannon was largely able to circle round Foster's New York caucus heads, CEC member Philip Aronberg and Jewish Federation leader H. I. Costrell, with Foster and Bittelman occupied on party assignment outside New York. He signed a joint opposition-group statement with them, for instance, that appeared in the *Daily Worker* on 2 October 1928, reiterating the minority's position that the Lovestone leadership was pushing programmatically to the right and demanding a cessation of the majority's factional persecution of the Cannon-Foster forces.

The schooled Stalinist and former Cannon friend, Clarence Hathaway, only recently returned from the Soviet Union, then led the charge to flush Cannon out in small-group encounters, caucus assemblies, New York membership meetings, and specially convened interrogations that took place between 2–5 October 1928. Pushed in the Cannon-Foster caucus meetings as to his positions, Cannon prevaricated and refused to be cornered by motions designed to expose him. Somewhat slippery, then, Cannon was, in the eyes of his inquisitors, a problem in their midst, but not one they could easily dispense with. Whether they were tied to his ability to best articulate the minority's oppositional stand, or whether they decided to hand Cannon sufficient rope to hang himself, is not known decisively. The Opposition caucus unanimously elected Cannon to speak as its representative at a critical 3 October 1928 membership meeting in New York, where reports of the Sixth Congress of the Comintern would be made to the ranks.

Cannon addressed the gathering, but left immediately following Lovestone's majority statement, escaping the waiting noose. Abern and Shachtman remained, and they were quickly confronted by a motion put to the assembly by members of the Foster-Cannon group. It called for endorsement of the Sixth Congress decisions, acknowledging reservations around questions pertaining to the American party. Defiant, the two young Left Oppositionists refused to vote on such a resolution, not being ready, they said, "to endorse the Comintern decisions on the Trotsky Question." A number of those present, including former Cannon loyalists Gomez and Hathaway, as well as ranking Foster partisans, demanded another, less public, discussion with Cannon and his two young allies.

At this final get-together, on 4 October 1928, Cannon was the subject of scrutiny. He refused to embrace the notion of "socialism in one country," insisted that he would not condemn Trotsky's so-called "Thermidorian theory," and would not agree that the Comintern treatment of the Trotsky Question had been adequate. Cannon's mind, he stated, was "open" on the issue of Trotsky, and he was reexamining the programmatic implications of various writings. Nevertheless, he maintained a position that he would later reiterate: "Not a single person . . . can truthfully say that I advocated or did anything in connection with the Trotsky question contrary to what had been decided by the party." Faced with a resolution that assailed Trotsky and the Left Opposition as "counter-revolutionary," and saw holding contrary views or "spreading doubts on the question" as "incompatible with membership in a Communist party," Cannon abstained, Shachtman voted against, and Abern voted in favor. Some tactical differences still separated the men: Shachtman claimed that he held the most uncompromising views, Abern feared a premature split, and Cannon wanted to preserve a little time in the war for position. This was also, of course, a bit of tactical guile. It did not entirely fool the reconfigured Foster group, for they gave the Trotskyist trio the heave-ho from their caucus the next evening, but it perhaps kept them enough off balance that Gomez, Hathaway, and Company dragged their feet in preferring charges before the party's Central Executive Committee.[35]

Neither Bittelman nor Foster was in New York as these meetings unfolded. However much Foster might have been inclined to hedge his bets, Bittelman, an increasingly inveterate "Comintern man" who considered Stalin to be Trotsky's superior, would have known that there was but one way forward and that, moreover, it was Foster's only chance to permanently resecure some of the ground that seemed always to be slipping away to Lovestone. Bittelman understood that ingratiating the Foster group with Stalin's Comintern demanded "outing" Cannon. "Otherwise," Bittelman raged in Chicago, "our name in Moscow will be mud." As for Foster, who never managed to forget Cannon's supposed betrayal of him in 1925, this possibly carried the bonus of a tasty revenge, eaten pleasantly cold.

That Lovestone and his factional entourage at the helm of the Communist Party were unaware of the events unfolding, in which Cannon, Shachtman, and Abern were increasingly unable to keep their programmatic endorsement of the Left Opposition secret, was of course untrue. The walls of the Communist Party domicile in this period indeed had ears. There is abundant evidence that the Lovestone majority, too, was preparing an anti-Trotskyist housecleaning. In the case of the Cannon nucleus, though, Lovestone's lot enjoyed the moment in which they could keep Foster squirming under the spotlight of aiding and abetting the counterrevolution. This all bought the emerging New York Left Opposition a precious two weeks, which they used to reconnect and solidify different relations with Spector and Eastman, and possibly to make tentative overtures to Chicago supporters Arne Swabeck and Albert Glotzer. Most importantly, this time allowed Cannon, Karsner, Shachtman, and Abern (with Spector a critical, but distant, correspondent) to discuss the publication possibilities, especially the prospects for a Left Opposition newspaper, that were central to their getting the programmatic word out among rank-and-file communists. The Trotskyist cat was, however, now very much out of the political bag.[36]

Before the Court of Lovestone

At a 16 October 1928 Political Committee meeting of the Central Executive Committee of the Communist Party, Foster, Bittelman, and Aronberg preferred anti-Trotskyist charges against Cannon, Shachtman, and Abern. The charges closed with a declaration of the minority's commitment to "wage [a] merciless fight against this Trotskyist manoeuvre of Comrade Cannon and to wage this fight as an organic part of its general struggle against the Right danger and the Right wing of our Party (the Lovestone group)." For their part, Lovestone, Pepper, Minor, and Stachel had the same mindset, and immediately set out to expose the Foster group's culpability in sheltering this clot of Trotskyists from the disciplining leadership of the party for an ostensibly momentous two weeks.[37]

After Foster and Bittelman made lengthy defensive statements before the Political Committee, the body got down to the main business at hand, demanding that Cannon explain himself. Pepper pressed Cannon on whether he agreed in full with the decisions of the Communist International, knowing that there were statements on Trotskyism's counterrevolutionary nature in various places. Cannon simply insisted that he had proposed no revision of Comintern policy. Asked bluntly by Aronberg, "Did Comrade Cannon ask any comrade to study Eastman's book on the Trotsky question?" Cannon offered the terse reply: "I did not." Outnumbered at least ten to one, Cannon stood up for Abern and Shachtman, moving that they be allowed to come before the Committee to defend themselves, and also insisted that removing himself and his two co-workers from their International Labor Defense posts would compromise the work of that body. It was all, predictably, for naught. The meeting ended with a motion to remove the three suspected Trotskyists from their ILD positions. Warned that continuation of their oppositional factional activity would be met with further disciplinary action, including removal from the Political Committee, Cannon, Shachtman, and Abern were instructed to appear before them again in two days' time to "explain their attitude." The matter was referred to the Central Control Commission for further investigation, and the oppositionists had to pledge not to reveal the nature of the proceedings to party members.[38]

In the approximately ten days that followed, Cannon, Shachtman, and Abern were, in effect, put on trial (it was technically a hearing to assess the validity of charges) before the Political Committee, although there was likely some procedurally muddled involvement of the Control Commission as well. What had originated as a closed Political Committee discussion gradually expanded into a larger and quite difficult-to-control body, which Cannon estimated grew, at its peak, to 100 comrades. The ranks were often unruly, and on occasion had to be reminded by the chair "to keep order or we cannot continue the meeting." Meetings were held, lasting for hours, on October 16, 18 (two sessions, afternoon and evening, the latter almost certainly extending past midnight and into October 19), and 27, 1928, and the stenographic record of the hearings totaled more than 100 pages.[39]

Leading the charge was Cannon's old Minnesota friend, Clarence "Charlie" Hathaway. His allegations placed a strong accent on how Cannon's evasiveness on the Trotsky question translated into a direct assault on the Communist International.[40] Trotsky's critique of the Communist International's policy vis-à-vis the Chinese Revolution, Cannon thought "more or less correct." On the Comintern's characterization of Trotskyism as counterrevolutionary, and on specific ECCI allegations of particular Trotskyist acts that demanded condemnation, Cannon now supposedly expressed "doubts." All of this Hathaway then related to Cannon's behavior at the Sixth Congress. Cannon's position, Hathaway described as "ILDism," a variant of "Loreism." This "theory" held that the party was "carrying on too many struggles, . . . trying to organize too many unions." Instead, Hathaway claimed that Cannon's position was that "we must . . . place more emphasis on concrete constructive work and that the ILD was the outstanding example." In Hathaway's view, which set the tone for the Foster-Bittelman group's position throughout the hearings, Cannon's Trotsky-ism was nothing more than a right-wing maneuver aimed at diverting the minority from its struggle against the Right Danger pinpointed by the Com-intern as the key battle for all communists, and identified in the United States with Lovestone. Gomez followed suit, largely parroting Hathaway, and a parade of others, prominent among them Aronberg and Costrell, provided endless, and endlessly contested, testimony on meeting dates and utterances in the 2–6 October 1928 period. That the two accusers first out of the condemna-tory gate were Hathaway, an old trade union ally of Cannon's, and Gomez, whom Cannon had been shielding throughout September and October from the Lovestone faction's persecutions regarding financial improprieties in the Anti-Imperialist Department was, of course, no accident.

With Cannon's expulsion virtually assured, Lovestone, Stachel, and others found themselves equally concerned with discrediting what was now their only opposition, the reconfigured minority that had coalesced around Foster-Bittelman. Tempers most often flared, then, not on the part of Cannon, Shacht-man, and Abern, who remained quite cool and dispassionate, but among the minority non-Cannonist ranks. They resented Lovestone's handling of the pro-ceedings, which often seemed to shut them up, veer in obviously threatening factional directions, and allow Cannon and Company far too much leeway in pursuing interrogations of their actions and misrepresentations.

As the hearings wore on in marathon sessions, Cannon, Shachtman, and Abern tired of the tactic of exposing their accusers, and the tone hardened: "I say Gomez lied about what took place in Moscow and I want to call other com-rades and see whether they spoke the truth." Cannon registered questions about the Communist Party's financial obligations to himself and his co-workers in the International Labor Defense. He also tried to protest, through a motion to the Control Commission, that the party had sent a "bodyguard" from the Keystone Detective Agency to the ILD offices, but his demand that such an offensively questionable act be the subject of inquiry and investigation was quickly swept under a procedural rug.[41]

Foster played little role in the early stages of the Political Committee pro-ceedings, being centrally involved in other, public party activities, but his patience, too, was waning. At the meeting of 27 October 1928, Cannon recalls him declaring with indignation: "It is absolutely clear already that there is a Trotskyite faction in the party and that the three leaders of it are sitting right here." Stachel, incapable of turning off the taps of factional possibility, supposedly adopted a posture of solemn concern: "These comrades have been a long time in the movement," he lectured, "and we must proceed very carefully before we make a decision." "Longer than you remember," Cannon quipped.

It was then that Cannon, Shachtman, and Abern dropped their final political bombshell. Communist Party ranks across the country were now aware of the hearings and no tactical advantage could be gained by stalling for more time. Cannon and his small New York group had contacted other party members in Chicago and elsewhere, preparing a nineteen-point programmatic statement, which they now released to the Political Committee. The document, which would later be boldly titled, "For the Russian Opposition! *Against Opportunism and Bureaucracy in the Workers Communist Party of America!*" was a decisive declaration to fight within party circles on the basis of a Left Opposition program. Premising their stand on largely accepting the old opposition's "The Right Danger in the American Party," excepting some passages on the world situation and the role of American imperialism, Cannon, Shachtman, and Abern railed against the Lovestone and Foster factions and cast their lot irretrievably with Trotsky, deploring the theoretical and programmatic deviations of "socialism in one country." Refusing to accept any arbitrary decisions made against them by the Communist Party, the newly declared Trotskyists insisted that they had helped to found and build the party and that they would continue to work for the party. The first act in their labors was to demand the dissemination of their ideas.

After reading the joint Cannon-Shachtman-Abern declaration, Cannon was interrogated closely by approximately a dozen comrades. Among the leading questioners were Bittelman, Stachel, Swift/Pepper, and, for the first time, Lovestone. Cannon responded by presenting himself as "a humble student and follower of the Russian Revolution, . . . unwilling to make offhand answers to conflicting questions." If, on occasion, Cannon lied directly (as, for instance, in his statements that he had had no contact with Max Eastman), he for the most part answered truthfully, if with a careful eye to nuances that nudged interpretation in his self-interested direction. Once this skirmishing subsided, Cannon and his two allies could hardly have been surprised when they were summarily tossed out of the revolutionary party that they had dedicated their lives to building. As Cannon recalled, "We were expelled and out of there a few minutes later. The 'jury' didn't bother to leave the box." The next day, the small nucleus of Trotskyists had a mimeographed "statement circulating throughout the party."[42]

A national mass mailing of their programmatic statement was accompanied by an open letter, dated October 28, from Cannon to all party members. In it Cannon explained that he, Shachtman, and Abern had endorsed the platform of the Russian Opposition, and that the trio had been expelled by the Political Committee, which refused to publish their documents of dissidence. Adamant that, as communists, they were bound to the Communist Party even as its leading body expelled them, Cannon committed himself, Shachtman, and Abern to fight for the ideas of Trotskyism and reinstatement to the Communist Party, asking for support from all who shared their views. In a key passage, Cannon linked the suppression of the struggle for thought and program in the party to its bureaucratic degeneration:

> Such methods which substitute bureaucratic control for ideological and political leadership have permeated our Party to an alarming degree, adversely affecting its policies, choking its inner life, weakening its influence, blocking its growth.... The proletarian masses of the Party must awaken to this danger and take up the fight against it. They must break through the bureaucratic crust that has formed itself on top of the Party. They must demand full information on all sides of the question so that they can decide for themselves intelligently and not merely from wrong and non-Leninist conceptions of formal discipline.[43]

Emphasizing "from the very beginning that [the central issue was] not simply a question of democracy," the Cannon opposition stressed "the program of Marxism." Utilizing the discontent around the lack of inner-party democracy that the Konikow forces in Boston had accented, Cannon, Shachtman, and Abern consciously strove to "get a sympathetic hearing and then immediately began pounding away on the rightness of Trotskyism on all the political questions."[44]

"Three Generals without an Army": Under Attack

By the time the full and conflicting accounts of the expulsion appeared in newsprint, with statements being published in both the *Daily Worker* and the new Trotskyist propaganda organ, *The Militant,* in mid-November, a new chapter in the history of the American revolutionary Left had commenced. Lovestone's lieutenant, Bertram Wolfe, dubbed Cannon, Shachtman, and Abern the "three Generals without an Army," a characterization not all that far off the mark, although its condescending male chauvinism, characteristic of the "hearings" and expulsions as a whole, wrote one crucial player, Rose Karsner, entirely out of the political war. Cannon recalled that he, Shachtman, and Abern "felt pretty lonely" as they departed, for the last time, the Political Committee meeting of 27 October 1928. Nevertheless, the slightly more than two-week interval separating the technical expulsion of Cannon and his comrades from the public announcement to the party ranks was something of a lull before the ugly storm that would eventually overwhelm the Trotskyist effort to create a Left Opposition appealing to the Communist Party's membership. In these weeks, *The Militant* was launched, funded by Eastman and some Chicago comrades and printed by an old Italian Wobbly, Joe Cannata, who both suggested the name and was generous in extending credit to the dissident communists. Shachtman recalled that the original response was anything but virulent. Old friends and comrades would talk about issues of political program; though some were hostile, there appeared to be openings to discuss Trotskyist criticisms, and it was possible to sell papers to party members.[45] Whittaker Chambers, well on his way to becoming an anti-communist informer, was one party member who furtively sidled up to Shachtman in late 1928, eager, supposedly, to translate some of Trotsky's German-language writing for the *Militant*. The trusting Left Oppositionists gave Chambers their only copy of a document. They never saw it again: Chambers ran to the Central Committee with it.[46]

As the word spread of the existence of the Cannon-Shachtman-Abern-Karsner group, recruits came their way. A previously expelled New York body of Hungarians, led by Louis Basky, had connected with Solntsev and a small, isolated cluster of Left Oppositionists at Amtorg, becoming followers of Trotsky. Cannon thought them a veritable "army" when they joined with him. More unstable, because they were not really Trotskyists in Cannon's view, was an assembly of Italian followers of the ultraleft dissident, Amadeo Bordiga, who worked with the emerging American Left Opposition until Trotsky and Bordiga had an eventual falling-out in 1930–1932 over the extremism of Bordiga's "communist abstentionist" approach to electoral activity. By ones and twos, moreover, Cannon's corps won the odd Communist Party member to their views.

This bringing-together of a Left Opposition by bits and pieces proceeded in the first week of November, with documents being sent to contacts in the Midwest and the mining milieu, where Cannon had decade-old ties to local militants. Some of it elicited positive responses; a miner long associated with opposition to the John L. Lewis trade union bureaucracy wrote: "It shows once more the necessity of rank and file rule instead of a few leaders whom can utilize their positions for personal advantage and machine rule. . . . The slogans must be as in the old UMW:—'save the Party!' 'Lovestoneism must go!' 'For a Communist Party of the Workers!'"[47]

Cannon and the Left Opposition appeared to be gaining some ground. Lovestone thus moved off the stand of relative moderation he had found it useful to occupy, for anti-Foster factional purposes, during the Political Committee hearings reviewing the charges against Cannon, Shachtman, and Abern. Pepper, writing under the name "Swift," prepared an early statement:

> The Trotskyist group around Cannon, Lore, and Eastman is an open ally of the
> capitalists, the Government, the Socialist Party, the A.F. of L., in their attempts
> to destroy the Communist Party. . . . The complete liquidation of Trotskyism in
> our Party can be achieved only by an uncompromising, relentless struggle
> against all manifestations of the right danger, by means of merciless self-
> criticism, by a complete mobilization of all Party forces against the renegades,
> near Social Democrats, splitters, and liquidators.

Cannon was now the head of a counterrevolutionary conspiracy, and it was
necessary to cut off all relations with him and any supporters. Philadelphia
communist, Herbert Benjamin, described the worsening climate of late 1928:
"All friendships were completely ended, terminated, broken up, and so on, and
there was no talking. And finally there were violent attacks upon the Trotskyists
. . . attempts to prevent them from holding meetings of any kind, of seizing their
records, seizing any properties. . . . It was the most ruthless and unethical kind
of action, and was considered tolerable, permissible, in your relations with
opponents." Shachtman later expressed his shock at how quickly the Lovestone
machine orchestrated a campaign of violence, meant to create an atmosphere
in which the Trotskyists were ostracized as a diseased contingent, contact with
which was prohibited for all rank-and-file communists. Most disturbing were
the organized groups of New York party members, often wielding furriers'
knives, who formed vigilante squads that would jostle and threaten the expelled
oppositionists on public streets as they distributed literature and sold the Trotskyist press. Cannon, Shachtman, and Abern now faced resistance and resentment that crossed over into the territory of physical intimidation.[48]

How Communist Party Repression Organized
Early American Trotskyism

This escalation in the nature of the official Communist Party response to the
ideas and organizational development of a Left Opposition was paralleled by a
closing of the internal ranks of the Lovestone-led party. Antoinette Konikow
was one of the first on the firing line. Lovestone took the initiative in stamping
out the influence of the dissident doctor in Boston. Konikow had been moving
in similar directions as Cannon and his small band of supporters, albeit in isolation. Lovestone traveled to Boston sometime in September or October to
speak on "the Trotsky question," and found Konikow set in her opposition to
his leadership and the CEC, and resistant about voting for party resolutions
until she had availed herself of the opportunity to read the appropriate documents. The Boston local of the Communist Party preferred charges against her
as the Political Committee hearings against Cannon, Shachtman, and Abern

were winding down. Summoned by registered letter to New York on 30 October 1928 to appear before a similar Polcom tribunal on November 2, Konikow declined to grace the Lovestone circle with her presence, castigating the lack of inner-party democracy and deploring the degeneration of the Communist International and its American affiliate: "[T]he Party has taken an outrageously wrong standing on the Trotsky situation in Soviet Russia . . . a result of the servile submission to the Stalin faction." Considering it her party right to "work for Trotsky's ideas" and "arouse sentiment for the Opposition," Konikow signed her rebuttal, "A comrade of thirty-nine years services in the Socialist cause." She was, of course, perfunctorily and unanimously expelled, Lovestone offering a final, and telling, statement:

> My opinion is that it is obvious from her letter that she is the worst kind of a Trotskyite, biologically as well as politically. The sooner that we throw her out the better for the Party. We don't think that Cannon will welcome the strength she will bring to his banner. He will welcome her as an ally but she has no influence, she has no following in the Boston section. I don't think she has any influence amongst the sympathizers even.

Lovestone underestimated the Russian-born revolutionary.

Within a month, Konikow had gathered together a small Boston group of dissidents in the Independent Communist League, which published its *Bulletin No. 1* in December 1928. A programmatically underdeveloped document, the *Bulletin* appealed for financial help from committed communists and explored what was wrong with the Communist Parties of the United States and the Soviet Union. It focused almost entirely on questions of democracy and the imposition of unanimity in a climate of factional intrigue. Konikow clearly despised Lovestone, the *Bulletin* declaring that his "political trickery and crookedness is admitted by his own supporters." In bolting from the factional logjam that Lovestone and others had bottlenecked the Communist Party with by the late 1920s, Konikow and her Boston associates ended throwing up their hands in despair over the inhibitions against free discussion, which they felt was the only antidote to the debilitating factionalism of American communism. Although the Independent Communist League brought issues associated with Trotsky's Left Opposition into view for Boston's revolutionary socialists, alluding to the repression that Trotsky supporters faced within the Soviet Union, publishing excerpts from the 27 October 1928 statement by Cannon, Shachtman, and Abern, and advising all comrades to read Eastman's compilation of Trotsky statements in *The Real Situation in Russia,* the group's first and only *Bulletin* failed to address the programmatic criticism of fundamentals that was the very core of Cannon's and Spector's break from

Stalinism, Trotsky's *Draft Program*. Konikow and her Boston group were, of course, quick to get in touch with Cannon and others in New York after their parallel expulsions, but as late as December 20, Shachtman would be writing to Spector intimating that an actual meeting with the Boston Left Oppositionist had not yet taken place. He could not easily put his hands on a copy of *Bulletin No. 1*, promising to forward the densely packed leaflet when he secured one. Meanwhile, in Shachtman's characterization, the Independent Communist League statement did "not amount to much and has an entirely wrong line, very similar to Lore's." That said, there was clearly ground for immediate common cause with Konikow, and indeed she would prove a generous benefactor and programmatic supporter of the Cannon group in the financially pressed and politically challenging times of Trotskyism's United States beginnings.[49]

The curtain of repression lowered on many others besides Konikow, forcing some into the Cannon ranks. A well-known radical, and a secret member of the Workers (Communist) Party since 1926–1927, Scott Nearing, came under fire for remarking that "the ILD was the most successful [Party] organization, [and] that the Party was trying to do too much," words that bespoke a coded Cannonism to those in the know in the closing months of 1928.[50] A contingent of Finns, headed by Elis Sulkanen, was hauled before the Political Committee and interrogated as to its role in promoting Cannon and Trotsky in a nonparty mass organization, the Brooklyn Finnish Workers Club. Questioned as to his views on studying material supplied "by the Trotsky Opposition to Cannon," Sulkanen replied, "You put this the wrong way. I don't say I have to study the matter of Cannon. I say I have to be familiar with what is happening."

"But you also said Cannon has at present a new viewpoint."

"Looks like it," the Finn responded tersely.

"And you have to study that viewpoint?" asked Bertram Wolfe incredulously.

"Certainly," said Sulkanen matter-of-factly.[51]

Every prominent Cannon faction member that the Political Committee could locate was sent a letter demanding that he or she respond to the statement Cannon, Shachtman, and Abern issued on 27 October 1928. Allowed one week to reply, comrades who neglected or were unable to offer a declaration to the Political Committee were sent another letter; if that too failed to elicit a response, they were then expelled. Specific national sections, such as the Italian and Greek, were encouraged by the Lovestone leadership to conduct foreign-language witch hunts and ferret out Trotskyists in their midst, turning over recommendations for expulsion to Lovestone lieutenants such as William Weinstone and Benjamin Gitlow. This mid-November 1928 deluge of correspondence produced disciplinary action and a number of excommunications, as well as letters denouncing Cannon, *The Militant*, and Trotskyism. Some rank-and-file communists clearly found it difficult to choose sides, given the history of factionalism and the incompleteness of their programmatic understanding. A number would write to the trio of expelled New York communists, asking to have access to their documents and statements. In the worsening climate of late 1928, this was judged heretical. In conjunction with the Lovestone majority's insistence on placing resolutions assailing Trotskyism and its three adherents before most party locals, this anti-Trotsky/anti-Cannon overdrive thus led to much disgruntlement, some of which ended in the nascent American Left Opposition securing the allegiance of critical forces.[52]

Chicago and Minneapolis: Centers of a New Movement

Two centers of Trotskyist development would be Chicago and Minneapolis. Shachtman's young friend, Albert Glotzer, and the older trade union Cannon ally, Arne Swabeck, had been privy to Cannon's Trotskyist turn even before the expulsion, and they were the first Chicago comrades to see a copy of Trotsky's *Draft Program*. When Hathaway came to the Windy City communist stronghold to beat the drums of anti-Trotskyism, Glotzer and Swabeck found that they knew far more than he did about the programmatic issues at stake in the Stalinized Comintern. They regarded Hathaway's arguments as "feeble," their slight familiarity with Trotsky's document providing them with the wherewithal to give the Lenin School graduate "a very rough time." On 22 November 1928, these two Cannon supporters wrote a withering letter to the Central Executive Committee of the Communist Party and the National Executive Committee of the Young Workers League. They detailed the programmatic lapses of the Lovestone-Pepper leadership and protested the mass expulsions that had decimated the proletarian ranks of the party throughout the industrial Midwest, citing with especial vehemence recent developments in Minneapolis, where seventeen comrades had been expelled, among them Vincent Ray Dunne, Oscar Coover, C. R. Hedlund, and Carl Skoglund. Other locales, such as Cannon's old stomping grounds of Kansas City, where A. A. "Shorty" Buehler, a pioneer communist since the days of the underground Communist Labor Party, was given the boot, also provided a basis for protest. Glotzer and Swabeck could not have been surprised by their subsequent expulsion, but they were caught rather unawares when three of their Chicago comrades (Judd, Zalisko, and Bergeson), sickened by the display of factional heavy-handedness, voted against the extreme discipline and put their own heads in the anti-Trotskyist guillotine.[53]

In the Twin Cities, the situation for the Left Opposition was anything but certain, and Cannon, at the point of his expulsion, had next to no contact with the leading comrades in Minneapolis-St. Paul. There the usual blend of Communist Party resolution bullying and Clarence Hathaway thickheadedness virtually organized a Left Opposition by default. Vincent Ray Dunne, Skoglund, Coover, and C. R. Votaw were suspended early in the Lovestone-orchestrated sweep through the Communist Party's Ninth District, and a combination of Hathaway's cajoling and begging only steeled an emerging contingent of dissidents in the belief that something was severely wrong in the now merged Houses of Lovestone and Stalin. C. R. Hedlund and the youth leader Carl Cowl then led a Twin Cities rebellion, pressing a motion protesting the suspensions. They lost, but their efforts garnered more than a dozen further supporters for the growing oppositional forces, which issued a circular letter to all communists in the district. At first this group, which apparently did not yet include the younger Dunne brothers Miles and Grant, chose to fight on the grounds of democracy, decency, open access to documents, and proper procedures, largely ignoring Trotskyism and the programmatic issues raised by the Russian Left Opposition and by Cannon and his supporters. Through a careful correspondence with Cowl, Cannon managed to steer the Twin Cities comrades onto the tracks of a principled political opposition, one that bridged dissidence from Moscow through New York to Minneapolis via the ideas of Trotsky's *Draft Program*. By the end of November, some twenty-seven Minneapolis-St. Paul comrades had been expelled, most of them lining up with Cannon. The proletarian Trotskyists of the Twin Cities would come to rank among Cannon's staunchest supporters.

Outside of this Minnesota stronghold, New York, New Haven, Philadelphia, Akron, Cleveland, St. Louis, Detroit, Chicago, Kansas City, and the coalfields of southern Illinois and Colorado were the sparse recruiting grounds of the "singlejack agitation" of the United States Left Opposition in the autumn of 1928, drawing converts in singles and pairs, or, more rarely, in threes and fours. It was, in Cannon's words, "a long and toilsome process." By the end of November, Cannon, Shachtman, Abern, and Karsner could almost count recruits to the Trotskyist cause on their collective fingers and toes, the total of the supporting ranks being approximately one hundred.[54]

To the north, Maurice Spector fared even worse, and after his 11 November 1928 expulsion, which followed a Lovestone-orchestrated course similar to the events in New York, few converts were won to the nascent Trotskyist movement. Spector anticipated that a group of twenty-five to thirty might form in Toronto, and Cannon put on a brave front to the comrades, reporting that "Spector is making headway and already has a solid group with him." But the prospects in Canada were, if anything, less heartening than in the United States.[55]

Trotskyism and the Communist Party: An Uncertain Future, 1928

Cannon, a soldier of the revolution who had been ignominiously discharged on 27 October 1928, now at least had a battalion behind him. Carrying only their program of renewing communist practice and principle with them into battle, Cannon and his guerilla forces were embarking on a protracted campaign that would often see them down and out, but never routed. If hopes of victory ran high for Cannon and others as 1928 came to a close, and an opening battle seemed to have been won, the war for Marxist, Leninist, and Trotskyist position in the years to come would be long, hard, and always contested. As perhaps the foremost Trotskyist in the United States on the eve of the Great Depression, Cannon faced his time in the trenches unaware of just how difficult the next decades would prove.

James P. Cannon, the United States Revolutionary Movement, and the End of an Age of Innocence

Revolution and Reaction

The revolutionary Left in the United States has never had an easy time of it. Opposed, at times quite vehemently, by capital and the state, it has also had an uphill battle in its efforts to lift the ideological weights of supposed affluence and democracy from the shoulders of dissidence. It has also been plagued by various sins of omission and commission, errors the movement itself has promulgated taking their toll. But those who have advocated the fundamental socioeconomic transformation of the American order have nevertheless been a presence in the United States past, and one not without influence.

In the first decades of the twentieth century, the forces of labor radicalism appeared to be gathering strength, and the storm of left-wing agitation threatened the economic and political bastions of power to such an extent that constituted authority unleashed the terrors of a repressive onslaught the likes of which had never before been seen. An atmosphere of vigilante lynch law was licensed throughout the land, exposing revolutionaries to the rough justice of the patriotic mob, culminating in patently illegal deportations, beatings, the liberal use of tar and feathers, public violence and humiliation, even execution. State-sanctioned raids on radical headquarters, mass arrests, show trials, and the exile of aliens dominated the landscape of class relations in the years from 1917 to 1921, leaving the ranks of the Industrial Workers of the World, the Communist Labor Party, the Communist Party of America, and the various wings and enclaves of anarchist and socialist thought and activism reeling, reaching for new perspectives. The Socialist Party of America felt the debilitating reverberations of the time, as did the DeLeonite Socialist Labor Party and countless foreign-language federations, sporting associations, and cultural clubs harboring Old-World radicals. This was never purely and simply a national panic, it being no accident that it arose in a time of war and momentous world events. Much of the irrational fear that spread like wildfire in widening public circles was fueled by the hatreds and phobias generated in certain quarters with the realization of workers' power in revolutionary Russia in 1917.[1]

Communism's First Decade: The End of an Age of Revolutionary Innocence

Out of the ferment of repression and change would be born a United States communist movement. Throughout the 1920s, this movement represented the promise of proletarian revolution, seemingly realized in the newly arrived Soviet state, and was, for all of its internal divisions, a leading edge of the labor Left, as well as an important force in defending civil rights for oppressed minorities and class-war prisoners. It had, to be sure, certain blind spots, including an inadequate appreciation of the critical areas of race and gender that are now rightly central in radical politics. On the whole, though, the communism of the 1920s was a momentous advance for the revolutionary Left, albeit one that would soon stumble and eventually fall backward. As much as the bright and shining red star of the Communist International was a guiding beacon for the United States revolutionary movement, for instance, its faltering bureaucratization and, from the mid-1920s on, increasing Stalinization, spelled the end of a particular age of innocence for the Left.

By *innocence* I imply no pejorative condescension, for I use the term positively, designating a basic freedom from corruption and capitulation to that which is wrong and ill-advised. Neither am I starry-eyed in my assessment, however, for *innocence* does not imply a lack of problems and difficulties. Quite the contrary. It is possible, however, to understand the shortcomings of the pre-communist revolutionary Left and, at the same time, appreciate the steps forward it was struggling to make. In the same vein, though no scholar can look at the 1920s experience of the United States revolutionary Left, concentrated in Communist Party organizations, and fail to see some fundamentally hard-nosed politics, much of which was certainly less than exemplary in the forms it assumed, it is crucial also to recognize what was indeed a record of activity honorable in its core intentions, even its belief in the authority and staying power of a distant, but revered, Revolution and its Russian leadership. It may thus seem strange to many to claim that this was a period of revolutionary innocence, but I do so with conviction. My meaning lies in a view of the origins of the American revolutionary Left, including the uneasy formative years of United States communism, at odds with contemporary judgment but very much aligned with James P. Cannon's absolute insistence on looking at this period in a certain way. "It was not as though a gang of bandits combined together and then began to fight over the spoils," he wrote of the first years of the Workers (Communist) Party. "There were no spoils," he exclaimed with vehemence. "The overwhelming majority of people came to pioneer Communism with serious purposes and sincere motives to organize a movement for the emancipation of the workers of the whole world. They were prepared to make sacrifices and take risks for their ideal, and they did so."[2]

Thus, when I refer to an age of revolutionary innocence, I am accentuating the character of a particular period in United States radicalism, one relatively uncorrupted by many of the cauterized complicities and worldly-wise knowledges that have calloused the politics of our time, undermining belief in the possibility of thoroughgoing transformation, dismissing the broad capacity of working-class people to effect material change, containing the expansiveness of radicalism in various liberal accommodations to "the art of the possible." In contrast, in its origins the American revolutionary Left was remarkably open and wide-ranging; resilient in its assent to new experiences; welcoming, in a culture often parochial and chauvinistic, of international currents; and vibrant in its demand to free the channels of politics, culture, economic organization, and everyday social life to the fast-flowing meanings of exhilarating possibility.[3]

A young Jim Cannon was nothing if not an expression of this revolutionary embrace of extending the human condition. How else is it possible to explain how a Catholic-raised youth from Rosedale, Kansas, found himself, in the space of a decade, moving out of the circles of pool-hall gangs and the constricted horizons of their worldview, through high school debates over arbitration of industrial disputes and female suffrage, into close contact with the leaders of the Industrial Workers of the World and conversations with Max Eastman at the New York offices of the *Masses*? Moreover, this did not end with the party-building of the 1920s: Cannon, a Bolshevik leader by this time, and a figure stamped with the unmistakable marks of the native-born proletarian agitator, nevertheless cultivated relations with some of the more cosmopolitan and theoretical elements in the communist movement, such as Alexander Bittelman, just as he rubbed shoulders with the cultural wing of the revolutionary Left, reviewing books by Mike Gold, drinking and breaking bread with the likes of Tom Tippett and Joseph Freeman, and impressing a youthfully radical Claude McKay with his acumen at a Comintern gathering in Moscow. In the later words of James and Grace Lee Boggs and Freddy and Lyman Paine, Cannon represented "a proletarian quality which we could never have absorbed through, for example, someone like William Z. Foster." Cannon was a "proletarian type," to be sure, but he coexisted easily with intellectuals and bohemians, as long as "they did not become too flighty." He sensed that "there was more to life, to history, to politics, and to revolution than just the proletariat," although, of course, he had a basic understanding of the working class as the pivotal force in social change.[4]

Cannon's capacity to bring together a proletarian quality and the political exuberance of revolutionary commitment was at the heart of the Left's age of innocence in early twentieth-century America. Once the decade of the 1920s had run its course, something of this innocence had been lost. This, too, was not a bad thing, and again, Cannon was very much of this moment. Eventually, the problematic drift of bureaucratization and triumphant Stalinization of the Comintern lowered a final curtain on the innocence of the revolutionary Left in 1928. It was no longer possible to trust in what Cannon and others had put so much radical faith, and he and others now knew it. This constellation of programmatic clarification understandably took time to sink into the consciousness of revolutionaries and to be implemented practically. When it was, a new day had dawned for the American revolutionary Left, which entered a period of development discernibly different from its youthful past.

Stalinism at Work

That the innocence had come to an end was, surely, evident with the Stalinist response to the emergence of a Trotskyist current in the United States, namely, the Cannon-headed contingent first known as "the Opposition Group in the Workers (Communist) Party of America." Fundamental criticisms of the Soviet leadership were raised publicly by Bolsheviks for the first time, as Cannon and his small group of supporters issued statements, "For the Russian Opposition!"; serialized Trotsky's *Draft Program of the Comintern*, with its blistering assault on deviations of principle that had characterized Soviet policy in the late 1920s; and railed against opportunism and bureaucracy in the Workers (Communist) Party of America. "It created a tremendous sensation," recalled Cannon. "For a few weeks they did not know what to do about it."

Then, of course, the word came down from the Lovestone-led party headquarters that it was time to silence the "counter-revolutionaries." Two Hungarian women who were selling the opposition paper outside the New York Workers Center on Union Square in mid-December 1928 were physically accosted, verbally abused, and labeled prostitutes, *The Militant* torn from their hands. Police were called as a crowd of hundreds gathered and the women were chased from the square. Ten days later, the Cannon-Karsner residence was burglarized; the break-in was repeated three weeks thereafter, in mid-January 1929, with documents and other materials stolen. As Cannon spoke across the country, his address, "The Truth about Trotsky and the Russian Opposition," was routinely invaded by bands of party workers, sixty to a hundred strong, some of them wielding blackjacks or furriers' knives and their gloved fingers outfitted with brass knuckles. The purpose was disruption, intimidation, and the closing-down of meetings. Drawing on old Wobbly connections and others in the radical movement committed to basic understandings of civil liberties and freedom of expression, the oppositionists formed Workers Defense Guards to protect the podium, and continued to promote their message and program of communist renewal. At Minneapolis, pioneer Trotskyists Oscar Coover and Carl Skoglund were beaten by a contingent of Lovestone and Foster supporters; a New York Labor Temple rally to protest Trotsky's deportation from Russia was the scene of staged riots, beatings, a knife slashing, and the summoning of 100 police and undercover "dicks" associated with the Industrial and Bomb squads. This initial U.S. Stalinist response to the programmatic critique of Trotskyism was a sorry repudiation of the elementary tenets of workers' democracy. Its violence, gang-sterism, and thuggery broke with past traditions of the Left. The extremism of the anti-opposition discourse would preface the language of "Third Period" sectarian denunciation, but even with the mellowing tone of the Popular Front, Communist Party anathema toward Trotskyists would not lessen.[5]

Nor was this passing of innocence evident only in Stalinism's harsh moves against Cannon and the incipient Left Opposition. No sooner had Lovestone and his majority in the Workers (Communist) Party eliminated Cannon and his allies than they too came under attack, the assault emanating unmistakably from Moscow. Many issues were at stake, including Lovestone's conceptual inclinations. They militated against his acceptance of the timing of the Comintern's push for a Left turn in global politics with their understanding of "American exceptionalism" and the immediate staying power of an upwardly moving technical revolution within United States capitalism, which promised to usher in an unprecedented age of affluence, peace, and prosperity. In Stalin's eyes, this linked the American party leadership with the Right Opposition of Nikolai Bukharin, the vanquishing of which was yet another part of Stalinist "cleansing" of the Soviet Party and movement into decisive control of the Comintern. The Stalin appointee V. M. Molotov soon replaced Bukharin, and served as little more than the Great Leader's deputy.

From 19 November 1928, when Stalin made "the Right Danger" and its chief architect, Bukharin, the main target of retribution in an address before a plenum of the Soviet Communist Party, Lovestone's days were numbered. A terse letter of November 21 from the Political Secretariat of the Communist International took Lovestone to task for his self-congratulatory campaign against party opponents, demanded a more self-critical posture, and concluded by instructing the Americans to postpone their party convention until February 1929. Lovestone was now cut off from adequate information at the Moscow center of communist influence. No Bukharin or Zinoviev was there to cover his back. Moreover, the United States Communist Party head had aligned with the now notorious Pepper, whose refusal to accede to a direct Comintern order to return to Moscow put an end to his stature as an authoritative link to the established, if spent, forces of world revolution and left him in extremely bad odor in Stalinist circles. Lovestone thus blundered through the last days of 1928. His emissary to Moscow, Bertram D. Wolfe, could do little to resurrect the situation.

As the voting for delegates to attend the March convention of the American communists took place in February 1929, Lovestone's greatest majority triumph unfolded, with more than 90 percent of those sent to the party love-in lined up behind him. But the victory was bitterly ironic. Comintern directives insisted on "balancing" the existing factions, suggested making William Z. Foster the organizational secretary, and told everyone in no uncertain terms that Lovestone's leadership was now unacceptable. In the end, Lovestone, Wolfe, and Benjamin Gitlow defied Stalin and the Comintern, refusing to knuckle under to a series of potted statements on the "complete correctness" of various Stalinist addresses and sign self-denunciatory declarations of unconditional political submission. By the end of June, they were unceremoniously expelled. The overwhelming majority of delegates who had lined up behind Lovestone at the raucous Sixth Convention of the Communist Party of the United States of America in March 1929 regarded their former leader as a renegade right-wing deviationist three months later.

With all of the major leaders of the American party now either expelled or thoroughly compromised and accommodated to Stalin's ultimate authority, Foster occupied a figurehead leadership that, combined with health problems in the early 1930s, finally secured the grey eminence of Comintern back rooms and political tightrope walking, Earl Browder, the undisputed leadership of United States communism, at least for a time. No one who looked seriously and closely at the internal regime of the CPUSA, circa 1930, could remain untroubled by how much the party had been reconfigured through Stalinist dictate.[6]

Cannon and the Struggle for a Left Oppositionist Practice

That the revolutionary Left of the 1920s is not much remembered is one of a number of true tragedies of American radicalism. Although its age of innocence came to an end with the expulsions of James P. Cannon and others late in 1928, the origins of the United States revolutionary Left were indeed an unmistakable accomplishment.

At the time of his expulsion from the Workers (Communist) Party in the last months of 1928, James P. Cannon was a mere thirty-eight years of age. For such a young man, Cannon had lived many lives, all of them, from late adolescence on, associated with the revolutionary movement. Educated as much in the debates and activities of the Left as in any formal or conventional schooling, Cannon passed through certain grades: the agitational nursery of pre-World War I socialism and revolutionary industrial unionism; the clandestine classrooms of an underground left wing, in which Cannon first styled himself a Marxist and faced the difficult organizational questions of a nascent communist movement, as well as the hard knocks of orchestrated state repression and the harsh, ideologically mounted antagonism of bellicose patriotism; and the college of communism, where the lessons learned were not just in the irreconcilable antagonisms of the class struggle, but also in the back-and-forth of party factionalism and, ultimately, the primacy of political program. Unlike so many others on the revolutionary Left, however, Cannon ultimately faced the end of his age of innocence squarely. Refusing to compromise or abandon the ideals of his past, he reoriented to the Workers (Communist) Party that he had helped to found and build, the movement that had sustained him materially and socially and that inspired his hopes for the future. Expulsion was inevitable, as Cannon well knew. He was soon forced to set out on the difficult path of regrouping and regenerating the revolutionary Left, his opposition conceived as one of winning his former comrades back to a politics of world revolution.

It was not an easy choice, and the task was indeed daunting. Much had to be remade afresh, including, somewhat, Cannon himself. When the Kansas revolutionary's curtain of innocence lowered, he had many bad habits to shed. Any new movement forged in the crucible of United States communism's failures would have to overcome them as well. Cannon was well aware of this, writing in 1943, "When I came out of the nine years of the CP I was a first-class factional hoodlum. If not, how would I ever have survived? All I knew when somebody started a fight, let him have it. That existence was all I knew....I was wrong about many things, including my methods and my impatience and rudeness with comrades in repulsing them."[7] In 1966, reflecting on the history of the Socialist Workers Party (SWP), Cannon recalled that his training in the school of American Stalinism caused him to remember "a lot from doing things the wrong way":

> Probably the hardest lesson I had to learn from Trotsky, after ten years of bad schooling through the Communist Party faction fights, was to let organizational questions wait until the political questions at issue were fully clarified, not only in the National Committee but also in the ranks of the party. It is no exaggeration, but the full and final truth, that our party owes its very existence

today to the fact that some of us learned this hard lesson and learned also how to apply it in practice.[8]

Others nevertheless seem convinced that Cannon never shed his Stalinist, bureaucratic skin, and that his subsequent history, as the preeminent leader of the forces of United States Trotskyism, and a major figure in the Trotskyist Fourth International, founded in September 1938 but in the making for a decade before its formal constitution, was merely a reproduction of the sordid lessons learned in the Comintern of the 1920s.[9] For instance, in critiques of Cannon much is often made of his early embrace of the Zinoviev policy of Bolshevization, articulated baldly in the theses of the Fifth Comintern Congress in 1924. Cannon quoted favorably the CI's advocacy of a particular kind of highly centralized Bolshevik party. That this contradicted the actual experience of Russian Bolshevism under Lenin, who was himself occasionally isolated in the ranks of a minority, largely escaped notice in the Comintern of the time, where bureaucratic heavy-handedness was increasingly evident. Cannon did, to be sure, gravitate too uncritically to this authoritarian conception of party practice, which was laden with coded meanings as to the early struggle against Trotsky and would, of course, create dangerous preconditions favorable to the gestation of Stalinism. Nonetheless, antagonists of Cannon's advocacy of such Bolshevization seldom grapple seriously with *why* the American revolutionary found elements of the Fifth Congress's pronouncements appealing.

By late 1924, Cannon had seen firsthand the debilitating consequences of factionalism in the U.S. party. Referring to factionalism as a plague, Cannon noted that "[a]t least one-half of the energy of the party has been expended in factional struggles, one after another." Cannon understandably reacted to this state of affairs, accepting too easily Zinoviev's demand for Communist Party centralization, an exhortation that warped original Leninist understandings of democratic centralism. Even as he drifted in this unhealthy direction, though, Cannon refused to concede too much to bureaucratism. He argued, "Of course, this condition cannot be eliminated by formal decree. We cannot eliminate factions, and factional struggles by declaring them undesirable. . . . The problem of factions, tendencies, and groups is not an organizational problem merely," and concluded, "it is a political problem and for political problems there are no mechanical solutions." Decades later, Cannon was adamant that although an unprincipled and unrelenting factionalism could indeed enervate a Bolshevik organization, the flip side of this troubling issue was equally problematic: "[I]f a party can live year after year without any factional disturbances," he wrote in 1966, "it may not be a sign of *health* it may be a sign that the party's *asleep;* that it's not a real live party. In a party, you have differences . . . that's a sign of life." Reflecting on Zinoviev's sad denouement as an unduly bureaucratizing influence in the Comintern, Cannon would later comment that in revolutionary politics you cannot "dispose of people too quickly, too cavalierly. You can't build cadre if you do that."[10]

British Trotskyists, with whom Cannon always had somewhat strained relations, as he cast his lot early within an intense history of division with the highly problematic but at one time quite energetic and talented figure, Gerry Healy, have seldom warmed to Cannon, and draw for explanations of their antagonism on this mid-1920s history. Al Richardson insisted that Cannon was formed in the bureaucratism of Zinoviev's "school of party building," the pitfalls of which the American revolutionary never managed to transcend.[11] This seems to fit well with the claims of Max Shachtman,[12] whose 1940 break from Cannon in a faction fight over the question of orthodox Trotskyism's defense of the Soviet Union as a degenerated workers' state resulted in extensive allegation of Cannon's deficiencies as a bureaucratically conservative revolutionary leader, shaped by the mid-1920s Zinoviev-led Comintern and frozen, in Sean Matgamna's words, in the pre-1940 logic of Trotskyism.[13] However, it underestimates evidence that Cannon himself was more supple in his understanding of the multiplicity of Zinoviev's roles. Even in Cannon's most aggressive defense of Zinoviev, for instance, he was not blinkered about the Comintern head's shortcomings. "I have no doubt whatever that in all his big actions, including his most terrible errors, he was motivated fundamentally by devotion to the higher interests of the working class of the whole world—to the communist future of humanity," Cannon wrote to Draper of Zinoviev in 1955. Recognizing that Zinoviev's "greatest fault as a politician" was reliance "on maneuverism when principled issues were joined in such a way to exclude the efficacy of maneuver," Cannon thought Zinoviev struggled to offer sage counsel to the faction-ridden American communists of the 1920s, whom he urged to forge new relations of cooperation. "Peace is better," proved a Zinoviev axiom that Cannon clearly took to heart.[14] Some critics, such as former Trotskyist Tariq Ali, are little more than uninformed and glibly unconcerned with matters of historical accuracy in their caricatures of Cannon's contribution to a history of suppressing factional opponents.[15]

There were times when Cannon's organizational orientations were also questioned in the United States. Trotsky himself cautioned Cannon, in the 1939–1940 debates with Max Shachtman, James Burnham, and Martin Abern, that there was a pressing need to conduct programmatic struggle on the basis of an even-handed political discussion, avoiding mechanical resolutions, precipitous splits, purges, or expulsions. Knowing full well that reconciliation of the minority to the majority, with a consolidation of political agreement around questions of the SWP regime and the nature of the Soviet Union as a degenerated workers' state, including the requisite political implications for a program of involvement in the class struggle, was likely an impossibility, Cannon's inclination might well have been to advocate a "cold split," in which the opposing forces simply went their separate organizational ways. In the end, though, Cannon avoided such an easy route, and let the factional dispute run its deep course; as a consequence, he oversaw a unique educational undertaking, in which comrades were introduced to the value of programmatic coherence.[16] If he was at times disgusted by the unfolding events—Cannon wrote to Trotsky that in debating Shachtman "I crawl on my belly through the mud for the sake of the Fourth International"— and closed the final split with Shachtman and Company with an imperious aside to his close friends among the majority allies, the old organizational warhorse nevertheless endured much in the interests of open party debate.[17]

For all the allegations of bureaucratism, then, few Leninist parties have the record of open debate and political exchange evident in the organizations that Cannon led from 1928 through the mid-1950s. From an early, and until recently quite misunderstood and unappreciated, Shachtman-Cannon clash in the Communist League of America, 1931–1933,[18] through a series of factional formations involving Shachtman, Burnham, Abern, C. L. R. James, Felix Morrow, Albert Goldman, Bert Cochran, and others, United States Trotskyism was a seething cauldron of programmatic debate and difference. From its inception on New Year's Day, 1938, Cannon's Socialist Workers Party was seldom free of the rancor of dissidence, and major political controversies and oppositional alignments erupted in 1939–1940, 1943–1946, and 1952–1953. Given that these years were punctuated by war, Cold War, the beginnings of McCarthyism, and the jailings of a crucial contingent of SWP leaders, including Cannon, this is a remarkable record of principled openness, political discussion, and internal party debate.

One of Cannon's last formal political engagements with the Socialist Workers Party was a mid-1960s plea for not resorting to disciplinary procedures and constitutional revisions that would have overly "centralized" the party and suppressed the circulation of dissident ideas:

> In the present political climate and with the present changing composition of the party, democratic centralism must be applied flexibly. At least ninety percent of the emphasis should be placed on the democratic side and not on any crackpot schemes to "streamline" the party to the point where questions are unwelcomed and criticism and discussion stifled. That is a prescription to kill the party before it gets a chance to show how it can handle and assimilate an expanding membership of young people, who don't know it all to start with, but have to learn and grow in the course of explication and discussion, in a free democratic atmosphere.[19]

Such words are not the ideas of an unreconstructed "Zinovievist," although, of course, their utterance when Cannon was no longer effectively heading the Socialist Workers Party must be balanced against his practice when he handled the leadership reins of the organization more directly.

As Paul LeBlanc has argued, and as C. L. R. James (whose history in the SWP was always marked by his dissidence and minority status) long ago acknowledged, there is little actual evidence of bureaucratic mishandling by Cannon and the majority that he led.[20] Four former followers of James recalled,

> James used to say of Cannon that he was not the kind of man who would trample on a minority. He would not line up his majority against you unless you got too far out of line and forced him to do it. Everybody who has a political party has to do that at a certain point. You can't let it be torn apart from whim. So Cannon was a man who had a great deal to teach us about how to live within the party. He was the kind of chairman who could sit back and not have to interfere with everything going on. He was not an insecure person.[21]

Cannon, it would seem, does not fare so badly when judged by any reasonable standard of revolutionary leadership's responsibilities. In the face of state repression and political ostracism outside of his ranks, and factional provocation and basic violations of Leninist party discipline inside them, Cannon's record is undoubtedly one of relative openness and considerable achievement.

Cannon's Legacy: The Theory and Practice of Building a Revolutionary Party

What, in the end, would be Cannon's contribution, and what was his historical meaning with respect to the United States revolutionary Left? Much, of course, relates to Cannon's organizational accomplishment in building a revolutionary Trotskyist current in the United States and in consolidating the Fourth International. In a subsequent volume I will explore this important history in the detail it deserves. Yet it is also the case that Cannon's pre-Trotskyist years are of fundamental importance. Indeed, nothing that Cannon accomplished in his post-1930 years as a Left Oppositionist can be understood without an appreciation of his first thirty-eight years at the center of what were the origins of the American revolutionary Left, in its age of admirable innocence.

Theoretically, Cannon shied away from claims to have left an acute mark on the pages of analytic Marxism. While he was an extremely effective writer of the agitational school, his prose, though hardly lacking in verve, did not have the academic appeal of the writing of a Shachtman or a James, just as it seldom ventured onto the broad canvas of international events and analytic subjects that were painted by others with such bold interpretive strokes.[22] Cannon's purpose was to develop and sustain orthodox Trotskyism and cultivate the organizational apparatus of the movement of the historical Left Opposition. In this, however, Cannon was more theoretical than others give him credit for, and just possibly more theoretical than he himself knew, for he had an unerring eye for the way in which those incapable of communist organizational discipline gave themselves over to flights of problematic fantasy in their supposed theoretical sophistication and cosmopolitan internationalism. A theory not grounded in particular actualities, capable of being applied to the political terrain of a given reality is, after all, necessarily limited. As Cannon would argue, in 1966, drawing on Trotsky's observation of the early days of the Left Opposition, when many dazzling but mercurial figures played with the ideas of a new international movement, "they have understood all the formulas and they can repeat them by rote, but they haven't got them in their flesh and blood. . . . When you get the formulas of Marxism in your flesh and blood that means you have an *irresistible* impulse and drive *to put theory into action.*"[23]

Cannon's major contribution, most particularly in the period that this book has explored, was the fusion of theory and practice that is the touchstone of all revolutionary endeavor. It jelled not so much on the page of any text as in the organization of a revolutionary working-class party. This was no mere bureaucratic accomplishment, nor was it separable from a broad conceptualization—or even theoretical acuity—relating to the nature of class, capitalism, and culture in early twentieth-century America. Few leaders in the United States communist movement of the 1920s grasped as fully as Cannon the necessity for the revolutionary project to engage with the actual conditions of the working class in the world's most advanced capitalist nation. For Cannon, that working class was not a monolithic, homogeneous mass, a proletarian essence marching inevitably to class victory and ultimate power. Rather, the working class was divided, layered in differentiations of ethnicity, race, skill, and region (gender, too, we might add, although Cannon, like so many of his time, paid too little attention to this realm). Such heterogeneity was also reflected in the organizational forms adhered to by workers (industrial vs. craft unionism), and Cannon, in contrast to most early communist leaders, was insistent that revolutionaries approach and interact with the plethora of working-class mobilizations in the United States astutely rather than dogmatically: he would countenance no routinized dismissal of any body of workers, organized or unorganized, IWW-affiliated or American Federation of Labor-led.

Divisions also manifested themselves in the executive corps of the revolutionary Left, which often appeared decidedly fractious. Precisely because Cannon understood well that the U.S. working class *and* the leaderships it spawned—not only within trade union officialdoms, but also in radical ethnic bodies and socialist and communist parties—were fragmented in their reflection of particular material origins, he grappled with the absolute necessity of creating a vanguard party that could unite the working class in struggle. He insisted on bringing together the strands of politics that others, for purposeful, self-interested ends, were prone to separate and privilege. Cannon grasped that the difficult path to that end could be constructed only by cultivating, educating, and developing particular leaders, who too often saw *their* territories as narrowly construed turfs of work designated "trade union," "foreign-language federation," "party press," or "political committee." In the process, Cannon struggled with a major difficulty in revolutionary practice: integrating difference and creating a larger sense of totality.

Thus, within a party perpetually riven by factional division, Cannon fought for a *collective* leadership that would bridge and eventually overcome various entrenched oppositions: petty-bourgeois intellectuals versus proletarian organizers; urbane, immigrant Marxists versus midwestern soapbox agitators; cultured editors and theoreticians versus hard-nosed combatants in the class struggle; underground ultralefts versus advocates of a legal mass party; Cominternists versus Americanizers. In this battle to overcome differences of ideas and identities by ongoing illustration of the potential revolutionary gains to be achieved by patiently struggling to transcend limitations and build a revolutionary presence in all sectors of working-class life, Cannon refused certain notions of how a communist party could be developed. It would never, given the diversity of its origins, grow under a titled "hereditary" leadership (Ruthenberg), whatever the executive strengths of specific individuals. Nor would a revolutionary party in the United States flourish in a bifurcated split of mechanical designations of particular historical streams or traditions, in which trade union "rights" were allocated to one wing (Foster) and political acumen to another (Lovestone). In his own contribution to mass party work, Cannon charted a course in the International Labor Defense that fought to overcome such distinctions in successful united-front endeavors. Not only did ILD activity persistently link revolutionary politics with trade union issues, by defending victimized strikers arrested on picket lines or workers charged with other violations against property and propriety, it also bridged the separations of English-speaking, native-born workers and radicals and their "alien," immigrant, foreign-language, even African American, counterparts, who so often needed defense campaigns mobilized on their behalf. In establishing and sustaining a mechanism by which the revolutionary Left could defend class-war prisoners and strike blows against state-sanctioned violence and the horrific reign of lynch law, Cannon extended the practice of communism, guided by a theoretical appreciation of the ways in which capital and the state exacerbated historic divisions in the American working class.

Most critically, unlike almost all other revolutionary leaders associated with the formative years of United States communism, Cannon persistently forged viable, if often transitory, coalitions of individuals who with their collective and usually time-bound capabilities moved the revolutionary project forward. In this he took a theoretical appreciation of the inherent fragmentation of United States class forces/leadership, and parlayed it into a practical appreciation both of what needed doing at a particular stage of the development of the revolutionary forces, and an astute realization of who might have something to offer at specific moments of impasse. Through his blocs with Ruthenberg or the Lovestone of the early 1920s, his relations with Foster, Browder, Bittelman, Weinstone, Swabeck, and Dunne at various points in the decade, as well as in his cultivation and mentoring of Shachtman and Abern, or the close, if limited, work conducted with underground Letts, Finnish cooperators, and socialist Jews in the New York needle trades, Cannon made principled alliances to secure United States communism yet another necessary advance or strategic foothold. His critical eye not only on shortcomings and deficiencies, but also on potential contributions and discrete strengths, Cannon, like no other figure in the revolutionary ranks, built the Workers (Communist) Party out of the unevenly developed human material available to revolutionaries at the time. Whereas jaundiced critics see this Cannon practice as one of opportunistic horse-trading, perhaps a more appropriate judgment is that early communism's native son struggled to create combinations of political integrity within a revolutionary movement whose leadership was invariably differentiated. This was the necessary, if not sufficient, condition for the creation of a vanguard party. This collective leadership, which Cannon alone among the leading cadre of the Workers' Party conceived as central and worked to create, was arguably a means of transcending the divisions with which the revolutionary left wing was branded at birth.

It was, of course, Cannon's impassioned belief that without this revolutionary party, the working class would never be more than the diversity of its many parts. Not until very late in 1928 was Cannon able to grasp that the organization he had struggled so arduously to bring into being and sustain now faced an ultimately more threatening barrier than all of the fractious differentiations and difficulties of the past: that of the Stalinist betrayal of the program of world revolution that had animated so many revolutionaries in the United States since 1917. Up until this point, it could be argued, Cannon had never seen himself as *the* leader, but as a figure struggling for positions and principles, as a means to forge the combined leadership corps necessary to advance the possibility of a proletarian order in a United States where the working class was born somewhat shackled in its pluralist diversity. Though there is no question that Cannon's place in the ranks of revolutionaries changed with his expulsion from the Workers (Communist) Party in 1928 (he was thereafter inevitably a bigger fish in a smaller pond), Cannon retained something of this valuable humility.

Communist Continuity: The Significance of Revolutionary Subjectivity

Unlike C. L. R. James, for instance, Cannon never fell prey to an overblown assessment of his own grandiose place in the universe. As James and Grace Lee Boggs and Freddy and Lyman Paine note, by "1953 C. L. R. was already becoming a Marxist egocentric, something which, strangely enough, Cannon never became. Cannon never tried to ballyhoo Cannon."[24] Unlike Shachtman and Lovestone, Cannon did not abandon what was innocent and idealistic in his revolutionary youth, believing in the American revolution until the day of his death, and making no compromise with the forces of capitalist reaction. As he commented before an assembly of comrades on the occasion of his sixtieth birthday, "The mark of a man's life is his capacity to march to the music of his youth." Everyone's younger self, Cannon believed, is the "better self." "In my own youth I saw the vision of a new world," the old revolutionary recalled in 1950, "and I have never lost it. I came out of Rosedale, Kansas forty years ago, looking for truth and justice. I'm still looking for it."[25]

Often Cannon's manner, almost certainly picked up and consciously developed in his days as a soapboxer for the Industrial Workers of the World, assimilated complex analytic issues to a language of everyday Americanism that understated his intuitive grasp of centrally important theoretical abstractions. He offered imaginative conceptual reconciliations of communist practice in the labor movement and Leninist understandings of such difficult American dilemmas as dual unionism, for instance, displaying a creative intelligence that the party's trade union figurehead, William Z. Foster, would have found difficult to negotiate.[26] Cannon advanced the theory of the Left significantly by engaging Stalinism critically and persistently and with the principle of a revolutionary for whom there would be no complicity with ideologues of the Right, and no accommodations with capitalism. This was an especially important contribution in a United States in which the combination of a mid-century "God That Failed" syndrome and a repressive McCarthyism could easily disfigure the politics of anti-Stalinism. All too often, in these years, criticism of the Soviet Union and its supporters congealed into a virulent anti-communism. In thwarting this, Cannon denied Stalinism an easy resting place, by constantly calling attention to how it had assailed not only socialism, but also the analysis and the activity of all revolutionary movements.[27] Out of this Cannonesque ability to fuse practical, organizational matters with an appreciation of theoretical concerns, posed in the homespun speech of a native son, came a series of insights and significant contributions. All of this conditioned Cannon's instinctual suspicions of the early 1930s international imbroglio of trade union opportunism and political dilettantism represented by Pierre Naville and others in France, from which Trotsky recoiled but to which Max Shachtman was drawn by his attractions to cliquish cosmopolitanism, becoming a powerful presence in the factional controversies of the early Communist League of America.[28] Cannon's capacities also figured forcefully in the accomplishments of trade union intervention in the robust 1934 Minneapolis general strike, and the exemplary articulation of a labor defense strategy in the courts when Cannon and others faced state repression in the early to mid-1940s.[29]

None of this, however significant its history, and yet to be studied in much detail,[30] would have been possible were it not for Cannon's experience in the United States revolutionary Left in its age of innocence up to 1928. In this living school of revolutionary activism, Cannon was educated in what would be his life's work, the advocacy and realization of the American revolution. Cannon stands out on the revolutionary Left as a singular figure whose *consistent* commitment was to the possibility of the United States working class creating a revolution. This was the overriding guiding formulation that lay behind his movement out of the pre-World War I Socialist Party and into the ranks of the revolutionary Industrial Workers of the World. Pushed to reconsider some basic programmatic and theoretical propositions by the achievements of the Bolsheviks in 1917, it was precisely this same abiding belief in the possibility of revolution, now enhanced by the realization of the importance of a political party, that galvanized Cannon to reenter the Socialist Party left wing and to work in the communist underground during the dangerous years of repression following World War I. As the founding chairman of the Workers' Party, Cannon struggled to knit together a coalition of communists committed to an above-ground, legal, *Americanized* communist party, capable of intersecting with the mass struggles of U.S. workers. At the core of every factional struggle Cannon waged in the communist movement throughout the 1920s, as well as in his class-war-prisoner defense activity in the International Labor Defense, nothing loomed larger than the making of this cherished American revolution. By the mid- to late 1940s, Cannon had developed his "Theses on the American Revolution," and authored an eloquent pamphlet, *The Coming of the American Revolution* (1947), which, though overly sanguine about the prospects of economic collapse and radical possibility, kept the flame of proletarian revolt burning in an epoch that snuffed out many lesser lights of radicalism.[31] Unlike almost any other communist leader, Cannon kept his finger on the pulse of American popular culture, understanding that one had to be critically cognizant of the forms of consumerism and mass leisure-time appeals, if the class sensibilities of any period were to be appreciated and the possibilities of revolutionary advance charted systematically.[32]

In a series of 1952–1953 SWP lectures at the Los Angeles Friday Night Forum, collectively called "America's Road to Socialism," Cannon offered creative glimpses of what socialism would look like once it came to fruition in the climate of advanced capitalism that was always meant to be its spawning ground. In these lectures he reiterated the revolutionary optimism and innocence that had enthused the socialist promise of his youth: "All will be artists. All will be workers and students, builders and creators. All will be free and equal. Human solidarity will encircle the globe and conquer it, and subordinate it to the uses of man." Yet Cannon well knew how far the United States was from socialism: "It is our destiny, here and now, to live in the time of the decay and death agony of capitalism," he admitted. "It is our task to wade through the blood and filth of this outmoded, dying system." Bringing this system to its knees and ushering in a new, egalitarian order was, for Cannon, "the highest privilege today," an exercise of human citizenship governed not by the manifestoes of acquisition and the politics of individual betterment, but by the anticipation of what Jack London had once called "the Golden Future." Quoting the romantic revolutionary poet, William Morris, Cannon called on his younger comrades to continue his life's fight:

> Join in the only battle
> Wherein no man can fail,
> For whoso fadeth and dieth,
> Yet his deeds shall still prevail.[33]

Cannon thus established his place in history because among his peers he ultimately stood out as a figure who countenanced no concession to defeat, and accepted no debasement of revolutionary program. This was of particular significance in 1928. Cannon would not barter principle for a continued place in the established ranks of the United States Communist Party, about to capitalize greatly on the collapse of capitalism associated with the Great Depression, which brought into being a "Red Decade" of radical revival. Instead, Cannon kept alive what was heroic and exemplary in the revolutionary Left's innocence: the insatiable desire for working-class socialism and the belief that it was possible for America's laboring people to win the ultimate struggle. Moving past this innocence, the Rosedale radical actually named, analyzed, and struggled against the pivotal programmatic degeneration of Stalinism which, by 1929, could no longer be misconstrued. If this movement out of the problematic connotations of innocence took longer, on Cannon's part, than some contemporary critics might think warranted, it nevertheless led to a decisive rupture. Out of this came a new revolutionary internationalism, one that rekindled the fires of the American revolution.

Because Cannon was a Wobbly who insisted that he had learned something from the Russian Revolution,[34] he is not championed in circles where the Industrial Workers of the World remain much in vogue but the legacy of 1917 is regarded with loud disfavor. The anarchist tradition, within which Cannon conducted much united-front work, especially in the defense of class-war prisoners, at the same time as he polemicized against it in debates on the Left, has little time for such an unambiguous Leninist. A Stalinist school of falsification has managed to write Cannon out of the history of the Communist Party in the 1920s, which takes considerable effort. Most New Left scholarship in the United States has a deeply ingrained hostility to Trotskyism, so much so that Cannon is remarkably absent in accounts of the American radical tradition emanating from this quarter.[35]

If the United States revolutionary Left is to be reborn, which is the only hope for turning back the tides of reaction, not only in America, but around the world, Cannon and his age of innocence have to be rediscovered. We need to bring back the spirit of that moment long past, and learn from the likes of Cannon how to adapt it to our time, with its new challenges and possibilities. The lessons that Cannon learned, about communist discipline and the necessity of a party of struggle and resolute Left opposition, appear to have been forgotten, or thrown into disrepute by, of all things, the very Stalinism that supposedly confirms the failures of socialism and the oppressive autocracy of vanguard organization. History, however, is unfortunately not some linear progress of knowledge gained and perspective clarified. It also contains defeats and reversals. Those of us on the Left have lived through such setbacks over the course of the last fifty years. We can never, of course, turn the clock back, but we can demand that the large time-piece's hands, passing over old numbers, be scrutinized with a sense of the past and its meanings for our presents and our futures. Failing this, we see nothing but relentless and purposeless movement, a treadmill on which the revolutionary movement marches endlessly to no avail. When we learn to look to the past, not for absolute lessons, but for traditions, insights, organizational forms, and strategic directions that we want to magnify, the better to understand how to transcend the defeatism of routine, Cannon and his history have much to tell us.

Harry Braverman, a political opponent of Cannon's in the faction wars of the Trotskyist movement in the 1950s, captured something of this when he remembered Cannon's place on the revolutionary Left:

He spoke to us in the accents of the Russian Revolution and of the Leninism which had gone forth from the Soviet Union in the twenties and thirties. But there was in his voice something more which attracted us. And that was the echoes of the radicalism of the pre-World War I years, the popular radicalism of Debs, Haywood and John Reed. And he spoke with great force and passion. I have thought of this from time to time in recent years when I have been struck by the cool style popular with academics and the older style of oratory of which Cannon was an excellent practitioner.

Max Shachtman conceded a part of the same point, emphasizing Cannon's "understanding of the American working class, and how the Communist movement had to operate, had to adjust itself to the realities of the American working class. . . . He knew what the American worker was, how he lived, how he thought, what he aspired to. He had that feeling, so to speak, organically—not from studying it in the book or a thesis or a document of any other sort. Without being a nationalist, he wanted to make the Communist movement in this country an American movement in the best sense of the word." As Shachtman acknowledged, with respect to the days he spent with Cannon in the Communist Party in the 1920s, Cannon also had "leadership qualifications, . . . the ability to bring people together . . . and hold them together." A rare quality, Shachtman suggested, leadership is something that you either have or you don't have, an illusive feature of the revolutionary movement that no tracts teach and no places provide. "Well, Cannon had it," his old comrade and eventual political critic concluded, "[a]nd much of the antagonism he aroused . . . was due simply to the fact that he had it and [others] didn't."[36]

Cannon summed up his beliefs briefly in 1950. His words do not have the ring of theoretical fashion that many demand in our times, the cool distance of academic abstraction. They are hot in their passions, speaking, innocently and powerfully, to the revolutionary ideal:

I believe in people and their unlimited capacity for improvement and progress through cooperation and solidarity. I believe in freedom, equality and the brotherhood of man. That is what we really mean when we say socialism. I believe in the power of fraternity and the love of comrades in the struggle for socialism. Walt Whitman said: "I will build great cities with the love of comrades." I would go farther and say: we will build a great new world.[37]

This may seem, to many in our time, a small, sentimental statement, but it is the revolutionary largesse that is the foundation of everything that socialism stands for. It grew to be a powerful influence in the origins of the American revolutionary Left in the opening three decades of the twentieth century. Jim Cannon played a large role in sustaining this transformative subjectivity. He embodied a politics of communist continuity in the recreation of institutions and the appeal of new, disciplined forms of political organization, in the search for a program guiding class struggle in the United States, and in the final repudiation of the left wing's degeneration within the constraints of Stalinism. We need to get back to much of this *historic* accomplishment, which is revolutionary Marxism's primary accumulation, before we race forward to fresh, future victories. A revived revolutionary movement needs more of the "hotness" that Cannon embodied, in the face of the various "cools" that now predominate in many quarters. As Trotsky once said, "Those who cannot defend old positions will never conquer new ones."[38]

Notes

Introduction

1. Among many studies that might be cited: Werner Sombart, *Why Is There No Socialism in the United States?* (White Plains, NY: M. E. Sharpe, 1976), a reprint of the original 1906 German publication; John H. M. Laslett and Seymour Martin Lipset, eds., *Failure of a Dream? Essays in the History of American Socialism* (Garden City, NY: Anchor Press, 1974); Eric Foner, "Why Is There No Socialism in the United States," *History Workshop Journal* 17 (Spring 1984), 57–80; Jean Heffer and Jeanine Rovet, eds., *Why Is There No Socialism in the United States?* (Paris: École des Hautes Études en Sciences Sociales, 1988). See, as well, the special issue of *Historical Materialism* 11 (December 2003), on "The American Worker."

2. As an introduction only, see James Weinstein, *The Decline of Socialism in America, 1912–1925* (New York: Vintage, 1969); Christine Stansell, *American Moderns: Bohemian New York and the Creation of a New Century* (New York: Henry Holt, 2000); Alan Dawley, *Struggles for Justice: Social Responsibility and the Liberal State* (Cambridge, MA: Harvard University Press, 1994), 139–294. Lenin on the *Appeal to Reason* is quoted in Theodore Draper, *The Roots of American Communism* (New York: Viking, 1957), 75.

3. Draper, *Roots of American Communism*, 129; Max Eastman, *Love and Revolution: My Journey Through an Epoch* (New York: Random House, 1964), 604.

4. Joseph Freeman, *An American Testament: A Narrative of Rebels and Romantics* (New York: Farrar & Rinehart, 1936), vii–viii, x, 667–68.

5. Eastman, *Love and Revolution*, 599–605; James D. Bloom, *Left Letters: The Culture Wars of Mike Gold and Joseph Freeman* (New York: Columbia University Press, 1992), 71–110.

6. James P. Cannon, *The History of American Trotskyism: From Its Origins (1928) to the Founding of the Socialist Workers Party (1938)—Report of a Participant* (New York: Pathfinder, 1972), 13–14; James P. Cannon, *Notebook of an Agitator* (New York: Pathfinder, 1973), 294–97.

7. Possibly the one area where Stalinism is addressed most frontally is in the cultural realm, where the studies of literary radicalism undertaken by Alan Wald have persistently engaged with the meaning of Stalinism and anti-Stalinism. See, for instance, Alan Wald, *Writing from the Left: New Essays on Radical Culture and Politics* (London: Verso, 1994). My accent throughout this book on Stalinism's "incremental creep" over the course of the years from 1923 to 1929 counters tendencies to see Stalinism as "made" in 1928–1929. I thus qualify significantly, in terms of periodization, the view of older studies such as Kermit E. McKenzie, *Comintern and World Revolution, 1928–1943: The Shaping of Doctrine* (London and New York: Columbia University Press, 1964), 9.

8. As one prominent example, see, for instance, Eric Hobsbawm, *Interesting Times: A Twentieth Century Life* (London: Allen Lane, 2002); and the extraordinarily perceptive review by Perry Anderson, "The Age of EJH," *London Review of Books*, October 3, 2002, 24.

9. The Trotsky quote is from Leon Trotsky, *Stalin: An Appraisal of the Man and His Influence* (New York: Harper & Brothers, 1941), 421. For a succinct interpretive introduction to Stalinism's historical emergence and meaning, see Alec Nove, *Stalinism and After* (London: George Allen & Unwin, 1975).

10. See, for instance, Michael Lowy, *The Politics of Combined and Uneven Development: The Theory of Permanent Revolution* (London: Verso, 1981).

11. For the accounts of Comintern history drawn upon in these paragraphs, see Isaac Deutscher, *The Prophet Unarmed: Trotsky, 1921–1929* (New York: Vintage, 1959), 140–48; Kevin McDermott and Jeremy Agnew, *The Comintern: A History of International Communism from Lenin to Stalin* (Basingstoke, UK: Macmillan, 1996), 41–67; Isaac Deutscher, "The Tragedy of the Polish Communist Party," in *Marxism, Wars & Revolutions: Essays from Four Decades* (London: Verso, 1984), 91–127; P. Minc (Aleksander), *The History of A False Illusion—Memoirs on the Communist Movement in Poland (1918–1938)*, trans. and ed. Robert Michaels (Lewiston, NY: Edwin Mellen Press, 2002). A useful collection of documents is Helmut Gruber, ed., *Soviet Russia Masters the Comintern: International Communism in the Era of Stalin's Ascendancy* (Garden City, NY: Anchor, 1974). See Tim Rees and Andrew Thorpe, eds., *International Communism and the Communist International, 1919–1943* (Manchester, UK: Manchester University Press, 1998), for recent essays particularly antagonistic to the Comintern.

12. Suffice it to say that I find unhelpful suggestions that conflate Bolshevism/Leninism with Stalinism. Discussion of Stalinism must, I suggest, begin with recognition that Stalinism marked a *programmatic* departure from Bolshevism and the ideas and theoretical premises of Lenin. This view is rejected by many, including Leszek Kolakowski, *Main Currents of Marxism: The Breakdown*, vol. 3 (Oxford: Clarendon Press, 1978), 1–25, a text that also understates the differentiation of Trotskyism and Stalinism. Trotskyism, as a particular historical variant of Bolshevism, arose in the late 1920s as an analysis of such shifts in program and presented itself as an effort to revive Leninism in the age of Stalinism, returning the revolutionary project to its communist and internationalist roots. Views circulating within certain anarchist, socialist-feminist, and New Left circles, in which hostility to Lenin and the idea of a vanguard party lead into claims that Trotskyist critiques of Stalinism simply reproduced a "Stal-

inist revolutionary personality" within the Left, and thereby handicapped efforts to overcome Stalinism, also understate important differentiations. See, for arguments of the sort I am opposing: Earl Browder to Theodore Draper, 16 March 1959, Series III, Box 18, Earl W. Browder Papers, George Arents Research Library for Special Collections, Syracuse University, Syracuse, New York (hereafter cited as Browder Papers); Kevin Morgan, "Parts of People and Communist Lives," in, *Party People, Communist Lives: Explorations in Biography*, ed. John McIlroy, Kevin Morgan, and Alan Campbell (London: Lawrence & Wishart, 2001), esp. 23–26; Sheila Rowbotham, Lynne Segal, and Hilary Wainwright, *Beyond the Fragments: Feminism and the Making of Socialism* (London: Merlin, 1979), 22; Tariq Ali, *Street-Fighting Years: An Autobiography of the Sixties* (Glasgow: Fontana/Collins, 1988), 246–47.

13. See, for instance, Mark Naison, *Communists in Harlem During the Depression* (Urbana: University of Illinois Press, 1983); Robin D. G. Kelley, *Hammer and Hoe: Alabama Communists During the Great Depression* (Chapel Hill: University of North Carolina Press, 1990); Theodore Rosengarten, *All God's Dangers: The Life of Nate Shaw* (New York: Alfred Knopf, 1974); Nell Irvin Painter, *The Narrative of Hosea Hudson: His Life as a Negro Communist in the South* (Cambridge, MA: Harvard University Press, 1979).

14. Much is written on communists and the arts, but note the recent extensive overview in Michael Denning, *The Cultural Front: The Laboring of American Culture in the Twentieth Century* (London: Verso, 1996).

15. The Abraham Lincoln Brigade, a battalion of Americans that included a number of communists and fought on the republican side during the Spanish Civil War, is the subject of much writing, including Arthur Landis, *The Abraham Lincoln Brigade* (New York: Citadel Press, 1967); James Yates, *Mississippi to Madrid: Memoir of a Black American in the Abraham Lincoln Brigade* (Seattle: Open Hand Publishers, 1989); Robin D. G. Kelley, *Race Rebels: Culture, Politics, and the Black Working Class* (New York: Free Press, 1994), 123–58.

16. See, for instance, Van Gosse, "'To Organize in Every Neighborhood, in Every Home': The Gender Politics of American Communists Between the Wars," *Radical History Review* 50 (1991): 110–41; Elsa Jane Dixler, "The Woman Question: Women and the American Communist Party, 1929–1941"(PhD diss., Yale University, 1974), chap. 3, 127–95.

17. Again, the writing that touches on such mobilizations is extensive. See, for example, Roger Keeran, *The Communist Party and the Auto Workers Unions* (Bloomington: Indiana University Press, 1980); Harvey Levenstein, *Communism, Anticommunism and the CIO* (Westport, CT: Greenwood Press, 1981); Bert Cochran, *Labor and American Communism: The Conflict That Shaped American Unions* (Princeton, NJ: Princeton University Press, 1977); Steve Rosswurm, ed., *The CIO's Left-Led Unions* (New Brunswick, NJ: Rutgers University Press, 1992); Roy Rosenzweig, "Organizing the Unemployed: The Early Years of the Great Depression," *Radical America* 10 (July–August 1976): 37–62; Dan T. Carter, *Scottsboro: A Tragedy of the American South* (Baton Rouge: Louisiana State University Press, 1969).

18. Rosalyn Baxandall, "The Question Seldom Asked: Women and the CPUSA," in *New Studies in the Politics and Culture of U.S. Communism*, ed. Michael Brown, et al.

(New York: Monthly Review Press, 1993), 141–62, raises a number of issues that are further addressed and extended in emphasis on "the personal" in Kathleen A. Brown and Elizabeth Faue, "Social Bonds, Sexual Politics, and Political Community in the U.S. Left, 1920s–1940s," *Left History* 7 (Spring 2000): 9–45; Kathleen A. Brown, "The 'Savagely Fathered and Unmothered' World of the Communist Party, U.S.A.: Feminism, Maternalism, and 'Mother Bloor,'" *Feminist Studies* 25 (Fall 1999): 537–70.

19. In the case of United States communism, consider Mary Inman, *In Woman's Defense* (Los Angeles: Committee to Organize the Advancement of Women, 1941); and the history of Antoinette Konikow, discussed in chapter 11 of this book. Early communist feminists included Clara Zetkin (Germany), Alexandra Kollontai (Russia), and Dora Montefiore (Britain). For this international history of women and communism, see Philip S. Foner, ed., *Clara Zetkin: Selected Writings* (New York: International, 1984); Cathy Porter, *Alexandra Kollontai* (London: Virago, 1980); Karen Hunt, "Dora Montefiore: A Different Communist," in McIlroy, Morgan, and Campbell, *Party People*, 29–50.

20. For an early overview, see Wilson Record, *The Negro and the Communist Party* (Chapel Hill: University of North Carolina Press, 1951). A major autobiography, Harry Haywood, *Black Bolshevik: Autobiography of an Afro-American Communist* (Chicago: Liberator Press, 1978), conveys something of the sweep of communist and African-American experience. Intellectual histories of merit include Harold Cruse, *The Crisis of the Negro Intellectual: From Its Origins to the Present* (New York: William Morrow, 1967); Cedric J. Robinson, *Black Marxism: The Making of the Black Radical Tradition* (London: Zed Press, 1983). A recent study of significance is Mark Solomon, *The Cry Was Unity: Communists and African Americans, 1917–1936* (Jackson: University Press of Mississippi, 1998). On the relational significance of the Communist Party, black Americans, and the development of the U.S. Left, see Michael Goldfield, "Recent Historiography of the Communist Party, U.S.A.," in *The Year Left: An American Socialist Yearbook, 1985*, ed. Mike Davis, Fred Pfiel, and Michael Sprinker (London: Verso, 1985), 315–56, which stresses the importance of communist work among black Americans in the programmatically skewed "Third Period" (1929–1934). For a documentary collection detailing these years, see Philip S. Foner and Herbert Shapiro, eds., *American Communism and Black Americans: A Documentary History* (Philadelphia: Temple University Press, 1991). I review two books relevant to the meaning of the 1928 Black Belt nation thesis—Barbara Foley, *Spectres of 1919: Class & Nation in the Making of the New Negro* (Urbana: University of Illinois Press, 2003) and Max Shachtman, *Race and Revolution,* ed. and introduced by Christopher Phelps (New York: Verso, 2003)—in Bryan D. Palmer, "Race & Revolution," *Labour/Le Travail* 54 (Fall 2004): 193–221.

21. See R. W. Postgate, *The Workers' International* (New York: Harcourt, Brace & Howe, 1920); Lewis L. Lorwin, *Labor and Internationalism* (New York: Macmillan, 1929); Victor Silverman, *Imagining Internationalism in American and British Labor* (Urbana: University of Illinois, 1999).

22. For a classic New Left-influenced statement that sidesteps both the origins and continuities of Stalinization, see Maurice Isserman, *Which Side Were You On? The American Communist Party during the Second World War* (Middletown, CT: Wesleyan

University Press, 1982). For an accounting of this New Left historiography, see Bryan D. Palmer, "Rethinking the Historiography of United States Communism," *American Communist History* 2 (December 2003): 147–52.

23. Communist memoirs are discussed critically in Palmer, "Rethinking the Historiography," 147–52, and more sympathetically in Roy Rosenzweig, "Oral History and the Old Left," *International Labor and Working-Class History* 24 (Fall 1983), esp. 32–33. See, as important statements, Al Richmond, *A Long View from the Left: Memoirs of an American Revolutionary* (Boston: Houghton Mifflin, 1973); Peggy Dennis, *The Autobiography of an American Communist: A Personal View of Political Life* (Westport/Berkeley: Lawrence Hill/Creative Arts, 1977); Steve Nelson, James R. Barrett, and Rob Ruck, *Steve Nelson: American Radical* (Pittsburgh: University of Pittsburgh Press, 1981); Dorothy Healey and Maurice Isserman, *Dorothy Healey Remembers: A Life in the American Communist Party* (New York: Oxford University Press, 1990). Geoff Eley's comment is in "International Communism in the Heyday of Stalin," *New Left Review* 157 (January–February 1986): 92.

24. See Richard Crossman, ed., *God That Failed: A Confession* (New York: Harper & Brothers, 1949); Deutscher, "The Ex-Communist's Conscience," in *Marxism, Wars & Revolution*, 49–59.

25. Draper, *Roots of American Communism*; Theodore Draper, *American Communism and Soviet Russia: The Formative Period* (New York: Viking, 1960).

26. Draper's equivalent in Great Britain, perhaps, would be Henry Pelling, *The British Communist Party: A Historical Profile* (London: A. & C. Black, 1958). Recent revisionist historiography on the British CP rejects Pelling's stress on the party's subordination to Moscow, and argues, albeit not from a social history/rank-and-file perspective, that the British Party was the master of its own fate. For an example of this scholarship, see Andrew Thorpe, *The British Communist Party and Moscow, 1920–1943* (Manchester, UK: Manchester University Press, 2000). For a critical response, see John McIlroy and Alan Campbell, "'Nina Ponomareva's Hats': The New Revisionism, the Communist International, and the Communist Party of Great Britain," *Labour/Le Travail* 49 (Spring 2002): 147–87; John McIlroy and Alan Campbell, "'For a Revolutionary Workers' Government': Moscow, British Communism and Revisionist Interpretations of the Third Period," *European Historical Quarterly* 32 (2002): 535–69.

27. See, for example, Isserman, *Which Side Were You On?* vii–viii; Isserman, "Three Generations: Historians View American Communism," *Labor History* 26 (Fall 1985): 538–45; Gary Gerstle, "Mission from Moscow: American Communism in the 1930s," *Reviews in American History* 12 (December 1984): 559–66; Walzer, "The New History of American Communism," *Reviews in American History* 11 (June 1983): 259–67. Draper responded to the New Left–influenced histories in what has to be considered a cranky two-part essay, originally published in the *New York Review of Books* and later consolidated as an afterword to the 1986 republication of his *American Communism and Soviet Russia*, 445–82. See, originally, Draper, "American Communism Revisited," *New York Review of Books* 32 (May 9, 1985), 35–43; Draper, "Popular Front Revisited," *New York Review of Books* 32 (May 30, 1985), 38–47. Subsequent issues of the *NYRB* (August 15

and September 26, 1985) contained a series of letter exchanges that pitted Draper against almost all of the New Left-influenced combatants. Note as well Sean Wilentz, "Red Herrings Revisited: Theodore Draper Blows His Cool," *Voice Literary Supplement* (June 1986), 6. A further installment appeared in Draper, "The Life of the Party," *New York Review of Books* 41 (January 13, 1994), 47.

28. Among their earlier writings, see Harvey E. Klehr, *Communist Cadre: The Social Background of the American Communist Party Elite* (Stanford, CA: Hoover Institution Press, 1978); Klehr, *The Heyday of American Communism: The Depression Decade* (New York: Basic, 1984); Harvey Klehr and John Earl Haynes, *The American Communist Movement: Storming Heaven Itself* (New York: Twayne, 1992); John Earl Haynes, *Dubious Alliance: The Making of Minnesota's DFL Party* (Minneapolis: University of Minnesota Press, 1984).

29. *Bibliography on the Communist Problem in the United States* (New York: Fund for the Republic, 1955); John Earl Haynes, *Communism and Anti-Communism in the United States: An Annotated Guide to Historical Writing* (New York: Garland, 1987).

30. See especially Harvey Klehr and Ronald Radosh, *The Amerasia Spy Case: Prelude to McCarthyism* (Chapel Hill: University of North Carolina Press, 1996); John Earl Haynes, *Red Scare or Red Menace? American Communism and Anti-Communism in the Cold War Era* (Chicago: Ivan R. Dee, 1996); Harvey Klehr, John Earl Haynes, and Fridrikh Igorevich Firsov, *The Secret World of American Communism* (New Haven: Yale University Press, 1995); Harvey Klehr, John Earl Haynes, and Kryrill M. Anderson, *The Soviet World of American Communism* (New Haven: Yale University Press, 1998); John Earl Haynes and Harvey Klehr, *Venona: Decoding Soviet Espionage in America* (New Haven: Yale University Press, 1999); James G. Ryan, "Socialist Triumph as a Family Value: Earl Browder and Soviet Espionage," *American Communist History* 2 (2002): 125–42. Of course, the "spy" phenomenon cut both ways. See, for instance, Daniel J. Leab, *I Was a Communist for the FBI: The Unhappy Life and Times of Matt Cvetic* (University Park: Pennsylvania State University Press, 2000). For the New Left-influenced case against McCarthyism, see Ellen Schrecker, *No Ivory Tower: McCarthyism and the Universities* (New York: Oxford University Press, 1986); Ellen Schrecker, *Many Are the Crimes: McCarthyism in America* (Boston: Little, Brown, 1998). For Klehr and Haynes on McCarthyism, see *Secret World of American Communism*, 16.

31. See Ronald Radosh and Joyce Milton, *The Rosenberg File: A Search for the Truth* (New York: Holt, Rinehart & Winston, 1983).

32. Maurice Isserman, "Notes from the Underground," *The Nation* (June 12, 1995), 846; Isserman, "Guess What—They Really Were Spies," *Forward* (January 29, 1999); Isserman, "They Led Two Lives," *New York Times Book Review* (May 9, 1999), 35; Sean Wilentz, "Seeing Red," *New York Times Book Review* (January 21, 1996), 15–17.

33. Note the discussions in John Earl Haynes, "The Cold War Debate Continues: A Traditionalist View of Historical Writing on Domestic Communism and Anti-Communism," *Journal of Cold War Studies* 2 (2000): 76–115; John Earl Haynes and Harvey Klehr, "The Historiography of American Communism: An Unsettled Field," *Labour History Review* 68 (April 2003): 61–78. One indication of the strong survival of a New

Left-inspired attempt to present the communist experience in bold strokes of opposition to Draper is Randi Storch, "'The Realities of the Situation': Revolutionary Discipline and Everyday Political Life in Chicago's Communist Party, 1928–1935," *Labor: Studies in Working-Class History of the Americas* 1 (Fall 2004): 19–44. The revisionist/traditionalist historiographic opposition is paralleled in a skewed way in Great Britain through an attempt to argue that the interpretation of communism poses an essentialist/realist dichotomy. This misreading, in which essentialists supposedly accent Moscow domination while realists stress that "events within British communism have to be examined in the light of the real events and people who made them," is untenable on a range of levels and fundamentally obscures the significance of Stalinism. See, for statements embracing this analytic opposition, Nina Fishman, "Essentialists and Realists: Reflections on the Historiography of the CPGB," *Communist History Network Newsletter* 11 (August 2001): 7–16; Harriet Jones, "Conference Report: Is CPGB History Important?," *Labour History Review* 67 (December 2002): 347–55. For a rejection of this position, see Alan Campbell and John McIlroy, "Is CPGB History Important? A Reply to Harriet Jones," *Labour History Review* 68 (December 2003): 385–90, and the subsequent related avalanche of rejoinder and commentary in *Labour History Review* 69 (December 2004): 349–80.

34. Fraser M. Ottanelli. *The Communist Party in the United States: From the Depression to World War II* (New Brunswick, NJ: Rutgers University Press, 1991), seems to fit this pattern. It stresses (see pp. 3–4) the need to balance rank-and-file-oriented histories of U.S. communism with appreciation of Comintern influences, crediting Draper with some insights and acknowledging the importance of social history findings. The resulting book is, however, very much premised on avoidance of the significance of Stalinism, and this is possible because Ottanelli misunderstands developments of the 1920s. In spite of characterizing the decade according to a periodization drawn from James P. Cannon's understandings (outlined in *The First Ten Years of American Communism—Report of a Participant* [New York: Pathfinder, 1973], 16–19), Ottanelli misses Cannon's grasp of the relationship of factionalism and Stalinization within the linked histories of the Communist International and the U.S. party. Ottanelli thus skims the surface of the 1920s, and claims that, "By 1930 the factionalism that had caused havoc in the Party throughout most of its short existence had ended. The Party was united around a new leadership which was to head it for the next fifteen years. . . . The new decade presented Communists with new challenges and opportunities which, having put factional strife behind them, they felt ready to seize" (9, 15–16). Klehr, *Communist Cadre*, 89, captures the significance of the ending of factionalism more correctly and more succinctly: "The Stalinization of the CPUSA was complete, and organized opposition to the party leadership ceased."

35. As an introduction only, see Susan Weissman, *Victor Serge: The Course Is Set on Hope* (London: Verso, 2001); Christopher Phelps, *Young Sidney Hook: Marxist and Pragmatist* (Ithaca, NY: Cornell University Press, 1997), esp. 140–233; Alan Wald, *The New York Intellectuals: The Rise and Decline of the Anti-Stalinist Left from the 1930s to the 1980s* (Chapel Hill: University of North Carolina Press, 1987), 128–63; Alan Wald, *James T. Farrell: The Revolutionary Socialist Years* (New York: New York University Press,

1978), 61–75; Preliminary Commission of Inquiry, *The Case of Leon Trotsky* (New York: Harper, 1937); Commission of Inquiry, *Not Guilty* (New York: Harper, 1938); Albert Glotzer, *Trotsky: Memoir & Critique* (Buffalo: Prometheus Books, 1989), 235–81. Ellen Schrecker, *Many Are the Crimes,* uncovers the ugliness of McCarthyism well, and even relates how the CPUSA succumbed to its rabid anti-communist foes in part because of policies embraced by the party. This might be seen as an implicit critique of Stalinism, but a serious probing of her book's relational understanding of Stalinism and Trotsky- ism reveals blind spots and a cavalier approach to the politics of this relation. Schrecker actually evades discussion of Stalinism by conflating *all* elements of a highly differen- tiated anti-Stalinist Left and assimilating them to a generalized "intelligence service" for McCarthyism's repressive anti-communist network. It is undeniable that elements of what had been an anti-Stalinist Left in the 1930s moved decidedly to the right (Love- stone is perhaps the best example) and by the 1950s had made common cause with official anti-communism, including the Central Intelligence Agency and the State Department. To claim, however, that *all* on the anti-Stalinist Left had such a trajectory, and involved themselves in such distasteful politics, is not sustained by evidence. Vir- tually everything Schrecker says about Trotskyists in the 1930s and 1940s is skewed, and much of it relies on a problematic source, Constance Ashton Myers, *The Prophet's Army: Trotskyists in America, 1928–1941* (Westport, CT: Greenwood, 1977). See Schrecker, *Many Are the Crimes,* 75–81, 104, 451, n. 88, and the criticism of Schrecker in Julius Jacobson, "Revising the History of Cold War Liberals," *New Politics* 7 (Winter 2000): 166–73. Note for the Lovestoneites: Robert J. Alexander, *The Right Opposition: The Lovestoneites and the International Communist Opposition of the 1930s* (Westport, CT: Greenwood, 1981); Ted Morgan, *A Covert Life: Jay Lovestone—Communist, Anti- Communist, and Spymaster* (New York: Random House, 1999).

36. The preceding paragraphs quote from Draper, *Roots of American Communism,* 3, 10, 394–95.

37. Draper, *American Communism and Soviet Russia,* 5, 440.

38. See James P. Cannon, "A Critical Review of Theodore Draper's History," in Can- non, *First Ten Years,* 311–33. I read Cannon's reviews of the two volumes, originally pub- lished separately, as being far more drawn to *The Roots of American Communism,* for which Cannon's praise is effusive, than to *American Communism and Soviet Russia,* as to which Cannon tackles more vociferously Draper's problematic argument that American communism's "original sin" of attaching itself to the Russian Revolution "led it inexorably, from one calamity to another, and to eventual defeat and disgrace" (p. 329). Although Cannon never drew a distinction between Draper's two volumes, it is implicit in the differences in tone and substantive critique that characterize the two separate reviews. This is merited, I would suggest, because there is a shift in Draper's language and substantive argument between the two volumes. For other former com- munists' critiques of Draper, see Herbert Benjamin, "Outline of Unpublished Manu- script: A History of the Unemployed Movement and Its Struggles During the Great Depression" (n.d., 1970s?), 108, deposited in Columbia Oral History Project, Columbia University, New York, New York; and Earl Browder, quoted in Isserman, *Which Side*

Were You On?, ix; Browder to Draper, 16 March 1959, Series III, Box 18, Browder Papers. Wolfe is quoted in Bertram D. Wolfe, *A Life in Two Centuries: An Autobiography* (New York: Stein & Day, 1981), 229; Lovestone in Paul Le Blanc, "The Rise of American Communism," unpublished manuscript, citing Jay Lovestone, "Testimony of Jay Lovestone, Secretary, Independent Labor League of America," *Investigation of Un-American Propaganda Activities in the United States: Hearings Before a Special Commitee on Un-American Activities (Dies Committee), House of Representatives, 75th–76th Congresses* (Washington, DC: Government Printing Office, 1939–1940); Trotsky in Eastman, *Love and Revolution,* 348–49.

39. *Steve Nelson, American Radical,* 246; Rosenzweig, "Oral History and the Old Left," 32–33. The problem with Nelson's formulation of issues of communist discipline and their relation to Stalinism is not so much conceptual as historical. Lenin's development of party discipline and the emergence of a machinery of Bolshevism in the pre-Revolution and immediate post-1917 years undoubtedly presented opportunities for Stalin to seize that machinery and change its meaning by severing the party from its historic relation to revolutionary ideas. In this sense, as Trotsky noted, Stalin was in part a creation of the Bolshevik machine, which in turn came to be taken over by an individual who personified its negation. To pose the issue of the revolutionary party and its degeneration in this way, in the Soviet Union of 1921–1926, is one thing, but to suggest that this interpretation is easily transferable to the experience of United States communism in the 1930s ignores the extent to which the Soviet Party, the Comintern, *and* the United States Communist Party had already succumbed to Stalinization by this late date. See Trotsky, *Stalin,* xv. Note on Draper and the New Left: Walzer, "New History of American Communism,"259–60, 266; Gerstle, "Mission from Moscow," 561, 563–64. Draper's broadside rejoinder, a two-part *NYRB* essay, is republished in the 1986 edition of *American Communism and Soviet Russia,* 445–82. Draper's later attack on Eric Foner's *The Story of American Freedom,* "Freedom and Its Discontents," *New York Review of Books* 46 (September 23, 1999), may have been prompted by some legitimate concerns, but it seemed shrill given the limited treatment Foner afforded the Popular Front (*Story of American Freedom,* 210–18), and it exposed Draper's capability to overreach himself in polemical rejection of all arguments that claimed the need for a critical engagement with the deficiencies evident in American democracy. This led Draper to whitewash the role of Sidney Hook and the American Committee for Cultural Freedom in the ugliness of 1950s anti-communism. See Jacobson, "Revising the History of Cold War Liberals."

40. The central texts here are Klehr, Haynes, and Firsov, *Secret World of American Communism;* and Klehr, Haynes, and Anderson, *Soviet World of American Communism.*

41. McIlroy, Morgan, and Campbell, the editors of *Party People* commence with the statement that "Communist historiography has in the main been impoverished by its disregard of biography" (p. 5). Kevin Morgan's opening chapter, "Parts of People and Communist Lives" (pp. 9–28), makes a case for the contributions of biography, and subsequent chapters provide glimpses of the potential of biography. In Canada, the first truly sophisticated biographical treatment appeared only recently: David Frank,

J. B. McLachlan: A Biography (Toronto: Lorimer, 1999). On the lack of biography in international communist historiography, note especially Perry Anderson, "Communist Party History," in *People's History and Socialist Theory,* ed. Raphael Samuel (London: Routledge & Kegal Paul, 1981), 150–56; and the essays in E. J. Hobsbawm, *Revolutionaries: Contemporary Essays* (New York: Pantheon, 1973), 3–54. In *Bibliography on the Communist Problem,* the entry on biography constituted slightly more than one page in a 474-page text. Other bibliographies, such as Joel Seidman, *Communism in the United States: A Bibliography* (Ithaca, NY: Cornell University Press, 1969), are not organized in a way that allows access to biographical material. John Earl Haynes, *Communism and Anticommunism,* repeats entries throughout various sections, but, even allowing for this exaggeration in the biographical realm, contains a total of 50 pages out of 321 that relate in the loosest way to biographical writing. Extremely useful are recent compilations such as Mari Jo Buhle, Paul Buhle, and Dan Georgakas, eds., *Encyclopedia of the American Left* (Urbana: University of Illinois Press, 1992).

42. Edward P. Johanningsmeier, *Forging American Communism: The Life of William Z. Foster* (Princeton, NJ: Princeton University Press, 1994); James R. Barrett, *William Z. Foster and the Tragedy of American Radicalism* (Urbana: University of Illinois Press, 1999). The advances of these texts over a past treatment of Foster, written by his secretary and research assistant over the course of the 1950s, are monumental. See Arthur Zipster, *Workingclass Giant: The Life of William Z. Foster* (New York: International, 1981). Note as well James G. Ryan, *Earl Browder: The Failure of American Communism* (Tuscaloosa: University of Alabama Press, 1997); Ted Morgan, *A Covert Life.*

43. Note Klehr, *Communist Cadre,* 110–11.

44. Note that Cannon receives no entry in Mari Jo Buhle, Paul Buhle, and Harvey Kaye, eds., *The American Radical* (New York: Routledge, 1994). Until now, the main writing on Cannon, aside from the publications of his own writings and speeches within the Trotskyist movement, has been Les Evans, ed., *James P. Cannon As We Knew Him: By Thirty-Three Comrades, Friends, and Relatives* (New York: Pathfinder, 1976); Wald, *New York Intellectuals,* 164–92; and the extremely useful introductions and other material in *James P. Cannon and the Early Years of American Communism: Selected Writings and Speeches, 1920–1928* (New York: Prometheus Research Library, 1992); *Dog Days: James P. Cannon vs Max Shachtman in the Communist League of America, 1931–1933* (New York: Prometheus Research Library, 2002).

45. Consider, for instance, that Draper originally titled chapter 4 of his *American Communism and Soviet Russia,* "Cannon's Coup," and that the preceding chapter, a 62-page typescript entitled "Hungarian Pepper," subsequently appeared as "Roads to Chicago." Cannon's focus on Pepper in his letters to Draper, published as *First Ten Years,* is evident (pp. 74–94). As I wrote this book, I found myself unconsciously retracing some of Draper's early steps, albeit in different shoes. See "Memorandum: To Theodore Draper from Earl Browder," uncorrected ms. of volume 2 of history, 16 March 1959, 32-page typescript, esp. 7–15. For Browder's earlier comments on volume 1, which again engage with Cannon's views, see Browder to Draper, 24 January 1956, 14 February 1956, 19–20 February 1956, 29 February 1956, 1 March 1956, 9 March 1956, 17

April 1956, 4 May 1956, all Browder documents in Series I, Box 3, Browder Papers. This correspondence ends (4 May 1956) with the statement: "I am going to go over Cannon's stories, not for their lapses and inaccuracies, but their positive contribution to the knowledge of facts about the party's early history—and this contribution is quite a valuable one." That left-handed compliment aside, Browder's rivalry with Cannon—indeed, his animus toward Cannon—is unmistakable.

46. Theodore Draper, "Preface," in Cannon, *First Ten Years*, 9–12.

Chapter 1: Rosedale Roots

1. On midwives, physicians, and the requirement of birth reporting in working-class districts of Kansas City, Kansas, see "Armourdale: A City within a City—The Report of a Social Survey of Armourdale, a Community of 12,000 People Living in the Industrial District of Kansas City, Kansas," *Bulletin of the University of Kansas* 20, no. 12 (June 15, 1919): 30. The state of Kansas did not require birth certificates until 1911. Cannon's birthdate is generally recognized as 11 February 1890, although it is occasionally designated 12 February. I follow the dating of his death certificate, located in James P. Cannon Papers, Microfilm Edition, 1994, "Death Certificate," Reel 1, State Historical Society of Wisconsin, Madison, Wisconsin (hereafter JPC Papers).

2. I am suggesting the complications of ethnicity, birthplace, and culture/politics in United States class formation. Cannon hints at the complexities of class development, for he would, as the son of foreign-born parents, adapt seemingly effortlessly to the status of a native son (admittedly easier for an Irish-American than for Poles, Ukrainians, Finns, Italians, or European Jews). His family background was a hybrid of radical/conservative, and like many in similar domestic settings in the Irish-American milieu, it contained cross-currents of gendered traditionalism/dissent. Ultimately, Cannon rejected much of the conservatism of the particular small-town Irish-American setting in which he was reared and, in the process, cultivated an identity as a native son and a revolutionary. See Herbert G. Gutman and Ira Berlin, "Class Composition and the Development of the American Working Class, 1840–1890," in Herbert G. Gutman, *Power & Culture: Essays on the American Working Class*, ed. Ira Berlin (New York: Pantheon, 1987), 380–94; David M. Emmons, *The Butte Irish: Class and Ethnicity in an American Mining Town, 1875–1925* (Urbana: University of Illinois Press, 1989), esp. 77; Mary Murphy, *Mining Cultures: Men, Women, and Leisure in Butte, 1914–1941* (Urbana: University of Illinois Press, 1997), esp. 93.

3. In nearby Argentine, one source reported that the prolonged railway strike of 1894 "severely [a]ffected the town." *Centennial History of Argentine, Kansas City, Kansas, 1880–1980, Includes the History of Argentine, Turner, and Shawnee Township* (Kansas City, KS: Simmons Funeral Home, 1980), 12.

4. Among the many sources that provide perspective, see Lewis Mumford, *The Brown Decade: A Study of the Arts in America* (New York: Harcourt, Brace, 1931); David Montgomery, *The Fall of the House of Labor: The Workplace, the State, and American Labor Activism, 1865–1925* (Cambridge, UK: Cambridge University Press, 1987), 171–213; Almont Lindsey, *The Pullman Strike: The Story of a Unique Experiment and a Great*

Labor Upheaval (Chicago: University of Chicago Press, 1942); Nick Salvatore, *Eugene V. Debs: Citizen and Socialist* (Urbana: University of Illinois Press, 1982), 231.

5. See Charles P. Deatherage, *Early History of Greater Kansas City, Missouri and Kansas* (Kansas City, MO: Chapman & Hall, 1927).

6. *Kansas City (The Heart of America)—What Is It—Where Is It—How Is It?* (Kansas City, MO: n.p., 1915). See, as well, Henry C. Haskell, Jr., and Richard B. Fowler, *City of the Future: A Narrative History of Kansas City, 1850–1950* (Kansas City, MO: Frank Glenn, 1950).

7. See, among many accounts, R. C. Miller, "Background of Populism in Kansas," *Mississippi Valley Historical Review* 11 (1924–1925): 478–85; Carroll D. Clark and Roy L. Roberts, *People of Kansas: A Demographic and Sociological Study* (Topeka: Kansas State Planning Board, 1936), 6–48.

8. On Kansas populism, note especially O. Gene Clanton, *Kansas Populism: Ideas and Men* (Lawrence: University of Kansas Press, 1969); Scott G. McNall, *The Road to Rebellion: Class Formation and Kansas Populism, 1865–1900* (Chicago: University of Chicago Press, 1988). Other useful studies, insightful for their general comment on populism and labor in this period, include Chester McArthur Destler, *American Radicalism, 1865–1901* (Chicago: Quadrangle, 1961); Lawrence Goodwyn, *Democratic Promise: The Populist Moment in America* (New York: Oxford University Press, 1976).

9. Elizabeth N. Barr, "The Populist Uprising," in *A Standard History of Kansas and Kansans*, vol. II, ed. William E. Connelley (Chicago: American Historical Society, 1928), 1150–51.

10. Quoted in "Industrial Slavery: Lorenzo D. Lewelling, Speech in Kansas, 1894," in Norman Pollack, ed., *The Populist Mind* (Indianapolis: Bobbs-Merrill, 1967), 5.

11. Clanton, *Kansas Populism*, 18.

12. One source mistakenly names Cannon's mother as Ruth, although it later corrects this error. See "Cannon Biography, ca. February 1971," Reel 1, JPC Papers. Ann Hackett is the name that appears on James P. Cannon/Lista Makimson, Certificate of Marriage, State of Illinois, County of Tazewell, June 5, 1913, vol. 3, 267, provided by Christine Webb, County Clerk.

13. Jeanne Morgan, "Journal from James P. Cannon's Office, 1954–56: Notes kept by secretary for personal memento, without Cannon's knowledge," January 24, 1956 (in possession of the author, with thanks to Jeanne Morgan and Alan Wald; hereafter Morgan diary).

14. On Bolton, see various passages in E. P. Thompson, *The Making of the English Working Class* (London: Victor Gollancz, 1963); Patrick Joyce, *Work, Society, and Politics: The Culture of the Factory in Later Victorian Britain* (Brighton, Sussex, UK: Harvester Press, 1980); Walter Greenwood, *Lancashire* (London: Robert Hale, 1951), 96–107.

15. John K. Walton, *Lancashire: A Social History, 1558–1939* (Manchester, UK: Manchester University Press, 1987), 105.

16. Rose Karsner to James P. Cannon, No. 27/April 3, 1944; No. 40/May 9, 1944, JPC Papers. The information on family matters is being conveyed through Rose by Cannon's sister, Agnes.

17. On this process, see the Lancashire study John Foster, *Class Struggle and the Industrial Revolution: Early Industrial Capitalism in Three English Towns* (London: Weidenfeld & Nicholson, 1974).

18. See Joyce, *Work, Society, and Politics.*

19. Consider W. J. Lowe, *The Irish in Mid-Victorian Lancashire: The Shaping of a Working Class Community* (New York: Peter Lang, 1989); E. C. Midwinter, *Social Administration in Lancashire, 1830–1860* (Manchester, UK: Manchester University Press, 1969).

20. On the Knights of Labor in Rhode Island, see Paul Buhle, "The Knights of Labor in Rhode Island," *Radical History Review* 17 (Spring 1978): 39–73. For Cannon's membership in L.A. 2971, see "Prospect Assembly Banquet," *Providence Journal*, February 5, 1887 (I am grateful to Scott Molloy of the Rhode Island Labor History Society for providing me with this reference). For the Central Falls (population 2,500–8,000) data, see Jonathan Garlock, *Guide to Local Assemblies of the Knights of Labor* (Westport, CT: Greenwood Press, 1982), 476–78, 651. For the John T. Cannon of the Machinists, almost certainly a relative of John Cannon, and perhaps his younger brother Jim, see *20th Century Illustrated History of Rhode Island and the Rhode Island Central Trades and Labor Union and Its Affiliated Organizations . . .* (Providence: Rhode Island Central Trades and Labor Union, 1901), 534; "Many Interruptions Disturbed the Harmony of the Meeting of the Economic League," *Providence Journal*, May 23, 1902 (again, I am indebted to Scott Molloy for these sources). Cannon's son learned of his father's involvement in the Providence labor movement from Tommy Powers, head of the IWW Textile Workers' Union, when he attended the Seventh Convention of the IWW in 1912. See Harry Ring interview with Cannon, April 4, 1973, 4–5 (in possession of the author; hereafter Ring interview). On Powers, who moved that the 1905 founding convention of the IWW close nominations for chair after Haywood was moved for nomination, see *Proceedings of the First Convention of the Industrial Workers of the World, founded at Chicago, June 27–July 8, 1905* (New York: New York Labor News, 1905), 27–28. Powers spoke often before the original IWW convention, but note especially his speech on textile workers, pp. 570–74.

21. This reconstruction of family developments, ages, and movements is pieced together from various sources. Among the most reliable are Rose Karsner to Jim Cannon, No. 27/April 3, 1944; No. 40/May 9, 1944, Reel 6, JPC Papers; Ring interview with Cannon, April 4, 1973, 4–6; 1895 State of Kansas Census, City of Rosedale, Township of Shawnee, Wyandotte County, K-165, vol. 406, 21a–21b.

22. Morgan diary, January 24, 1956; Ring interview with Cannon, April 4, 1973, 4–5. This pattern of metal-working plants succumbing was common in the period. In the nearby industrial district of Argentine, a silver smelter failed in the same period, causing much distress among the local working-class population. See *Centennial History of Argentine*, 4–12. Reference to John Cannon's Knights of Labor toast to "The Ladies" is in "Prospect Assembly Banquet," *Providence Journal*, February 5, 1887.

23. Sandra Van Meter McCoy and Jan Hults, *1001 Kansas Place Names* (Lawrence: University of Kansas Press, 1989).

24. *Kansas City (The Heart of America)*, 10; *Kansas State Federation of Labor: Industrial History and Official Yearbook, 1909* (Wichita: McCormick Press, issued for the Executive Board of the Kansas State Federation of Labor, 1909), 85; Kate L. Cowick, *The Story of Kansas City* (Kansas City, KS: Central High School Press, 1926), 4.

25. Justice Neale Carman, *Foreign Born Units of Kansas. I. Historical Atlas and Statistics* (Lawrence: University of Kansas Press, 1962), 302, 307. For the importance of the foreign-born in American working-class formation, see Ira Berlin and Herbert G. Gutman, "Class Composition," 380–94.

26. Leon Fink, *Workingmen's Democracy: The Knights of Labor and American Politics* (Urbana: University of Illinois Press, 1983), 114–17.

27. Fink, *Workingmen's Democracy*, 307; "Armourdale—A City within a City," 10–12; Ring interview with Cannon, April 4, 1973, 1. For a thorough account of the demographic character of Kansas, which explores both the understated presence of foreign-born people and the centrality of urbanization in the post-1890 years, see Clark and Roberts, *People of Kansas*, 49–90.

28. Clark and Roberts, *People of Kansas*, 60.

29. Fink, *Workingmen's Democracy*, 117–48. Fink's study shows how a brokering of political patronage could produce conservatism in the Irish-American milieu, whereas David Emmons, in *Butte Irish*, explores how an economic brokering of jobs led to a similar dampening of radicalism.

30. "Armourdale—A City within a City," 11, 21–27; Margaret Landis, *The Winding Valley and the Craggy Hillside: A History of the City of Rosedale, Kansas* (Kansas City, KS: Arrowhead Instant Printing, 1976), 65, 120. Two maps, available in the Map Division, New York Public Library, are useful for comparisions of a chronological sort. *Rascher's Map of Kansas City, Kansas Containing Also Bonner Springs, Calorific, New Philadelphia, Vance, Argentine, Rosedale* (Chicago: Rascher Map Publishing Company, April 1889) shows a largely undeveloped Rosedale in the late 1880s, whereas *The Berry Company's Map of Kansas City, Kansas, Showing Rosedale, Kans., and New City Limits* (Kansas City, KS: Berry Company, 1911) indicates a much more developed residential community, but still one in which the large factories of Armourdale are not present.

31. These paragraphs draw on [Emily Turnbull], "What Walta Ross Knew of Jim and Rose's Families," November 29, 1993, Typescript, 1, Prometheus Research Library, New York, New York; Ring interview with Cannon, April 4, 1973, 11; and on the Rosedale Local Assembly of the Knights of Labor, Garlock, *Guide*, 149. Alan Wald, *The New York Intellectuals: The Rise and Decline of the Anti-Stalinist Left from the 1930s to the 1980s* (Chapel Hill: University of North Carolina Press, 1987), 167, notes that Cannon lost his thumb, "presumably in a work-related accident," but Frank Lovell told Emily Turnbull that Cannon lost the thumb accompanying his father to a building site, where John had temporary work as a carpenter. [Emily Turnbull], "What We Know of James P. Cannon, 1890–1921," Typescript, 1, Prometheus Research Library, New York, New York.

32. This was Cannon's view of his mother. See the recollections of Harry Ring in Les Evans, ed., *James P. Cannon As We Knew Him: By Thirty-three Comrades, Friends, and Relatives* (New York: Pathfinder, 1976), 165.

33. 1895 State of Kansas Census, City of Rosedale, Township of Shawnee,Wyandotte County, K-165, vol. 406, 17a–b, 18a–b, 21a–b.

34. Ring interview with Cannon, April 4, 1973, 5; Affectionate Father John Cannon to My Dear Son, 3 August 1931; 12 December 1931, Reel 3, JPC Papers, which indicate that Jim's stepsiblings Mary and Tom had migrated to the Oakland area. On Edward, his residential separation from his father, and his occupational shifts, see *Hoye's Rosedale, Kansas, Directory,* for the years 1903–1907. Frank Lovell, a seaman and close political comrade of Cannon's, recalled that Cannon had "a brother" who was a member of the Marine Cooks and Stewards Union and was in general sympathy with socialist politics. This must have been Tom, eight years Jim's senior. He apparently dropped in to see Cannon at the West Coast offices of the Socialist Party sometime in 1936–1937, during the maritime strike. Lovell had never heard Cannon mention him. Bryan Palmer interview with Frank Lovell, New York, April 1, 1994; minuted telephone conversation with Alan Wald (relating to Lovell's recollections of Cannon brother), July 21, 1997; notes on a conversation with Frank Lovell, February 18–19, 1998; Lovell to Palmer, 29 June 1997. On the maritime strike, see James P. Cannon, *Notebook of an Agitator* (New York: Pathfinder, 1973), 97–126.

35. Rose to Jim, 3 April 1944, Reel 6, JPC Papers, citing the authority of Agnes, Jim's older sister, and the most knowledgeable source of family history. This is the source that notes that John Cannon may have served as a "Police Judge and Justice of the Peace" for a time. John Cannon was always listed as employed in "real estate" in any census consulted between 1895–1915. See, for example, 1895 Census, State of Kansas, City of Rosedale, Township of Shawnee, Wyandotte Country, K-165, vol. 406, 21b; 1915 Census, State of Kansas, City of Rosedale . . . , K-270, vol. 341, sec. 1, 18. The 1905 state census listed Edward Cannon as a "real estate agent." Note as well the advertisements for John Cannon's Insurance Agency and John Cannon and Sons, Insurance Agency in *The Inter-State News,* October 27, 1911, 6; *Mt. Marty Annual, Rosedale High School,* vol. 3 (Rosedale, Kansas, 1910), a yearbook for the local high school. Rosedale entries in city directories (apparently not available for the earlier years), always list John Cannon as in the real estate business between 1903–1912. See, for typical examples: *Hoye's Rosedale, Kansas Directory, 1903* (Kansas City, MO: Hoye Directory, 1903), 7, 26; *Forty-first Annual 1911 Kansas City, Kansas, Directory, Including Rosedale* (Kansas City, MO: Gate City Directory, 1911), 517, 542.

36. Ring interview with Cannon, April 4, 1973, 6–9, 11; Morgan diary, January 24, 1956.

37. Ring interview with Cannon, April 4, 1973, 13–14.

38. Bryan Palmer interview with Walta Ross (Cannon stepdaughter), Del Mar, CA, April 18, 1996; recollections of Carl Cannon (son), Mathew Ross (grandson), and Art Sharon and Sam Gordon (comrades) in Evans, *As We Knew Him,* 47, 218, 89, 66, respectively.

39. The following paragraphs draw on the manuscript "Iron City," ca. 1958(?), Reel 46, JPC Papers. The manuscript follows broken paginations, has no clearly discernible finish, but is separated into four chapters comprising 38 pages. It is followed by a two-page outline of what was clearly meant to be a larger novel, "The Story of Max

Dezettel," integrating the "Iron City" material into its themes. This latter project probably encompassed more than fictionalized autobiography, but Cannon clearly commenced this literary endeavor by drawing on his family experience and childhood in Rosedale. Joseph Hansen's recollections in Evans, *As We Knew Him*, 12, make a one-line allusion to Cannon having started a novel.

40. For illuminating discussions of Irish working-class enclaves in this period, see Emmons, *Butte Irish* and Murphy, *Mining Cultures.* Comment on the Irish in more urban, slum conditions is associated with recent studies of another leading communist, and one-time Cannon ally, William Z. Foster. See Edward P. Johanningsmeier, *Forging American Communism: The Life of William Z. Foster* (Princeton, NJ: Princeton University Press, 1994), 10–30; James R. Barrett, *William Z. Foster and the Tragedy of American Radicalism* (Urbana: University of Illinois Press, 1999), 9–29.

41. In 1890, 6.4 percent of the Kansas state population was classified as "Negro." Kansas City alone, which would have included Rosedale, accounted for almost 30 percent of the entire black population of the state at this time, or roughly 12,500 African Americans. Most of this population had come into being over the course of the 1880s and 1890s, giving rise to intensified racial tensions in the state. See Clark and Roberts, *People of Kansas*, 58–60; Fink, *Workingmen's Democracy*, 112–48.

42. JPC to Carl Cannon, 9 June 1963, Reel 22, JPC Papers.

43. For a classic fictional account of a second-generation immigrant youth and the mother-father-son engagements of the urban slum, see Henry Roth, *Call It Sleep* (New York: Avon, 1964), a reprinted edition of a 1934 publication.

44. "Turtle Creek" chap. III of "Iron City," 17, Reel 46, JPC Papers.

45. Ring interview with Cannon, April 4, 1973, 1–2. It has recently been claimed, on the authority of extremely dubious Soviet, KGB-related, sources that Cannon's sister was married to Dr. Philip Rosenbliett (Rosenblit), a figure in the early communist underground of 1920–1923 who was later connected to Whittaker Chambers and the courier system of Soviet espionage. The evidence of Rosenbliett's courier status in the first years of American communism, and his later spy activity in the 1930s, may well have some foundation, as indicated in Allen Weinstein, *Perjury: The Hiss-Chambers Case* (New York: Knopf, 1978), 64, 122–23; Harvey Klehr, John Earl Haynes, and Fridrikh Igorevich Firsov, *The Secret World of American Communism* (New Haven: Yale University Press, 1995), 25–26. Nevertheless, any connection of Rosenbleitt to Cannon through marriage to his sister is clearly untrue, as are many of the assertions made in the questionable documentation cited in Sam Tanenhaus, *Whittaker Chambers: A Biography* (New York: Random House, 1997), 133–34, where indexed references to Cannon also confuse him with the *New York Post* journalist, Jimmy Cannon. The most likely explanation for this mistaken identity relating to Cannon's sister is that the Soviet source was a fabrication. However, a faint possibility is that Cannon's sister-in-law, a sibling of his common-law spouse Rose Karsner, was married to Dr. Rosenbliett. Karsner did have a sister, on the periphery of the communist movement, who went with her husband to the Soviet Union in the 1930s, where they both disappeared; the sister ultimately died in a camp in 1950 or 1951. Morgan diary, "About Rose Karsner," February 3, 1954.

46. Jeanne Morgan to Bryan Palmer, 24 September 1997; Morgan diary, February 4, 1954. Cannon's experience with flood has already been demonstrated in his fictionalized "Iron City," but he would have been aware as well of the great flood of 1903. See "Armourdale—A City within a City," 9; *Pictorial Souvenir of the Armourdale Flood, 1903* (Kansas City, KS: R. B. Hansford & F. W. Allen, 1903); S. W. Rider, ed., *The New Empire Kansas City Flood Edition, 1903* (Kansas City, MO: New Empire Company, 1903); W. R. Hill, *The Great Flood of 1903* (Kansas City, MO: Enterprise Publishing, 1903); *Centennial History of Argentine*, 12–13. The Kansas-Missouri twang is commented on in Sam Gordon's recollections in Evans, *As We Knew Him*, 54; Wald, *New York Intellectuals*, 168; and with denigration in Benjamin Gitlow, *I Confess: The Truth about American Communism* (New York: E.P. Dutton, 1940), 161.

47. Evans, *As We Knew Him*, 46.

48. "Turtle Creek," chap. III of "Iron City," 18, Reel 46, JPC Papers.

Chapter 2: Youth's Discoveries

1. Harry Ring interview with James Cannon, April 4, 1973, 12, 14 (in possession of the author; hereafter Ring interview); "Biographical Note Material," February 18, 1971, Reel 1, James P. Cannon Papers, Microfilm Edition, 1994, State Historical Society of Wisconsin, Madison, Wisconsin (hereafter JPC Papers); James P. Cannon, "The Stalinist Ideology 1. Back in the Packing House," in *The Road to Peace* (New York: Pioneer Publishers, 1951), 27.

2. See, for the Chicago muckraking context of Sinclair's "jungle," James R. Barrett's account of packinghouse workers and his edited version of Sinclair's classic text: James R. Barrett, *Work and Community in the Jungle: Chicago's Packinghouse Workers, 1894–1922* (Urbana: University of Illinois Press, 1990); Upton Sinclair, *The Jungle*, ed. and introduced by James R. Barrett (Chicago: University of Illinois Press, 1988). The packinghouse bosses, if Chicago was any example, were notoriously anti-union, and working conditions and wages were poor, as low as 12.5 cents an hour. See William Z. Foster, *Pages from a Worker's Life* (New York: International, 1939), 152–53; James R. Barrett, *William Z. Foster and the Tragedy of American Radicalism* (Urbana: University of Illinois Press, 1999), 69. For Kansas City, Kansas, details on meatpacking in particular and labor unions in general, see *Kansas State Federation of Labor: Industrial History and Official Yearbook, 1909* (Wichita: McCormick Press, issued for the Executive Board of the Kansas State Federation of Labor, 1909), esp. 82–85; Kate L. Cowick, *The Story of Kansas City* (Kansas City, KS: Central High School Press, 1926), 2–4, 27.

3. For residency information in this period, I have relied on *Hoye's Rosedale, Kansas Directory, 1903* (Kansas City, MO: Hoye Directory Company, 1903), 7; *Hoye's Kansas City, Kansas, Directory, 1904* (Kansas City, MO: Hoye Directory, 1904), 358; *Thirty-fifth Annual Issue, 1905, Hoye's Kansas City Directory including . . . Rosedale, Kansas* (Kansas City, MO: Hoye Directory Company, 1905), 366.

4. For information on wages, hours, and child labor in Chicago's meatpacking industry, see Barrett, *Work and Community in the Jungle*, 50, 72, 90–95.

5. 1905, State of Kansas Census, City of Rosedale, Wyandotte County, Shawnee Township. Bryan Palmer interview with Frank Lovell, March 30, 1994, indicates that Cannon worked on the railroads, but only for a short period; this interview addresses the issue of seniority and night work. Quote from Farrell Dobbs recollection in Les Evans, ed., *James P. Cannon As We Knew Him: By Thirty-three Comrades, Friends, and Relatives* (New York: Pathfinder, 1976), 34. Other reference to railroad work in this period is in "Biographical Note Material," February 18, 1871, JPC Papers; [Emily Turnbull], "What We Know of James P. Cannon, 1890–1921," Typescript, 1, Prometheus Research Library, New York, New York. It is possible that the name Missouri, Kansas, and Texas, or Katy/KT, was a worker designation of a line that went by another official name, there being many rail lines in the Kansas City area that linked Missouri-Kansas and the Texas/Pacific regions.

6. *Hoye's Kansas City Directory, 1905*, 366, lists James P. Cannon as employed in engraving, and see as well Ring interview with Cannon, May 10, 1973, 14. For a statistical profile of the state's industry and labor conditions at this time, see State of Kansas, *Bulletin of the Bureau of Labor and Industry, 1905* (Topeka, KS: State Printing Office, 1906).

7. For suggestive comment, note Carl Cannon's memorial remembrance of his father in Evans, *As We Knew Him*, 46–47; Ring interview with Cannon, April 11, 1973, 5–7, 12–13; and the pseudo-fictional final chapter of "Iron City," ca. 1958, entitled "Drink," Reel 46, JPC Papers.

8. James P. Cannon, *The First Ten Years of American Communism—Report of a Participant* (New York: Pathfinder, 1973), 139.

9. 1910 Federal Census, State of Kansas, County of Wyandotte, Township of Shawnee, City of Rosedale. Upon the breakup of the John and Frances Cannon marriage, Frances took her son John/Jack and migrated to England. See Jack to My Dear Brother Jim (Montreal), 4 May 1929; Frances Cannon to Dear Jim (Scarborough, England), 21 April 1932, Reel 3, JPC Papers. John Cannon was obviously something of a charmer, but Frances, an older woman of some independence, was less long-suffering than her predecessor, Ann.

10. Ring interview, April 4, 1973, 10; April 11, 1973, 5. Residence and employment information for the young Jim Cannon in these years is from *Hoye's Kansas City, Kansas Directories*, 1906–1910.

11. Theodore Draper, *The Roots of American Communism* (New York: Viking, 1957), 305.

12. The preceding paragraphs draw on Ring interviews with Cannon, April 4, 1973, 3, 9; April 11, 1973, 1–4, 13–15; May 10, 1974, 3; Jeanne Morgan, "Journal from James P. Cannon's Office, 1954–56: Notes kept by secretary for personal memento, without Cannon's knowledge," January 24, 1956 (in possession of the author; hereafter Morgan diary); "Cannon Biography: letter dated 14 March 1962," "Biographical Note Material, 18 February 1971," "John T. Amendt interview with Cannon, April 1970," all in Reel 1, JPC Papers; JPC to Carl Cannon, 9 June 1963, Reel 22, JPC Papers. Cannon's warm remembrance of his father's socialist activity, which must have been developed after his

mother's death, is found in John Cannon's obituary: James P. Cannon, "Farewell to a Socialist Pioneer," *The Militant,* June 7, 1947, reprinted in Cannon, *Notebook of an Agitator* (New York: Pathfinder, 1973), 165–67. For Shachtman's views, see "The Reminiscences of Max Shachtman," Number 488, Oral History Research Office, 1963, 321, Columbia University, New York, New York.

13. For Foster's reading, see Barrett, *William Z. Foster,* 15–16.

14. Sam Gordon recollection in Evans, *As We Knew Him,* 79–80, but note that Ring interview, April 4, 1973, 1, indicates that Cannon remembered this conversation quite differently, suggested that it was initiated by Gordon, and expressed a lack of amusement with the Truman-Cannon comparison. Cannon's Kansas contemporary, Earl Browder, was apparently solicited by the Pendergast machine. See James G. Ryan, *Earl Browder: The Failure of American Communism* (Tuscaloosa: University of Alabama Press, 1997), 12. In later years Cannon would on occasion be likened to a "ward heeler" and a "Tammany Hall boss." See Gordon recollection in Evans, *As We Knew Him,* 79; Benjamin Gitlow, *I Confess: The Truth about American Communism* (New York: E.P. Dutton, 1940), 161–62; Constance Ashton Myers, *The Prophet's Army: Trotskyists in America, 1928–1941* (Westport, CT: Greenwood, 1977), 8.

15. On Christian socialism, see John Rae, *Contemporary Socialism* (New York: Scribner's Sons, 1891); Jessie Wallace Hughan, *American Socialism of the Present Day* (New York: John Lane, 1911); Albert T. Mollegen, "The Religious Basis of Western Socialism," in Donald Drew Egbert and Stow Persons, eds., *Socialism and American Life,* vol. 1 (Princeton, NJ: Princeton University Press, 1952), 97–123; Howard H. Quint, *The Forging of American Socialism: Origins of the Modern Movement* (Indianapolis: Bobbs-Merrill, 1964), 103–41; Paul Buhle and John Cort, "Christian Socialism," in *Encyclopedia of the American Left,* ed. Mari Jo Buhle, Paul Buhle, and Dan Georgakas (Urbana: University of Illinois Press, 1992), 131–33.

16. Ring interview with Cannon, May 10, 1973, 2–4; Morgan diary, January 24, 1956; Arthur M. Lewis, *Evolution: Social and Organic* (Chicago: Charles H. Kerr, 1910). Unlike Foster (see Barrett, *William Z. Foster,* 16), Cannon was little influenced by Herbert Spencer, whom Lewis had pilloried in *Evolution.* This suggests a generational divide separating nineteenth-century eclectic radicalism, and perhaps even the libertarian anarchism of Benjamin Tucker, which often drew from the wellspring of Spencer's theories, and twentieth-century socialist and communist thought, which was generally more distanced from Spencer.

17. The most recent full-scale treatment is J. Anthony Lukas, *Big Trouble: A Murder in a Small Western Town Sets Off a Struggle for the Soul of America* (New York: Simon & Schuster, 1997).

18. For the text, see *Debs: His Life, Writings and Speeches, with a Department of Appreciations* (Girard, KS: The Appeal to Reason, 1908), 309–12. For Cannon's attachment, see James P. Cannon, "Eugene V. Debs and the Socialist Movement of His Time," in Cannon, *First Ten Years,* 245–76, and his obituary of Debs, "Eugene V. Debs," *Labor Defender,* December 1926, reprinted in Cannon, *Notebook of an Agitator,* 46, and Ring interview with Cannon, April 11, 1973, 4; April 18, 1973, 5–6.

19. Ring interview with Cannon, April 4, 1973, 10; April 11, 1973, 3–4; April 18, 1973, 1–9.

20. On the Rosedale SP, see Ring interview with Cannon, April 11, 1973, 1. For a wider appreciation, note Ira Kipnis, *The American Socialist Movement: 1897–1912* (New York: Monthly Review Press, 1972); David Shannon, *The Socialist Party of America: A History* (Chicago: Quadrangle, 1967); and James Weinstein, *The Decline of Socialism in America, 1912–1925* (New York: Vintage, 1969), among other studies.

21. Margaret Landis, *The Winding Valley and the Craggy Hillside: A History of Rosedale, Kansas* (Kansas City, KS: Arrowhead Instant Printing, 1976), 29–30.

22. Reba Hansen recollection in Evans, *As We Knew Him,* 234; Ring interview with Cannon, April 11, 1973, 7–13. Cannon's irregular attendance was noted in the high school yearbook with some affection by a student who obviously admired Jim and appreciated the lengths to which he had been forced to go to seek out his education. *Rosedale High School,* vol. 3 (Rosedale, KS, 1910), 74: "But still Mr. Cannon was with us." On Jim's salesman phase, there is no evidence save for a listing in *1910 Kansas City, Kansas Directory,* 489.

23. Ring interview with Cannon, April 4, 1973, 8–12; Reba Hansen recollection in Evans, *As We Knew Him,* 234; Morgan diary, January 27, 1954, 20; February 4, 1954; March 1955; *Rosedale High School,* vol. 3 (Rosedale, KS, 1910), 41, 71–74, 81; *Rosedale High School,* vol. 4 (Rosedale, KS, 1911), 72 (referencing Shylock performance, which Cannon never recalled in any interviews); *Mt. Marty Annual, Rosedale High School,* vol. 5 (Rosedale, KS, 1912), 106 (on the founding of the debating society); "Biographical Note Material," February 18, 1971, Reel 1, JPC Papers.

24. Ring interview with Cannon, April 11, 1973, 5, 7, 12; Reba Hansen recollection in Evans, *As We Knew Him,* 234.

25. Ring interview with Cannon, April 11, 1973, 12.

26. *Rosedale High School,* vol. 3, 72, 81, on Makimson's faculty sponsorships. Melvern, like Rosedale now a dead city, was also first settled in the early 1870s, and was located in Osage County, Kansas. See Mary E. Montgomery, *Lesser Known or Extinct Towns of Kansas,* vol. 12 Mea-My (Topeka, KS: Kansas State Historical Society, no date).

27. Much of this is speculation based on admittedly thin evidence. There is simply very little to go on vis-à-vis Cannon's sexuality: he offered little, and those who interviewed him during his lifetime did not probe. But see Reba Hansen recollection in Evans, *As We Knew Him,* 234–35.

28. Ibid.

29. Ibid. For Wald's accent on this issue of age, see the positions of nuanced difference put forward in a series of three statements, all of which rely solely on the brief, and problematic, statement in Reba Hansen's recollections, and therefore get basic facts of age and age at marriage wrong. *The New York Intellectuals: The Rise and Decline of the Anti-Stalinist Left from the 1930s to the 1980s* (Chapel Hill: University of North Carolina Press, 1987), 168; Wald, "The End of American Trotskyism, Part 2," *Against the Current* (January/February 1995): 35; George Breitman, Paul Le Blanc, and Alan Wald, *Trotskyism in the United States: Historical Essays and Reconsiderations* (Atlantic Highlands, NJ:

Humanities Press, 1996), 256–85, esp. 266. In the more politically poised statement in *Against the Current*, the issue of Cannon's age and marital relations was raised to criticize the tendency to strip Cannon of any human dimension and to present him as a mere "political machine," a tendency Wald apparently saw in *James P. Cannon and the Early Years of American Communism: Selected Writings and Speeches, 1920–1928* (New York: Prometheus Research Library, 1992). Unfortunately, Wald's choice of language in this article, which he dropped in the reprint of the piece in the collection he produced with Breitman and Le Blanc, tended to paint the complications of Cannon's life at this time into a rather unattractive corner, posing the issue thus: "he ran off with his high school teacher who was twice his age."

30. For pictures of Lista Makimson, see *Rosedale High School*, vol. 3, 9, 71.

31. *Mt. Marty Annual, Rosedale High School*, vol. 5 (1912), 134.

32. For Makimson's proper age I rely on Federal Manuscript Census, State of Kansas, Wyandotte County, June 7–8, 1900, 92a–b, which records Lista's age as 17 and year and month of birth, information offered when she was resident with her parents and there was no reason to distort the truth. Later censuses, which first record a mistaken younger age and then state a proper age, include: State Manuscript Census, City of Rosedale, Wyandotte County, Shawnee Township, 1915, vol. 341, sec. 1, 18 (listing both Jim and Lista as 25); and Federal Manuscript Census, State of Kansas, Wyandotte County, January 3, 1920, where Cannon is identified as 29 and Makimson as 36. Lista shared a Kansas City, Missouri, residence with her father Frank; she was employed at the Rosedale High School, he at the Rosedale factory of Arms & Kidder. Living together suggests a level of mutual dependency that might well have contributed to Lista's reluctance to establish a visible and sustained relationship with Jim. See *Forty-first Annual Issue, 1911, Kansas City Directory, including . . . Rosedale, Kansas* (Kansas City, MO: Gate City Directory, 1911), 1063.

33. Arthur M. Lewis, *The Art of Lecturing* (Chicago: Charles H. Kerr, n.d.), quote from 107.

34. Ring interview with Cannon, May 10, 1973, 1–10; Morgan diary, January 20, 1954.

35. Ring interview with Cannon, April 11, 1973, 12.

36. Cannon, "Eugene V. Debs and the Socialist Movement of His Time," in *First Ten Years*, 257–65. In this same essay, Cannon recalls with pride his father's commitment to the revolutionary wing of socialism, associated with Debs: "Debs was an ever-present influence in the home where I was raised. My father was a real Debs man—all the way through. . . . Debs never deviated from the class-struggle line in his own public agitation. . . . He was opposed to middle-class intellectuals and preachers occupying positions of leadership in the party" (pp. 251, 268). Yet, as we have seen, by the time Jim joined the SP in 1908, his father was no longer a manual worker, and his place in the Rosedale SP must have furthered those cross-class processes that an older Cannon would later see as the death knell of the early Socialist Party.

37. There were no socialist educationals or study groups in the Rosedale SP local. Ring interview with Cannon, April 11, 1973, 17.

38. *Rosedale High School*, vol. 4 (1911), 73.

392 . NOTES TO PAGES 52-54

Chapter 3: Hobo Rebel/Homeguard

1. See Cannon, "Farewell to a Socialist Pioneer," *The Militant,* June 7, 1947, reprinted in James P. Cannon, *Notebook of an Agitator* (New York: Pathfinder, 1973), 165.

2. Les Evans, ed., *James P. Cannon As We Knew Him: By Thirty-three Comrades, Friends, and Relatives* (New York: Pathfinder, 1976), 234.

3. A John Cannon was present for at least a part of the founding convention of the Industrial Workers of the World in Chicago in 1905, although he did not vote. See *Proceedings of the First Convention of the Industrial Workers of the World, Founded at Chicago, June 27–July 8, 1905* (New York: New York Labor News, 1905), 611.

4. On Cannon's introduction to the IWW, see Harry Ring interviews with James P. Cannon, April 11, 1973, 11–13, 22; May 10, 1973, 2 (in possession of the author; hereafter Ring interview); "Cannon Biography," from 14 March 1962 letter, in "Biographical Miscellany," Reel 1, James P. Cannon Papers, Microfilm Edition, 1994, State Historical Society of Wisconsin, Madison, Wisconsin (hereafter JPC Papers). A bricklayer, Halcro was probably involved in what would later come to be the Building Construction Workers' Industrial Union No. 330 of the Department of General Construction. See *One Big Union of the I.W.W. (Chart Included)* (Chicago: Industrial Workers of the World, n.d., original 1915?), 14.

5. See various outlines of "The Story of the Renegade," "The Renegade," and "Trails of Glory," all quite incomplete and abbreviated fiction/play manuscripts in Reel 47, JPC Papers. The Industrial Workers of the World Hall was at 211 East Missouri Avenue. See *Forty-first Annual Issue, 1911 Kansas City Directory . . . Classified Business and Miscellaneous Directory* (Kansas City, MO: Gate City Directory, 1911), 2119.

6. Cannon penned a number of table-of-contents-like lists of "Story of the Renegade" (where Dezettel was fictionalized as Don Scott) and "The Story of Max Dezettel," as well as a ten-page beginning entitled "The Renegade" (where the pseudonym for Dezettel was Dan McGlynn). These different versions are all about the same individual, however, and contain the same section headings or chapter titles, as well as similar statements. All are in Reel 47, JPC Papers. On Dezettel, see Theodore Draper, *American Communism and Soviet Russia: The Formative Period* (New York: Viking, 1960), 68, which gets some minor matters of chronology with respect to Dezettel and Cannon wrong; Edward P. Johanningsmeier, *Forging American Communism: The Life of William Z. Foster* (Princeton, NJ: Princeton University Press, 1994), 71, 79, 84; William Z. Foster, *From Bryan to Stalin* (London: Lawrence & Wishart, 1937), 73, 83, 85; and for the Chicago context, Harold Seidman, *Labor Czars: A History of Labor Racketeering* (New York: Liveright, 1938), esp. 26–33. On Dezettel and Spokane, see *Solidarity,* August 3, 1911. For the context of corrupt Chicago labor officialdom, see William Z. Foster, *Misleaders of Labor* (Chicago: Trade Union Educational League, 1927), 163–80; Royal E. Montgomery, *Industrial Relations in the Chicago Building Trades* (Chicago: University of Chicago Press, 1927), esp. 21–41, 209–29. On Fitzpatrick and the progressives, who wrested control of the Chicago Federation of Labor away from "Skinny" Madden a decade before World War I, see David Brody, "John Fitzpatrick," in *Dictionary of American Biography,* Supplement IV, ed. John Garraty (New York: Scribner's,

1974), 279–80; John Keiser, "John Fitzpatrick and Progressive Unionism" (PhD diss., Northwestern University, 1965); Elizabeth McKillen, *Chicago Labor and the Quest for Democratic Diplomacy, 1914–1924* (Ithaca, NY: Cornell University Press, 1995), esp. 46–53; Eugene Staley, *History of the Illinois State Federation of Labor* (Chicago: University of Chicago Press, 1930), 307–542.

7. *Proceedings of the First Convention of the IWW,* 575–76; Elizabeth Gurley Flynn, *The Rebel Girl: An Autobiography—My First Life, 1906–1926* (New York: International, 1973), 77.

8. Many standard sources could be cited, but note the classic early statement, Paul F. Brissenden, *The I.W.W.: A Study of American Syndicalism* (New York: Russell & Russell, 1957), 83–259. For treatment of anarchists at the founding convention of the IWW, see Salvatore Salerno, *Red November, Black November: Culture and Community in the Industrial Workers of the World* (Albany: State University of New York Press, 1989), 69–92; other factions are outlined in Ben H. Williams, "American Labor in the Jungle: Saga of the One Big Union" (unpublished memoir, Archives of Labor History and Urban Affairs, Wayne State University, Detroit, Michigan), a synopsis of which appears in Melvyn Dubofsky, *We Shall Be All: A History of the Industrial Workers of the World* (Chicago: Quadrangle, 1969), 82–83. On Daniel DeLeon, see L. Glen Seretan, *Daniel DeLeon: The Odyssey of an American Marxist* (Cambridge, MA: Harvard University Press, 1979).

9. On IWW syndicalism, see Dubofsky, *We Shall Be All,* 146–70. Certainly Cannon thought that he had simply assimilated a kind of Wobbly "syndicalism." See Ring interview with Cannon, April 11, 1973, 20–21.

10. Andre Tridon, *The New Unionism* (New York: H. B. Huebsch, 1913); David Montgomery, "The 'New Unionism' and the Transformation of Workers' Consciousness in America, 1909–1922," in *Workers' Control in America: Studies in the History of Work, Technology, and Labor Struggles* (Cambridge, UK: Cambridge University Press, 1979), 91–112.

11. See Dubofsky, *We Shall Be All,* 91–170; Fred W. Thompson and Patrick Murfin, eds., *The I.W.W.: Its First Seventy Years, 1905–1975* (Chicago: Industrial Workers of the World, 1976), 23–52; James R. Green, *Grass-Roots Socialism: Radical Movements in the Southwest, 1895–1943* (Baton Rouge: Louisiana State University Press, 1978), 204–13; Joyce Kornbluh, ed., *Rebel Voices: An I.W.W. Anthology* (Ann Arbor: University of Michigan Press, 1968), 1–64.

12. For introductions, see Dubofsky, *We Shall Be All,* 173–97; Kornbluh, *Rebel Voices,* 94–125; Brissenden, *The I.W.W.,* 260–82.

13. Philip S. Foner, ed., *Fellow Workers and Friends: IWW Free-Speech Fights as Told by Participants* (Westport, CT: Greenwood, 1981), 178; "The Fall of Kansas City," *The Agitator* 2, December 1, 1911, 1; James P. Cannon, "The Renegade," 2–3, Reel 47, JPC Papers.

14. John Graham Brooks, *American Syndicalism: The I.W.W.* (New York: Macmillan, 1913), 21, 105. See, as well, Robert Franklin Hoxie, *Trade Unionism in the United States* (New York: Appleton-Century, 1936), 139–76; Samuel P. Orth, *The Armies of Labor* (New Haven: Yale University Press, 1921), 188–209; Kornbluh, *Rebel Voices,* 65–93. Cannon's account of Frank Little, in *Notebook of an Agitator,* 32–36, presents a view of the itinerant organizer as a "tradition of the American revolution."

15. Ring interview with Cannon, April 11, 1973, 17–20; May 5, 1973, 18; James P. Cannon, "The Lives of Two Revolutionaries—Remarks by James P. Cannon at a Banquet in Los Angeles, 15 December 1962," in Cannon, *Speeches for Socialism* (New York: Pathfinder, 1971), 280. On the Sunday Forum, see as well Earl Browder, "'No-Man's Land': A Political Autobiography," unpublished manuscript, 10, 33–34, Earl W. Browder Papers, George Arents Research Library for Special Collections, Syracuse University, Syracuse, New York (hereafter Browder Papers). On DeLeon, see Seretan, *Daniel DeLeon;* James P. Cannon, "The IWW: The Great Anticipation," in Cannon, *The First Ten Years of American Communism—Report of a Participant* (New York: Pathfinder, 1973), 277–310. Note, as well, Justus Ebert, *Trade Unionism in the United States— 1742–1905, Bulwark of Capitalism or Framework of Socialism?* (New York: New York Labor News, n.d., ca. 1905); *American Industrial Evolution—From the Frontier to the Factory, Its Social and Political Effects* (New York: New York Labor News, 1907); and the discussion of DeLeon and the SLP's significance in Joan London, *Jack London and His Times: An Unconventional Biography* (New York: Book League of America, 1939), esp. 113–20; Stanely Frost, *Labor and Revolt* (New York: E.P. Dutton, 1920), 129.

16. The preceding paragraphs draw on Ring interview with Cannon, May 10, 1973, 1–6, 14–15; "Cannon Biography," from a 14 March 1962 letter; Hansen interview with Cannon, "Autobiographical Material," October 5, 1956, 15–16, Reel 1, JPC Papers; "An Old Wobbly's Story by William Chance," interview with James P. Cannon, no date; John T. Amendt interview with James P. Cannon, April 1970, 4–5, all in Reel 1, JPC Papers; "Trails of Glory," Scene 1, Reel 47, JPC Papers; Cannon, "The Lives of Two Revolutionaries," 283–84; *Songs of the Workers: To Fan the Flames of Discontent* (Chicago: Industrial Workers of the World, 1970). On residency and clerk employment, see *Forty-second Annual Issue, 1912, Kansas City Directory, including . . . Rosedale, Kansas* (Kansas City, MO: Gate City Directory, 1912), 324.

17. For a tribute to Leppert, see Frank Dawson, "The Hobo Agitator," *Solidarity,* May 17, 1913. The teaming up of Leppert and Cannon, as something of an apprenticeship, was almost certainly set up by Vincent St. John, possibly with input from Tom Halcro.

18. Ring interviews with Cannon, April 11, 1973, 20–22; April 18, 1973, 10; Hansen interview with Cannon, October 5, 1956, 2. Cannon remembered the IWW local as No. 65, but *Report of the Seventh Annual Convention, Industrial Workers of the World, Chicago, Illinois, September 16–26, 1912,* establishes that Cannon was a delegate from No. 61.

19. See the brief description of the conference in Dubofsky, *We Shall Be All,* 260–61. For Lawrence, see ibid., 227–53; Kornbluh, *Rebel Voices,* 158–96; Ring interview with Cannon, April 18, 1973, 11–14.

20. Ring interviews with Cannon, April 18, 1973, 14–15; April 10, 1973, 10; [Emily Turnbull], "What We Know of James P. Cannon, 1890–1921," Typescript, 1, Prometheus Research Library, New York, New York; James P. Cannon, "The IWW: The Great Anticipation," in Cannon, *First Ten Years,* 290; *Proceedings of the Seventh Annual Convention, Industrial Workers of the World, Chicago, Illinois, September 16–26, 1912,* 17, 28, 31, 34. Cannon would later be a strong advocate of a paid, professional corps of communist

organizers, but he balanced this with an appreciation of never allowing such figures to rise materially above their constituency. Given the Wobbly rank-and-file, he thus endorsed St. John's system of voluntary organizers in the IWW. See James P. Cannon, "In the Spirit of the Pioneers," *Labor Action*, November 28, 1936, reprinted in *Notebook of an Agitator*, 104.

21. James P. Cannon, "Spirit of the Pioneers," reprinted in Cannon, *Notebook of an Agitator*, 104; Cannon, "The IWW: The Great Anticipation," in *First Ten Years*, 291; Evans, *As We Knew Him*, comments of Farrell Dobbs (p. 35) and Art Sharon (p. 87); Ring interview with Cannon, June 13, 1973, 9. See as well Sideny Lens, *The Labor Wars: From the Molly Maguires to the Sitdowns* (New York: Anchor, 1974), 183; John S. Gambs, *The Decline of the I.W.W.* (New York: Columbia University Press, 1932), 91–92; Elizabeth Gurley Flynn, *I Speak My Own Piece: Autobiography of "the Rebel Girl"* (New York: Masses & Mainstream, 1955), 81–84.

22. Ring interviews with Cannon, April 18, 1973, 15–16; June 13, 1973, 9; Hansen interview with Cannon, October 5, 1956, 4, 7. The Jackson strike is an obscure event. On the IWW and early agitation in the Michigan automobile industry, where a 1913 Studebaker strike was perhaps the most significant event, see John S. Klemanski and Alan Di Gaetano, "Wobblies and Auto Workers: The Industrial Workers of the World in Detroit," *Detroit in Perspective* 6 (Spring 1982): 22–39; "Big News," *Masses* 5 (February 1914): 6; Philip S. Foner, *History of the Labor Movement in the United States: The Industrial Workers of the World, 1905–1917*, vol. 4 (New York: International, 1965), 383–90. On Williams, who served a term on the IWW's General Executive Board before taking over its Newcastle paper in 1909, see Dubofsky, *We Shall Be All*, 145–46.

23. Ring interview with Cannon, April 18, 1973, 15–16; Hansen interview with Cannon, October 5, 1956, 4. On Newcastle, see James Weinstein, *The Decline of Socialism in America, 1912–1925* (New York: Vintage, 1969), 43, 116; *Persecution or Solidarity—Shall the Master Class Destroy the Labor Press of Pennsylvania?* (New Castle, PA: Solidarity, 1910); Louis Duchez, "Class War in New Castle," *International Socialist Review* 10 (April 1910): 876–77; Jack B. Gearity, "New Castle Free Press Fight," *International Socialist Review* 12 (August 1911): 97–99; Frank Bohn, "Today's Victory and Tomorrow's Battle," *International Socialist Review* 12 (December 1911): 363–65.

24. Hansen interview with Cannon, October 5, 1956, 4–6; Carolyn Ashbaugh interview with James P. Cannon, March 25, 1974, 3, Reel 2, JPC Papers; Ring interviews with Cannon, April 18, 1973, 16; August 12, 1973, 9–12. The actual title of Goldman's lecture was "Love and the Family." See "Emma Goldman in New Castle," *Solidarity*, November 30, 1912. On Goldman, see Emma Goldman, *Living My Life* (2 vols.) (New York: Knopf, 1931) and, especially on the question of free love, Candace Falk, *Love, Anarchy, and Emma Goldman* (New York: Holt, Rinehart & Winston, 1984).

25. Ring interview with Cannon, May 10, 1973, 12–13, 17; J. P. Cannon, "Seventh Convention, Harmonious Gathering of Young Men Fighting for Industrial Freedom," *Solidarity*, September 28, 1912; J. P. Cannon, "The Seventh I.W.W. Convention," *International Socialist Review* 8 (November 1912): 424; "Cannonballs," *Solidarity*, December 7, 1912. Cannon would later comment, "The IWW itself was predominantly

a young workers movement. It had no special youth organization. And the drive and idealism of youth was a large part of its power and its merit. . . . They had to be young because it was a hard life." Finkel interview with Cannon, March 1974, 6, Reel 2, JPC Papers. Frank Lovell recalled that Cannon always maintained that "[o]nly the young can make a revolution." See Evans, *As We Knew Him*, 140. See also Ralph Chaplin's comments on migratory labor in Chaplin, *Wobbly: The Rough-and-Tumble Story of an American Radical* (Chicago: University of Chicago Press, 1948), 83–93, with the statement: "Youth has a logic all its own, and the I.W.W. was an organization of young men. Sometimes it pays to be out of step with the world. . . . We weren't willing and uncomplaining victims of exploitation—'work oxen,' 'wage plugs,' 'scissorbills.' We were rebels—and proud of it" (p. 89). See also Brissenden, *The I.W.W.*, 298; Brooks, *American Syndicalism*, 92–93.

26. Hansen interview with Cannon, October 5, 1956, 6–7. Quotes from Cannon, "In the Spirit of the Pioneers," in *Notebook of an Agitator*, 104–105. Ring interview with Cannon, June 13, 1973, 10, stressed the spontaneous character of the making of a contingent of migratory soapboxers.

27. For a broad-ranging discussion, see David Montgomery, *The Fall of the House of Labor: The Workplace, the State, and American Labor Activism, 1865–1925* (Cambridge, UK: Cambridge University Press, 1987), 112–70.

28. See, for instance, P. Schidrowitz and T. R. Dawson, eds., *History of the Rubber Industry* (Cambridge: W. Heffer & Sons, 1952).

29. For introductions, see Harold S. Roberts, *The Rubber Workers: Labor Organization and Collective Bargaining in the Rubber Industry* (New York: Harper & Brothers, 1944), 1–37; Leslie H. Marcy, "800 Per Cent and the Akron Strike," *International Socialist Review* 10 (April 1913): 711–24; Frederick M. Davenport, "Treating Men White in Akron Town," *Outlook* 126 (November 3, 1920): 407–11; Bryan D. Palmer, *Capitalism Comes to the Backcountry: The Goodyear Invasion of Napanee* (Toronto: Between the Lines, 1994), 19–29.

30. Marcy, "800 Per Cent and the Akron Strike"; "Rubber Workers Rebel," *International Socialist Review* 13 (March 1913): 654; "Rubber Workers: Show Symptoms of Revolt in the Biggest Center of the Rubber Goods Industry, Akron, Ohio," *Solidarity*, June 15, 1912; "Akron Preacher Tells of Conditions," *Solidarity*, February 22, 1913; Dubofsky, *We Shall Be All*, 286; Archie Green, *Wobblies, Pile Butts, and Other Heroes: Laborlore Explorations* (Urbana: University of Illinois Press, 1993), 151. The brief strike of 1912 is mentioned in Walter Knox, "To Akron Workers," *Solidarity*, February 8, 1913.

31. "Akron Rubber Workers," *Solidarity*, August 17, 1912; *Solidarity*, September 14, 1912.

32. Thompson and Murfin, *The I.W.W.*, 71.

33. "To Akron Workers," *Solidarity*, February 8, 1913; "20,000 Rubber Workers Revolt in Akron! IWW in Full Control," "How the Revolt Started," and "The Big Revolt," all in *Solidarity*, February 22, 1913; and various articles in the *Akron Beacon Journal*, February 12–14, 1913. Standard accounts of the strike include Foner, *History of the Labor Movement*, vol. 4, 373–83; Roberts, "Storm Over Akron: The 1913 Strike," in *Rubber Workers*, 38–78; Roy Wortman, "The IWW and the Akron Rubber Strike of 1913," in *At the Point*

of Production, ed. Joseph R. Conlin (Westport, CT: Greenwood, 1981), 49–60; Wortman, *From Syndicalism to Trade Unionism* (New York: Garland, 1985), 19–46. On the Preveys, a critical Socialist Party support in the strike, see Nick Salvatore, *Eugene Debs: Citizen and Socialist* (Urbana: University of Illinois Press, 1982), 255, 291, 294, 319, 321, 322, 327.

34. Thompson and Murfin, *The I.W.W.,* 6, 25–27, 43–45, 74; Dubofsky, *We Shall Be All,* 106–13, 237; "Govannitti [sic] Arrives to Lead the Strike," *Akron Beacon Journal,* February 15, 1913; Cary Nelson, *Repression and Recovery: Modern American Poetry and the Politics of Cultural Memory, 1910–1945* (Madison: University of Wisconsin Press, 1989), 62–66; Kornbluh, *Rebel Voices,* 184–95; William D. Haywood, *Bill Haywood's Book: The Autobiography of Big Bill Haywood* (New York: International, 1929, reprint 1969), 264–66; "Haywood Speaks in the Park," *Akron Beacon Journal,* March 5, 1913; "Haywood Tells Strikers the Fight Is Won, Attacks Senate Probe," *Akron Beacon Journal,* March 6, 1913; "Haywood Is Asked to Return," *Akron Beacon Journal,* March 10, 1913; "Haywood to the Rubber Strikers," *Solidarity,* March 15, 1913; Salerno, *Red November, Black November,* 26.

35. Frank Dawson, "The Akron 'Fiasco,'" *Solidarity,* April 26, 1913; Alfred Winslow Jones, *Life, Liberty and Property: A Story of Conflict and a Measurement of Conflicting Rights* (New York: Octagon Books, 1964), 76–77.

36. "Serious Charge Against Couple: Both Wore Long Badges of Red Ribbon When in Court," *Akron Beacon Herald,* February 21, 1913; "Many Rubber Workers Take Advantage of Strike to Embark in Matrimony," *Akron Beacon Herald,* February 28, 1913.

37. Dawson, "Hobo Agitator." Reference to the commissary appears in "Rubber Workers Repudiate Fiery Organizers of the IWW Movement," *Akron Beacon Journal,* February 28, 1913; "Haywood Is Announced," *Akron Beacon Journal,* March 4, 1913.

38. "Youngstown Editor Is Arrested During Picketing of Goodrich Company," *Akron Beacon Journal,* February 26, 1913; "Midney Fined," *Akron Beacon Journal,* February 27, 1913; "Midney Calls Himself a Martyr; Bessemer Attacks Judge Vaughn," *Akron Beacon Journal,* February 27, 1913; "Midney's Fine Is Paid by Bessemer," *Akron Beacon Journal,* March 6, 1913; Hansen interview with Cannon, October 5, 1956, 7.

39. "Pollack Is Out of Strike Ranks. He Says He Resigned; Strikers Say They Kicked Him Out," *Akron Beacon Journal,* March 5, 1913; Green, *Wobblies, Pile Butts, and Other Heroes,* 151; Haywood, *Bill Haywood's Book,* 266; Thompson and Murfin, *The I.W.W.,* 71–74; James W. Reed, Affidavit in "Spies Control I.W.W. in Akron," *Solidarity,* January 17, 1914; "No Defense Offered by Akron Spies," *Solidarity,* January 24, 1914. On the strained relations of Wobblies and AFL officials, and conservative unionism's critique of the IWW strike, see articles in *Akron Beacon Journal,* February 17, 19, and 20 and March 1, 14, 15, and 24, 1913.

40. See numerous articles in *Akron Beacon Journal,* February 24—March 31, 1913; John A. Fitch, "The IWW: An Outlaw Organization," *Survey* 30 (June 7, 1913): 357; Vincent St. Stephens (Secretary, Chamber of Commerce), "Communication: The IWW in Akron," *Survey* 30 (August 9, 1913): 613–14; Haywood, *Bill Haywood's Book,* 265; Selig Perlman and Philip Taft, *History of Labor in the United States, 1896–1932,* vol. 4 (New

York: Macmillan, 1935), 277–78; "Scene at Akron by a Travelling Man," *Solidarity,* March 22, 1913; Dawson, "The Akron 'Fiasco.'"

41. See "First Serious Disorders of Rubber Strike," *Akron Beacon Journal,* March 8, 1913; Roberts, *Rubber Workers,* 62–63.

42. See *Akron Beacon Journal,* February 24—March 31, 1913. Orth, *Armies of Labor,* 207, stresses that the theatrics of the strike leaders and acts of violence alienated "the public." For more on the role of the state, arbitration, and William Green, see J. E. Good, "How Akron Was Vindicated," *Leslie's Illustrated Weekly,* May 22, 1913, 558; James Boyle, *The Minimum Wage and Syndicalism: An Independent Survey of the Two Latest Movements Affecting American Labor* (Cincinnati: Stewart & Kidd, 1913), 127–30; Bruce Minton and John Stuart, "William Green of Coshocton, O.," *New Masses,* May 18, 1937, 4.

43. Hansen interview with Cannon, October 5, 1956, 7–8; Evans, *As We Knew Him,* 235 (Reba Hansen recollection); Ring interviews with Cannon, April 18, 1973, 16; May 10, 1973, 10–11. See, as well, Joseph Robert Conlin, *Bread and Roses Too: Studies of the Wobblies* (Westport, CT: Greenwood, 1969), 5–6; Stewart Bird, Dan Georgakas, and Deborah Shaffer, *Solidarity Forever: An Oral History of the IWW* (Chicago: Lake View Press, 1985), 88–89.

44. The first substantial *Solidarity* report on the Akron struggle was sent by George Swasey, "20,000 Rubber Workers Revolt in Akron!" *Solidarity,* February 22, 1913, and Cannon would later co-author articles with this experienced agitator. Cannon's first *Solidarity* report was "Rubber Workers Ranks Unbroken: Big Akron Factories Tied Up and Speedy Victory Is Expected," *Solidarity,* March 1, 1913.

45. See, among the signed statements: Cannon, "20,000 Workers Strike in Akron," *Industrial Worker,* February 27, 1913; Cannon and Swasey, "Rubber Workers on the Firing Line," *Industrial Worker,* March 6, 1913; Cannon, "A Test of Strength," *Solidarity,* March 8, 1913. Among the unsigned statements that Cannon could perhaps have had a hand in drafting are: "Violence in Akron," *Solidarity,* March 15, 1913; "Sixth Week of Strike," *Solidarity,* March 22, 1913; "Haywood Returns to Akron, Ohio," *Solidarity,* March 22, 1913; "Akron Strike," *Solidarity,* March 29, 1913; "Akron Strikers Are Still Out," *Industrial Worker,* March 13, 1913; "Police Start Violence in Akron Strike," *Industrial Worker,* March 20, 1913; "The Battle at Akron Must Be Won!" *Industrial Worker,* March 27, 1913; "The Akron Strike," *Industrial Worker,* April 3, 1913. Besides the IWW press, Cannon also apparently wrote for the socialist *New York Call.* See Ring interview with Cannon, May 10, 1973, 12–13; *New York Call,* April 19, 1913, cited in Perlman and Taft, *History of Labor,* 277–78.

46. "A Test of Strength," *Solidarity,* March 8, 1913.

47. For a brief biography of Prevey—Canadian-born and of rural background, an optician by profession, and a personal friend of Debs, see *Ohio Socialist,* November 19, 1919. Prevey is described as "Joan of Arc" in "First Serious Disorders of Rubber Strike," *Akron Beacon Journal,* March 8, 1913.

48. Cannon's quote of Haywood's speech is from John T. Amendt interview with James P. Cannon, April 1970, in Reel 1, JPC Papers. Cannon's speaking activities are noted in "Pollack Is Out of Strike Ranks," *Akron Beacon Journal,* March 5, 1913; "Senate

Strike Probers Busy in Columbus," *Akron Beacon Journal*, March 7, 1913. Compare this to Haywood, *Bill Haywood's Book*, 265; "Haywood to the Rubber Workers," *Solidarity*, March 15, 1913; Ring interview with Cannon, April 18, 1973, 16–17; Hansen interview with Cannon, October 5, 1956, 10; "Haywood Returns to Akron, Ohio," and "Scene at Akron, Ohio, by a Travelling Man," *Solidarity*, March 22, 1913; and articles in *Akron Beacon Journal*, March 13–15, 1913. Cannon comments on Haywood's oratory and the Reindeer Hall speech in his obituary of Haywood, originally printed in the *Daily Worker*, May 22, 1928, reprinted in Cannon, *Notebook of an Agitator*, 61, where the recollection is accurate save for the highly exaggerated estimate of the crowd accompanying Haywood to the hall as numbering 10,000. See as well Cannon, "W. D. Haywood: A Pioneer of Revolutionary Unionism," *Labor Unity*, June 1928, 13–14.

49. Cannon, *First Ten Years*, 260; "Comrades Who Will Control the City Government of St. Mary's, Ohio, for the Next Two Years," *International Socialist Review* 12 (December 1911): 376–77; Frank Dawson, "St. Mary's Fighting Mayor," *International Socialist Review* 13 (June 1913): 874–76; "Strike May Be Called Off Sunday," *Akron Beacon Journal*, March 29, 1913; "Akron Girls in Newcastle," *Solidarity*, March 15, 1913; *Industrial Worker*, April 17, 1913.

50. Cannon, "Rubber Workers Ranks Unbroken," *Solidarity*, March 1, 1913.

51. On Paterson, see Steve Golin, *The Fragile Bridge: Paterson Silk Strike, 1913* (Philadelphia: Temple University Press, 1988); Martin Green, *New York, 1913: The Armory Show and the Paterson Strike Pageant* (New York: Collier, 1988); Linda Nochlin, "The Paterson Strike Pageant of 1913," *Art in America* 52 (May–June 1974): 67–68; Kornbluh, *Rebel Voices*, 197–226; Steven Watson, *Strange Bedfellows: The First Avant-Garde* (New York: Abbeville Press, 1991), 166–87, 401–2, 410; Dubofsky, *We Shall Be All*, 263–90.

52. On saloon closings, see "Saloons May Now Reopen," *Akron Beacon Journal*, March 3, 1913. On prayer, see "Opening Prayer of the Meetings," *Akron Beacon Journal*, February 24, 1913, and more generally, Donald E. Winters, Jr., *The Soul of the Wobblies: The IWW, Religion, and American Culture in the Progressive Era, 1905–1917* (Westport, CT: Greenwood, 1985).

53. For the view of the strike as a disastrous defeat, see Dubofsky, *We Shall Be All*, 286–87, whose conclusion that, "Such was the splendor of this Akron rubber workers' local that within the IWW it was never heard from again," is overstated. For future reference to Akron's IWW LU 470, see "A Message from 470, Akron, Ohio," *Solidarity*, July 12, 1913; "No Defense Offered by Akron Spies," *Solidarity*, January 24, 1914; "Suggestions to Akron Workers," *Solidarity*, November 8, 1913; Thompson and Murfin, *The I.W.W.*, 73–74, while admitting the failures of the strike, are more generous in their final assessment. Note, as well, "Akron Strike Not a Failure," *Industrial Worker*, April 24, 1913; "Rubber Slavery at Akron," *Industrial Pioneer* 3 (August 1925): 3–5, 44.

54. "Rubber Strike Is Called Off: Organizers Speed and White Urge Workers to Practice Sabotage," *Akron Beacon Journal*, March 31, 1913.

55. The unsigned Dawson article can be attributed to him because of its consistency of style and information with the two signed statements. See "The Battle at Akron

Must Be Won!" *Industrial Worker,* March 27, 1913; Frank Dawson, "Akron Rubber Barons Are Weakening," *Industrial Worker,* April 3, 1913; Frank Dawson, "The Akron 'Fiasco,'" *Solidarity,* April 26, 1913. Publication of the latter article, which was written at the very end of March when the strike was declared over, was delayed for three weeks. For telegrams dated March 31, declaring the strike over, see *Industrial Worker,* April 10, 1913.

56. James P. Cannon, "C.E. Ruthenberg," from *Labor Defender,* April 1927, reprinted in Cannon, *Notebook of an Agitator,* 49.

57. Flynn's perspective is outlined in "The Truth About the Paterson Strike," in Kornbluh, *Rebel Voices,* 214–26. Just after Cannon's departure from Cleveland, Rose Charvat attempted to organize a Housemaids Union and Rose Pastor Stokes lectured on socialism. See William Ganson Rose, *Cleveland: The Making of a City* (Cleveland: World Publishing, 1950), 716–17.

58. The preceding paragraph draws upon Hansen interview with Cannon, October 5, 1956, 8–9; Ring interview with Cannon, April 4, 1973, 7. For a discussion of hoboes, see Frank Tobias Higbie, *Indispensable Outcasts: Hobo Workers and Community in the American Midwest, 1880–1930* (Urbana: University of Illinois Press, 2003). Note, as well, the discussion of hoboes gleaned from the life of anarchist Anton Johansen in Hutchins Hapgood, *The Spirit of Labor* (New York: Dutton, 1907), esp. 9–166.

59. Hansen interview with Cannon, October 5, 1956, 11; "Strike at Rock Island," *Solidarity,* May 1, 1913.

60. Bessie Morgan, "Rebels Wanted in Peoria," *Industrial Worker,* April 17, 1913; James P. Cannon, "More Rebels Needed in Peoria," *Solidarity,* May 31, 1913; Editorial, "Peoria and San Diego," *Solidarity,* June 14, 1913. The comment on the sexual politics of the Peoria IWW is found in Ring interview with Cannon, April 4, 1973, 7; and more obliquely in Hansen interview with Cannon, October 5, 1956, 11. It is possible that the Bessie Morgan who filed the first call for rebels was one of the women St. John wanted removed from authority in the Peoria IWW local. Cannon claimed that the issue was not a "moral one," that the organization did not care what went on outside of IWW circles, but that when a local's capacity to function well was undermined by matters of a sexual sort, it was time to restore a more stable regime.

61. Ring interview with Cannon, April 4, 1973, 7; Hanson interview with Cannon, October 5, 1956, 12; Thompson and Murfin, *The I.W.W.,* 64–65; Cannon, "More Rebels Needed in Peoria," *Solidarity,* May 31, 1913; Cannon, "Peoria's Folly," *Solidarity,* June 7, 1913; Rudolf Pfeiffer, "Jail Peoria Reds for "Conspiracy,'" *Industrial Worker,* May 29, 1913; and various articles in *Peoria Evening Star,* May 23–June 4, 1913.

62. Cannon, "More Rebels Needed in Peoria," *Solidarity,* May 31, 1913; Ring interview with Cannon, October 10, 1973, 7; Hansen interview with Cannon, October 5, 1956, 12; Cannon, "Peoria's Folly," *Solidarity,* June 7, 1913; Cannon, "Hell Popping in Peoria," *Industrial Worker,* June 5, 1913; "Rebels Are Rambling from Jungle to Jail," *Industrial Worker,* June 5, 1913; "One Hundred Men Ready to Hand Peoria a Jolt," *Industrial Worker,* June 12, 1913; "Catching 'Em Coming and Going," *Solidarity,* June 28, 1913. Also note various articles in *Peoria Evening Star* and *Peoria Journal,* May 24–30, 1913.

63. Cannon, "More Rebels Needed in Peoria," *Solidarity,* May 31, 1913; Cannon, "Peoria's Folly," *Solidarity,* June 7, 1913; "More IWW Men Coming—Agitators in This City

Have Summoned Help from Denver—Trial of Second Man Slow," *Peoria Evening Star,* May 23, 1913; Cannon, "Frank Little," in *Notebook of an Agitator,* 35; Hansen interview with Cannon, October 5, 1956, 12–13; Ring interview with Cannon, October 10, 1973, 7; Farrell Dobbs in Evans, *As We Knew Him,* 36–37. For more on Little, see Dubofsky, *We Shall Be All,* 186–87, 391–92; Arturo Giovannitti, "When the Cock Crows—to the Memory of Frank Little, Hanged at Midnight," *Masses* 9 (October 1917): 18–20; and the "Frank Little Memorial Number," *Labor Defender,* August 1926, which contained Cannon's original "Frank Little" statement.

64. See especially "'Can' Members of the IWW—Ordered to Leave City—Couldn't Wish Rudolph Pfeiffer on Them," *Peoria Evening Star,* June 12, 1913; "Fight for Freedom in Peoria," *Industrial Worker,* June 12, 1913; John Arscott, "Peoria Fight for Free Speech Is Postponed Until This Fall," *Industrial Worker,* July 10, 1913; "Another San Diego," and "Peoria and San Diego," *Solidarity,* June 14, 1913; Frank Little telegram in *Industrial Worker,* June 19, 1913; "Catching 'Em Coming and Going," June 28, 1913; Hansen interview with Cannon, October 5, 1956, 13–14; "Nine More Arrests Made: Sheriff Minor and Chief Rhoades Summarily Break up Incendiary Street Meeting," *Peoria Evening Star,* May 31, 1913; "IWW Prisoners Go on New Strike," *Peoria Journal,* June 3, 1913. Fred Moore, the lawyer sent to Peoria by St. John, would later defend the IWW figures arrested in 1918. See Dubofsky, *We Shall Be All,* 383, 427; Harrison George, *The IWW Trial: Story of the Greatest Trial in Labor's History by One of the Defendants* (Chicago: IWW, n.d., Arno reprint, 1969). For a later assessment of the Peoria debacle, see A Sympathizer, "Continue the Fight at Home," *Solidarity,* September 6, 1913.

65. Hansen interview with Cannon, October 5, 1956, 14; Ring interview with Cannon, June 13, 1973, 8; "IWW Organizers," *Solidarity,* September 6, 1913; John Panzer, "The Spokane Free Speech Fight," Jack Whyte, "His Honor Gets His," and E. F. Doree, "Gathering the Grain," in Kornbluh, *Rebel Voices,* 98–100, 104–5, 243–47; Dubofsky, *We Shall Be All,* 216–17.

66. Reba Hansen in Evans, *As We Knew Him,* 234–35.

67. Ibid., 235; Hansen interview with Cannon, October 5, 1956, 13; "Certificate of Marriage, Cannon/Makimson," June 5, 1913, Pekin, Tazewell Country, Illinois.

68. For background on this immigrant workforce, see Leroy Hodges, "Immigrant Life in the Ore Region of Northern Minnesota," *Survey* 27 (September 7, 1912): 703–9.

69. For background, see numerous articles in *Duluth Herald* and *Duluth News Tribune,* August 1–7, 1913.

70. The preceding two paragraphs draw on Bird, Georgakas, and Shaffer, *Solidarity Forever,* 177. Thompson and Murfin, *The I.W.W.,* 77–78, state that Cannon and Laukki preceded Little in organizing the Duluth-Superior strikers, but this is contradicted by Cannon's recollection (Ring interview with Cannon, October 5, 1913, 12), which states that he was notified of the strike after it broke out, and travelled to Duluth from Minneapolis, and by Frank Little, "Rebels Wanted in Duluth," *Solidarity,* August 9, 1913, a dispatch dated Duluth, 29 July. On Laukki, see Michael G. Karni, "Finnish Immigrant Leftists in America: The Golden Years, 1900–1918," and David Montgomery, "Nationalism, American Patriotism, and Class Consciousness among Immigrant Workers in the United States in the Epoch of World War I," in *"Struggle a Hard Battle": Essays on*

Working-Class Immigrants, ed. Dirk Hoerder (Dekalb: Northern Illinois University Press, 1986), 214–22 and 342–43; George, *The IWW Trial,* 154–55. There is some comment on the later history of what is referred to as Duluth's "People's College" in John S. Gambs, *The Decline of the I.W.W.* (New York: Columbia University Press, 1932), 163–64. The Mesabi Range would later be the site of an important 1916 Wobbly agitation. See Dubofsky, *We Shall Be All,* 319–31.

71. The preceding paragraphs draw upon *Duluth Herald* and *Duluth News Tribune,* August 7–11, 1913; James P. Cannon, "Kidnapped Organizer Rescued by Strikers," *Solidarity,* August 16, 1913; Cannon/Doree, "Telegram," *Industrial Worker,* August 14, 1914.

72. Cannon, "Frank Little," in *Notebook of an Agitator,* 34.

73. On the Eighth Annual 1913 Convention, undoubtedly a low point in IWW rancors, and the centralizer-decentralizer battle, see Dubofsky, *We Shall Be All,* 287–90; Chaplin, *Wobbly,* 137–38, which identifies the convention as having taken place in September, which was the norm; and the exceedingly hostile account in Robert Franklin Hoxie, *Trade Unionism in the United States* (New York: D. Appleton, 1924), 139–76, esp. for quotes on procedures, 143, 149.

74. Farrell Dobbs in Evans, *As We Knew Him,* 35–36.

75. Cannon would later, in 1959, frame his remembrance of the IWW in terms of the unfavorable context in which all class conflict developed. Of the Duluth-Superior strike he commented: "There we ran up against company thugs dressed up in police uniforms who sometimes outnumbered the pickets. . . . This was a common experience of the IWW and socialist attempts to organize in the steel industry or anyplace else. The most you could do was conduct a guerrilla attack at a single locality. The idea of a general strike, which was our ideal and our program, was far from realization." James P. Cannon, "Sixty Years of American Radicalism," speech delivered to a meeting of the West Coast Vacation School and Camp, Labor Day, 1959, reprinted in Cannon, *Speeches for Socialism* (New York: Pathfinder, 1971), 89.

76. Thompson and Murfin, *The I.W.W.,* 77–78; Frank Little, "Duluth Strike Still On," *Solidarity,* August 30, 1913, from dispatch dated 18 August 1913; *Duluth Herald* and *Duluth News Tribune,* August 11–18, 1913.

77. W. Morgan Perl, ed., *History of Wyandotte County Kansas and Its People,* vol. 1 (Chicago: Lewis Publishing, 1911), 389, notes that women teachers in the high school averaged an annual salary of $68. *Forty-third Annual Issue, 1913, Kansas City, Missouri, City Directory* (Kansas City, MO: Gate City Directory, 1913), lists a Lista Makimson residing at 1022 Garfield Avenue, Kansas City, Missouri, employed as a welfare investigator.

78. Max Dezettel, "Lockout in Kansas City," *Syndicalist* 3 (August 1–15, 1913), 52; Oscar Erickson, "Free Speech Fight in Kansas City," and Earl R. Browder, "The Relation of Economic Power to Free Speech," *The Toiler* 1/2 (October 1913). This latter newspaper, edited by Dezettel, indicated that the Kansas City Free Speech League had a room in the Schutte Building, 1209 Grand Avenue. On Person and the epic shop crafts battle, see Carl E. Person, *The Lizard's Trail: A Story from the Illinois Central and Harriman Lines Strike of 1911 to 1915 Inclusive* (Chicago: Lake Publishing, 1918); Carl Person, "In the County Jail," *The Toiler* 2/2 (February 1914); Otto Cook, "Carl Person," *The Toiler* 2/3 (March 1914).

79. For representative articles in *The Toiler*, see Earl R. Browder, "How Can I Bring About the General Strike," 2/1 (January 1914); Browder, "Why Should the Toilers Capture the State," 2/3 (March 1914). On residence, see *Forty-fourth Annual Issue, 1914, Kansas City, Missouri, City Directory* (Kansas City, MO: Gate City Directory, 1914), 452; and Manuscript Census, State of Kansas, Schedule 1, Rosedale, 1915, vol. 341, sec. 1, 18.

80. Cannon, *First Ten Years*, 98–100, 109–10; Draper, *American Communism and Soviet Russia*, 68; James G. Ryan, *Earl Browder: The Failure of American Communism* (Tuscaloosa: University of Alabama Press, 1997), 12.

81. On the Wheatland riot, see Dubofsky, *We Shall Be All*, 294–300; Carleton H. Parker, *The Casual Laborer and Other Essays* (New York: Harcourt, Brace & Howe, 1920); Gregory R. Woirol, *In the Floating Army: F.C. Mills on Itinerant Life in California, 1914* (Urbana: University of Illinois Press, 1992). The arrested Wheatland "leaders" were "Blackie" Ford and Herman D. Suhr. It is possible that Max Dezettel headed a Kansas City support campaign in their interests. See Cannon, outline of "The Story of the Renegade," Reel 47, JPC Papers.

82. Cannon, "Free Speech Fight in Kansas City," *International Socialist Review* 14 (February 1914): 510. Foner, *Fellow Workers and Friends*, 178–82, contains two significant letters describing jail terms, but its brief account of the struggle reproduces some misinformation, especially material taken at face value from the daily press. Brief overview appears in Foner, *History of the Labor Movement*, vol. 4, 209–10. For a more thorough, Wobbly-oriented account, see: "The I.W.W. and the Police," *Solidarity*, December 27, 1913; "The Kansas City Fight," *Solidarity*, January 3, 1914; "Free Speech and Police Brutality in Kansas City," *Solidarity*, January 10, 1914; "I.W.W. Gaining Favor in K.C.," *Solidarity*, January 31, 1914; "Fight in Kansas City at Critical Stage," *Solidarity*, February 21, 1914; "Kansas City Tries to Deport I.W.W. Men," *Solidarity*, February 28, 1914; "K.C. Rebels are Standing Firm," *Solidarity*, March 7, 1914; "Carolyn Lowe Leads Free Speech Fight," *Workers Chronicle* 4 (January 23, 1914): 5; "Fight to the Death in Kansas City! Free Speech at All Costs," *Voice of the People* 3 (February 26, 1914): 2.

83. See Dubofsky, *We Shall Be All*, esp. 196–97; Foner, *History of the Labor Movement*, vol. 4, 210–13.

84. Cannon, "Free Speech Fight in Kansas City," 510; "Free Speech and Police Brutality in Kansas City," *Solidarity*, January 10, 1914.

85. Kornbluh, *Rebel Voices*, 407; Nels Anderson, *The Hobo: The Sociology of the Homeless Man* (Chicago: University of Chicago Press, 1923), 96–97, 100–101; John S. Gambs, *Decline of the I.W.W.*, 112–13; Cannon, "Trails of Glory," scene II, 5–6, Reel 46, JPC Papers; Ring interview with Cannon, July 13, 1973, 11. Note, as well, Hapgood, *Spirit of Labor*, 54–118, 348–49, outlining the "settling down" of the hobo anarchist, Anton Johannsen.

86. Carl Cannon was listed as five years old in the Fourteenth Federal Census of the United States, State of Kansas, County of Wyandotte, Rosedale, the enumerator taking the data on January 3, 1920. Cannon's recollection of singing to his son is in Ring interview with Cannon, May 10, 1973, 4–5; the same source, at 5–6, mentions his Joe Hill memorial speech. Hill's Utah conviction for murder and subsequent execution were

covered in some detail in the *Kansas City Star,* November 19–25, 1915. Cannon's appreciation of song, with comment on his voice, is also noted in Jeanne Morgan, "Journal from James P. Cannon's Office, 1954–56: Notes kept by secretary for personal memento, without Cannon's knowledge," April 10, 1955 (in possession of the author). One hostile commentator noted of Cannon: "In the I.W.W. he had gained a reputation for his languid laziness and his aptness in singing and reciting hobo and I.W.W. ditties." See Benjamin Gitlow, *I Confess: The Truth about American Communism* (New York: E.P. Dutton, 1940), 161. For Kansas City campaigns, see Carolyn Ashbaugh interview with James P. Cannon, June 25, 1974, Reel 2, JPC Papers; "K.C. Forward," *Solidarity,* May 16, 1914; "Local 61 Proposes Amendments," *Solidarity,* September 12, 1914; "The Ninth I.W.W. Convention," *Solidarity,* October 3, 1914; "Thanksgiving Spread in K.C.," and "K.C. Has Big Time," *Solidarity,* December 5, 1914; "Big Doin's in K.C.," *Solidarity,* November 13, 1915; Cannon, *First Ten Years,* 98–100; 108–10; Ring interview with Cannon, August 15, 1973, 9–10; Browder, "'No-Man's Land,'" 33–34, Box 10, Browder Papers; William Z. Foster, *Pages from a Worker's Life* (New York: International, 1939), 148–51.

87. Ring interview with Cannon, May 30, 1973, 1–7. For an account of the Cannon family's difficulties in Rosedale during World War I, an admittedly exaggerated source is Joe Hansen, "How the Trotskyists Went to Jail: Rosedale and World War I," *Fourth International* 5 (February 1944): 44. It is impossible to separate out Cannon's recollections of this period from Hansen's hyperbole, but whatever the embellishment the period certainly registered with Cannon as one of popular hostility to "war resisters." Indications of how an ugly patriotism was directed against the IWW in Kansas City are found in "Patriotism in the Middle West," *Masses* 9 (June 1917): 19–21. On conscientious objection and World War I, which Cannon would later come to see as a wrong approach to opposing capitalist war, see Norman Thomas, *The Conscientious Objector in America* (New York: B. W. Huebsch, 1923).

88. On the repression of 1914–1919, see Max Lowenthal, *The Federal Bureau of Investigation* (London: Turnstill Press, 1951), 93–102; Dubofsky, *We Shall Be All,* 349–444, and p. 143, which outlines St. John's 1914–1915 departure from the IWW; Ring interview with Cannon, May 30, 1973, 3–6; Clayton R. Koppes, "The Industrial Workers of the World and County-Jail Reform in Kansas, 1915–1920," *Kansas Historical Quarterly* 41 (Spring 1975): 63–86. The turn to agricultural workers is evident in Kornbluh, *Rebel Voices,* 227–50; Henry E. McGuckin, *Memoirs of a Wobbly* (Chicago: Charles H. Kerr, 1987), 69–87; Cannon's quote appears in James P. Cannon, "The I.W.W.—The Great Anticipation," in Cannon, *First Ten Years,* 293–96.

89. Ring interviews with Cannon, April 12, 1973, 5; May 30, 1973, 11.

90. Theodore Draper, *The Roots of American Communism* (New York: Viking, 1957), 306. Solon De Leon, ed., *The American Labor Who's Who* (New York: Hanford Press, 1925), 36, refers to Cannon's education at the Kansas City Law College. See also Bernard K. Johnpoll and Harvey Klehr, eds., *Biographical Dictionary of the American Left* (Westport, CT: Greenwood, 1986); "The Reminiscences of Max Shachtman," Number 488, Oral History Research Office, 1963, 322, Columbia University, New York, New York.

91. Ring interview with Cannon, September 12, 1973, 17–18. Cannon had seen Emma Goldman in Newcastle, but she also spoke in Kansas City in 1915, as did Alexander Berkman, and Cannon recalled seeing both of them. See Carolyn Ashbaugh interview with James P. Cannon, March 25, 1974, 8, Reel 2, JPC Papers.

92. Mari Jo Buhle, *Women and American Socialism, 1870–1920* (Urbana: University of Illinois Press, 1983), 162–65.

93. Note the comments on Lenin in Joan Sangster, *Dreams of Equality: Women on the Canadian Left, 1920–1950* (Toronto: McClelland & Stewart, 1990), 18.

94. Reba Hansen in Evans, *As We Knew Him,* 234–35.

95. Women, too, even the most radical, were wrapped up in similiar contradictions, as is evident in Emma Goldman's complex relations with Alexander Berkman and Ben Reitman. See her account of this in *Living My Life.* Relevant comment appears in Hapgood, *Spirit of Labor,* a source in which much is made of "radical manhood." One anarchist woman noted that she wanted "to be a beautiful woman, merely to be able to make men unhappy, for in that way only can men amount to anything!" (p. 330).

96. Consider, for instance, Francis Shor, "Masculine Power and Virile Syndicalism: A Gendered Analysis of the IWW in Australia," *Labour History* 63 (1992): 83–99; Colleen O'Neill, "Domesticity Deployed: Gender, Race, and the Construction of Class Struggle in the Bisbee Deportation," *Labor History* 34 (1993): 256–73.

97. For suggestive readings in this highly problematic area, see two essays by Todd McCallum: "'Not a Sex Question'? The One Big Union and the Politics of Radical Manhood," *Labour/Le Travail* 42 (Fall 1998): 15–54; "The Strange Tale of Tom Cassidy and Catherine Rose, or Free Love, Homosexuality, and the One Big Union," *Journal of the Canadian Historical Association* 9 (1998): 125–54. "The I.W.W. and the Police—Why We Go to Jail," *Solidarity,* December 27, 1913.

98. The preceding paragraphs draw on the 10-page, incomplete typescript by Cannon, "The Renegade," in Reel 47, JPC Papers. Note the comments in Hapgood, *Spirit of Labor,* 365, where a packinghouse organizer denounces "hen-pecked husbands," claiming that union wives are often in the same camp as superintendents and scabs: "We are between the devil and the deep blue sea, and the woman is the devil."

99. But see, as examples of what could pass for comment on women and politics in the radical movement, R. B. Tobias and Mary E. Marcy, *Women as Sex Vendors, or Why Women Are Conservative (Being a View of the Economic Status of Women)* (Chicago: Charles H. Kerr, 1918); J. H. Greer, *The Social Evil and the Remedy* (Chicago: Charles H. Kerr, ca. 1910). Note as well Anton Johannsen's recollections of gender ideology in anarchist "free love" circles, where it was apparently commonplace to refer to "natural, womanly conservatism," and for radical women to chastise men for being "slaves to their wives." However, it was also the case that in strike situations, when wives complained that husbands were not bringing their strike benefits home, union executives could decide to pay such funds directly to wives. Hapgood, *Spirit of Labor,* 230–31, 254.

100. The preceding paragraph draws on Cannon's later appreciation and critique of the IWW, James P. Cannon, "The IWW," *Fourth International* 16 (Summer 1955): 75–86,

reprinted as a pamphlet, *The I.W.W.: The Great Anticipation* (New York: Pioneer Publishers, 1956), and in "The I.W.W.—The Great Anticipation," in Cannon, *First Ten
Years, 277–310.*

101. Chaplin, *Wobbly,* 347; Finkel interview with Cannon, March 1974, 26; Arne
Swabeck, unpublished typescript (written for but not published in Evans, *As We Knew
Him*), Reel 2, JPC Papers; Frank Lovell in Evans, *As We Knew Him,* 130.

Chapter 4: Red Dawn

1. Harrison George, *The Red Dawn: The Bolsheviki and the I.W.W.* (Chicago: IWW
Publishing, 1918); Harrison George, *The IWW Trial: Story of the Greatest Trial in Labor's
History by One of the Defendants* (Chicago: I.W.W., n.d. [1918], Arno reprint, 1969). See
also Theodore Draper, *The Roots of American Communism* (New York: Viking, 1957), 110,
416. On the jail, George, and the response of the IWW prisoners to the Bolshevik Revo-
lution, see Ralph Chaplin, *Wobbly: The Rough-and-Tumble Story of An American Radical*
(Chicago: University of Chicago Press, 1948), 205–38, 245, 298; Harry Ring interview with
James P. Cannon, April 12, 1974, 16 (in possession of the author; hereafter Ring interview).

2. For the Kansas context, see *Solidarity,* April 17, 1917; "Patriotism in the Middle
West," *Masses* 9 (June 1917): 19–21; Clayton R. Koppes, "The Kansas Trial of the IWW,
1917–1919," *Labor History* 16 (Summer 1975): 338–58, with the wider repression detailed
in Melvyn Dubofsky, *We Shall Be All: A History of the Industrial Workers of the World*
(Chicago: Quadrangle, 1969), 349–444; George, *The I.W.W. Trial;* Mary Heaton Vorse,
A Footnote to Folly: Reminiscences of Mary Heaton Vorse (New York: Farrar & Rinehart,
1935), 155–65.

3. Note the legal challenge to this repression in *The Case of the Chicago Socialists*
(Chicago: n.p., n.d [1918]), a 618-page brief for the plaintiffs in error deposited in the
United States Court of Appeals for the Seventh Circuit, October Term, 1918.

4. See, for instance, Paul L. Murphy, *World War I and the Origin of Civil Liberties in
the United States* (New York: Norton, 1979); Robert K. Murray, *Red Scare: A Study in
National Hysteria, 1919–1920* (New York: McGraw-Hill, 1966); William Preston, Jr.,
Aliens and Dissenters: Federal Suppression of Radicals, 1903–1933 (New York: Harper &
Row, 1966), esp. 35–237.

5. Cannon's most explicit statement on Rosedale and World War I is Joseph Hansen's
"How the Trotskyists Went to Jail," *Fourth International* 5 (February 1944): 44–45,
although I believe its statements, attributed to Cannon, may either have been exagger-
ated due to the context of Cannon going to jail, or overstated by Hansen. Note also
James P. Cannon, *The History of American Trotskyism: From Its Origins (1928) to the
Founding of the Socialist Workers Party (1938)—Report of a Participant* (New York:
Pathfinder, 1972), 64; James P. Cannon, *The First Ten Years of American Communism—
Report of a Participant* (New York: Pathfinder, 1973); Ring inteviews with Cannon, May
30, 1973, 1–10; January 3, 1974, 8–9. On Cannon's living arrangements and employment,
note State of Kansas, Census, Schedule 1, Rosedale, 1915, vol. 341, sec. 1, 18; Fourteenth
Census of the United States, Kansas, Wyandotte Country, Rosedale, January 3, 1920,
which indicates Cannon living at Bertha Wasson's boardinghouse, where fourteen

individuals, in all, resided; *Forty-fourth Annual Issue, 1914, Kansas City, Missouri, City Directory* (Kansas City, MO: Gate City Directory, 1914), 452; *Fiftieth Edition, 1920, Kansas City Missouri, City Directory and Business Catalogue* (Kansas City, MO: Gate City Directory, 1920), 818. On Browder, see James G. Ryan, *Earl Browder: The Failure of American Communism* (Tuscaloosa: University of Alabama Press, 1997), 12–15.

6. As noted in chapter 3, Cannon considered the idea of a law career. See Theodore Draper, *Roots of American Communism*, 306; Solon De Leon, ed., *The American Labor Who's Who* (New York: Hanford Press, 1925), 36; "The Reminiscences of Max Shachtman," Number 488, Oral History Research Office, 1963, 321, Columbia University, New York, New York; Ring interviews with Cannon, May 10, 1974, 4–5; February 23, 1974, 16–17.

7. Cannon, *First Ten Years*, 300; Ring interview with Cannon, May 30, 1973, 4; Dubofsky, *We Shall Be All*, 423–41.

8. Cannon always guarded against a cavalierly one-sided dismissal of the meaning of the pre-communist Socialist Party. Aware of the SP's defects, Cannon nevertheless acknowledged its important historic message of anti-capitalism, its role in the founding of the IWW, and the pivotal significance of a small minority of youthful socialists in sustaining the early communist movement. See James P. Cannon, "Sixty Years of American Radicalism," speech delivered to a meeting of the West Coast Vacation School and Camp, Labor Day, 1959, reprinted in Cannon, *Speeches for Socialism* (New York: Pathfinder, 1971), 83–104. Trotsky's characterization is in Leon Trotsky, *My Life: An Attempt at an Autobiography* (New York: Scribner's, 1931), 274.

9. Consider, for instance, Nick Salvatore, *Eugene V. Debs: Citizen and Socialist* (Urbana: University of Illinois Press, 1982), 251–56, 280–88; Alexander Trachtenberg, ed., *The Socialists and the War* (New York: Garland reprint, 1973); John Graham, ed., *"Yours for the Revolution": The Appeal to Reason, 1895–1922* (Lincoln: University of Nebraska Press, 1990), 246–88; Rose Pastor Stokes, *"I Belong to the Working Class": The Unfinished Autobiography of Rose Pastor Stokes*, ed. Herbert Shapiro and David L. Sterling (Athens: University of Georgia Press, 1992), 141–50; Arthur Zipster and Pearl Zipster, *Fire and Grace: The Life of Rose Pastor Stokes* (Athens: University of Georgia Press, 1989), 160–75; David Shannon, *The Socialist Party of America: A History* (Chicago: Quadrangle, 1967), 81–125; Draper, *Roots of American Communism*, 80–96; James Oneal and G. A. Werner, *American Communism: A Critical Analysis of Its Origins, Development and Programs* (New York: E.P. Dutton, 1947), 33–46; and, for a "Third Period" reading of this context, Alexander Bittelman, "From Left Socialism to Communism," in *Fifteen Years of the Communist Party* (New York: Workers Library, 1934), 8–22. On the SP and Article 2, sec. 6, directed at Haywood, the IWW, and the prohibition on sabotage, see William D. Haywood, *Bill Haywood's Book: The Autobiography of Big Bill Haywood* (New York: International, 1929, reprint 1969), 254–60; Ira Kipnis, *The American Socialist Movement: 1897–1912* (New York: Monthly Review Press, 1972), 391–420; Philip S. Foner, *History of the Labor Movement in the United States: The Industrial Workers of the World, 1905–1917*, vol. 4 (New York: International, 1965), 391–414.

10. Note the tension that runs through Cannon's appreciation and critique of

the Socialist Party of this period in Cannon, *First Ten Years,* esp. 96–97, 262–67; Ring interviews with Cannon, May 30, 1973, 1–3, 20–21; April 12, 1974, 5–7.

11. On the Hillquit campaign, see James Weinstein, *The Decline of Socialism in America, 1912–1925* (New York: Vintage, 1969), 149–55. For Cannon's response, see Ring interviews with Cannon, May 30, 1973, 20–21; April 12, 1974, 6–7.

12. James P. Cannon, "The IWW: The Great Anticipation," in *First Ten Years,* 292, 300–301. For the mixed response of the IWW to the Russian Revolution, see Chaplin, *Wobbly,* 285–88; Dubofsky, *We Shall Be All,* 462–65; Draper, *Roots of American Communism,* 110–13.

13. Consider, for instance, the pre-1918 holdings of one IWW member's library: Larry Peterson, "The Intellectual World of the IWW: An American Worker's Library in the First Half of the Twentieth Century," *History Workshop Journal* 22 (Autumn 1986): 153–72. Draper discusses influences in *Roots of American Communism,* 65–79. On Walling and Lenin, see William English Walling, *Russia's Message: The True World Import of the Revolution* (New York: Doubleday, Page, 1908), and the brief comment in James Boylan, *Revolutionary Lives: Anna Stransky & William English Walling* (Amherst: University of Massachusetts Press, 1998), 129, 145.

14. Ring interviews with Cannon, May 10, 1973, 18; May 30, 1973, 7; April 12, 1974, 5; James P. Cannon, "The Russian Revolution—Twenty-Eight Years After," *The Militant,* November 17, 1945, reprinted in James P. Cannon, *The Struggle for Socialism in the "American Century": Writings and Speeches, 1954–1947* (New York: Pathfinder, 1977), 194–202; James P. Cannon, "The First Days of American Communism," *Fourth International* 5 (February 1944): 38–39; with the quote from Cannon, *First Ten Years,* 102.

15. Cannon refers to Fraina as having been influenced first by DeLeon in his 1957 *International Socialist Review* of Draper's *The Roots of American Communism,* reprinted in Cannon, *First Ten Years,* 317. See also Paul Buhle, *A Dreamer's Paradise Lost: Louis C. Fraina/Lewis Corey (1892–1953) and the Decline of Radicalism in the United States* (Atlantic Highlands, NJ: Humanities Press, 1995), 5. Louis Boudin's *The Theoretical System of Karl Marx in the Light of Recent Criticism* (Chicago: Charles H. Kerr, 1907) originally appeared as articles in the *International Socialist Review* from May 1905 through October 1906. On Ludwig Lore, see Draper, *Roots of American Communism,* 76, 77, 79, 85, 100, 120; Paul Buhle, "Ludwig Lore and the *New Yorker Volkszeitung:* The Twilight of the German-American Socialist Press," in *The German-American Radical Press: The Shaping of a Left Political Culture, 1850–1940,* ed. Elliott Shore, Ken Fones-Wolf, and James P. Danky (Urbana: University of Illinois Press, 1990), 168–81. Note Lore's article on Trotsky in *One Year of Revolution, Celebrating the First Anniversary of the Founding of the Russian Soviet Republic* (New York: Socialist Publication Society, November 7, 1918). Buhle credits Draper's *Roots of American Communism* with having "recalled Fraina from obscurity" in Paul Buhle, *Marxism in the United States: Remapping the History of the American Left* (New York: Verso, 1991) 1, n. 29, 283, but it would be more correct to say that it was Cannon who pushed Draper to this recognition. See Cannon, "Fraina—The Founder," in *First Ten Years,* 46–50, this writing being, in its origins, a letter to Draper.

16. Among the signed articles produced by Fraina in *Class Struggle* were: "The War and America," 1 (May–June 1917), 22–24; "Socialists and War," 1 (July–August 1917), 75–99; "Labor and Democracy," 1 (September–October 1917), 57–62; "The I.W.W. Trial," 1 (November–December 1917), 1–5; "The Proletarian Revolution in Russia," 2 (January–February 1918), 29–67; "Laborism and Socialism," 2 (September–October 1918), 410–31; "Problems of American Socialism," 3 (February 1919), 26–47.

17. See N. I. Hourwich, "The Fundamentals of Bolshevism," *The Revolutionary Age,* December 7, 1918.

18. See, for instance, N. Lenin and Leon Trotsky, *The Proletarian Revolution in Russia,* ed. with an introduction, notes, and supplementary chapters by Louis C. Fraina (New York: Communist Press, 1918); "The Trend of Socialism in Europe," and N. Lenin, "Why Soviet Russia Made Peace," *Revolutionary Age,* November 20, 1918; "Withdraw from Russia," and John Reed, "The Origins of Workers' Control of Industry in Russia," *Revolutionary Age,* November 23, 1918; Ludwig Lore, "The German Revolution in Action," and Eadmonn MacAlpine, "Sinn Fein—and the New Struggle," *Revolutionary Age,* November 27, 1918, an issue that commenced serializing Trotsky, *My Diary;* "Workers' Control of Industry," *Revolutionary Age,* June 21, 1919. Note, as well, Fraina, "The Problems of Reconstruction," *Revolutionary Age,* November 27, 1918. Useful documents from this period appear in Albert Fried, *Communism in America: A History in Documents* (New York: Columbia University Press, 1997), 13–36; Bernard K. Johnpoll, ed., *A Documentary History of the Communist Party of the United States,* vol. 1 (Westport, CT: Greenwood, 1994).

19. The preceding paragraphs draw on Ring interviews with Cannon, May 10, 1917, 19; May 30, 1917, 8–9; Draper, *Roots of American Communism,* 86–91, 131–39; Trotsky, *My Life,* 276; Weinstein, *Decline of Socialism,* 177–233. Note the cavalier personalizations in Benjamin Gitlow, *The Whole of Their Lives: Communism in America—A Personal History and Intimate Portrayal of Its Leaders* (New York: Scribner's Sons, 1948), 6–17, 25. On Katayama, see Hyman Kublin, *Asian Revolutionary: The Life of Sen Katayama* (Princeton, NJ: Princeton University Press, 1964). On Eastman's *Liberator,* see Max Eastman, *Love and Revolution: My Journey Through an Epoch* (New York: Random House, 1964), 69–78; and Richard Fitzgerald, "*Masses, Liberator,*" in *The American Radical Press, 1880–1960,* ed. Joseph R. Conlin, vol. 2 (Westport, CT: Greenwood, 1974), 532–38. Volume 1 of Conlin's book contains statements on *Class Struggle* by David E. Brown (pp. 138–44) and *The Revolutionary Age* by Martin Glaberman and George P. Rawick (pp. 155–58).

20. For general statements, see David Montgomery, *Workers' Control in America: Studies in the History of Work, Technology, and Labor Struggles* (Cambridge, UK: Cambridge University Press, 1979); Montgomery, "Immigrants, Industrial Unions, and Social Reconstruction in the United States, 1916–1923," *Labour/Le Travail* 13 (Spring 1984): 101–14; Montgomery, "Labor and the Republic in Industrial America: 1860–1920," *Mouvement social* 111 (April–June 1980): 213; Montgomery, "Nationalism, American Patriotism, and Class Consciousness among Immigrant Workers in the United States in the Epoch of World War I," in *"Struggle a Hard Battle": Essays on Working-Class Immigrants,* ed. Dirk Hoerder (Dekalb: Northern Illinois University

Press, 1986), 327–52; James Oneal and G. A. Werner, *American Communism: A Critical Analysis of Its Origins, Development and Programs* (New York: E.P. Dutton, 1947), 46; P. K. Edwards, *Strikes in the United States, 1881–1974* (Oxford: Basil Blackwell, 1981), 1–51, 84–133; James R. Barrett, *William Z. Foster and the Tragedy of American Radicalism* (Urbana: University of Illinois Press, 1999), 71–101; Jeremy Brecher, *Strike!* (San Francisco: Straight Arrow Books, 1972), 101–43; Philip S. Foner, *History of the Labor Movement in the United States: Postwar Struggles, 1918–1920,* vol. 8 (New York: International, 1988); Harvey O'Connor, *Revolution in Seattle* (New York: Monthly Review Press, 1964); David Jay Bercuson, *Confrontation at Winnipeg: Labour, Industrial Relations, and the General Strike* (Kingston, Canada: McGill-Queen's University Press, 1974).

21. Alexander Bittelman, "Things I Have Learned: An Autobiography," 365, Boxes 1–2, Collection 62, unpublished manuscript in Alexander Bittelman Papers, Tamiment Institute, New York, New York. See also the section on the SP and the left wing in Alexander Bittelman, *Fifteen Years of the Communist Party,* 8–22, an earlier version of which Cannon comments on favorably in Cannon, *First Ten Years,* 101–4.

22. Membership figures from Daniel Bell, *Marxian Socialism in the United States* (Princeton, NJ: Princeton University Press, 1967), 79, and comment on elections in Weinstein, *Decline of Socialism,* 119–76. The initial manifesto and program of the left wing appeared in many publications, including *The Ohio Socialist,* February 26, 1919. See also Oneal and Werner, *American Communism,* 47–53.

23. Ryan, *Earl Browder,* 1–16; Earl Browder, "'No-Man's Land': A Political Autobiography," unpublished manuscript, chaps. 1–5, Box 10, Earl W. Browder Papers, George Arents Research Library for Special Collections, Syracuse University, Syracuse, New York (hereafter Browder Papers); Chaplin, *Wobbly,* 274, 314; Cannon, *First Ten Years,* 110; Draper, *Roots of American Communism,* 307–9; and on the Gompers-endorsed Kansas City "Labor Forward Movement," see C. F. Steckhahn, "The Labor Forward Movement of Greater Kansas City," *The Toiler* 2/4–5 (April–May 1914).

24. Cannon, *First Ten Years,* esp. 109–14; Ring interview with Cannon, May 30, 1973, 11.

25. For a wider discussion of Mooney, see Richard H. Frost, *The Mooney Case* (Stanford: Stanford University Press, 1968); and Curt Gentry, *Frame-Up: The Incredible Case of Tom Mooney and Warren Billings* (New York: Norton, 1967), which notes of the Kansas City defense campaign: "By now the juggernaut that would be known as the Mooney Defense was moving full steam, with defense groups in most of the major cities. The one in Kansas City, for example, was organized by Berkman and headed by young radicals Earl Browder and James P. Cannon" (p. 175). The Mooney defense campaign was a defining touchstone for those of the revolutionary Left. See "Mooney, Strikes, and the AFL," *Revolutionary Age,* November 27, 1918; Oneal and Werner, *American Communism,* 60.

26. Browder, "'No-Man's Land,'" chap. 3, esp. 33–38, contrasted with Ryan, *Earl Browder,* 14–16; Draper, *Roots of American Communism,* 309. Browder claims that Cannon threatened to sabotage the birth of *Workers' World,* but that the two revolutionaries brokered a "trade-off" in which Cannon forced Browder to accept an ultimatum. Browder was to be the first editor of the newspaper, but Cannon was to secure delegate

status to the National Conference of the left wing of the Socialist party, meeting in New York at the end of June 1919. Browder, claiming that he was not prepared to see *Workers' World* scuttled, agreed. Indeed, Browder was the first editor of the Kansas City paper and Cannon did attend the conference of the left wing as a delegate. The difficulty of Browder's claim lies in its narrative chronology. The first issue of *Workers' World* appeared on April 4, 1919. The call for a National Conference of the left wing, reported in the first issue publication of this revolutionary wing of the SP, the *New York Communist,* appeared April 19, 1919, and could not have reached Kansas City until well after the middle of April. Thus, Cannon could not possibly have blackmailed Browder into securing his election as a delegate to a convention with the threat that he would stop the publication of a newspaper that was already appearing under Browder's editorship. On the timing of the call for a left-wing conference, see Draper, *Roots of American Communism,* 164; Weinstein, *Decline of Socialism,* 164; *Revolutionary Radicalism: Its History, Purpose and Tactics with an Exposition and Discussion of the Steps Being Taken and Required to Curb It Being the Report of the Joint Legislative Committee Investigating Seditious Activities, Filed April 24, 1920, in the Senate of the State of New York— Part I: Revolutionary and Subversive Moments at Home and Abroad,* vol. 1 (Albany, NY: J.B. Lyon, 1920), 683. Serious scrutiny of Browder's memoirs often establishes the impossibility of his representations. Cannon's views are presented in Ring interview with Cannon, May 30, 1973, 11–12, 17–18; Cannon, *First Ten Years,* 110–11, 127, 304–5. On the Workers Educational League, with its offices in the Kansas City, Missouri, Schutte Building, see *Fiftieth Edition, 1920, Kansas City Missouri City Directory and Business Catalogue* (Kansas City, MO: Gate City Directory, 1920), 844, 2161.

27. Browder's remembrance that he edited the paper up to his imprisonment, and "[t]hereafter Cannon got out two issues and the paper ceased publication," distorts the balance of editorial responsibility greatly. Cannon's editorial involvement, in terms of actual numbers of issues he managed, likely surpassed Browder's, and certainly totalled twelve or more, possibly reaching a maximum of twenty. Contrast Browder, "'No-Man's Land,'" chap. 3, 37; and Draper, *Roots of American Communism,* 443, n.9; Theodore Draper, *American Communism and Soviet Russia: The Formative Period* (New York: Viking, 1960), 68. Walter Goldwater, *Radical Periodicals in America, 1890–1950* (New Haven: Yale University Library, 1964), 47–48, notes thirty-five issues.

28. Typical of later Communist Party-sponsored publications, Ella Reeve Bloor, *We Are Many: An Autobiography* (New York: International, 1940), 158–66, addresses the Kansas City paper, *Workers' World,* and her contribution to it, in a way that manages to avoid mention of Cannon.

29. "The Street Car Strike," *Workers' World,* April 4, 1919, an unsigned article likely written by Browder, assumes the defeat of the strike, concluding, "The situation seems to be hopeless." For more on this strike, which involved equal pay for women "conductorettes," see Foner, *History of the Labor Movement,* vol. 8, 108–16; Maurine Weiner Greenwald, *Women, War and Work: The Impact of World War I on Women Workers in the United States* (Westport, CT: Greenwood, 1980), 174–75. Background on the street-railway workers is in N. G. Cook, "Street Railway Employees of KC," *The Toiler* 2/6 (July

1914). The long quote is from "Dedication/Why the *Workers' World?" Workers' World,* April 4, 1919.

30. "Bob Minor Is Coming," "We Look to the East," [ABP], *Workers' World,* September 19, 1919; Draper, *Roots of American Communism,* 443, n.9; Browder, "'No-Man's Land,'" chap. 3, 36–37; Tom Mann, "The Power of United Labor," *The Toiler* 1/2 (November 1913); Paul Buhle, *Marxism in the USA: From 1870 to the Present Day* (London: Verso, 1987), 121.

31. Ring interviews with Cannon, May 10, 1973, 19–20; May 30, 1973, 12; Draper, *Roots of American Communism,* 166–67, 424–25, n.5; Draper, *American Communism and Soviet Russia,* 18; Emmet Larkin, *James Larkin: Irish Labor Leader, 1876–1947* (Cambridge, MA: M.I.T. Press, 1965), 231–33; Ted Morgan, *A Covert Life: Jay Lovestone— Communist, Anti-Communist, and Spymaster* (New York: Random House, 1999), 16–17; James P. Cannon, "C.E. Ruthenberg," *Labor Defender,* April 1927, reprinted in Cannon, *Notebook of an Agitator* (New York: Pathfinder, 1973), 49. Cannon discerned four specific groups at the June 1917 convention: the foreign-language-federation delegates, whom he judged distant from American conditions; figures such as Fraina, whom he respected, and Ruthenberg, whose stature was known to him but whose personality left him cold; a hair-splitting contingent of native-born American sectarians from Michigan; and the Reed-Gitlow-Larkin-Katterfeld-Wagenknecht "American" contingent. See Cannon, *First Ten Years,* 55, and on his self-description, 103. There is much discussion of Reed in a new treatment of New York's World War I bohemian milieu, but it too easily slides over his leftward political development in this period, especially in terms of his Bolshevism. See Christine Stansell, *American Moderns: Bohemian New York and the Creation of a New Century* (New York: Henry Holt, 2000). For standard accounts of Reed, see Granville Hicks, *John Reed: The Making of a Revolutionary* (New York: Macmillan, 1936); Robert Rosenstone, *Romantic Revolutionary: A Biography of John Reed* (New York: Knopf, 1975).

32. Ruthenberg's statement is in C.E. Ruthenberg, "News and Views," *Ohio Socialist,* April 9, 1919. On Lenin and Hourwich, see Paul Buhle, *Marxism in the United States: Remapping the History of the American Left* (London: Verso, 1991), 112. Stoklitsky is quoted in Weinstein, *Decline of Socialism,* 203.

33. Draper, *Roots of American Communism,* 167–69; Weinstein, *Decline of Socialism,* 201; Ring interview with Cannon, May 10, 1973, 21; Benjamin Gitlow, *I Confess: The Truth about American Communism* (New York: E.P. Dutton, 1940), 32–33; Cannon, *First Ten Years,* 42–43, 55. Browder makes a number of dubious claims about Cannon in this period in "'No-Man's Land,'" chap. 3, 36–38. See also Ralph Korngold, "Revolutionary Romanticists," *Cleveland Citizen,* May 19, 1919, quoted in Weinstein, *Decline of Socialism,* 206. See *Revolutionary Radicalism,* vol. 1, 684, for the composition of various positions/committees; this source also reproduces the convention Manifesto (pp. 716–38). For other accounts of the left wing, see Oneal and Werner, *American Communism,* 47–64; Arne Swabeck, unpublished, untitled, and unpaginated typescript, chap. 5, "The Socialist Party Split," Autobiographies File, Prometheus Research Library, New York, New York; Shannon, *Socialist Party of America,* 126–49; and, for one of the few

accounts from a member of the foreign-language-federation faction, Alexander Bittelman, "Things I Have Learned," 310–21, which does not situate Cannon prominently.

34. Membership figures from Bell, *Marxian Socialism*, 33. The foreign-language federations are presented one-sidedly as mere bastions of otherworldly sectarianism in most accounts of the United States Left, from Draper, *Roots of American Communism* to Weinstein, *Decline of Socialism*. Oneal and Werner, *American Communism*, 44–45, at least gesture toward a more complex understanding. The most accessible general counter to this Draper-Weinstein view is Buhle, *Marxism in the United States*, 58–154. Buhle effectively challenges the inattention to the foreign-language-section ranks, but in some ways his general critique is the mirror image of the Draper-Weinstein distortion, bypassing too easily the *politics* and *leaderships* of the Socialist Party's foreign-born left wing. But see, for suggestive and more specific alternative presentations, various essays in Paul Buhle and Dan Georgakas, eds., *The Immigrant Left in the United States* (Albany: State University of New York Press, 1996), especially Mary E. Cygan, "The Polish American Left," (pp. 148–84) and Maria Woroby, "The Ukrainian Immigrant Left in the United States, 1880–1950," (pp. 185–206). Note particularly Michael G. Karni, "Finnish Immigrant Leftists in America: The Golden Years, 1900–1918," and David Montgomery, "Nationalism, American Patriotism, and Class Consciousness among Immigrant Workers in the United States in the Epoch of World War I," in *"Struggle a Hard Battle,"* ed. Hoerder, 199–226, 327–52; Karni, "Finnish-American Co-operativism: The Radical Years, 1917–1930," in Scott Cummings, ed., *Self-Help in Urban America: Patterns of Minority Economic Development* (Port Washington, NY: Kennikat Press, 1980), 145–59; Peter Kivisto, *Immigrant Socialists in the United States: The Case of Finns and the Left* (London: Associated University Presses, 1984); David John Ahola, *Finnish-Americans and International Communism: A Study of Finnish-American Communism from Bolshevization to the Demise of the Third International* (Washington, DC: University of America Press, 1981); Henry Bengston, *On the Left in America: Memoirs of the Scandinavian-American Labor Movement* (Carbondale: Southern University Illinois Press, 1999); Joseph Stipanovich, "Immigrant Workers and Immigrant Intellectuals in Progressive America: A History of the Yugoslav Socialist Federation, 1900–1918" (PhD diss., University of Minnesota, 1977); Stipanovich, "Collective Economic Activity Among Serb, Croat, and Slovene Immigrants in the United States," in *Self-Help in Urban America*, ed. Cummings, 160–76; Thomas Capek, *The Cechs (Bohemians) in America: A Study of their National, Cultural, Political, Social, Economic, and Religious Life* (New York: AMS Press reprint, 1969 [1920]), esp. 137–54, 265–78; Shannon, *Socialist Party of America*, 44–47. On repression and infiltration of the Russian Socialist Workers' Federation and other bodies, see Bruce R. Schubert, "The Palmer Raids in Connecticut: 1919–1920," *Connecticut Review* 5 (1971): 53–69; Weinstein, *Decline of Socialism*, 232; Louis F. Post, *The Deportation Delirium of Nineteen Twenty* (Chicago: Charles H. Kerr, 1923), esp. 22–33.

35. Ring interview with Cannon, April 19, 1974, 1–2. On the *Masses* and Eastman, see Eastman, *Love and Revolution*; William L. O'Neill, ed., *Echoes of Revolt: The Masses, 1911–1917* (Chicago: Quadrangle, 1966). Baldwin's remembrance of Cannon is in Les

Evans, ed., *James P. Cannon As We Knew Him: By Thirty-three Comrades, Friends, and Relatives* (New York: Pathfinder, 1976), 48–51.

36. Buhle, *Marxism in the United States,* 117–19; also Melech Epstein, *The Jew and Communism, 1919–1941* (New York: Trade Union Sponsoring Committee, 1959), 34–35.

37. The preceding paragraphs draw on an array of sources. Details of the Chicago Conference, splits, and other developments can be gleaned from Weinstein, *Decline of Socialism,* 177–233; Draper, *Roots of American Communism,* 164–96, 332; Draper, *American Communism and Soviet Russia,* 9–28; Shannon, *Socialist Party of America,* 126–49; Oneal and Werner, *American Communism,* 59–79; Larkin, *James Larkin,* 219–49; Gitlow, *I Confess,* 11–58; Gitlow, *Whole of Their Lives,* 3–52; Irving Howe and Lewis Coser, *The American Communist Party: A Critical History (1919–1957)* (Boston: Beacon Press, 1957), 42–44; Vernon L. Pederson, *The Communist Party in Maryland, 1919–1957* (Urbana: University of Illinois Press, 2001), 13–16. The Communist Party and the Communist Labor Party statements appear in *Revolutionary Radicalism,* vol. 1, 739–817. Other contemporary commentary can be found in issues of the left-wing press, for instance: various articles in *The Ohio Socialist,* July 2, 1919; July 9, 1919; July 30, 1919; August 13, 1919; September 10, 1919; September 17, 1919; September 24, 1919. Note especially, reprinted from the *Liberator,* Max Eastman, "The Three Chicago Conventions," *Ohio Socialist,* October 8, 1919; as well as a later comment, Nathan Moser, "The Socialist Party and Communist Party Conventions," *The Marxian* 1 (October 1921): 22–27. For Cannon's commentary, see Cannon, *First Ten Years,* 42–43, 55, 103–4; Ring interviews with Cannon, May 10, 1973, 19–20; May 30, 1973, 12–13; Cannon, *History of American Trotskyism,* 5–10. Engels is quoted in Engels to Sorge, 2 December 1893, in Fran Mecklenburg and Manfred Stassen, eds., *German Essays on Socialism in the Nineteenth Century* (New York: Continuum, 1990), 75; also in Alan Johnson, "Editorial Introduction: The American Worker and the Absurd Truth about Marxism," *Historical Materialism* 11 (Fall 2003): 9. See, as well, Johnpoll, *Documentary History of the Communist Party,* 179, 186, 188–90; Montgomery, "Nationalism, Patriotism, and Class Consciousness," 342; Buhle, *Marxism in the United States,* 119. I am especially indebted to an unpublished paper by John Holmes, "American Jewish Communism and the Left-Wing Movement in the Needle Trades: A Forgotten Page of Labor History," for clarifications concerning London, Bittelman, and the fractured nature of the Jewish Federation. For other useful statements on the Jewish Socialist Federation, see Tony Michels, "Socialism with a Jewish Face: The Origins of the Yiddish-Speaking Communist Movement in the United States, 1907–1923," in Gennady Estraikh and Mikhail Krutikov, eds., *Yiddish and the Left* (Oxford: Legenda, European Humanities Research Centre, 2001), 24–55; Eugene Victor Orenstein, "The Jewish Socialist Federation of America, 1912–1921: A Study of Integration and Particularism in the American Jewish Labor Movement" (PhD diss., Columbia University, 1978). On gender, radicalism, and the garment trades in this period, see Daniel E. Bender, *Sweated Work, Weak Bodies: Anti-Sweatshop Campaigns and the Languages of Labor* (New Brunswick, NJ: Rutgers University Press, 2003).

38. Cannon, *First Ten Years,* 42–43; Ring interviews with Cannon, May 10, 1973, 19–21; May 30, 1973, 17–18; Cannon, *History of American Trotskyism,* 7–8; "The Party and the

Workers' World," and "Platform and Program of Communist Labor Party," *Workers' World*, September 19, 1919. See also Fried, *Communism in America*, 31–33, for the CLP platform and program. Given the *Workers' World*, August 22, 1919, statement on the need to reduce "theory to the simplest possible language . . . having for its primary purpose the unification of the labor movement under the control of the rank and file," the CLP was the only possible option for the Kansas City left wing. Again, Browder's presentation ("'No-Man's Land,'" chap. 3, 37–38) of Cannon in this period, as well as the development of the two communist parties after the Chicago Conventions, contains allegations that are factually untrue, chronologically garbled, impossible, and clearly the result of subsequent animus.

39. Ring interviews with Cannon, May 10, 1973, 19–21; May 30, 1973, 17–18; "Tri-State Conference," *Workers' World*, September 19, 1919; Gertrude Crumb Harmon, W. H. Tilley, A. L. Kuntz, J. L. Creviston, Effie Main, Ernest I. McNutt, and J. P. Cannon, "Statement of the Kansas Membership by the Temporary State Executive Committee of the Communist Labor Party," *Workers' World*, September 26, 1919; "Kansas and Missouri Hold Conventions," and "Communist Labor Party National Office Bulletin," *Ohio Socialist*, October 1, 1919; "Hands Off Soviet Russia! A Call to the American Working Class. By the Communist Labor Party," *Class Struggle* 3 (November 1919): 354–55. Commentators other than Cannon found the CLP more in touch with American realities than the foreign-language-federation-dominated CP, describing it as having "a certain atmosphere of reality, a sense of work to be done, a freedom from theological dogma on the one hand and machine politics on the other, which is new in American socialism and hopeful." See Max Eastman, "The Three Chicago Conventions," *Ohio Socialist*, October 8, 1919.

40. See "The Street Car Strike," *Workers' World*, April 4, 1919.

41. For Cannon's recollections of Howat, sometimes reaching back to 1919, see James P. Cannon, "A Talk with Alex Howat," reprinted from *Labor Herald*, in *Maritime Labor Herald*, June 9, 1923; Cannon, "The Story of Alex Howat," reprinted from *The Liberator*, April 1921, in *James P. Cannon and the Early Years of American Communism: Selected Writings and Speeches, 1920–1928* (New York: Prometheus Research Library, 1992), 78–84. Among the sources that present background on and the development of Howat, with comment on Kansas mining strikes, the UMWA hierarchy, the Kansas Industrial Law Court, and other union rebellions, are Melvyn Dubofsky and Warren Van Tine, *John L. Lewis: A Biography* (New York: Quadrangle, 1977); McAlister Coleman, *Men and Coal* (New York: Farrar & Rinehart, 1943); Alan Singer, "Communists and Coal Miners: Rank-and-File Organizing in the United Mine Workers of America," *Science & Society* 55 (Summer 1991): 132–57; Sylvia Kopald, *Rebellion in the Labor Unions* (New York: Boni & Liveright, 1924); Edward Dean Wickersham, "Opposition to the International Officers of the United Mine Workers: 1919–1933" (PhD diss., Cornell University, 1951); Julia E. Johnsen, "Kansas Court of Industrial Relations," *The Reference Shelf* 1 (December 1922): 1–70, reprinted (New York: Wilson, 1922); *Kansas Court of Industrial Relations* (Research Report No. 67) (New York: National Industrial Conference Board, 1924); John Dorsey, "The Industrial Court—Dead," *Labor Herald* 1 (March 1922): 10–11;

Revolutionary Radicalism, "Constructive Movements and Measures in America," vol. 4, 4241–54; James Gray Pope, "Labor's Constitution of Freedom," *Yale Law Journal* 106 (January 1977): 941–1031.

42. On the character of the November-December battle in the nation's coal fields, see Foner, *History of the Labor Movement,* vol. 8, 141–49; Dubofsky and Van Tine, *John L. Lewis,* 32–33, 40–41, 48, 50–51, 55, 57, 60; Cecil Carnes, *John L. Lewis: Leader of Labor* (New York: Robert Speller, 1936), 28–46; John Laslett, *Labor and the Left: A Study of Socialist and Radical Influences in the American Labor Movement, 1881–1924* (New York: Basic Books, 1970), 224–25; Singer, "Communists and Coal Miners," 134–38.

43. Cannon, "A Talk with Alex Howat"; Cannon, *First Ten Years,* 111; Ring interviews with Cannon, May 30, 1973, 4–5, 18; September 12, 1973, 6; October 10, 1973, 6–7; April 12, 1973, 8; "Miners Go Back—But as Rebels," *The Toiler,* December 17, 1919; "Baker Arrested Now Free on Bonds," *The Toiler,* December 31, 1919; Scott Nearing, "The Spirit of Mid-Western Labor," *The Toiler,* January 21, 1920; J. L. Creviston, "Talking It Over with the Miners," *The Toiler,* February 13, 1920; "Grand Jury Indicts Baker and Cannon," *The Toiler,* May 7, 1920; *Communist Labor,* May 15, 1920; JPC to Theodore Draper, 10 June 1963, Reel 22, JPC Papers. On Baker, see the note in *The Toiler,* March 12, 1920; Charles Baker, "Strangling American Workers," *The Toiler,* April 2, 1920.

44. Dubofsky and Van Tine, *John L. Lewis,* 113–21; Laslett, *Labor and the Left,* 224; "Irresponsible and Running Wild," *The Toiler,* March 12, 1920; Bill Smith, "The Kansas Court of Industrial Slavery," *The Toiler,* March 19, 1920; Johnsen, "Kansas Court of Industrial Relations," 19–30; *Kansas Court of Industrial Relations,* 52–63, 76–77.

45. Noah F. Whitaker, "Go to Kansas," *The Toiler,* April 16, 1920.

46. For general accounts, see Draper, *Roots of American Communism,* 202–4, 206–7, 211–12; Murray, *Red Scare;* Preston, *Aliens and Dissenters;* Robert W. Dunn, ed., *The Palmer Raids* (New York: International, 1948); Howard Abramowitz, "The Press and the Red Scare, 1919–1921," in *Popular Culture and Political Change in Modern America,* ed. Ronald Edsforth and Larry Bennett (Albany: State University of New York Press, 1991), 61–80.

47. Cannon, *History of American Trotskyism,* 9; Gitlow, *I Confess,* 65–66; Draper, *Roots of American Communism,* 204, 207, 443, n.9; Murray, *Red Scare,* 217; Bloor, *We Are Many,* 158–66. *The Toiler* published numerous articles on the "red scare" from December 1919 to June 1920.

48. Ring interviews with Cannon, May 10, 1974, 4–5; February 23, 1974, 16–17.

49. See, for example, "Let 'Organization' Be Your Answer," *The Toiler,* January 7, 1920.

50. On the repressive assault on the CLP, see "On Killing Us Dead," and "Casualties," *Communist Labor,* March 25, 1920; "Spies," *Communist Labor,* May 1, 1920; "Trials but No Tribulations," *Communist Labor,* May 15, 1920. It is possible that this repression adversely affected the judgment of revolutionaries responsible for putting out party propaganda. Thus, the third issue of *The Communist,* February 25, 1920, featured a one-third page, front-page, graphic of an offensive racist sort. Attorney-General Palmer was depicted as a warlike Indian chief, bedecked in full-length headdress, clutching a blood-dripping scalp in a hand held high over his head, and a menacing knife in the other. Dancing atop

the caption "The Scalp Dancer—'Heap Big Scalp, Heap Big Office,'" the illustration was, even acknowledging the early period of communism and undeveloped perspectives on the oppression of native peoples, remarkably obtuse.

51. "Caesar—Beware the Ides of March," *Communist Labor*, March 25, 1920; "Capitalism Your Days Are Numbered," and Lettish Group of Communists, "From Ellis, Island, New York," *Communist Labor*, February 25, 1920; "Down Tools May First, 1920," *Communist Labor*, May 1, 1920.

52. See the comments of Cannon, *History of American Trotskyism*, 9; Cannon, *First Ten Years*, 315–16; Gitlow, *I Confess*, 65–66; Draper, *Roots of Soviet Communism*, 207.

Chapter 5: Underground

1. See Jeanne Morgan, "Journal from James P. Cannon's Office, 1954–56: Notes kept by secretary for personal memento, without Cannon's knowledge," entries for January 25, 1954; January 26, 1954; April 25, 1955 (in possession of the author; hereafter Morgan diary); Joseph Hansen interview with Cannon, "Autobiographical Material," October 5, 1956, 15–16, Reel 1, James P. Cannon Papers, Microfilm Edition, 1994, State Historical Society of Wisconsin, Madison, Wisconsin (hereafter JPC Papers).

2. James P. Cannon, "The Lives of Two Revolutionaries—Remarks by James P. Cannon at a Banquet in Los Angeles, 15 December 1962," in Cannon, *Speeches for Socialism* (New York: Pathfinder, 1971), 284–87.

3. See Theodore Draper, *American Communism and Soviet Russia: The Formative Period* (New York: Viking, 1960), 21; Theodore Draper, *The Roots of American Communism* (New York: Viking, 1957), 204–9; Ted Morgan, *A Covert Life: Jay Lovestone—Communist, Anti-Communist, and Spymaster* (New York: Random House, 1999), 18–23; Robert K. Murray, *Red Scare: A Study in National Hysteria, 1919–1920* (New York: McGraw-Hill, 1966), 212–17; James P. Cannon, *The History of American Trotskyism: From Its Origins (1928) to the Founding of the Socialist Workers Party (1938)—Report of a Participant* (New York: Pathfinder, 1972), 9; Alexander Bittelman, "History of the Communist Movement in America," in *Investigation of Communist Propaganda, Hearings before a Special Committee to Investigate Communist Activities in the United States*, pt. 5, vol. 4 (Washington, DC: Government Printing Office, 1930), 443.

4. Cannon, "Lives of Two Revolutionaries," 285–87.

5. C.E. Ruthenberg, "Communism in the Open Again," *The Liberator* (February 1923): 13; Edwin P. Hoyt, *The Palmer Raids, 1919–1920: An Attempt to Suppress Dissent* (New York: Seabury Press, 1969), 19; Arne Swabeck, unpublished, unititled, and unpaginated typescript, chap. 5, "The Socialist Party Split," Autobiographies File, Prometheus Research Library, New York, New York; "The Reminiscences of Max Shachtman," Number 488, Oral History Research Office, 1963, 320–24, Columbia University, New York, New York; Vera Buch Weisbord, *A Radical Life* (Bloomington: Indiana University Press, 1977), 83.

6. The state, predictably, regarded the factions of the early communist movement as a unified bloc of subversion. See Max Lowenthal, *The Federal Bureau of Investigation* (London: Turnstill Press, 1951), 113–19.

7. See a number of articles in *Ohio Socialist,* September 17, 1919; September 24, 1919; October 15, 1919; November 19, 1919; Draper, *Roots of American Communism,* 198–201; James R. Barrett, *William Z. Foster and the Tragedy of American Radicalism* (Urbana: University of Illinois Press, 1999), 112–13; Swabeck, unpublished autobiography, chaps. 4–6; Harry Ring interviews with James P. Cannon, May 30, 1973, 10–11, 13–14; April 12, 1974, 3 (in possession of the author; hereafter Ring interview). There is much on the Communist Party and the Communist Labor Party in *Revolutionary Radicalism: Its History, Purpose and Tactics with an Exposition and Discussion of the Steps Being Taken and Required to Curb It Being the Report of the Joint Legislative Committee Investigating Seditious Activities, Filed April 24, 1920, in the Senate of the State of New York* (Albany, NY: J.B. Lyon, 1920), esp. vol. 1, 739–817. Alexander Bittelman's memoir, "Things I Have Learned: An Autobiography," Boxes 1–2, Collection 62, unpublished manuscript in Alexander Bittelman Papers, Tamiment Institute, New York, New York, contains one of the best statements of a foreign-language-federation figure relating to the CP milieu and its relations with the CLP; see chap. 12, "I Join in Founding the Communist Party of America," 322–64, esp. 329, 331–32.

8. For a full discussion of the general context, see Draper, *Roots of American Communism,* 198–219. For reprints of the Communist Party's articles in *The Communist* in this period, see *Revolutionary Radicalism,* vol. 2, 1147–57. Note also Ring interview with Cannon, May 30, 1973, 13–14. On Charles E. Ruthenberg, see the many accounts of Ruthenberg's Socialist Party activity in the Cleveland *Socialist News,* vol. 1, no. 1, December 5, 1914, through vol. 1, no. 52, November 27, 1915. The official party hagiography is Oakley Johnson, *The Day Is Coming: The Life and Work of Charles E. Ruthenberg, 1882–1927* (New York: International Publishers, 1957), a depiction challenged by Draper's *Roots of American Communism* and Cannon's *The First Ten Years of American Communism—Report of a Participant* (New York: Pathfinder, 1973), esp. for personal characteristics, 123. There is also much on Ruthenberg in Benjamin Gitlow, *I Confess: The Truth about American Communism* (New York: E.P. Dutton, 1940); *Revolutionary Radicalism,* vol. 1, 24, 632–33, 684, 700, 749, 757, 763–66, and vol. 2, 1153, 1322. Cannon's obituary of Ruthenberg appeared in *Labor Defender,* April 1927, and is reprinted as "C.E. Ruthenberg," in James P. Cannon, *Notebook of an Agitator* (New York: Pathfinder, 1973), 49–53. Ironically, given Ruthenberg's back-and-forth relation to the foreign-language-federations leaders, his original inclination was espoused in a 1912 Socialist Party missive deploring the lack of party discipline exercised over immigrant socialists. See *Socialist Party National Proceedings, 1912* (Chicago: Socialist Party, 1912), 89, cited in Paul Buhle, *Marxism in the United States: Remapping the History of the American Left* (New York: Verso, 1991), 133.

9. Draper, *Roots of American Communism,* 205; Betty Yorburg interview with Max Shachtman, Socialist Movement Project, Oral History Research Office, Columbia University, No. 651 [1967], 15 May 1965, 6–7; "The Reminiscences of Max Shachtman," Number 488, Oral History Research Office, 1963, 10, Columbia University, New York, New York; Peter Drucker, *Max Shachtman and His Left: A Socialist's Odyssey through the "American Century"* (Atlantic Highlands, NJ: Humanities Press, 1994), 10.

10. Among the Left newspapers Cannon likely had passing acquaintance with were a trio of San Francisco/Oakland papers—*The World, Western Worker,* and *Rank and File*—and two Cleveland-based papers, the *Ohio Socialist* and *The Toiler.* See *Revolutionary Radicalism,* vol. 1, 805–6, and vol. 2, 1348–50.

11. "Capitalism—Your Days Are Numbered," *Communist Labor,* February 25, 1920; "Caesar—Beware of the Ides of March," "The Fluttering of Twilight Butterflies," "Debs Does Not Know," and Karl Radek, "To the Memory of Karl Liebnecht," *Communist Labor,* March 25, 1920; "Down Tools May First, 1920," "The Outlaw Strike," "Lenin as Scholar and Writer," *Communist Labor,* May 1, 1920; "A Call to the Workers of All Countries to Help Save Soviet Russia," "Lenin—The Man and His Work," "The Winds of Reaction," *Communist Labor,* May 15, 1920; "The Growing Colossus," "Railroad Workers' Double Strike," "Class Lines at the Centralia Trial," "Labor in South Africa," "Trade Unionism, Industrial Unionism and Workers' Committees," and "Railroad Workers—Fight On," *Voice of Labor,* April 20, 1920. For comment on Centralia, see, as well, Melvyn Dubofsky, *We Shall Be All: A History of the Industrial Workers of the World* (Chicago: Quadrangle, 1969), 455–56; Ralph Chaplin, *The Centralia Conspiracy* (Chicago: Industrial Workers of the World, 1920).

12. "Lettish Group of Communists, Ellis Island, 13 January 1920," *The Toiler,* January 21, 1920; "The Question of Unity of the Communist Labor Party and the Communist Party," *The Toiler,* February 27, 1919; "The Communist Party Splits," *The Toiler,* May 14, 1920. Cannon had considerable regard for the Letts, admiring their Bolshevik resolve. Ring interview with Cannon, April 12, 1974, 2.

13. Max Bedacht to Theodore Draper, 9 December 1954, Box 10, Folder 15, Theodore Draper Research Files, Robert W. Woodruff Library, Emory University, Atlanta, Georgia, cited in *James P. Cannon and the Early Years of American Communism: Selected Writings and Speeches, 1920–1928* (New York: Prometheus Research Library, 1992), 30.

14. Alexander Bittelman, "Things I Have Learned," 357–58.

15. Gitlow, *I Confess,* 161.

16. For the call for a unity conference, see *Communist Labor,* May 15, 1920. The major accounts of the conference, including statements, publication of the United Communist Party Program, and various commentaries, appeared in *The Communist,* June 12, 1920, the most detailed depiction of the proceedings being Y. F., "The Convention of Revolutionists," reprinted as "United Communist Party Formed by Communist Groups," *The Toiler,* June 25, 1920. "Y. F." was I. E. Ferguson, of the Ruthenberg group that split from the foreign-language-federations-dominated Communist Party. A Canadian who graduated from the University of Chicago Law School, farmed in Wyoming, and ran for office on a Republican ticket, Ferguson was won to Socialist Party politics in Chicago in 1917, and with little experience in either the Left or the labor movement managed to become a prominent communist for a brief period. He dropped out of revolutionary activity in the early 1920s, retiring from politics to practice law. See Draper, *Roots of American Communism,* 432, n. 19; Irving Howe and Lewis Coser, *The American Communist Party: A Critical History (1919–1957)* (Boston: Beacon Press, 1957), 65. Note, as well, for reprints of some statements in *The Communist* and of

materials relevant to the formation of the United Communist Party, *Revolutionary Radicalism,* vol. 2, 1858–70, 1873–99.

17. "Convention of Revolutionists," *The Communist,* June 12, 1920.

18. Ring interviews with Cannon, May 10, 1973, 21–22; May 30, 1973, 14–15. Cannon's count of delegates and recollection of the convention meeting for two weeks are slightly off in this oral testimony. Draper's account in *Roots of American Communism,* 218–22, is accurate; in contrast, an abbreviated statement in what is perhaps the official history, William Z. Foster, *History of the Communist Party of the United States* (New York: International 1952), 177–78, is of limited use.

19. "Convention of Revolutionists," and "Program of the United Communist Party," *The Communist,* June 12, 1920. Further statements coming out of the convention appeared subsequently, including "The Communist Challenge: Proclamation of the United Communist Party of America," *The Communist,* July 3, 1920.

20. Is it possible that Cannon adopted the name of the Wobbly critic of Akron, Frank Dawson, out of respect for Dawson's analysis of that IWW strike? See Frank Dawson, "The Akron 'Fiasco,'" *Solidarity,* April 26, 1913. Given that Dawson also wrote favorably on Cannon's hobo travelling companion, George Leppert (see Frank Dawson, "The Hobo Agitator," *Solidarity,* May 17, 1913), and that Cannon's perspectives on the strike as it unfolded meshed with those of Dawson, it is also remotely possible that Cannon was in fact Dawson in 1913, and continued this pseudonym at the founding of the United Communist Party. There is no evidence for this, save that the IWW writer Frank Dawson appears to have disappeared after 1913, that there are similarities in tone and content if one compares Cannon's and Dawson's 1913 IWW journalism, and that Cannon appears under the *nom de guerre* of Dawson in 1920.

21. "Convention of Revolutionists," *The Communist,* June 12, 1920; Ring interviews with Cannon, May 10, 1973, 21–22; May 30, 1973, 14–15; April 5, 1974, 3–4; Cannon, *First Ten Years,* 197–98. For later Cannon statements on trade union/IWW issues, see "The IWW at Philadelphia," *The Toiler,* August 27, 1920; "Who Can Save the Unions," *The Toiler,* May 7, 1921, both reprinted in *James P. Cannon and the Early Years of American Communism,* 71–74, 88–89.

22. Alan Singer, "Communists and Coal Miners: Rank-and-File Organizing in the United Mine Workers of America During the 1920s," *Science & Society* 55 (Summer 1991): 136–37.

23. For a brief reference to the Belleville District Defense League, see David M. Schneider, *The Workers' (Communist) Party and American Trade Unions* (Baltimore: Johns Hopkins, 1928), 40, citing *United Mine Workers' Journal,* October 15, 1919, 5.

24. "CEC Meeting," *The Communist,* June 12, 1920; Ring interviews with Cannon, May 10, 1973, 21–23; May 30, 1973, 15–16; April 5, 1974, 3–4; Alan Wald, *The New York Intellectuals: The Rise and Decline of the Anti-Stalinist Left from the 1930s to the 1980s* (Chapel Hill: University of North Carolina Press, 1987), 197–98. Cannon claimed to have received the highest number of votes, but he was slightly mistaken.

25. So much so that from this point on Cannon would be subject to Department of Justice, Federal Bureau of Investigation interest, although actual surveillance would

not take place until later. The first reports on Cannon were filed in 1922, but a subsequent profile reached back to the Bridgman conference in which the CP and the CLP united to form the UCP. In error about the location of the gathering, which it placed in Chicago, this outline of Cannon's involvement in the revolutionary movement rightly identified him as a member of the IWW, the CLP, the CEC of the UCP, a St. Louis district organizer of the UCP, "associate editor" of *The Toiler*, and national chairman of the Workers' Party. But it may well have slipped up in its association of Cannon and a defense of underground communist principles of "revolutionary violence," possibly confusing Cannon with another Kansas City delegate to an earlier Chicago conference—or it may just have been an agent's conscious feeding of overblown rhetoric to masters who wanted to be quoted the most subversive language. See "James P. Cannon, or Joseph P. Cannon, alias Cook," n.d. (ca. 1925), U.S. Department of Justice, Federal Bureau of Investigation, Freedom of Information/Privacy Act Files, Washington, DC (hereafter FBI File). It should be noted that there was some early confusion with the FBI files about Cannon's actual identity, and in some documents he is held to be Joseph P. Cannon, a more moderate labor figure of no consequence on the revolutionary Left.

26. For Lista's living arrangements in the Frank Makimson household, see *Forty-first Annual Issue, 1911, Kansas City Directory, including Independence, Missouri, Kansas City, Kansas, Rosedale, Kansas* (Kansas City, MO: Gate City Directory Company, 1911), 1063. On the Makimson family's hostility to Cannon, possibly conditioned by Jim's and Lista's later separation, but likely of long-standing duration, note the assessment of Walta Ross, conveyed to Emily Turnbull in "What Walta Ross Knew of Jim and Rose's Families," November 29, 1993, Prometheus Research Library, New York, New York. On Cannon's return to Rosedale in 1947 for his father's funeral, see James P. Cannon, "Farewell to a Socialist Pioneer," *The Militant*, June 7, 1947, reprinted in *Notebook of an Agitator*, 165–67. For Cannon's qualms about being a parent and a revolutionary, see Ring interview with Cannon, May 10, 1974, 1–5. Among some of the old-time Kansas City radicals, the attachment to Cannon would be lifelong. See, for instance, Shorty A. A. Buehler to Jim, 30 December 1929; 3 February 1930; 9 February 1930, Reel 3, JPC Papers.

27. "Program of the United Communist Party," *The Communist*, June 12, 1920; "The Communist Challenge," *The Communist*, July 3, 1920. Note also the less abrasive but still quite intransigent statement, "Debs and the Socialist Party," in *The Toiler*, July 2, 1920.

28. Ring interviews with Cannon, May 10, 1973, 22–23; May 30, 1973, 16; Cannon, *First Ten Years*, 43. For the context and background on Walker, see Eugene Staley, *History of the Illinois State Federation of Labor* (Chicago: University of Chicago Press, 1930); John Laslett, *Labor and the Left: A Study of Socialist and Radical Influences in the American Labor Movement, 1881–1924* (New York: Basic Books, 1970), 192–240; Melvyn Dubofsky and Warren Van Tine, *John L. Lewis: A Biography* (New York: Quadrangle, 1977), 30–66; Schneider, *The Workers' (Communist) Party*, 38–41; Mother Jones to John H. Walker, 22 March 1921 and Mother Jones to My dear Powderly, 23 November 1921, in Edward M. Steel, ed., *The Correspondence of Mother Jones* (Pittsburgh: University of Pittsburgh Press, 1985), 221, 235.

29. Lista and the children apparently moved with Cannon to Cleveland, although evidence for this is scanty given the limited time they were there. See Ring interview with Cannon, April 12, 1974, 10.

30. For Debs's electoral votes in the presidential campaigns of 1904 (408,000), 1908 (421,000), 1912 (900,000 and 6 percent), and 1920 (923,000), see Ira Kipnis, *The American Socialist Movement, 1897–1912* (New York: Monthly Review, 1972), 163, 213, 367; James Weinstein, *The Decline of Socialism in America, 1912–1925* (New York: Vintage, 1969), 115.

31. "Boycott the Election! Proclamation of the United Communist Party of America," *The Communist,* n.d. [No. 9: Russian Revolution Anniversary Number]. See, as well, *Revolutionary Radicalism,* vol. 2, 1879–80. The last dated number of *The Communist,* which appeared every two weeks, was no. 5, August 15, 1920, so no. 9 likely appeared sometime shortly after October 15, 1920, and certainly before the first week of November 1920. On this dating, see Draper, *Roots of American Communism,* 433, n. 27.

32. Cannon, *History of American Trotskyism,* 10–12. See, as well, Cannon, *First Ten Years,* 43; and for a general overview of this period and subsequent developments, Howe and Coser, *The American Communist Party,* 41–95.

33. *Ohio Socialist,* October 15, 1919.

34. *Ohio Socialist,* October 29, 1919.

35. Herbert Benjamin, "Outline of Unpublished Manuscript: A History of the Unemployed Movement and Its Struggles During the Great Depression," [n.d., 1970s?], 150–52, 213–14, deposited in Columbia Oral History Project, Columbia University, New York, New York.

36. *The Toiler,* November 26, 1919; December 3, 1919; December 10, 1919; February 20, 1920.

37. See, among many possible citations: *The Toiler,* December 10, 1919; December 31, 1919; January 7, 1920; February 13, 1920; March 12, 1920; Scott Nearing, "The Spirit of Western Labor," *The Toiler,* January 21, 1920; "Craft Unionism—An Admitted Failure," and "The 'Outlaws,'" *The Toiler,* April 23, 1920; "For the Workers Councils," *The Toiler,* August 6, 1920.

38. See the "Proletarian Science History" course articles in *The Toiler,* March 19, 1920; March 26, 1920; April 2, 1920; May 7, 1920.

39. *The Toiler,* April 30, 1920.

40. "The IWW at Philadelphia," *The Toiler,* August 27, 1920; "Another Renegade," *The Toiler,* December 11, 1920; "Who Can Save the Unions?" *The Toiler,* May 7, 1921, all reprinted in *James P. Cannon and the Early Years of American Communism,* 71–77, 88–89, which also contains useful introductions contextualizing this writing.

41. Among the many articles that might be cited from *The Toiler* in this period, note particularly: Mollie Stiner [sic: Steimer], "Freedom for All Class War Prisoners," August 27, 1920 (on Steimer, see Lowenthal, *The Federal Bureau of Investigation,* 111–12); Mary Heaton Vorse, "Shadows of the Sweatshop," January 1, 1921; Mary Heaton Vorse, "Sacco and Vanzetti," January 8, 1921; Benjamin Gitlow, "Prison Greetings to the Strik-

ing Clothing Workers," "A Lesson for Labor," and reprint of Mary Heaton Vorse article from *The Liberator*, January 15, 1921; Robert Minor, "Who Are the Traitors," February 25, 1921; Minor, "Stedman's Red Raid," May 21, 1921 (later published as a pamphlet, Minor, *Stedman's Red Raid* (Cleveland: Toiler Publishing, 1921); Gus Schaefer, "Facts of Hobo Life," July 9, 1921; "The Illinois Miners' Strike," August 13, 1921. Draper, *Roots of American Communism*, 443, n. 7, draws the lineage of the *Ohio Socialist* and *The Toiler* through to the *Worker* and eventually the *Daily Worker*, established as the major organ of U.S. communism in 1924. Cannon, of course, relished noting that he had in fact been the editor of the communist paper that would eventually become the mainstay of the American Stalinist party. See Ring interview with Cannon, May 10, 1973, 23, which also contains the quote on editing and the ways in which party work took him away from many of the technical responsibilities.

42. "Two Letters on Trade Unionism," and "The Editor Replies," *The Toiler*, November 6, 1920; note also the brief allusion to this exchange in Howe and Coser, *American Communist Party*, 78–79. Also, M. P. Black, "Another Letter on Trade Unions," and "Editor Replies," and "Answer by the Editor," *The Toiler*, November 20, 1920; Fred Hurtig, "Within or Without," and "Editor Replies," *The Toiler*, January 15, 1921. Note, as well, from a slightly later period, Rose Wortis, "Problems of American Trade Unionism," *The Marxian* 2 (November 1921): 27–31.

43. James R. Barrett, *William Z. Foster and the Tragedy of American Radicalism* (Urbana: University of Illinois Press, 1999), 103–8; Louis Levine, *The Women's Garment Workers: A History of the International Ladies Garment Workers Union* (New York: B.W. Huebsch, 1924), 355–57; Lewis L. Lorwin, *Labor and Internationalism* (New York: Macmillan, 1929), 216–18; Draper, *American Communism and Soviet Russia*, 25, 125; James Oneal and G. A. Werner, *American Communism: A Critical Analysis of Its Origins, Development and Programs* (New York: E.P. Dutton, 1947), 94–98. The twenty-one points are reproduced in *Revolutionary Radicalism*, vol. 2, 1647–53, and the Comintern debate around them in John Riddell, ed., *Workers of the World and Oppressed Peoples Unite! Proceedings and Documents of the Second Congress, 1920: The Communist International in Lenin's Time*, vol. 2 (New York: Pathfinder, 1991), 291–419.

44. Issues of *The Toiler* carried advertisements for IWW-sponsored events, such as the July 5, 1920, picnic and mass meeting, to be addressed by John Sandgreen, editor of the *One Big Union Monthly*, on the subject of "The Truth about Industrial Unionism." See *The Toiler*, July 2, 1920.

45. James P. Cannon, "Open Shop Fight a Conflict of Classes," *Truth*, May 6, 1921; "Who Can Save the Unions?" *The Toiler*, May 7, 1921, reprinted in *James P. Cannon and the Early Years of American Communism*, 88–89.

46. See the statement by Milner in *The Toiler*, February 25, 1921.

47. *The Toiler*, November 13, 1920.

48. See Ring interview with Cannon, April 5, 1974, 4.

49. For comments from *The Toiler* on working in this clandestine period, see "How American Communists Work Underground," May 21, 1921, although this article may

well have appeared after Cannon's tenure as editor lapsed. The Lusk Committee estimated that *The Toiler* had a circulation of 1,500 in New York City alone. See *Revolutionary Radicalism,* vol. 2, 2006.

50. James P. Cannon, "The Story of Alex Howat," *The Liberator,* April 1921, and Cannon, "The Political Prisoners," *The Red Album* (Cleveland: Toiler, May 1, 1921), both reprinted in *James P. Cannon and the Early Years of American Communism,* 78–87.

51. *The Toiler,* September 17, 1921. It is impossible to know where Allison's editorship ended and recommenced, and where Cannon's commenced and stopped. Allison was originally on the masthead, and with the communist movement driven underground, no new editor would have been named. The Lusk Committee thus considered Allison the editor, naming him as such when it reprinted an article dated January 7, 1920. It is, of course, possible that Cannon was the editor at that time; another possibility is that he had finished up his Cleveland sojourn and was taking up responsibilities in New York. See *Revolutionary Radicalism,* vol. 2, 1348–50.

52. James P. Cannon, "Sixty Years of American Radicalism," speech delivered to a meeting of the West Coast Vacation School and Camp, Labor Day, 1959, reprinted in Cannon, *Speeches for Socialism,* 92.

53. Robert Miner, "John Reed Is Dead," *The Toiler,* October 30, 1920; W. F. Haycook, "John Reed, Martyr to Liberty," *The Toiler,* November 20, 1920; John Reed, "The World Congress of the Communist International," *The Communist,* no. 10 (n.d. [ca. November 1920]); Draper, *Roots of American Communism,* 284–93; Granville Hicks, *John Reed: The Making of a Revolutionary* (New York: Macmillan, 1936), 365–402. Reed's last days in Moscow were consumed with the burning issues of the American communist movement, that of unification of the revolutionary Left and issues relating to trade union policy. See statements by Zinoviev reproduced in *Revolutionary Radicalism,* vol. 1, 647–51; and the full account of Reed's (and Fraina's) interventions at the 1920 Second Congress in John Riddell, ed., *Workers of the World,* vols. 1 and 2.

54. Draper, *Roots of American Communism,* 293–97; Paul Buhle, *A Dreamer's Paradise Lost: Louis C. Fraina/Lewis Corey (1892–1953) and the Decline of Radicalism in the United States* (Atlantic Highlands, NJ: Humanities Press, 1995), 87–116. For *The Toiler*'s take on the early allegations of Fraina as spy, see the statement of skepticism in "The 'Spy' Story," *The Toiler,* July 2, 1920. Much has recently been made of Comintern funds and the United States communist movement. This seems overblown, although it is undeniable that money did pass from the Soviets to revolutionaries such as Reed and Fraina, and the flow of funds continued, of course, into later periods. See Harvey Klehr, John Earl Haynes, and Fridrikh Igorevich Firsov, *The Secret World of American Communism* (New Haven: Yale University Press, 1995), 21–40 on the years 1917–1925.

55. *James P. Cannon and the Early Years of American Communism,* 11. Not that office skills were that developed in the underground. "I always thought an office was a desk, you know, with your own pencils," Cannon confessed in the 1950s. See Morgan diary, entry for May 14, 1956.

56. Louis Francis Budenz, *This Is My Story* (New York: McGraw Hill, 1947), 85.

57. Les Evans, ed., *James P. Cannon As We Knew Him: By Thirty-Three Comrades, Friends, and Relatives* (New York: Pathfinder, 1976), 168 (Harry Ring recollection); Ring interview with Cannon, April 12, 1974, 10–11, 15; Morgan diary, entry for August 30, 1955; "Bob Minor Is Coming," *Workers' World*, December 19, 1919.

58. Budenz, *This Is My Story*, 85; Louis Budenz, *The Techniques of Communism* (New York: Regency, 1954).

59. Draper, *Roots of American Communism*, 306–11; Cannon, *First Ten Years*, 109–11; James G. Ryan, *Earl Browder: The Failure of American Communism* (Tuscaloosa: University of Alabama Press, 1997), 21–23; Philip J. Jaffe, *The Rise and Fall of American Communism* (New York: Horizon, 1975), 29; Earl Browder, "'No-Man's Land': A Political Autobiography," Box 10, chap. 6, 117–34, Earl Browder Papers, George Arents Research Library for Special Collections, Syracuse University, Syracuse, New York (hereafter Browder Papers); Earl R. Browder, "Letters from the Mine Workers Convention," *The Toiler*, October 8, 1921; Earl R. Browder, "The Red Trade Union International: The First World Congress of Revolutionary Unions," *The Toiler*, October 15, 1921. Browder's unpublished characterizations of Cannon contain his usual transparent animosities and are not without contradictions and inconsistencies. For more on the first congress of the RILU, see James R. Barrett, *William Z. Foster and the Tragedy of American Radicalism* (Urbana: University of Illinois Press, 1999), 103–9, 122–23.

60. Draper, *Roots of American Communism*, 306; Cannon, *First Ten Years*, 111.

61. Cannon, *History of American Trotskyism*, 15.

62. Foster, *History of the Communist Party*, 180–81; Ring interview with Cannon, April 5, 1974, 1–4; Draper, *Roots of American Communism*, 251; Cannon, *History of American Trotskyism*, 11; Cannon, *First Ten Years*, 318; *Revolutionary Radicalism*, vol. 1, 647–51.

63. For Cannon's comments, see Ring interviews with Cannon, May 30, 1973, 19–20; April 12, 1974, 2–3; and for a brief general statement note *James P. Cannon and the Early Years of American Communism*, 12.

64. "Communist Unity," *The Communist*, no. 14 (n.d.), and now publishing under the subtitle "Official Organ of the United Communist Party of America, Section of the Communist International"; "The Third International Has Acted," "Communist Compromise," "Labor's Bill of Rights and Sovietism," and "Communist Tactics," *The Communist*, no. 16. These concerns continued in later articles in *The Toiler*. See, for instance, Ness Edwards, "Some Thoughts on Tactics," *The Toiler*, August 13, 1921.

65. Ring interview with Cannon, May 30, 1973, 19; Cannon, *First Ten Years*, 44–45; Cannon, *History of American Trotskyism*, 173–74; Draper, *Roots of American Communism*, 270–74, 333; Donald Drew Egbert and Stow Persons, eds., *Socialism and American Life*, vol. 1 (Princeton, NJ: Princeton University Press, 1952), 338–40; Arne Swabeck, "Unpublished Reminiscence of James P. Cannon" (written for, but not appearing in, Evans, *As We Knew Him*), Reel 1, JPC Papers; Henry Bengston, *On the Left in America: Memoirs of the Scandinavian-American Labor Movement* (Carbondale: Southern University Illinois Press, 1999), 120, 130–34, 202, n. 1; Evelyn Reed, "Rose Karsner Cannon Is

Dead, a Foremost Woman Trotskyist," *Militant*, February 18, 1968; Evelyn Reed interview with Rose Karsner (n.d., ca. 1960), Rose Karsner Cannon Papers, in Reel 61, JPC Papers; Oneal and Werner, *American Communism*, 103–8; Melech Epstein, *Jewish Labor in the U.S.A.—An Industrial, Political, and Cultural History of the Jewish Labor Movement* (n.p.: KTAV Publishing House, 1969), vol. 2, 112–14. For the general Comintern position, see *Theses and Statutes of the Third (Communist) International, Adopted by the Second Congress, July 17th–August 7th, 1920* (Moscow: Publishing Office of the Communist International, May 1920, reprinted by United Communist Party of America).

66. "The Reminiscences of Max Shachtman," Number 488, Oral History Research Office, 1963, 24–25, Columbia University, New York, New York; Drucker, *Shachtman and His Left*, 14–15.

67. Bittelman, "Things I Have Learned," 357–59; Gitlow, *I Confess*, 161; Sam Gordon in Evans, *As We Knew Him*, 79; Bertram D. Wolfe, *A Life in Two Centuries: An Autobiography* (New York: Stein & Day, 1981), 266. Bittelman's wording perhaps requires clarification. Divisions would remain among Jewish groups on the revolutionary Left in the years 1921–1924, but Cannon had helped to bring two major sections into a common revolutionary organization.

68. Cannon would address an American Labor Alliance convention at the Manhattan Labor Temple, 243 East 84th Street, stating that the purpose of the gathering was "to unify all revolutionary elements." See "James Patrick Cannon," searched December 9, 1941, 2a, FBI File. See also Bittelman, "Things I Have Learned," 351; Cannon, *History of American Trotskyism*, 15; Cannon, *First Ten Years*, 104, 113, 116, 118, 123 (in a later critique of the Alliance, accenting the ways it managed to reproduce sectarianism); Oneal and Werner, *American Communism*, 93 (on the lack of discipline and direction in the underground); Draper, *Roots of American Communism*, 273, 336–40; Browder, "'No-Man's Land,'" chap. 6, 117; Morgan, *A Covert Life*, 26; "American Labor Alliance to Charter City Locals and Organize a Political Party," *The Marxian* 2 (November 1921): 108–9.

69. A. Raphael (Alexander Bittelman) and J. P. Collins, writing in the Communist Party of America's underground journal, *The Communist*, October 1921, 3, 21, cited in Draper, *Roots of American Communism*, 353, 451, nn. 1–2.

70. For a succinct membership accounting, see Howe and Coser, *American Communist Party*, 91–93. See, as well, Cannon, "Sixty Years of American Radicalism," 93; and on his determination, Cannon, *First Ten Years*, 43–44.

71. "Report of the Executive Secretary, Meeting of the Central Executive Committee of the Workers Party of America," June 29, 1922, Reel 1a, 4–5, in Documents from Russian Center for the Preservation and Study of Contemporary History, Microfilm Copies Held, Prometheus Research Library, New York, New York. This same source establishes the precarious economic foundation of early American communism, where yearly deficits often surpassed $10,000. On communist newspapers and the dominance of foreign-language publications, see Solon De Leon, *American Labor Press Directory* (New York: Rad School of Social Science, 1925), 20–22.

72. Foster, *History of the Communist Party*, 194; Draper, *Roots of American Communism*, 335–41; Cannon, *First Ten Years*, 45–46; "New Workers' Party to Be Organized,"

Truth, December 3, 1921; *Workers' Council*, December 15, 1921; *The Toiler*, December 24, 1921.

73. James Cook (Cannon) et al, to the Communist International, "For a Party of the Masses (The Struggle Against Sectarianism)" (n.d., ca. November 1921), in Reel 3, Documents from Russian Center for the Preservation and Study of Contemporary History, Microfilm Copies Held, Prometheus Research Library, New York, New York.

74. Minutes of the Meeting of the American Commission of the 4th Congress of the Communist International, Wednesday, November 27, 1922, 13–19, Reel 2, in Documents from Russian Center for the Preservation and Study of Contemporary History, Microfilm Copies Held, Prometheus Research Library, New York, New York. For a pristine statement of Katterfeld's (Carr's) privileging of the underground apparatus, see J. Carr, Executive Secretary, CEC, Communist Party of America to Comrades, 1 August 1921, Box 39, Folder 1, "Workers' Party Documents and Clippings Pertaining to Hardman's Expulsion," J. B. S. Hardman Papers, Tamiment Institute, New York University, New York, New York.

75. Browder, "'No-Man's Land,'" Series III, Box 10, chap. 7, 172–73, and Earl Browder to Theodore Draper, 24 January 1956; 19 February 1956, Series I, Box 3, Browder Papers, suggest that a compromise had been worked out, in which Browder concurred, between the controlling underground and those advocating a legal party. Cannon's role in putting this agreement together was obviously important, although Browder neglects to mention this. Browder to Theodore Draper, 7 February 1956, Series I, Box 3, Browder Papers, states: "Formally the underground 'goose' caucus executive committee held firm control, and Cannon was a sort of 'chairman-of-the-arrangements committee' on its behalf. . . . Lovestone represented most actively the New York 'liquidators'; Cannon was performing miracles of 'diplomacy' operating between the two camps." This indicates Cannon's centrality, although its effort to paint Cannon as somehow placatory toward undergroundism is a rather fantastic reading of the record, which contains no other evidence confirming Browder's view. These letters also put forward the view that Cannon's role as a liquidator in Moscow was insignificant, and no one in the party treated all that seriously the comings and goings to Russia. At best, this is a strange reconstruction of events and their significance.

76. There is something of this kind of condescension in Weinstein, *Decline of Socialism*, ch. 6, "The Workers' Party: Prescriptive Antidote to an Infantile Disorder, 1921–1922," 258–71.

77. Cannon, *History of American Trotskyism*, 13–14; Ring interview with Cannon, April 5, 1974, 2.

Chapter 6: Geese in Flight

1. On the African Blood Brotherhood (ABB), founded by Cyril V. Briggs in 1919 as a materialist alternative to the black separatism of Marcus Garvey, see Theodore Draper, *American Communism and Soviet Russia: The Formative Period* (New York: Viking, 1960), 323–33; Harry Haywood, *Black Bolshevik: Autobiography of an Afro-American Communist* (Chicago: Liberator Press, 1978), 122–31; Mark Naison, *Communists in*

Harlem During the Depression (Urbana: University of Illinois Press, 1983), 3, 5–7, 17–18; Theman Taylor, "Cyril Briggs and the African Blood Brotherhood: Effects of Communism on Black Nationalism, 1919–1935" (PhD diss., University of California—Santa Barbara, 1981); Cedric J. Robinson, *Black Marxism: The Making of the Black Radical Tradition* (London: Zed Press, 1983), 279, 296–301, 311, 342–43; Robin D. G. Kelley, "'Afric's Sons with Banner Red': African American Communists and the Politics of Culture, 1919–1934," in Kelley, *Race Rebels: Culture, Politics, and the Black Working Class* (New York: Free Press, 1994), 103–22; Winston James, *Holding Aloft the Banner of Ethiopia: Caribbean Radicalism in Early Twentieth-Century America* (New York: Verso, 1998), 122–84; Wayne F. Cooper, *Claude McKay: Rebel Sojourner in the Harlem Renaissance—A Biography* (Baton Rouge: Louisiana State University Press, 1987), 106–9, 142–43, 175–78, 184, 402; Mark Solomon, *The Cry Was Unity: Communists and African Americans, 1917–1936* (Jackson: University Press of Mississippi, 1998), 3–21; Barbara Foley, *Spectres of 1919: Class & Nation in the Making of the New Negro* (Urbana: University of Illinois Press, 2003), 61–68. The ABB was the foundation of early African American communism with Briggs, Richard B. Moore, Otto Huiswoud, and Harry Haywood prominent in its history.

2. See, for accounts of delegates and the convention, Theodore Draper, *The Roots of American Communism* (New York: Viking Press, 1957), 341–43; James Oneal and G. A. Werner, *American Communism: A Critical Analysis of Its Origins, Development and Programs* (New York: E.P. Dutton, 1947), 118; James Weinstein, *The Decline of Socialism in America, 1912–1925* (New York: Vintage, 1969), 258–71. The uninvited Marx-Engels Institute of New York delegate is mentioned in "The 'Workers' Party,'" *The Communist*, February 1922, monthly organ of the underground Communist Party of America.

3. See "New Workers' Party to Be Organized," *Truth* (Duluth), December 3, 1921; Oneal and Werner, *American Communism*, 116–17; David Montgomery, *The Fall of the House of Labor: The Workplace, the State, and American Labor Activism, 1865–1925* (Cambridge, UK: Cambridge University Press, 1987), esp. 370–464.

4. On Cannon's views of Salutsky, see James P. Cannon, *The History of American Trotskyism: From Its Origins (1928) to the Founding of the Socialist Workers' Party (1938)—Report of a Participant* (New York: Pathfinder, 1972), 172–75; James P. Cannon, *The First Ten Years of American Communism—Report of a Participant* (New York: Pathfinder, 1973), 44. For Salutsky/Hardman and the process of negotiation that culminated in the Workers' Council/Jewish Socialist Federation elements joining the Workers' Party, see Eugene Victor Orenstein, "The Jewish Socialist Federation of America, 1912–1921: A Study of Integration and Particularism in the American Jewish Labor Movement" (PhD diss., Columbia University, 1978), 227–73. There is no corroborating evidence for Salutsky's claim, made through Melech Epstein, that Cannon suggested to the Workers' Council leaders that they would be "taken care of financially and provided with sufficient 'space' for their talents." See Melech Epstein, *The Jew and Communism, 1919–1941* (New York: Trade Union Sponsoring Committee, 1959), 98. Salutsky/Hardman remained in the Workers' Party, functioning on its CEC until his expulsion in the summer of 1923. He continued to oppose undergroundism and saw it

as critically important in the party during the period 1921–1923. For documentation relating to this, see Box 39, Folder 1, "Workers' Party Documents and Clippings Pertaining to Hardman's Expulsion," J. B. S. Hardman Papers, Tamiment Institute, New York University, New York, New York.

5. Alexander Bittelman, "Things I Have Learned: An Autobiography," 357–59, Boxes 1–2, Collection 62, unpublished manuscript in Alexander Bittelman Papers, Tamiment Institute, New York, New York; Cannon, *First Ten Years*, 90–91. See, as well, Paul Buhle, *Marxism in the United States: Remapping the History of the American Left* (New York: Verso, 1991), 82–84.

6. See Draper, *Roots of American Communism*, 339–40. Much is made—on perhaps small and dubious evidence—of the funding of early American communism by the Comintern in Harvey Klehr, John Earl Haynes, and Fridrikh Igorevich Firsov, *The Secret World of American Communism* (New Haven: Yale University Press, 1995), 21–25.

7. The speech, reprinted in *The Toiler*, January 7, 1922; *Voice of Labor*, January 6, 1922, has been anthologized in *James P. Cannon and the Early Years of American Communism: Selected Writings and Speeches, 1920–1928* (New York: Prometheus Research Library, 1992), 90–94. Its warm reception is commented on in Thomas J. O'Flaherty, "Flashlights on the Convention," *The Toiler*, January 7, 1922; Bittelman, "Things I Have Learned," 358; Oneal and Werner, *American Communism*, 119. William Z. Foster, *History of the Communist Party of the United States* (New York: International 1952), 188–93, contains a brief account of the Workers' Council role in the preconference period and a discussion of the Workers' Party's founding convention. It is marred by some factual errors and, like almost all official CPUSA sources, manages to write Cannon out of the proceedings. Note, as well, Albert Fried, *Communism in America: A History in Documents* (New York: Columbia University Press, 1997), 40–42.

8. Foster's coming-out statement was undoubtedly his pamphlet *The Russian Revolution* (Chicago: Trade Union Educational League, 1921), described as the result of a fourteen-week stay in Soviet Russia, with Foster serving as a correspondent of the Federated Press during the spring and summer of 1921. See, as well, Draper, *Roots of American Communism*, 342; Foster, *History of the Communist Party*, 191–93; *The Toiler*, January 14, 1922. On Foster's movement to communism in this period, see Edward P. Johanningsmeier, *Forging American Communism: The Life of William Z. Foster* (Princeton, NJ: Princeton University Press, 1994), 150–74. For the TUEL, see Earl K. Beckner, "The Trade Union Educational League and the American Labor Movement," *Journal of Political Economy* 33 (April 1925): 410–31.

9. Foster, *History of the Communist Party*, 193; Draper, *Roots of American Communism*, 343–44, 450, n. 32; *The Worker*, May 27 & June 17, 1922; Martin Abern, "Who's Red—and Why?" *The Young Worker*, June–July 1922, 9–10; Abern, "Culture, Science and Working-Class Education," *The Young Worker*, August–September 1922, 5–6; Abern, "Into the Fight, Young Workers!" and "The Red Raids," *The Young Worker*, October 1922, 10–14, 16; *Manifesto, Program, Resolutions, and Constitution, Young Workers League of America, Adopted by the First National Conference, 12–15 May 1922* (Chicago: Young Workers League of America, 1922).

10. For the twenty-one points, see Robert V. Daniels, *A Documentary History of American Communism: Volume 2—Communism and the World* (Hanover: University Press of New England, 1984), 44–47.

11. The Program and Constitution of the Workers' Party is printed in *The Toiler,* January 7, 1922. For the seventeen-member CEC and the seven alternates, as well as major offices, see Draper, *Roots of American Communism,* 342, 450, n. 28; *James P. Cannon and the Early Years of American Communism,* 11. On the unconstitutional expansion of the CEC from seven to seventeen, see Oneal and Werner, *American Communism,* 122, an issue posed differently in Harvey E. Klehr, *Communist Cadre: The Social Background of the American Communist Party Elite* (Stanford, CA: Hoover Institution Press, 1978), 11. On Prevey and Baker, see Bernard K. Johnpoll, ed., *A Documentary History of the Communist Party of the United States,* vol. 1 (Westport, CT: Greenwood, 1994), 169, 179, 186, 188–90, 194. The Ohio duo did not last in the communist milieu, Cannon explaining to a comrade: "Charley Baker and Margaret Prevey could not be assimilated into the Communist Party." James P. Cannon to Joseph Siminoff, 22 September 1924, in Loose File, Documents from Russian Center for the Preservation and Study of Contemporary History, Microfilm Copies Held, Prometheus Research Library, New York, New York (hereafter Russian Center, PRL).

12. Max Eastman had condemned the communist project in a preconference article in *The Liberator,* October 1921, quoted in Oneal and Werner, *American Communism,* 123–24.

13. Quoted in "The 'Workers' Party,'" in the organ of the underground, "left opposition" CP, *The Communist,* February 1922, 15. This report denigrated the Marx-Engels Institute (located at 208 East 12th Street) delegate as "low-brow," but the Institute, whose guiding spirit was Harry Waton, produced the important theoretical journal, *The Marxian.* Though shortlived, appearing for only two issues in October–November 1921, *The Marxian* demanded a level of familiarity with Marxist classics rare in United States communist circles.

14. Foster, *History of the Communist Party,* 191; O'Flaherty, "Flashlights on the Convention"; Oneal and Werner, *American Communism,* 123, citing *The Proletarian,* December 1921; Cannon, *First Ten Years,* 55, 103. On Batt, see as well James R. Barrett, *William Z. Foster and the Tragedy of American Radicalism* (Urbana: University of Illinois Press, 1999), 103; Earl Browder, "'No-Man's Land': A Political Autobiography," Series 3, Box 10, chap. 6, 166, Earl W. Browder Papers, George Arents Research Library for Special Collections, Syracuse University, Syracuse, New York (hereafter Browder Papers). For Harry M. Wicks, not to be confused with the British Bolshevik, Harry Wicks, see the discussion in Draper, *American Communism and Soviet Russia,* 434–35, 530–31, nn. 72–73. Wicks faced charges as an anti-communist spy in 1923, but was exonerated. In 1937 similar allegations were made on the basis of evidence from the Chicago Federation of Labor, and at this time Wicks was expelled from the Communist Party. Draper claims, on the basis of an exploration of Wicks's private papers, that there was no convincing evidence for these charges, and by 1937 Stalinist purges were sufficiently unscrupulous that it must be said that Wicks's guilt or innocence remains unproven.

That said, Wicks always carried with him a whiff of the untrustworthy. See Benjamin Gitlow, *I Confess: The Truth about American Communism* (New York: E.P. Dutton, 1940), 547. Wicks's final statement, *Eclipse of October* (London: Holborn, 1958), is not terribly useful in unraveling these issues.

15. For a brief account of this November–January conflict, see Draper, *Roots of American Communism,* 339–40, 353–55; on the confusing array of publications named *The Communist* in this period, see as well, 432, n. 21, 451, n. 4.

16. "Our Attitude Towards the Workers' Party," *The Communist,* January 1922, 1–2.

17. Draper, *Roots of American Communism,* 353–55; "Emergency Convention: The Fifth Convention of the Communist Party of America," *The Communist,* February 1922, 1–3; Gitlow, *I Confess,* 133; William F. Dunne Papers, "Manuscript—History of the Communist Party," Box 63, 6, Tamiment Institute, New York, New York.

18. "Emergency Convention," *The Communist,* February 1922, 1–3, with pages 3–5 containing "Constitution of the C.P. of A." On Minor's role, see Draper, *Roots of American Communism,* 340, 354–55, citing J. Ballister (Robert Minor), "The Blight of Purity," *The Communist* (Workers' Party), July 1922, 9. Dunne, "Manuscript—History of the Communist Party," Box 63, 6, ridiculed Minor and the Goose Caucus as offering at this convention a "Fish Pond" thesis, whereby "one could dip in and pull out something to suit anyone—except a Marxist-Leninist."

19. Minutes of the Central Executive Committee Meeting, February 22, 1922: Unfinished District Matters, District 2, 20, Reel 1a, Russian Center, PRL, noted a communication from a "non-member" charging Cook (Cannon) with having made statements advocating the liquidation of the Communist Party. The CEC exonerated Cannon of any wrongdoing, but in sections of the ultraleft underground he was less likely to receive support.

20. The preceding paragraph draws on "Emergency Convention," and "The 'Workers' Party,'" *The Communist,* February 1922, 1–3, 14–16; Davis, Executive Secretary, CEC/CPA, "Manifesto of the Communist Party of America on the Workers' Party: To the Workers of America," and Edwin Trent, "Fooling the Workers into Communism," *The Communist,* March 1922, 14–15; Minutes of the Meeting of the American Commission of the Fourth Congress of the Communist International, Wednesday, November 27, 1922, 13–22, in Russian Center, PRL.

21. The preceding paragraphs draw on Draper, *Roots of American Communism,* 353–58; Draper, *American Communism and Soviet Russia,* 22; Cannon, *First Ten Years,* 46, 67; Harry Ring interview with James P. Cannon, April 12, 1974, 3 (in possession of the author; hereafter Ring interview); Cannon, *History of American Trotskyism,* 18–19; Foster, *History of the Communist Party,* 194; Irving Howe and Lewis Coser, *The American Communist Party: A Critical History (1919–1957)* (Boston: Beacon Press, 1957), 97; Gitlow, *I Confess,* 133–34, 142–43, 147, 547.

22. Draper, *Roots of American Communism,* 388; Undated "Report of the C.P. of A. (Minority Group) Convention," hand pagination 94–97, Reel 1a, Russian Center, PRL. It is likely that this gathering, which elected the Boston Lettish ultraleftist "Sullivan" to attend the Fourth Congress of the Communist International, took place sometime

after the supposed Comintern "Special Representative" John Pogany/Pepper (Lang) arrived in the United States. Pepper, who is dealt with extensively in chapter 7, attended this convention, but was clearly subordinate to Valetski.

23. For a youth section statement appealing for unity in the midst of the intense factionalism of the spring of 1922, see H. Seligson and E. Elston, "Appeal for Revolutionary Unity," *The Young Worker* (May 1922), 11–12. Note also "Statement to the Membership of the C. P.of A. by the C.E.C," 24 April 1922, signed by Cannon and fourteen others, in 1a, Russian Center, PRL. The Central Executive Committee of the Communist Party remained staunch in its commitment to the underground party. See "Some CEC Decisions, from the 6th and 7th Meetings," Undated, Reel 1a, hand pagination, 99, Russian Center, PRL: "The underground organization is an absolute necessity for the performance of revolutionary, com work in this country. . . . It must be the controlling body of any open org that may be set up, to spread com among the broad masses." Also, from the same collection, "Rules of Procedure for the C.E.C. of the C.P. of A.," undated, 9–10.

24. Les Evans, ed., *James P. Cannon As We Knew Him: By Thirty-three Comrades, Friends, and Relatives* (New York: Pathfinder, 1976), 169 (Harry Ring recollection); Cannon, *First Ten Years*, 80–81, 305.

25. Cannon, *First Ten Years*, 45, 53, 78, 80–81, 115. Ted Morgan, *A Covert Life: Jay Lovestone—Communist, Anti-Communist, and Spymaster* (New York: Random House, 1999), 3–29, covers the period of the Cannon-Lovestone combination, but provides limited commentary on its significance. Lovestone, a student with little involvement in actual movements of class struggle, managed to produce a book-length overview of the employers' offensive, the role of the state and its courts, and working-class conflict in the early 1920s. His collaboration with Cannon in this period must have colored his perspective. See Jay Lovestone, *The Government-Strikebreaker: A Study of the Role of the Government in the Recent Industrial Crisis* (New York: Workers' Party of America, 1923). Gitlow, *I Confess*, 152, suggests that John Pepper put the Workers' Party up to having Lovestone write this book in order to reestablish Lovestone's credentials as a potential party leader. Lovestone's stature had been compromised by widespread knowledge that he had testified against a comrade during the post-World War I "Red Scare." Ruthenberg had supposedly advised Lovestone to testify, rationalizing this stand with the view that the state could gain nothing of advantage from Lovestone openly recounting certain facts. This may or may not have been the case, but a view of Lovestone as a stool pigeon persisted in certain communist circles, well into the 1920s.

26. To my knowledge, the only collection of such correspondence is in Reel 7, Russian Center, PRL: see, for examples: Cannon to Comrades, 3 March 1922; 16 March 1922; 17 March 1922; 22 April 1922; Cannon to All District Organizers (n.d. [March 1922?]); 4 March 1922; Cannon to all Federation Secretaries, 22 March 1922; Cannon to Editors, 27 March 1922; Cannon to All Branches, 21 April 1922.

27. Theodore Draper interview with James P. Cannon, April 24, 1956, series 3, no. 7, Theodore Draper Research Files, Robert W. Woodruff Library, Emory University, Atlanta, Georgia, cited in *James P. Cannon and the Early Years of American Commu-*

nism, 14–15. On Ruthenberg's release, see Gitlow, *I Confess,* 128–30, and for his assuming the National Secretary's post, *The Worker,* May 20, 1922. On Cannon and Ruthenberg, see Cannon, *First Ten Years,* 122–23, 126, 183, 194, which stresses Ruthenberg's formality *and* ability. "Definitely not the palsy-walsy type" though, Cannon concluded colloquially. A cryptic comment on Harrison's departure from the communist movement is found in Klehr, *Communist Cadre,* 88.

28. "Cannon and Baker Freed," and "Workers Party Organizational News," *The Worker,* February 11, 1922; Ring interview with Cannon, May 30, 1973, 18–20; Cannon, *First Ten Years,* 74. For a brief statement on this context of political economy, definitely favorable to Cannon's strategic push for legalization of the communist party, but one in which there remained significant pockets of coercive ugliness, see *James P. Cannon and the Early Years of American Communism,* 12–14. "U.S. vs. James P. Cannon and Charles Baker," January 30, 1922, U.S. Department of Justice, Federal Bureau of Investigation, Freedom of Information/Privacy Act File, Washington, DC (hereafter FBI File), indicates that on January 23, 1922, "a demurrer to the indictment in this case was sustained and Cannon and Baker released." For treatment of the 1916 and 1922 contrasts, see Montgomery, *Fall of the House of Labor,* 257–464, esp. 407–10; for the shopmen's national railroad strike, see Colin J. Davis, *Power at Odds: The 1922 National Railroad Shopmen's Strike* (Urbana: University of Illinois Press, 1997).

29. "James P. Cannon, National Chairman, Workers' Party," January 30, 1922, Kansas City, Missouri, FBI File. The informer noted that Cannon claimed 148 delegates had convened to establish the Workers' Party, clearly an exaggeration.

30. See Oneal and Werner, *American Communism,* 127–30. For a conservative response, see Blair Coan, *The Red Web* (Chicago: Northwest Publications, 1925), 89–90.

31. James P. Cannon and Caleb Harrison, "Workers' Party Calls on All Labor for Big United Front: Open Letter to the Conference of Progressive Political Action," *The Worker,* March 4, 1922, also in "To the Labor Press," Reel 7, 25–31, Russian Center, PRL.

32. "James Patrick Cannon," Searched December 9, 1941, 7a, FBI File. On the 1922 coal strike, see Melvyn Dubofsky and Warren Van Tine, *John L. Lewis: A Biography* (New York: Quadrangle, 1977), 82–85; Lovestone, *The Government-Strikebreaker,* 74–133.

33. See Cannon to All Party Editors, 27 March 1922, Reel 7, 49, Russian Center, PRL. Goldman's antagonism to the Soviet Union was ultimately presented in Emma Goldman, *My Disillusionment in Russia* (New York: Doubleday, Page, 1923).

34. James P. Cannon to Frank Miner (Minneapolis Trades and Labor Assembly), 17 April 1922, in "Cannon Working Files, 1919–1924 & 1925–1928," Prometheus Research Library, New York, New York; Mary Heaton Vorse, "Sacco and Vanzetti," *The Toiler,* January 8, 1921; Mary Heaton Vorse, *A Footnote to Folly: Reminiscences of Mary Heaton Vorse* (New York: Farrar & Rinehart, 1935). On Sacco and Vanzetti, see, among other sources, Paul Avrich, *Sacco and Vanzetti: The Anarchist Background* (Princeton, NJ: Princeton University Press, 1991).

35. James P. Cannon and Caleb Harrison, "Proclamation of the Workers Party for International May Day, 1922," *The Worker,* April 29, 1922; Cannon and Harrision, "WORKERS OF AMERICA! Choose! Capitalism and Chains! OR Social Revolution

and Freedom!" 65–69, Reel 7, Russian Center, PRL. See also Cannon and Harrison, "To All Locals and Branches of the Workers Party—Important: May Day Demonstrations," 16 March 1922, Russian Center, PRL, Reel 7, 45–46, as well as other correspondence relating to May Day.

36. "First of May Festival Concert and Ball," *The Worker,* April 22, 1922; "May Day Is Party's Red Letter Day," *The Worker,* May 13, 1922.

37. "Prison Doors of New York Swing Open!" and "Coming Out Celebration," *The Worker,* May 6, 1922; Cannon, *First Ten Years,* 75.

38. Cannon, *First Ten Years,* 81, 115, 46, 50, 305–7; Cannon, *The I.W.W.: The Great Anticipation* (New York: Pioneer, 1956); Charles Shipman, *It Had to Be Revolution: Memoirs of an American Radical* (Ithaca, NY: Cornell University Press, 1993), 139; Dorothy Gallagher, *All the Right Enemies: The Life and Murder of Carlo Tresca* (New Brunswick, NJ: Rutgers University Press, 1988), 93–94; Elizabeth Gurley Flynn, *The Rebel Girl: An Autobiography—My First Life (1906–1926)* (New York: International, 1982), 206–7.

39. For positive endorsement, see Alexander Bittelman, "Things I Have Learned," 365, chap. 12, 357–59; "The Reminiscences of Max Shachtman," Number 488, Oral History Research Office, 1963, 24–25, Columbia University, New York, New York. More negative assessment appears in Earl Browder, "'No-Man's Land,'" chap. 6, 117; Louis Francis Budenz, *This Is My Story* (New York: McGraw Hill, 1947), 85; Gitlow, *I Confess,* 161–62; "Emergency Convention," *The Communist,* February 1922; Edwin Trent, "Fooling the Workers into Communism," *The Communist,* March 1922.

40. "The 'Workers' Party,'" *The Communist,* February 1922, 16; Oneal and Werner, *American Communism,* 121.

41. J. P. Morray, *Project Kuzbas: American Workers in Siberia (1921–1926)* (New York: International, 1983), 74–84; Charles Wood, "H.S. Calvert's Giant Task in Industry: Once a Worker in a Ford Factory He Has Engaged to Develop a Russian Territory Bigger Than New Jersey," *New York World,* February 12, 1922; Howe and Coser, *American Communist Party,* 95; Joseph R. Conlin, *Big Bill Haywood and the Radical Union Movement* (Syracuse: Syracuse University Press, 1969), 196, 200; William D. Haywood, *Bill Haywood's Book: The Autobiography of Big Bill Haywood* (New York: International, 1929, reprint 1969), 364; Tom Barker, "Red Russia and the IWW," *Industrial Pioneer* 1 (April 1921): 3–5; Barker, "Petrograd in July, 1921," *Industrial Pioneer* 1 (October 1921): 39–40.

42. For the best succinct statements on this convoluted set of alignments, see Draper, *Roots of American Communism,* 358–62; Howe and Coser, *American Communist Party,* 96–99.

43. See Katterfeld's (Carr's) comments in Minutes, American Commission, November 27, 1922, Reel 2, 15; Cannon to All Branch and Local Secretaries, "Trade Union Education League," 21 April 1922, Reel 7, 75, both in Russian Center, PRL.

44. Cannon's snapshot assessment of Amter is in *First Ten Years,* 191–93.

45. On this evolving factionalism, see Draper, *American Communism and Soviet Russia,* 22–23; Cannon, *First Ten Years,* 74–75; and Draper, *Roots of American Communism,* 360–62, 452–53, nn. 18–23, citing especially Central Executive Committee of the C.P. of A., "Theses on Relations of the C.P. to an L.P.P.," Damon (Ruthenberg) and Marshall

(Bedacht), "Problems of Communist Organization in the U.S.," J. Ford (Amter) and A. Dubner (Jakira), "Theses on the Relations of No. 1 and No. 2," J. Ballister (Minor), "The Blight of Purity," *The Communist,* July 1922, 1–3, 23–24, 12–13, 8–10. Note Katterfeld's discussion of the relations of Numbers One and Two in Minutes, American Commission, September 27, 1922, Reel 2, 17–18, Russian Center, PRL.

46. Gitlow, *I Confess,* 133, 153; Howe and Coser, *American Communist Party,* 98. Cannon did not know how the Goose Caucus was named, noting in Ring inteview with Cannon, April 12, 1974, 11: "Somebody maybe used that expression derisively and it stuck." See as well, Earl Browder, "'No-Man's Land,'" chap. 7, 168.

47. See "Report of Delegate of 'Opposition' Faction," and "Sullivan" statement in Minutes, American Commission, November 27, 1922, Reel 2, 38–45, 46–59, Russian Center, PRL. "Sullivan" was the leading Boston Lett deeply committed to the underground, arguing against liquidation.

48. Ibid., 54, 58, citing James A. Marshall (Bedacht), "That Centrist," *The Communist* 9, July 1922, 4.

49. I am indebted to communications with Ed Johanningsmeier for clarifications on these matters. It is easy to draw the conclusion from the existing secondary literature that Foster was the Profintern's key figure in the United States from the moment of his involvement in the first Congress of the RILU. See Barrett, *William Z. Foster,* 105–9; Johanningsmeier, *Forging American Communism,* 164–65; James G. Ryan, *Earl Browder: The Failure of American Communism* (Tuscaloosa: University of Alabama Press, 1997), 22–25; Draper, *Roots of American Communism,* 316. This is not entirely mistaken, but it had been agreed at the first Congress of the RILU that ultimate authority within the American Bureau of the Profintern rested with the Communist Party. Although Foster was apparently provided with instructions on how to function as "special representative" of the RILU in the United States, Cannon also received (addressed to Cook) an undated communication, probably written late in 1921, that designated his appointment as "special representative of the Red International of Labor Unions in the United States." This document stipulated that "the work of carrying out the decisions of the First Congress of the R.I.L.U. is entrusted to your supervision alone." Browder (Dixon) was to be Cannon's assistant and alternate. See To Comrade Cook, "Instructions for Work in the United States" (n.d. [ca. November 1921?]), Reel 3, Russian Center, PRL. For the Cannon-Browder-Foster cooperation, see, for instance, the TUEL pamphlet, the first volume of "the Little Red Library," W. Z. Foster, J. P. Cannon, and E. R. Browder, *Trade Unions in America* (Chicago: Daily Worker Publishing, n.d. [ca. 1925]). Cannon on the "united front" is quoted in Cook to Dixon, 18 June 1922, cited in Edward P. Johanningsmeier, "The Profintern and the 'Syndicalist Current' in the United States," unpublished paper presented to Real Socialism and the Second World Workshop, Center for Russian and Eastern European Studies, University of Toronto, May 1–2, 2004. For general context, see Reiner Tosstorff, "Moscow versus Amsterdam: Reflections on the History of the Profintern," *Labour History Review* 68 (April 2003): 82–93.

50. "Sessions of the Anglo-American Colonial Group," June 15, 1922; June 22, 1922; June 29, 1922 (from which long quotes are drawn); July 4, 1922; July 10, 1922; August 25,

1922; August 26, 1922; August 29, 1922; August 31, 1922 (on the Secretary and the ECCI); September 7, 1922, all from Reel 10, Russian Center, PRL. In all, twenty sessions of this group appeared to have been held.

51. "One Cook and One Dixon," Report of May 25, 1922, New York, FBI File; Ruthenberg to EC of CI, 9 May 1922, Reel 2, Russian Center, PRL; Cook to Dixon, 18 June 1922, Reel 3, Russian Center, PRL; Cannon, *First Ten Years*, 64–65; Ring interview with Cannon, June 13, 1973, 1–6.

52. Ring interview with Cannon, June 20, 1973, 14; April 12, 1974, 4; Draper, *Roots of American Communism*, 381–82; Cannon, *History of American Trotskyism*, 16–17; Cannon, *First Ten Years*, 65–66; Bittelman, "Things I Have Learned," chap. 13, "My First Visit to Soviet Russia," 365, 375–76, 388; Cook to the Members of the Presidium, Moscow, 12 August 1922 (misdated 1920), Reel 3, Russian Center, PRL.

53. See Cook to the Members of the Presidium, Moscow, 12 August 1922 [misdated 1920], citing "Extracts from a private letter just received from Comrade Marshall [Bedacht]," and Cook to Secretariat, 16 August 1922, as well as the statement against factionalism in the undated (but signed/sealed by a number of leading figures, including Cannon/Cook) "Statement to the Membership of the C.P.A. by the C.E.C.," 34 in Reels 3, 1a, Russian Center, PRL; Gitlow, *I Confess*, 132–46; Draper, *Roots of American Communism*, 363–75; Cannon, *First Ten Years*, 57, 66, 73–76, containing some relatively charitable comment on Valetski/Walecki. For Trotsky's more condemnatory assessment, see Leon Trotsky, *The Challenge of the Left Opposition (1928–1929)* (New York: Pathfinder, 1981), 187, stressing his opportunism. On what Cannon described as the "surprising . . . transformation of the character of the modest, gentle artist that I had known before I left [Minor]," into the "nastiest factionalist of all . . . the dirtiest fighter . . . in the Goose Caucus," see Ring interview with Cannon, April 12, 1974, 8–13. Dunne dubbed Minor "the skunk." For an account of Rose Pastor Stokes that bypasses much, see Arthur Zipster and Pearl Zipster, *Fire and Grace: The Life of Rose Pastor Stokes* (Athens: University of Georgia Press, 1989).

54. For a sampling of the documents seized and accompanying anti-communist commentary, see R. M. Whitney, *Reds in America* (New York: Beckwith Press, 1924). Note as well Morgan, *A Covert Life*, 27–29; Cannon, *First Ten Years*, 74; Draper, *Roots of American Communism*, 373–75; Howe and Coser, *American Communist Party*, 99–102.

55. Cook to the Members of the Presidium, 12 August (1922), Reel 3, Russian Center, PRL.

56. Howe and Coser, *American Communist Party*, 100–101; Johanningsmeier, *Forging American Communism*, 182–92; Gitlow, *I Confess*, 151; "First Meeting of Adjustment Committee," 12 August 1922, hand pagination, 32, Reel 1a, Russian Center, PRL.

57. Valetski was the only appointee who had any experience with conditions in the United States, and this put Cannon and his faction at a decided disadvantage, for they understood that "he leaned quite strongly to the left." See Ring interview with Cannon, June 20, 1973, 15; Cannon, *First Ten Years*, 66, 73, 76; Gitlow, *I Confess*, 135, 139–40.

58. Cannon, *First Ten Years*, 67–68; Draper, *Roots of American Communism*, 381–87; Ring interview with Cannon, April 19, 1974, 3; Claude McKay, *A Long Way from Home*

(New York: Lee Furman, 1937), 162, 178–79. In *First Ten Years,* 192, Cannon refers to Amter in 1924 as being "the standing representative of the American CP on the Executive Committee of the Communist International for a long time before that," so, if this is correct, it is likely that Amter was one of the Goose Caucus advocates at the American Commission in November 1922. Gitlow, *I Confess,* 152, claims that John Pepper won Amter over to the necessity of legalization and sent him to Moscow to discredit Katterfeld, but this is challenged implicitly in Cannon, *First Ten Years,* 61. There is no evidence of Amter's opposition to Katterfeld at the American Commission meetings. For background on Claude McKay, see Wayne F. Cooper, *Claude McKay: Rebel Sojourner in the Harlem Renaissance—A Biography* (Baton Rouge: Louisiana State University Press, 1987), 102–33 (on his work with Sylvia Pankhurst's *Workers' Dreadnaught*), 134–70 (on his association with Eastman's *Liberator*), and 106–9, 142–43, 175–78, 184, 402 (on the African Blood Brotherhood and communism). Note as well Solomon, *Cry Was Unity,* 8, 9, 20, 27–28, 40–43; James, *Holding Aloft the Banner of Ethiopia,* 180; Foley, *Spectres of 1919,* 42–43.

59. Max Eastman, *Love and Revolution: My Journey Through an Epoch* (New York: Random House, 1964), 333; Vera Buch Weisbord, *A Radical Life* (Bloomington, IN: University Press, 1977), 322; Milton Cantor, *Max Eastman* (New York: Twayne, 1970), 86; Daniel Aaron, *Writers on the Left: Episodes in American Literary Communism* (New York: Columbia University Press, 1992), 123; Ring interview with Cannon, April 19, 1974, 3–4; Cannon, *History of American Trotskyism,* 16–17; Cannon, *First Ten Years,* 69–70; Draper, *Roots of American Communism,* 383–84; Arne Swabeck, unpublished, untitled, and unpaginated typescript, chap. 6, "From Chicago to Moscow," Autobiographies File, Prometheus Research Library, New York, New York. Cannon's recollection of his arguments before Trotsky is a strikingly accurate rendition, given the almost thirty-five years that had passed, of what appeared on that "single sheet of paper." For a translation of Bedacht's German copy, which Cannon could not have seen in the interval, note Cannon, Bedacht, and Swabeck, "The American Question" (ca. November 1922), a document also signed by two Young Communist League delegates (one of whom was Abern), three TUEL representatives (likely including Johnstone and Wortis), and one Communist Party of America regional organizer, in *James P. Cannon and the Early Years of American Communism,* 95–97. The one area where Cannon's later recollections telescope his arguments somewhat is around the issue of the labor party, which is dealt with in chapter 7 of this book, where it converges with the political significance of Comintern representative John Pepper.

60. "James P. Cannon," Cleveland, Ohio, April 23, 1923, FBI File.

61. Short statements of Carr, Trachtenberg, and Katayama, Minutes, American Commission Meeting, Evening, November 27, 1922; Carr statement (with Cook heckling), Minutes, American Commission, 89; Claude McKay to the Mandate Commission, 20 November 1922 + undated document of petition; Sasha (Rose Pastor Stokes) to Secretariat and Mandate Commission, 8 November 1922, Reel 2, Russian Center, PRL. For McKay's views on a range of issues, with a clear indication of his stand on racism in the communist milieu, and the subsequent Comintern effort to address "the Negro

Question," see McKay to Wallunyus, 28 November 1922; McKay to Kolaroff, 23 December 1922, Reel 3, 77–78, 88–90, Russian Center, PRL. These letters indicate McKay's pique at Rose Pastor Stokes's obstruction of his recognition before the American Commission and his resentment that "the Negro Question" was given short shrift. "If I spoke out boldly and seem in conflict with the American comrades, it is because I know they have spent all their time in petty squabbles while the big work of reaching the American Labor movement & the Negroes is left undone." See as well McKay, *Long Way from Home*, 153–90; Cooper, *Claude McKay*, 171–92; and Leon Trotsky, "A Letter to Comrade McKay," in *The First Five Years of the Communist International*, vol. 2 (New York: Monad, 1972), 354–56, dated 13 March 1923.

62. Cannon, *First Ten Years*, 77.

63. Carr (Katterfeld), Minutes, American Commission, November 27, 1922, Reel 2, 10–19, Russian Center, PRL.

64. The preceding paragraphs draw on McKay, *Long Way from Home*, 174; and, for a useful account of McKay's Fourth Congress activity, Cooper, *Claude McKay*, 171–92. For Katterfeld's speech and the united front, see as well Draper, *Roots of American Communism*, 382; Bittelman, "Things I Have Learned," 374. The pivotal statement on the united front is *Resolutions and Theses of the Fourth Congress of the Communist International, Held in Moscow, Nov. 7 to Dec. 3 1922* (London: Communist International/Communist Party of Great Britain, 1923), 35–45. United-front issues blurred into the underground-liquidationist contrasts in discussions over trade union questions. See, for instance, "Trades Union Question," *Fourth Congress of the Communist International: Abridged Report of Meetings held in Petrograd and Moscow, Nov. 7–Dec. 3, 1922* (London: Communist International/Communist Party of Great Britain, 1923), 225–35, which pitted Lansing (Swabeck) against the spokesman for the United Labor Council of America (Kutcher), a New York-based body that endorsed the Profintern but resisted its directives to work within the mainstream American Federation of Labor unions.

65. Draper, *Roots of American Communism*, 383, notes that, "Bedacht [Marshall] spoke for the Liquidators," which he did, but it was Cannon (Cook) who led off and offered the more decisive statement. Cannon's *First Ten Years*, 70, is truer to the documentary record: "Nothing was hurried. There was a full and fair debate, in a calm and friendly atmosphere. Nobody got excited but the Americans. Katterfeld and I were given about an hour each to expound the conflicting positions of the contending factions. Rose Pastor Stokes, Bedacht, and others were called upon to supplement the remarks of the main reporters on both sides. A representative of the seceding underground leftist group was also given the floor."

66. The preceding paragraphs draw upon Cook (Cannon) statement, "American Commission, 27 November 1922," Reel 2, 21–34, Russian Center, PRL. The last two pages of this document contain the short statement written for Trotsky, and though differing slightly in translation, it is essentially the same as what appears in *James P. Cannon and the Early Years of American Communism*, 95–97.

67. Sullivan statement, "American Commission" (n.d. [ca. November 27–29, 1922]; "The American Movement (Report of Delegate of 'Opposition' Faction), n.d. [ca.

November 27–29, 1922], both in Minutes, American Commission, Reel 2, 38–60, Russian Center, PRL.

68. Minutes, American Commission, Morning 30 November 1922, Reel 2, 96–100; Marshall (Bedacht), Lansing (Swabeck), and Huiswoud (Billings) statements, "American Commission, 30 November 1922 Evening," 128–33, 157–60, 161–66, Russian Center, PRL. Huiswoud's interventions were among the most sarcastic. Quite combative, he tussled with Radek over minor matters. Darker skinned than Huiswoud, McKay was regarded as a "genuine" African American in the Soviet Union. Huiswoud mocked this and in the process revealed an arrogance over McKay's insufficiencies as a communist. McKay responded with animosity, referring to Huiswoud as "the mulatto delegate." Substantively, McKay promoted the Cannon liquidationist view to Radek, Trotsky, and other leading Bolsheviks, and in the case of a discussion with Radek clearly bested Huiswoud, who retreated into sectarianism. See McKay, *Long Way from Home*, 159–84; and for a more benign view, Zipster and Zipster, *Fire and Grace*, 236–37. Cannon's recollection of Huiswoud suggests that the West Indian delegate did not register much of an impression: "There was also a Negro delegate whose name has escaped me, who seemed to support the leftist faction." Cannon, *First Ten Years*, 67. Solomon, *Cry Was Unity*, 38–43, is more favorable towards Huiswoud.

69. Carr (Katterfeld) statement, Minutes, American Commission, 30 November 1922, Evening, Reel 2, 32–37, Russian Center, PRL.

70. Statements by MacDonald, Katayama, Gordon, Sasha (Rose Pastor Stokes), Carr (Katterfeld), Trachtenberg, Cook (Cannon), in Minutes, American Commmission, December 1, 1922, Reel 2, 27–53a, Russian Center, PRL; Ring interview with Cannon, June 20, 1973, 1, 14; Ian Angus, *Canadian Bolsheviks: The Early Years of the Communist Party of Canada* (Montreal: Vanguard, 1981), 101; Draper, *Roots of American Communism*, 385–88; Cannon, *First Ten Years*, 73.

71. Ring interview with Cannon, June 20, 1973, 15; Cook (Cannon) statement, Minutes, American Commission, December 1, 1922, and undated, corrected two-page typescript, Reel 2, 46, 44c–d (also labeled 255–56), Russian Center, PRL; Cannon, *First Ten Years*, 70–71. See also "To the Communist Party," ECCI to CPUSA, 12 December 1922, Box 11, Folder 1, Martin Abern Papers, Wayne State Archives of Labor History and Urban Affairs, Wayne State University, Detroit, Michigan. Cannon may have been right that the Comintern ruled against the underground, but he undoubtedly placed too much significance on this in terms of its endorsement of specific legalization/liquidationist positions. It was telling, for instance, that except for detailed exploration of "the Negro Question," the United States figured so marginally in the published statements that came out of the Fourth Congress. Note the lack of attention to the American Commission discussions in *Resolutions and Theses of the Fourth Congress* and *Fourth Congress of the Communist International: Abridged Report*. For a respectful comment on Cannon's critical role, see McKay, *Long Way from Home*, 178.

72. On Cannon and Zinoviev, see *First Ten Years*, 69, 186–87; Cannon, *History of American Trotskyism*, 17–18; Ring interview with Cannon, June 20, 1973, 7–8; and the useful comments of Zinoviev's multiple roles historically in James P. Cannon, "A Reply

to Goldman in Three Points," October 7, 1945, in Cannon, *The Struggle for Socialism in the "American Century": Writings and Speeches, 1945–1947* (New York: Pathfinder, 1977), 186–87; Bittelman, "Things I Have Learned," 373–76.

73. *The Worker,* January 6 and 20, 1923; Draper, *Roots of American Communism,* 389–90, 457, n. 32.

74. Karl Marx, "The Eighteenth Brumaire of Louis Bonaparte," in Marx and Engels, *Selected Works* (Moscow: Progress, 1968), 97.

Chapter 7: Pepper Spray

1. James P. Cannon, *The First Ten Years of American Communism—Report of a Participant* (New York: Pathfinder, 1973), 85; Minutes of the C.E.C. Meeting, January 26, 1923, Reel 1b, 38, in Documents from Russian Center for the Preservation and Study of Contemporary History, Microfilm Copies Held, Prometheus Research Library, New York, New York (hereafter Russian Center, PRL).

2. For a depiction of the communist movement in this period, see Theodore Draper, *The Roots of American Communism* (New York: Viking, 1957), 390–93; Robin D. G. Kelley, *Hammer and Hoe: Alabama Communists During the Great Depression* (Chapel Hill: University of North Carolina Press, 1990), 13–14; "Report of the Central Executive Committee of the Workers' Party," 1923, 12, 14, in Series II, Box 20, Earl W. Browder Papers, George Arents Research Library for Special Collections, Syracuse University, Syracuse, New York (hereafter cited as Browder Papers); C.E. Ruthenberg, "Report of the Executive Secretary, Meeting of the Central Executive Committee of the Workers' Party of America," June 29, 1922, and Minutes of the Meeting of the Central Executive Committee, October 21, 1922, both in Reel 1a, Russian Center, PRL.

3. See Scott Nearing, "What Can the Radicals Do?" Magazine Section, *New York Call,* February 4, 1923; James P. Cannon, "Scott Nearing and the Workers' Party," *The Worker,* February 24, 1923; Draper, *Roots of American Communism,* 394; Bert Cochran, *Labor and American Communism: The Conflict That Shaped American Unions* (Princeton, NJ: Princeton University Press, 1977), 21; Theodore Draper, *American Communism and Soviet Russia: The Formative Period* (New York: Viking, 1960), 27, citing Ruthenberg article in *Daily Worker,* Magazine Section, March 5, 1924, and 122–23. Nearing applied for membership in the Workers' Party in 1924, was rejected, but was admitted in 1926–1927, only to be expelled in 1930. Cannon was assigned the early task of engaging with Nearing and combatting some of his ideas. See "Application of Former SP Leaders," in Minutes of the Central Executive Committee, February 15–16, 1924, and "Scott Nearing," in Minutes of the Political Committee, August 4, 1924, in Reel 1c, and, for the CEC's rejection of Nearing, "Scott Nearing's Application," in Minutes of the CEC, February 5, 1925, Reel 1d, all in Russian Center, PRL; "Scott Nearing and Party Policy," *Daily Worker,* May 10, 1924, magazine supplement; "Foster's Reply to Nearing," *Daily Worker,* May 17, 1924, magazine supplement; *Daily Worker,* January 8, 1930. Note, as well, Stephen J. Whitfield, *Scott Nearing: Apostle of American Radicalism* (New York: Columbia University Press, 1974), esp. 156–71.

4. Cannon's New York City home address comes from Report on James P. Cannon, Kansas City, Missouri, June 17, 1923, U.S. Department of Justice, Federal Bureau of

Investigation, Freedom of Information/Privacy Act File, Washington, DC (hereafter FBI File).

5. Cannon, *First Ten Years,* 85.

6. James P. Cannon, "A Talk with Alex Howat," *Labor Herald* 2 (June 1923): 10, and *Maritime Labor Herald* (Glace Bay, Nova Scotia), June 9, 1923; Alexander Howat, "Fighting Industrial Slavery," *Labor Herald* 1 (January 1923): 15–16, as well as numerous articles by John Dorsey in the *Labor Herald,* 1922–1923; Melvyn Dubofsky and Warren Van Tine, *John L. Lewis: A Biography* (New York: Quadrangle, 1977), 113–25.

7. James P. Cannon, "The I.W.W. and the International," *Voice of Labor,* May 26, 1923 and June 2, 1923. As background, see George Hardy et al., "Policy of the Workers' Party in Regard to the I.W.W.," 1–22, April 12, 1923, Adopted by the Political Committee, May 11, 1923, Reel 1b, Russian Center, PRL; Minutes of the Conference to Form the Council of Action, June 5, 1923, Series II, Box 15, Browder Papers.

8. Minutes of the C.E.C, January 26 & February 10, 1923, Reel 1b, Russian Center, PRL. When former Goose Caucus leader Edward I. Lingren faced party discipline for what was clearly a misunderstanding over personal/defense campaign funds, Cannon attempted unsuccessfully to pass a motion securing the missing $400 through a CEC commitment to guarantee return of the money. On the *Liberator* appointment, see Minutes of the Meeting of the Executive Council, March 8, 1923, Reel 1b, Russian Center, PRL. Quote from James P. Cannon to Charley (Scott), n.d., Reel 6, Russian Center, PRL. On Scott, see Harry Ring interview with James P. Cannon, April 12, 1974, 2–4 (in possession of the author; hereafter Ring interview); Benjamin Gitlow, *I Confess: The Truth about American Communism* (New York: E.P. Dutton, 1940), 172, 174, 468, 535–36.

9. Ruthenberg to Zinoviev, Fourth Congress Communist International, Moscow, 24 November 1922; Minutes of the Meeting of the C.E.C., 31 October 1922—Jewish Federation Controversy; and the Cannon-chaired Minutes of the Administrative Council, 21, 23 March 1923: Situation in "The Freiheit," in Reels 2, 1a, 1b, Russian Center, PRL.

10. Alexander Bittelman, "Things I Have Learned: An Autobiography," chap. 13, 393, 395, Collection 62, Boxes 1–2, unpublished manuscript in Alexander Bittelman Papers, Tamiment Institute, New York, New York; for Cannon's brief statement on the Olgin-Bittelman contests, see Cannon, *First Ten Years,* 90–92.

11. I am indebted to John Holmes, currently at work on a PhD dissertation focusing on Noah London and the Jewish Federation, for suggesting this factional context of Cannon's initial distance from the crisis in the Jewish section, which manifested itself in a struggle for control over the *Freiheit.* For an account of Salutsky/Hardman, who played a pivotal role in bringing the last wave of Jewish socialists into the communist movement in the 1920–1922 years, who inspired the founding of the *Freiheit* only to find himself unable to join its staff, and who was eventually expelled from the Workers' Party in 1923, see Eugene Victor Orenstein, "The Jewish Socialist Federation of America, 1912–1921: A Study of Integration and Particularism in the American Jewish Labor Movement" (PhD diss., Columbia University, 1978), 227–73.

12. Noah London penned a Yiddish article, the title translating into English as "Don't smother the child with too much love (about the discussion on party discipline),"

Freiheit, May 29, 1923, which presents a humorous assault on Pepper's role in the Jewish section crisis. My thanks to John Holmes for making me aware of this article and offering a summary of its contents.

13. Bittelman, "Things I Have Learned," 386–89; Cannon, *First Ten Years,* 76–77.

14. Albert Glotzer, "Reminiscences of James P. Cannon," Reel 1, James P. Cannon Papers, Microfilm Edition, 1994, State Historical Society of Wisconsin, Madison, Wisconsin (hereafter JPC Papers).

15. Minutes of the C.E.C, February 10, 1923, Reel 1b, Russian Center, PRL.

16. The young woman Clarissa (Chris, Crissie, C. S.) Ware was older than Lovestone; had experienced marriage, childbirth, and divorce; was in charge of the Research Department of the Workers' Party; wrote for and was on the editorial staff of *The Liberator;* and published articles in a number of other communist periodicals. Popular in Party circles, Ware authored a pamphlet on the oppression and discrimination faced by foreign-born workers in the United States: *The American Foreign-Born Workers* (New York: Workers Party, ca. 1924). She had sexual relations with Lovestone and Ruthenberg simultaneously, but rebuffed the former to support the latter. Pepper, to complete the complicated triangle, supposedly attempted to "win the affections" of Ware as she delivered research materials to him at the party's underground uptown headquarters. Ruthenberg was apparently less than pleased. Clarissa Ware's life ended tragically: she died of complications resulting from an abortion. Whether the unborn child had been fathered by Lovestone or Ruthenberg (or neither) is unknown. Scorned by Ware, Lovestone responded with maudlin attempts to rekindle the relationship and, when that failed, with misogynist rationalizations. Ruthenberg was apparently distraught at Ware's funeral, but quickly patched up his working alliance with Lovestone and Pepper. The Workers' Party obituary lauded Ware as "the woman of the Communist society of tomorrow—frank, unafraid, intellectually capable, yet glorious in her womanhood." It attributed her death to "an operation for pancrititis." See C. S. Ware, "Makers of America," *The Liberator* (May 1923): 39–40; "Clarissa S. Ware," *The Liberator* (October 1923): 7; Gitlow, *I Confess,* 153–54; Ted Morgan, *A Covert Life: Jay Lovestone—Communist, Anti-Communist and Spymaster* (New York: Random House, 1999), 34–38; Joseph Freeman, *An American Testament: A Narrative of Rebels and Romantics* (New York: Farrar & Rinehart, 1936), 313–15.

17. Earl Browder, "'No-Man's Land': A Political Autobiography," chap. 7, 173–74, Series III, Box 10, Browder Papers, claims that Ruthenberg "loathed Cannon most profoundly." This was most likely a Browder exaggeration. See also Cannon, *First Ten Years,* esp. 120–23; Earl Browder to Theodore Draper, 14 February 1956, Series I, Box 3, Browder Papers. When Ruthenberg himself came to comment on the factional alignments of this period, the document most often cited (as in Draper, *American Communism and Soviet Russia,* 43, 450, n. 34) is a later letter written to the ECCI explaining the emergence of the factional crisis in the U.S. Workers' Party. This document lends credence to Browder's claims, on some levels, but it certainly understates Cannon's role, ignoring critical documents. The curious nature of this letter, however, is that it was provided to Draper by Browder, and is a *copy* of Ruthenberg's letter, *in Browder's hand.*

See Browder to Draper, 1 March 1956, providing copy of Ruthenberg to ECCI, 11 April 1924, Series I, Box 3, Browder Papers.

18. The preceding two paragraphs draw upon Bittelman, "Things I Have Learned," 388–98; Cannon, *First Ten Years,* 78, 84–85, 90–92, 123, 192; Gitlow, *I Confess,* 160; Morgan, *A Covert Life,* 27–28, 50; Ring interview with Cannon, April 12, 1974, 13–14; James P. Cannon, *The History of American Trotskyism: From Its Origins (1928) to the Founding of the Socialist Workers' Party (1938)—Report of a Participant* (New York: Pathfinder, 1972), 29.

19. Cannon, *First Ten Years,* 63, 78–79, 85. Draper, *American Communism and Soviet Russia,* 78, suggests that the Central Executive Committee deliberately sent Cannon as far from the inner-party activity as was possible, posting him to speak in Portland on the date of a critical convention, "a circumstance which [Cannon] did not think had been accidental." Draper cites *Daily Worker,* December 11, 1924, but the article cited, Cannon's "The CEC, the Minority and Comrade Lore: How the Minority Fought Lore When They Controlled the Party," reprinted in *James P. Cannon and the Early Years of American Communism: Selected Writings and Speeches, 1920–1928* (New York: Prometheus Research Library, 1992), 257–63, is perhaps not the best source to rely on. Cannon was bending the polemical stick in the midst of a factional eruption, and he was citing, for partisan purposes, how Lore had been elevated to major party committees while Cannon was excluded from them. This discounts Cannon's desire to be on tour, understates his lack of involvement in the CEC as a matter of choice, and neglects the fact that the dating of his West Coast speech and such critical steering committee meetings could hardly have been easily set for the partisan purposes Cannon suggests. See, for another view, Browder to Draper, 14 February 1956; 24 January 1956, Series I, Box 3, Browder Papers.

20. The best source for this tour remains approximately twenty reports filed between February 16, 1923 and July 11, 1923 on "James P. Cannon," FBI File. See, as well, Draper, *American Communism and Soviet Russia,* 78–79; Cannon, *First Ten Years,* 63–64, 85–86; "To Tell the Story of Russia in 1922," *The Worker,* February 10, 1923; "Cannon Tells about Unions in Red Russia," *The Worker,* February 17, 1923; "Cannon Tour Meeting with Approval," *The Worker,* February 17, 1923; *The Worker,* April 21, 1923, which lists Cannon's speaking engagements in industrial Pennsylvania and Ohio; *The Worker,* July 19, 1923; Ian Angus, *Canadian Bolsheviks: The Early Years of the Communist Party of Canada* (Montreal: Vanguard, 1981), 132; "Cannon Hits Morality of the Kept Press," *The Worker,* April 21, 1923.

21. "James P. Cannon," Bridgeport and Hartford, March 14–15, 1923; Lynn and Peabody, March 4–5, 1923, FBI File; James P. Cannon, "The Russian Revolution—The Inspiring Force in the American Labor Movement," *The Worker,* November 3, 1923; Cannon, *The Fifth Year of the Russian Revolution* (New York: Workers' Party of America, 1923), reprinted in *James P. Cannon and the Early Years of American Communism,* 98–116. For an announcement of the appearance of Cannon's pamphlet, *Russia Today, 1923!* as well as an enthusiastic review by Elmer T. Allison under the title "Russia Now!" see *The Worker,* June 2, 1923.

22. "James P. Cannon," Portland, Oregon, July 3–4, 1923, FBI File.

23. "James P. Cannon," Bridgeport and Hartford, March 14–15, 1923; Minneapolis, May 20, 1923, FBI File.

24. "James P. Cannon," Denver, June 19, 1923; Franklin, Kansas, June 17, 1923; Pittsburgh, Searched December 9, 1941, 5, FBI File.

25. "James P. Cannon," Searched December 9, 1941, referring to March 23, 1923, 4a, FBI File. Particular attention was paid to military matters, and Cannon's references to Soviet arms or planes were often noted. See, for instance, ibid., 4a, 6.

26. "James P. Cannon," Cleveland, April 24, 1923; Bridgeport and Hartford, March 14–15, 1923; Minneapolis, May 20, 1923; Toledo, May 22, 1923; Butte, July 9–14, 1923; Portland, July 3–4, 1923; Spokane, July 11, 1923, FBI File.

27. Officially the lecture tour was lauded as a landmark event. As early as mid-April, the Executive Council was claiming that Cannon's meetings had generated 5,600 new subscribers to the *Worker*. See Minutes of the Meeting of the Executive Council, April 17, 1923, Reel 1b, Russian Center, PRL. "Report of the Central Executive Committee of the Workers' Party, 1923," in Series II, Box 20, Browder Papers, stated: "Comrade Cannon made a speaking tour lasting five months which took him to every part of the country. His meetings were universally successful and we reached thousands of workers thru his addresses" (p. 12).

28. Cannon, *First Ten Years,* 86.

29. See "What Kind of Party?" *The Worker,* March 3, 1923, reprinted in *James P. Cannon and the Early Years of American Communism,* 117–23; "James P. Cannon," Toledo, May 11, 1923, FBI File.

30. "James P. Cannon," Lynn and Peabody, March 14, 1923; Portland, July 3–4, 1923; Cleveland, Searched December 9, 1941, 5, FBI File.

31. Cannon therefore overstated his opposition to the Farmer-Labor Party scheme significantly in Ring interview with Cannon, October 17, 1973, 1–2, claiming: "When I got back from Russia I took one good look at it and saw it was a false alarm. I began a little agitation in the Party to retreat from that false step they'd made." See also Cannon, *First Ten Years,* 62–63, 85; Alexander Bittelman, "Things I Have Learned," 399–400, Boxes 1–2.

32. See Cannon to Ruthenberg, 25 May 1923, reprinted under the title, "Don't Pack the July 3 Conference," in *James P. Cannon and the Early Years of American Communism,* 124–26; "James Patrick Cannon," Searched December 9, 1941, referring to Chicago, May 1, 1923, 5a, FBI File.

33. Draper, *American Communism and Soviet Russia,* 57–61; E. H. Carr, *The Bolshevik Revolution, 1917–1923,* vol. 3 (Hamondsworth, UK: Penguin, 1966), 334–36; Helmut Gruber, ed., *International Communism in the Era of Lenin: A Documentary History* (Garden City, NY: Doubleday, 1972), 117–52, 267–96; Freeman, *American Testament,* 629–30; Oscar Jaszi, *Revolution and Counter-Revolution in Hungary* (London: P.S. King & Son, 1924); Baron Albert Kaas and Fedor de Lazarovics, *Bolshevism in Hungary* (London: Grant Richards, 1931); Elemer Malusz, *The Fugitive Bolsheviks* (London: Grant Richards, 1931). For Trotsky's comments on Pepper, see Leon Trotsky, *The Challenge of the Left Opposition (1928–1929)* (New York: Pathfinder, 1981), 173, 177–78, 379, 413, 440,

445, and esp. 202, 210, 184–86; Trotsky, *The First Five Years of the Communist International,* vol. 1 (New York: Monad, 1972), 230–32, 323, 351; Trotsky, *The Third International After Lenin* (New York: Pathfinder, 1970), 120–21; Freeman, *American Testament,* 629–30.

34. On Pepper, see Thomas Sakmyster, "A Hungarian in the Comintern: Jozsef Pogany/John Pepper," in Kevin Morgan, Gidon Cohen, and Andrew Flinn, eds., *Agents of the Revolution: New Biographical Approaches to the History of International Communism in the Age of Lenin and Stalin* (Bern: Peter Lang, 2005), 57–72; Malcolm Sylvers, "Pogany/Pepper: Un representative du Komintern apres du Parti Communiste des Etats-Unis," *Cahiers d'histoire de l'Institut de Recherche Marxiste* 28 (Summer 1987): 119–31; Irving Howe and Lewis Coser, *The American Communist Party: A Critical History (1919–1957)* (Boston: Beacon Press, 1957), 115–18.

35. Draper, *American Communism and Soviet Russia,* 59.

36. Gitlow, *I Confess,* 136.

37. Draper, *American Communism and Soviet Russia,* 38. Pepper's original writings, to take the *Liberator,* as an example, were of the sort that would appeal to the remnants of the Goose Caucus that he had integrated into his factional base. See, for instance, the flailing of the dead horse of the Socialist Party: John Pepper, "The S.P.—Two Wings without a Body," *The Liberator* (May 1923): 32–33; "Bon Voyage, Hillquit!" *The Liberator* (June 1923): 9–10. Note, finally, that speaking under the pseudonym Lang, Pepper attempted to add a series of amendments to a resolution denying the threat of liquidationism. The passed resolution and Lang's failed amendments are found in "First Meeting of the Adjustment Committee," August 1, 1923, 32, in Reel 1a, Russian Center, PRL, and they would have unmistakable appeal to former Goose Caucus members inasmuch as they stressed the dependency of the legal party on the "absolute necessity" of the illegal body: "The basis of a sound function of a number two is the existence of a number one."

38. See Draper, *American Communism and Soviet Russia,* 59–61; Cannon, *First Ten Years,* 74–83; Ring interview with Cannon, April 12, 1974, 13–16; James P. Cannon, *The Left Opposition in the U.S. 1928–1931: Writings and Speeches* (New York: Monad, 1981), 67, 108, 116, 136, 168–71. Browder, who claimed to have regarded Pepper as abnormal and expressed surprise that both Cannon and Foster could marvel at his oratory, stated: "To put it in the most primitive terms, to me John Pepper was the incarnation of the Devil, and my memories of 1923 are most fresh and vivid when they are associated with Pepper." See Browder to Draper, 9 March 1956, 20 February 1956, Series I, Box 3, Browder Papers.

39. For background on Fitzpatrick, see David Brody, "John Fitzpatrick," in *Dictionary of American Biography,* Supplement IV, ed. John Garraty (New York: Scribner's, 1974), 279–80; David Brody, *Steelworkers in America: The Nonunion Era* (New York: Harper Torchbooks, 1969), 214–15, 239–41, 249, 258, 276; James R. Barrett, *Work and Community in the Jungle: Chicago's Packinghouse Workers, 1894–1922* (Urbana: University of Illinois Press, 1990), 191–92, 200–207, 228; Elizabeth McKillen, *Chicago Labor and the Quest for Democratic Diplomacy, 1914–1924* (Ithaca, NY: Cornell University Press,

1995), 46–53. The major study is unpublished: John Keiser, "John Fitzpatrick and Progressive Unionism, 1915–1925" (PhD diss., Northwestern University, 1965). A reactionary, anti-communist comment on the CPPA is in Blair Coan, *The Red Web* (Chicago: Northwest Publishing, 1925), 94.

40. On this general farmer-labor party evolution the literature is extensive. See, for a sampling of commentary, Eugene Staley, *History of the Illinois State Federation of Labor* (Chicago: University of Chicago Press, 1930), 361–90; Stanley Shapiro, "'Hand and Brain': The Farmer-Labor Party of 1920," *Labor History* 26 (Summer 1985): 405–22; James Weinstein, *The Decline of Socialism in America, 1912–1925* (New York: Vintage, 1969), 272–323; *James P. Cannon and the Early Years of American Communism*, 21–23; James R. Barrett, *William Z. Foster and the Tragedy of American Radicalism* (Urbana: University of Illinois Press, 1999), 83–101, 123–25; Edward P. Johanningsmeier, *Forging American Communism: The Life of William Z. Foster* (Princeton, NJ: Princeton University Press, 1994), 111, 116–17, 125–28, 155–56, 196–200; David Montgomery, *The Fall of the House of Labor: The Workplace, the State, and American Labor Activism, 1865–1925* (Cambridge, UK: Cambridge University Press, 1987), 434–37.

41. For the WP account of the Cleveland Conference of the CPPA, see C.E. Ruthenberg, "The Cleveland Skirmish," *The Liberator* (January 1923): 9–11; William F. Dunne, "The Cleveland Farce," *Voice of Labor*, December 22, 1922. A dissident party critique, stressing the ineffectual nature of the WP's CPPA intervention, is in J. B. Salutsky to H. Rosenfeld, 17 February 1923, Box 39, Folder 1, "Workers' Party Documents and Clippings Pertaining to Hardman's Expulsion," J. B. S. Hardman Papers, Tamiment Institute, New York University, New York, New York. Just who the delegates of the Workers' Party/Young Communist League were to the Cleveland Convention is somewhat open to question. Certainly Ruthenberg was one. Foster is often cited as the second delegate: see William Z. Foster, *History of the Communist Party of the United States* (New York: International, 1952), 214; Johanningsmeier, *Forging American Communism*, 197; Barrett, *William Z. Foster*, 124. But the evidence for this seems weak, and Foster played no major role in the Cleveland gathering. It is possible that he was there as an observer, later elevating his position to that of proposed delegate.

42. Howe and Coser, *American Communist Party*, 119, citing *New Majority*, December 22, 1922; Browder to Draper, 20 February 1956, Series I, Box 3, Browder Papers.

43. For a brief account, see David Montgomery, "The Farmer-Labor Party," in *Working for Democracy: American Workers from the Revolution to the Present*, ed. Paul Buhle and Alan Dawley (Urbana: University of Illinois Press, 1985), 73–82. See, as well, Charles Edward Russell, *The Story of the Nonpartisan League: A Chapter in American Evolution* (New York: Harper & Brothers, 1920).

44. "The American Question," in *James P. Cannon and the Early Years of American Communism*, 95; Cannon (Cook) statement and Katterfeld (Carr) statement, "American Commission Meeting," Minutes, Evening, November 27, 1922, 16–17, 22, and Cook statement at "Meeting of the Anglo-American Colonial Group," June 29, 1922, 48, as well as "Pullman" statement, "American Commission Meeting," Minutes, Morning, December 1, 1922, 205, Reels 2 and 1a, Russian Center, PRL.

45. Browder insists that this implied no inequality, but a united front of equals. Of long-standing practice, this relationship nevertheless depended upon communists' willingness to suppress their organizational affiliation with the Workers' Party: their relations with the Fitzpatrick-Nockels group were in some senses premised on an unwritten, unstated agreement *not* to raise the red flag too high in the CFL's house. See Browder to Draper, Memorandum uncorrected mss. of vol. 2 history, March 16, 1959, 2, Series III, Box 18, Browder Papers.

46. For this context, see Draper, *American Communism and Soviet Russia,* 38–42; Johanningsmeier, *Forging American Communism,* 196–99; Barrett, *William Z. Foster,* 123–25. Browder claimed to be able to discern the hand of Pepper in fomenting the inner-party gossip relating to the Chicago Federation and the Workers' Party trade unionists: see Browder to Draper, 20 February 1956, Series I, Box 3, Browder Papers. For Pepper's promotion of the Farmer-Labor Party, see John Pepper, "The Declaration of Independence of the American Working Class," *The Liberator* (July 1923): 8–10; and the extremely influential John Pepper, *For a Labor Party: Recent Revolutionary Changes in American Politics* (Chicago: Workers Party, 1923), which was first published as a Workers' Party political statement in October 1922 and then went through a number of editions under Pepper's signature. (Unless otherwise indicated, future citations to this pamphlet refer to the edition that Pepper revised *after* the July 3 founding conference of the Federated Farmer-Labor Party.) See also John Pepper, *"Underground Radicalism": An Open Letter to Eugene Debs and to All Honest Workers within the Socialist Party* (New York: Workers Party, 1923), quoted in Howe and Coser, *American Communist Party,* 111. For his article on Foster, see John Pepper, "William Z. Foster—Revolutionary Leader," *Worker,* April 14, 1923. Other articles by Pepper are cited in Draper, *American Communism and Soviet Russia,* 40–41; *Worker,* May 12, 1923, May 19, 1923. Swabeck reported to Draper that Fitzpatrick had used the words "back seat," a phrasing Browder denied. See Arne Swabeck, unpublished, unititled, and unpaginated typescript, chap. 7, "Misguided Labor Party Maneuvers," Autobiographies File, Prometheus Research Library, New York, New York; Browder to Draper, Memorandum uncorrected mss. vol. 2 history, March 16, 1959, 9, Series III, Box 18, Browder Papers.

47. Barrett, *William Z. Foster,* 125–26; Jay Fox, *Amalgamation* (Chicago: Trade Union Educational League, 1923); Earl Browder, "Progress of the Amalgamation Movement," *Labor Herald* 1 (October 1923): 3–6; Browder, "Amalgamation Movement Sweeps Onward," *Labor Herald* 1 (November 1922): 11; Browder, "Eleven States Demand Amalgamation," *Labor Herald* 1 (December 1922): 7; Edward B. Mittelman, "Basis for American Federation of Labor Opposition to Amalgamation and Politics at Portland," *Journal of Political Economy* 32 (February 1924): 86–100; Earl K. Beckner, "The Trade Union Educational League and the American Labor Movement," *Journal of Political Economy* 33 (August 1925): 410–31; W. Z. Foster, "Amalgamation or Annihilation," *Labor Herald* 1 (April 1922): 6–8, 30; W. Z. Foster, J. P. Cannon, and E. W. Browder, *Trade Unions in America* (Chicago: Daily Worker Publishing, 1925); David M. Schneider, *The Workers' (Communist) Party and American Trade Unions* (Baltimore: Johns Hopkins, 1928); Montgomery, *Fall of the House of Labor,* 453; James Oneal and G. A. Werner,

American Communism: A Critical Analysis of Its Origins, Development and Programs (New York: E.P. Dutton, 1947), 164–79. For the TUEL program, see "The Principles and Program of the Trade Union Educational League," *Labor Herald* 1 (March 1922): 1–7. The monthly *Labor Herald,* published from March 1922 through October 1924, is an excellent source on the TUEL.

48. Browder attributes this to Ruthenberg and, indirectly, to himself: see Browder to Draper, 14 February 1956, Series I, Box 3; Browder to Draper, 19 June 1959, "Notes on Theodore Draper," Series III, Box 18, Browder Papers; Browder, "'No-Man's Land,'" chap. 8, "A Battle Won," 173–84, Series III, Box 10, Browder Papers.

49. See Draper, *American Communism and Soviet Russia,* 36–38; Foster, *History of the Communist Party,* 215; Bittelman, "Things I Have Learned," 399–403; "Labor Party Referendum," *The Liberator* (April 1923): 5; "The Coming Labor Party," *The Liberator* (June 1923): 6–7; *For a Labor Party: A Statement by the Workers Party* (New York: Workers Party of America, 1st ed., October 15, 1922); John Pepper, "Gompers Refuses to Recognize the US Government," *Labor Herald* 2 (June 1923): 20–22; John Pepper, "The Declaration of Independence of the American Working Class," *The Liberator* (July 1923): 8–10; William Z. Foster, "The Significance of the Elections: Three Stages of Our Labor Party Policy," and Alexander Bittelman, "In Retrospect: A Critical Review of Our Past Labor Party Policy in Light of the Present Situation," in *Workers Monthly,* December 1924, 51–54, 85–92; William Z. Foster, "A Political Party for Labor," *Labor Herald* 1 (December 1922): 3–6; Earl Browder, "The League's Labor Party Referendum," *Labor Herald* 2 (June 1923): 12–13; "To All Local Unions of All Trades in the US," *Labor Herald* 2 (March 1923): 12; Howe and Coser, *American Communist Party,* 118–20.

50. For a highly critical and somewhat simplified presentation of the Workers' Party–Federated Farmer-Labor Party relation, see Oneal and Werner, *American Communism,* 150–63. J. B. Salutsky, expelled from the WP in August 1923, was highly critical of the party's politics in this period, referring to Pepper as a "would-be Lenin" and castigating his "glorious Labor Party strategy." At a hearing relating to Salutsky's expulsion, Cannon asked, "Are you in favor of the Workers' Party stand on the question of a Labor Party?" "No," answered Salutsky. "My position is: a Labor Party embracing the mass of organizations of Labor would be of value. There is no chance for such today." Box 39, Folder 1, "Workers' Party Documents and Clippings Pertaining to Hardman's Expulsion," J. B. S. Hardman Papers, Tamiment Institute, New York University, New York, New York.

51. On Zinoviev and the Comintern, see Carr, *The Bolshevik Revolution,* vol. 3, 420–21. Note as well the discussion of Trotsky's positions in Leon Trotsky, *The Challenge of the Left Opposition (1923–1925)* (New York: Pathfinder, 1974), and his contrasting development of the theory of permanent revolution, with its attention to the peasantry in ways that do not subordinate working-class leadership. See Leon Trotsky, *The Permanent Revolution* (1930) reprinted as *The Permanent Revolution and Results and Prospects* (New York: Pathfinder, 1969); Michael Lowy, *The Politics of Combined and Uneven Development: The Theory of Permanent Revolution* (London: Verso, 1981), esp. 30–99; Baruch Knei-Paz, *The Social and Political Thought of Leon Trotsky* (Oxford: Clarendon, 1978), 127–74. For Pepper's contribution, see *For a Labor Party,* 18–19; and

many essays in communist publications, including: "The Declaration of Independence of the American Working Class," *The Liberator* (July 1923): 8–10; "The Workers Party and the Federated Farmer-Labor Party," *The Liberator* (August 1923): 10–14; "Facing the Third American Revolution," *The Liberator* (September 1923): 9–12; "Shall We Assume Leadership?" *The Liberator* (October 1923), 9–11; also Hal S. Ware, "The Farmers in the New Party," *Labor Herald* 2 (August 1923): 8; Howe and Coser, *American Communist Party*, 119. The Fitzpatrick forces are the subject of comment in *James P. Cannon and the Early Years of American Communism*, 21–23; Weinstein, *Decline of Socialism*, 272–89; Keiser, "John Fitzpatrick and Progressive Unionism," 106–33. On Lovestone and American exceptionalism, see Draper, *American Communism and Soviet Russia*, 268–81; Jay Lovestone, "Imperialism and the American Working Class," *Workers Monthly*, March 1926, 203–5; Morgan, *A Covert Life*, 63–87.

52. J. P. Cannon to C.E. Ruthenberg, 25 May 1923, reprinted as "Don't Pack the July 3 Conference," in *James P. Cannon and the Early Years of American Communism*, 124–26; *The Second Year of the Workers' Party of America: Report of the Central Executive Committee to the Third National Convention, December 30, 31 1923 and January 1, 1924—Theses. Program. Resolutions.* (Chicago: Workers Party of America, 1924), 23; Earl Browder to Theodore Draper, 20 February 1956, Series I, Box 3; Browder to Draper, 19 June 1959, "Notes on Theodore Draper," Series III, Box 18, Browder Papers; J. Louis Engdahl, "Landslide Vote for a Labor Party," *Labor Herald* 2 (May 1923): 24. See also Cannon to Charles Scott (n.d. [ca. July–August 1923]), quoted in Johanningsmeier, *Forging American Communism*, 200, also in Reel 6, Russian Center, PRL.

53. The suggestion that Ruthenberg, for instance, at first took cognizance of the fears of the Chicago Workers' Party trade unionists relating to a split with Fitzpatrick seems to rest largely on the problematic communication, C.E. Ruthenberg to ECCI, Chicago, 11 April 1924, and accompanying a letter of Browder to Draper, Yonkers, 1 March 1956, Series I, Box 3, Browder Papers. See Draper, *American Communism and Soviet Russia*, 42–43; Johanningsmeier, *Forging American Communism*, 199; Barrett, *William Z. Foster*, 137. The critical omission in Ruthenberg's letter to the ECCI is any mention of Cannon's May 25, 1923 communication, pleading not to pack the July 3 Conference, cited in full in *James P. Cannon and the Early Years of American Communism*, 124–26. Ruthenberg's stature in the party in future years, as "the founder," no doubt contributes to this aura. Yet both Cannon and Foster had mixed views of Ruthenberg, and even Browder acknowledges that Ruthenberg's contributions, up to 1923, were "purely literary." See Browder to Draper, 19 June 1959, "Notes on Theodore Draper," Series III, Box 18, Browder Papers; Cannon, *First Ten Years*, 80; Bittelman, "Things I Have Learned," 395–98.

54. Browder to Draper, 20 February 1956, Series 1, Box 3; Browder to Draper, 19 June 1959, Series III, Box 18, Browder Papers; Draper, *American Communism and Soviet Russia*, 41, 74; *Second Year of the Workers' Party*, 23–24. Sections of the Ruthenberg letter are quoted at length in Report of the Central Executive Committee of the Workers' Party, 1923, 7–11, Series II, Box 20, Browder Papers.

55. Browder to Draper, 14 February 1956, Series I, Box 3, Browder Papers; Bittelman, "Things I Have Learned," 398; Cannon, *First Ten Years*, 84–85.

56. See, among other sources, McKillen, *Chicago Labor,* 193–213; Draper, *American Communism and Soviet Russia,* 29–51; Weinstein, *Decline of Socialism,* 272–89; Foster, *History of the Communist Party,* 216–17; Browder to Draper, 20 February 1956, Series I, Box 3, Browder Papers; Howe and Coser, *American Communist Party,* 116; *Second Year of the Workers' Party,* 19; Pepper, *For a Labor Party,* 75; "F.L.P. Disowns New Party: Workers' Party Takes Advantage of Its Position as a Guest to Start a Dual Movement," *New Majority,* July 14, 1923; Bittelman, "Things I Have Learned," 399–403.

57. See Bittelman, "Things I Have Learned," 399–403, for Pepper's post-convention mood, as well as a critique of Pepper's two-stage understanding of world and American revolution in the early to mid-1920s. For articles by Pepper, see "The Workers Party and the Federated Farmer-Labor Party," *The Liberator* (August 1923): 10–14; "Facing the Third American Revolution," *The Liberator* (September 1923): 9–12; "Shall We Assume Leadership?" *The Liberator* (October 1923): 9–11; "The New Wave of World Revolution," *The Liberator* (November 1923): 10–13; "The First Mass Party of American Workers and Farmers," *International Press Correspondence* 3, July 26, 1923, 352–54; "The Slogan of the Workers' and Farmers' Government," *International Press Correspondence* 3, August 16, 1923, 602–4; "A Revolt of Farmers and Workers in the United States," *International Press Correspondence* 3, August 23, 1923, 616–18; "The Workers Party at a Turning Point," *International Press Correspondence* 3, September 27, 1923, 698–99.

58. Browder to Draper, 29 February 1956, Series I, Box 3, Browder Papers; James G. Ryan, *Earl Browder: The Failure of American Communism* (Tuscaloosa: University of Alabama Press, 1997), 26; Earl Browder, "'No-Man's Land,'" chap. 9, "A War Lost," 199–201.

59. Report of the Central Executive Committee of the Workers' Party, 1923, 7, in Series II, Box 20, Browder Papers.

60. See Draper's account of the stillbirth of the Federated Farmer-Labor Party in *American Communism and Soviet Russia,* 75; and for retrospective comment, Joseph Manley, "Goodbye 'Class' Farmer-Labor Party," *Daily Worker,* December 5, 1924. See also Montgomery, *Fall of the House of Labor,* 436–37. Swabeck confirms the sorry realization that the Workers' Party had captured, not a mass movement, "but only our close political allies and friends." See Arne Swabeck, unpublished, unititled, and unpaginated typescript, chap. 7, "Misguided Labor Party Maneuvers," Autobiographies File, Prometheus Research Library, New York, New York. On the Minnesota 1924 election, see Weinstein, *Decline of Socialism,* 290–323.

61. Cannon, *First Ten Years,* 86–87, which is not all that distant from the description in Bittelman, "Things I Have Learned," 403. On Cannon's view of Foster and his limitations, see *First Ten Years,* 84, 88–89, 92, 112–13, 120, 123–24. This interpretation, though different from the views of Foster's two major recent biographers, Barrett, *William Z. Foster,* esp. 138, and Johanningsmeier, *Forging American Communism,* 200–202, is also, I think, congruent with their accounts.

62. Cannon, *First Ten Years,* 89, 117, 119. Previous accounts of the communists and the Farmer-Labor Party often miss the nuances of intraparty struggle. See, for instance, Oneal and Werner, *American Communism,* 150–63. More attentive to differentiations within the Workers' Party is Howe and Coser, *American Communist Party,* 112–39.

63. Staley, *History of the Illinois State Federation of Labor,* 383–86; Barrett, *William Z. Foster,* 139–40; Johanningsmeier, *Forging American Communism,* 202–5; *New Majority,* September 22, 1923.

64. On gender in the garment trades and the factional context of the needle trades, see Daniel E. Bender, *Sweated Work, Weak Bodies: Anti-Sweatshop Campaigns and the Languages of Labor* (New Brunswick, NJ: Rutgers University Press, 2003), an imaginative book that nevertheless understates significantly the traditional *political* component of factionalism; Louis Levine, *The Women's Garment Workers: A History of the International Ladies Garment Workers Union* (New York: B.W. Huebsch, 1924), 354–59; Edward B. Mittelman, "Basis for American Federation of Labor Opposition to Amalgamation and Politics at Portland," *Journal of Political Economy* 32 (February 1924): 86–100; David M. Schneider, *The Workers' (Communist) Party and American Trade Unions* (Baltimore: Johns Hopkins, 1928); James P. Cannon, "What Happened at Portland?" *Worker,* November 24, 1923, reprinted in *James P. Cannon and the Early Years of American Communism,* 179–82; Cannon to Scott (n.d.), quoted in Johanningsmeier, *Forging American Communism,* 200, and in Reel 6, Russian Center, PRL; Ring interview with Cannon, April 12, 1974, 2–3; Draper, *American Communism and Soviet Russia,* 25; William F. Dunne, "Labor's Chamber of Commerce," *Labor Herald* 2 (November 1923): 3–5; Montgomery, *Fall of the House of Labor,* 433–34; Dunne to Browder (n.d.), quoted in Johanningsmeier, *Forging American Communism,* 205–6; Alex Howat to Dear Bill, Pittsburgh, KS, 8 November 1923, "Speeches/Expulsion—AFL Convention, Portland, 1923," Box 18, William F. Dunne Papers, Tamiment Institute, Bobst Library, New York University, New York, New York; Barrett, *William Z. Foster,* 141; Earl Browder, "Reactionaries Smashing Ladies Garment Workers," *Labor Herald* 2 (November 1923): 13–16. At an October meeting of the Organization and Political Committee, a committee of Pepper, Lovestone, Foster, Cannon, and Ruthenberg was constituted to reply to the Dunne expulsion, with Cannon, Ruthenberg, and Foster to sign the document as a "public announcement of [Foster's] membership in the party and on the C.E.C." Minutes of the Organization and Political Committee, October 9, 1923, Reel 1b, Russian Center, PRL. That document, "The Communists in the Trade Unions: Statement by the Central Executive Committee of the Workers Party of America" (n.d.), Loose File, Russian Center, PRL, appeared shortly thereafter. Note as well Minutes of the Organizational and Political Committee, August 13, 1923, Reel 1b, Russian Center, PRL.

65. Cannon, *First Ten Years,* 92–93; Cannon to Scott (n.d.), Reel 6, Russian Center, PRL.

66. James P. Cannon, "The Albany 'Conversion,'" *Worker,* August 11, 1923. Considerable irony existed in the Albany exclusion, given a previous Socialist Party accent on the expulsion from the New York state legislature of five Socialist assemblymen. See Louis Waldman, *Albany: The Crisis in Government—The History of the Suspension, Trial and Expulsion from the New York State Legislature in 1920 of Five Socialist Assemblymen by Their Political Opponents* (New York: Boni & Liveright, 1920).

67. James P. Cannon, "Things As They Are," *Worker,* August 11, 1923; "Things As They Are—Words and Deeds," *Worker,* August 18, 1923.

68. Cannon to Scott (n.d.), Reel 6, Russian Center, PRL.

69. The preceding paragraphs draw on Browder to Draper, 29 February 1956, Series I, Box 3, Browder Papers; Bittelman, "Things I Have Learned," 397, 403–4; Cannon, *First Ten Years*, 90, 92, 123; Cannon, *History of American Trotskyism*, 29–30; Morgan, *A Covert Life*, 38.

70. Cannon, *First Ten Years*, 90–93; Draper, *American Communism and Soviet Russia*, 87–88; Browder to Draper, 19 February 1956, Series I, Box 3, Browder Papers; Cannon to London, 29 April 1924, Reel 3, JPC Papers.

71. Draper, *American Communism and Soviet Russia*, 88–90; Bittelman, "Things I Have Learned," 395–410; Cannon, *First Ten Years*, 88, 117–20. Gitlow, *I Confess*, 184–85, presents Foster as the initiator of these inner-party moves, seeing Cannon in an entirely secondary light, but this is a reversal of the actual relations.

72. Cannon, *First Ten Years*, 87–88; Draper, *American Communism and Soviet Russia*, 81–82. For the Cannon articles, see "The Workers Party—Today and Tomorrow," comprising statements in the *Worker*, August 25, September 1, September 8, September 15, September 22, 1923, reprinted in *James P. Cannon and the Early Years of American Communism*, 127–49. Note also Arne Swabeck, Unpublished typescript (written for but not published in Les Evans, ed., *James P. Cannon As We Knew Him: By Thirty-three Comrades, Friends, and Relatives* [New York: Pathfinder, 1976]), JPC Papers; Cannon to Scott (n.d.), Reel 6, Russian Center, PRL.

73. Minutes of the C.E.C., August 24, 1923; Minutes of the Executive Council, November 13, 1923, Reel 1b, Russian Center, PRL.

74. Cannon, *First Ten Years*, 87–88; Draper, *American Communism and Soviet Russia*, 81–82; Minutes of the Organization and Political Committee, August 2, 1923, Reel 1b, Russian Center, PRL.

75. Howe and Coser, *American Communist Party*, 127–30; Draper, *American Communism and Soviet Russia*, 79–85; Charles Shipman, *It Had to Be Revolution: Memoirs of an American Radical* (Ithaca, NY: Cornell University Press, 1993), 150–51; John Pepper, "Facing the Third American Revolution," *The Liberator* (September 1923): 9–12; "Shall We Assume Leadership?" *The Liberator* (October 1923): 9–11, 28; Pepper, "*Underground Radicalism*"; Cannon, *First Ten Years*, 122–23; Minutes of the C.E.C. Meeting, November 5–6, 1923; Minutes of the Executive Council, November 13, 1923, Reel 1b, Russian Center, PRL. The hyperbole of Pepper's formulation is also commented on in Arne Swabeck, unpublished, unititled, and unpaginated typescript, chap. 7, "Misguided Labor Party Maneuvers," Autobiographies File, Prometheus Research Library, New York, New York; Browder to Draper, Memorandum uncorrected mss. vol. 2 history, March 16, 1959, 17, Series III, Box 18, Browder Papers.

76. John Pepper in *Worker*, May 26, 1923, quoted in Howe and Coser, *American Communist Party*, 104.

77. Draper, *American Communism and Soviet Russia*, 88; Solon De Leon, ed., *The American Labor Who's Who* (New York: Hanford Press, 1925), 33; Weinstein, *Decline of Socialism*, 290–91; Johanningsmeier, *Forging American Communism*, 207; Browder, "'No-Man's Land,'" chap. 9, "A War Lost," contains some comment on Burman.

78. This document, a seventeen-page mimeograph, which Draper secured from Charles Zimmerman (Draper, *American Communism and Soviet Russia*, 457, n. 33), is reprinted in *James P. Cannon and the Early Years of American Communism*, 153–78.

79. In any case, such theses were largely irrelevant: LaFollette eventually repudiated communist support and scuttled the Minnesota Farmer Labor Party's efforts to launch a third party. Also, new winds were blowing from the Comintern, all of them quite discernibly hostile to farmer-laborism by the end of 1924. Draper, *American Communism and Soviet Russia*, 85–86; *Second Year of the Workers' Party*, 47–56; Minutes of the Executive Council, November 13, 1923; "Resolution on Trade Unions Adopted by the Executive Council"; Minutes of Political and Organization Committee, October 23, 1923; Minutes of the Political Committee, October 25, 1923, Reel 1b, Russian Center, PRL; Weinstein, *Decline of Socialism*, 318–21.

80. Draper, *American Communism and Soviet Russia*, 88–91.

81. See the following Cannon articles: "Party in Ohio Plans to Push Fight Forward," *Worker*, September 22, 1923; "Militants in 2nd TUEL Conference Pledge Struggle for Class War Victims," *Worker*, September 22, 1923; "The Communists in the Trade Unions," *Voice of Labor*, October 26, 1923; "Lewis' Policies Victimize Maryland Miners," *Voice of Labor*, November 30, 1923; "The Russian Revolution—The Inspiring Force in the American Labor Movement," *Worker*, November 3, 1923. See also James P. Cannon and Robert Minor, Letter to the 15th Convention of the I.W.W., 15 November 1923, "Cannon Files, 1919–1928," Prometheus Research Library, New York, New York. On the miners, note William Z. Foster, "The Progressive Miners' Conference," *Labor Herald* 2 (July 1923): 3–6; Thomas Myerscough, "The Coming Miners' Convention," *Labor Herald* 2 (January 1924): 3–5.

82. Cannon, *First Ten Years*, 93–94.

83. Minutes of the Political Committee, October 13, 1923; Minutes of the Political and Organization Committee, October 23, 1923, Reel 1b, Russian Center, PRL.

84. Minutes of the Meeting of the Organization Committee, October 25, 1923; November 21, 1923, Reel 1b, Russian Center, PRL; "Report of Jay Lovestone on the Convention of the Communist Party of Mexico" (n.d. [January 1924?]); Minutes of Political Committee, January 10, 1924, Reel 1c, Russian Center, PRL.

85. Anne Chester to Rose and Jim, 20 October 1966, and Albert Glotzer, "Reminiscences of James P. Cannon," Reels 1 and 62, JPC Papers; Sam Gordon in Evans, *As We Knew Him*, 58.

86. James P. Cannon, "The Lives of Two Revolutionaries—Remarks by James P. Cannon at a Banquet in Los Angeles, 15 December 1962," in Cannon, *Speeches for Socialism* (New York: Pathfinder, 1971), 287–88.

87. For the "Roumanian materialist" designation used by Jim to describe Rose, see Mathew Ross entry in Evans, *As We Knew Him*, 217. For the hippie/digger contrast, see Jeanne Morgan, "Journal from James P. Cannon's Office, 1954–56: Notes kept by secretary for personal memento, without Cannon's knowledge," Introductory Notes, 3 (in possession of the author; hereafter Morgan diary). Also, Rose to Reba (n.d. [ca. 1965]), Reel 62, JPC Papers.

88. The preceding paragraphs draw upon Evelyn Reed, "Rose Karsner Cannon Is Dead, a Foremost Woman Trotskyist," *Militant,* February 18, 1968; Bryan D. Palmer interview with Walta and Marshall Ross, Del Mar, CA, April 18, 1996; Reed interview with Rose, typescript (n.d. [ca. 1960]), Reel 61, Rose Karsner/James P. Cannon Papers; George R. Kirkpatrick, *War—What For?* (West Lafayette, OH: Published for the Author, 1911); Emily Turnbull, "What Walta Ross Knew of Jim's and Rose's Families," typescript, November 29, 1993, Prometheus Research Library, New York, New York; Morgan diary, entries for January 23 and February 3, 1954.

89. Reed interview with Rose, 1960, Reel 61; Rose Karsner, "Introductory Address made at the Debs Centennial Meeting," Los Angeles, CA, November 4, 1955, Reel 63, Rose Karsner/James P. Cannon Papers.

90. *Rose Greenberg Karsner v. David Fulton Karsner* (N.Y. Supreme Court, Manhattan, June 9, 1921 and December 9, 1921); Rose Karsner to Dear Gene, 31 August 1921, 7 September 1921, Reel 61, Rose Karner/James P. Cannon Papers.

91. Rose Karsner to Dear Gene, 7 September 1921, Reel 61, Rose Karsner/James P. Cannon Papers.

92. Reed interview with Karsner, Reel 61, JPC Papers; Reba Hansen in Evans, *As We Knew Him,* 236–37; Palmer interview with Walta and Marshall Ross, April 18, 1996; Palmer interview with Milt Zaslow (Mike Bartel), Solana Beach, CA, April 18, 1996. For Walta Karsner's poem, see "Xmas Time," *The Liberator* (December 1923): 29. One of Rose Karsner's first published pieces was "White Terror in Europe: Can America Be Far Behind?" *Workers' Monthly,* December 1924, 82; on her work with the various Soviet and International Workers' aid bodies, see Ring interview with Cannon, September 15, 1973, 2. Note also the back covers of various issues of *The Liberator,* where Friends of Soviet Russia appeals were made: February 1923, May 1923, June 1923, July 1923, August 1923, September 1923, October 1923. On the Karsner, Munzenberg, and FSR relationship, see Sean McMeekin, *The Red Millionaire: A Political Biography of Willi Munzenberg, Moscow's Secret Propaganda Tsar in the West* (New Haven: Yale University Press, 2003), esp. 168, 338.

93. Albert Glotzer's copy of *Second Year of the Workers' Party,* 10, which lists Rose Karsner as a fraternal delegate attending the national convention as a representative of the Friends of Soviet Russia, marks her as associated with the Cannon-Foster faction (copy in possession of the author).

94. Draper, *American Communism and Soviet Russia,* 90; *Second Year of the Workers' Party,* 9, 56–61; Browder to Draper, 20 February 1956, Series I, Box 3, Browder Papers; Gitlow, *I Confess,* 188. For a precise statement on membership, claiming a growth from approximately 12,400 in 1922 to roughly 15,200 in 1923 (of whom almost 6,900 were "industrial"), see "Report of the Central Executive Committee of the Workers' Party, 1923," in Series II, Box 20, Browder Papers; *Daily Worker,* January 13, 1924; also *Second Year of the Workers' Party,* 29–31, where the delegates to the convention, fifty-two in total, are listed on 9. The same document also lists a number of fraternal delegates and organizations entitled to fraternal representation, including John Pepper and all members of the CEC not formally accredited as delegates. See, as background, "Letter

from the EECI to the Workers Party of America," July 12, 1923, Series II, Box 20, Browder Papers.

95. Such figures are rough estimations at best, and could not account for variations resulting from specific issue voting. That the alignments were somewhat open and an issue to participants involved is indicated in Albert Glotzer's copy of *Second Year of the Workers' Party*, where the list of voting delegates (9) is marked with three different symbolic connotations indicating factional alignment. Glotzer clearly knew most accurately the Foster-Cannon forces, whom he designated as constituting, among others, eleven of the twelve delegates from the Illinois and Minnesota districts, the core areas of Workers' Party trade union strength. Just how the delegates lined up for the Ruthenberg-Pepper-Lovestone group or the Lore group was less easily identifiable, but the key players were obviously discernible, and were so marked by Glotzer. Glotzer also marked the lengthy list of fraternal delegates, where the dominance clearly lay with the Ruthenberg-Pepper-Lovestone faction.

96. Gitlow, *I Confess*, 186; Draper, *American Communism and Soviet Russia*, 90–91. Lore's subsequent recollection of the event, which confirms that Lovestone offered him a seat on the CEC and that the suggestion originated with Ruthenberg, is in "Speech by Lore" (n.d. [December 1924?]), Reel 3, Russian Center, PRL.

97. This figure was later cited in Comintern appeals authored by Foster. See a letter by Foster, dated Moscow, 24 March 1924 in Foster's FBI file, provided to me by James R. Barrett. Much of the heading of the letter, including the body to which it is addressed, is illegible.

98. For the conference, Pepper's appeal to Lore, and the eventual committee breakdowns, see Draper, *American Communism and Soviet Russia*, 91–92, 457–58, n. 49. Bittelman, "Things I Have Learned," 416, confirms that it was Pepper's appeal to Lore that lay behind the decision to send the labor party thesis to Moscow for a final decision. Note as well Swabeck, unpublished autobiography, chap. 7, "Misguided Labor Party Maneuvers." On Shachtman, Abern, and Glotzer, see especially Peter Drucker, *Max Shachtman and His Left: A Socialist's Odyssey through the "American Century"* (Atlantic Highlands, NJ: Humanities Press, 1994), 16–24; Albert Glotzer, *Trotsky: Memoir & Critique* (Buffalo: Prometheus Books, 1989), 17–19; Martin Abern, "Report of Comrade Abern, Fraternal Delegate to the Third Congress of the Young Communist League," January 29, 1923, Reel 1b, Russian Center, PRL. Into the summer and fall of 1924, Cannon remained the main party leadership representative within the National Executive Committee of the Young Workers' League. See Minutes of the NEC, YWL, July 19, 1924; August 16, 1924; November 27, 1924, Reel 1c, Russian Center, PRL. Cannon's resignation as national chairman, Foster's election to the national chairman's post, and Pepper's opposition are recorded in Minutes of the C.E.C., February 15–16, 1924, Reel 1c, Russian Center, PRL.

99. Drucker, *Shachtman and His Left*, 16; Glotzer, "Reminiscences of Cannon," Reel 1, James P. Cannon Papers; "J.P. Cannon," Hartford, CT, March 14–15, 1923, FBI File.

100. Browder to Draper, 24 January 1956, Series I, Box 3, Browder Papers; Cannon, *First Ten Years*, 126. The most jarring misreadings of events and alignments appear in

Browder, "'No-Man's Land,'" chaps. 8–9, "A Battle Won" and "A War Lost," 185–204 [pagination varies], Series III, Box 10, Browder Papers. In this unpublished account, Browder makes himself the architect of all that was good in the 1923 events. See also Earl Browder to Dear Comrade [New York], 24 December 1923, Series I, Box 8, Browder Papers; and, from more than thirty years later, Browder to Draper, 9 March 1956, Series 1, Box 3, Browder Papers.

Chapter 8: Stalinist Suspensions

1. Benjamin Gitlow, *I Confess: The Truth about American Communism* (New York: E.P. Dutton, 1940), esp. 215–36; Peggy Dennis, *The Autobiography of an American Communist: A Personal View of a Political Life, 1925–1975* (Westport, CT/Berkeley, CA: Lawrence Hill/Creative Arts, 1977), 32; James Oneal and G. A. Werner, *American Communism: A Critical Analysis of Its Origins, Development and Programs* (New York: E.P. Dutton, 1947), 198–222; Paul Buhle, *Marxism in the USA: From 1870 to the Present Day* (London: Verso, 1987), 133–34. The blind spot in this approach to faction and communist activity in the mid- to late 1920s is that it uniformly draws from the recollections and experience of those who *failed* to break decisively from the Stalinist degeneration of the Comintern, and thus elaborates a perspective blinkered in its ability to analyze the unfolding history. This problem appears as well in the two excellent biographies of William Z. Foster, both of which provide useful accounts of this period: James R. Barrett, *William Z. Foster and the Tragedy of American Radicalism* (Urbana: University of Illinois Press, 1999), 148–62; Edward P. Johanningsmeier, *Forging American Communism: The Life of William Z. Foster* (Princeton, NJ: Princeton University Press, 1994), 214–48. See, as well, Bertram D. Wolfe's discussion in *A Life in Two Centuries: An Autobiography* (New York: Stein & Day, 1981), 373–92; Albert Glotzer, "Reminiscences of James P. Cannon," Reel 2, James P. Cannon Papers, Microfilm Edition, 1994, State Historical Society of Wisconsin, Madison, Wisconsin (hereafter JPC Papers), and the extensive discussions of factionalism in Theodore Draper, *The Roots of American Communism* (New York: Viking, 1957); Draper, *American Communism and Soviet Russia* (New York: Viking, 1960).

2. Minutes of the Central Executive Committee Meeting, May 2, 1924, Reel 1c, in Documents from Russian Center for the Preservation and Study of Contemporary History, Microfilm Copies Held, Prometheus Research Library, New York, New York (hereafter Russian Center, PRL).

3. James P. Cannon, *The First Ten Years of American Communism—Report of a Participant* (New York: Pathfinder, 1973), 137–38, 153; Harry Ring interview with James P. Cannon, September 5, 1973, 7 (in possession of the author; hereafter Ring interview). See also James P. Cannon, "The Problem of Party Leadership," November 1, 1943, published in Cannon, *The Socialist Workers Party in World War II: Writings and Speeches, 1940–1943* (New York: Pathfinder, 1975), 374. The problem of parties of the Left Opposition emerging out of a context of Stalinism that deformed them was noted by Trotsky in 1930–1931. See Leon Trotsky, "The Crisis in the German Left Opposition," February 17, 1931, published in *Writings of Leon Trotsky [1930–1931]* (New York: Pathfinder, 1973), 147.

4. Buhle, *Marxism in the USA*, 133–34.

5. Cannon, *First Ten Years*, 18–34; James P. Cannon, *The History of American Trotsky-ism: From Its Origins (1928) to the Founding of the Socialist Workers' Party (1938)—Report of a Participant* (New York: Pathfinder, 1972), 20–39.

6. Cannon, *History of American Trotskyism*, 24–28.

7. For such characterizations, see Benjamin Gitlow, *The Whole of Their Lives: Communism in America—A Personal History and Intimate Portrayal of Its Leaders* (New York: Scribner's Sons, 1948), 109–11; Gitlow, *I Confess*, 409–10, 324–26; Cannon, *History of American Trotskyism*, 29–30.

8. Alexander Bittelman, "Things I Have Learned: An Autobiography," 407, Boxes 1–2, Collection 62, unpublished manuscript in Alexander Bittelman Papers, Tamiment Institute, New York, New York. See, as well, Gitlow, *Whole of Their Lives*, 106.

9. On McSorley's, see Hutchins Hapgood, "McSorley's Saloon: An Ancient Landmark, a Relic of One Phase of American Life That Has Passed," *Harper's Weekly* (October 25, 1913), 13–17; Joseph Mitchell, *Up in the Old Hotel and Other Stories* (New York: Pantheon, 1992), esp. 3–22; Grant Holcomb, "John Sloan and McSorley's Wonderful Saloon," *American Art Journal* 15 (Spring 1983): 4–20; Timothy J. Gilfoyle, *City of Eros: New York City, Prostitution, and the Commercialization of Eros, 1790–1920* (New York: Norton, 1992), 244. In general, see Jon M. Kingsdale, "The 'Poor Man's Club': Social Functions of the Urban Working-Class Saloon," *American Quarterly* 25 (October 1973): 472–89. On John's, see Bittelman, "Things I Have Learned," 511, and regular advertisements that appeared in communist publications, declaring it "The Favorite Restaurant of Radicals and Their Friends." See, for instance, *Workers Monthly*, December 1926. On Chicago sociability, see Ring interview with Cannon, February 13, 1974, 15.

10. Cannon's connections to Max Eastman and the *Liberator* group have been touched on in earlier chapters, and those connections would continue into the later 1920s and beyond, although the two were always troubled by political difference. Cannon maintained an interest in the cultural realm throughout his life, in ways that differentiated him from Foster. The latter, whose early anarchistic attachments and loose Chicago relationship (around World War I) with the Bohemian Jack Jones and his Dil[l] Pickle Club somewhat paralleled Cannon's New York *Liberator* relations, quickly put such cultural radicalism behind him as he consolidated his authority as a voice of trade union strategy in the Workers' Party. On the Dil[l] Pickle Club, see Barrett, *William Z. Foster*, 73; Roger A. Bruns, *The Damndest Radical: The Life and World of Ben Reitman, Chicago's Celebrated Social Reformer, Hobo King, and Whorehouse Physician* (Urbana: University of Illinois Press, 1987), 230–42.

11. Undated correspondence, Joseph Freeman to Mike Gold, Mike Gold Papers, Special Collections Library, University of Michigan at Ann Arbor, Ann Arbor, Michigan (the quote graciously provided to me by Alan Wald).

12. Bittelman, "Things I Have Learned," 510.

13. Gitlow, *I Confess*, 187.

14. For a brief overview of this period, see *James P. Cannon and the Early Years of American Communism: Selected Writings and Speeches, 1920–1928* (New York: Prometheus

Research Library, 1992), 29–41. Arne Swabeck comments on Cannon's struggle against "unprincipled factionalism" in Swabeck, Unpublished typescript (written for but not published in Les Evans, ed., *James P. Cannon As We Knew Him: By Thirty-Three Comrades, Friends, and Relatives* [New York: Pathfinder, 1976]), JPC Papers. For "collective leadership," see "Conference on Moderating Factionalism," February 7, 1927, reprinted in *James P. Cannon and the Early Years of American Communism*, 383–91. For the American perception of the shadowy presence of Stalin, whose public role in the Comintern was quite minimal in the early to mid-1920s, note Cannon's remarks to Harry Ring in Ring interview with Cannon, June 20, 1973, 15–17.

15. Lisa McGirr, "Black and White Longshoremen in the IWW: A History of the Philadelphia Marine Transport Workers Industrial Local 8," *Labor History* 37 (Summer 1995): 377–402; Melvyn Dubofsky, *We Shall Be All: A History of the Industrial Workers of the World* (Chicago: Quadrangle, 1969), 437, 448; Ben Fletcher, "Philadelphia's Waterfront Unionism," *The Messenger*, June 1923, 740–41.

16. James P. Cannon, "The IWW and the Red International of Labor Unions," *Worker*, December 1, 1923, and Cannon, "The IWW Convention," *Labor Herald* 2 (January 1924): 24–26, both reprinted in *James P. Cannon and the Early Years of American Communism*, 183–95. See, as well, James P. Cannon and Robert Minor, "Letter to the 15th Convention of the I.W.W., 15 November 1923," in "Cannon Files, 1919–1928," Prometheus Research Library, New York, New York; Cannon to Charles Johnson [Scott], 14 February 1924; 25 March 1924, Reel 6, Russian Center, PRL. On the Cannon-Edwards debate, see "Communist, I.W.W. Clash to Big Crowd: Cannon-Edward Debate before Big Throng," *Daily Worker*, April 14, 1924. For background, see the assembled documents: "Joint Meeting of T.C. for W.U. and T.U.E.L. for reorgansing the minority for work in the I.W.W.," "Statement Regarding the I.W.W. Minority," "Reply to Statment Regarding the Minority," all of which were apparently developed in the Comintern, involving George Hardy, in April 1923, and which were seemingly appended to "Policy of the Workers Party in Regard to the I.W.W. (Adopted by the Political Committee on May 11th [1924])," a one-page statement that obviously drew upon Cannon's perspective. All documents in Reel 1b, Russian Center, PRL, where the May 11, 1924 statement is numbered 1, and the documents following, 2–17. See, as well, Minutes of the Red International Affiliation Committee for the IWW, February 4, 1924, Series II, Box 15, Earl W. Browder Papers, George Arents Research Library for Special Collections, Syracuse University, Syracuse, New York (hereafter cited as Browder Papers). On Cannon's view of Foster's mechanical approach in general, see *First Ten Years*, 120.

17. "Cannon Lauds Herrin Miners' Strike at Klan," *Daily Worker*, February 12, 1924. For background, see Melvyn Dubofsky and Warren Van Tine, *John L. Lewis: A Biography* (New York: Quadrangle, 1977), 84–85, 100; "Herrin under Martial Law," *Daily Worker*, February 12, 1924. For the ultimate defeat of the militant miners, see Thurber Lewis, "Class and Klan in Herrin," *Workers Monthly*, March 1925, 198–200.

18. See "Get Cannon Speech in Daily Worker Saturday," *Daily Worker*, July 30, 1924; James P. Cannon, "Our Aims and Tactics in the Trade Unions," *Daily Worker*, Magazine

Supplement, August 2, 1924, reprinted in *James P. Cannon and the Early Years of American Communism*, 213–22.

19. See the correspondence around lecture tours and speakers for party functions in small locales in James P. Cannon to All CCCs in Districts One-Ten Inclusive, and District 15, 29 January 1924; 30 January 1924; JPC to Editor, 1 March 1924; JPC to J. Klekunas, 29 January 1924, Reel 7, Russian Center, PRL.

20. See, for instance, James P. Cannon to T. O'Flaherty, 26 January 1924; Cannon to John J. Ballam, 24 April 1924; Cannon to Joseph Zach, 24 October 1924, Reel 7, Russian Center, PRL.

21. Among many sources, see "James Connolly Memorial Meeting," *Daily Worker*, June 4, 1924; "Party Activities of Local Chicago," *Daily Worker*, June 17, 1924; "Train Speakers for the Campaign in Special Classes," *Daily Worker*, July 17, 1924; "Party Activities in Chicago," *Daily Worker*, July 18, 1924; "Anti-Capitalist War Week Plans of Party Grow," *Daily Worker*, July 23, 1924; "Party Activities in Chicago," August 12, 1924; "Chicago Workers Party Offers Classes in Communist History, Economics and World Imperialism," *Daily Worker*, September 29, 1924.

22. On Stokes, see Mari Jo Buhle, *Women and American Socialism, 1870–1920* (Urbana: University of Illinois Press, 1983), 321. The most recent biography, Arthur Zipster and Pearl Zipster, *Fire and Grace: The Life of Rose Pastor Stokes* (Athens: University of Georgia Press, 1989), has next to nothing on this Workers' Party women's work, and appears to misdate and misconstrue the Cannon-Stokes correspondence; see especially p. 271. Note as well Draper, *American Communism and Soviet Russia*, 177; *The Toiler*, February 2, 1922; *Truth* [Duluth], June 23, 1922. For the Comintern position and Lenin's publications, see "Woman and the Communist International, Theses Adopted at the Third Congress," *Communist* 1 (November 1921): 12–15; Lenin, "The Emancipation of Women," in *The Forge* [Seattle], May 1, 1920; *Worker*, March 11, 1922. For the activities of women in the Workers' Party, there is some background in the following sources, although they are more focused on the 1930s: Rosalyn Baxandall, "The Question Seldom Asked: Women and the CPUSA," in *New Studies in the Politics and Culture of U.S. Communism*, ed. Michael E. Brown et al. (New York: Monthly Review, 1993), 141–62; Van Gosse, "'To Organize in Every Neighborhood, In Every Home': The Gender Politics of American Communists Between the Wars," *Radical History Review* 50 (1991): 110–41; Elsa Dixler, "The Woman Question, Women, and the American Communist Party, 1929–1941" (unpublished PhD diss., Yale University, 1974).

23. Minutes of the Central Executive Committee, March 18, 1924, 5; October 10–11, 1924, 7–8; Minutes of the Executive Council, September 29, 1924, 3, Reel 1c, Russian Center, PRL. A later 1925 document, relating to the Foster-Cannon (majority) and Ruthenberg-Lovestone (minority) positions on a range of issues, including the Farmer-Labor Party, reprinted a majority thesis supposedly "explaining" the attraction to "women's work": "Their theory (the minority) is that the Workers Party can at present appeal only to a small section of theoretically convinced communists and in order to approach with communist propaganda large masses of workers our party must form new special political organizations, such as women's councils and a farmer labor

party." Undated, untitled document beginning "The decision of the Communist International is in FAVOR OF THE MINORITY," Reel 3, Russian Center, PRL.

24. The preceding paragraphs draw on Rose Pastor Stokes to Dear Comrade Cannon, 13 August 1924; Stokes to Cannon, 5 September 1924; Kate Gitlow to C.E. Ruthenberg, 1 September 1924; Cannon to Gitlow, 10 September 1924; Statement (n.d. [ca. October–November 1924]), "The Woman Question," all in "Cannon Files, 1919–1928," Prometheus Research Library, New York, New York (hereafter Cannon PRL Files); James P. Cannon to Jeanette D. Pearl, 22 September 1924; 20 October 1924, Russian Center, PRL. On the 1924 election, in which the Workers' Party decision to run open candidates was a highly contested, factionalized decision, see Draper, *American Communism and Soviet Russia,* 86, 101, 117–20, 128, 206, 227; Barrett, *William Z. Foster,* 144–45; and Ring interview with Cannon, October 17, 1973, 4.

25. Cannon to Stokes, 4 August 1924; 28 August 1924; Stokes to Cannon, 13 August 1924; 5 September 1924, Cannon PRL Files.

26. For the continuity of complaint around the issue of women, reaching into 1928, see Porter to Stachel, "Re Women's Relief Organizations," 6 June 1929; Poyntz to Porter, 11 June 1928, Reel 2c, Russian Center, PRL.

27. Note Ring interview with Cannon, September 12, 1973, 16–17. Poyntz, a dynamic speaker and powerful educational presence in the early communist movement, built her main base around the International Ladies Garment Workers Union, where she founded the educational department in 1915–1919, and her later directorship of the New York Workers' School. Unmarried, though linked romantically at one time with the associate editor of the *Freiheit,* Shachno Epstein, Poyntz was a highly educated, cultured, middle-class woman who nevertheless had little of the privileged bearing about her, mixing well with female needle-trades workers and other party rank-and-filers. Affiliated with Ludwig Lore, Poyntz was not necessarily adept at organizing, but she was a fiery agitator, "a stormy petrel" in Gitlow's words. Feared as an unrelenting factional opponent, she often stood her ground against the dominant men in the party hierarchy, and was known to have torn political and personal strips off them in heated mid-1920s battles. (This resulted in a factional statement of attack, linking Poyntz to the Cannon-Foster bloc. See "The Statement on Juliet Stuart Poyntz," undated [September 1924?], Reel 7, Russian Center, PRL.) Klehr notes that she was an alternative delegate to the national conference. By the 1930s, according to Elizabeth Bentley, she was a major clandestine operative in the communist movement, and one of her pseudonyms was Juliet Glazer. She disappeared in 1937, rumored to have been a victim of GPU liquidation. Unfortunately, the most detailed statements on her come from Gitlow, whose characterizations and accounts of her later GPU assassination must be taken with the proverbial grain of salt, and, for her later activity, from Bentley, whose reliability is also somewhat suspect. See Solon De Leon, ed., *The American Labor Who's Who* (New York: Hanford Press, 1925), 188; Draper, *Roots of American Communism,* 193; Draper, *American Communism and Soviet Russia,* 88; Gitlow, *I Confess,* 184, 186, 190, 199–200, 204–5, 233, 245, 249–55, 267, 357; Benjamin Gitlow, *Whole of Their Lives,* 115, 331–41; Harvey E. Klehr, *Communist Cadre: The Social Background of the American Communist Party Elite* (Stan-

ford, CA: Hoover Institution Press, 1978), 71, 73; Melech Epstein, *Jewish Labor in the U.S.A.—An Industrial, Political, and Cultural History of the Jewish Labor Movement* (n.p.: KTAV Publishing House, 1969), 338–39; Elizabeth Bentley, *Out of Bondage: The Story of Elizabeth Bentley* (New York: Devin-Adair, 1951). For various statements on women and communism in this period, see Vera Buch Weisbord, *A Radical Life* (Bloomington, IN: University Press, 1977); Baxandall, "The Question Seldom Asked"; Kathleen A. Brown, "The 'Savagely Fathered and Unmothered World' of the Communist Party, U.S.A: Feminism, Maternalism, and Mother Bloor," *Feminist Studies* 25 (Fall 1999): 537–70; Joan Sangster, *Dreams of Equality: Women on the Canadian Left, 1920–1950* (Toronto: McClelland & Stewart, 1989). A recent feminist tendency to slight the kinds of issues discussed here and to concentrate treatment on the personal realm has recovered aspects of the experience of communist women while obscuring the importance of politics and faction, certainly central issues in the Workers' Party of the mid-1920s. See, for instance, Kathleen A. Brown and Elizabeth Faue, "Social Bonds, Sexual Politics, and Political Community on the U.S. Left, 1920s–1940s," *Left History* 7 (Spring 2000): 9–45.

28. Ring interiew with Cannon, October 5, 1973, 7–8; Zipster and Zipster, *Fire and Grace*, 229, 233, 258; Sean McMeekin, *The Red Millionaire: A Political Biography of Willi Munzenberg, Moscow's Secret Propaganda Tsar in the West* (New Haven: Yale University Press, 2003), esp. 114–18.

29. See, for instance, James P. Cannon to Noah London, 24 April 1924, in Cannon PRL Files; Cannon to London, 29 April 1924, Reel 3, JPC Papers; "Statement of N. London at the Convention of the Jewish Section of the Workers Party," no date (1925?), in Loose File, Russian Center, PRL; and Minutes of the Central Executive Committee: FSR Representative in Berlin, March 18, 1924, Reel 1c, Russian Center, PRL.

30. Note Paul Buhle, *Marxism in the United States: Remapping the History of the American Left* (New York: Verso, 1991), 139. More subtle is the brief statement in Michael Goldfield, "Recent Historiography of the Communist Party, USA," in *The Year Left: An Ameican Socialist Yearbook,* ed. Mike Davis, Fred Pfeil, and Michael Sprinker, vol. 1, 1985 (New York: Verso, 1985), 328–30.

31. As a suggested corrective to this bypassing of important steps forward among revolutionaries around race in the pre-1928 years, see the fascinating conceptual discussion in Barbara Foley, *Spectres of 1919: Class & Nation in the Making of the New Negro* (Urbana: University of Illinois Press, 2003), and the historical outline in Mark Solomon, *The Cry Was Unity: Communists and African Americans, 1917–1936* (Jackson: University Press of Mississippi, 1998).

32. Cannon and Swabeck had been asked by the Secretariat of the ECCI to submit a statement on conditions in the United States. Directly queried on specific areas of working-class repression (death sentences, suppression of strikes and riots, vigilante attacks on workers, and imprisonment and deportation), the American delegates responded and added a statement of "supplementary information": "the lynchings of negroes in the southern part of the country at a rate of 1–2 a week." See James Cook and J. Lansing, Untitled statement on "Our Bill to the Bourgeoisie," 199, Reel 3, Russian Center, PRL.

33. *Resolutions and Theses of the Fourth Congress of the Communist International, held in Moscow Nov. 7 to Dec. 3 1922* (London: Communist Party of Great Britain/Communist International, 1922), 84–87; *Fourth Congress of the Communist International, Abridged Report of Meetings held at Petrograd & Moscow, Nov. 7–Dec. 3, 1922* (London: Communist Party of Great Britain/Communist International, 1922), 257–62; Draper, *Roots of American Communism,* 387; Draper, *American Communism and Soviet Russia,* 326–28; Zipster and Zipster, *Fire and Grace,* 236–37; J. Steklov, "The Awakening of a Race," *International Press Correspondence,* November 24, 1922, 825–26; William Z. Foster, *The Negro People in American History* (New York: International, 1954), 452–60; Claude McKay to Comrade Wallunyus, 28 November 1922, Reel 3, Russian Center, PRL. The most thorough recent treatments of this preface to a communist-African American bond are Earl Ofari Hutchinson, *Blacks and Reds: Race and Class in Conflict, 1919–1990* (East Lansing: Michigan State University Press, 1995), 12–28; Solomon, *Cry Was Unity,* 3–51; Winston James, *Holding Aloft the Banner of Ethiopia: Caribbean Radicalism in Early Twentieth-Century America* (New York: Verso, 1998), 122–84; Oscar Berland, "The Emergence of the Communist Perspective on the 'Negro Question' in America, 1919–1931," *Science & Society* 64 (Summer 2000): 194–217.

34. As background, see "Resolution on Negro Question," *The Second Year of the Workers Party of America, held in Chicago, Illinois, Dec. 30, 31, 1923 and Jan. 1, 2 1924* (Chicago: Workers Party, 1924), 125–26. On the February 1924 congress, see Philip S. Foner and James S. Allen, eds., *American Communism and Black Americans: A Documentary History, 1919–1929* (Philadelphia: Temple University Press, 1987), 38, 53–63.

35. For a brief discussion of the early "Negro Committee" that paved the way for the American Negro Labor Congress, see Minutes of the Executive Council, March 10, 1925, Reel 1e, Russian Center, PRL.

36. See Solomon, *Cry Was Unity,* 52–67; Hutchinson, *Blacks and Reds,* 29–42; *James P. Cannon and the Early Years of American Communism,* 42–49; Draper, *American Communism and Soviet Russia,* 329–32; Robert Minor, "The First Negro Workers' Congress," *Workers Monthly,* December 1925, 68–73; Lovett Fort-Whiteman, "American Negro Labor Congress," *International Press Correspondence,* August 27, 1925, 983; M. Rabinovitch, "American Negro Labor Congress," *International Press Correspondence,* December 10, 1925, 1305–6; Harry Haywood, *Black Bolshevik: Autobiography of an Afro-American Communist* (Chicago: Liberator Press, 1978), 143–48. On Fort-Whiteman and Fletcher, see Earl R. Browder, "A Negro Labor Organizer," *Workers Monthly,* May 1925, 294; Haywood, *Black Bolshevik,* 146. The indiscretion of being insufficiently critical of Trotsky, to the point of endorsing some of his views, undoubtedly ended Fort-Whiteman's influence in 1927–1928. See material on the "Negro Question," Reel 9, Russian Center, PRL.

37. The enthusiasms of the original report on the ANLC—see Robert Minor, "The First Negro Workers' Labor Congress," *Workers Monthly,* December 1925, 68–73—should be measured against subsequent judgments: James W. Ford, *The Negro and the Democratic Front* (New York: International, 1938), 82; Solomon, *Cry Was Unity,* 66.

38. See, for instance, James, *Holding Aloft the Banner of Ethiopia,* 157–84; Theman Taylor, "Cyril Briggs and the African Blood Brotherhood: Effects of Communism on

Black Nationalism, 1919–1935" (PhD diss., University of California, Santa Barbara, 1981). On Padmore, see James R. Hooker, *Black Revolutionary: George Padmore's Path from Communism to Pan-Africanism* (New York: Praeger, 1970); Cedric J. Robinson, *Black Marxism: The Making of the Black Radical Tradition* (London: Zed Press, 1983), esp. 362–83; and Padmore's *The Life and Struggles of Negro Toilers* (London: RILU Magazine for the International Trade Union Committee of Negro Workers, 1931).

39. James, *Holding Aloft the Banner of Ethiopia*, 177–80; Haywood, *Black Bolshevik*, 121, 125–26; James S. Allen, "Organizing in the Depression South: A Communist's Memoir," *Nature, Society, and Thought* 12 (2000): 51–52. For the limitations on race, a legacy within white revolutionary circles (native-born and foreign-language federation) of the Socialist Party, see Foley, *Spectres of 1919*, 20–121. On black communists and Stalinist loyalties, see Nell Irvin Painter, *The Narrative of Hosea Hudson: His Life as a Negro Communist in the South* (Cambridge, MA: Harvard University Press, 1979), esp. 25–26.

40. Allen, "Organizing in the Depression South," 18.

41. Minutes of the Central Executive Committee, May 2, 1924, Reel 1c; Minutes of the Secretariat, June 4, 1924, Reel 3, Russian Center, PRL.

42. Haywood, *Black Bolshevik*, 138–42.

43. Harvey Klehr and William Tompson, "Self-Determination in the Black Belt: Origins of a Communist Policy," *Labor History* 30 (Summer 1989): 354–65. Haywood, *Black Bolshevik*, 218–80, presents the views of a leading advocate of the Black Belt thesis, as well as a history of its early development. Draper, *American Communism and Soviet Russia*, 342–56, offers a useful overview of the Stalinist origins of the theory. John Pepper, who earlier in the 1920s had rejected strongly all nationalist solutions to the "Negro Question" in America, adapted to the new line and pushed it in particularly blunt directions. See Pepper, *American Negro Problems* (New York: Workers Library, 1928), a pamphlet developed from an article in *The Communist*, October 1928, 628–38. See also, Gitlow, *I Confess*, 480–82; Wilson Record, *The Negro and the Communist Party* (Chapel Hill: University of North Carolina Press, 1951), 58–59; Earl Browder, C. A. Hathaway, Harry Haywood, and the Communist International, *The Communist Position on the Negro Question: Equal Rights for Negroes: Self-Determination for the Black Belt* (New York: Workers Library, ca. 1932); Robinson, *Black Marxism*, 301–24; Hutchinson, *Blacks and Reds*, 43–58; and Solomon, *Cry Was Unity*, 68–91. Useful comment appears in James, *Holding Aloft the Banner of Ethiopia*, 286, which suggests that the Black Belt nation thesis had "little appeal to the Negro people." For a brilliantly suggestive critique of what is designated the "metonymic nationalism" that would register in the Black Belt nation thesis, see Foley, *Spectres of 1919*, which notes that "this insistence in the 'soilness' and 'rootedness' of black folks did not entirely refute the racists, but instead ended up reproducing various features of the dominant ideology by reinforcing essentialist notions of racial difference" (esp. ix, but also 160–68). An enlightening and relevant discussion is Christopher Phelps, "Introduction," in Max Shachtman, *Race and Revolution* (New York: Verso, 2003), ix–lxv.

44. Jay Lovestone, "The Great Negro Migration," *Workers Monthly*, February 1926, 179–84. The position that radicalization of American blacks was dependent upon

migration from the agricultural south to the urban, industrial capitaist north met with a chilly response from most communist African Americans.

45. Note a passage of Dunne's speech at the Third Congress of the RILU (1924), in which he opposed strongly Lozovsky's suggestion that where AFL unions refused to admit black workers, the WP should organize separate unions. Dunne commenced his intervention with the statement, "The fact that the black workers are unorganized is not due to racial antagonism, but is because the American workers are unorganized in general." Published originally only in German, this passage is translated in *James P. Cannon and the Early Years of American Communism,* 47. See, as well, Bill Dunne, "American Negro Situation" (n.d.), Reel 9, Russian Center, PRL.

46. For Haywood's positive view of Dunne, no doubt enhanced in hindsight by Dunne's embrace of the Black Belt thesis at the Sixth Congress of the Comintern in 1928, see Haywood, *Black Bolshevik,* 228, 258, 261–62, 271, 275, 277.

47. See, for instance, Ted Morgan, *A Covert Life: Jay Lovestone—Communist, Anti-Communist, and Spymaster* (New York: Random House, 1999), 87.

48. Quoted in *James P. Cannon and the Early Years of American Communism,* 47–48.

49. Dunne's major statements of the mid-1920s include William F. Dunne, "Negroes in American Industries," *Workers Monthly,* March 1925, 206–8, 237; "Negroes in American Industry," *Workers Monthly,* April 1925, 257–60; "The Negroes as an Oppressed People," *Workers Monthly,* July 1925, 395–98; "The NAACP Takes a Step Backward," *Workers Monthly,* August 1926, 459–61; "Our Party and the Negro Masses," *Daily Worker,* August 13, 1925.

50. J. Swift [John Pepper], "Policies on Negro Work," Attached to Political Committee Minutes, May 30, 1928, Reel 2c, Russian Center, PRL. For a full accounting of the various divergent positions on the "black question" that emerged at the Sixth Congress, and out of which would develop the Black Belt thesis, see Draper, *American Communism and Soviet Russia,* 345–53. Note, as well, Minutes of the Negro Commission, August 11, 1928, Reel 9, Russian Center, PRL.

51. See Max Shachtman, "Communism and the Negro," and Christopher Phelps, "Introduction," in Shachtman, *Race and Revolution.*

52. Harry Haywood, *Negro Liberation* (New York: International, 1948), 216; Robert A. Hill, "Racial and Radical: Cyril V. Briggs, *The Crusader* Magazine, and the African Blood Brotherhood, 1918–1922," introduction to the reprint edition of the *Crusader* (New York: Garland, 1987), xxvi. On Huiswoud's opposition, see Harold Cruse, *The Crisis of the Negro Intellectual: From Its Origins to the Present* (New York: William Morrow, 1967), 140–43; Huiswoud, "World Aspects of the Negro Question," *The Communist,* February 1930, 132–47, an article polemicized against by Haywood, "Against Bourgeois Liberal Distortion of Leninism on the Negro Question in the United States," *The Communist,* August 1930, 694. See also Painter, *Hosea Hudson,* 16–17, 26–28, 101–3; Ruth Needleman, *Black Freedom Fighters in Steel: The Struggle for Democratic Unionism* (Ithaca, NY: Cornell University Press, 2003), 27, 184, 193–94; Mark Naison, *Communists in Harlem During the Depression* (Urbana: University of Illinois Press, 1983), 18–22, 45–47. For a pointed Socialist Party critique of the Black Belt Nation thesis, see

Norman Thomas, "For the Socialists," in "Symposium for 1932 Presidential Candidates," *Opportunity* 10 (November 1932): 340.

53. Dunne called the thesis a "contribution," accepting that its stress on racism in the party was a useful corrective and suggesting that "self-determination" was part of a revolutionary program, rather than an immediate demand. See Solomon, *Cry Was Unity*, 73, quoting a Comintern source.

54. James P. Cannon, "The Russian Revolution and the American Negro Movement," in Cannon, *First Ten Years*, 232–37.

55. See, for instance, Dan T. Carter, *Scottsboro: A Tragedy of the American South* (Baton Rouge: Louisiana State University Press, 1969); Naison, *Communists in Harlem*; Robin D. G. Kelley, *Hammer and Hoe: Alabama Communists During the Great Depression* (Chapel Hill: University of North Carolina Press, 1990); Goldfield, "Recent Historiography of the Communist Party USA," esp. 328–31; Michael Denning, *The Cultural Front: The Laboring of American Culture in the Twentieth Century* (London: Verso, 1996); Robin D. G. Kelley, "'Afric's Sons with Banner Red': African Amercian Communists and the Politics of Culture, 1919–1934," and "'This Ain't Ethiopia, But It'll Do': African Americans and the Spanish Civil War," in *Race Rebels: Culture, Politics, and the Black Working Class* (New York: Free Press, 1994), 103–58, esp. 115; Solomon, *Cry Was Unity*, 95–310.

56. "Communist Party—Lovestone Factionalism, 1929," containing an undated letter to the ECCI from Jay Lovestone [ca. 1924?] in Series II, Box 3, Browder Papers.

57. Seidel to My Dear Comrade Cannon, 24 August [1924], Reel 7, Russian Center, PRL.

58. Minutes of the Executive Council, December 14, 1923; December 21, 1923, Reel 1b; Minutes of the Central Executive Committee, January 3, 1924; February 15–16, 1924; March 17, 1924; March 18, 1924, Reel 1c, Russian Center, PRL; Meeting of the Executive Council, January 25, 1924; Minutes of the Political Committee, January 22, 1924; January 28, 1924; February 8, 1924; March 25, 1924; April 2, 1924; Minutes of Joint Meeting of the Political and Educational Committees, January 25, 1924, Reel 1c, Russian Center, PRL.

59. Minutes of the Central Executive Committee, February 15–16, 1924, Reel 1c, Russian Center, PRL.

60. See Cannon, *First Ten Years*, 89; Cannon, *History of American Trotskyism*, 29.

61. Cannon, *First Ten Years*, 131, 153. On Bela Kun and the oppposition of Landler and Lukacs, I am indebted to an unpublished paper by Paul Le Blanc, "Spider and Fly: The Leninist Philosophy of Georg Lukacs." An extremely useful contextualization also appears in John Rees, "Introduction," in Lukacs, *A Defence of History and Class Consciousness* (London: Verso, 2000), 1–38, a book that publishes Lukacs's *Tailism and the Dialectic*. See, as well, the admittedly compromised discussion in Franz Borkenau, *World Communism: A History of the Communist International* (Ann Arbor: University of Michigan Press, 1962), 108–33, 174–75. Also Miklos Molnar, *A Short History of the Hungarian Communist Party* (Boulder, CO: Westview Press, 1978), 10–30; Agnes Szabo, "The Hungarian Party of Communists in the Social Relationships of the Counter-Revolutionary Regime, 1919–1933," in *Studies in the History of the Hungarian Working-Class Movement, 1867–1966*, ed. Henrik Vass (Budapest: Akademiai Kiadu, 1975),

155–84. Zinoviev's penchant for "beating down" opposition "in the blustering manner which was to become customary with him," was evident in his Comintern dealings with the French section as early as 1922. See Tom Kemp, *Stalinism in France: Volume I, the First Twenty Years of the French Communist Party* (London: New Park, 1984), 52.

62. Cannon to London, 29 April 1924, Reel 3, JPC Papers.

63. Foster to Zinoviev, Moscow, 9 March 1924, letter in the William Z. Foster files of U.S. Department of Justice, Federal Bureau of Investigation, Freedom of Information/Privacy Act Files, Washington, DC (hereafter FBI File). My thanks to James R. Barrett for providing me with a copy of this document.

64. Foster, Cannon, et al., "To the Executive Committee of the Communist International," March 27, 1924, Loose File, Russian Center, PRL; Cannon, *First Ten Years*, 117, 125–26; Cannon to Scott, 14 February 1924; 25 March 1924, Reel 6, Russian Center, PRL.

65. See Jane Degras, ed., *The Communist International, 1919–1943: Documents*, vol. 2 (London: Frank Cass, 1971), 188–99, 215–17, 222–23.

66. James P. Cannon, "The Bolshevization of the Party," *Workers Monthly*, November 1924, 34–37. For a general statement on Bolshevization, see Theodore Draper, *American Communism and Soviet Russia*, 153–85. Especially negative is the depiction of Bolshevization in Kemp, *Stalinism in France*.

67. See Cannon, *First Ten Years*, 130–31; *History of American Trotskyism*, 36–37. Leon Trotsky's *The New Course* (Ann Arbor: University of Michigan Press, 1972), was unavailable, having been written in 1923. The decisive statement would not come until later in the 1920s and beyond, with the publication of Trotsky's analysis of the tragedy of the Chinese Revolution of 1925–1927. See especially Leon Trotsky, "The Results and Prospects of the Chinese Revolution . . . ," in *The Draft Program of the Communist International: A Criticism of Fundamentals* (New York: The Militant, 1929), 76–139; Trotsky, "The Basic Strategic Mistake of the Fifth Congress," in *The Strategy of the World Revolution* (New York: Communist League of America, 1930), 23–30; Trotsky, *Problems of the Chinese Revolution* (New York: Pioneer, 1932). For later invaluable accounts, see Jean Chesneaux, *The Chinese Labor Movement, 1919–1927* (Stanford, CA: Stanford University Press, 1968); Harold R. Isaacs, *The Tragedy of the Chinese Revolution* (Stanford, CA: Stanford Univesity Press, 1961); Wang Fan-Hsi, *Chinese Revolutionary: Memoirs, 1919–1949* (Oxford: Oxford University Press, 1980).

68. For Trotsky's account of Lenin's death and the shift of power, see Leon Trotsky, *My Life: The Rise and Fall of a Dictator* (London: Thornton Butterworth, 1930), 428–41.

69. Lore later commented on the sharp factional alliances growing weaker in this period, noting, "We felt that the majority was beginning to leave the sound sane way and was coming dangerously near to adopting the Pepper policy of adventurism." See "Speech by Lore" (n.d. [December 1924]), Reel 3, Russian Center, PRL. Note the overstated claim in Albert Weisbord, *The Conquest of Power: Liberalism, Anarchism, Syndicalism, Socialism, Fascism, and Communism*, vol. 2 (New York: Covici Friede, 1937), 984.

70. See Charles A. Madison, "Robert M. LaFollette: The Radical in Politics," in *American Radicals: Some Problems and Personalities*, ed. Harvey Goldberg (New York: Monthly Review Press, 1957), 91–110; R. David Myers, "Robert M. LaFollette," in *The*

American Radical, ed. Mari Jo Buhle, Paul Buhle, and Harvey J. Kaye (New York: Routledge, 1994), 159–66.

71. Pepper's perspective was developed in a series of statements in the *Worker,* December 22, 1923; *Daily Worker,* March 7, 1924; March 8, 1924; March 13, 1924. For the Foster-Cannon position, see Foster, Cannon, and Bittelman, "Present Economic and Political Situation and Our Immediate Tasks," Memorandum to the ECCI and adopted by the CEC of the Workers Party on March 16, 1924, original in Loose File, Russian Center, PRL, reprinted in *Daily Worker,* March 22, 1924, magazine section.

72. For this LaFollette maze, see Bittelman, "Things I Have Learned," 410–15; Draper, *American Communism and Soviet Russia,* 96–104; Irving Howe and Lewis Coser, *The American Communist Party: A Critical History (1919–1957)* (Boston: Beacon Press, 1957), 130, 132–35, 139–43; Oneal and Werner, *American Communism,* 180–97. A succinct discussion appears in David Montgomery, "The Farmer-Labor Party," in *Working for Democracy: American Workers from the Revolution to the Present,* ed. Paul Buhle and Alan Dawley (Urbana: University of Illinois Press, 1985), 76–78. For a selection of Central Executive Committee discussions, see Minutes of the Central Executive Committee Meeting, January 3, 1924; February 15–16, 1924; March 17, 1924, Reel 1c, Russian Center, PRL.

73. On Lore's background, see Paul Buhle, "Ludwig Lore," in *Encyclopedia of the American Left,* ed. Mari Jo Buhle, Paul Buhle, and Dan Georgakas (Urbana: University of Illinois Press, 1992), 434–35; Paul Buhle, "Ludwig Lore and the *New Yorker Volks- zeitung:* The Twilight of the German-American Socialist Press," in *The German- American Radical Press: The Shaping of a Left Political Culture, 1850–1940,* ed. Elliott Shore, Ken Fones-Wolf, and James P. Danky (Urbana: University of Illinois Press, 1990), 168–81; Paul Buhle, *A Dreamer's Paradise Lost: Louis C. Fraina/Lewis Corey (1892–1953) and the Decline of Radicalism in the United States* (Atlantic Highlands, NJ: Humanities Press, 1995), 72; Trotsky, *My Life,* 236; Draper, *Roots of American Communism,* 76–77, 79–82, 85, 100, 120, 132, 139, 143, 154, 180–81.

74. Note Trotsky's "Paul Levi and Some 'Lefts,'" in Trotsky, *The First Five Years of the Communist International,* vol. 2 (New York: Monad, 1972), 85–90, and the suggestion in *James P. Cannon and the Early Years of American Communism,* 35, that Lore and the *Volkszeitung* supported Levi, an expelled figure in the German communist movement.

75. Draper, *American Communism and Soviet Russia,* 106–7, quotes Lore's attack on the Comintern from the *New Yorker Volkszeitung,* March 5, 1924.

76. See Gitlow, *I Confess,* 201–2.

77. Although unsigned, an 11 January 1924 letter to Dear Comrade Lore, in which a Central Executive Committee member asks for clarification and confirmation of Lore's supposed criticism of the author's "political putchism or adventurism" bears the mark of Pepper. It is in Reel 3, Russian Center, PRL.

78. See Gitlow, *I Confess,* 198–203; Draper, *American Communism and Soviet Russia,* 106–9, cites the magazine supplement, *Daily Worker,* December 6, 1923; December 13, 1923; March 7, 1924. See, as well, Minutes of the Executive Council, March 7, 1924; Minutes of the Central Executive Committee, March 17, 1924; March 18, 1924, Reel 1c,

Russian Center, PRL; Bittleman, "Things I Have Learned," 421. For a brief, and uncomplimentary, account of Zinoviev that credits the Comintern head in this period with the first public use of "Trotskyism" as a term of abuse, suggesting further that Zinoviev "brought on himself the principal odium of the campaign against Trotsky, and allowed Stalin to reap its advantages," see E. H. Carr, *Socialism in One Country, 1924–1926*, vol. 1 (Harmondsworth, UK: Penguin, 1970), 167–73, esp. 166; see also Degras, *The Communist International*, vol. 2, 140–41.

79. For a posthumous statement on how this hit the Foster-Cannon bloc and the entire CEC, see Alexander Bittelman, *Daily Worker*, August 29, 1925, magazine supplement, quoted in Draper, *American Communism and Soviet Russia*, 113.

80. Trotsky's condemnation, dated May 20, 1924, and thus developing out of the "American Commission" discussion at the Fifth Congress, was relentless: "In America the conciliationist illusions of the petty bourgeoisie, primarily the farmers, and the petty-bourgeois illusions of the proletariat take the form of the Third Party. . . . For a young and weak Communist Party, lacking in revolutionary temper, to play the role of solicitor and gatherer of 'progressive voters' for the Republican Senator LaFollette is to head toward the political dissolution of the party in the petty bourgeoisie. . . . [T]he inspirers of this monstrous opportunism, who are thoroughly imbued with skepticism concerning the American proletariat, are impatiently seeking to transfer the party's center of gravity into a farmer milieu—a milieu that is being shaken by the agrarian crisis." Though he went unnamed, Pepper was obviously the architect of this "monstrous opportunism" that Trotsky targeted, the appeal to the "agrarian revolution" having been central to Pepper's 1923 American writings on farmer-labor party activity. See Leon Trotsky, "Author's 1924 Introduction," in *The First Five Years of the Communist International*, vol. 1 (New York: Monad, 1972), 12–14. Trotsky would later name Pepper more directly in his 1928 book, *The Third International After Lenin* (New York: Pathfinder, 1970), 120–21. Note, as well, William F. Dunne, "Manuscript—History of the Communist Party," Folder 63, 5, William F. Dunne Papers, Tamiment Institute, Bobst Library, New York University, New York, New York, in which Dunne correctly locates a Trotsky animus to Pepper, but confuses a later Sixth Congress of the Comintern (1928) denunciation of Pepper with Trotsky's critique.

81. See Alexander Bittelman and James P. Cannon, "Reply to the Thesis of Comrades Lore and Olgin," *Daily Worker* magazine supplement, April 12, 1924, reprinted in *James P. Cannon and the Early Years of American Communism*, 196–206. This article actually cited Trotsky positively in an inconsequential, passing manner. As such, it represents a last stand of innocence in the Workers' Party. Within months, mention of Trotsky was much more difficult, and generally involved criticism. See, for instance, Alexander Bittelman, "Lenin, Leader and Comrade," *Workers Monthly*, January 1925, 99–101. Cannon also defended the Third Party alliance/two splits notion before the South Slavic branch, but the opaque nature of the position did not translate easily in the *Daily Worker* account and Cannon had to offer a subsequent clarification of his arguments that repudiated the journalistic account of his speech. See "Third Party Will Weaken Our Foe, Says Cannon," *Daily Worker*, April 21, 1924; James P. Cannon, "Letter to the

Editors of the *Daily Worker*," *Daily Worker*, April 22, 1924. It is not known if Comintern intervention prompted this revision of the record, but Cannon's speech did become the basis of critique in the American Commission statement that came out of the Fifth Congress. Cannon was able to successfully deflect the Comintern critique on the grounds that the position he put forward was in absolute accord with the positions developed in the Central Executive Committee, and that there was no basis for suggesting that he was doing anything but presenting official Workers' Party policy. See "Resolution on Comrade Cannon's Statement" (n.d. [April–May 1924]); Minutes of the Executive Council, April 1, 4, 1924, Reel 1c, Russian Center, PRL; Cannon, *History of American Trotskyism*, 35–36; Ring interview with Cannon, October 17, 1973, 2–4.

82. Draper, *American Communism and Soviet Russia*, 104–13; Barrett, *William Z. Foster*, 142–44; Johanningsmeier, *Forging American Communism*, 208–10. For a sense of the tenor of the American Commission at the Fifth Congress of the Communist International, see "Meeting of American Commission," April 29, 1924; May 7, 1924; May 17, 1924, Reel 1b, Russian Center, PRL. Radek and Zinoviev are quoted in "Excerpts from the Report of the American Commission in the Presidium of the EC of the CI on 20 May 1924," Reel 1b, Russian Center, PRL. Foster reported to the CEC in Minutes of the Central Executive Committee, June 7, 1924, Reel 1c, Russian Center, PRL.

83. James P. Cannon, "The Bolshevization of the Party," *Workers Monthly*, November 1924, 34–36, is one of the more rigid statements on Bolshevization and was originally a Sunday-evening talk at New York's Workers' School, headed by Juliet Stuart Poyntz, a member of the Lore group. Cannon later noted that this speech was "ordered published in the *Workers Monthly*," indicating that he possibly realized he was being sent into a stronghold of the Lore group to promote a Comintern directive that might meet resistance. On this, see James P. Cannon, William Z. Foster, et al., "A Statement on Two and a Half Internationalism," *Daily Worker*, December 27, 1924, magazine supplement, reprinted in *James P. Cannon and the Early Years of American Communism*, quote from 286. See, as well, Cannon, *First Ten Years*, 188–90; and Cannon's four articles: "New Party Industrial Registration," *Daily Worker*, July 25, 1924; "All Ready for the Industrial Registration," *Daily Worker*, August 16, 1924; "Industrial Registration in Full Swing," *Daily Worker*, September 6, 1924; "Using the Party Registration," *Daily Worker*, October 25, 1924. Minutes of the Political Committee, August 11, 1924, Reel 1c, Russian Center, PRL, contain a report by Cannon on industrial registration, with the statement on education in Minutes of the Executive Council, October 14, 1924, 5, Reel 1c, Russian Center, PRL. Also on education, see Cannon, "Developing the Party Educational Work," *Daily Worker*, November 15, 1924; Cannon, "How to Organize and Conduct a Study Class," *Daily Worker*, December 13, 1924, magazine supplement, reprinted in *James P. Cannon and the Early Years of American Communism*, 264–67. On his address to miners, see "Our Aims and Tactics in the Trade Unions," *Daily Worker*, August 2, 1924, reprinted in *James P. Cannon and the Early Years of American Communism*, 213–22. Lenin's "Five Years of the Russian Revolution and the Prospects of the World Revolution: Report to the Fourth Congress of the Communist International, 13 November 1922," is in Lenin, *Collected Works*, vol. 33 (Moscow: Progress, 1966), 418–32.

For excerpts and commentary, see Prometheus Research Series #1, *Guidelines on the Organizational Structure of Communist Parties, on the Methods and Contents of Their Work* (New York: Prometheus Research Library, August 1988).

84. See James P. Cannon, "The St. Louis Conference of the C.P.P.A," *Labor Herald* (March 1924): 25–26.

85. James P. Cannon, "St. Paul—June 17th," *Labor Herald* (May 1924): 88–91. See as well William F. Dunne, "Workers and Farmers on the March," *Labor Herald* (April 1924): 38–40; Joseph Manley, National Secretary, Federation Farmer Labor Party, "Farmers! Workers! Organize Your Party" (n.d. [May 1924?]), in "International Labor Defense," File No: 62–2608, sec. 3, FBI File.

86. "Lafollette," *Daily Worker,* July 11, 1924; "Train Speakers for the Campaign in Special Class," *Daily Worker,* July 17, 1924; "Party Activities in Chicago," *Daily Worker,* July 18, 1924; James P. Cannon, "Communist Candidates and the Farmer-Labor Party," *Daily Worker,* July 29, 1924. Cannon, *First Ten Years,* 129–30 attributes the policy change to Foster and Bittelman, suggesting that the latter's theoretical influence was at its greatest in this period. It was quite clear, though, that Cannon himself went along with the Foster-Bittelman orientation, albeit in ways that stressed, not a principled repudiation of the labor party per se, but the necessity of premising its emergence on "mass sentiment" within the trade unions. See, as well, Bittelman, "Things I Have Learned," 413–29; Minutes of the Executive Council, April 14, 1924; April 28, 1924; May 27, 1924; September 22, 1924; "Statement by Comrade Foster" (n.d. [July–August 1924]), Reel 1c, Russian Center, PRL; Cannon to Hansen [Seattle], 22 July 1924, Loose File, Russian Center, PRL; Draper, *American Communism and Soviet Russia,* 113–18; Barrett, *William Z. Foster,* 143–46.

87. Alexander Bittelman, "Who Is Bankrupt?" unpublished, undated manuscript (1924–1925) in "Bittelman," Series III, Box 29, Browder Papers; Cannon, *First Ten Years,* 129–30; numerous articles in *Daily Worker,* August 28–October 30, 1924; "Red Nights," flyer from Theodore Draper Research Files, Robert W. Woodruff Library, Emory University, Atlanta, Georgia, copy in "From 1924—About Cannon," file at Prometheus Research Library, New York, New York.

88. Minutes of the Political Committee, November 5, 1924; J. P. Cannon (discussion on Ruthenberg Report), n.d. (November 1924?); untitled document noting Cannon (Ida's transcription first), n.d. (1924–1925), Reel 3; Minutes of the Central Executive Committee, November 21–22, 1924, Reel 1c, Russian Center, PRL; Cannon, *First Ten Years,* 129. Cannon published his *Daily Worker* articles addressing the election in the first week of December; both are reprinted in *James P. Cannon and the Early Years of American Communism,* 244–56. Alternative factional theses on the election appeared in the *Daily Worker,* November 26, 1924 (Foster-Cannon) and November 28, 1924 (Ruthenberg-Lovestone).

89. Browder to Lozovsky, 24 November 1924, quoted in Barrett, *William Z. Foster,* 149.

90. The most serious statements on the part of the Cannon-Foster group were those of Alexander Bittelman, "In Retrospect: A Critical Review of Our Past Labor Party Policy in the Light of the Present Situation,"*Workers Monthly,* December 1924, 85–90;

"Communism Versus LaFolletteism,"*Daily Worker*, Special Magazine Supplement, October 18, 1924. See, as well, "The Problem of the Labor Party," *New International* 2 (March 1935): 33–37.

91. George W. Lawson, *History of Labor in Minnesota* (Saint Paul: Minnesota Federation of Labor, 1955), 59–61; James Weinstein, *The Decline of Socialism in America, 1912–1925* (New York: Vintage, 1969), 320–23.

92. Minutes of the Political Committee, August 11, 1924; August 18, 1924, Reel 1c, Russian Center, PRL.

93. For the Comintern cable delaying the convention and inviting the factions to Moscow, see Minutes of the Political Committee, November 12, 1924, Reel 3, Russian Center, PRL. Anti-Trotskyism was evident in the same period, pushed by Lovestone but acquiesced in by the Cannon-Foster group. See Minutes of the Political Committee, December 7, 1924, Reel 3, Russian Center, PRL. The Comintern issued a directive barring any party press from publishing Trotsky's *1917* or any of its chapters. See *Daily Worker*, December 13, 1924. As late as March 1925, Trotsky's book on Lenin was available for sale in party bookstores, but the common response within key committees was that there "be no advertising campaigns or special endeavors to widen [the book's] circulation and that the Party Press be instructed accordingly." See Minutes of the Executive Council, March 10, 1925, Reel 1e, Russian Center, PRL. The book referred to in all of this documentation as *1917* was almost certainly Leon Trotsky, *Lenin* (New York: Minton, Balch & Company, 1925).

94. Minutes of the Political Committee, December 9, 1924, Reel 3, Russian Center, PRL.

95. See Moissaye J. Olgin, "Lore and the Comintern," *Daily Worker*, magazine supplement, December 6, 13, and 20, 1924; Minutes of the Political Committee, December 16, 1924, Reel 3, Russian Center, PRL; James P. Cannon, "The CEC, the Minority, and Comrade Lore: How the Minority 'Fought' Lore When They Controlled the Party," *Daily Worker*, December 11, 1924; Cannon, Foster, et al., "Two and a Half Internationalism," both reprinted in *James P. Cannon and the Early Years of American Communism*, 257–63, 284–86; "Incomplete Text of Speech delivered by Comrade Lore at CEC Meeting, 12 May 1925," Reel 1d, Russian Center, PRL; Gitlow, *I Confess*, 204–5. Noah London provided a statement to the Jewish Federation of the Workers' Party that suggested the divisions created in the aftermath of the assault on Lore. It contains a weak criticism of Cannon. See "Statement of Noah London at the Convention of the Jewish Federation of the Workers' Party" n.d. (1925?), Loose File, Russian Center, PRL. For documents that detail Cannon's and London's relations, see James P. Cannon to Noah London, 24 April 1924, Cannon PRL Files; Cannon to London, 29 April 1924, Reel 3, JPC Papers.

96. Quotes in the preceding paragraph draw from the public document by Cannon, Foster, Bittelman, "A Year of Party Progress—Being a Record of Difficulties Overcome, of Party Achievements, and the Part Played Therein by the CEC and the Minority," *Daily Worker*, December 27, 1924, magazine supplement, reproduced in *James P. Cannon and the Early Years of American Communism*, 268–83; and from Cannon's more private, internal statement, "J.P. Cannon (Discussion on Ruthenberg Report), n.d. (November–December 1924?), Reel 3, Russian Center, PRL. Cannon could appreciate

advances in the trade union sphere, but he was well aware that there remained factional differences over this issue. See, for instance, the Ruthenberg group's reluctance to endorse motions supported by the Foster-Cannon group relating to a Paterson silk strike and the TUEL: Minutes of the Political Committee, November 12, 1924, Reel 3, Russian Center, PRL.

97. Ring interview with Cannon, April 26, 1974, 20, states bluntly: "I didn't notice any crookedness in the Comintern until 1925, I guess."

98. Minutes of the Central Executive Committee, May 3, 1924, Reel 1c, Russian Center, PRL.

99. See Acting Secretary to the ECCI (Attention: Organizational Department), 13 January 1925, with enclosures, in William Z. Foster file, Federal Bureau of Investigation, courtesy of James R. Barrett; Cannon to Krumbein, telegram, 14 January 1924; "Report of Sub Committee on Italian Federation Submitted Unanimously by Cannon, Bedacht, and Bittelman" n.d. (January 1925), Reel 5, Russian Center, PRL.

100. Bryan D. Palmer interview with Walta and Marshall Ross, Del Mar, CA, April 18, 1996. For a suggestion of a competition between Cannon and Lovestone for Rose's affections, see Ann Chester to Rose and Jim, 20 October 1966, Reel 62, Rose Karsner Cannon/James P. Cannon Papers. There is little hint in any of the comment on Lovestone from the ranks of Workers' Party figures, or in the recent biography, Morgan, *A Covert Life*, that Lovestone would have been capable of an affectionate relationship with children. That Cannon and Karsner would entrust Lovestone with Walta's trip to Chicago also suggests dimensions of the human relationships that existed within factional oppositions, and that are seldom apparent in conventional commentary, political or historical.

101. Minutes of the Executive Council, September 17, 1924; September 22, 1924, Reel 1c, Russian Center, PRL.

102. J. P. Cannon to Comrade Schapp, New York, 2 October 1924, Reel 7, Russian Center, PRL. Lista was moving to an apartment at 360 West 15th Street.

103. The only statement on this that I have been able to locate is Reba Hansen's recollection in Evans, *As We Knew Him*, 236–37. However, the complete passage betrays some difficulties, and possibly confuses Jim and Rose meeting casually in 1921 at the Unity Convention atop Mount Overlook at Woodstock, New York, with the consummation of a sexual relationship. It also notes that Cannon claimed he had been in Chicago a year without any sexual contact with a woman, when other statements indicate that he and Rose were indeed sharing accommodations sometime in 1924. See James P. Cannon, "The Lives of Two Revolutionaries—Remarks by James P. Cannon at a Banquet in Los Angeles, 15 December 1962," in Cannon, *Speeches for Socialism* (New York: Pathfinder, 1971), 287–88.

104. Minutes of the Political Committee, December 9, 1924, Reel 3, Russian Center, PRL.

105. Cannon had been the central figure in education since the CEC took over the direction of the New York Workers' School and appointed Poyntz director in April 1924. See Minutes of the Executive Council, April 14, 1924, Reel 1c, Russian Center, PRL.

There is no doubt from the minutes that Poyntz was a factional appointment, with Lovestone attempting to secure the placement of another director, the former ultra-leftist, Harry M. Wicks. Cannon presented a series of reports on Bolshevization and education thereafter. See, for instance, Cannon, "Report of the Education Director," in Minutes of the Central Executive Committee, November 21–22, 1924, and Cannon, "Educational Work in New York," in Minutes of the Executive Council, October 14, 1924, both in Reel 1c, Russian Center, PRL; Cannon, "Educational Work," in Minutes of the Political Committee, November 12, 1924, Reel 3, Russian Center, PRL. Poyntz had been targeted for a speech during a Paterson silk strike in Minutes of the Executive Council, September 17, 1924, Reel 1c, Russian Center, PRL, but the anti-Lore climate of December 1924 assured her demise, and her resignation was offered by Cannon in Minutes of the Political Committee, December 9, 1924, Reel 3, Russian Center, PRL.

106. Draper, *American Communism and Soviet Russia*, 127; see also the hard-hitting statement directed to the membership of New York's powerful District No. 2: *For a Communist Party of Action: Against Liquidating the Workers (Communist) Party! Against Substituting the Workers (Communist) Party by a Sham Farmer-Labor Party! An Appeal to the Members of District No. 2, Workers Party* (New York: Co-operative Press, n.d. [1925]). On the convention, see Minutes of the Central Executive Committee, January 7–8, 1925, Reel 1d, Russian Center, PRL; Gitlow, *I Confess*, 262–63.

107. Document declaring James P. Cannon, Assistant Executive Secretary, Workers (Communist) Party of America, Member CEC, delegate to the Enlarged Section, ECCI, January 14, 1925, Reel 2, Russian Center, PRL.

108. See Arthur Bliss Lane to J. E. Hoover, 5 March 1925; 30 March 1925 (enclosures); 11 June 1925, 25 June 1925, in William Z. Foster file, FBI File, courtesy of James R. Barrett.

109. Cannon, *First Ten Years*, 131–32; Peter Drucker, *Max Shachtman and His Left: A Socialist's Odyssey Through the "American Century"* (Atlantic Highlands, NJ: Humanities Press, 1994), 24–25; "The Reminiscences of Max Shachtman," 71–84, 1963, Number 488, Oral History Research Office, Columbia University, New York, New York; "Rose Karsner Cannon Is Dead, a Foremost Woman Trotskyist," *Militant*, March 18, 1968; Ring interview with Cannon, August 15, 1973, 2–3.

110. The writing on this 1924–1925 turn is voluminous, but see Trotsky, *Third International After Lenin*, 116–26; Draper, *American Communism and Soviet Russia*, 129–33; Isaac Deutscher, *The Prophet Unarmed—Trotsky: 1921–1929* (New York: Oxford University Press, 1959), esp. 73–270; E. H. Carr, *Socialism in One Country*, vol. 2 (Baltimore: Penguin, 1970), esp. 11–246. See, as well, Trotsky, *My Life*, 417–98. For selections of the documents passed by the Fifth Congress, in which increasing weight is placed on peasant revolution in the East, the durability and ultimate significance of the Soviet state as the embodiment of "socialism in one country," and the increasing rigidity of Bolshevization instructions (tending toward bureaucratism and even "conspiracy" organization within the Comintern), see Degras, *The Communist International*, vol. 2, 172–234.

111. For the debate over Pepper's seating, see "American Commission: Session of 13 February 1925, with remarks by Comrades Foster, Lovestone, and Cannon," Reel 2, Russian Center, PRL. Cannon's remarks are reprinted in "Pepper: Menace to Party

Unity," in *James P. Cannon and the Early Years of American Communism*, 319–20. The only discussions I have been able to locate around delegate election are ambiguous. They focus on the majority, where Cannon and Williamson were elected as party delegates to the ECCI, with the understanding that Foster, too, would be seated. There was further discussion about Lore attending. See Minutes of the Central Executive Committee, January 7–8, 1925, Reel 1d, Russian Center, PRL.

112. See the reproduction and commentary on Cannon and Foster, "Controversial Questions in the Workers Party of America," n.d. (February–March 1925); and James P. Cannon, "The Situation Is Different in America," *International Press Correspondence*, 16 April 1925, in *James P. Cannon and the Early Years of American Communism*, 287–318, 321–22; also, *For a Communist Party of Action!* (1925).

113. Reel 2, Russian Center, PRL contains a plethora of documentation from the American Commission. Among the items indicative of the tenor and content of the debate: "American Commission: Meeting of 4 March 1925: Cannon," 141-45-50, 161-63 (from which quotes were taken), 181–82 (quote), 183–200; James P. Cannon, "The CEC Majority and the United Front"; "The Foster Lore Majority and the United Front"; "The CEC Majority's Conception of the Conflict Between Trotskyism and Leninism" (the previous three documents being one-page statements and compilations of quotations in loose form); "American Commission: Meeting of 8 March 1925: Foster," 19 pp; "American Commission: Meeting of 8 March 1925: Cannon," 121–30; "American Commission: Meeting of 8 March 1925: Ruthenberg," 371-72-60; "American Commission: Sixth Session, 5 April 1925: Cannon," 30–33; Foster and Cannon, "Recommendations to the American Commission," n.d. (February–April 1925), reprinted in *James P. Cannon and the Early Years of American Communism*, 317–19, which was an appendix to Foster's and Cannon's "Controversial Questions in the Workers Party of America"; Ruthenberg, Pepper, and Lovestone to Humbert Droz, Chairman, American Commission, 19 March 1925.

114. Cannon, *First Ten Years*, 131–32; Morgan, *A Covert Life*, 48–51; Draper, *American Communism and Soviet Russia*, 133–40. The relations were complicated by Lovestone, who befriended Bukharin and attracted the affections of a Comintern official's lover, Lou Geisler. See, however, "Protocol of the Sub-Commission on the Question of Federation Conventions of the W.P. of A., First Session," March 5, 1925, Reel 2, Russian Center, PRL, for some indications of the Foster-Cannon faction's gains.

115. See Foster to Zinoviev, 22 March 1925, Reel 20, JPC Papers.

116. See the final text of the Comintern decision, published in *Daily Worker*, May 19, 1925. Note, as well, Alfred Wagenkencht to MA [Abern?], 1 May 1925, Reel 20, JPC Papers.

117. Cannon, *First Ten Years*, 131–33; Draper, *American Communism and Soviet Russia*, 133–40; Howe and Coser, *American Communist Party*, 152–56. See "American Commission: 6th Session, 5 April 1925: Cannon," and "American Commission: 7th Session, 6 April 1925: Cannon—Amendment to the Organizational Proposal [Pepper]," Reel 2, Russian Center, PRL, both documents reproduced in *James P. Cannon and the Early Years of American Communism*, 324–28.

118. The travel itinerary was reported in Lane to Hoover, 25 June 1925, William Z. Foster file, FBI File, courtesy James R. Barrett.

119. See Drucker, *Shachtman and His Left*, 25.

120. See, for instance, Minutes of the Executive Council, March 10, 1925, Reel 1e, Russian Center, PRL.

121. Gitlow, *I Confess*, 244. Vera Buch Weisbord recalled that Foster in this period seemed "overwrought, easily provoked, and contentious," in contrast to Ruthenberg, with whom she allied and thought to be "more mature, mellow, and stable, more detached from the petty power struggle." See Weisbord, *A Radical Life*, 98.

122. Cannon labeled one Lore supporter, the ILGWU figure Charles Zimmerman, as "a dangerous opportunist who has to be watched." See *James P. Cannon and the Early Years of American Communism*, 36. Zimmerman ended up in Lovestone's Right Opposition in the post-1929 period. See Robert J. Alexander, *The Right Opposition: The Lovestoneites and the International Communist Opposition of the 1930s* (Westport, CT: Greenwood, 1981); Morgan, *A Covert Life*, 110, 111, 124, 133, 304, 364.

123. See, for instance, "Bittelman," unpublished, undated [1924–1925] manuscript, "Who Is Bankrupt?" Series III, Box 29, Browder Papers, an uncompromising attack on Ruthenberg and his position on the farmer-labor party.

124. Cannon, *First Ten Years*, 130–31; Wagenknecht to MA [Abern?], 1 May 1925, Reel 20, JPC Papers.

125. Minutes of the Central Executive Committee, May 12, 1925, Reel 1d, Russian Center, PRL. There were, of course, factional maneuverings to deprive specific individuals of their vote, especially in the youth section. See Oscar Carlson to CEC of the WP, 15 May 1925, Reel 20, JPC Papers.

126. "Incomplete Text of the Speech delivered by Comrade Lore at the CEC meeting of 12 May 1925," Reel 1d, Russian Center, PRL; Gitlow, *I Confess*, 246–48. Lore's relationship with Trotsky reached back to 1917–1918, but it was more one of genuine revolutionary respect than of political integration and knowledge of the programmatic points of issue emerging in the Comintern and demarcating "Trotskyist" position. For Lore's early views of Trotsky, see his essay in *One Year of Revolution, Celebrating the First Anniversary of the Founding of the Russian Soviet Republic* (New York: Socialist Publication Society, November 7, 1918).

127. Gitlow, *I Confess*, 249–53, which establishes the Poyntz-Ruthenberg connection through the "ideological bag man," Jack Stachel. Gitlow quotes Poyntz's speech, although I have been unable to secure a copy. However, Poyntz did place a document before the CEC, which contains a similar line of argument, albeit one less knockabout in its jocular jibes at the Foster-Cannon group. See J. S. Poyntz, "Resolution Submitted to CEC Meeting," May 12, 1925, Reel 1d, Russian Center, PRL. This document confirms her Comintern loyalties, her antagonism to Trotskyism, her membership in what she designates the Foster, Lore, Cannon majority of the CEC (which she chastises for its syndicalist, right-wing tendencies), and her insistence that Lore must "acknowledge his errors *in toto*." It presents Poyntz as unerringly on the side of "correct policy," battling the sectarian, unMarxian, and undialectical positionings of Bittelman and Foster in

their "rejection of the slogan of the labor party and independent working-class politi-cal action." See, as well, the compilation of quotes and a small fragment from Poyntz's speech assembled, for factional purpose, by someone in the minority in "On Juliet Poyntz," n.d. (May–June 1925), Reel 7, Russian Center, PRL.

128. Minutes of the Central Executive Committee, May 12, 1925, Reel 1d, Russian Center, PRL. Much was made of the Lovestone-Winitsky affair, in which Lovestone had appeared as a state witness against another communist in a 1920 trial. See Morgan, *A Covert Life*, 19–23; Draper, *Roots of American Communism*, 203–4; Gitlow, *I Confess*, 150.

129. Minutes of the Central Executive Committee: Cannon submission, May 13, 1925; Alexander Bittelman, "Preamble," and "Resolution on Needle Trades Situation," at Meeting of the Central Executive Committee, May 13, 1925; Minutes of the Central Executive Committee: Foster Submission [on Poyntz], May 13, 1925, all in Reel 1d, Russian Center, PRL.

130. Minutes of the Central Executive Committee, May 14, 1925, Reel 1d, Russian Center, PRL; Abern, Browder, Burman, Bittelman, Cannon, Dunne, Foster, "Statement of the C.E.C. on Resolution of the E.C.C.I," *Daily Worker,* May 19, 1925; Gitlow, *I Con-fess,* 244.

131. Quoted in Morgan, *A Covert Life,* 52. For the stalemated positions of the major-ity and the minority, see the Ruthenberg-circulated documents from both factions in "Ruthenberg to All Party Branches: To the American Commission," 26 May 1925, which includes a letter from Ruthenberg, Lovestone, and Pepper, 24 March 1925, and a 28 March 1925 rejoinder from Foster and Cannon, a copy of which is in Cannon PRL Files.

132. On Gusev (also spelled Gussev), born Yakov Davidovich Drabkin, see Paul Le Blanc, *Lenin and the Revolutionary Party* (Atlantic Highlands, NJ: Humanities Press, 1990), 112–17, 328–30; Leon Trotsky, *Stalin: An Appraisal of the Man and His Influence* (New York: Harper & Brothers, 1941), 63, 272, 276, 310–14, 323, 333, 348; Gitlow, *I Con-fess,* 256–64; Morgan, *A Covert Life,* 52–53; Howe and Coser, *American Communist Party,* 156–57; Draper, *American Communism and Soviet Russia,* 140–42; Wolfe, *A Life in Two Centuries,* 368, 376–89; Victor Serge, *Memoirs of a Revolutionary, 1901–1941* (London: Oxford University Press, 1963), 212. On the superiority of the Ruthenberg-Lovestone faction over the Foster-Cannon group with respect to maneuvering, see the brief statement in Weisbord, *The Conquest of Power,* 1111–12.

133. Cannon, *First Ten Years,* 133–35; Gitlow, *I Confess,* 260–61; "Reminiscences of Max Shachtman," 100–101. For the Parity Commission's record in this preconvention period, see Minutes of the Session of the Parity Commission, July 7, 8, 16, and 23, 1925; "The Lore Question," n.d. (July 1925); "Declaration of the Parity Commission," n.d. (July 1925); "Differences in Regard to the Nine Points," n.d. (July 1925); "Arrangements for the Election of Delegates to the Convention," n.d. (July 1925), all in Reel 1c, Russian Center, PRL. The most sympathetic account of Gusev, no doubt colored by later col-laborations, is Earl W. Browder, "'No-Man's Land': A Political Autobiography," unpub-lished manuscript, chap. 10, 8–9, Box 10, Browder Papers.

134. Gitlow, *I Confess,* 264–70; Wolfe, *A Life in Two Centuries,* 378–80; Howe and Coser, *American Communist Party,* 158; Minutes of Fourth National Convention of

Workers (Communist) Party of America, First Session—August 21, 1925, 1–2, Reel 1c, Russian Center, PRL, lists all delegates and fraternal delegates.

135. Cannon, *First Ten Years*, 134; Bittelman, "Things I Have Learned," 438; Draper, *American Communism and Soviet Russia*, 142–43; Gitlow, *I Confess*, 269–73; Wolfe, *A Life in Two Centuries*, 380–87; C.E. Ruthenberg, "From the Third Through the Fourth Convention of the Workers (Communist) Party," *Workers Monthly*, October 1925, 533; "Workers Party Convention Organized—Cannon's Statement," *Daily Worker*, August 25, 1925. For Cannon's loyal statement, see James P. Cannon, "The Achievements of the Parity Commission," *Daily Worker*, August 11, 1925, reprinted in *James P. Cannon and the Early Years of American Communism*, 343–46; for his prominent role in the convention, including addresses on Bolshevization, see Minutes of Fourth National Convention of the Workers (Communist) Party of America, Sessions 1 through 11, August 21–27, 1925, Reel 1c, Russian Center, PRL. Browder claims that Cannon masterminded the majority's "offensive" in the district conventions. See Browder, "'No-Man's Land,'" chap. 10, 11.

136. Minutes of Fourth National Convention, Fifth Session, August 24, 1925, Reel 1c, Russian Center, PRL, indicate that Cannon moved a motion at 12:50 that a committee of three (Cannon, Foster, Bittelman) wait on the minority to inform it that the session was now two hours late in starting and all delegates were requested to convene. Lovestone's comments are in an undated, untitled transcript, designated "Lovestone," Reel 1d, Russian Center, PRL. See also Draper, *American Communism and Soviet Russia*, 143; Gitlow, *I Confess*, 273–75; "Reminiscences of Max Shachtman," 86–88; Drucker, *Shachtman and His Left*, 25; William Z. Foster, *History of the Communist Party of the United States* (New York: International 1952), 223; Barrett, *William Z. Foster*, 150; and Browder, "'No-Man's Land,'" chap. 10, 12.

137. I reproduce the actual telegram, grammatical errors included. The issue of who within the Communist International was responsible for the cable is unknown: Zinoviev, Stalin, Bukharin, and Pepper have all been mentioned. For speculation, see Wolfe, *A Life in Two Centuries*, 382–84; Bittelman, "Things I Have Learned," 440–41; AB to Dear Comrade, Moscow, 15 November 1925, Reel 20, JPC Papers; William Z. Foster, "James P. Cannon: Renegade," unpublished typescript in possession of the author, courtesy of James R. Barrett; Johanningsmeier, *Forging American Communism*, 397–98, n. 20. The actual cable, as well as a partial written version, are in two documents, Reel 5, Russian Center, PRL: "Lydia Gibson, Brompton Place, Chicago," n.d. (August 27–28, 1925), written pagination, 10; "Delivery No. 495, Moscow 11:35 AM/1925 Aug 27 PM 8:12 To Lydia Gibson, 521 Brompton Place, Chicago," written pagination, 11. Gitlow, *I Confess*, 276–77, has another version, and the final, cleaned-up presentation of the demands appeared in C.E. Ruthenberg, "From the Third through the Fourth Convention of the Workers (Communist) Party," *Workers Monthly*, October 1925, 536.

138. Gitlow, *I Confess*, 277–78; Morgan, *A Covert Life*, 54; Wolfe, *A Life in Two Centuries*, 383–84.

139. Cannon, *First Ten Years*, 124–25, 135; Gitlow, *I Confess*, 277–78; Wolfe, *A Life in Two Centuries*, 383; Draper, *American Communism and Soviet Russia*, 144–45.

140. Gitlow, *I Confess*, 260, 275; Wolfe, *A Life in Two Centuries*, 381; Foster, "James P. Cannon: Renegade."

141. Weisbord, *A Radical Life*, 98.

142. Cannon, *First Ten Years*, 135–37; Gitlow, *I Confess*, 278–79 (Gitlow claims that the 50–50 split was in fact Green/Gusev's proposal); Wolfe, *A Life in Two Centuries*, 385; Ring interview with Cannon, October 10, 1973, 11. For a Ruthenberg faction member's sympathies with Dunne, see Weisbord, *A Radical Life*, 99.

143. Gitlow, *I Confess*, 278; Draper, *American Communism and Soviet Russia*, 145–47; *The Fourth National Convention of the Workers (Communist) Party of America: Report of the Central Executive Committee to the 4th National Convention Held in Chicago, Illinois, August 21–30 1925* (Chicago: Daily Worker Publishing, 1925), 165–66.

144. Foster, *History of the Communist Party*, 223.

145. Cannon, *First Ten Years*, 137–38; Draper, *American Communism and Soviet Russia*, 147–52; *Daily Worker*, October 3, 1925. Browder's account of the entire process whereby Cannon and Foster were maneuvered by Gusev is the one factual discussion that diverges from other recollections. Browder notes that as a member of the Foster-Cannon group, he welcomed the cable from the Comintern, a rather striking admission or reconstruction of his position at the time. See Browder, "'No-Man's Land,'" chap. 10, 12–18, Box 10.

146. Minutes of the Politbureau/Political Committee, September 2, 10, & 14, 1925; October 6, 9, 10, 19, 22, 24, & 30, 1925; November 11, 14, & 27, 1925, Reel 1d, Russian Center, PRL; Drucker, *Shachtman and His Left*, 26; Ring interview with Cannon, February 13, 1974, 14–15; James P. Cannon, "Cannon Replies to Henry Askeli," *Daily Worker*, August 8, 1925, magazine supplement, reprinted in *James P. Cannon and the Early Years of American Communism*, 333–42, and the brief discussion of the early Finnish controversy in Howe and Coser, *American Communist Party*, 157–58; Cannon and Dunne, "On Trade Union Policy," in *James P. Cannon and the Early Years of American Communism*, 359–61; and the undated document, likely from September–November 1925, entitled "II The Trade Union Work and the Trade Union Educational League," Reel 1d, Russian Center, PRL, which argued that the TUEL was an isolated bloc of party trade union factions and party sympathizers, functionally illegal in many labor organizations. Cannon and Dunne were apparently evolving a perspective on trade union questions in this period, in which broadening the TUEL was a major initiative. They placed an accent on building a strong, broad left wing in the unions through trade union work, labor party campaigns, and organization of the unorganized. See the reprinted statement of Cannon before the American Commission of the ECCI's Sixth Plenum, March 18, 1926, reprinted in *James P. Cannon and the Early Years of American Communism*, 367–68, and also p. 51 of that same source.

147. "Reminiscences of Max Shachtman," 95–96, quoted in *James P. Cannon and the Early Years of American Communism*, 40.

148. Minutes of the Politbureau, October 9, 1925, Reel 1d, Russian Center, PRL; *Daily Worker*, October 3, 4, & 6, 1925; Draper, *American Communism and Soviet Russia*, 149; Bittelman, "Things I Have Learned," 440–41.

149. James P. Cannon, "Our Party and the Communist International," *Daily Worker*, October 8, 1925, reprinted in *James P. Cannon and the Early Years of American Communism*, 347–58.

150. "Unify the Party!" *Daily Worker*, November 16, 1925, being a resolution signed by Bedacht, Lovestone, Ruthenberg, Cannon, Dunne, and the National Executive Committee of the Young Workers League. Foster was the only member of the Political Committee who did not endorse the statement, and in the Foster-controlled Chicago District Committee the resolution was voted down nine to eight. See *James P. Cannon and the Early Years of American Communism*, 362–66; Johanningsmeier, *Forging American Communism*, 224–25. On the Lovestone-Cannon tour, see Browder, "'No-Man's Land,'" ch. 10, 15; Foster, "James P. Cannon: Renegade"; "Reminiscences of Max Shachtman," 100; *Daily Worker*, November 16, 1925; December 3, 1925; December 15, 1925. Stachel and Cannon had written in opposition to Foster's Comintern appeal in October 1925, and Stachel provides an undated, but extremely detailed, account of being "on the road" to combat Fosterism, with Cannon providing a series of extremely effective speeches. See Draper, *American Communism and Soviet Russia*, 149, citing *Daily Worker*, October 8, 1925; Jack to Dear Comrades, n.d. (October–December 1925?), Reel 9, Russian Center, PRL.

151. "Meditation," n.d. (December 1925?), Reel 9, Russian Center, PRL. No authorship is provided, but the piece has the feel of an Earl Browder production.

152. James P. Cannon to Dear Comrades, 16 December 1925, Reel 3, JPC Papers; Minutes of the Politbureau, October 10, 1925; "II Trade Union Work and the TUEL," both in Reel 1d, Russian Center, PRL; "Our Trade Union Policy," and "Broaden the TUEL," in *James P. Cannon and the Early Years of American Communism*, 359–61, 367–68. For the Foster group's response to what Bittelman considered "the silliness of the charges of Green and Cannon and Ruthenberg," see AB to Dear Comrade, 16 November 1925; No author [Bittelman?] to Dear Comrade, 3 December 1925, both in Reel 20, JPC Papers. The latter letter also outlines the critique of the TUEL launched by Cannon, Dunne, Swabeck, and Abern.

Chapter 9: Labor Defender

1. For the 1924 figures, see Minutes of the Central Executive Committee, June 7, 1924, Reel 1c, in Documents from Russian Center for the Preservation and Study of Contemporary History, Microfilm Copies Held, Prometheus Research Library, New York, New York (hereafter Russian Center, PRL). On other membership figures, the difficulty of accurate counts, the dual stamp system, and Bolshevization, see Theodore Draper, *American Communism and Soviet Russia: The Formative Period* (New York: Viking, 1960), 187–94; Charles Shipman, *It Had to Be Revolution: Memoirs of an American Radical* (Ithaca, NY: Cornell University Press, 1993), 139. For a discussion of Party organization at this time, see Jay Lovestone, *The Party Organization, Workers (Communist) Party of America* (Chicago: Daily Worker Publishing, n.d. [ca. 1925–1926]); and *The Communist International Between the Fifth & Sixth World Congresses, 1924–1928* (London: Communist Party of Great Britain, 1928), with the entry on the United States,

333–51, which also contains membership figures and discussion of various sectors of communist work.

2. James P. Cannon, *The History of American Trotskyism: From Its Origins (1928) to the Founding of the Socialist Workers' Party (1938)—Report of a Participant* (New York: Pathfinder, 1972), 24.

3. For Cannon's shifting relationship on trade union questions, involving movement away from Foster and an increasing tendency to bloc with Ruthenberg-Lovestone, see "On Trade Union Policy," October 10, 1925, and "Unify the Party!" November 16, 1925, both in *James P. Cannon and the Early Years of American Communism: Selected Writings and Speeches, 1920–1928* (New York: Prometheus Research Library, 1992), 359–68.

4. David Montgomery, *The Fall of the House of Labor: The Workplace, the State, and American Labor Activism, 1865–1925* (Cambridge, UK: Cambridge University Press, 1987), 432–35; David J. Saposs, *Left-Wing Unionism: A Study of Radical Policies and Tactics* (New York: International, 1926), 80; William Z. Foster, *American Trade Unionism: Principles, Organization, Strategy, Tactics* (New York: International, 1947), 142; William Z. Foster, *History of the Communist Party of the United States* (New York: International 1952), 204; James R. Barrett, *William Z. Foster and the Tragedy of American Radicalism* (Urbana: University of Illinois Press, 1999), 140–42; Philip S. Foner, *History of the Labor Movement in the United States: The T.U.E.L. to the End of the Gompers Era*, vol. 9 (New York: International, 1991); Philip S. Foner, *History of the Labor Movement in the United States: The T.U.E.L.*, vol. 10 (New York: International, 1994).

5. Jay Fox, *Amalgamation* (Chicago: Trade Union Educational League, 1923). Note as well the 1922 four-page statement, "The Need of the Hour: Amalgamation of the Sixteen Standard Railroad Unions—A Practical Plan Proposed by Minnesota Railroad Shop Crafts Legislative Committee," in United States Department of Justice, Federal Bureau of Investigation, Freedom of Information/Privacy Acts Section, "International Labor Defense," File Number 62-2608, secs. 1–3, Washington, DC (hereafter cited as "International Labor Defense," FBI File).

6. See, for instance, Irving Bernstein, *The Lean Years: A History of the American Worker, 1920–1933* (Baltimore, MD: Penguin, 1966), 84–90.

7. On background, see David J. Goldberg, *A Tale of Three Cities: Labor Organization in Paterson, Passaic, and Lawrence, 1916–1921* (New Brunswick, NJ: Rutgers University Press, 1989). Treatments of Passaic and Weisbord include Draper, *American Communism and Soviet Russia*, 223–33; Selig Perlman and Philip Taft, *History of Labor in the United States, 1896–1932*, vol. 4 (New York: Macmillan, 1935), 555–58; Morton Seigel, "The Passaic Strike of 1926" (PhD diss., Columbia University, 1953); Paul Murphy, et al., eds., *The Passaic Textile Strike of 1926* (Belmont, CA: Wadsworth, 1974); Vera Buch Weisbord, *A Radical Life* (Bloomington, IN: University Press, 1977); Dee Garrison, *Mary Heaton Vorse: The Life of an American Insurgent* (Philadelphia: Temple University Press, 1989), 196–203; Marsha Stone Asher, "Recollections of the Passaic Textile Strike of 1926," *Labor's Heritage* 2 (April 1990): 4–23; Bert Cochran, *Labor and American Communism: The Conflict That Shaped American Unions* (Princeton, NJ: Princeton University Press, 1977), 30–33; and the self-serving Benjamin Gitlow, *The Whole of Their Lives:*

Communism in America—A Personal History and Intimate Portrayal of Its Leaders (New York: Scribner's Sons, 1948), 132–33; Benjamin Gitlow, *I Confess: The Truth about American Communism* (New York: E.P. Dutton, 1940), 363–77. On Weisbord's role in the West New York Strike, including his secretaryship of the United Front Committee of Textile Workers there, see Draper, *American Communism and Soviet Russia,* 485, n. 29, citing *Daily Worker,* October 29, 1925.

8. As early as mid-November 1925, the Ruthenberg-Cannon alliance had called for a fundamental revision of the trade union policy of the Workers (Communist) Party, and in urging revolutionaries to aid all activities of the left wing within the trade union movement Cannon, Dunne, Bedacht, Lovestone, and Ruthenberg acknowledged that the official name under which a progressive-oppositional bloc in the unions was constituted was unimportant. This was an implicit downplaying of the importance of the TUEL. See "The basis for the unification of the party . . . ," in Minutes of the Politbureau, November 14, 1925, Reel 1d; "Cannon Summing Up of TU Res" (from the December 1926 Workers (Communist) Party Plenum), Reel 6, Russian Center, PRL, especially pp. 46–49. See also James P. Cannon, "The Passaic Strike," in Cannon, *The First Ten Years of American Communism—Report of a Participant* (New York: Pathfinder, 1973), 140–45; Harry Ring interview with James P. Cannon, October 17, 1973, 18–19 (in possession of the author; hereafter Ring interview). On the continuity of tensions within the Ruthenberg-Cannon bloc, Dear Comrades, 20 July 1926, Loose File, Russian Center, PRL, relating largely to problems of "unity" in the Chicago district. For other statements and the final Trade Union Resolution at the December 1925 Plenum, see "J.W. Johnstone, TU Res," December 26, 1925; "Browder, TU Res," December 26, 1925; "Dunne, TU Res," December 27, 1925; "Cannon—37 Questions," December 28, 1925; "Resolution on the Trade Union Work of the Party," n.d. (December 1925), all in Reel 1d, Russian Center, PRL.

9. W. A. Swanberg, *Norman Thomas: The Last Idealist* (New York: Scribner's Sons, 1976), 101–2; Cannon, "The Passaic Strike," 140–45; Ring interview with Cannon, October 17, 1973, 18–19; Perlman and Taft, *History of Labor,* vol. 4, 557; Mary Heaton Vorse, "The War in Passaic," *The Nation,* March 17, 1926, 280–81; Vorse, "Passaic—The Hell Hole," *Daily Worker,* February 27, 1926; Edward P. Johanningsmeier, *Forging American Communism: The Life of William Z. Foster* (Princeton, NJ: Princeton University Press, 1994), 227–28. For the Minutes of the Meetings of the Central Executive Commitee, Textile Committee, Passaic, starting with those of February 2, 1926, see Reel 1h, Russian Center, PRL. Often present were Benjamin Gitlow, Weisbord, Jack Stachel, Vorse, and Don Zack. Cannon played no role in these meetings.

10. See Ruth Fischer, *Stalin and German Communism: A Study in the Origins of State Policy* (Cambridge, MA: Harvard University Press, 1948); John M. Cammett, *Antonio Gramsci and the Origins of Italian Communism* (Stanford, CA: Stanford University Press, 1967), 156–86; Giuseppe Fiori, *Antonio Gramsci: Life of a Revolutionary* (London: New Left Books, 1970), 167–206; Fernando Claudin, *The Communist Movement: From Comintern to Cominform* (New York: Monthly Review Press, 1975), 154, 165; Robert J. Alexander, *International Trotskyism, 1929–1985: A Documented Analysis of the Movement* (Durham, NC: Duke University Press, 1991), 586.

11. Draper, *American Communism and Soviet Russia,* 223–33; Cannon, *First Ten Years,* 240–45; Ring interview with Cannon, October 17, 1973, 18–19. *The Christian Century,* August 5, 1926, quoted in Irving Howe and Lewis Coser, *The American Communist Party: A Critical History (1919–1957)* (Boston: Beacon Press, 1957), 241; Minutes of the Political Committee, July 15, 1926; August 6, 1926, Reel 1f, Russian Center, PRL.

12. William Z. Foster, *From Bryan to Stalin* (London: Lawrence & Wishart, 1937), 202; Foster, *History of the Communist Party,* 250.

13. Weisbord, *A Radical Life,* 121; Minutes of the Political Committee, August 11, 1926, Reel 1f, Russian Center, PRL; "The Reminiscences of Max Shachtman," 104–6, 1963, Number 488, Oral History Research Office, Columbia University, New York, New York.

14. Cannon, *First Ten Years,* 140.

15. Lozovsky quoted in Johanningsmeier, *Forging American Communism,* 228.

16. Cannon, *First Ten Years,* 143–44.

17. James P. Cannon, "Defend Weisbord! Appeal to the Workers of America by the International Labor Defense," *Daily Worker,* April 17, 1926; Cannon, "Free Weisbord! Campaign On—ILD Gathers All Resources for Big Fight," *Daily Worker,* April 18, 1926; "United Front in Passaic Defense," telegram, April 22, 1926, "Cannon Working Files, 1925–1928," Prometheus Research Library, New York, New York (hereafter Cannon PRL Files), also in Reel 6, Russian Center, PRL; Cannon to Ruthenberg, 25 May 1926, Reel 7, Russian Center, PRL; James P. Cannon, "The United Front at Passaic," *Labor Defender,* June 1926, 83–85. See also Mary Heaton Vorse, *Passaic* (Chicago: International Labor Defense, 1926); J. O. Bentall, "The Passaic Textile Strike Encounters the Courts," *Labor Defender,* April 1926, 57–58; Max Shachtman, "Passaic Fights On," *Labor Defender,* July 1926, 103–4.

18. For Cannon's summary of the importance of these defense struggles, see James P. Cannon, "The Trial of the Stalinist Leaders," in Cannon, *Speeches for Socialism* (New York: Pathfinder, 1971), 133–42; this is the text of a speech delivered in New York City in 1949 and published originally in *The Militant,* February 14, 1949. See also Ring interview with Cannon, September 5, 1973, 1; Carolyn Ashbaugh interview with James P. Cannon, March 25, 1974, 16–17 (in possession of the author).

19. Peggy Dennis, *The Autobiography of an American Communist: A Personal View of a Political Life, 1925–1975* (Westport, CT/Berkeley, CA: Lawrence Hill/Creative Arts, 1977), 40; Mike Davis, *City of Quartz: Excavating the Future in Los Angeles* (London: Verso, 1990), 30–36; Louis Adamic, *Laughing in the Jungle* (New York: n.p., 1932); Carey McWilliams, *Louis Adamic and Shadow-America* (Los Angeles: Arthur Whipple, 1935); Steve Nelson, James R. Barrett, and Robert Ruck, *Steve Nelson, American Radical* (Pittsburgh: University of Pittsburgh Press, 1981), 21; Fred E. Beal, *Proletarian Journey: New England, Gastonia, Moscow* (New York: Hillman-Curl, 1937), 109–223; Liston Pope, *Millhands and Preachers: A Study of Gastonia* (New Haven: Yale University Press, 1942), 302; Peter Drucker, *Max Shachtman and His Left: A Socialist's Odyssey Through the "American Century"* (Atlantic Highlands, NJ: Humanities Press, 1994), 30.

20. Ed Delaney and M. T. Rice, *The Bloodstained Trail: A History of Militant Labor in the United States* (Seattle, WA: Industrial Worker, 1927), 152–61. See also Upton Sinclair, *Oil!* (New York: Grosset & Dunlap, 1927), 508–10.

21. David M. Chalmers, *Hooded Americanism: The History of the Ku Klux Klan* (Chicago: Quadrangle, 1968); Larry L. Gerlach, *Blazing Crosses in Zion: The Ku Klux Klan in Utah* (Logan: Utah State University Press, 1982); Emerson H. Loucks, *Ku Klux Klan in Pennsylvania: A Study in Nativism* (Harrisburg, PA: n.p., 1936), 43–58, cited in Montgomery, *Fall of the House of Labor,* 463.

22. William Preston, Jr., *Aliens and Dissenters: Federal Suppression of Radicals, 1903–1933* (Urbana: University of Illinois Press, 1994), 234–35.

23. Carey McWilliams, *Southern California Country: An Island on the Land* (New York: Duell, Sloan & Pearce, 1946), 292.

24. Still valuable is G. Louis Joughin and Edmund M. Morgan, *The Legacy of Sacco and Vanzetti* (New York: Harcourt, Brace, 1948); Delaney and Rice, *The Bloodstained Trail,* esp. 7–12, 166–71.

25. Cannon to Noah London, 29 April 1924, Box 3, File 1, James P. Cannon Papers, Microfilm Edition, 1994, State Historical Society of Wisconsin, Madison, Wisconsin (hereafter JPC Papers). At this point Cannon had strong views that the labor defense organization should be under "the direct control and supervision of the CEC." In the future he would have a more united-front orientation, advocating a less rigid relationship of party-defense organization.

26. See Karsner to Sabo, 16 January 1924 [Friends of Soviet Russia], Reel 7, Russian Center, PRL; Earl Browder to the ECCI, 14 January 1925 [Karsner credentials, International Red Aid], Reel 9, Russian Center, PRL; Sean McMeekin, *The Red Millionaire: A Political Biography of Willi Munzenberg, Moscow's Secret Propaganda Tsar in the West* (New Haven: Yale University Press, 2003), 168.

27. As a brief introduction to these organizations, see Draper, *American Communism and Soviet Russia,* 174–82; McMeekin, *Red Millionaire.* The National Defense Committee/Labor Defense Council initiatives of earlier years are a much neglected area of Workers' Party history. An invaluable source is the United States Department of Justice, Federal Bureau of Investigation, Freedom of Information/Privacy Acts Section, "International Labor Defense," File Number 62-2608, secs. 1–3, Washington, DC (cited as "International Labor Defense," FBI File). These files contain a wide array of agents' reports, leaflets, and other materials relating to the defense campaigns of the early 1920s. See also *The Burns's and Daugherty's Attack Upon Labor and Liberty: Defend Your Liberty!* (Chicago: Labor Defense Council, 1923?), a twenty-six-page pamphlet. The *New York Vokszeitung,* July 6, 1924, reported that the Labor Defense Council was intending to publish a regular "Encyclopedia of Labor Informants" in which the "special friends" of the Workers' Party, the IWW, and various socialist organizations would be listed alphabetically, photographs run when possible, and aliases, working methods, and special characteristics fully described.

28. See Drucker, *Shachtman and His Left,* 30; William Z. Foster, James P. Cannon, Rose Karsner, "Resolution on American Section of Red Aid," n.d. (March–April 1925?), Reel 6, Russian Center, PRL; Ring interviews with Cannon, August 15, 1973, 2–3; September 5, 1973, 3–4; Cannon, *First Ten Years,* 159–63; William D. Haywood, "A Message from Big Bill Haywood," *Labor Defender,* June 1926, 86; James P. Cannon, "The Trial of

the Stalinist Leaders," in Cannon, *Speeches for Socialism,* 133–42; Ashbaugh interview with Cannon, 16–18.

29. Ring interview with Cannon, August 15, 1973, 4–5. For original reports on International Red Aid and the proposal to form the International Labor Defense, see Minutes of the Executive Council, May 20, 1925; Minutes of the Executive Council, May 22, 1925; Minutes of the Executive Council, May 26, 1925; Minutes of the Executive Council, August 7, 1925, all in Reel 1e, Russian Center, PRL.

30. The preceding paragraphs draw on Ring interviews with Cannon, August 15, 1973, 5–6; September 5, 1973, 4–7; Cannon, *First Ten Years,* 159; Elizabeth Gurley Flynn, *The Rebel Girl: An Autobiography—My First Life (1906–1926)* (New York: International, 1973); Rosalyn Fraad Baxandall, *Words on Fire: The Life and Writing of Elizabeth Gurley Flynn* (New Brunswick, NJ: Rutgers University Press, 1987), 143–44, 278–79, n. 90; Jim to Rose, telegram, 20 March 1926; James P. Cannon to S. Tempkin, 1 August 1925; James P. Cannon to Executive Committee of MOPR, 17 October 1927, Reel 6, Russian Center, PRL; *Labor Defense: Manifesto, Resolutions, Constitution—Adopted by the First National Conference, held in Ashland Auditorium, Chicago, June 28, 1925* (Chicago: International Labor Defense, 1925), 5; Anton Johannsen, "Matt Schmidt," *Labor Defender,* July 1926, 113; on the pressing need for funds, James P. Cannon, "International Defense Calls on All Organizations to Make Returns on Coupons Sent," *Daily Worker,* July 7, 1925; Cannon, "Emergency Call," *Daily Worker,* December 7, 1925; on Lucy Parsons, Ashbaugh interview with Cannon, March 25, 1974, and Carolyn Ashbaugh, *Lucy Parsons: American Revoutionary* (Chicago: Charles H. Kerr, 1976), 251; on Howat, *Labor Defender,* February 1926, 22. For a listing of the eventual three executive officers (Flynn as chairman; Edw. C. Wentworth, vice chairman; and Cannon as executive secretary) and fifty-four other national officers (all of those notables already mentioned, with the exception of Howat), see the leaflet, "What Is International Labor Defense? Why You Should Join It," which was published after the Third National Conference of the ILD in 1927, in Box 11, Folder 15, Martin Abern Papers, Wayne State Archives of Labor History and Urban Affairs, Walter P. Reuther Library, Wayne State University, Detroit, Michigan. For the response of state agents to the formation of the ILD, note the reports from Los Angeles, where the emergence of a branch in September 1925 was immediately reported to J. Edgar Hoover in the Department of Justice. Confusions in such early reports abounded. The machinists' leader Andrew T. McNamara was confusedly identified as a "dynamiter" and the ILD was described conclusively as "controlled by the American Civil Liberties Union." See correspondence dated 15 September 1925; 29 September 1925, "International Labor Defense," FBI File; and, in the same source, J. F. Eckhart to Director, Bureau of Investigation, Cincinnati, 14 November 1925.

31. Draper, *American Communism and Soviet Russia,* 180–81; Ring interview with Cannon, August 15, 1973, 8, 10.

32. Minutes of the Political Committee, June 26, 1925, Reel 1c, Russian Center, PRL, reprinted in *James P. Cannon and the Early Years of American Communism,* 329–30.

33. Rose Karsner to Comrade Ruthenberg, 4 July 1826; 28 July 1926, both in Reel 7, Russian Center, PRL. It is clear that in the early years of the ILD, Ruthenberg, on behalf

of the Central Executive Committee of the Workers (Communist) Party, appropriated funds sent by the Soviet MOPR and earmarked for the ILD, for the general needs of the party, including funding the cash-strapped *Daily Worker*. See, for explicit statement of this, Ruthenberg to Comrade Piatnitski, Moscow, 4 March 1926, Fond 515, OP151, Delo594, Comintern Archives, Moscow, courtesy of Herbert Romerstein.

34. "Statement on I.L.D. by George Maurer," January 24, 1926; "Resolution on International Labor Defense," n.d. (December 1925–January 1926?), both in Reel 1f, Russian Center, PRL. Maurer had launched his attack with Cannon in Russia. Cannon cabled Rose to "avoid serious complications with George." See Jim to Rose Karsner, telegram, 20 March 1926, Reel 6, Russian Center, PRL.

35. See Minutes of the Sub-Committee on ILD, February 16, 1926; "Sub-Committee Report on I.L.D.," including "Financial Report," and "Statement by Rose Karsner at subcommittee of ILD regarding printing of financial detailed statements," n.d. (February 1926), 15 pp., Reel 2f, Russian Center, PRL; J. P. Cannon to All Locals, "The Organization of Money Making Affairs for ILD," 27 July 1926, Reel 6, Russian Center, PRL.

36. Gitlow, *I Confess*, 223–27, 283–85, but for coverage of Gitlow's and Whitney's cases and protest around them, see Al Richmond, *Native Daughter: The Story of Anita Whitney* (San Francisco: Whitney 75th Anniversary Committee, 1942), 90–150; *Labor Defense: Manifesto, Resolutions, Constitution—Adopted by the First National Conference, held in Ashland, Auditorium, Chicago, 28 June 1925* (Chicago: International Labor Defense, 1928), 8; "Anita Whitney Sentenced to San Quentin," "Cases I.L.D. Is Defending or Cooperating with Existing Defense Organizations," and "Ben Gitlow Returns to Sing Sing," *Labor Defender*, January 1926, 11–13; "Sub-Committee Report on I.L.D.," section titled "Gitlow-Whitney," n.d. (1926), Reel 9, Russian Center, PRL; *James P. Cannon and the Early Years of American Communism*, 329–30.

37. Draper, *American Communism and Soviet Russia*, 181.

38. Cannon, *First Ten Years*, 160.

39. Ring interview with Cannon, August 15, 1973, 5–7; Ashbaugh interview with Cannon, March 25, 1974, 20; Ralph Chaplin, *Wobbly: The Rough-and-Tumble Story of an American Radical* (Chicago: University of Chicago Press, 1948), esp. 333, 346, 348, 358.

40. Rose Karsner to Dear Comrade Tomkin, 3 August 1925, Reel 6, Russian Center, PRL.

41. Ring interviews with Cannon, September 5, 1973, 7; August 15, 1973, 7; Cannon, *History of American Trotskyism*, 32; "The Reminiscences of Max Shachtman," 115; Albert Glotzer, "Reminiscences of James P. Cannon," unpaginated manuscript, Reel 2, JPC Papers.

42. Ring interview with Cannon, September 5, 1973, 8; "Students Hear Opposing Ideals," *Kansas City Journal*, 15 June 1926. For Cannon correspondence, see Cannon to Eugene Debs, 15 July 1925, reprinted as "The I.L.D. Will Grow Quickly," in *James P. Cannon and the Early Years of American Communism*, 331–32; Cannon to Clara Zetkin, 17 October 1927, Reel 6, Russian Center, PRL; James P. Cannon to Eugene V. Debs, 15 July 1926; Cannon to Debs, 26 January 1926; Debs to Cannon, 26 January 1926; Cannon to Debs, 27 May 1926; Elizabeth Gurley Flynn and James P. Cannon to Eugene V. Debs, 8 September 1926, all in Reel 3, JPC Papers.

43. The preceding paragraphs draw on Karsner to Tomkin, 3 August 1925, Reel 6, Russian Center, PRL; Abern comments on ILD, "Organizational Conference, Workers Party of America," February 20–22, 1926; James P. Cannon to All Locals, "The Organization of Money Making Affairs for the ILD," 27 January 1926, Reel 1g, Russian Center, PRL; for "Building the I.L.D," and "Voices from Prison," virtually any issue of the *Labor Defender* for 1926, which will also contain the publication of donations. Other indications of Cannon's and Karsner's strict accountancy in terms of finances are found in James P. Cannon to All Locals, "The Organization of Money Making Affairs for ILD," 27 July 1926, Reel 6; "Statement by Rose Karsner at Sub-Committee of ILD regarding printing of financial detailed statement," n.d. (1926), Reel 7; "Sub-Committee Report on the I.L.D.," subsection, "Financial Report," n.d. (1926), Reel 9, Russian Center, PRL; Cannon, *First Ten Years,* 161; "Reminiscences of Max Shachtman," 117. On Abern, see Martin Abern, "Workers Party Press Service—Second National Convention of the Young Workers League," n.d. (1926?); Martin Abern to Dear Comrade, National Office, Organization Department, 29 March 1926, Reel 9, Russian Center, PRL. For the "elimination" of Abern, see unsigned factional letter [Ruthenberg group] to Dear Comrades, 20 July 1926, Loose File, Russian Center, PRL; also on Abern, Ring interviews with Cannon, September 5, 1973, 8; February 23, 1974, 1–8; and for the unadulterated praise of Abern's most admiring comrade, "Reminiscences of Max Shachtman," 14, 42–47. For organizational activities, see "Debs Memorial Meeting," and "Flynn on Tour," *Labor Defender,* December 1926, 214; "The Bishop Brown Tour," and "The New York Bazaar of I.L.D.," *Labor Defender,* March 1927, 46–47; "The Tour of James P. Cannon against the Frame-Up System," *Labor Defender,* November 1927, 165; "The Chicago I.L.D. Bazaar," *Labor Defender,* December 1927, 191.

44. For an introduction to *Labor Defender,* see Milton Canton, "Labor Defender, Chicago and New York, 1926–1937/Equal Justice, New York, 1937–1942," in *The American Radical Press, 1880–1960,* ed. Joseph R. Conlin (Westport, CT: Greenwood Press, 1974), 248–59. Cannon's introductory remarks on the launching of the *Labor Defender* appear in Cannon, "The Labor Defender and the I.L.D.," *Labor Defender,* January 1926, 7.

45. Ring interview with Cannon, August 15, 1973, 12–13; Drucker, *Shachtman and His Left,* 27. Cannon and O'Flaherty had an easygoing relationship, one in which jokes over party matters and factionalism were clearly commonplace. See, for instance, Cannon to Dear Comrade Tom [O'Flaherty], signed "Yours diplomatically," 29 January 1924, Loose File, Russian Center, PRL.

46. Drucker, *Shachtman and His Left,* 26–30; "Reminiscences of Max Shachtman," 116; JPC (Lover-husband) to Rose Dear, Berlin, 25 May 1927, Reel 3, JPC Papers; Ring interviews with Cannon, May 10, 1973, 23–24; September 5, 1973, 7–8; Jim to Rose Karsner, telegram, 2 February 1926; 26 February 1926, Reel 6, Russian Center, PRL. On Munzenberg, see Stefan Berger, "Willi Munzenberg," in *Biographical Dictionary of European Labor Leaders: M–Z,* ed. A. Thomas Lane (Westport, CT: Greenwood, 1995), 679–80; Stephen Koch, *Double Lives: Stalin, Willi Munzenberg, and the Seduction of the Intellectuals* (London: HarperCollins, 1995); McMeekin, *Red Millionaire.*

47. C.E. Ruthenberg to All Party Branches, 17 July 1925; ILD Leaflet entitled, "The Paris Commune, March, 1871," announcing a Paris Commune Celebration for March 23, 1926, enclosed in a March 13, 1926, communication to the Bureau of Investigation, all documents in "International Labor Defense," FBI File; "Sub-Committee Report on the I.L.D," n.d. (February 1926?), Reel 9, Russian Center, PRL.

48. Money for this relief work was raised in all sorts of ways. One particularly extensive campaign was the ILD coupon book, containing detachable coupons, bearing the likenesses of class-war prisoners, families and children of imprisoned workers, and pen-and-ink drawings of prison scenes. These coupons, in the denominations of ten cents, twenty-five cents, fifty cents, and one dollar, were sold in workplaces, unions, fraternal societies, and neighborhoods. They designated that the bearer had contributed a specific amount to the International Labor Defense Christmas Fund, and constituted an official receipt. For a copy of this coupon book and an accompanying circular letter, see Memorandum for —, November 22, 1927; Alfred Wagenknecht and Elizabeth Gurley Flynn, "International Labor Defense—An Important Xmas Appeal Addressed Personally to You," n.d. (November 1927?); and ILD Leaflet, "Christmas—Extend Your Hand Through Prison Bars"; ILD Coupon Book, all in "International Labor Defense," FBI File. Cannon presented and promoted this ILD work in the highest committees of the Workers (Communist) Party. See, for instance, his focus on defense work in Minutes of the Political Committee, November 30, 1926; December 3, 1926; December 17, 1926, all in Reel 1g, Russian Center, PRL. A later pamphlet indicates the kinds of advice for workers facing the courts that was often put forward by the ILD in the 1920s. See *Under Arrest! Workers' Self-Defense in the Courts* [pamphlet no. 5] (New York: ILD, n.d.).

49. The preceding paragraphs draw upon *Labor Defense: Manifesto, Resolutions, Constitution;* "What Is International Labor Defense—Why You Should Join It"; Warren K. Billings, "The Value of Money to the Man Inside," *Labor Defender,* December 1926, 212–13; James P. Cannon, "A Christmas Fund of Our Own," *Daily Worker,* October 17, 1927; Ring interviews with Cannon, August 15, 1973, 1; September 5, 1973, 4–9; Draper, *American Communism and Soviet Russia,* 181; "Reminiscences of Max Shachtman," 108–15; Arne Swabeck, unpublished, untitled, and unpaginated typescript, chap. 8, "Storm Signals from the Comintern," Autobiographies File, Prometheus Research Library, New York, New York.

50. *Labor Defender* articles and other material on these cases were numerous. See, for representative statements only: For the Rakosi case, James P. Cannon, telegram, "ILD Wires Kellogg on Karolyi Ban," *Daily Worker,* October 23, 1925; "Story of Fight to Save Mathias Rakosi," *Labor Defender,* January 1926, 8–10; Marin Abern, "Save the Victims of Horthy!" *Labor Defender,* May 1927, 84; Ring interview with Cannon, August 15, 1973, 11, which mentions Bullitt. On other international agitational work, Cannon, "Shall the U.S. Government Be Mussolini's Bloodhound?" *Daily Worker,* December 10, 1926; Cannon telegram, "ILD Protests Imprisonment of Polish Workers," *Daily Worker,* August 23, 1926; Max Shachtman, "American Imperialism Shall Not Throttle the Chinese Revolution," *Labor Defender,* July 1927, 104–5; "Under the Heel of Fascism," *Labor Defender,*

February 1927, 19; "Labor Defense in Pictures," "Halt the Lithuanian Hangmen! An Appeal of the International Red Aid," and "Trial of the Czechoslovak Deputies," *Labor Defender,* March 1927, 34, 42, 45; "China's Struggle for Freedom," "China Surges Forward toward Freedom," Martin Abern, "Beat Back the Fascist Terror," "Labor Defense Thruout the World," and "Against the Hungarian Special Court," *Labor Defender,* May 1927, 66–78; "Labor Defense in Pictures," *Labor Defender,* June 1927, 87; James P. Cannon telegram, "Labor Defense Cables Protest," *Daily Worker,* May 10, 1928 (calling for release of Bela Kun); Charles Yale Harrison, "The Long Arm of Mussolini," *Labor Defender,* November 1927, 166–67; John M. Keith Report of Washington, DC, Lithuanian Legation demonstration, May 20, 1926, "International Labor Defense," FBI File. Cannon's perspective on international work, immigrant labor, and the ILD came into play in his worry that too many foreign-language-federation organizations might detract from the work of the defense body. See Cannon to F. V. Zalpis, 28 October 1927, Reel 7, Russian Center, PRL.

51. James P. Cannon, Executive Secretary, ILD, "Emergency Call," *Daily Worker,* December 7, 1925; Cannon, "Send $1,500,000 More to Miners—Hold Successful Labor Defense Conference," *Daily Worker,* September 8, 1926; Thurber Lewis, "The Frame-Up of the Zeigler Miners," *Labor Defender,* January 1926, 5–6; Max Shachtman, "Framing the Zeigler Coal-Diggers," *Labor Defender,* February 1926, 19–20. On Cannon, the ILD, and interest in the miners, see, as well, Glotzer, "Reminiscences of James P. Cannon," Reel 2, JPC Papers.

52. James P. Cannon, "Defend Weisbord! Appeal to the Workers of America by the International Labor Defense," *Daily Worker,* April 17, 1926; Cannon, "Free Weisbord! Campaign On—ILD Gathers All Resources for Big Fight," *Daily Worker,* April 18, 1926; Cannon, "The United Front at Passaic," *Labor Defender,* June 1926, 83–85. For other ILD statements on Passaic, see Max Shachtman, "Passaic Fights On!" *Labor Defender,* July 1926, 103–4; Cyril Briggs, "Rally Labor for Passaic Strike Prisoners," *Labor Defender,* May 1927, 69–71; "The Fight Is Not Over in Passaic," *Labor Defender,* July 1927, back cover appeal; James P. Cannon to All Locals and Branches of International Labor Defense, 10 September 1927, Reel 7, Russian Center, PRL.

53. For an original listing of some of these, see "Report of the American Class War Prisoners," n.d. (ca. 1925), Reel 7; "Meeting of Executive Committee of International Labor Defense," November 26, 1926, Reel 1h, Russian Center, PRL; "Cases I.L.D. Is Defending or Cooperating with Existing Defense Organizations," *Labor Defender,* January 1926, 12. For a sampling of subsequent articles on these cases, see Austin Lewis, "Ford and Suhr," *Labor Defender,* February 1926, 21–24; James Lacey, "The Boston Checker Frame-up," and "Ford's Acquittal Arouses Workers to New Fight against Persecutions," *Labor Defender,* March 1926, 39–41; "Chicago Greets Trumball—Now Let's Free Crouch," *Labor Defender,* April 1926, 51–52, 56; Robert W. Dunn, "'Sedition' in Pennsylvania," *Labor Defender,* May 1926, 69–70; "The Ruthenberg Appeal," *Labor Defender,* June 1926, 90–92; Esther Lowell, "Another Blasphemy Case in Massachusetts?" *Labor Defender,* July 1926, 195; Sam A. Darcy, "The Appeal of Paul Crouch," *Labor Defender,* August 1926, 134, 139; Max Shachtman, "George Papcun Is Convicted,"

Labor Defender, September 1926, 147–48; "The Three Fall River Anarchists and Enea Sormenti," *Labor Defender*, February 1927, 26–27.

54. Elmer Beach, "The Prosecution of the Daily Worker," *Labor Defender*, July 1927, 102; "Free Speech in Pennsylvania: An I.L.D. Meeting in Greenville Broken Up by Steel Trust Agents," *Labor Defender*, December 1926, 209; J. Louis Engdahl, "Our Press Is in Danger," *Labor Defender*, August 1927, 119; Max Shachtman, "One for All and All for One," *Labor Defender*, April 1928, 84; Drucker, *Shachtman and His Left*, 30. Cannon would later make two contributions to defending the revolutionary press: James P. Cannon, "Militant Labor Urged by ILD to Save 'Daily,'" *Daily Worker*, September 3, 1927; Cannon, "Vitality of the Revolutionary Press," *Daily Worker*, supplement, June 13, 1928.

55. "Frame-Up in New Jersey," *Labor Defender*, December 1926, 212; Hollace Ransdell, "The State versus Thomas Regan, Textile Striker," *Labor Defender*, April 1927, 54; "A Good Strike Is a Crime: The Imprisonment of the I.F.U. and the I.L.G.W.U. Members in N.Y.," *Labor Defender*, June 1927, 87; Helen Black, "Giving the Furriers Hell," *Labor Defender*, August 1927, 117; Ben Rubin, "The Mineola Frame-up," *Labor Defender*, November 1927, 170; George J. Sand, "The Colorado Battle Line," and Hugo Oehler, "The Fight in Berwind Canyon," *Labor Defender*, December 1927, 179–80.

56. George Maurer, "The Deportation of Emanuel Vajtauer," *Labor Defender*, February 1927, 23; M. Krasich, "Another Victim of Class Justice," *Labor Defender*, October 1927, 150.

57. James P. Cannon, "Shall the U.S. Government Be Mussolini's Bloodhound?" *Daily Worker*, December 10, 1926; Max Shachtman, "Enea Sormenti," Carlo Tresca, "The Fascist Menace in the United States of America," and James P. Cannon, "The Sormenti Case: A Challenge to American Labor," *Labor Defender*, January 1927, 2–9; "Under the Heel of Fascism," and "Halt Sormenti's Deportation," *Labor Defender*, February 1927, 19–22; Enea Sormenti, "Maintain American Tradition of Political Asylum," *Labor Defender*, April 1927, 52; Ettore Frisina, "Why Greco and Carillo?" *Labor Defender*, December 1927, 183. On the subsequent history of Vidale, his aliases, his relationship with Modotti, and his actions, see Dorothy Gallagher, *All the Right Enemies: The Life and Murder of Carlo Tresca* (New Brunswick, NJ: Rutgers University Press, 1988); Draper, *American Communism and Soviet Russia*, 179; Isaac Don Levine, *The Mind of an Assassin* (New York: Farrar, Straus, & Cudahy, 1959), 71; "Reminiscences of Max Shachtman," 449–52; David Wingeate Pike, *In the Service of Stalin: The Spanish Communists in Exile, 1939–1945* (Oxford: Clarendon Press, 1993), 53; Patricia Albers, *Shadows, Fire, Snow: The Life of Tina Modotti* (New York: Clarkson Potter, 1999); Letizia Argenteri, *Tina Modotti: Between Art and Revolution* (New Haven: Yale University Press, 2003).

58. On Sacco and Vanzetti the sources are now extensive, and include a number of older texts by Felix Frankfurter, Oswald Fraenkel, and others. The anarchist context is developed in two statements: Paul Avrich, *Sacco and Vanzetti: The Anarchist Background* (Princeton, NJ: Princeton University Press, 1991), and Nunzio Pernicone, "Carlo Tresca and the Sacco-Vanzetti Case," *Journal of American History* 66 (December 1979): 535–47. The former book develops the views of the *Galleanisti*; the latter deals

directly with the issues associated with questions over Sacco's guilt. The major revisionist treatment, in which the case for guilt is made most strongly, is Francis Russell, *Tragedy in Dedham: The Story of the Sacco-Vanzetti Case* (New York: McGraw-Hill, 1977 [originally published 1962]), and the subsequent clash of interpretations is best captured in the opposing essays: Francis Russell, "The End of the Myth: Sacco and Vanzetti Fifty Years Later," *National Review* 29 (August 19, 1977): 938–41; Carey McWilliams, "Massachusetts Pays Its Debts," *The Nation* 225 (August 20–27, 1977): 133–35. Russell, in *Tragedy in Dedham,* 332, states (without citation of a source) that Cannon would, subsequent to his expulsion from the Communist Party, "admit privately . . . that he felt Sacco was guilty." In this he no doubt was linking Cannon to Tresca and Max Eastman, long-time friends, whom Russell also claims questioned Sacco's innocence. Such a perspective, as established in Pernicone's "Carlo Tresca and the Sacco and Vanzetti Case," ignores the context of 1920–1927, when there is no evidence to indicate such belief. Note, as well, Max Eastman, "Is This the Truth about Sacco and Vanzetti?" *National Review* 11 (October 21, 1961): 261–64; Bertram D. Wolfe, *A Life in Two Centuries: An Autobiography* (New York: Stein & Day, 1981), 413–19; and Francis Russell, *Sacco and Vanzetti: The Case Resolved* (New York: Harper & Row, 1986), 132–33, where Russell's source on Cannon's statement is the one-time Socialist Workers Party member, James Burnham, who, after his departure from the SWP, moved decidedly to the right. Cannon wrote to the *New Republic* to express his revulsion at Russell's position and his astonishment that he would be cited as someone who thought either Sacco or Vanzetti guilty. He wanted no part in any "white-wash" of Sacco's and Vanzetti's executioners. See Cannon to the Editors, *New Republic,* 9 April 1963; Cannon to Tom Kerry, 10 April 1963; Justice Michael A. Musmanno to James P. Cannon, 13 May 1963, all in Reel 11, JPC Papers. That said, Cannon did acknowledge, in private (Comintern) communist circles, that there was a *public* question about innocence in the Sacco-Vanzetti case that differentiated it from other frame-ups on which the ILD worked in defense campaigns. See James P. Cannon, "Statement to MOPR, 3rd Session," August 27, 1928, Reel 6, Russian Center, PRL. The political points and breadth of the movement, as well as some comment on workers' struggles, are reasonably well articulated in Drucker's brief discussion of Shachtman's views in Drucker, *Shachtman and His Left,* 29–30; Max Shachtman, *Sacco and Vanzetti: Labor's Martyrs* (Chicago: International Labor Defense, 1927); "ILD Endorses Sacco, Vanzetti Protest Strikes," *Daily Worker,* August 6, 1927; "100,000,000 for Sacco and Vanzetti," *Labor Defender,* September 1927, 131, 143; James P. Cannon, "The International Campaign for Sacco and Vanzetti," *Labor Defender,* February 1927, 24–25. On labor struggles, see Montgomery, *Fall of the House of Labor,* 463–64.

59. Mary Heaton Vorse, "Sacco and Vanzetti," *The Toiler,* January 8, 1921. See also Garrison, *Mary Heaton Vorse,* 171–72. At a March 1923 meeting in Chelsea, Massachusetts, Cannon supposedly urged the audience to support Sacco and Vanzetti, who were "red-blooded workers with communistic principles, needed for work in the future." See Boston File No. 199/53, March 6–7, 1923, "International Labor Defense," FBI File, sec. 1.

60. The core statements, four from the *Daily Worker* and seven from the *Labor Defender*, are gathered together and reprinted in James P. Cannon, *Notebook of an Agitator* (New York: Pathfinder, 1973), 3–31. See, as well, "Statement of International Labor Defence on the Sacco-Vanzetti Case," *Daily Worker*, May 14, 1926; James P. Cannon, "Real Murderer Confesses in Vanzetti Case," and ILD Statement, "Echoes of Sacco, Vanzetti Move Stirs Congress," *Daily Worker*, June 19, 1926; "A Reply to an Infamous Slander," *Labor Defender*, January 1927, 6; "Save Sacco and Vanzetti from Death! International Labor Defense Calls on All Labor to Protest," *Daily Worker*, April 7, 1927; "ILD Warns of New Menace for Sacco and Vanzetti—Analyzes Attempts to Disrupt Campaign," *Daily Worker*, May 4, 1927, which is almost the same as James P. Cannon, "Life and Feedom for Sacco and Vanzetti," *Labor Unity*, May 15, 1927; "ILD Answers Felicani Slander; Socialists Curbed Mass Protests," *Daily Worker*, September 2, 1927; James P. Cannon, "Boston and Cheswick," *Daily Worker*, October 3, 1927; Cannon, "Shall It Be Again? Yesterday, Sacco and Vanzetti—Today, Greco and Carillo," *Daily Worker*, November 12, 1927; Cannon, "The Red Month of November," *Labor Defender*, November 1927, 168–69. Note as well Ring interview with Cannon, September 5, 1973, 2.

61. "Meeting of the Executive Committee of International Labor Defense," November 26, 1926 and Minutes of the Second Annual Conference of the International Labor Defense, New England District, November 28, 1926, Reel 1h, Russian Center, PRL; James P. Cannon, "The International Campaign for Sacco and Vanzetti," *Labor Defender*, February 1927, 24–25, 28; Cannon, "Free Sacco and Vanzetti: From the Supreme Court of the Capitalists to the Supreme Court of the Laboring Masses," *Labor Defender*, May 1927, 67; Eugene V. Debs, "Sacco and Vanzetti—An Appeal to American Labor," *Labor Defender*, July 1926, 99; "100,000,000 for Sacco and Vanzetti," *Labor Defender*, September 1927, 131, 143; "ILD Endorses Sacco-Vanzetti Protest Strikes," *Daily Worker*, August 6, 1927; photomontage entitled "Police!" *Labor Defender*, September 1927, 135; photomontage entitled "For Sacco and Vanzetti the Whole World Over," and "The N.Y. Sacco and Vanzetti Meeting," *Labor Defender*, August 1927, 114–16; Eugene Lyons, *The Life and Death of Sacco and Vanzetti* (New York: International, 1927); Drucker, *Shachtman and His Left*, 28. For the ILD "Sacco and Vanzetti Must Not Die" poster, see the inside front cover of the special "Save Sacco and Vanzetti" issue of *Labor Defender*, July 1927. On ILD activity, note Shipman, *It Had to Be Revolution*, 166; Rose Karsner to C. Berger (Buffalo), 20 July 1927, and copies to many other locales, Reel 19; R. W. [Dunn] to Dear Friend, May 1927 [draft of a letter relating to finances]; "Statement by Robert W. Dunn, Treasurer of the New York Sacco-Vanzetti Emergency Committee," n.d. (May 1927?); leaflet, Eugene V. Debs, *Sacco and Vanzetti: Must Not Die* (Chicago: International Labor Defense, 1927); undated 1927 New York press clipping, "One Hour Strike and Union Square Meeting Planned Here as Sacco-Vanzetti Protest,"; press clipping, "NY Committee to Back Strike Plea for Sacco-Vanzetti," April 18, 1927, referring to a Harlem strike-support meeting called under the auspices of the American Negro Labor Conference, planning a half-day worldwide work stoppage for June 15, 1927; "Demonstrate—Strike: Save Sacco and Vanzetti," a leaflet calling for a July 7, 1927 strike/protest meeting under the auspices of the Sacco-Vanzetti Emergency

Committee; draft for ILD Leaflet, "Workers of America—Strike to Free Sacco and Vanzetti," n.d.; "More Support Comes to Sacco and Vanzetti," ILD press release on united-front conferences, May 28, 1926; Rose Karsner to All ILD Secretaries, "Re Labor Delegations . . . Sacco-Vanzetti Conferences," 27 June 1927; "Sacco-Vanzetti Conference of Chicago," press release, n.d. (June 1927?); ILD Bulletin No. 2, "Report of Sacco-Vanzetti Protest Campaign . . . Conferences . . . Signatures to Petitions . . . Protest Mass Meetings and Demonstrations," July 1927; Minutes of the Sacco-Vanzetti Conference, July 9, 1927, New York, all in "Sacco and Vanzetti General File, 1926," Reel 18, International Labor Defense Papers, Emory University, Atlanta Georgia (hereafter ILD Papers); "Another 'Forward' Bluff Is Called" (on finances), *Daily Worker,* November 10, 1926; "Over 110,000 Appeals, 200 Cables and Over 50,000,000 People Dare to Protest," *Daily Worker,* May 19, 1927. "Sacco and Vanzetti General," Reel 18, ILD Papers, contains an extensive collection of ILD press releases.

62. Bartolomeo Vanzetti to Friends of the International Labor Defense, 23 May 1926, in *Labor Defender,* July 1926, 114; Sacco N. & B. V. to Dear Cannon, 11 April 1927, Reel 18, ILD Papers.

63. ILD Bulletin No. 2, "What Happened in New York City," July 1927, Reel 18, ILD Papers; "The New York Sacco and Vanzetti Meeting," *Labor Defender,* August 1927, 115–16.

64. James P. Cannon, "Sacco and Vanzetti Must Not Burn on the Electric Chair," *Labor Defender,* June 1927, 89.

65. James P. Cannon, "A Living Monument to Sacco and Vanzetti," *Labor Defender,* October 1927, 152–53; Shachtman, *Sacco and Vanzetti: Labor's Martyrs;* "The Funeral of Sacco and Vanzetti," *Labor Defender,* October 1927, 148; Leonard Craig, "State Troopers Again Amuck," *Labor Age* 16 (November 1927): 18–20; "Sacco and Vanzetti Shall Not Die! Monster Mass Protest Meeting, Saturday 3 PM, July 30th," and "Statement for Immediate Release by James P. Cannon, International Labor Defense," n.d. (August 23, 1927?), both in "Sacco and Vanzetti General File," Reel 18, ILD Papers, which also contain numerous telegrams detailing the activities of August 1927, among them: Labor Defense to MOPR, Moscow, 29 July 1927; Robert Zelms to Rose Karsner, 30 July 1927; Cannon to Congressman Bob LaFollette Jr. et al., 5 August 1927; Cannon to Attached List, 15 August 1927; Rose [Baron] to Cannon, 15 August 1927; M. Zelisko to Cannon, 18 August 1927; Johnston to Cannon, 18 August 1927; Sacco-Vanzetti Defense Committee to International Labor Defense, 19 August 1927; Cannon to Sacco-Vanzetti Defense Committee, Boston, 20 August 1927; Cannon to ILD Executive, 23 August 1927; Cannon to Sacco-Vanzetti Defense Committee, 24 August 1924. For one international statement, see *Lest We Forget! The Trial and Execution of Two Brave Men—Sacco and Vanzetti* (London: National Committee, International Class War Prisoners Aid, September 1927).

66. "Strikers and Sacco Demonstrators Arrested in Massachusetts," November 7, 1928; "List of Speakers at Sacco-Vanzetti Memorial, Union Square," August 22, 1928; "Sacco-Vanzetti Memorials Countrywide," August 21, 1928; Cannon to Sacco-Vanzetti

Defense Committee, Boston, 24 August 1924, all in Reel 18, ILD Papers; Beal, *Proletarian Journey,* 98–106.

67. Note the Cannon-authored *Labor Defender* statements from 1926–1927 reproduced in *Notebook of an Agitator,* commemorating the lives of Little, Debs, and Ruthenberg. The *Labor Defender* issues of December 1926 and April 1927 memorialized Debs and Ruthenberg respectively, with the former listing Debs memorial meetings undertaken by the ILD in twenty-two cities, noting Cannon's speeches (p. 214). For more on the Workers (Communist) Party response to Debs's death, see Minutes of the Political Committee, October 21, 1926, and "Resolution on the Policy to Be Pursued by the Party towards the Traditions of Eugene V. Debs," n.d. (October 29, 1926?), both in Reel 1g, Russian Center, PRL.

68. See James P. Cannon, "Third Annual ILD Conference to Link Sacco-Vanzetti Murders with Famous Haymarket Cases," *Daily Worker,* September 27, 1927; Cannon, "Call for the Third Annual Conference of the International Labor Defense," *Labor Defender,* October 1927, 160; Cannon, "The Cause That Passes through a Prison: For the Second Annual Conference of the International Labor Defense," *Labor Defender,* September 1926, 154–55; Cannon, "The Cause of the Martyrs," *Daily Worker,* magazine section, October 8, 1927; Cannon, "The Red Month of November—For the Third Annual Conference of International Labor Defense,"*Labor Defender,* November 1927, 168–69; and Cannon, "The Third Conference of International Labor Defense," *Labor Defender,* December 1927, 184–85.

69. See James P. Cannon to Dear Friend, 21 October 1927, a four-page folder titled inside, "1887—The Haymarket Martyrs // Sacco and Vanzetti—1927: It Must Not Happen Again!" in "International Labor Defense," FBI File. These documents may well have been forwarded to the Department of Justice, November 24, 1927, with a letter that read: "Gentlemen: I have just received the inclosed, and herewith send it to your department. In my judgement it bespeaks anarchy."

70. For full details on the Third Annual Conference of the ILD, see Agenda and Minutes, Third Annual Conference of the International Labor Defense, November 12–13, 1927, in Reel 2b, Russian Center, PRL.

71. "The Tour of James P. Cannon against the Frame-Up System," *Labor Defender,* November 1927, 165; James P. Cannon, "The Workers Party and the 1928 Election Drive," *Daily Worker,* March 24, 1928; Cannon, "Points West—Impressions on the Road," *Daily Worker,* March 24, 1928; Cannon, "Colorado, The Realm of the Rockefellers," *Daily Worker,* March 26, 1928, Cannon, "To Revive Case of Billings, Mooney, Frame-Up Victims—'Center on Masses' is Message from Cell," *Daily Worker,* April 12, 1928; Cannon, "A Visit with Billings at Folsom Prison," and Cannon, "A Talk with the Centralia Prisoners," *Labor Defender,* June 1928, reprinted in *Notebook of an Agitator,* 63–71; Martin Abern, "International Labor Defense Activities (1 January–1 July 1928)," July 23, 1928, reprinted in *James P. Cannon and the Early Years of American Communism,* 536; and Cannon, "The Voice of the Communist Movement," *Daily Worker,* June 26, 1928. For fuller histories of the Mooney-Billings and Centralia cases, see Curt

Gentry, *Frame-Up: The Incredible Case of Tom Mooney and Warren Billings* (New York: Norton, 1967); Richard H. Frost, *The Mooney Case* (Stanford, CA: Stanford University Press, 1968); Ralph Chaplin, *The Centralia Conspiracy* (Chicago: Industrial Workers of the World, 1920). One of the Centralia prisoners, Eugene Barnett, published his auto-biography, "A Rebel Worker's Life," in serialized form in the *Labor Defender,* from January 1927 through January 1928, and later repudiated IWW claims that the Centralia prisoners had rejected the ILD. See "Barnett Corrects the IWW," *Labor Defender,* September 1929, 184. On the Colorado miners, the ILD, and the memory of the Ludlow massacre of 1914, see Zeese Papanikolas, *Buried Unsung: Louis Tikas and the Ludlow Massacre* (Lincoln: University of Nebraska Press, 1982); Barron B. Beshoar, *Out of the Depths: The Story of John R. Lawson, a Labor Leader* (Denver: Trades & Labor Assembly, 1943); Max Shachtman, "Remember the Ludlow Massacre!" *Labor Defender,* December 1927, 182, an issue that contained the first of many ILD reports on the Colorado miners' struggles of 1927–1928: George J. Saul, "The Colorado Battle Line," and Hugo Oehler, "The Fight in Berwind Canyon," 179–81.

72. "Reminiscences of Max Shachtman," 108–17; Cannon, *First Ten Years,* 159. Albert Glotzer, "Reminiscences of James P. Cannon," unpublished/unpaginated manuscript, Reel 2, JPC Papers, confirms this positive assessment of Cannon and the ILD. Cannon would not likely have resisted a Workers (Communist) Party or Comintern subsidy to the ILD, and in fact such monies likely were on occasion forthcoming. At the very least, Cannon and other ILD functionaries were paid by the Workers' Party. Nevertheless, he would certainly not have wanted the nonpartisan character of the defense body compromised, and he understood that any such organization worthy of mass support would also have to raise funds on its own. There is no basis for the claim recently made in McMeekin, *Red Millionaire,* 202, 347, that Cannon and the ILD raised $500,000 for Sacco-Vanzetti, "most of which was filched by the American Communist Party."

73. See James P. Cannon, "Shall It Be Again? Yesterday Sacco and Vanzetti—Today, Greco and Carillo," *Daily Worker,* November 12, 1927; Ettore Frisina, "Why Greco and Carillo," *Labor Defender,* December 1927, 183; Cannon, "Greco and Carillo on Trial," *Labor Defender,* January 1928, 12–13; Cannon, "The Acquittal of Greco and Carillo," *Labor Defender,* February 1927, 28–29.

74. For a list of Cannon's publications, see *James P. Cannon and the Early Years of American Communism,* 607–10.

75. James P. Cannon, "Fun on Commerce Street—A Review of Gold's 'Hoboken Blues,'" *Daily Worker,* February 2, 1928. Cannon had no personal animosity toward Gold and the cultural wing of the Workers (Communist) Party in this period, and enjoyed socializing in this milieu when the opportunity arose. There was, however, a distinction between the artistic and the political wings of the Left, and the latter was certainly dominant. See Joseph Freeman, *An American Testament: A Narrative of Rebels and Romantics* (New York: Farrar & Rinehart, 1936), 310. For more on Gold, see John Pyros, *Mike Gold: Dean of American Proletarian Literature* (New York: Dramatika Press, 1979); Alan Wald, *Writing from the Left: New Essays on Radical Culture and Poli-*

tics (London: Verso, 1994); Michael Denning, *The Cultural Front: The Laboring of American Culture in the Twentieth Century* (London: Verso, 1996).

76. "A Fraternal Order for the U.S. Workers," *Daily Worker*, March 30, 1928. See also Cannon, *First Ten Years*, 139.

77. James P. Cannon, "The Workers Party and the 1928 Election Drive," *Daily Worker*, March 24, 1928; Cannon, "Our Communist Nominating Convention," *Daily Worker*, May 23, 1928; Cannon, "Opening the Election Campaign," *Daily Worker*, June 5, 1928.

78. James P. Cannon, "Tasks Face Every Workers Party Member," *Daily Worker*, March 23, 1928, reprinted as "Party Work and Accountability," *Party Organizer* 3 (March–April 1928), and also in *James P. Cannon and the Early Years of American Communism*, 494–96. See also "Organization of Propaganda Meetings," *Daily Worker*, May 14, 1928, reprinted in *Party Organizer* 3 (May–June 1928).

79. James P. Cannon, "Trade Union Questions," *The Communist*, July 1928, reprinted in *James P. Cannon and the Early Years of American Communism*, 512–20. Note as well the growing discontent of the Cannon group over the linked trade union and ILD issues of late 1928, expressed by Martin Abern and Arne Swabeck in reports on textiles and mining, reprinted in *James P. Cannon and the Early Years of American Communism*, 542–58.

80. James P. Cannon, "William D. Haywood—Soldier to the Last," *Daily Worker*, May 22, 1928; Cannon, "William D. Haywood: A Pioneer of Revolutionary Unionism," *Labor Unity*, June 1928, 13–14.

81. *James P. Cannon and the Early Years of American Communism*, 58; Ted Morgan, *A Covert Life: Jay Lovestone—Communist, Anti-Communist, and Spymaster* (New York: Random House, 1999), 69; "Meeting of the Convention Arrangements Committee," July 31, 1927; "Convention Preparations Committee," August 4, 1927; Minutes Convention Arrangements Committee, August 4, 1927; William Z. Foster, "Speech on Credentials Committee Report," September 1, 1927, all in Reel 1h, Russian Center, PRL. Reel 7 of the same source contains routine ILD correspondence between Cannon and Foster in this period. For a brief account of ILD work in this period, see as well, Albert Glotzer, "Reminiscences of James P. Cannon," Reel 2, JPC Papers; and Minutes of the Political Committee, April 7, 1927, April 21, 1927, April 22, 1927, all in Reel 1h, Russian Center, PRL; and Minutes of the Political Committee, August 4, 1927, August 11, 1927, August 13, 1927, August 23, 1927; "Sacco and Vanzetti Murdered by the Capitalist Class; Manifesto of the Central Executive Committee of the Workers (Communist) Party on the Brutal Murder of Our Comrades, Nicola Sacco and Bartolomeo Vanzetti," August 23, 1927; Minutes of the Political Committee, August 24, 1927, all in Reel 2a, Russian Center, PRL.

82. See James P. Cannon, "Labor Defense Cables Protest," *Daily Worker*, May 10, 1928; Max Shachtman to Albert Glotzer, 20 March 1928, Reel 21, JPC Papers; Shipman, *It Had to Be Revolution*, 166–67; Cannon, "Refute Slander of IWW Officials," *Daily Worker*, May 16, 1928; Abern, "International Labor Defense Activities (1 January–1 July 1928)," in *James P. Cannon and the Early Years of American Communism*, 536–41. Abern's meticu-

496 . NOTES TO PAGES 283–87

lous accounting of matters both financial and political is in contrast with Gitlow's rather cavalier and caustic dismissal of the ILD in *I Confess*, 470–71.

83. James P. Cannon to Rose Dear, Berlin, 25 May 1927, Reel 3, JPC Papers.

Chapter 10: Living with Lovestone

1. James P. Cannon, "The Degeneration of the Communist Party and the New Beginning," *Fourth International* 15 (Fall 1954): 122, also in James P. Cannon, *The First Ten Years of American Communism—Report of a Participant* (New York: Pathfinder, 1973), 18–19.

2. Theodore Draper, *American Communism and Soviet Russia: The Formative Period* (New York: Viking, 1960), 489–90, n. 4; Ted Morgan, *A Covert Life: Jay Lovestone—Communist, Anti-Communist, and Spymaster* (New York: Random House, 1999), 3–83; quote from Cannon, *First Ten Years*, 173.

3. Cannon, *First Ten Years*, 179–80.

4. Alexander Bittelman, "Things I Have Learned: An Autobiography," 440–42, Boxes 1–2, Collection 62, unpublished manuscript in Alexander Bittelman Papers, Tamiment Institute, New York, New York; James P. Cannon to Theodore Draper, 19 July 1955, Reel 25, James P. Cannon Papers, Microfilm Edition, 1994, State Historical Society of Wisconsin, Madison, Wisconsin (hereafter JPC Papers); *James P. Cannon and the Early Years of American Communism: Selected Writings and Speeches, 1920–1928* (New York: Prometheus Research Library, 1992), 49–50; Cannon, *First Ten Years*, 203; James R. Barrett, *William Z. Foster and the Tragedy of American Radicalism* (Urbana: University of Illinois Press, 1999), 152. On the Bukharin-Lovestone friendship and Bukharin's partisanship with respect to the Ruthenberg group, see Morgan, *A Covert Life*, 48–50, 66–75; Cannon, *First Ten Years*, 129, 132; Draper, *American Communism and Soviet Russia*, 258; Edward P. Johanningsmeier, *Forging American Communism: The Life of William Z. Foster* (Princeton, NJ: Princeton University Press, 1994), 224, 235–36 (which also contains evidence of Stalin's low esteem for Foster in certain areas, [p. 243]). For an introduction to trade union questions and communist politics in this period, see Draper, *American Communism and Soviet Russia*, 215–33.

5. Cannon, *First Ten Years*, 150–51.

6. For the American Commission, see "First Session, American Commission, Zinoviev's Secretariat, Kremlin," February 16, 1926, which contains introductory statements by Ruthenberg, Foster, and Browder; "Second Session, American Commission," February 18, 1926, which contains statements by Cannon and Bittelman; "Third Session, American Commission," February 19, 1926, which contains statements by Dunne and Brown (England); and a further session, "American Commission," March 12, 1926, containing statements by Ruthenberg, Foster, Bittelman, Browder, Dunne, and Cannon. Early prefatory documents, indicating the high level of factional animosity, include Bedacht, Cannon, and Pepper to the Secretary of the American Commission, 30 January 1926; Foster and Bittelman to the American Commission, n.d. (but likely late January/early February 1926), all in Reel 3, in Documents from Russian Center for the Preservation and Study of Contemporary History, Microfilm Copies Held,

Prometheus Research Library, New York, New York (hereafter Russian Center, PRL). See Earl Browder to Theodore Draper, 16 March 1959, 23–24, Series III, Box 18, Earl W. Browder Papers, George Arents Research Library for Special Collections, Syracuse University, Syracuse, New York (hereafter Browder Papers), for an unusually self-serving statement.

7. Reel 1d, Russian Center, PRL, contains a series of documents, including statements by Cannon, on the debate around the trade union question developed in the December 1925 plenum. In the absence of Foster and Bittelman, Browder was the Foster group's designated spokesman. For the final majority outcome, see "Resolutions on Trade Union Work of the Party," n.d. (December 1925/January 1926?).

8. On the Foster group's account of this, see No author [Bittelman?] to Dear Comrade, 3 December 1925, Reel 20, JPC Papers.

9. On the subsequent recognition, by all sides, that folding the once-impressive *Labor Herald,* a TUEL organ with at least the potential to convey some level of separation from the Workers (Communist) Party, into the *Workers Monthly,* was an "error," see Alexander Bittelman, "An Answer to Bedacht's Charge That Foster Is Non-Marxian; That He Is Not a Communist," Part III, 2, 1926, Roll 2/R 3345, in Max Shachtman Papers, Tamiment Institute, New York University, New York, New York; Ruthenberg, "First Session, American Commission," February 16, 1926, 30, Reel 3, Russian Center, PRL.

10. For the December 1925 decision on reconstructing the TUEL, see Draper, *American Communism and Soviet Russia,* 217–23, the Comintern background appearing in "A Letter from the Comintern and the Profintern on Trade Union Work," *Daily Worker,* August 14, 1925. Cannon's American Commission address is in "Second Session, American Commission," February 18, 1926, 5–7, 10–13, Reel 3, Russian Center, PRL.

11. Cannon, "Second Session, American Commission," February 18, 1926, 20–32, Reel 3, Russian Center, PRL. For the bloc of Ruthenberg-Cannon against Foster, see Ruthenberg, Cannon, et al, "Facts Repudiating Foster," February 17, 1926, 70, Reel 5, Russian Center, PRL.

12. Dunne, "Third Session, American Commission," February 19, 1926, 20–30; Dunne and Dunne interjection, "American Commission," March 12, 1926, 9–11, 35, Reel 3, Russian Center, PRL.

13. Cannon, "American Commission," March 12, 1926, 31–33, Reel 3, Russian Center, PRL.

14. Minutes of Political Committee, April 15, 1926; Minutes of Plenum of Central Executive Committee, May 26–28, 1926; "The Work Before the Party in the Light of the Comintern Decision," and "The Trade Union Work and the Trade Union Educational League," n.d. (May 1926?), all in Reel 1f, Russian Center, PRL. Ruthenberg group meetings, one in early April of a more rank-and-file character, another in late May composed of more established cadre, are minuted in "Present about 35 Comrades," April 4, 1926; "Party Meeting, Tuesday," May 25, 1926, both in Reel 1h, Russian Center, PRL.

15. Contrast Draper, *American Communism and Soviet Russia,* 235–36, with *James P. Cannon and the Early Years of American Communism,* 52, 54. The quote on Cannon's December 1925 perspective is from Cannon to Comrades, 16 December 1925, Reel 1,

498 · NOTES TO PAGES 290–91

JPC Papers. Cannon's voting record on the Political Committee in the immediate aftermath of his April 1926 return from Moscow is detailed in: Minutes of the Political Committee, April 27, 1926, May 11, 1926, May 24, 1926, June 2, 1926, all in Reel 1f, Russian Center, PRL.

16. See Jay Lovestone, "Daily Worker—Management Committee Report," and "Motion by Foster," in Minutes of the Political Committee, April 27, 1926 (Cannon not present); Moritz J. Loeb to *Daily Worker* Management Committee, CEC, 8 June 1926; Sam Darcy to CEC, 10 June 1926; Ruthenberg statement, "*Daily Worker* Situation and Location of Party Headquarters," Minutes of the Political Committee, June 29, 1926, all in Reel 1f, Russian Center, PRL.

17. See Jay Lovestone, "Resolution on the Location of Party Headquarters," Alexander Bittelman, "Resolution on the *Daily Worker* and Location of Party Headquarters," motion by Cannon (and subsequent procedural discussion), and amended "Resolution on the Location of Party Headquarters," all in Minutes of the Political Committee, August 6, 1926; Statement of the Political Committee, "The Party Headquarters Should Be Moved to New York," and Central Executive Committee, "Why Headquarters Should Be Moved to New York" (both Ruthenberg-Lovestone statements); Cannon and Dunne, "Statement on the Question of Moving Party Headquarters," and Foster, Bittelman, and Johnstone, "On the Question of Moving the Party Headquarters to New York," n.d. (July–August 1926); for the Soviet cable, "On the Question of Moving," Minutes of the Political Committee, August 18, 1926, which also contain discussion of the resignation of the manager of the *Daily Worker*, Moritz Loeb; and Cannon statement in "On Moving," Minutes of the Political Committee, August 26, 1926, all in Reel 1f, Russian Center, PRL. For background on the *Daily Worker* and Loeb, see Moritz J. Loeb, "Torchbearers," *Workers Monthly*, November 1924, 19–20.

18. For discussion of the British General Strike within the Political Committee in the Workers (Communist) Party, see William Z. Foster, "Resolutions and Motions on the Tasks of the Party in the British Strike," and "The Tasks of the Party in the British Strike," Minutes of the Political Committee, May 11, 1926; "Statement on CI Decision and the Tasks of the Party," Minutes of the Political Committee, May 24, 1926, Earl Browder, "Weaknesses and Mistakes of the WPA on the Question of the British General Strike," n.d., all in Reel 1f, Russian Center, PRL. Note, for the public position of the American party, Robert Minor, "The British General Strike," *Workers Monthly*, July 1926, 393–96, 400. See, as well, Leon Trotsky, *The Strategy of the World Revolution* (New York: Communist League of America (Opposition), 1930), 50–56.

19. C. [Clarence Hathaway] to Jim, 4 July 1926; Bud to Dear Jim, Bill, et al, Detroit, 14 August 1926; R. Baker to Ruthenberg, 4 August 1926; Reynolds to Ruthenberg, 14 August 1926, all in Reel 1, JPC Papers.

20. Bill Dunne to Jim, 3 August 1926, Reel 1, JPC Papers.

21. The cable is reproduced in Draper, *American Communism and Soviet Russia*, 237. See also "Cable-Moving," Minutes of the Political Committee, October 13, 1926, Reel 1g; "Question of Moving *Daily Worker* and Party Headquarters," Minutes of the Central Executive Committee Plenum, November 10–12, 1926, Reel 1f, Russian Center, PRL. See,

as well, Morgan, *A Covert Life*, 62–64; Benjamin Gitlow, *I Confess: The Truth About American Communism* (New York: E.P. Dutton, 1940), 307.

22. As background to the context outlined in the preceding paragraphs, see Moshe Lewin, *Lenin's Last Struggle* (New York: Pantheon, 1968). On rising anti-Trotskyism in the Comintern and the upper reaches of the United States Workers (Communist) Party, see Bertram D. Wolfe, *A Life in Two Centuries: An Autobiography* (New York: Stein & Day, 1981), 406–12; Morgan, *A Covert Life*, 62–63; Leon Trotsky, *My Life* (New York: Pathfinder, 1970), 526–29; Draper, *American Communism and Soviet Russia*, 237–43; *James P. Cannon and the Early Years of American Communism*, 53–54; "The Reminiscences of Max Shachtman," 53–54, Number 488, 1963, Oral History Research Office, Columbia University, New York, New York; Peter Drucker, *Max Shachtman and His Left: A Socialist's Odyssey Through the "American Century"* (Atlantic Highlands, NJ: Humanities Press, 1994), 36; James P. Cannon, *The History of American Trotskyism: From Its Origins (1928) to the Founding of the Socialist Workers' Party (1938)—Report of a Participant* (New York: Pathfinder, 1972), 46; Cannon, *First Ten Years*, 181; Bittelman, "Things I Have Learned," 458–69; Arne Swabeck, unpublished, unititled, and unpaginated typescript, chap. 9, "Misguided Labor Party Maneuvers," Autobiographies File, Prometheus Research Library, New York, New York; Harry Ring interview with James P. Cannon, April 19, 1974, 4–6 (in possession of the author; hereafter Ring interview); Max Eastman, *Love and Revolution: My Journey Through an Epoch* (New York: Random House, 1964), 442–45, 510–16; Max Eastman, *Since Lenin Died* (London: Labour Publishing, 1925); C. M. Roebuck, "Since Eastman Lied," *Workers Monthly*, June 1925, 369–72; N. Krupskaya, "Lenin and Trotsky," *Workers Monthly*, September 1925, 516; Max Eastman to *The New Masses*/Comrades, 21 January 1928, Reel 2c, Russian Center, PRL. On Cannon's relationship with Eastman, which had a long history, and considerable affection, Maurice Spector to Max Shachtman, 27 April 1930, Roll 8/Reel 3351, Max Shachtman Papers, Tamiment Institute, New York University, New York, New York (hereafter MS Papers). For Political Committee materials, see "Reported Speech by Stalin Repudiating World Revolution Branded as Falsehood," in Minutes of the Political Committee, September 14, 1926; "New York Times—Max Eastman," Minutes of the Political Committee, October 16, 1926 (Cannon not present); "CPSU and Zinoviev as Chairman of Comintern," "Plenum of ECCI," and "Resolution on the Situation in the Communist Party of the Soviet Union and the Withdrawal of Comrade Zinoviev from Work in the Comintern," Minutes of the Political Committee, October 29, 1926, all of the latter in Reel 1g, Russian Center, PRL. For an early Cannon speech alluding to Trotsky, see "Report on James P. Cannon, Kansas City, Missouri," June 17, 1923, U.S. Department of Justice, Federal Bureau of Investigation, Freedom of Information/Privacy Act File, Washington, DC.

23. See, among other sources, Minutes of the Second Annual Conference, International Labor Defense, Ashland Auditorium, Chicago, Illinois, September 5–6, 1926; Minutes of the National Committee, (ILD), September 7, 1926, Reel 2f, Russian Center, PRL.

24. See Johanningsmeier, *Forging American Communism*, 228–29; Melech Epstein, *Jewish Labor in the USA: 1914–1952* (New York: Trade Union Sponsoring Committee,

1953), 119, 134, 153; Joe Rapaport, *The Life of a Jewish Radical* (Philadelphia: Temple University Press, 1981), 76, 123; Barrett, *William Z. Foster*, 126–28.

25. Barrett, *William Z. Foster*, 152–53. For highly critical accounts of communist-garment trades relations in this period, see Melech Epstein, *The Jew and Communism, 1919–1941* (New York: Trade Union Sponsoring Committee, 1959), 121–33; Melech Epstein, *Jewish Labor in the U.S.A.—An Industrial, Political, and Cultural History of the Jewish Labor Movement* (n.p.: KTAV Publishing House, 1969), vol. 2, 124–83.

26. Irving Howe and Lewis Coser, *The American Communist Party: A Critical History (1919–1957)* (Boston: Beacon Press, 1957), 247–51; Barrett, *William Z. Foster*, 153; John Laslett, *Labor and the Left: A Study of Socialist and Radical Influences in the American Labor Movement, 1881–1924* (New York: Basic Books, 1970), 128–29; Bert Cochran, *Labor and American Communism: The Conflict That Shaped American Unions* (Princeton, NJ: Princeton University Press, 1977), 38–42; Elaine Leeder, *The Gentle General: Rose Pesotta, Anarchist and Labor Organizer* (Albany, NY: SUNY Press, 1993), 32–33. For an imaginative statement on the gendered nature of these developments, in which a largely female workforce and predominantly male leadership figured significantly, see Daniel E. Bender, *Sweated Work, Weak Bodies: Anti-Sweatshop Campaigns and the Languages of Labor* (New Brunswick, NJ: Rutgers University Press, 2003), 155–80. Bender, however, barely scratches the surface of the traditional politics of communist-socialist divergence in the needle trades, so intent is he on reading union relations as entirely governed by gender.

27. The preceding paragraphs owe a great deal to unpublished work by John Holmes, who has explored the needle trades' "civil war" and its historiography in impressive detail. See, especially, Holmes, "Jewish Communism and Garment Unionism in the 1920s: Historical Interpretations" (1995); "American Jewish Communism and the Left-Wing Movement in the Needle Trades: A Forgotten Page of Labor History" (n.d.). The unfortunately influential denigration of the 1926 strike in Benjamin Stolberg's *Tailor's Progress* (New York: Garden City, 1944), is also challenged in David Gurowsky, "Factional Disputes Within the ILGWU, 1919–1928" (PhD diss., SUNY at Binghamton, 1978); Rose Wortis, "A Perversion of ILGWU History," *Political Affairs* 24 (January 1945): 78–89, although these rejoinders sidestep much. An account of developments in Sidney Hillman's Amalgamated Clothing Workers plays on the theme of emerging Stalinism lightly in its title, "Socialism in One Union." See Steve Fraser, *Labor Will Rule: Sidney Hillman and the Rise of American Labor* (New York: Free Press, 1991), 198–237. Accenting the forty-hour week is Ben Gitlow, "The Furriers Strike—A Victory for the 40-Hour Week," *Workers Monthly*, July 1926, 406–9. For Cannon and Dunne, see Dunne, "The ILGWU Convention," *Workers Monthly*, February 1926, 171–76; "On Trade Union Policy," October 10, 1925 and "For Industrial Groups on a Broader Basis Than the TUEL," October 29, 1926, in *James P. Cannon and the Early Years of American Communism*, 359–61, 382.

28. See Cannon, "For Industrial Groups on a Broader Basis than the TUEL," in *James P. Cannon and the Early Years of American Communism*, 382; for Cannon's trade union and defense initiatives, see Minutes of the Political Committee, November 30, 1926,

December 3, 1926, December 6, 1926, December 17, 1926; William Z. Foster to the Political Committee, 23 December 1926; "Speech by Comrade Dunne on Trade Union Resolution," December 27, 1926, all in Reel 1g, Russian Center, PRL. A series of detailed letters, some possibly authored by Bertram D. Wolfe, outline the debates that took place in the Central Executive Committee plenum: Phil [Frankfield] to Pete [Shapiro], 12 November 1926; Unsigned to Birch, 15 November 1926; Unsigned to Jack, 17 November, 1926; and "Plenum," by Bert [Wolfe], all in Reel 1f, Russian Center, PRL.

29. Proposed Letter by Lovestone to the CC of the WP and the YWL, 17 December 1926, Reel 9; "Meeting Between Russian and American Delegations to the VII Enlarged Plenum ECCI," December 24, 1926; "Outline for Statement on Present Situation in the US," n.d. (December 1926); "Points to Be Dealt with in Letter by Presidium to American Party," n.d. (and later decision no letter to be sent); "Fakes of Fosterism," Parts I & II, n.d. (November–December 1926?), all in Reel 1f, Russian Center, PRL.

30. See Minutes of the Political Committee, January 12, 1927, January 20, 1927, January 27, 1927, all in Reel 1h, Russian Center, PRL.

31. See "Conference on Moderating Factionalism," February 7, 1927, and citation of co-authored Ruthenberg-Cannon statement, appended to Minutes of Political Committee, February 24, 1927, in *James P. Cannon and the Early Years of American Communism*, 383–91, 56.

32. See Jack to Dear Comrades, n.d. (but internal evidence suggests November–December 1925), Reel 9; and for Stachel's reasonable positions on Cannon and factionalism in the aftermath of the Sixth Plenum of the ECCI, see "Party Meeting, Tuesday," May 25, 1926, Reel 1h, Russian Center, PRL.

33. Cannon, *First Ten Years*, 175–76; Draper, *American Communism and Soviet Russia*, 236, where the claim is made that the Weinstone-Cannon alliance was first broached in communications of August 19, 1926 and September 14, 1926, with Cannon initiating the contact. This would have meant that Cannon approached Weinstone directly after hearing from Dunne that New York was largely controlled by Weinstone, Stachel, and Wolfe. See Dunne to Jim, 3 August 1926, Reel 1, JPC Papers. On Weinstone's apparent disaffection from the Ruthenberg-Lovestone group, see "A Burglary—Its Political Meaning," *The Militant*, January 1, 1929; and for another somewhat jaundiced interpretation of the Cannon-Weinstone relation, Gitlow, *I Confess*, 404–6. For indications of a possible Cannon-Dunne alliance with Weinstone based on a reading of the needle-trades events of 1925–1926, compare and contrast the Dunne and Weinstone contributions (ILGWU/Furriers) to "The Left-Wing at Two Conventions," *Workers Monthly*, February 1926, 171–78.

34. For reports of this positive work, see Cannon to Comrades, 10 January 1927; 15 January 1927, Reel 1, JPC Papers.

35. For accounts of this period, see Bittelman, "Things I Have Learned," 475; Draper, *American Communism and Soviet Russia*, 243–49; Morgan, *A Covert Life*, 65–66; Cannon, *First Ten Years*, 158–59, 166–69, 173; James P. Cannon to Theodore Draper, 22 July 1955; 26 July 1955, Reel 25, JPC Papers, also published in *International Socialist Review* 17 (Summer 1956): 89–92, 107 and (Fall 1956): 127–30; Gitlow, *I Confess*, 405–15; Minutes of

the Political Committee, March 5, 1927, March 22–23, 1927, both in Reel 1h, Russian Center, PRL.

36. See, for instance, Minutes of the Political Committee, April 7, 1927, April 21, 1927, April 22, 1927, all in Reel 1h, Russian Center, PRL.

37. See "Weinstone's Speech under Polcom Report by Lovestone at Plenum," May 27, 1927, Roll 2, Reel 3345, MS Papers.

38. Ballam embraced the Cannon unity program at the same time as Weinstone. Although Cannon had a low opinion of Ballam, he had no reason to exclude him. See Cannon, *First Ten Years,* 177. For Ballam's shift to Cannon, see Weinstone for B [Dunne], n.d. (1927), Reel 20, JPC Papers.

39. The bulk of the preceding paragraphs draw upon Draper, *American Communism and Soviet Russia,* 253–57; Gitlow, *I Confess,* 417–19; Cannon, *First Ten Years,* 168–69; Morgan, *A Covert Life,* 67–68. On Swabeck and the Cannon group, see Arne Swabeck to Max Bedacht, 17 May 1927, Reel 9, Russian Center, PRL. For the Cannon-Weinstone group's telegram to Moscow, see Cannon, Dunne, Ballam, Swabeck, Abern, Reynolds, and Weinstone to Comintern, n.d. (23 March 1927?), Reel 1, JPC Papers. Gitlow reproduces variants of the Moscow cables, and Draper cites the original communication. See, as well, Minutes of the Political Committee, March 22–23, 1927, April 8, 1927, April 25, 1927, April 27, 1927, all in Reel 1h, Russian Center, PRL; and in the same source, Executive Session, May 9, 1927, on the motions regarding Lovestone's and Gitlow's departure for Moscow and Cannon's call for censure. For the general statement on the party's political platform at this time, see *The Platform of the Class Struggle: National Platform of the Workers (Communist) Party* (New York: Workers Library, 1928).

40. Cannon, *First Ten Years,* 178–79, discusses the character of this alliance.

41. See, for instance, "Theses on the Party Factional Situation," ca. May 1927, and "Letter to the American Commission," June 16, 1927, both in *James P. Cannon and the Early Years of American Communism,* 451.

42. "Theses on the Party Factional Situation," in *James P. Cannon and the Early Years of American Communism,* 451; quoting the *Daily Worker* letter, Morgan, *A Covert Life,* 66.

43. Dunne became something of a whipping boy at the 1927 American Commission. His liquidationist position on the TUEL was central to this critique, but so too was an article he had published in the *Daily Worker,* March 24, 1927, in which he differentiated personnel within the AFL labor bureaucracy, seemingly favoring William Green over Mathew Woll. Cannon stated before the American Commission that he had voted against Dunne within party committees "on all these points upon which comrade Dunne is criticized." Cannon's distancing himself from Dunne at this time might well have strained relations between them. See unsigned circular, Cannon group, "Report from Moscow," June 26, 1927, and transcripts of Cannon's remarks before American Commission, "Lovestone Faction an Obstacle to Party Unity," n.d. (June 1927), both in *James P. Cannon and the Early Years of American Communism,* 470; Minutes of the Political Committee, April 25, 1927, Reel 1h, Russian Center, PRL. For the actual critique of Dunne, see, "Resolution on the American Question," Final Text, Endorsed by the Presidium of ECCI, July 1, 1927, 5, Roll 2, R 3345, in MS Papers.

44. See Jim, Bill, and Will Cablegram, 28 June 1927, in Dear Comrades circular, June 29, 1927, Reel 5, Russian Center, PRL.

45. See, for instance, Leon Trotsky, *Problems of the Chinese Revolution* (Ann Arbor: University of Michigan Press, 1967); Jean Chesneaux, *The Chinese Labor Movement, 1919–1927* (Stanford, CA: Stanford University Press, 1968), esp. 237–412; Wang Fan-hsi, *Chinese Revolutionary: Memoirs, 1919–1949*, trans. and intro. Gregor Benton (Oxford: Oxford University Press, 1980); unsigned circular, Cannon group, June 27, 1927, "Report from Moscow," and transcripts of Cannon's remarks to the American Commission, "Lovestone Faction an Obstacle to Party Unity," n.d. (June 1927), both in *James P. Cannon and the Early Years of American Communism*, esp. 455, 463. For the Lovestone group's perspective on Trotsky, China, and other issues of central concern to the Comintern, see the later statement of Bertram D. Wolfe, Director, National Agit-prop Department, Workers (Communist) Party of America, "Speaker's Outline for Discussion of the Controversy in the Communist Party of the Soviet Union," Roll 2, Reel 3345, MS Papers. This document was originally presented to a February 1928 CEC plenum of the Workers (Communist) Party.

46. Cannon, *First Ten Years*, 170–72; Gitlow, *I Confess*, 429–31; Morgan, *A Covert Life*, 68–69; unsigned circular, Cannon group, June 26, 1927, "Report from Moscow," in *James P. Cannon and the Early Years of American Communism*, 452–60, original in Roll 2, R 3345, MS Papers.

47. See the transcripts of Cannon's statements in "Lovestone Faction an Obstacle," in *James P. Cannon and the Early Years of American Communism*, 461–70. For the Foster group's assessment of the Cannon group, see Dear Comrade (n.d., 1927), commencing "The following is an analysis of the last Plenum. . . . Four outstanding features characterize the Plenum. . . . 3. The political bankruptcy of the Cannon group and its right wing inclinations," in Roll 2, R 3345, MS Papers.

48. "The Resolution of the Comintern on the American Question," Endorsed by the Presidium of the Executive Committee of the Communist International, July 1, 1927, reprinted in *Daily Worker*, August 3, 1927; summarized in Draper, *American Communism and Soviet Russian*, 259–61; and conveyed originally to the Cannon-Weinstone-Foster bloc supporters in the United States in National Committee Opposition Bloc to Dear Comrades, 1 July 1927, Reel 5, Russian Center, PRL, a copy of which is also in Roll 2, R 3345, MS Papers. See, as well, "Resolution on the American Question," Final Text, Endorsed by Presidium of the ECCI, July 1, 1927, in Roll 2, R 3345, MS Papers. For positive comment on the Cannon-Weinstone-Foster bloc, accenting Cannon's repudiation of Lovestone and trajectory away from Foster, see Herbert Benjamin, "Outline of Unpublished Manuscript: A History of the Unemployed Movement and Its Struggles During the Great Depression," n.d. (1970s?), 107–10, deposited in Columbia Oral History Project, Columbia University, New York, New York.

49. Draper, *American Communism and Soviet Russia*, 261; "Agreement for the Carrying Out of the Resolution on the American Question Adopted by the Presidium of the Executive Committee of the Comintern," n.d. (July 1927), signed by Lovestone, Gitlow, Pepper, Cannon, Foster, Weinstone, and Braun (Ewert); and Foster, Cannon, Weinstone,

"Declaration," July 7, 1927, in Reel 5, Russian Center, PRL. The Ewert statement on buffer groups is in "Report from Moscow," in *James P. Cannon and the Early Years of American Communism*, 454; see, as well, Cannon, *First Ten Years*, 179, 182. An earlier draft appears in "Letter Signed by Cannon Caucus," n.d. (July 1927?), Reel 9, Russian Center, PRL. The "Agreement for the Carrying Out of the Resolution of the American Question," is also in Roll 2, Reel 3345, MS Papers.

50. Cannon, *First Ten Years*, 172–73, 155–57. See also Arne Swabeck, unpublished, unititled, and unpaginated typescript, chap. 10.

51. On the preceding paragraphs, see National Committee Opposition Bloc to Dear Comrades, 1 July 1927; undated circular, Dear Comrades, containing cablegrams from Opposition Bloc (July 1927); "Opposition Cables which circulated in mimeographed form as a Factional Statement, submitted to the PolCom by the Acting Secretary [Bedacht], and subsequently also submitted by Johnstone," n.d. (July 1927); Weinstone, Cannon, Dunne, Ballam, Abern, Swabeck, Reynolds, Gomez, "Outline of Statment on Liquidation of Factions and Unification of the Party," n.d. (July 1927); Abern et al. to Kuusinen, cablegram, n.d. (July 1927), all in Reel 5, Russian Center, PRL; "Statement of Protest Against the Unauthorized and Factional Tour of Comrade Wolfe and Impermissable Factional Attacks of Comrade Bedacht," attached to Minutes of Political Committee, June 9, 1927; Minutes of the Political Committee, July 7 & 11, 1927; "Statement by Comrades Abern, Swabeck, and Johnstone to Accompany Publication of the Second Cable from the CI," n.d. (July 1927); "Statement by Bedacht on the Three Opposition Cables Attached," n.d. (July 1927); Charles Krumbein et al., to the Political Committee of the Workers (Communist) Party of America, 12 July 1927, Attached to the Minutes of Polcom, July 14, 1927, Reel 2a, Russian Center, PRL; *Daily Worker*, July, 8–9, 12, & 30, 1927; Alexander Bittelman, "Answer to Bedacht's Charge That Foster Is Non-Marxian," n.d. (June–August 1927), in Roll 2, R 3345, MS Papers, which also contains a July 23, 1927, circular from the Cannon-Weinstone-Foster bloc, "Dear Comrades," which condemns the Lovestone group's factionalism; Cannon, *First Ten Years*, 171; Draper, *American Communism and Soviet Russia*, 262–64, with the cablegram from the Comintern chastising the National Committee of the Opposition Bloc, reprinted from *Daily Worker*, July 8, 1927; "Introduction," *James P. Cannon and the Early Years of American Communism*, 57–58; Morgan, *A Covert Life*, 69. Bittelman, "Things I Have Learned," 474, also contains Bittelman's recollection of the Trotsky-Zinoviev opposition, which he judged too strident in its attacks on Stalin and the Soviet Party (pp. 458–69).

52. Cannon, *First Ten Years*, 171–72. See as well Draper's account in *American Communism and Soviet Russia*, 264. One of the first Political Committee meetings that Cannon and Foster attended upon their return was that of July 27, 1927, in which the circulation of factional documents was a topic of heated discussion. At that meeting, and in immediate subsequent meetings where issues such as Foster's secretaryship were raised, Cannon and Foster were always outvoted four to three by the Lovestone majority. See Minutes of the Political Committee, July 27, 1927, July 28, 1927, August 4, 1927, Reel 2a, Russian Center, PRL.

53. The preceding paragraphs draw on a wide array of sources, not all cited here. But see Cannon's "Speech at the 5th National Convention of the Workers (Communist) Party, New York, 3 September 1927," Reel 5, Russian Center, PRL. The "Agreement for the Carrying Out of the Resolution on the American Question," n.d. (July 1927), signed by majority and minority representatives and Ewert (Braun, the Comintern representative), Reel 5, Russian Center, PRL, stated in clause 4 that the CEC to be elected at the 1927 convention was to have thirty-five members and "that the minority should have 13 members." As this stipulation occurred before it was possible to know which majority and minority delegates would attend the convention and vote, the only conclusion to be drawn is that the CEC's composition was determined before the convention. See, as well, Gitlow, *I Confess*, 449–50; Draper, *American Communism and Soviet Russia*, 266–67, 492–93, n. 33, which contains a list of all CEC members drawn from *Daily Worker*, September 8, 1927; Cannon, *First Ten Years*, 179, 182.

54. Minutes, Session of September 6, 1927, Reel 1h, Russian Center, PRL.

55. Draper, *American Communism and Soviet Russia*, 266–67; Minutes of Central Executive Committee, September 8, 1927, Reel 1h, Russian Center, PRL.

56. Draper's *American Communism and Soviet Russia*, 269–78, covers succinctly most of the ground addressed in these paragraphs; p. 298 addresses the issue of Panken support and the subsequent Comintern critique. See as well "Introduction," *James P. Cannon and the Early Years of American Communism*, 58–59, and 476–93; Minutes of the Political Committee, October 12, 1927; [Bill Dunne Statement], November 23, 1927; Minutes of the Political Committee, December 14, 1927; Minutes of the Secretariat, December 28, 1927, all in Reel 2a, Russian Center, PRL. Cannon's most explicit statement on the Jacob Panken affair came subsequently, at a February plenum of the CEC of the Workers (Communist) Party. See Cannon, "Workers Entering New Path of Struggle," February 5, 1928, reprinted in *James P. Cannon and the Early Years of American Communism*, esp. 485–89. Both Dunne and Swabeck commented on the Panken affair in their "Discussion at the Plenum" remarks, recorded in "Attached CEC Plenum," February 4–7, 1928, Reel 2b, Russian Center, PRL, which also contain Dunne's comments on the "anti-pus campaign." Note, for the evolution of the Lovestone-Wolfe positions, articles by Lovestone in *Daily Worker*, July 3, 1926; July 10, 1926; *Our Heritage from 1776* (New York: Workers School, 1926); Lovestone, "The Spirit of the First American Revolution," *Workers Monthly*, November 1926, 614–17; Lovestone, "More about the First American Revolution," *Workers Monthly*, January 1927, 713–15; Lovestone, "Perspectives for Our Party," *Communist* 6 (May 1927): 201–6; *Communist* 6 (June 1927): 287–94; Bertram D. Wolfe, "Whose Revolution Is It?" *Workers Monthly*, July 1926, 387–92. The Lovestonesque view of American exceptionalism undoubtedly conditioned counteranalysis. See, for instance, the preliminary draft statement, William Z. Foster, "Capitalist Efficiency, Socialism," appended to Minutes of the Political Committee, January 18, 1928, Reel 2c, Russian Center, PRL.

57. See Draper, *American Communism and Soviet Russia*, 278–90, 498, n. 19; Cannon, *First Ten Years*, 184–203. For the Political Committee discussions of the Left Opposition in the CPSU, and Cannon's voting record, see Minutes of the Political Committee,

October 7, 1927, which contain "Resolution on the Opposition of the CPSU and the Comintern"; November 16, 1927, which contain "On the Expulsion of Trotsky and Zinoviev"; November 30, 1927; December 14, 1927; June 9, 1928, all in Reel 2a, Russian Center, PRL. Quotes are from Lozovsky's "Results and Prospects of the United Front," *The Communist International,* March 1928, 146; Cannon's article, "Trade Union Questions," *The Communist,* July 1928, is reprinted in *James P. Cannon and the Early Years of American Communism,* 512–20. On "Save the Union," see Arne Swabeck, unpublished, unititled, and unpaginated typescript, chap. 11; Melvyn Dubofsky and Warren Van Tine, *John L. Lewis: A Biography* (New York: Quadrangle, 1977), 127, 130, 171; Johanningsmeier, *Forging American Communism,* 236–42; John Brophy, *A Miner's Life* (Madison: University of Wisconsin Press, 1964), 229–30. A National Save the Union Conference was scheduled by United Mine Workers of America dissidents for April 1, 1928, and Foster and others pushed for a program that would develop communist capacity to seize control of the union machinery, organize the unorganized, and secure actual leadership of the union. From March–April through August 1928, the mining situation occupied a central place in Political Commitee and other Workers (Communist) Party body discussions. See, for example, various documents and discussions appended and central to Minutes of the Political Committee, March 7, 1928, April 30, 1928, May 16, 1928, June 9, 1928, July 8, 1928, July 31, 1928, all in Reels 2c and 2d, Russian Center, PRL.

58. Cannon, *First Ten Years,* 196.

59. Note, for instance, the often ILD-influenced agitational initiatives Cannon and Abern pushed in the Political Committee from September 15, 1927 through June 27, 1928: Minutes of the Political Committee, September 15, 1927, October 12, 1927, November 2, 1927, November 30, 1927, February 21–22, 1928, April 11, 1928, April 20, 1928, June 9, 1928, June 15, 1928, June 27, 1928, July 16, 1928, July 23, 1928, in Reel 2f, Russian Center, PRL. Among the issues Cannon and Abern promoted were the cases of the Michigan communists, Lithuanian anti-Fascist organization, defense of the anthracite miners, broad party support for the ILD, and Sacco-Vanzetti memorial organizing.

60. Vaughn Davis Bornet, *Labor Politics in a Democratic Republic: Moderation, Division, and Disruption in the Presidential Election of 1928* (Washington: Spartan Books, 1964), 103–4; Johanningsmeier, *Forging American Communism,* 236–42.

61. For the Lovestone-Wolfe February CEC plenum attack on Trotsky and the Left Opposition, see "The Opposition in the CPSU," Attached CEC Plenum, February 4–7, 1928, Reel 2b; and "Resolution on the Opposition in the Communist Party of the Soviet Union, Passed at the February Plenum of the CEC, 1928," Reel 9, Russian Center, PRL.

62. As an indication of the revived Lovestone interest in the Labor Party, see Jay Lovestone, "The Labor Party Campaign," n.d. (1928), Reel 2c, Russian Center, PRL; and "Prospects for Trade Union Committee for Labor Party," an undated series of lists of potential Labor Party supporters in various districts and occupational sectors, Reel 2b, Russian Center, PRL.

63. See Minutes of the CEC Plenum, May 1928, Reel 2b, Russian Center, PRL.

64. See James P. Cannon, "Tasks Face Every Workers Party Member," *Daily Worker,* March 23, 1928; Cannon, "Our Communist Nominating Convention," *Daily Worker,*

May 23, 1928; "Third ILD Conference to Link Sacco-Vanzetti Murders with Famous Haymarket Cases," *Daily Worker*, September 27, 1927; "Militant Labor Urged by ILD to Save 'Daily,'" *Daily Worker*, September 3, 1927, reprinted as James P. Cannon, "Call for Third Annual Conference for International Labor Defense," *Labor Defender*, October 1927; Cannon, *First Ten Years*, 185, 195; Cannon, *History of American Trotskyism*, 43–47; Morgan, *A Covert Life*, 70–71; and the reprinted publications of Cannon in *James P. Cannon and the Early Years of American Communism*, 476–505.

65. Draper, *American Communism and Soviet Russia*, 293–96; Cannon, *First Ten Years*, 195–201; Cannon, *History of American Trotskyism*, 46–48; Bittelman, "Things I Have Learned," 510–14; Minutes of the Central Executive Committee Plenum, February 4–7, 1927, May 1928, Reel 2b, Russian Center, PRL; Minutes of the Political Committee, March 19, 1928, Reel 2h, Russian Center, PRL; Max Shachtman to Albert Glotzer, 20 March 1928, Reel 21, JPC Papers; Gitlow, *I Confess*, 459.

66. On Rose, women's work, and miners' relief, see "Policy on the Helper," April 1928; Porter (Wagenknect) to Stachel, 6 June 1928; Poyntz to Porter, 11 June 1928, both letters attached to Minutes of the Political Committee, June 27, 1928, all in Reel 2c, Russian Center, PRL. Note also Johanningsmeier, *Forging American Communism*, 238–39; Carl Meyerhuber, *Less Than Forever: The Rise and Decline of Union Solidarity in Western Pennsylvania, 1914–1948* (Selinsgrove, PA: Susquehanna University Press, 1987), 92–93, 100; Linda Nyden, "Black Miners in Western Pennsylvania, 1925–1931: The National Miners Union and the United Mine Workers of America," *Science and Society* 41 (Spring 1977): 78–87.

67. On Dunne and drinking, see Gitlow, *I Confess*, 419; Foley to Wolfe, 7 November 1927; Dunne to Secretariat, 8 November 1927, attached to Minutes of the Secretariat, November 30, 1927, Reel 2a, Russian Center, PRL. On O'Flaherty, who suffered a bout with alcoholism and eventually left the United States to try his hand at writing—he was a brother of the famous Irish author Liam O'Flaherty—see Tom O'Flaherty to Martin Abern, 14 July 1933, in which O'Flaherty notes that he is "still off tobacco and alcohol." This correspondence is in Box 12, Folder 14, Martin Abern Papers, Wayne State Archives of Labor History and Urban Affairs, Walter P. Reuther Library, Wayne State University, Detroit, Michigan. See, as well, Drucker, *Shachtman and His Left*, 27; Minutes of the Political Committee, February 22, 1928, July 16, 1928, Reels 2c and 2d, Russian Center, PRL. Cannon enjoyed alcohol, but his "spree" drinking, as he told Sam Gordon in the late 1920s or early 1930s, "was to get away from some insurmountable problem he didn't want to think about for a while." See Sam Gordon recollection in Les Evans, ed., *James P. Cannon As We Knew Him: By Thirty-three Comrades, Friends, and Relatives* (New York: Pathfinder, 1976), 58.

68. The personal lives of Rose and Jim in this period are opaque, but I draw upon Palmer interview with Walta and Marshall Ross, Del Mar, CA, April 18, 1996; Palmer interview with Milt Zaslow (Mike Bartel), Solana Beach, CA, April 19, 1996; Emily Turnbull, "What Walta Ross Knew of Jim and Rose's Families," typescript, November 29, 1993, Prometheus Research Library, New York, New York; *Rose Greenberg Karsner v. David Fulton Karsner*, (N.Y. Supreme Court, Manhattan, June 9, 1921 & December 9,

1921), Reel 61; and "Playday House," leaflet dated January 1930, listing Rose K. Cannon (Kindergartener), Michelle Chargin (Montessori School Teacher), and Esther E. Karsner (Sculptor), Reel 61, JPC Papers; Cannon, *First Ten Years*, 187–88.

69. Cannon's most explicit retrospective statement on his silence in this period appears in *History of American Trotskyism*, esp. 43–47.

70. For the textile sector and the International Ladies Garment Workers Union issues, see Minutes of the Political Committee, April 11, 1928, July 16, 1928; Swabeck to Gitlow, 23 July 1928, 31 July 1928; Gitlow, "Statement on the Textile Situation," August 8, 1928, all in Reels 2c and 2d, Russian Center, PRL.

71. See Minutes, National Election Campaign Committee, May 16, 1928, Reel 2e, Russian Center, PRL.

72. On Cannon's original reticence, and final statement of acceptance, with respect to the Sixth Congress, see Minutes of the Political Committee, June 13, 1928, reprinted in *James P. Cannon and the Early Years of American Communism*, 507. For the official party position on the presidential election, see Jay Lovestone, *1928: The Presidential Election and the Workers* (New York: Workers Library, 1928).

73. "Introduction," and "I Will Go to the Sixth Congress," in *James P. Cannon and the Early Years of American Communism*, 61, 506; Cannon, *First Ten Years*, 200–201; Cannon, *History of American Trotskyism*, 48–49. For the composition of the final twenty-member delegation to the Sixth Congress, see "To the Mandate Commission," Moscow, July 3, 1928, Reel 9, Russian Center, PRL. Draper, in *American Communism and Soviet Russia*, 298–99, presents this period as one in which the American oppositionists were on the rise and Lovestone in retreat, but this reads the results of the Sixth Congress backward, and while it does perhaps capture something of a mood upswing in terms of those hostile to Lovestone, it neglects to appreciate the divisions emerging between Foster and his group, and Cannon's malaise.

Chapter 11: Expulsion

1. See Theodore Draper, *American Communism and Soviet Russia: The Formative Period* (New York: Viking, 1960), 300–302; Isaac Deutscher, *The Prophet Unarmed: Trotsky, 1921–1929*, vol. 2 (New York: Oxford University Press, 1959), 425–26, 444; E. H. Carr and R. W. Davies, *Foundations of a Planned Economy, 1: 1926–1929* (Harmondsworth, UK: Penguin, 1974), 497; Fernando Claudin, *The Communist Movement: From Comintern to Cominform* (Harmondsworth, UK: Peregrine, 1977), 77; Milorad M. Drachkovitch and Branko Lazitch, "The Communist International," in *The Revolutionary Internationals, 1864–1943*, ed. Milorad M. Drachkovitch (Stanford, CA: Hoover Institution on War, Revolution, and Peace, 1966), esp. 184–87; Susan Weissman, *Victor Serge: The Course Is Set on Hope* (London: Verso, 2001), 109–36; Stephen Cohen, *Bukharin and the Bolshevik Revolution: A Political Biography* (New York: Knopf, 1973), 277; Max Shachtman, et al., *The Fate of the Russian Revolution: Lost Texts of Critical Marxism*, vol. 1, ed. Sean Matgamna (London: Phoenix Press, 1998), 24–28.

2. "The Reminiscences of Max Shachtman," 1963, Number 488, Oral History Research Office, Columbia University, New York, New York; Max Shachtman, "twenty-

five Years of American Trotskyism: Part I, The Origins of American Trotskyism," *New International* 20 (January–February 1954): 16. That Cannon was well aware of Comintern officials' disregard for buffer groups is evident in "Letter signed by Cannon Caucus," n.d. (June 1927?), Reel 9, in Documents from Russian Center for the Preservation and Study of Contemporary History, Microfilm Copies Held, Prometheus Research Library, New York, New York (hereafter Russian Center, PRL). This document is a preliminary draft of a fuller statement that is reprinted in *James P. Cannon and the Early Years of American Communism: Selected Speeches and Writings, 1920–1928* (New York: Prometheus Research Library, 1992), 452–60.

3. On Hathaway, a native-born midwestern revolutionary whose development bore some resemblance to Cannon's, see Joseph Freeman, *An American Testament: A Narrative of Rebels and Romantics* (New York: Farrar & Rinehart, 1936), 618–21.

4. James P. Cannon, *The History of American Trotskyism: From Its Origins (1928) to the Founding of the Socialist Workers' Party (1938)—Report of a Participant* (New York: Pathfinder, 1972), 47–48; James P. Cannon, *The First Ten Years of American Communism—Report of a Participant* (New York: Pathfinder, 1973), 204–8; Draper, *American Communism and Soviet Russia*, 306–7.

5. Lovestone controlled thirteen of the twenty voting delegates: Lovestone, Pepper, Engdahl, Toohey, Poyntz, Zam, Phillips, Wicks, Knutson, Fort-Whiteman, Tallentire, Weinstone, and Wolfe. The combined Cannon-Foster opposition totalled seven voting delegates: Cannon, Foster, Dunne, Bittelman, Gomez, Johnstone, and Siskind. See "To the Mandate Commission," July 3, 1928, Reel 9, Russian Center, PRL; for a typical vote lineup, see Minutes of the Meeting of the Full Delegation in Room 37, The Lux, July 20, 1928, Reel 2b, Russian Center, PRL. On the Lovestone group's hegemony entering the Sixth Congress proceedings, see Robert Hessen, ed., *Breaking with Communism: The Intellectual Odyssey of Bertram D. Wolfe* (Stanford, CA: Hoover Institute, 1990), 7.

6. The preceding paragraphs draw on Cannon, *First Ten Years*, 199–200, 206–7; *James P. Cannon and the Early Years of American Communism*, 62; Manny [Gomez] to Dear Comrades [For Marty, Max, and Arne only], Moscow, 8 July 1928, Reel 9, Russian Center, PRL; Charles Shipman [Gomez], *It Had to Be Revolution: Memoirs of an American Radical* (Ithaca, NY: Cornell University Press, 1993), 169–75; Draper, *American Communism and Soviet Russia*, 268–314; Harry Haywood, *Black Bolshevik: Autobiography of an Afro-American Communist* (Chicago: Liberator Press, 1978), 184–91, 228; Earl Browder to Theodore Draper, 16 March 1959, 25, Series III, Box 18, Earl W. Browder Papers, George Arents Research Library for Special Collections, Syracuse University, Syracuse, New York (hereafter cited as Browder Papers); Minutes of the Bureau Meeting of the American Delegation, July 16, 1928, Reel 2b, Russian Center, PRL; Ted Morgan, *A Covert Life: Jay Lovestone—Communist, Anti-Communist and Spymaster* (New York: Random House, 1999), 72–76. Cannon denied that Lovestone and others knew of any "Corridor Congress" suggestion that Stalin was moving against Bukharin (Cannon, *First Ten Years*, 208), while Draper, *American Communism and Soviet Russia*, 309, accepts Lovestone's later claim in "The Truth about the 'Corridor Congress,'" *Revolutionary Age*, December 15, 1929, that he had attempted to repudiate the hallway gossiping about

differences within the Soviet leadership. Alexander Bittelman, in "Things I Have Learned: An Autobiography," 488–90, Boxes 1–2, Collection 62, unpublished manuscript in Alexander Bittelman Papers, Tamiment Institute, New York, New York, alludes to the rumors of an internal Soviet struggle, citing anti-Bukharin feeling circulating in the Congress lobbies. Dunne claimed that upon his early arrival, he "had a fairly good idea of the situation. Bukharin's right opportunist bloc was on the way to defeat." William F. Dunne Papers, "Manuscript—History of the Communist Party," 22, Box 63, Tamiment Institute, New York, New York. See also Benjamin Gitlow, *I Confess: The Truth about American Communism* (New York: E.P. Dutton, 1940), 507; Harry Wicks, *Keeping My Head: The Memoirs of a British Bolshevik* (London: Socialist Platform, 1992), 101–5.

7. Cannon, *History of American Trotskyism*, 48–49; Cannon, *First Ten Years*, 207; Morgan, *A Covert Life*, 72–76; Minutes of the Bureau Meeting of the American Delegation, July 16, 1928, Reel 2b; Minutes of the Meeting of the Anglo-American Secretariat, July 14, 1928; "Discussion at Joint Meeting of Enlarged Anglo-American Secretariat with Bureau of American Delegation," July 23, 1928, Reel 9; Lovestone, Cannon, Petrovsky, et al., "Draft of Cable to American Party," Reel 6, Russian Center, PRL; Political Committee Minutes, July 16 & 26, 1928, Reel 2d, Russian Center, PRL.

8. Manny [Gomez] to Dear Comrades [for Marty, Max, and Arne only], Moscow, 8 July 1928, Reel 9, Russian Center, PRL. There is a rather cavalier attempt to disassociate Lovestone from some supposedly "full-flower" American exceptionalist position in Harvey Klehr and John Earl Haynes, *The American Communist Movement: Storming Heaven Itself* (New York: Twayne, 1992), 45; Harvey Klehr, "Leninism and Lovestoneism," *Studies in Comparative Communism* 8 (1974): 9. Far more useful is the brief discussion in Draper, *American Communism and Soviet Russia*, 268–81. Note, as well, the account in chapter 10 of this book.

9. The most accessible version of "The Right Danger in the American Party" appears in a five-part serialization: *The Militant*, November 15, 1928–January 15, 1929. For a summary of the Sixth Congress Lovestone-versus-Foster battle, see Irving Howe and Lewis Coser, *The American Communist Party: A Critical History (1919–1957)* (Boston: Beacon Press, 1957), 164–67. On Lovestone's 1928 presidential campaign methods, which included spending thousands of dollars to hire "professional" canvassers and urging an array of ploys to get communists on the ballot in as many states as possible, see Morgan, *A Covert Life*, 71.

10. Cannon, *First Ten Years*, 210–15; Draper, *American Communism and Soviet Russia*, 306–11; Edward P. Johanningsmeier, *Forging American Communism: The Life of William Z. Foster* (Princeton, NJ: Princeton University Press, 1994), 242–45; Gitlow, *I Confess*, 504; Minutes of Meeting of Anglo-American Secretariat, July 14, 1928, Reel 9, Russian Center, PRL; Alexander Bittelman, "Things I Have Learned," 434–35, 487–510. Bertram D. Wolfe, *A Life in Two Centuries: An Autobiography* (New York: Stein & Day, 1981), 439, has a particularly self-serving and unconvincing brief comment on "the Bittelman Rebellion." See also, Comrade Foster, July 1928 Congress of ECCI, Moscow, in Box 11, Folder 12, Martin Abern Papers, Wayne State Archives of Labor History and Urban Affairs, Walter P. Reuther Library, Wayne State University, Detroit, Michigan.

11. Cannon, *First Ten Years,* 199–215.

12. On Spector's importance, the starting point is Ian Angus, *Canadian Bolsheviks: The Early Years of the Communist Party of Canada* (Montreal: Vanguard, 1981), 179–224; William Rodney, *Soldiers of the International: A History of the Communist Party of Canada, 1919–1929* (Toronto: University of Toronto Press, 1968), includes a useful biographical note in a closing appendix. For an abbreviated intellectual history statement, see Ian McKay, "For a New Kind of History: A Reconnaissance of 100 Years of Canadian Socialism," *Labour/Le Travail* 46 (Fall 2000): 87–95. I draw more upon Canadian Securities and Intelligence Service, Access to Information Act, File of Maurice Spector, born March 19, 1898, died 1968 (hereafter cited as CSIS/Spector). (I thank Gregory S. Kealey for making this CSIS file on Spector available to me.) For a hint of Spector's public assessment of the German situation, see Maurice Spector's two-part article, "Letter of E.C.C.I. to German Communist Party," *The Worker,* November 7 & 14, 1925; and Spector, "Ebert Dies and Cheats the Gallows," *The Worker,* March 14, 1925. (I thank Ian McKay for making his notes on *The Worker* available to me.) On the Canadian Party and Trotskyism, see Tim Buck, *Thirty Years: The Story of the Communist Movement in Canada, 1922–1952* (Toronto: Progress, 1975), 67; "Jack Macdonald Joins the Left Opposition," *The Militant,* May 28, 1932; John Manley, "Moscow Rules: International and Indigenous Forces in the Formation and Implementation of the Communist Party 'Line' in Canada, 1921–1931," unpublished paper presented to the Annual General Meeting of the Canadian Historical Association, Halifax, Canada, May 30, 2003; Stewart Smith, *Comrades and Komsomolkas: My Years in the Communist Party of Canada* (Toronto: Lugus, 1993), 108; Robert J. Alexander, *International Trotskyism, 1929–1985: A Documented Analysis of the Movement* (Durham, NC: Duke University Press, 1991), 144, citing a Spector obituary, *Intercontinental Press,* September 16, 1968, 754, and drawing, in part, on an interview with Spector, Detroit, May 31, 1958. See, as well, "The Reminiscences of Max Shachtman," 150–51. To the extent that *The Worker* under Spector's editorship addressed the Left Opposition, it was very much to echo official Comintern views, or, on occasion, to reproduce opposition documents or offer statements on expulsion. This was largely a phenomenon of the last quarter of 1927, and it carried into 1928. See *The Worker,* August 6, 1927; September 17, 1927; October 15, 1927; December 3, 1927. I thus consider Draper's statement in *American Communism and Soviet Russia,* 362, relating to 1927, that "[i]n the entire Western hemisphere there was at this time only one real Trotskyist—Maurice Spector, a Canadian," an exaggeration. For more detail, see Bryan D. Palmer, "Maurice Spector, James P. Cannon, and the Origins of Canadian Trotskyism," *Labour/Le Travail* 56 (Fall 2005): 91–148.

13. Cannon's recollection of these events, and their confirmation in a Draper-Spector interview, is outlined in Cannon, *First Ten Years,* 220–21; Draper, *American Communism and Soviet Russia,* 362–67.

14. As an example of one such document, see Bolsheviks-Leninists (Opposition) of the Factories and Workshops of Moskow, "To the VI Congress of the Communist International," n.d., Reel 9, Russian Center, PRL.

15. Cannon, *History of American Trotskyism,* 49; Cannon, *First Ten Years,* 210. The publishing history in the United States of Trotsky's *Draft Program* is as follows. The

Comintern-translated portion of the entire draft, secs. 1 and 3, was read by Cannon and Spector and published in the United States as Leon Trotsky, *The Draft Program of the Communist International: A Criticism of Fundamentals* (New York: The Militant, 1929). Section 2, which contained much of relevance to the American situation, with Trotsky's critique of farmer-laborism, was unavailable for a year, appearing as *The Strategy of the World Revolution* (New York: Communist League of America, 1930). Trotsky's *The Third International After Lenin* (New York: Pioneer, 1936 [reprint, New York: Pathfinder, 1970]), finally made the complete version of the draft available more than six years later.

16. Shipman [Gomez], *It Had to Be Revolution,* 171; Arne Swabeck, unpublished, unititled, and unpaginated typescript, chap. 12, Autobiographies File, Prometheus Research Library, New York, New York; *James P. Cannon and the Early Years of American Communism,* 64; Rodney, *Soldiers of the International,* 141. Deutscher, *Prophet Unarmed,* 443–44, notes that Stalin was dropping broad hints to foreign delegates at the Sixth Congress that indicated his willingness to initiate a rapprochement with Trotsky. Stalin's "Corridor Congress" emissaries talked about Trotsky's possible rehabilitation. It is therefore not beyond possibility that Trotsky's *Draft Program* was deliberately made available to select elements, with the purposes of both flushing out suspected Trotskyist sympathizers *and* laying the groundwork for a "left" assault on Bukharin. If this was indeed the case, Spector certainly, and possibly Cannon, would be likely targets in the Stalinist maneuvering. A number of international delegates, many of whom would become hardened in their Stalinism over the 1930s, apparently saw Trotsky's *Draft Program* and expressed their admiration for the document's Marxist analysis. Draper insists that Cannon was wrong in thinking that the Stalinist bureaucracy merely slipped up in allowing the document into select circulation. See Draper, *American Communism and Soviet Russia,* 365, 516, n. 20. For a contrasting assessment, more accepting of Cannon's views, see Sam Gordon statement in Les Evans, ed., *James P. Cannon As We Knew Him: By Thirty-three Comrades, Friends, and Relatives* (New York: Pathfinder, 1976), 55–56.

17. See Trotsky, *The Draft Program of the Communist International: A Criticism of Fundamentals* (New York: The Militant, 1929). For a discussion of Spector's Congress interventions on the war question, see Rodney, *Soldiers of the International,* 140–41. As editor of *The Worker,* Spector had been addressing the war drive since 1926. See "Locarno Brews New World War," *The Worker,* April 10, 1926; "Dominions Involved in Imperialist Wars," *The Worker,* April 10, 1926; Maurice Spector, "A.F.L. Adjunct of U.S. War Department," *The Worker,* October 29, 1927; Spector, "Soviet Delegation Proposes Total World Disarmament at Geneva Conference of Powers," *The Worker,* December 10, 1927. (My appreciation to Ian McKay for making his notes on *The Worker* and Spector's journalism available to me.) Of course, Trotsky's *Draft Program,* and especially its powerful analysis of Comintern failure in China, was a distillation of important discussion and debate within Left Opposition circles, which were never monolithic. For introductions to this context of Russian dissidence in this period, see Weissman, *Victor Serge,* esp. 74–113; Deutscher, *Prophet Unarmed,* 271–395; Roland Gaucher, *Opposition in the U.S.S.R., 1916–1967* (New York: Funk & Wagnalls, 1969), 98–122.

18. Cannon, *First Ten Years*, 210–12, 225; Cannon, *History of American Trotskyism*, 49–50; Angus, *Canadian Bolsheviks*, 207–8. Rightly or wrongly, at least one later communist commentator thought that Cannon could have achieved leadership of the party in 1928 had he abandoned principles in this moment and negotiated his way through the falling fortunes of both Lovestone and Foster. See Herbert Benjamin, "Outline of Unpublished Manuscript: A History of the Unemployed Movement and Its Struggles During the Great Depression," n.d. (1970s?), 112, interview with Roger Goodman, 1975, deposited in Columbia Oral History Project, Columbia University, New York, New York.

19. Peter Drucker, *Max Shachtman and His Left: A Socialist's Odyssey Through the "American Century"* (Atlantic Highlands, NJ: Humanities Press, 1994), 36–37; Smith, *Comrades and Komsomolkas*, 108–12.

20. For Cannon's absences, see, for instance, Minutes of the Meeting (4) of the Full American Delegation, July 21, 1928; undated note, signed Bill Dunne, Jack Johnstone (on Cannon's proxy vote); "Roll Call," undated record of voting delegation, with Cannon the only member of the group of twenty unaccounted for, Reel 2b; Dunne, Hathaway, et al., to Dear Comrades, 31 August 1928, Reel 6, Russian Center, PRL. Oddly, the Minutes of the American Delegation, August 22, 1928, and Minutes of the American Delegation, August 23, 1928, Reel 2b, Russian Center, PRL, do not record Cannon as present *or* absent, but do indicate his involvement in motions and voting. It is possible that this is the result of poor minute taking in recording Cannon's presence, or that it reflects absence but proxy votes/motions. The August 22 minutes record Cannon abstaining on a number of motions.

21. See Cannon, *History of American Trotskyism*, 50; Gitlow, *I Confess*, 508; Theodore Draper interview with Manuel Gomez, February 18, 1964, Series 3, Number 9, Theodore Draper Research Files, Robert W. Woodruff Library, Emory University, Atlanta, Georgia, cited in *James P. Cannon and the Early Years of American Communism*, 63. On the Cannon-Dunne relationship in terms of Cannon's early Trotskyist turn, see James P. Cannon to Albert Glotzer, 14 August 1929; Cannon to Glotzer, 24 August 1929; Albert Glotzer to Max Shachtman, 13 September 1929, James P. Cannon Papers, Microfilm Edition, 1994, State Historical Society of Wisconsin, Madison, Wisconsin (hereafter JPC Papers). On Spector and Neumann, see Rodney, *Soldiers of the International*, 139; Angus, *Canadian Bolsheviks*, 208; Ruth Fischer, *Stalin and German Communism: A Study in the Origins of State Policy* (Cambridge, MA: Harvard University Press, 1948), 445–46; Gitlow, *I Confess*, 436, 527. On arranged meetings between Stalin/Molotov and members of the American delegation, see Shipman [Gomez], *It Had to Be Revolution*, 172; Johanningsmeier, *Forging American Communism*, 243; Wolfe, *A Life in Two Centuries*, 459; Morgan, *A Covert Life*, 74–75; Draper, *American Communism and Soviet Russia*, 309–12; Gitlow, *I Confess*, 502–4; *Stalin's Speeches on the American Communist Party* (New York: Central Committee, Communist Party, USA, 1929). On the attacks by American Lovestoneite Harry Wicks on Cannon's drawing on Trotsky in an address before the Congress, see the account of Wicks's British namesake, Wicks, *Keeping My Head*, 102; Draper, *American Communism and Soviet Russia*, 366,

434–35, 530–31, nn. 72–73, citing Wicks, *International Press Correspondence*, August 13, 1928, 850; and H. M. Wicks, *Eclipse of October* (London: Holburn, 1958), v. Wicks would also appear before the final Political Committee hearings at which Cannon, Shachtman, and Lovestone were eventually expelled and question Cannon on his Sixth Congress speech: Political Committee Minutes, October 27, 1928, Roll 2/R3345, Max Shachtman Papers, Tamiment Institute, New York University, New York, New York (hereafter MS Papers).

22. The published version of Cannon's speech appeared in *International Press Correspondence*, August 11, 1928, and is reprinted (and dated July 25, 1928) as a transcript of that speech in "Against the Opportunism of the Lovestone Majority," *James P. Cannon and the Early Years of American Communism*, 521–25. The actual transcript of the Cannon speech, dated July 28, 1928, is in "CI Congress, 7–28–28—Comrade Cannon," Reel 6, Russian Center, PRL, and differs in the sharpness of its assault on the Lovestone leadership and in the pointedness of its conclusions, from the previously cited published versions.

23. "Discussion of the Enlarged Anglo-American Secretariat," August 17, 1928, Reel 9, Russian Center, PRL.

24. Bill Dunne, C. A. Hathaway, D. A. Gorman, Sam Don, Max Salzman, Harry Heywood [sic], Manuel Gomez to Dear Comrades, Moscow, 31 August 1928, Reel 6, Russian Center, PRL. Gitlow, *I Confess*, 508, repeats that Cannon wanted to put together a Foster-Cannon-Weinstone faction. On Foster's indications that he might be amenable to closer relations with Cannon (and Dunne) at this time, see Cannon, *First Ten Years*, 215. The Shachtman/Abern critique of Cannon's retreat into the "mass activity" of the ILD was supposedly voiced to Maurice Spector in February 1928. See Draper, *American Communism and Soviet Russia*, 363. Dunne's animosity to Cannon clearly hardened over the course of the last two weeks of August 1928. In an informal communication to Cannon group comrades (probably of August 10, 1928), Dunne detailed what he perceived to be the need for "amalgamation of the groups," and warned that "the split up condition of the opposition is a big handicap." He stressed that such division "may be easily decisive if it is not remedied at once." In addition, Dunne noted that the "tense international situation, the plots here, etc., are turning the attention away from our commission which is bad for us. It makes the leaders hard to see also." Bill to Dear Comrades, n.d. (notation of Friday 10), Reel 9, Russian Center, PRL. See, as well, Manny [Gomez] to Dear Comrades (for Marty, Max, and Arne only), Moscow, 8 July 1928, Reel 9, Russian Center, PRL, for an indication of how Cannon had certainly been bypassed in the setting of a political agenda for the combined opposition forces.

25. A later Lovestone-faction circular would claim that Foster admitted in October 1928 that "Cannon had written whole sections of the document." Such a claim, of course, served specific factional purpose. See No author to Dear Comrades, 28 November 1928, Reel 2d, Russian Center, PRL.

26. On the minority opposition's dissent from Paragraph 49 ("The International Situation and the Tasks of the Communist International") of Bukharin's Congress Theses, dealing with the United States, see "Reservations and Attack on VI Congress by

Opposition," Reel 6, Russian Center, PRL, a typescript prepared by the Lovestone faction. This associates the final opposition document with Foster and Cannon by prefacing the statement with a note that it had been tabled in the name of these comrades, although they did not appear as signatories at the bottom of the dissenting theses. Draper, *American Communism and Soviet Russia*, 312–13, 502, n. 25, indicates that in the published version of the Congress Theses, Paragraph 49 was, through renumbering, designated No. 52. See *International Press Correspondence*, November 21, 1928, 1538–39. The spearhead of the minority opposition statement was Jack Johnstone, and it was signed by Dunne, Gomez, Bittelman, Siskind, and Epstein, but not Foster or Cannon. Cannon later told Theodore Draper that he remembered nothing about the minority's protest against Paragraph 49, and downplayed its significance. See Cannon, *First Ten Years*, 210. On Bittelman's "Motion on the Statement of the British, American, Canadian, Latin American Delegations to the Congress on the Russian Question," see Minutes of American Delegation, August 23, 1928, Reel 2b, Russian Center, PRL.

27. The preceding paragraph draws upon James P. Cannon to Young, 13 August 1929; Cannon to Albert Glotzer, 14 August 1929; Cannon to Glotzer, 24 August 1929; Glotzer to Max Shachtman, 13 September 1929, Reel 3, JPC Papers; Minutes of the Political Committee of the Central Executive Committee, December 5, 1928, Reel 2e, Russian Center, PRL; Mit Gruss to Maurice Spector, 5 November 1928, Reel 6, Russian Center, PRL. There are faint suggestions of Dunne trying to bridge the chasm separating Trotskyism and the Comintern in the late 1920s with positions he developed within the American delegation discussions on the colonial question. Dunne's defeated motions stressed that the defeat of imperialism could only come through "the hegemony of the proletariat with the Communist Party at its head." See Minutes of the American Delegation, August 22, 1928, Reel 2b, Russian Center, PRL. Contrast this with the later position of Dunne, elaborated in the 1940s, in which the period of the late 1920s was associated with Trotskyist efforts to take over the Communist International and implement a "left program" of "permanent revolution . . . red imperialism . . . subjugation of the [Soviet Union] peasantry." See William F. Dunne, "Manuscript—History of the Communist Party," in Box 63, 1–2, esp. 21–23, William F. Dunne Papers, Tamiment Institute, Bobst Library, New York University, New York, New York. For one Dunne statement at the Sixth Congress, see Dunne, July 24, 1928, ECCI Sixth World Congress, Moscow, in Box 11, Folder 12, Martin Abern Papers, Wayne State Archives of Labor History and Urban Affairs, Walter P. Reuther Library, Wayne State University, Detroit, Michigan. For Dunne's stint in the Far East, see "The Red Tide in the Homeland of Genghis Khan," a report by Dunne while attending the Trade Union Congress of the Mongolian People's Revolutionary Party, in Box 29, William F. Dunne Papers, Tamiment Institute, Bobst Library, New York University, New York, New York. On Dunne's coming to favor Stalin, see Shipman [Gomez], *It Had to Be Revolution*, 172.

28. The preceding paragraphs draw on Howe and Coser, *American Communist Party*, 164–69; Draper, *American Communism and Soviet Russia*, 308–14; Morgan, *A Covert Life*, 73–76; Shipman [Gomez], *It Had to Be Revolution*, 172–73; Gitlow, *I Confess*, 502–1; Bittelman, "Things I Have Learned," 512–14; Cannon, *First Ten Years*, 208–9; James G.

Ryan, *Earl Browder: The Failure of American Communism* (Tuscaloosa: University of Alabama Press, 1997), 35–37; Johanningsmeier, *Forging American Communism*, 243–47. For a Lovestone faction assessment, see [Weinstone?] to Johnny, 31 July 1928; for a later, rather self-serving judgment and construction of the meaning of the Sixth Congress and its aftermath, see Wolfe, *A Life in Two Centuries*, 422–41. On the Cannon-Foster group judgment, see [No Author] to Dear Comrades, 2 August 1928; Dunne and Bittelman to Dear Comrades, 1 September 1928, all in Reel 9, Russian Center, PRL. On the skirmishes in the Political Committee in New York in July and August 1928, where O'Flaherty and Gomez came under attack, see Political Committee Minutes, July 16 & 23, 1928, Reel 2d; and Harry to Manny, 10 August 1928, Reel 9, Russian Center, PRL. The Gomez case came to a head in mid-October 1928. See "Motions Adopted by Control Commission Re Case Manuel Gomez, 19 October 1928," and the lengthy discussion recorded in Political Committee Minutes, November 1, 1928, Reel 2d, Russian Center, PRL. On the mass work in the labor defense and industrial union sectors, see *James P. Cannon and the Early Years of American Communism*, 68–69, 535–58; Swabeck, unpublished autobiography, chap. 11; and a series of Political Committee Minutes, July–September 1928, Reel 2d, Russian Center, PRL. The latter also contain discussion of anti-imperialist work, headed by the then-Cannon factional figure, Gomez. See Shipman [Gomez], *It Had to Be Revolution*, 153–69. On Foster in this period, see James R. Barrett, *William Z. Foster and the Tragedy of American Radicalism* (Urbana: University of Illinois Press, 1999), 157–62.

29. On this episode of smuggling Trotsky's *Draft Program* out of the Soviet Union, on which Cannon was relatively tight-lipped throughout his life, see Sam Gordon in Evans, *As We Knew Him*, 55–56; Wicks, *Keeping My Head*, 158–59; "Reminiscences of Max Shachtman," 152–55; Shachtman, "Twenty-Five Years of American Trotskyism," 16; Rodney, *Soldiers of the International*, 141; Cannon, *First Ten Years*, 220–21; Draper, *American Communism and Soviet Russia*, 367; Cannon, *History of American Trotskyism*, 51; Alexander, *International Trotskyism*, 440; Sam Bornstein and Al Richardson, *Against the Stream: A History of the Trotskyist Movement in Britain, 1924–1938* (London: Socialist Platform, 1986); 37, 64; *James P. Cannon and the Early Years of American Communism*, 64.

30. The preceding paragraphs draw on Cannon, *First Ten Years*, 220–26, and also 15–34, which reprints Cannon's article, "The Degeneration of the Communist Party—and the New Beginning," *Fourth International* 15 (Fall 1954): 121–27; Cannon, *History of American Trotskyism*, 52; Evelyn Reed, "Rose Karsner Cannon Is Dead, a Foremost Woman Trotskyist," *The Militant*, March 18, 1968; Sam Gordon in Evans, *As We Knew Him*, 57; Shachtman, "Twenty-Five Years of American Trotskyism," 15; "Reminiscences of Max Shachtman," 152–56; Harry Ring interview with James P. Cannon, October 24, 1973, 11 (in possession of the author; hereafter Ring interview); *James P. Cannon and the Early Years of American Communism*, 66; Drucker, *Shachtman and His Left*, 36–47.

31. The preceding paragraphs draw upon Alan Wald, *The New York Intellectuals: The Rise and Decline of the Anti-Stalinist Left from the 1930s to the 1980s* (Chapel Hill: University of North Carolina Press, 1987), 113–14; E. B. Solntsev, "Lettre a Trotsky (1),

Berlin, 8 novembre 1928," *Cahiers Leon Trotsky* 7/8 (1981): 43–53; Draper, *American Communism and Soviet Russia*, 368–69; Max Eastman, *Love and Revolution: My Journey Through an Epoch* (New York: Random House, 1964), 510–15; Leon Trotsky, *The Real Situation in Russia*, trans. Max Eastman (New York: Harcourt, Brace, 1928); Albert Glotzer, *Trotsky: Memoir & Critique* (Buffalo: Prometheus Books, 1989), 160–62. Trotsky's public reconciliation with Eastman, and his explanation of why he had to denounce Eastman at the time of the publication of "Lenin's Testament," discussed briefly in chapter 10 of this book, appears in Trotsky to Nicolai Ivanovich [Muralov], Alma-Ata, 11 September 1928, reprinted in "Trotsky on Max Eastman," *New International* 1 (November 1934): 125–26. This document of Trotsky's attempted reconciliation of Eastman was worked through by Solntsev, who delivered it into Eastman's hands. Jay Lovestone would sign a copy of Trotsky's *The Real Situation in Russia* to the young Cannon supporter, Albert Glotzer, with the inscription "This book has been my *Ruination*. There is but one devil, and this Trotskyism. [Signed] Hades," and "To a former comrade, Al—To a selfish, conceited, perverted Trotskyite, from one who knows. [Signed] Jay Lovestone" (copy in possession of the author). See also Cannon, *First Ten Years*, 222; Ring interview with Cannon, April 19, 1974, 8–12; Victor Serge, *Russia Twenty Years After* (Atlantic Highlands, NJ: Humanities Press, 1996 [1937]), 101–2, 107, 109, 191, the latter page quoting a Trotsky-Serge correspondence that detailed Trotsky's being "deeply affected" by Solntsev's death.

32. On Konikow, see the extensive discussion of her history that appeared upon her death in 1946 in *The Militant*, July 13, 1946; Antoinette Konikow, "The First Trotskyist Group in New England," *Socialist Appeal*, October 22, 1938; Konikow, "Antoinette Konikow Views 50 Years of Her Activity," *Socialist Appeal*, November 5, 1938; Cannon, *First Ten Years*, 190–91; Dianne Feeley, "Antoinette Konikow: Marxist and Feminist," *International Socialist Review* 33 (January 1972): 42–46; Feeley, "Konikow, Antoinette Bucholz," in *Encyclopedia of the American Left*, ed. Mari Jo Buhle, Paul Buhle, and Dan Georgakas (Urbana: University of Illinois Press, 1992), 405; Alexander King, *Is There Life After Birth?* (New York: Simon & Schuster, 1963), 141–47. Among her publications that relate to material covered in the preceding paragraph, see *New York Call*, June 1, 1913, August 16, 1914; Konikow, "The Doctor's Dilemma in Massachusetts," *Birth Control Review* (January 1931): 21–22. Konikow's fullest statement on birth control would be *Physicians' Manual of Birth Control* (New York: Buchholz Publishing, 1931). I spell Konikow's maiden name Buchholz in light of the publisher of this account, which was labeled "For members of the Medical Profession only." Linda Gordon, *Woman's Body, Woman's Right: Birth Control in America* (New York: Penguin, 1977), 212, 232, 240, 265–69.

33. Eastman, *Love and Revolution*, 515–16; Wald, *New York Intellectuals*, 113–14; "Reminiscences of Max Shachtman," 170–75; Ring interview with Cannon, April 19, 1974, 6–12; Draper, *American Communism and Soviet Russia*, 370; Gitlow, *I Confess*, 491; Drucker, *Shachtman and His Left*, 39; Angus, *Canadian Bolsheviks*, 209; Mit Gruss to Spector, 5 November 1928, Reel 6, Russian Center, PRL.

34. The Cannon-Spector correspondence of this period was part of a documentary record burglarized from the Cannon-Karsner apartment in two separate raids, one of

December 23, 1928, in which the thieves were disturbed in the midst of their work, and another, which finished the job, on January 14, 1929. Sections of letters were reproduced in the communist press, and the correspondence itself ended up in Jay Lovestone's files and in Moscow, some of which I draw on in the preceding and following paragraphs. For the theft of documents, see Jack Stachel, "Report to the Political Committee," December 25, 1925, in *James P. Cannon and the Early Years of American Communism*, 561–71; Gitlow, *I Confess*, 491; Draper, *American Communism and Soviet Russia*, 372, 517–18, n. 39; Ring interview with Cannon, October 24, 1973, 11–13; Angus, *Canadian Bolsheviks*, 209; "A Burglary—Its Political Meaning," *The Militant*, January 1, 1929; *Daily Worker*, December 27, 1929. For reprints of segments of the correspondence, see *Daily Worker*, January 8, 1929; *The Worker* (Toronto), January 19, 1929. Quotes in the preceding paragraph from these sources as well as: Spector to Cannon, October 9 & 16, 1928; Mit Gruss to Spector, 5 November 1928, Reel 6; Spector to Cannon, 7 November 1928, Reel 9, Russian Center, PRL. Ian McKay cites Maurice Spector to James P. Cannon, 27 November 1928, Box 430, Folder, "Cannon, James," Jay Lovestone Papers, Hoover Institute on War, Revolution and Peace, Stanford University, Palo Alto, CA, listing thirteen specific sets of documents Spector brought back from Europe. See McKay, "Revolution Deferred: Maurice Spector's Political Odyssey, 1928–1941," 8, n. 22, unpublished paper presented to the Canadian Historical Association, May 2003. On Fischer and Maslow, see Franz Borkenau, *World Communism: A History of the Communist International* (Ann Arbor: University of Michigan Press, 1962); Fischer, *Stalin and German Communism*.

35. For the preceding paragraphs, see Draper, *American Communism and Soviet Russia*, 370; *Daily Worker*, October 4, 1928; "Reminiscences of Max Shachtman," 156–60; Howe and Coser, *American Communist Party*, 162–63; George Spiro, *Marxism and the Bolshevik State: Workers' Democratic World Government Versus National-Bureaucratic "Soviet" and Capitalist Regimes* (New York: Red Star Press, 1951), 172; "Statement of Cannon, Aronberg, and Costrell," *Daily Worker*, October 2, 1928; Drucker, *Shachtman and His Left*, 39; Johanningsmeier, *Forging American Communism*, 246; Barrett, *William Z. Foster*, 159–60; Cannon, *History of American Trotskyism*, 53–54; "Additional Information Concerning Trotskyist Tendencies in the American (USA) Party," For the Information of the ECCI, October 23, 1928, submitted by Engdahl; "Trotsky Opposition in the United States," submitted by Engdahl, For the Information of the ECCI, n.d. (November 13, 1928), Reel 9; Political Committee Minutes, October 16, 1928, Reel 2d, Russian Center, PRL.

36. The preceding paragraphs draw on Cannon, *History of American Trotskyism*, 52–53; Bittelman, "Things I Have Learned," 468–514; Swabeck, unpublished autobiography, chap. 12; Ryan, *Earl Browder*, 37; Drucker, *Shachtman and His Left*, 39–40; Glotzer, *Trotsky*, 22–24; Mit Gruss to Spector, 5 November 1928, Reel 6; Political Committee Minutes, Second Session, October 18, 1928, Reel 2d; Russian Center, PRL; William Z. Foster, "James P. Cannon: Renegade," unpublished manuscript (originally written for *Pages from a Worker's Life*, but not included in that volume, provided to the author by James R. Barrett).

37. These charges and the immediate and later skirmishing of the Lovestone and Foster factions are related in "For a Correct Bolshevik Line in the American Party Against the Right Danger and Against the Cannon Trotsky Opposition—Statement by the Minority of the Central Executive Committee of the Communist Party of America," n.d. (October 1928); Lovestone, "International Connections of Trotzkyism in America," n.d. (1928); "Reservations and Attack on VI Congress by Opposition: Statement October 2nd"; undated and untitled one-page document commencing, "The statement introduced by the Foster-Bittelman Opposition," all in Reel 6, Russian Center, PRL. Some of this material, from both factions, appears in *Daily Worker*, November 16, 1928. For the actual meeting, see Political Committee Minutes, October 16, 1928, Reel 2d, Russian Center, PRL. See also Cannon, *First Ten Years*, 222–23.

38. Minutes of the Political Committee, October 16, 1928, Reel 2d, Russian Center, PRL.

39. *James P. Cannon and the Early Years of American Communism*, 526, dates the hearings as October 16, 19, and 27, 1928. The transcripts of these Political Committee meetings indicate dates of October 16, 18, and 27, 1928, and in the paragraphs that follow I quote the following detailed stenographic transcripts: Political Committee Minutes, October 16, 1928, Reel 2d; October 18, 1928, First Session (#59, thirty pages); Second Session (forty-one pages), Reel 2d, Russian Center, PRL; Political Committee Minutes, October 27, 1928 (#63, thirty-four pages), Roll 2/R3345, MS Papers.

40. Political Committee Minutes, October 27, 1928, Roll 2/R3345, MS Papers.

41. The preceding paragraphs rely on the extensive stenographic reports of the Political Committee Minutes of October 1928, especially Sessions 1 and 2, in Reel 2d, Russian Center, PRL. See, as well, Cannon, *First Ten Years*, 222; Cannon, *History of American Trotskyism*, 54; "Reminicences of Max Shachtman," 161–68. For Bittelman's later qualms about expelling Cannon, see Bittelman, "Things I Have Learned," 510–11.

42. The preceding paragraphs draw on Draper, *American Communism and Soviet Russia*, 371; Cannon, *History of American Trotskyism*, 54–55; Cannon, *First Ten Years*, 223; Political Committee Minutes, October 27, 1928, Roll 2/R3345, MS Papers, which also contain a draft of the Cannon-Shachtman-Abern statement and a copy of the letter Cannon wrote to comrades on 28 October 1928, explaining the expulsion and appealing for the creation of an American Left Opposition, subsequently published in *The Militant*. Announcement in the Communist Party press was delayed for more than two weeks, until after the presidential election campaign. See *Daily Worker*, November 16, 1926, which contains the official Party position, "The Struggle Against Trotskyism and the Right Danger," as well as the Cannon-Shachtman-Abern statement to the Political Committee. For the full statement see "For the Russian Opposition!" and "Concerning Our Expulsion," *The Militant*, November 15, 1928. Cannon's final statements before the hearings acknowledged past doubts over Trotskyism, but state unequivocally that the struggle for Trotskyism is now the only course, and that the Foster opposition to Lovestone's rightward trajectory can only lead to assimilation by the very Right Danger it supposedly resists. See Cannon, "I Stand on My Record," *James P. Cannon and the Early Years of American Communism*, 526–34. For their part, the Foster-Bittelman-Aronberg

group, having done Lovestone's bidding in ridding the Communist Party of Cannon, was reduced to begging the Comintern to rectify what to them was an unacceptable outcome of the hearings they had brought into being, cabling Moscow: "Polcom Majority refuses to publish Minority statement against Trotskyism and Right Danger while at same time carries on widespread campaign against us as Trotskyites. This is part of general plan to crush minority and solidify right wing." See Foster, Bittelman, Aronberg to Plathnicky/Comintern/Moscow, 24 November 1928, Reel 9, Russian Center, PRL.

43. James P. Cannon to the Party Members, 28 October 1928, Reel 2d, Russian Center, PRL.

44. Cannon, *History of American Trotskyism*, 57.

45. Cannon, *History of American Trotskyism*, 55; "Reminiscences of Max Shachtman," 170–75.

46. James P. Cannon, *Notebook of an Agitator* (New York: Pioneer Publishers, 1958), 303.

47. Cannon, *History of American Trotskyism*, 55–58; "Reminiscences of Max Shachtman," 170–75; Draper, *American Communism and Soviet Russia*, 372; William Z. Foster, *History of the Communist Party of the United States* (New York: International 1952), 270; Gerry Allard to Shachtman, Cannon & Abern, 4 November 1928, Frederick, Colorado; Joe Giganti to Marty [Abern], 4 November 1928; Joseph Giganti to Political Committee, Workers (Communist) Party, New York, Chicago, 24 January 1929 (misdated 1928), all correspondence in Reel 9, Russian Center, PRL. Gitlow, *I Confess*, 571, estimates the number of Trotskyists drawn to Cannon in this period as about fifty. On Bordiga, see Alexander, *International Trotskyism*, 586–87; E. H. Carr, *Twilight of the Comintern, 1930–1935* (New York: Pantheon, 1982), 240–44.

48. Pepper/Swift, "Statement Proposed by Swift," n.d. (November 1928?), Reel 2d, Russian Center, PRL; Herbert Benjamin, "Outline of Unpublished Manuscript," 107–10; "Reminiscences of Max Shachtman," 176; Arne Swabeck, unpublished autobiography, chap. 13.

49. For Konikow's letter and Lovestone's remarks, see Minutes of the Political Committee, November 2, 1928, Reel 2d, Russian Center, PRL. Konikow's letter is reproduced in *James P. Cannon and the Early Years of American Communism*, 559–60, and also in *Bulletin No. 1*, December 1928, Box 11, Folder 36, Martin Abern Papers (copy also in possession of the author). Shachtman's assessment of the *Bulletin* is in Shachtman to Spector, 20 December 1928, Reel 9, Russian Center, RPL; Konikow's financial generosity is alluded to in "Reminiscences of Max Shachtman," 170–75.

50. See Minutes of the Political Committee, November 8, 1928, Reel 2d, Russian Center, PRL.

51. Executive Secretary to Elis Sulkanen, 31 October 1928; Louis Engdahl, "Trotsky Opposition in the United States, For the Information of the ECCI," n.d. (November 1928), both in Reel 9, Russian Center, PRL. For a full account of the Finnish hearing, see Minutes of the Political Committee, November 2, 1928; Elis Sulkanen, et al., "Statement of our Point of View," n.d. (November 1928), Reel 2d, Russian Center, PRL.

52. See, for instance, Secretary of the Bureau Nazionale Frazione Italia, Workers Communist Party, to Ben Gitlow, 7 November 1928; Jay Lovestone to Tom O'Flaherty, 23 November 1928; Jay Lovestone to William F. Dunne, 26 November 1928; William

Mollenhauer to Comrade Lovestone, 20 November 1928; Philip A. Raymond, 22 November 1928; George G. Saul to Comrade Gitlow, 30 November 1928; Saul to Comrade Oehler, 22 November 1928, Reel 9, Russian Center, PRL; Alex Bail to Lovestone, 2 November 1928; B. Herman to Jay Lovestone, 22 October 1928, Philadelphia; Minutes of the Political Committee, November 14, 1928; Alfred E. Goetz to Jay Lovestone, 19 November 1928; T. Radwanski to the Polbureau, 21 November 1928; Allard to Cannon, 15 November 1928; No author to Allard, 30 November 1928; Summary and excerpts of letters to Cannon/Dear Comrades from Barney Mass, Leo Kameneff, E. Greenberg, Alex Haldman, Andrew Shelly, 21 November 1928; Maria Penyaska to Dear Comrades, 22 November 1928; Max Waldman to Cannon, 11 December 1928; Mass to Cannon, 3 December 1928, Reel 2d, Russian Center, PRL.

53. Drucker, *Shachtman and His Left*, 39–40; Glotzer, *Trotsky*, 23–24; Swabeck, unpublished autobiography, chap. 13; "Reminiscences of Max Shachtman," 190–91; "Statement of Arne Swabeck and Albert Glotzer," Chicago, November 22, 1928, Reel 9; No Author to Dear Comrades [Lovestone faction circular], 28 November 1928, Reel 2d, Russian Center, PRL.

54. Drucker, *Shachtman and His Left*, 39–40; Ring interview with Cannon, October 24, 1973, 11; Cannon, *History of American Trotskyism*, 62–63; Swabeck, unpublished autobiography, chap. 13; "Reminiscences of Max Shachtman," 190–91; "Statement on Expulsion of Cannon, Shachtman, and Abern and Suspension of Comrades Skoglund, Dunne, Coover, and Votaw in the Twin City Party Membership Meeting," November 18, 1928; Carl Cowl to Cannon, 16 November 1928; Cowl to Cannon, n.d. (November 1928); Cannon to Cowl, n.d. (November 1928); Dunne et al. to Comrade Hays et al., 24 November 1928; excerpts of a letter from Cowl to Cannon, 10 December 1928; "Statement to Members of the District #9, from the Expelled Group"; Minutes of a Meeting at Skoglund's, November 17, 1928; Meeting, Headquarters, Small Committee, November 19, 1928; Reel 2d, Russian Center, PRL; Foster, *History of the Communist Party*, 270. Draper, *American Communism and Soviet Russia*, 372, suggests that all the Minneapolis Dunne brothers (that is, excepting Bill), went with Cannon in 1928. They *ended up* with Cannon, to be sure, but it appears that only Vincent Ray Dunne was expelled from the Communist Party in 1928 and played any role in the origins of Trotskyism in Minneapolis.

55. See, for an introduction only, Spector to Cannon, 31 October–1 November 1928; Mit Gruss to Spector, 5 November 1928, Reel 6; Spector to Cannon, 7 November 1928; Cables Spector to Cannon, 8, 9, 12, & 14 November 1928; No Author to F. J. Flatman, Hamilton, 20 November 1928; Cannon to Spector, 1 December 1928; Spector to Cannon, 27 November 1928, 3, 5, 6, 10, & 14 December 1928; Cannon to Spector, 20 December 1928; transcript of letter, Cannon to Cowl, n.d. (November–December 1928), Reel 2d; Meeting of the Anglo-American Secretariat, December 22, 1928, Reel 9, Russian Center, PRL; Cannon, *History of American Trotskyism*, 63; Draper, *American Communism and Soviet Russia*, 373; Smith, *Comrades and Komsomolkas*, 110–11.

Conclusion

1. As an introduction, see William Preston, Jr., *Aliens and Dissenters: Federal Suppression of Radicals, 1903–1933* (New York: Harper & Row, 1966), 35–237.

2. James P. Cannon, *The History of American Trotskyism: From Its Origins (1928) to the Founding of the Socialist Workers' Party (1938)—Report of a Participant* (New York: Pathfinder, 1972), 26. The issue of spoils has been raised implicitly with reference to new revelations from the Soviet archives relating to Moscow's material support for the early communist movement in the United States. No doubt finances were provided, most of which were clearly expended on the basic overhead of the movement: offices, press, education, propaganda, and, especially in the earliest years, considerable legal defense costs. Professional revolutionaries such as Cannon certainly had some perquisites of Left office: trips to Moscow, tours of the country, meals and accommodations bankrolled to some extent, and a professional revolutionary's wage. This, however, was hardly a lucrative enterprise, and individual gain was negligible. Any skilled worker with stable employment would have easily amassed wealth and property far in excess of those whose wages were paid by the Communist Party. On Cannon and Foster and their disdain of acquisitive individualism, see, for instance, Reba Hansen in Les Evans, ed., *James P. Cannon As We Knew Him: By Thirty-three Comrades, Friends, and Relatives* (New York: Pathfinder, 1976), 234; Carl Cannon to James Cannon, 16 December 1954, Reel 17, James P. Cannon Papers, Microfilm Edition, 1994, State Historical Society of Wisconsin, Madison, Wisconsin (hereafter JPC Papers); Edward P. Johanningsmeier, *Forging American Communism: The Life of William Z. Foster* (Princeton, NJ: Princeton University Press, 1994), 322–23, 349. On the revival of concern with "Moscow Gold," see Harvey Klehr, John Earl Haynes, and Fridrikh Igorevich Firsov, *The Secret World of American Communism* (New Haven: Yale University Press, 1995), esp. 20–31.

3. For further congruent comment on this perspective, see James R. Barrett, *William Z. Foster and the Tragedy of American Radicalism* (Urbana: University of Illinois Press, 1999), 7; Eric J. Hobsbawm, "Problems of Communist History," in Hobsbawm, *Revolutionaries: Contemporary Essays* (New York: Pantheon, 1973), 3–10; and Roger Baldwin's recollection of Cannon in Evans, *As We Knew Him*, 48–50.

4. James Boggs, Grace Lee Boggs, Freddy Paine, and Lyman Paine, *Conversations in Maine: Exploring Our Nation's Future* (Boston: South End Press, 1978), 281–82.

5. Cannon, *History of American Trotskyism*, 66–73; "The Reminiscences of Max Shachtman," 175–94, 1963, Number 488, Oral History Research Office, Columbia University, New York, New York; *The Militant*, November 15, 1928 through April 15, 1929; William F. Dunne and Morris Childs, *Permanent Counter-Revolution: The Role of the Trotskyites in the Minneapolis Strikes* (New York: Workers Library, 1934); Moissaye J. Olgin, *Trotskyism: Counter-Revolution in Disguise* (New York: Workers Library, 1935); Philip J. Jaffe, *The Rise and Fall of American Communism* (New York: Horizon, 1975), 50–52.

6. Theodore Draper, *American Communism and Soviet Russia: The Formative Period* (New York: Viking, 1960), 377–441; Irving Howe and Lewis Coser, *The American Communist Party: A Critical History (1919–1957)* (Boston: Beacon Press, 1957), 144–74; Ted Morgan, *A Covert Life: Jay Lovestone—Communist, Anti-Communist, and Spymaster* (New York: Random House, 1999), 67–104; James G. Ryan, *Earl Browder: The Failure of American Communism* (Tuscaloosa: University of Alabama Press, 1997), 37–64. For the later politics of the Lovestoneites as a Communist Opposition in the 1930s, see Robert

J. Alexander, *The Right Opposition: The Lovestoneites and the International Communist Opposition of the 1930s* (Westport, CT: Greenwood, 1981).

7. James P. Cannon, "The Problem of Party Leadership," in Cannon, *The Socialist Workers Party in World War II: Writings and Speeches, 1940–1943* (New York: Pathfinder, 1975), 374.

8. James P. Cannon to the Secretariat, for NC Majority Only, 8 February 1966, reprinted as "Don't Try to Enforce a Nonexistent Law," in James P. Cannon, *Don't Strangle the Party!* (New York: Fourth Internationalist Tendency, 1991), 9.

9. For extreme statements, often wildly inaccurate, see George Marlen, *Earl Browder: Communist or Tool of Wall Street—Stalin, Trotsky, or Lenin* (New York: George Marlen, 1937), 144–55; Marlen, "Cannon's '*Struggle for a Proletarian Party*': An Exposure of a Political Career" (New York: Leninist League, n.d. [ca. 1943]). Note, as well, Philip Selznick, *The Organizational Weapon: A Study of Bolshevik Strategy and Tactics* (Glencoe, IL: Free Press, 1960), 167–68, accenting Cannon's Leninist lack of democracy; or Tim Wohlforth, *The Struggle for Marxism in the United States* (New York: Labor Publications, 1971), 42, which sees Cannon as capable only of taking "his basic political line as something given to him from abroad."

10. The preceding paragraphs draw on James P. Cannon, "The Bolshevization of the Party," *Workers Monthly,* November 1924, 35; James P. Cannon to Noah London, 29 April 1924, Box 3, File 1, JPC Papers; James P. Cannon, "Reasons for the Survival of the SWP and for Its New Vitality in the 1960s," in Cannon, *Don't Strangle the Party!* 16–17; Harry Ring interview with Cannon, June 20, 1973, 7–8 (in possession of the author). See, as well, Pierre Frank, *The Fourth International: The Long March of the Trotskyists* (London: Ink Links, 1979), 71–122; Paul Le Blanc, "James P. Cannon and the Fourth International," in Le Blanc, ed., *Revolutionary Traditions of American Trotskyism* (New York: Fourth International Tendency, 1988), 12–15.

11. See "Al Richardson's Reply to Paul Le Blanc" in *Revolutionary History* 4 (Spring 1993): 213. See also Sam Bornstein and Al Richardson, *War and the International: A History of the Trotskyist Movement in Britain, 1937–1949* (London: Socialist Platform, 1986); Al Richardson, "Introduction," in Alfred Rosmer, *Trotsky and the Origins of Trotskyism* (London: Francis Boutle, 2002), 11–18.

12. See especially Max Shachtman, "Twenty-Five Years of American Trotskyism: Part 1: The Origins of American Trotskyism," *New International* 20 (January–February 1954): 20–23.

13. For the factional divide of 1940, arguably a crucial moment in the fracturing of Trotskyism, see James P. Cannon, *The Struggle for a Proletarian Party* (New York: Pathfinder, 1943); Sean Matgamna, ed., *The Fate of the Russian Revolution: Lost Texts of Critical Marxism,* vol. 1 (London: Phoenix Press, 1998); Leon Trotsky, *In Defense of Marxism* (New York: Pathfinder, 1942). For a discussion of Cannon cast within the Shachtmanite disparagements, see Tim Wohlforth, *The Prophet's Children: Travels on the American Left* (Atlantic Highlands, NJ: Humanities Press, 1994).

14. James P. Cannon, "A Reply to Goldman in Three Points," in Cannon, *The Struggle for Socialism in the "American Century": Writings and Speeches, 1945–1947* (New

York: Pathfinder, 1977), 186–87; and for Cannon's famous 1955 "A Note on Zinoviev," in Cannon, *The First Ten Years of American Communism—Report of a Participant* (New York: Pathfinder, 1973), 186–87.

15. Tariq Ali, *Street Fighting Years: An Autobiography of the Sixties* (London: Fontana, 1988), 246–47. Ali's book, dedicated to Ernest Mandel, repudiates Cannon's *Struggle for a Proletarian Party* as a document that "shocked his sensibilities" because it seemed little more than "the single-minded and relentless pursuit of an oppositional current within the same organization until it was defeated, demoralized and expelled." Yet, Ali expresses no concern with what the fundamental issues raised by this oppositional current (composed of Shachtman, Burnham, Abern and many others) were. He is wrong to conclude that this opposition was demoralized, although Burnham did gravitate almost immediately to the right. Shachtman went on to found the Workers' Party, hardly an act of demoralization. Furthermore, these three opposition leaders were *not* expelled by Cannon, but split of their own accord, taking with them a good deal of the resources and a not inconsiderable contingent of the personnel of the young Socialist Workers Party. The faction fight that is in part recorded in Cannon's book is of course one of the most documented such organizational contests in the history of Trotskyism and, as such, provides exemplary lessons in how arguments around principled questions are raised. This contrasts markedly with the historical practice of Stalinism and social democracy, other currents on the Left in which effort to preserve the record of revolutionary debate is taken much less seriously.

16. This is certainly how Cannon understood the meaning of the published records of the 1939–1940 faction fight, as an example of subordinating "disciplinary measures to the bigger aims of political education." See Cannon to the Political Committee, 27 June 1967, reprinted in *Don't Strangle the Party*, 22.

17. For the conduct of the 1939–1940 factional debate, see Cannon, *Struggle for a Proletarian Party*; "Reminiscences of Max Shachtman," 318–20; Peter Drucker, *Max Shachtman and His Left: A Socialist's Odyssey through the "American Century"* (Atlantic Highlands, NJ: Humanities Press, 1994), 106–43; Leon Trotsky, *In Defense of Marxism* (New York: Pathfinder, 1973), 66–67, 158, 212–13; Albert Glotzer, *Trotsky: Memoir & Critique* (Buffalo: Prometheus Books, 1989), 285–89.

18. See Prometheus Research Library, *Dog Days: James P. Cannon vs. Max Shacthman in the Communist League of America, 1931–1933* (New York: Prometheus Research Library, 2002).

19. Cannon to Ed Shaw, Jean Simon, and Reba Hansen, 12 November 1966, reprinted in *Don't Strangle the Party*, 21.

20. Paul Le Blanc, "Leninism in the U.S. and the Decline of Trotskyism," in *Trotskyism in the United States: Historical Essays and Reconsiderations*, ed. George Breitman, Paul Le Blanc, and Alan Wald (Atlantic Highlands, NJ: Humanities Press, 1986), 177–81, citing J. R. Johnson (C. L. R. James), F. Forest (Raya Dunayeveskaya), Martin Harvey (Martin Glaberman), *Trotskyism in the United States, 1940–1947: Balance Sheet* (n.p.: Johnson-Forest Tendency, August 1947), 16.

21. Boggs, Boggs, Paine, and Paine, *Conversations in Maine*, 282. Note also the recollections of Harry Braverman, who split from Cannon in the "Cochran fight" in 1952–1953, in Evans, *As We Knew Him*, 203–6.

22. Contrast, for instance, James P. Cannon, *Notebook of an Agitator* (New York: Pathfinder, 1958), Cannon, *History of American Trotskyism*, and Cannon, *First Ten Years*, with Max Shachtman, *The Bureaucratic Revolution: The Rise of the Stalinist State* (New York: Donald, 1962); C. L. R. James, *World Revolution, 1917–1936: The Rise and Fall of the Communist International* (London: Secker & Warburg, 1937); James, *The Black Jacobins: Toussaint L'Ouverture and the San Domingo Revolution* (New York: Vintage, 1963 [original 1938]); James, *Mariners, Renegades and Castaways: The Story of Herman Melville and the World We Live In* (New York: C. L. R. James, 1953); James, *Beyond a Boundary* (New York: Pantheon, 1983 [original 1963]).

23. Cannon, "Reasons for the Survival of the SWP," 15.

24. Boggs, Boggs, Paine, and Paine, *Conversations in Maine*, 287.

25. Morgan, *A Covert Life*; Drucker, *Shachtman and His Left*; Harry Ring in Evans, *As We Knew Him*, 169; James P. Cannon, "Sixtieth Birthday Speech" (1950), in Cannon, *Speeches for Socialism* (New York: Pathfinder, 1971), 257, 259.

26. Consider Cannon, "The IWW and the Red International of Labor Unions," in *James P. Cannon and the Early Years of American Communism: Selected Writings and Speeches, 1920–1928* (New York: Prometheus Research Library, 1992), 183–89.

27. See, for instance, James P. Cannon, *American Stalinism and Anti-Stalinism* (New York: Pioneer, 1947); Cannon, *The Road to Peace: According to Stalin and According to Lenin* (New York: Pioneer, 1951); Cannon, *Notebook of an Agitator*, esp. 225–41, 288–97. For a problematic New Left statement, admirable in its critique of McCarthyism, but troubling in its assimilation of the entirety of anti-Stalinism to a generalized "intelligence" service for the anti-communist witch hunt, see Ellen Schrecker, *Many Are the Crimes: McCarthyism in America* (Boston: Little, Brown, 1998), xii, 75–76, 81.

28. Prometheus Research Library, *Dog Days*.

29. Note especially Cannon, *Socialism on Trial*, a 1973 reprint of this publication containing a critique of the SWP trial strategy by Grandizo Munis, and Cannon's rejoinder; Albert Goldman, *In Defense of Socialism: The Official Court Record of Attorney Albert Goldman's Final Speech for the Defense in the Famous Minneapolis "Sedition" Trial* (New York: Pioneer Publishers, 1944). On Cannon and the original Minneapolis truckers' strike, the sources are many, but see James P. Cannon, *The Communist League of America, 1932–1934: Writings and Speeches* (New York: Monad Press, 1958), esp. 328–40; Cannon, *Notebook of an Agitator*, 75–94; Cannon, *History of American Trotskyism*, 139–68.

30. Of the work on Cannon and Trotskyism in this period, the best remains that of Alan Wald, *The New York Intellectuals: The Rise and Decline of the Anti-Stalinist Left from the 1930s to the 1980s* (Chapel Hill: University of North Carolina Press, 1987), but Wald's excellent study is more in the way of a pioneering beginning than a full-scale historical exploration. Scholars generally agree that Constance Ashton Myers, *The*

Prophet's Army: The American Trotskyists, 1928–1941 (Westport, CT: Greenwood, 1977) is unreliable and flawed, whereas Robert J. Alexander, *International Trotskyism, 1929–1985: A Documented Analysis of the Movement* (Durham, NC: Duke University Press, 1991), contains a lengthy, but encyclopedia-like, entry on United States Trotskyism. Also important are the suggestive essays in George Breitman, Paul Le Blanc, and Alan Wald, *Trotskyism in the United States: Historical Essays and Reconsiderations* (Atlantic Highlands, NJ: Humanities Press, 1996).

31. For these and other statements, see Cannon, *Struggle for Socialism*.

32. Consider much of the writing in the articles published in Cannon, *Notebook of an Agitator*.

33. James P. Cannon, *America's Road to Socialism* (New York: Pioneer, 1953), 79. I am aware of the gender-specific language utilized, but allowing for the time in which it was written and an extension of its utilization of masculine forms to the entirety of humanity, the essential argument retains validity.

34. Frank Lovell in Evans, *As We Knew Him*, 130.

35. Mari Jo Buhle, Paul Buhle, and Harvey J. Kaye, eds., *The American Radical* (New York: Routledge, 1994), contains no entry on Cannon, and James Green, *Taking History to Heart: The Power of the Past in Building Social Movements* (Amherst: University of Massachusetts Press, 2000), has no mention of Cannon, although Louise Bryant, John Reed, William Z. Foster, Big Bill Haywood, Terence V. Powderly, Harry Bridges, and many others are cited.

36. Braverman in Evans, *As We Knew Him*, 203–7; "Reminiscences of Max Shachtman," 325, 327.

37. Cannon, "Sixtieth Birthday Speech."

38. Trotsky, *In Defense of Marxism*, 178.

Index

Abern, Martin, 139, 157, 200, 204, 248–49, 358–59; Cannon's expulsion and, 327, 329–30, 334, 337–46, 348; labor defense and, 267–68, 283

African Americans, 2, 212–19

African Blood Brotherhood (ABB), 135, 157, 213–16, 218

Akron (Ohio) rubber plants, 60–67

Albany Conference for Progressive Action, 189

Aleksander, *see* Pincus Minc

Ali, Tariq, 358

Allison, Elmer T., 123, 126, 131, 137, 140, 208

Amalgamated Clothing Workers, 243, 293

Amalgamated Textile Workers, 256

amalgamation, 181, 188, 207, 255

American Civil Liberties Union, 156, 263

American exceptionalism, 1, 183, 307–8

American Federation of Labor, 18, 26, 54, 62–63, 75, 94, 99, 102, 118, 128, 230, 240, 321, 361, 464n45; antagonism with IWW, 58, 206–7; farmer-laborism and, 180, 182, 189, 223; labor defense and, 255–59; Lovestone regime and, 293, 302, 310, 312; race and, 214, 217

Americanization: of communism, 152, 155–57, 163, 171–72, 187–88, 201; of Workers' Party, 193, 299, 307, 365

American Labor Alliance, 131, 135, 137

American Negro Labor Congress (ANLC), 213–14

American Revolution, 307

Amter, Israel, 151, 157

Amtorg, 331, 343

anarchism, 1, 3, 55, 62

anarcho-communists, 1

Anglo-Russian Trade Union Unity Committee, 292

anti-capitalism, 2, 18, 50, 136, 207

anti-communism, 188–89, 230; Draper and, 8–15, 19, 109–12; pogrom of 1919–1920, 88

Anti-Fascist Alliance of North America, 273

anti-imperialism, 214–15, 320

Anti-Imperialist League, 283

anti-labor legislation, 269

anti-lynching campaigns, 219

anti-racism, 212, 219

anti-radicalism, 180

anti-red dragnet, 109–12

anti-Semitism, 236

anti-Stalinism, 364, 372n7

anti-Trotskyism, 5–6, 226, 231–32, 237, 291, 323, 336–38, 347

anti-war movement, 7

Appeal to Reason, 1, 42, 45

Arbeiter Bildungs-Vereine, 135

Armourdale, 27, 29

Armour's packinghouse, 27, 40

Aronberg, Philip, 250, 336, 338–40

Ashkenudzie, George, 132, 141, 144

Avery Implements Works, 68

Bailey, Carl, 61

Baker, Charles, 109–10, 140, 146–47

Bakery Workers Industrial Union, 206

Baldwin, Roger, 101, 126

Ballam, John J., 132, 141–45, 155, 299, 306

Barnes, J. Mahlon, 80–81
Barrett, James R., 15
Basky, Louis, 343
Batt, Dennis E., 99, 135, 140
Bedacht, Max, 111, 171, 215, 242, 259, 264;
  Lovestone regime and, 291, 296–97, 306, 313;
  undergroundism and, 117–18, 126, 132;
  Workers' Party and, 143–45, 149, 151, 154,
  157–58, 160, 162
Bell, Tom, 288
Bellamy, Edward: *Looking Backward*, 42, 43
Belleville District Miners' Defense League,
  119–20
Benjamin, Herbert, 122, 344
Berger, Victor L., 88, 89, 102, 104,
Berkman, Alexander, 405n95
Bessemer, William "Red," 61
Billings, Warren K., 260, 263, 274, 280, 283
Bittelman, Alexander, 93–94, 104–5, 259, 264,
  326–28, 340–41, 352, 363; anti-Trotskyism
  and, 336–38; Corridor Congress and,
  318–21; factionalism and, 204–5, 210, 227,
  230, 232, 240–44, 248–50; Lovestone regime
  and, 287, 291, 296–97, 304, 307–8, 313;
  Pepper and, 169–70, 177, 190–91, 200; "The
  Right Danger in the American Party,"
  320–21, 327; undergroundism and, 113,
  130–32; Workers' Party and, 137, 140–41, 145,
  149, 154, 160
Black Belt nation thesis, 212, 216–19
black nationalism, 217
blacks, Workers' Party views on, 139, 212–19
Bloor, Ella Reeve "Mother," 80, 97, 111, 127, 131,
  275
Boggs, Grace Lee, 352, 364
Boggs, James, 352, 364
bohemians, New York, 126–27
Bolshevik Revolution, *see* Russian Revolution
Bolsheviks, 5, 16, 18, 117, 122, 224, 353; Goose
  Caucus and, 154–55, 159, 163–64; Pepper
  and, 170, 173, 175–76
Bolshevism, 4, 9, 91, 93, 235, 260, 357;
  monolithic, 6; United States, 17, 87, 93–94,
  98, 133; vs. Stalinism, 372n12
Bolshevization, 5–6, 299, 307, 357,
  473nn105,110; electoral campaigning and,
  229–31; factionalism and 227–28, 233; labor
  defense and, 252–55; Stalinism and, 222, 233,
  237, 244, 250
Bolton (England), 24–25
Bolton Irish Land League, 25
Bordiga, Amadeo, 343

Bouck, William, 229
Boudin, Louis, 224; *The Theoretical System of
  Karl Marx*, 92
bourgeoisie, 223–25, 226–27, 229
bourgeoisification, 302, 307–8
Brace, Donald, 331
Braverman, Harry, 367
Bridgman (Michigan) conference, 118–21,
  154–57, 176, 263, 421n25
Briggs, Cyril V., 157, 214, 272
British Communist Party, 375n26
Brooklyn Finnish Workers Club, 346
Brooks, John Graham, 55
Brophy, John, 311
Brotherhood of Timber Workers, 70
Browder, Earl, 16, 19–20, 75, 77, 88, 254, 287,
  295, 355, 363; Cannon's expulsion and, 318,
  321, 329; Cannon and, 94–96, 97, 106–7;
  factionalism and, 204, 232, 240; Pepper and,
  177, 178, 181, 184–86, 189; undergroundism
  and, 126, 127–28; Workers' Party and, 140,
  152, 154, 199–200
Browder, William, 88
Browderism, 10–11
Brown, William Montgomery, 268, 269
Bryan, William Jennings, 42
Bryant, Louise, 271
Buchholz, Antoinette, *see* Konikow
Buckeye, 60
Budenz, Louis Francis, 127
Buehler, A. A. "Shorty," 96, 347
Buhle, Paul, 102, 202–3
Bukharin, Nikolai, 92, 316–20, 323–25, 328,
  354–55; Comintern degeneration and, 225,
  236, 238; Lovestone regime and, 287, 289,
  292, 301, 307, 309–10; Workers' Party and,
  152, 157, 164
Bullitt, William C., 271
"bummery brigade," 56, 91
bureaucratic centrism, 220
bureaucratic utopianism, 220
bureaucratism, 150, 219–22
bureaucratization, 4, 7, 12, 14, 164, 201, 206,
  228, 351, 353, 359; Comintern and, 206,
  219–22, 231, 233, 254, 285
bureaucratized abstentionism, 308
Burman, Fahle, 193, 264, 290
Burnham, James, 358–59
business unionism, 177

Cannata, Joe, 343
Cannon, Ann (née Hackett; JPC's mother),

24, 26, 29–30, 31–32, 37, 44; death of, 39–40, 43; politics and, 42
Cannon, Agnes (JPC's aunt), 41
Cannon, Agnes (JPC's sister), 29, 31–32, 40, 41
Cannon, Carl (JPC's son), 77–78, 79, 111, 120, 133–34, 168, 195, 233, 314
Cannon, Catherine (JPC's grandmother), 25–26, 40
Cannon, Edward (JPC's half-brother), 25, 30, 31
Cannon, Emma (JPC's aunt), 41
Cannon, Frances (John Cannon's third wife), 41
Cannon, Jack (JPC's half-brother), 41
Cannon, James P.: adolescence of, 39–51; Akron strike and, 63–67, 84; alienation from IWW of, 79–80, 88–89; "America's Road to Socialism," 366; as editor of *The Toiler*, 123–26; as hobo rebel, 57–70, 77, 80; as member of the "homeguard," 77–80; as soapbox itinerant, 57–70; as trade union factionalist, 283; as Trotskyist, 336–42; birth of, 29; Bolshevism of, 91; boyhood of, 31–38; Browder and, 94–96, 97; bureaucratism and, 219–22; clandestine, 328–31; class-war prisoners and, 272–74; CLP and, 106–7, 109–12; *The Coming of the American Revolution*, 365; communist biography and Stalinism, 15–20; communist education and, 208; "Corridor Congress" and, 316–21; CP and, 16–18, 129–34; cultural criticism of, 281; debating and, 46–47, 56; diffidence of, 315; Duluth strike and, 71–75; William F. Dunne and, 250–51, 257, 327–28; early employment of, 39; early encounters with socialism of, 42–45; education of, 45–51; electoral campaigns of, 229–31; emergence of as potential communist leader, 117–21; entry into revolutionary movement of, 52; evolution from syndicalism to socialism of, 90; expulsion of, 3, 340–42, 356; factionalism and, 202–8, 210–11, 219–22, 236–51, 285–90, 297; Farmer-Labor party and, 186–88; *The Fifth Year of the Russian Revolution*, 173; "For the Russian Opposition!", 341, 353; Foster and, 188–92, 193–94, 199–201, 204, 207, 209, 212, 216, 219, 222–25, 229–30, 231, 233–34, 238–39, 241, 242, 244–46, 252, 268, 283, 299–304, 317–20, 327–29, 336; Gusev's views on, 243; "Hell Popping in Peoria," 69; ILD and, 260–71; imprisonment of, 69–71, 109–11, 113, 359;

Iron City, 32–38; IWW anticipation and, 85–86, 90–91; journalistic output of, 280–81; Kansas coal-miners' strike and, 107–9, 121; labor defense and, 254–68; legacy of, 360–64; legal communist party and, 145–51; Leninism and, 253–54; Lovestone and, 145, 170–71, 305–15, 338–42; marriage of, 71; oratorical skill of, 49–51, 130, 208; ostracism of, 78–79, 88; Peoria strike and, 67–70, 84; Pepperism and, 192–95; poetry and, 47; Political Committee hearings and, 338–44; reading and, 42, 43, 47; relationship with Max Eastman, 291–92; relationship with father, 43–44; relationship with Rose Greenberg Karsner, 195–98, 233–34, 283–84, 313–15; relationship with Lista Makimson, 48–51, 70–71, 84–85, 111, 120, 168, 195, 233–34, 314; relationship with mother, 43; religious background of, 31–32, 44; "The Renegade," 53, 82–84; Rosedale roots of, 21–38; Russian Revolution and, 91; Sacco-Vanzetti case and, 275–79; St. John and, 57–60; sexuality of, 48–49; soapbox apprenticeship and "career" of, 52–60; Soviet Union visits of, 152–65, 173, 235–39, 284, 286–90, 315–28; speaking tour of, 168–75; Spector and, 322–27; Star Casino convention and, 138–41; "Theses on the American Revolution," 365; thumb amputation of, 30; "Trails of Glory," 53, 77; "The Truth about Trotsky and the Russian Opposition," 353–54; UCP and, 118–21; Weinstone and, 299–304; women and, 47, 80–85, 208–12; *Workers' World*, 95–98; youthful rebelliousness of, 41, 47–48
Cannon, Jim (JPC's uncle), 25–27
Cannon, John (JPC's father), 24–27, 29–31, 32, 33, 36–37, 120; and death of second wife, 39–40; relationship with JPC, 43–44; socialism of, 42–43, 52; third marriage of, 41; working life of, 25–26, 29–31
Cannon, John T., *see* Jim Cannon
Cannon, Kate (John Cannon's first wife), 25–26; death of, 26
Cannon, Mary (JPC's half-sister), 25, 30
Cannon, Phillip (JPC's brother), 29, 31, 32, 41
Cannon, Ruth (JPC's daughter), 79, 111, 120, 133–34, 168, 195, 233, 314
Cannon, Thomas (JPC's half-brother), 25, 30
Carillo, Donato, 280
Centralia Seven, 280, 283
centralism, bureaucratic, 220, 222, 224, 299
Central Labor Council, 25, 94

Central Labor Union, 26

Central Trades and Labor Union of Rhode Island, 26

centrism, 152, 155

Chambers, Whittaker, 343, 386n45

Chaplin, Ralph, 86, 95, 263, 269

Charles H. Kerr publishing house, 49

chauvinism, 6

Cheka, 5

Cheyney, Ralph, 97

Chiang Kai-Shek, 325

Chicago Federation of Labor (CFL), 54, 177–78, 180–81, 184–87, 277

Chin, C. T., 214

Chinese Revolution, 6, 283, 301, 306, 325, 339

Chinese Students' Alliance, 214

Christian Century, The, 259

Christian socialism, 1, 43, 50

Citizens' Welfare League, 62, 64

civic boosterism, 28

clandestine communism, 126–28

class character, 219

class consciousness, 220

class formation, 381n2

class militancy, 93

class solidarity, politics of, 29–30

class struggle, 93–94, 138, 203, 212, 215, 307, 320, 362

Class Struggle, 92, 107

class-war leadership, 71–75

class-war prisoners, 269, 272–74, 282

Cleveland (Ohio), 121–26

Cochran, Bert, 359

Cold War, 9–10, 13–15, 18–19, 205, 359

Collar, Tilden, 315

collective leadership, 206–8, 211, 312, 327; regrouping of, 293–97

collectivism, 16–17

Comintern (Communist International/CI), 2, 3, 6, 7, 9, 11–14, 167, 169, 174, 193, 198, 199, 201, 297, 299–304, 305–6, 309, 312, 322–25, 351–55, 358; American Bureau of, 319; American Commission of, 157–58, 160–63, 169, 179, 184, 233–34, 237–39, 284, 287–90, 299–300, 320; Anglo-American Colonial Group of, 153, 320, 326; bureaucratization and, 206, 219–22, 231, 233, 254, 285; changes in, 225–28; degeneration of, 202, 235–39; Eighth Plenum of, 298, 299; Enlarged Executive Committee of, 232; Executive Committee (ECCI) of, 6, 143, 155, 159, 184, 220, 235–36, 287, 289, 322, 339; farmer-

laborism and, 175–76, 179, 182–84, 186; Fifth Congress of, 220, 222, 226–28, 357; Fifth Plenum of, 234, 236, 242; formation of, 5; Fourth Congress of, 157, 160, 182, 212, 227; Information Department of, 226; Antoinette Konikow and, 333–34; labor defense and, 261–62, 270, 273, 281; legalization of American communism and, 152–65; Lovestone and, 286–87; Negro Commission of, 217; Ninth Plenum of, 309; Presidium of, 319–21; Program Commission of, 319–20, 322–24; race issues and, 213, 215–17; "Resolution of the Comintern on the American Question," 302–4; Second Congress of, 124, 126; Seniorum Konvent of, 319–20, 328; Seventh Plenum of, 292, 296; Sixth ("Corridor") Congress of, 316–21, 323–24, 327–31, 336–37, 339; Sixth Plenum of, 251, 255, 258; Stalinization of, 18, 291–93, 299–304, 347; Third Congress of, 175, 225; Trotskyism and, 336–38; undergroundism and, 123–24, 128–29, 131–33, 141–44; Workers' Party and, 136, 138–39, 141, 150; WP factionalism and, 205, 207, 224–25, 239, 242–51

communism, American: 1, 86, 102; Americanization of, 152, 155–57, 163, 171–72, 187–88, 201; as native or foreign, 3; above-ground, 135–41; centers of new movement of, 347–48; clandestine, 126–28; development of new type of, 128–34; Draper and, 8–15; history of, 4, 7–8; legalization of, 137–65, 171; membership in, 252–53, 255; otherness of, 18; reductionist view of, 13; repression of, 109–12, 113; revolutionary, 7, 17; underground, 112, 113–34; women's commissions and, 208

Communist, The (CEC journal), 118–19, 129, 283, 306, 308, 311

Communist, The (underground journal), 141, 158

communist biography, lack of, 379n41

communist education, 208, 227–28

Communist International (Comintern/CI), *see* Comintern

Communist International, 237, 310

Communist Labor, 112, 117

Communist Labor Party (CLP), 104, 106–7, 109–12, 122, 347, 350; CP and, 114–19; Executive Committee of, 115–16

Communist League of America, 359, 365

Communist Party, French, 5

Communist Party, German, 5

Communist Party, Polish (KPP), 5, 7

Communist Party of America (CP), 2, 99, 135, 139, 142, 150, 158, 211; Cannon and, 16–18, 350; Central Executive Committee (CEC) of, 131–33, 141–43, 151, 155–56; CLP and, 114–19; dissolution of, 166; Draper and, 8–11, 14; Left Opposition, 132, 141–43; need for, 98–100; racism and, 7; Third International, 132, 143; union with UCP, 129; Unity Conference of, 116; Workers' School, 2; *see also* Communist Party, USA; Workers (Communist) Party; Workers' Party.

Communist Party of Canada, 323, 335

Communist Party of the Soviet Union, *see* Russian Communist Party

Communist Party, USA (CPUSA), 329–30, 334, 336–38, 340–41, 345–49, 355; Sixth Convention of, 355; *see also* Communist Party of the United States; Workers (Communist) Party; Workers' Party

communist studies: institutional, 9; political, 9

Conference for Progressive Political Action (CPPA), 147–48, 178, 180–83, 223, 228

Conservator, The, 197

Continental Congress of the Working Class, 54

Contreras, Carlos, *see* Vittorio Vitale

Coolidge, Calvin, 230

cooperationism, 96

co-operators, 1

Coover, Oscar, 347–48, 354

"Corridor Congress," 316–21

Costrell, H. I., 336, 340

councilism, 105

Council of People's Commissars, 319

Cowl, Carl, 348

Croatian Peasant Party, 235

Crouch, Paul, 272

Cuba, 6

Cut-Throats' Welfare League, 62

czarist autocracy, 4

Daily Worker, The, 123, 208, 210, 229, 232–33, 239, 245, 252, 259, 268–69, 271, 273, 275, 281–83, 290, 291, 300, 304, 307–8, 311, 313, 330, 336, 342

Darrow, Clarence, 45, 264, 280

David, Anna, 297

Davis, John M., 273

Dawson, Frank, 65–66

Debs, Eugene, 2, 16, 22, 89, 122, 174, 197, 264, 332; "Arouse, Ye Slaves!", 45; Cannon's early years and, 42, 45, 49, 50; Sacco-Vanzetti case and, 276, 278

DeLeon, Daniel, 54–56, 92, 332

"Democratic Centralization," 144

Democratic Party, 23, 28, 43

Dennis, Peggy, 202

Detroit Labor Council, 140

Deutscher, Isaac, 6–7

Dezettel, Max, 53–54, 75, 82–84

Dil(l) Pickle Club, 457n10

Dirba, Charles, 132, 141

Dobbs, Farrell, 40

Doree, E. F., 70, 73

Dos Passos, John, 281

Draper, Theodore, 2, 19–20, 41, 155, 234, 259, 265, 280, 290, 306; *American Communism and Soviet Russia,* 12–13, 19; "meanings" of, 8–11; *Roots of American Communism,* 12–13; three histories of, 11–15

Druso, M. A., 64

dual unionism, 207, 254, 257, 293, 312

Dubinsky, David, 294–95

DuBois, W. E. B., 223, 333

Duluth (Minnesota) dock strike, 71–75

Duluth, Mesabe & Northern Railway Company, 73

Dunne, Grant, 348

Dunne, Margaret, 315

Dunne, Miles, 348

Dunne, Vincent Ray, 40, 347–48

Dunne, William F., 97, 126, 177, 186, 189, 204, 245, 287–89, 291, 300, 326–27, 329, 363; collective leadership and, 293–96; Corridor Congress and, 317–18, 320–21; factionalism and, 241, 248–51; labor defense and, 255, 259, 264–65, 283; Lovestone regime and, 307–12, 314–15; race and, 216–18; split with Cannon, 327–28; Workers' Party and, 149, 151, 155, 200

Eastman, Eliena, 331–32

Eastman, Max, 101, 157, 159, 160, 197, 269, 291–92, 457n10; *The Real Situation in Russia,* 331, 334–35, 339, 341, 345; *Since Lenin Died,* 222, 291; "Stalin Falsifies History," 335; Trotskyism and, 331–32, 334–35, 338, 341, 343, 345, 352; *see also The Liberator*

Eberson, Esther, 197–98, 314

Ebert, Justus, 55, 77

ECCI, *see* Comintern, Executive Committee
economic expansion: 1890s, 22–23
Edwards, Forrest, 207
electoral campaigning, 229–31, 237, 279, 313, 336
Eley, Geoff, 8
Ellis, Fred, 268
Elore, 132
Emancipation of Labor, 332
Engdahl, J. Louis, 88, 131, 192, 245, 259, 310
Engels, Friedrich, 103, 118
England, 24–27
Epstein, Melech, 104
Epstein, Shachno, 460n27
espionage, 9–10
Espionage Law (1917), 88
Ettor, Joe, 70
Everett, Wesley, 117
Everhart, Max, *see* Arne Swabeck
Ewert, Arthur, 302–3
"Extreme Left," 99, 105, 124, 142, 149

factionalism, 13, 210–11, 266, 271, 292, 347, 357, 362, 365, 377n34; anti-Trotskyism and, 236–51; Bolshevization and, 229–31, 253–54; Cannon faction to end, 285–90, 297; collective leadership and, 206–8; foreign domination and, 202–6; Lore and, 224–25; Lovestone regime and, 307, 309, 311, 313, 315; Pepper and, 219–23; race and, 212, 215–18; Stalinism and, 299–300, 302–4; toll of, 280–84
Farmer-Labor Federation, 223
farmer-laborism 179, 183, 185, 222–23, 226, 230, 238–240, 295
Farmer-Labor Party, 177–88, 222–23, 226, 228, 229–31, 232, 234, 237–39
Farmers' Alliance, 23
Farmers' Mutual Benefit Association, 23
Farrington, Frank, 120
fascism, 6
Federated Commune Soviets, 123
Federated Farmer-Labor Party, 186, 189–90, 192–94, 199, 223, 230
Federated Press, 259
feminism, 1, 7, 209
Ferguson, Isaac, 103–4, 123, 126, 149, 419n16
fin de siècle context, 22–24
Finnish general strike (1905), 72
Finnish Socialist Federation, 105
Finnish socialists, 101, 132
Firestone, 60, 61

Fisher, Ruth, 335
Fitzpatrick, John, 54, 177–86, 188, 223, 231, 237, 277
Fletcher, Ben, 206–7, 213
Flynn, Elizabeth Gurley, 64, 66, 80, 264, 268
Ford, James, 216
Ford, Richard, 272
foreign-language federations, 96, 100–105, 115–16, 118, 129, 131–32, 135, 142, 151, 162, 166–67, 193, 219, 243, 300
Fort-Whiteman, Lovett, 213–14, 318
Foster, William Z., 15–20, 43, 53, 75, 86, 94, 96, 105, 118, 128, 156, 193, 290, 295, 297–98, 312, 324, 326, 340–41, 352, 355, 362–64; anti-Trotskyism and, 336–38; bloc with Cannon, 5, 46, 188–92, 193–94, 199–201, 204, 207, 209, 212, 216, 219, 229–30, 231, 233–34, 238–39, 241, 242, 244–46, 252, 268, 283, 317–21, 327–29, 336; Corridor Congress and, 319–21; factionalism and, 204–5, 210, 217, 219, 221, 226, 229–32, 235–43, 247–50, 287–88; farmer-laborism and, 177, 180, 182, 184–87; labor defense and, 254–55, 257–59, 263–65, 282; Lovestone regime and, 305–8; Pepper and, 169–71, 175; Stalinism and, 291–93, 299–304; temporary eclipse of, 321–22; TUEL and, 124, 138–39, 151–52, 254–55, 287–88, 310
Fourth International, 357, 360
Fox, Jay, 75, 255
Fraina, Louis, 91–93, 98–99, 104, 106, 126, 224; *The Proletarian Revolution in Russia*, 92; *The Revolutionary Age*, 92, 96
Fraternal Order of Eagles, 41
free love, 59, 80–82
Freeman, Joseph, 2–4, 127, 205, 352; *An American Testament*, 2
free speech, 54–57, 59, 69, 75–76, 81
Free Speech Committee, 71, 76
Freiheit, 105, 137, 154, 441n11
Friends of Soviet Russia (FSR), 198, 211, 262; Famine Scouts, 211; Women's Division of, 211
Friends of Soviet Russia and Workers Germany, 211
Fund for the Republic, 9, 13

Galleani, Luigi, 274
Garvey, Marcus, 215
gendered radicalism, 80–85, 105
George, Harrison, 87–88; *Red Dawn*, 87
German Communist Party, 322, 335

German Revolution, 5
Germany, 5, 87; fascism in, 6
Germer, Adolph, 88, 101, 102, 106
Ghent, W. H., 197
Gibson, Lydia, 214–15, 245–46
Giovannitti, Arturo, 61
Gitlow, Benjamin, 98–100, 103–4, 169, 171,
    199, 263, 265, 269, 283, 291, 294, 297–99, 305,
    310, 312, 346, 481n9; expulsion of, 355;
    factionalism and, 202–3, 225, 229, 232, 241,
    243, 247–48, 251; undergroundism and, 116,
    118, 123, 126, 130, 131; women's work and,
    208–10; Workers' Party and, 149, 151, 155–57
Gitlow, Kate, 208–10
Glassberg, Benjamin, 104
Glazer, Juliet, see Juliet Stuart Poyntz
Glotzer, Albert, 170, 200, 204, 338, 347, 455n95
Glover, Walter, 61
Gold, Ben, 276
Gold, Mike, 205, 352; Hoboken Blues, 281
Goldman, Albert, 359
Goldman, Emma, 59, 80–81, 148, 405n95
Gomez, Manuel (Charles Shipman), 283, 318,
    320, 324, 326–27, 329, 337, 340
Gompers, Samuel, 177, 180, 188, 236
Goodrich-Diamond, 60
Goodyear, 60
Goose Caucus, 142, 151–65, 169–71, 176, 181,
    201, 208, 210, 212
Goose-versus-Liquidator conflict, 154–65, 179
Gould, Jay, 28
Greater Kansas City region, 22–238
Great Southwestern Strike, 28
Greco, Calogero, 280
Green, William, 63, 66, 214
greenbackers, 23
Greenback Party, 183
Greenberg, Rose, see Karsner
Gurowsky, David, 295
Gusev, Sergei Ivanovich, 242–48, 268;
    relationship with Cannon, 247

Hackett, Ann (JPC's mother), see Ann
    Cannon
Halcro, Tom, 52–53
Hall, Otto, 214, 318
Hannan, Thomas F., 28
Hansen, Reba, 48, 52, 81
Harcourt, Alfred, 331
Harding, Warren, 147, 156
Harlem Renaissance, 216
Harrison, Caleb, 140, 145–46, 148

Hathaway, Clarence, 291, 317–18, 326–27,
    336–37, 339–40, 347–48
Hayes, Max, 178
Haymarket martyrs, 22, 88, 278–79, 307
Haynes, John Earl, 9–10, 15; The American
    Communist Movement, 9
Haywood, Harry, 214, 216–18, 318
Haywood, William D. "Big Bill," 16, 17, 57, 70,
    89, 91, 235, 281; Akron strike and, 61–62, 64,
    66; imprisonment of, 44–45; labor defense
    and, 257, 260, 262–63
Healy, Gerry, 358
Hedlund, C. R., 347–48
hegemony, 6, 260, 281
"Helper, The," 313
Hill, Joe, 77
Hillman, Sidney, 293
Hillquit, Morris, 89–90, 102, 104, 106
historiography, 8–15; revisionist vs.
    traditionalist, 377n33
Hitler, Adolf, 6, 8
hobo rebels, 55–60, 67–70, 77
Holmes, John, 105, 295
Holy Name Parish Catholic Church, 31
Holy Rollers, 56
"homeguard," 77–80
Homestead works, 22
Horthy, Admiral, 220, 231, 271
Hourwich, Nicholas I., 92, 99, 102, 104–5, 115,
    117
housewives' organizations, 7
Howat, Alexander, 108–10, 121, 123, 169, 172,
    264
Huiswoud, Otto, 157, 162, 212, 214–15, 218
Hungarian Communist Party, 220
Hungarian revolution, 175–76, 220
Hutcheson, William, 189
Hyman, Louis, 294

idealist mysticism, 155
Illinois State Federation of Labor, 121, 188
immigrant communists, 100–103
immigrant Marxists, 1
immigrant nationalism, 93
imperialism, 300–301, 305–6, 308, 320, 325
impossibilists, "red," 55
Independent Communist League, 345–46;
    Bulletin of, 345–46
individualism, 16, 23, 149
Industrial Court Law, 110
industrial frontier, 27–29
industrial organization, 50

Industrial Revolution, 24; twentieth-century, 60

industrial unionism, 54, 57, 75, 105, 119–20, 123; in Akron, 61–67; in Duluth, 71–75; in Peoria, 67–70; Russian Revolution and, 91; World War I and, 78–80

Industrial Worker, 65

Industrial Workers of the World (IWW/Wobblies), 16–19, 51, 85–86, 94, 99, 119, 123, 125, 150, 161, 167, 169, 206–7, 224, 307–8, 350, 352, 361, 364–65, 367; Akron rubber plants and, 61–67; antagonism with AFL, 58, 206–7; Bolshevism and, 87; Cannon's disillusionment with, 80–86, 88–89; Cannon's membership in, 52–86; Committee for the Red Trade Union International, 135; Defense Committee of, 272; Duluth strike and, 71–75; fragmentation of, 54; General Executive Board of, 52, 57; "great anticipation of," 85–86; Kansas City and, 75–78, 87–88; labor defense and, 254, 256–57, 260–61, 263, 265, 270, 273; Ninth National Convention of, 77, 79; Peoria strike and, 67–70; persecution of, 79, 87–88; Russian Revolution and, 91–92; Seventh National Convention of, 57; soapboxers of, 52–70; *Solidarity* newspaper, 58–59, 63, 67, 68, 77, 123, 146; Wichita case, 109; World War I and, 78–80; WP and, 207

Ingersoll, Robert G., 44

International Association of Machinists (IAM), 26–27

internationalism, 7, 16, 91, 150; proletarian, 6–7; revolutionary, 5

International Labor Defense (ILD), 18, 260, 261–68, 285, 289, 293, 305, 308, 311–12, 329–30, 334, 339–40, 346, 362; class-war prisoners and, 272–73; Executive Committee of, 264; factionalism and, 265, 280, 282–84; press and, 268–71; Sacco-Vanzetti case and, 275–80; Third Annual Conference of, 279

International Ladies Garment Workers Union (ILGWU), 105, 188, 224, 293–94, 460n27

International Red Aid (MOPR), 211, 240, 262–63, 292, 330

International Socialist Review, The, 42, 59

International Workers Defense Committee, 261

International Workers Relief/International Workers Aid, 198, 234, 262, 264

Interworld Church Movement, 124

Irish diaspora, 24–27

Irish Home Rule, 42

Iskra, 148

isolationism, 111

Isserman, Maurice, 10

Italian Defense Committee, 274

itinerant organizers, 57–60, 67–70

"I Will Win" heritage, 59

Jackson (Michigan) auto workers' strike, 58

Jakira, Abraham, 151, 171

James, C. L. R., 359–60, 364

James, Winston, 214

Jansen, Carl, *see* Charles Scott

Jefferson, Thomas, 307

Jewish Federation, 104–5, 170, 209, 232, 297

Jewish socialists, 137–38, 169–70

Johanningsmeier, Edward P., 15

Johannsen, Anton, 264

Johnson, Charles, *see* Charles Scott

Johnstone, Jack W., 157, 178, 181, 204, 248, 257, 310, 318, 320–21

joint action committee (JAC) (garment trades), 293–94

Jones, Jack, 457n10

"Jungle to Jail" movement, 69

Kamenev, Leon, 225, 236, 286, 291

Kansas, fin de siècle context of, 22–24

Kansas City (Kansas), 27–29, 40; demographics of, 27–28

Kansas City (Missouri), 75–79, 81; soapbox community of, 52–57

Kansas City revolutionary Left, 94–96

Kansas City Structural Steel, 27

Kansas coal-mining strike, 107–9, 121

Karolyi, Michael, 175

Karsner, David Fulton, 197–98

Karsner, Esther Eberson, *see* Eberson

Karsner, Rose Greenberg: personal life with Cannon, 129, 195–96, 198, 199, 201, 204, 208, 233–34, 235, 239, 283–84, 313–15; political activity, 129, 197, 208, 211, 235, 239, 240, 251, 262–65, 267, 269, 276, 330, 334, 338, 342, 343, 348

Karsner, Walta, 197–99, 233–34, 314

Katayama, Sen, 92, 158

Katterfeld, Ludwig E., 126, 129, 133, 143, 151, 154–55, 157–63, 179, 184

Kautsky, Karl, 92, 232

Keegan, "Baldy," 32

Kellogg, Frank, 271

Keracher, John, 141
Kipling, Rudyard, 47
Kirkpatrick, George R. 197; *War—What For?*, 197
Kjar, Nels, 178
Klehr, Harvey, 9–10, 15; *The American Communist Movement*, 9
Knights of Labor, 23, 25–26, 28, 30, 60
Konikow, Antoinette, 309, 332–34, 342, 344–46; *Voluntary Motherhood*, 333
Konikow, William, 332
KPP, *see* Communist Party, Polish
Kraska, George, 250
Krause, William F., 88
Krumbein, Charles, 115, 178, 184, 200, 232, 248, 250, 318
Kun, Bela, 175, 220–21, 225, 283
Ku Klux Klan, 207–8, 261, 272
Kuusinen, Ottomar V., 152, 157, 301

Labor Defender, 267, 268–72, 275–76, 278, 283, 330
labor defense, 7, 139, 254–60, 282, 305, 329; professionalization of, 260–68
Labor Defense Council, 263
Labor Defense Day, 269
"Labor Forward Movement," 94
Labor Herald, 139, 268, 289
labor movement, 25–26; oppression of, 29–30
Labor Party, 174–75, 177, 183, 239, 279; *see also* Farmer-Labor Party
labor reform, 28
Labor Unity, 275, 283
LaFollette, Robert M., 223, 226, 228–32, 235, 237–38, 453n79
LaFollette revolution, 192, 194, 223
Landler, Eugen/Jeno, 220
Larkin, Jim, 98, 100
Latvian immigrants, 102
Laukki, Leo, 72–73
Lavoratore, Il, 273
Law, Jack, 69
Lawrence (Massachusetts) textile strike, 57, 65
Lawson, Howard, 281
leadership struggles, 202–8, 210–11, 219–23, 228, 229–34, 236–51, 280–90, 292
League for Industrial Democracy, 259
Lease, Mary E., 23–24
LeBlanc, Paul, 360
Lee, Algernon, 197
Left Opposition: American, 132, 141–43,

329–30, 334–36, 338, 341, 343–44, 346–48, 354, 355–61; Trotskyist, 220, 222, 224, 226, 236, 292, 309, 312–13, 316–17, 322–25, 331–32, 334, 337, 345, 348, 361
legal communist party: development of, 141–45, 152–65
legalization, 137–41, 152–65, 171, 232
Legal Political Party (LPP), 144, 150; *see also* Workers' Party
Lenin, Krupskaya, 292
Lenin, Vladimir Ilyich, 1, 5, 13, 14, 81, 91–92, 97, 99, 117, 118, 122, 154, 158, 173, 176, 179, 183, 208, 222, 225, 227, 235, 242, 256, 292, 325, 357; *Left-Wing Communism*, 128, 142; "Letter to American Workers," 92
Leninism, 100, 125, 136, 144, 164, 207, 221–22, 224, 228, 233, 252–55, 261, 324, 348, 359–60, 364, 367; vs. Stalinism, 372n12
Leninist party, 5, 7
Leninization, 227
Lenin School, 317–18, 347
Leppert, George, 57–59, 62, 65, 70
Lever Act, 109–10, 120, 129, 140, 146
Levi, Paul, 224, 240
Lewelling, Lorenzo D., 24
Lewis, Arthur M., 44; *The Art of Lecturing*, 49
Lewis, Austin, 92
Lewis, John L., 62, 66, 108–10, 120–21, 148, 189, 207, 308, 311, 343
Lewis, Lena Morrow, 80–81
Liberator, The, 92–93, 127, 157, 169, 182, 198, 204, 225, 273, 289
Liebknecht, Karl, 117, 333
Liebstein, Jacob, *see* Jay Lovestone
Lifshutz, Dora, 178
Lincoln, Abraham, 7
Lingren, Edward I., 441n8
liquidationism, 140, 143, 151, 152, 154–55, 162, 175, 194, 201, 219, 243
Liquidators, conflict with Goose Caucus, *see* Goose Caucus
Lithuanian Workers' Literature Society, 185
Little, Frank, 16, 54, 69–70, 72–74, 84; murder of, 88; "Rebels Wanted in Duluth," 72
London, Jack, 136, 366; *The Iron Heel*, 43; *The People of the Abyss*, 43
London, Noah, 104, 191, 261, 441n11, 471n95
Loose-Wiles Company, 88
Lore, Ludwig, 92, 140, 150, 171, 191, 194, 199–200, 331–32, 460n27; factionalism and, 222, 224–25, 227, 231–32, 237, 239, 240–41, 244; Trotsky and, 224, 226–27

Lovestone, Jay (Jacob Liebstein), 14, 16, 17–18, 98, 195, 219, 233, 240–41, 242, 244, 254, 264–65, 268, 283, 285–315, 353–55, 363–64; "Against Factionalism," 311; "becoming Lovestone," 299–304; Cannon's expulsion and, 318–19, 321, 326–27, 328, 336–38, 340–41, 343–45, 347–48; combination with Cannon, 145, 170–71; coup of, 297–99; expulsion of, 355; *For a Labor Party*, 183; Pepper and, 170–72, 175, 177, 190–91, 199–201, 203–4, 206, 208, 237, 318; Political Committee hearings on Cannon, 338–44; race and, 216, 218; Ruthenberg and, 191, 199–201, 203–4, 206, 208, 213–14, 230, 234, 236–37, 248–51, 282; undergroundism and, 115, 126, 130, 131–32; Wolfe and, 317; Workers' Party and, 137, 140, 143–45, 149, 151

Lozovsky, Solomon, 138–39, 157, 164, 207, 225, 259, 287, 310–12, 321, 328, 464n45

Lukacs, Georg, 220; *History and Class Consciousness*, 220; *Tailism and the Dialectic*, 220

Lusk Committee, 129

MacDonald, Duncan, 229

Mahoney, William, 229–31

Mailey, Bertha, 197

Makimson, Lista: demise of relationship of with Cannon, 195, 233–34, 235, 314; difficulties in relationship of with Cannon, 84–85, 111, 120, 133–34, 168; early years with Cannon, 48–51, 75, 77–78; marriage of, 70–71; relationship with Tilden Collar, 315

Manley, Joe, 185–86

Mann, Tom, 97

Marine Transport Workers' International Union, 206

Martens, Ludwig C. A. K., 262

Marty, Albert, 46

Marx, Karl, 213; *Communist Manifesto*, 118

Marx-Engels Institute, 135, 140, 189

Marxian, The, 430n13

Marxism, 3, 50, 53, 55–56, 89, 91–92, 100, 117, 144, 176, 215–16, 218, 220, 222, 224, 325, 348, 360, 369

Maslow, Arkadi, 335

Masses, 101, 126–27, 197, 269, 331, 352

mass labor party, 230

Matgamna, Sean, 358

Maurer, George, 265–66

McCarthyism, 9, 359, 364, 378n35

McKay, Claude, 157–60, 212–13, 352, 439n68

McNamara, Andrew T., 263, 269

McNamara, James, 263–64

McNamara, John, 263–64

Mehring, Franz, 92

Menshevism, 93, 116, 140, 143, 154–55, 311

Mercantile and·Manufacturers' Association, 68

Merrick, John, 272

Midney, Frank, 62

Militant, The, 342–43, 346, 353

Minc, Pincus (Aleksander), 6–7

Minnesota Federation of Labor, 231

Minnesota Socialist, 197

Minnesota Union Advocate, 179

Minor, Bob, 97, 127, 132, 192, 207, 240, 307, 309, 338; race and, 213–15; Workers' Party and, 143, 148, 151, 155

Missouri, Kansas, and Texas (KT/Katy) Railroad, 40

Modotti, Tina, 274

Molotov, V. M., 326, 354

Montgomery, David, 93, 189

Mooney, Tom, 77, 95, 123, 260, 263, 274, 280, 283

Moore, Richard B., 214

Moore, Tom ("Overland Spike"), 67–70, 81

MOPR, *see* International Red Aid

Morgan, Bessie, 400n60

Morris, Mary, 330

Morris, William, 366

Morrow, Felix, 359

"Moscow authority," 228

Moscow domination, 7, 10–11, 12, 15, 180

Mothers League (Boston), 208

Mt. Marty Rosedale High School, 46–51, 75

Moyer, Charles, 17, 44–45, 260

Munzenberg, Willi, 198, 211, 269

Mussolini, Benito, 271, 273

National Committee Opposition Bloc, 304

National Farmer-Labor Party, 121

National Left-Wing Conference, 98–102

National Miners' Union, 312

Naville, Pierre, 365

Nearing, Scott, 97, 125, 167, 174, 264, 346; "The Labor Crisis in America," 125

"Negro Question," 160, 212–19, 438n61, 439n71

"Negro Workers' Congress," 214

Nelson, Steve, 14, 260

neoconservatism, 8

Neumann, Heinz, 326

Newcastle (Pennsylvania), 58–59, 64, 146

New Internationalist, The, 92

New Left, 8–12, 202
New Majority, 178, 188
New Masses, 2, 331
"New Negro," 216
New York Call, 197, 333
New York Communist, 411n26
New York Labor News, 55
Nockels, Edward, 177–78, 180–85, 188, 223, 231, 237
Non-Partisan League, 179, 181
non-partisanship, 182
Novy Mir, 102, 224
Nurse, Malcolm Meredith, *see* George Padmore

O'Flaherty, Liam, 268
O'Flaherty, Thomas, 140, 268, 283, 314, 329–30
O'Hare, Kate Richards, 42, 80
Ohio Socialist, 121–22, 423n41
Old Left, 10
Olgin, Moissaye J., 104, 137, 169–70, 191, 224, 226–27, 232
Omaha Socialist Party, 97
Oneal, James, 92, 202, 307; *The Workers in American History*, 307
"one big unionism," 88, 91, 93
Orchard, Harry, 44
Ottanelli, Fraser M., 377n34
"Overalls Brigade," 54
"Overland Spike," *see* Tom Moore
Owens, Edgar, 148

Padmore, George (Malcolm Meredith Nurse), 214
Paine, Freddy, 352, 364
Paine, Lyman, 352, 364
Palmer, A. Mitchell, 109–10
Palmer Raids, 110, 129, 138, 156, 196, 260
pan-Africanism, 214
Pancer, John, 70
Panken, Jacob, 308
Pankhurst, Sylvia, 157
Pan-Pacific Secretariat, 318
Paris Commune, 146, 269, 278
parochialism, 6–7, 31
Parsons, Albert, 264, 278
Parsons, Lucy, 264, 279, 311
Passaic (New Jersey) textile mills strike, 255–60, 272, 279, 287, 291
paternalism, 43; industrial, 25
Paterson (New Jersey) silk weavers' strike, 64, 65

patronage, 43
Patrons of Husbandry, 23
peace movement, 7
Pearl, Jeanette D., 208–10
peasant mobilization, 235
Pelling, Henry, 375n26
Pendergast, James, 43–44
Pendergast, Tom, 43–44
People's Party, 23
Peoria (Illinois), 67–70, 81
Pepper, John, 165, 188–95, 199–201, 254, 285, 302–3, 306, 310, 313, 318, 326, 328, 338, 341, 343, 347, 355, 432n25, 437nn58,59; bureaucratism and, 219–21; "The Declaration of Independence of the American Working Class," 182; emergence of, 170–72, 175–77; factionalism and, 203–4, 206, 208, 217, 224–25, 240–41, 242–43, 248; Farmer-Labor Party and, 180, 183–88, 223; Lovestone and, 170–72, 175, 177, 190–91, 199–201, 203–4, 206, 208, 237, 318; "Policies on Negro Work," 217; recall of, 225–27, 233; re-emergence of, 236–39; Ruthenberg and, 199–201, 203–4, 206, 208
Pepperism, 189, 191, 192–95; decline of, 199–201
Person, Carl E., 75
Petrovsky, G., 327
petty bourgeoisie, 223, 320
Pfeiffer, Rudolph, 68
Phillips, H. V., 214
Pilsudski nationalism, 155
Pogany, Joseph, *see* John Pepper
Polish immigrants, 102
Pope, Liston, 260
Popular Front, 10, 11
populism, 1, 3, 150; Kansas, 23–24, 27, 42
Populist Party, 183
postwar economic recovery, 147
Poyntz, Juliet Stuart, 224, 234, 240–41, 314, 460n27
Prashner, Albert B., 97
Pravda, 232
press: propaganda and, 268–71, 299; revolutionary, 96–98, 132
Prevey, Frank, 61, 397n33
Prevey, Marguerite, 61, 64, 140, 397n33
Procter & Gamble, 27
Profintern, *see* Red International of Labor Unions
progressive reform, 43
Project Kuzbas, 150, 152

proletarian internationalism, 6–7
proletarianism, 4, 204
Proletarian Party, 135, 140–41, 150
"Proletarian Rabble and Bummery," 54, 56, 91
proletarian revolt, international, 173
Proletarian Women (Detroit), 209
proto-Stalinism, 205
Providence (Rhode Island), 25–27

Rabinowitz, Matilda, 61, 64, 70, 80
race: in Kansas, 28; WP and, 212–19
racism, eradication of, 7, 215, 270, 437n61
Radek, Karl, 14, 152, 154, 157, 164, 222, 224, 227
Radic, Stejpan, 235
radicalism, American, 1–4, 16–19, 101;
    gendered, 80–85; literary, 372n7
Radosh, Ronald, 10
railroads, 22–23, 40, 147–48
Rakosi, Mathias, 271
Rand School of Social Science, 197
Red Decade (1930s), 2, 10
Red International of Labor Unions
    (Profintern/RILU), 128, 138–39, 140,
    152–54, 169, 207, 225, 287, 310; First
    Congress of, 152
"red scare," 88
Reed, John, 64, 98, 100, 116, 126, 257, 271; CLP
    and, 106–7; foreign-language federations
    and, 103–4; socialist revival and, 91, 92–93;
    Ten Days That Shook the World, 92
reformism, national, 325
Reitman, Ben, 405n95
Republican Party, 23, 28
revolutionary internationalism, 5
revolutionary leadership, 222
revolutionary socialism, 99
revolutionary subjectivity, significance of,
    364–69
Richardson, Al, 358
Right Opposition, 354
Ring, Harry, 30, 36, 58, 80, 260
Robinson, Boardman, 197
Rock Island Sash and Door Works strike, 67
Rosedale (Kansas), 16, 21–38; limits of
    socialism in, 50–51
Rosedale High School, see Mt. Marty
Rosedale Society of Debate, 46–47, 50–51
Rosenberg, Julius and Ethel, 10, 274
Rosenbliett (Rosenblit), Philip, 386n45
Rossiter, Clinton, 9
Rubicki, Steve, 178
Russell, Charles Edward, 90

Russian Communist Party (Communist Party
    of the Soviet Union), 226, 235, 310, 316, 331,
    335, 345, 354
Russian immigrants, 102
Russian Revolution, 5, 13, 17, 86, 90–94, 96, 99,
    106, 122, 127, 153–54, 198, 201, 206–7, 215, 221,
    236, 239, 260, 292, 331, 333, 351
Russian secret police (GPU), 326
Russian Socialist Workers' Federation, 100
Russification, 5
Ruthenberg, Charles E. (C.E.), 17, 61, 66,
    98–99, 103–4, 106, 189, 191, 192–94, 254,
    256–57, 259, 268, 278, 282, 290, 315, 318, 363;
    collective leadership and, 236–38, 293–97;
    death of, 297–99, 300; factionalism and,
    203–4, 206, 208–9, 219, 223, 225–26, 230, 234,
    241, 242–49, 285, 287–88; farmer-laborism
    and, 180, 183–86; labor defense and, 263–66;
    Lovestone and, 191, 199–201, 203–4, 206,
    208, 213–14, 230, 234, 236–37, 248–51, 282;
    Pepper and, 169–72, 176–77, 199–201, 203–4,
    206, 208; race and, 213–16; Stalinism and,
    291–93; undergroundism and, 114–17,
    122–23, 126, 131; Workers' Party and, 140,
    144, 146, 149–51, 156, 199–201
Rykov, Alexis I., 319

Sacco, Nicola, 123, 261, 263, 274–79, 280, 282,
    284, 298, 305, 308, 311
Sacco-Vanzetti Defense Committee, 148
Sacco-Vanzetti Emergency Committee, 276
St. John, Vincent "The Saint": 16, 57–60, 74,
    86; Akron strike and, 61, 63; Peoria strike
    and, 67, 70
Salutsky, J. B., 104, 131, 137, 170, 448n50
Salvation Army, 56
Sanger, Margaret, 223
"Save the Union" movement, 308, 310, 312
Schmidt, Matt A., 263
Scott, Charles, 169, 226
Scottsboro Boys mobilizations, 219
Seattle general strike, 93–94, 115
Sebestyen, Paul, 61
"Second Avenue intellectuals," 149
sectarianism, 102, 142, 149, 159, 179, 194, 220,
    222, 240, 271
sectionalism, 255, 302
self-determination, African American, 212,
    217–18
Serge, Victor, 316
Serrati, Giacinto Menatti, 240
Sessions, Alanson, 97

Shachtman, Max, 43, 116, 129–30, 200, 271, 280, 283, 292, 317, 327, 330, 334, 363, 365, 368; factionalism and, 204, 235, 239, 245, 248–50, 358–60; propaganda and, 268–69; Trotskyism and, 337–48

Sherman, Charles, 54

Shipman, Charles, see Manuel Gomez

shop delegates' movement, 105

Sigman, Morris, 293–95

Silver Bow Trades and Labor Council, 189

Simons, Algie M., 90

Sinclair, Upton, 174, 264; The Jungle, 43

single-taxers, 23, 55

Siskind, George, 320

Skoglund, Carl, 347–48, 354

Sloan, John, 197

Smith, Al, 229

soapboxers, 52–70, 75–76

social democracy, 3

socialism, 1, 3, 16; Christian, 44, 50; early encounters of Cannon with, 42–45; Iron Curtain, 6; limits of in Rosedale, 50–51; revolutionary, 99; utopian, 42

"socialism in one country," 6–7

Socialist Educational Society, 55

socialist humanity, 2

Socialist Labor Party (SLP), 55–56, 120, 140, 332, 350

Socialist Party of America, 2, 16, 17, 42, 54–55, 61, 68, 89–90, 94, 121, 122, 129, 135, 144, 148, 150, 167, 180, 188–89, 197–98, 212, 215–16, 229, 256, 281, 308, 326, 332–33, 350, 365; Chicago convention of, 99, 102–3, 106–7; divisions in, 100–105; emergency convention of, 99; Jewish Federation, 104–5; joining of by Cannon, 45, 50, 52; legal assault on, 88; Michigan branch of, 99; National Executive Committee of, 89, 103; Russian Federation, 99, 102, 105; Women's Commission of, 332

Socialist Party of Canada, 141, 169

Socialist Party of Great Britain, 141

Socialist Party of Kansas, Missouri, and Nebraska, 95–96

socialist reconstruction, 212

socialist revival, 89–93

Socialist Workers Party (SWP), 356–60, 366

Society for Technical Aid, The, 262

Solidarity, 58–59, 63, 67, 68, 77, 123, 146

Solntsev, Eleazer B., 331–32, 343

Sorge, Friedrich, 103

Sormenti, Enea, see Vittorio Vitale

Southwestern Interstate Coal Operators' Association, 108

Souvarine, Boris, 224

soviets, 121, 125, 181

Soviet Union, 5, 9, 11, 12, 86, 143, 148, 150, 180, 182, 203, 206, 219–22, 269, 292, 309–10, 316–21, 323–27, 364; Cannon's visits to, 152–65, 173, 175, 235–39, 284, 286–90, 315–28

Spanish Civil War, 6, 7, 273

Spector, Maurice, 291–92, 312, 334–35, 338, 348; Cannon and, 322–27, 329–30, 345–46

Speed, George, 61, 64, 70

spiritualism, 53, 83

Stachel, Jack, 250, 296, 297, 306, 308, 329, 338, 340–41, 475n127, 481n9

Staley, Eugene, 188

Stalin, Joseph, 4–7, 8, 11, 215, 221, 222, 224–26, 236, 242, 258, 287, 292, 300–301, 313, 316, 319–20, 324–26, 328, 334, 337–38, 348

Stalinism, 3, 8, 10–11, 12–15, 18–20, 164, 254, 258, 274, 286, 311, 327–28, 331, 346, 353–55, 357, 364, 366–67, 369, 378n35; definition of, 4–7; factionalism and, 202–51; Lovestone and, 299–304; vs. Bolshevism/Leninism/Trotskyism, 372n12

Stalinization, 206, 228, 291–93, 351, 353, 374n22

Star Casino convention, 136–41, 146, 148

Steimer, Mollie, 123

Steuenberg, Frank, 44

Stokes, J. Phelps, 90

Stokes, Rose Pastor, 155, 157, 208–11, 213, 438n61, 459n22

Stoklitsky, Alexander, 99, 102

Stolberg, Benjamin: Tailor's Progress, 295

strikes: Akron rubber-plant, 60–67; Boston police and telephone operators, 93; British general strike, 271, 291–92, 312; Chicago meatpacking, 93; Duluth dock, 71–75; Finnish general strike, 72; Great Southwestern, 28; Great Steel, 187; Jackson autoworkers, 58; Kansas City street railway workers, 97; Kansas coal miners, 107–9; Lawrence textiles, 57, 65; of 1922, 147–48; Ohio/Pennsylvania miners, 311–14; Passaic textile mills, 255–60, 272, 279, 287, 291, 310; Paterson silk weavers, 64, 65; Peoria, 67–70; Rock Island, 67; Seattle general strike, 93–94, 115; Superior dock strike, 71, 73; Williamson County miners, 207–8; Winnipeg general strike, 93–94

Strong, Anna Louise, 97

Suhr, Herman, 272

Sulkanen, Elis, 346
"Sullivan," 162
Sullivan, Thomas, 88
Sunday, Billy, 49
Superior (Wisconsin) dock strike, 71, 73
Supreme Revolutionary Military Council, 242
Swabeck, Arne (Max Everhart), 86, 175, 192,
    200, 204, 248, 288, 311, 329, 338, 347, 363;
    collective leadership and, 295–96; farmer-
    laborism and, 177, 178, 180–81, 184;
    Lovestone regime and, 306–9;
    undergroundism and, 115, 126, 129;
    Workers' Party and, 140, 157–58, 160, 162
Swasey, George H., 61
Swift's packinghouse, 27, 40
syndicalism, 1, 3, 53–54, 75, 94, 96, 105
Syndicalist, The, 75
Syndicalist League of North America, 53

Tammany Hall Socialism, 130, 143, 181, 229
Third Party Alliance, 223–24, 226–28
third-party formation, 178, 194, 229–30
Thomas, Norman, 229
Tippett, Tom, 352
Togliatti, Palmiro, 317
Toiler, The, 75, 121–26, 148
Tomsky, Mikhail P., 319
Topeka convention, 23
totalitarianism, 7
Trachtenberg, Alexander, 104, 131, 158, 169
Trades Union Economic League, 26
Trade Union Educational League (TUEL), 53,
    124, 194, 232, 241, 250, 300, 302, 308, 310,
    478n146; collective leadership and, 293–96;
    decline of, 223, 287–89; dual unionism and,
    254–55, 257; farmer-laborism and, 178,
    181–82, 184–85, 187; labor organization and,
    207; Needle Trades Committee of, 294;
    trade union combination and, 188–90;
    Workers' Party and, 138–39, 146, 150, 153,
    160, 174
trade unions, 1, 7, 17, 28, 54, 136, 148, 153, 157,
    167, 171–72, 201, 300, 302, 310, 313, 321, 362;
    American Commission and, 287–89;
    Cannon-Foster combination and, 188–92;
    collective leadership and, 293–95;
    factionalism and, 204, 219, 224, 232, 238–39,
    241; farmer-laborism and, 177, 180–81,
    183–84, 187; in Akron, 61–67; in Duluth,
    71–75; in Peoria, 67–70; labor defense and,
    254–60, 273, 281–83; TUEL and, 138–39;
    undergroundism and, 115, 119–20, 124–25, 129

"Tramp, The," 77–78
Traubel, Horace, 98, 197
Trautmann, William, 61, 64
Tresca, Carlo, 64, 273–74
Trotsky, Leon, 2, 5–6, 14, 89, 92, 97, 117, 152,
    160, 162, 173, 179, 183, 224, 231, 242, 273, 286,
    300, 331, 334–35, 343, 365, 369; banishment
    of, 316; The Draft Program of the
    Communist International, 323–27, 329–30,
    347–48, 353; Left Opposition and, 220, 222,
    226–27, 240–41, 309–12; Lore and, 224,
    226–27; meeting of with Cannon and
    Bedacht, 157–58, 164; Pepper and, 175–76,
    225; split of Stalin and, 235–38, 291–92;
    "Thermidorian theory" of, 337
Trotskyism, 3, 17, 19, 86, 201, 205, 237, 287,
    357–61, 367, 378n35; American Left
    Opposition and, 322–24, 329–30, 334, 348,
    353–54; American underground, 331–32;
    Communist Party repression and, 344–47;
    flushing out of, 336–42; vs. Stalinism,
    372n12
Trotsky-Zinoviev United Opposition Bloc,
    304
Truman, Harry, 44
Trumball, Walter, 272
Truth, 124
Tucker, Irwin St. John, 88
Twain, Mark, 32
Twining, Luella, 42, 80
"Two-and-a-Half" International, 232, 239
Tyler, Walter V., 58
Tyomies, 101

Uj Elore, 176
Ukrainian immigrants, 102
ultraleftism, 55, 100, 102, 162, 173, 175, 179, 194,
    201, 222; challenge to, 121–26;
    undergroundism and, 115, 128, 130, 134, 142,
    144
underground communist movement, 86,
    113–34, 176, 181, 190, 201, 210, 220, 222, 228,
    232, 271; division in, 114–17; "Emergency
    Convention" of, 142–43; liberation of,
    133–34, 136–37; Workers' Party and, 140–45,
    149, 151, 154, 159, 162–65
Undjus, Margaret, 208
unemployment, 7, 147–48, 219, 232, 316
Union Labor party, 23
United Communism, 203
United Communist Party (UCP), 118–21, 135;
    Central Executive Committee (CEC) of,

118–19, 127; Cannon and, 118–26; union with CP, 129; *see also* Communist Party

United Council of Working Class Women/Wives, 208–10

United Mine Workers' Journal, 119

United Mine Workers of America (UMWA), 121, 148, 169, 178, 217, 272, 291, 308; Kansas coal miners' strike and, 108–9; Ohio-Pennsylvania miners' strike and, 311–13, 315; Williamson County strike and, 207

United Textile Workers, 256, 258

United Toilers of America, 144–45, 150, 167, 176

United Workingmen Singers, 185

United Zinc and Chemical, 27

Universal Negro Improvement Association, 215

Urbahns, Hugo, 335

urban poverty, 25

Valetski, H., 144–45, 155, 157, 160–61, 163, 176

Vanzetti, Bartolomeo, 123, 261, 263, 274–79, 280, 282, 284, 298, 305, 308, 311

Vidale/Vidali, Vittorio, 273–74

Vietnam, 6

Voice of Labor, The, 117

Volkszeitung, New Yorker, 132, 224, 231–32, 240

Vorse, Mary Heaton, 127, 148, 208, 258, 481n9

Votaw, C. R., 348

Wagenknecht, Alfred, 98–99, 131, 151, 194, 211, 262, 313

wage slavery, 76, 213

Wald, Alan, 48

Walecki, H., *see* Valetski

Walker, John H., 121

Walling, William English, 90, 91

Ware, Clarissa, 171

War Fuel Administration, 108

Washington, George, 307

Washington Agreement, 108

Waton, Harry, 189, 430n13

Weeks, Rufus W., 197

Weinstone, William W., 126, 130, 132, 137, 140, 145, 204, 308, 320, 346, 363; bloc with Cannon, 296–99; bloc with Foster and Cannon, 299–304, 306

Weisbord, Albert, 256–60, 272, 310, 481n9

Weisbord, Vera Buch, 247, 259

Werner, G. A., 202

Western Federation of Miners (WFM), 17, 44, 57

Weston, George, 330

Wheatland riots, 76, 272

"white terror," 161, 262

Whitman, Walt, 98, 197

Whitney, Anita, 265

Whyte, Jack, 61, 64, 70

"Why We Go To Jail," 81

Wicks, Harry (British Bolshevik), 430n14

Wicks, Harry M., 141, 143, 169, 326, 430n14, 473n105

Wilentz, Sean, 10

Wilkins, Scott, 64–65

Williams, Ben, 58–59, 63, 77, 146

Williamson, John, 235, 237, 239

Wilshire's Magazine, 42

Wilson, William B., 109

Wilson, Woodrow, 87

Winnipeg general strike, 93–94

Wobblies, *see* Industrial Workers of the World

Wolfe, Bertram D., 14, 98–99, 126, 218, 241, 242, 247, 299, 306–10, 312, 317, 342, 346; expulsion of, 355

Wolfe, Ella, 242

women: as revolutionaries, 7; gendered radicalism and, 80–85; in political struggle, 7; Workers' Party views on, 139

women's rights, 75

women's work, 208–12

Worker, The, 146, 180, 191, 192–93, 322

Workers' Challenge, 143

Workers (Communist) Party, 16, 18, 252–53, 261, 270, 298, 326–28, 346, 353–54, 356, 364; class-war prisoners and, 272–73; collective leadership and, 293, 295–96; development of, 248, 251; factionalism and, 280–84; Konikow and, 332–33; labor defense and, 263–66, 268; Lovestone regime and, 305–15, 317–20; 1925 Plenum of, 257; Passaic strike and, 255–58; Stalinism and, 301–4; *see also* Communist Party of America; Communist Party, USA; Workers' Party

Workers' Council, 105, 129, 131–32, 135, 137, 140

Workers Defense Guards, 354

Workers' Dreadnaught, 157

Workers' Educational Association, *see* Arbeiter Bildungs-Vereine

Workers' Educational League, 96

Workers International Relief, 211, 262

Workers Monthly, 217, 232, 289, 306–7

Workers' Party, 3, 17, 18, 123, 160, 168–72, 174–77, 198, 199–201, 207–8, 226, 263, 363, 365; "All-Race Negro Congress" of, 213;

Workers' Party (*continued*)
Anti-Imperialist Department of, 340; anti-Trotskyism and, 231–32; Arrangements Committee of, 282; as center of American communism, 166–67; attitudes toward, 140–41; Bolshevization and, 252; Cannon-Foster combination and, 188–92; Central Control Commission of, 339–40; Central Executive Committee (CEC) of, 139–40, 146, 164, 169, 171–72, 180, 184–85, 189–93, 199, 209–12, 214, 216, 219, 221, 222, 225, 226–28, 229, 231–33, 238, 240–41, 244, 246–50, 287–90, 291–92, 294–95, 297–99, 301, 306, 309, 313, 336–37, 343–44, 347; Education Committee of, 227; Executive Council of, 164, 209, 225, 265; factionalism in leadership of, 202–8, 210–11, 219–23, 228, 229–34, 236–51, 280–90, 292; Farmer-Labor Party and, 178–88, 222–23, 228; founding of, 135–41, 153; Fourth Congress of, 238, 241; Industrial Department of, 232–33; IWW and, 206–7; Jewish Bureau of, 170, 209; Cannon and, 145–51, 154; Labor Defense Council, 156, 262; National Defense Committee of, 148, 262; Parity Commission of, 241–44, 248, 268; Pepperism and, 192–95; Political Committee of, 176, 184, 192, 230, 248–49, 265, 282–83, 290, 291–98, 305, 307, 311, 315, 338–44, 346; race issues and, 212–19; relief work and, 211–12; St. Paul conventions and, 223, 228–29, 231; Secretariat of, 171; Third Convention of, 194, 199–201, 224; Trade Union Committee of, 289, 294–95, 320; undergroundism and, 141–45; *Underground Radicalism*, 180–81; Women's Commission/Bureau of, 208; women's work and, 208–12; *see also*

Communist Party of America; Communist Party, USA; Workers (Communist) Party
workers' republic, formation of, 136
Workers' School, 227, 234
Workers' World, 95–98, 102, 106–7, 109, 111, 122, 410n26
working-class political action, 178, 183
Workingmen's Parties, 177
Workmen's Gymnastic Association, 185
Work People's College, 72
World War I, 4, 17, 53, 78–80, 87–90, 121, 175; Cannon as conscientious objector to, 78–79, 88
World War II, 6, 11
Wortis, Rose, 157, 189, 241, 294
Wyatt, Cal, 63

Young, Art, 197
Young Communist League, 156
Young People's Socialist League, 256
Youngstown Socialist, 62
Young Worker, The, 139, 200, 249
Young Workers' League, 139, 178, 200, 267; National Executive Committee of, 240, 347
youth organization, development of, 139
Yugoslav Socialist Federation, 100

Zack, Don, 481n9
Zack, Joseph, 250, 294
Zimmerman, Charles, 224, 240–41, 294
Zinoviev, Gregory, 5, 14, 129, 206, 242, 250, 309, 312, 316, 322, 333, 355, 357–58, 360; factionalism and, 220–22, 224–27, 235–36, 238, 285–86; farmer-laborism and, 176, 182–83, 194, 201; Stalinism and, 291–92; Workers' Party and, 152, 154, 157, 160, 163–64

BRYAN D. PALMER is the Canada Research Chair, Canadian Studies Program, Trent University; the editor of *Labour/Le Travail;* and the author of a number of books in social and working-class history, among them *Cultures of Darkness* and *Descent into Discourse.*

Worker City, Company Town: Iron and Cotton-Worker Protest in Troy and Cohoes,
  New York, 1855–84   *Daniel J. Walkowitz*
Life, Work, and Rebellion in the Coal Fields: The Southern West Virginia Miners,
  1880–1922   *David Alan Corbin*
Women and American Socialism, 1870–1920   *Mari Jo Buhle*
Lives of Their Own: Blacks, Italians, and Poles in Pittsburgh, 1900–1960
  John Bodnar, Roger Simon, and Michael P. Weber
Working-Class America: Essays on Labor, Community, and American Society
  Edited by Michael H. Frisch and Daniel J. Walkowitz
Eugene V. Debs: Citizen and Socialist   *Nick Salvatore*
American Labor and Immigration History, 1877–1920s: Recent European Research
  Edited by Dirk Hoerder
Workingmen's Democracy: The Knights of Labor and American Politics   *Leon Fink*
The Electrical Workers: A History of Labor at General Electric and Westinghouse,
  1923–60   *Ronald W. Schatz*
The Mechanics of Baltimore: Workers and Politics in the Age of Revolution, 1763–1812
  Charles G. Steffen
The Practice of Solidarity: American Hat Finishers in the Nineteenth Century
  David Bensman
The Labor History Reader   *Edited by Daniel J. Leab*
Solidarity and Fragmentation: Working People and Class Consciousness in Detroit,
  1875–1900   *Richard Oestreicher*
Counter Cultures: Saleswomen, Managers, and Customers in American Department
  Stores, 1890–1940   *Susan Porter Benson*
The New England Working Class and the New Labor History
  Edited by Herbert G. Gutman and Donald H. Bell
Labor Leaders in America   *Edited by Melvyn Dubofsky and Warren Van Tine*
Barons of Labor: The San Francisco Building Trades and Union Power in the
  Progressive Era   *Michael Kazin*
Gender at Work: The Dynamics of Job Segregation by Sex during World War II
  Ruth Milkman
Once a Cigar Maker: Men, Women, and Work Culture in American Cigar Factories,
  1900–1919   *Patricia A. Cooper*
A Generation of Boomers: The Pattern of Railroad Labor Conflict in Nineteenth-
  Century America   *Shelton Stromquist*
Work and Community in the Jungle: Chicago's Packinghouse Workers, 1894–1922
  James R. Barrett
Workers, Managers, and Welfare Capitalism: The Shoeworkers and Tanners of Endicott
  Johnson, 1890–1950   *Gerald Zahavi*
Men, Women, and Work: Class, Gender, and Protest in the New England Shoe
  Industry, 1780–1910   *Mary Blewett*
Workers on the Waterfront: Seamen, Longshoremen, and Unionism in the 1930s
  Bruce Nelson

German Workers in Chicago: A Documentary History of Working-Class Culture from
    1850 to World War I   *Edited by Hartmut Keil and John B. Jentz*

On the Line: Essays in the History of Auto Work
    Edited by Nelson Lichtenstein and Stephen Meyer III

Upheaval in the Quiet Zone: A History of Hospital Workers' Union, Local 1199
    Leon Fink and Brian Greenberg

Labor's Flaming Youth: Telephone Operators and Worker Militancy, 1878–1923
    Stephen H. Norwood

Another Civil War: Labor, Capital, and the State in the Anthracite Regions of
    Pennsylvania, 1840–68   *Grace Palladino*

Coal, Class, and Color: Blacks in Southern West Virginia, 1915–32
    Joe William Trotter, Jr.

For Democracy, Workers, and God: Labor Song-Poems and Labor Protest, 1865–95
    Clark D. Halker

Dishing It Out: Waitresses and Their Unions in the Twentieth Century
    Dorothy Sue Cobble

The Spirit of 1848: German Immigrants, Labor Conflict, and the Coming of the
    Civil War   *Bruce Levine*

Working Women of Collar City: Gender, Class, and Community in Troy, New York,
    1864–86   *Carole Turbin*

Southern Labor and Black Civil Rights: Organizing Memphis Workers
    Michael K. Honey

Radicals of the Worst Sort: Laboring Women in Lawrence, Massachusetts, 1860–1912
    Ardis Cameron

Producers, Proletarians, and Politicians: Workers and Party Politics in Evansville and
    New Albany, Indiana, 1850–87   *Lawrence M. Lipin*

The New Left and Labor in the 1960s   *Peter B. Levy*

The Making of Western Labor Radicalism: Denver's Organized Workers, 1878–1905
    David Brundage

In Search of the Working Class: Essays in American Labor History and Political
    Culture   *Leon Fink*

Lawyers against Labor: From Individual Rights to Corporate Liberalism
    Daniel R. Ernst

"We Are All Leaders": The Alternative Unionism of the Early 1930s
    Edited by Staughton Lynd

The Female Economy: The Millinery and Dressmaking Trades, 1860–1930
    Wendy Gamber

"Negro and White, Unite and Fight!": A Social History of Industrial Unionism in
    Meatpacking, 1930–90   *Roger Horowitz*

Power at Odds: The 1922 National Railroad Shopmen's Strike   *Colin J. Davis*

The Common Ground of Womanhood: Class, Gender, and Working Girls' Clubs,
    1884–1928   *Priscilla Murolo*

Marching Together: Women of the Brotherhood of Sleeping Car Porters
    Melinda Chateauvert

Down on the Killing Floor: Black and White Workers in Chicago's Packinghouses,
  1904–54   *Rick Halpern*
Labor and Urban Politics: Class Conflict and the Origins of Modern Liberalism
  in Chicago, 1864–97   *Richard Schneirov*
All That Glitters: Class, Conflict, and Community in Cripple Creek
  Elizabeth Jameson
Waterfront Workers: New Perspectives on Race and Class   *Edited by Calvin Winslow*
Labor Histories: Class, Politics, and the Working-Class Experience
  Edited by Eric Arnesen, Julie Greene, and Bruce Laurie
The Pullman Strike and the Crisis of the 1890s: Essays on Labor and Politics
  Edited by Richard Schneirov, Shelton Stromquist, and Nick Salvatore
AlabamaNorth: African-American Migrants, Community, and Working-Class
  Activism in Cleveland, 1914–45   *Kimberley L. Phillips*
Imagining Internationalism in American and British Labor, 1939–49
  Victor Silverman
William Z. Foster and the Tragedy of American Radicalism   *James R. Barrett*
Colliers across the Sea: A Comparative Study of Class Formation in Scotland
  and the American Midwest, 1830–1924   *John H. M. Laslett*
"Rights, Not Roses": Unions and the Rise of Working-Class Feminism, 1945–80
  Dennis A. Deslippe
Testing the New Deal: The General Textile Strike of 1934 in the American South
  Janet Irons
Hard Work: The Making of Labor History   *Melvyn Dubofsky*
Southern Workers and the Search for Community: Spartanburg County,
  South Carolina   *G. C. Waldrep III*
We Shall Be All: A History of the Industrial Workers of the World (abridged edition)
  Melvyn Dubofsky, ed. Joseph A. McCartin
Race, Class, and Power in the Alabama Coalfields, 1908–21   *Brian Kelly*
Duquesne and the Rise of Steel Unionism   *James D. Rose*
Anaconda: Labor, Community, and Culture in Montana's Smelter City
  Laurie Mercier
Bridgeport's Socialist New Deal, 1915–36   *Cecelia Bucki*
Indispensable Outcasts: Hobo Workers and Community in the American Midwest,
  1880–1930   *Frank Tobias Higbie*
After the Strike: A Century of Labor Struggle at Pullman   *Susan Eleanor Hirsch*
Corruption and Reform in the Teamsters Union   *David Witwer*
Waterfront Revolts: New York and London Dockworkers, 1946–61
  Colin J. Davis
Black Workers' Struggle for Equality in Birmingham
  Horace Huntley and David Montgomery
The Tribe of Black Ulysses: African American Men in the Industrial South
  William P. Jones
City of Clerks: Office and Sales Workers in Philadelphia, 1870–1920
  Jerome P. Bjelopera

Reinventing "The People": The Progressive Movement, the Class Problem,
    and the Origins of Modern Liberalism   *Shelton Stromquist*
Radical Unionism in the Midwest, 1900–1950   *Rosemary Feurer*
Gendering Labor History   *Alice Kessler-Harris*
James P. Cannon and the Origins of the American Revolutionary Left, 1890–1928
    Bryan D. Palmer

The University of Illinois Press
is a founding member of the
Association of American University Presses.

Composed in 10.5/13 Adobe Minion
with Meta display
by BookComp, Inc.
at the University of Illinois Press

University of Illinois Press
1325 South Oak Street
Champaign, IL 61820–6903
www.press.uillinois.edu

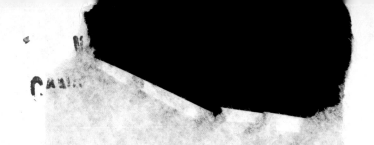